From the Land of Ever Winter to the American Southwest

From the Land of Ever Winter to the American Southwest

Athapaskan Migrations, Mobility, and Ethnogenesis

Edited by
Deni J. Seymour

THE UNIVERSITY OF UTAH PRESS
Salt Lake City

Copyright © 2012 by The University of Utah Press. All rights reserved.

 The Defiance House Man colophon is a registered trademark of the University of Utah Press. It is based upon a four-foot-tall, Ancient Puebloan pictograph (late PIII) near Glen Canyon, Utah.

16 15 14 13 12   1 2 3 4 5

LIBRARY OF CONGRESS CATALOGING-IN-PUBLICATION DATA

From the land of ever winter to the American Southwest :
Athapaskan migrations, mobility, and ethnogenesis / edited
by Deni J. Seymour.
         p. cm.
Includes bibliographical references and index.
ISBN 978-1-60781-175-6 (cloth : alk. paper)
1. Athapascan Indians — Southwest, New — Origin.
2. Athapascan Indians — Southwest, New — Migrations.
3. Athapascan Indians — Southwest, New — Antiquities.
4. Excavations (Archaeology) — Southwest, New. 5. Southwest,
New — Antiquities. I. Seymour, Deni J.
E99.A86F78 2012
978.004'972 — dc23
                                                    2011052823

Printed and bound by Sheridan Books, Inc., Ann Arbor, Michigan.

Contents

List of Figures   vii
List of Tables   xi

1. Athapaskan Migrations, Mobility, and Ethnogenesis: An Introduction   1
   Deni J. Seymour

2. Apachean Archaeology of Rocky Mountain National Park, Colorado, and the Colorado Front Range   20
   Robert H. Brunswig

3. Looking for Lovitt in All the Wrong Places: Migration Models and the Athapaskan Diaspora as Viewed from Eastern Colorado   37
   Kevin P. Gilmore and Sean Larmore

4. Tierra Blanca: A Complex Issue   78
   David T. Hughes

5. Isolating a Pre-differentiation Athapaskan Assemblage in the Southern Southwest: The Cerro Rojo Complex   90
   Deni J. Seymour

6. Emergence of the Navajo People   124
   David M. Brugge

7. Navajo Emergence in Dinétah: Social Imaginary and Archaeology   150
   Douglas D. Dykeman and Paul Roebuck

8. We Do Not Forget; We Remember: Mescalero Apache Origins and Migration as Reflected in Place Names   182
   David L. Carmichael and Claire R. Farrer

9. Finding and Not Finding Athapaskans in the Archaeological Record Using Percentage Stratigraphy   198
   Dale Walde

10. Variation in the Production of Ceramics by Athapaskans in the Western United States   225
    David V. Hill

11. DNA Evidence of a Prehistoric Athapaskan Migration
    from the Subarctic to the Southwest of North America   241
    Ripan S. Malhi

12. Linguistic Evidence Regarding the Apachean Migration   249
    Keren Rice

13. Apache Names in Spanish and Early Mexican Documents: What They
    Can Tell Us about the Early Contact Apache Dialect Situation   271
    Willem J. de Reuse

14. Southern Athapaskan Quotative Evidentials: A Discursive
    Areal Typology   286
    Anthony K. Webster

15. The Ancestral Chipewyan Became the Navajo and Apache:
    New Support for a Northwest Plains–Mountain Route to
    the American Southwest   303
    Bryan C. Gordon

16. Modeling Athapaskan Migrations   356
    Martin P. R. Magne

17. "Big Trips" and Historic Apache Movement and Interaction:
    Models for Early Athapaskan Migrations   377
    Deni J. Seymour

18. Issues in Athapaskan Prehistory   410
    Roy L. Carlson

    List of Contributors   427
    Index   429

Figures

2.1. Sites in Rocky Mountain National Park   23
2.2. Dismal River (Apachean) and Uncompahgre Brown (Ute) rim sherds   24
2.3. Recently documented Dismal River ceramic sites south of Rocky Mountain National Park   28
3.1. Generalized Athapaskan migration routes   39
3.2. Core and periphery of the Dismal River culture   40
3.3. Distribution of prehistoric Athapaskans based on ceramic wares   41
3.4. Dated western Dismal River sites in Colorado and Wyoming   46
3.5. Projectile points from western Dismal River sites   48
3.6. Small side-notched projectile points from Franktown Cave   49
3.7. Diagnostic proto-Apache bipointed bifaces   49
3.8. Sherds from the Eureka Ridge site   51
3.9. Sherd from Franktown Cave   51
3.10. Micaceous sherd from Arroyo del Arenal   51
3.11. Summed probability distribution for radiometric dates from western Dismal River sites   53
3.12. Comparison of archaeological radiocarbon dates for eastern Colorado with dates associated with western Dismal River sites   54
3.13. Reconstructed Palmer Drought Severity Index for areas in the western United States   55
3.14. Comparison of proxy population in eastern Colorado with paleoclimate episodes   56
3.15. Geographic distribution of cultures in the Plains and Rocky Mountains during the twelfth century   57
3.16. Geographic distribution of cultures in the Plains and Rocky Mountains during the thirteenth century   58
3.17. Geographic distribution of cultures in the Plains and Rocky Mountains during the fourteenth century   58
3.18. Geographic distribution of cultures in the Plains and Rocky Mountains during the fifteenth century   59
3.19. Geographic distribution of source areas of exotic lithic materials found at Dismal River sites in Colorado   60
3.20. Geographic distribution of cultures in the Plains and Rocky Mountains during the sixteenth and seventeenth centuries   62

3.21. Geographic distribution of cultures in the Plains and Rocky Mountains during the eighteenth century   62
4.1. Distribution of Tierra Blanca sites in the Texas Panhandle   79
4.2. Tierra Blanca site tipi ring structure   82
4.3. Tierra Blanca site, Structure 2   82
4.4. Fifth Green site excavations and features   84
5.1. Idealized distribution of mobile groups in the southern Southwest   92
5.2. The extractive method   97
5.3. Mountain spirit images at a Peloncillo Mountain Apache site   100
5.4. Headdress shape distributions in rock art   101
5.5. Apparent distributions in early Apache rock art   102
5.6A. Wind god image   102
5.6B. Buffalo-horned image   103
5.7. Apparent distributions in later Apache rock art   103
5.8A. Mountain spirit headdress image   104
5.8B. Intermediate headdress form   104
5.9. Side-notched arrow points from the Cerro Rojo site   109
5.10. Cerro Rojo complex flaked-stone tools   109
5.11. Cerro Rojo complex bifacial knife   110
5.12. Cerro Rojo complex wickiup ring outlines   112
6.1. Rod-frame halo on a gourd rattle   132
6.2. Fringe Mouth God with a rattle and a rod-frame halo   133
6.3. *Tablita*-like rod frame   133
6.4. Ladder-like rod frames to support features for headdresses   133
6.5. Pictograph of female Ye'ii performer   134
6.6. Female Ye'ii, Hunchback God, and deity resembling the Fringe Mouth God   134
6.7. Traditional Navajo forked-pole hogan   136
7.1. Navajo petroglyphs in Crow Canyon, Dinétah   151
7.2. Plan view of hogan from LA 55979   153
7.3. Map of the Dinétah region   159
7.4. Delgadito Canyon Navajo pictograph   165
8.1. Mountain Spirit rock art image   185
8.2. Locations of traditional Apache place names   188
8.3. Ancestral Apache site of Obsidian Cliff   189
9.1. Canadian Plains overview map   199
9.2. Sequence of cultural historical entities on the Canadian Plains   202
9.3. Projectile point types from the Gull Lake site   204
9.4. Distribution of Kehoe's projectile point types by assemblage   207
9.5. Schematic model of historical continuity frequency distributions   209
9.6. Schematic model of population replacement frequency distributions   209

Figures · ix

9.7. Projectile point measurement locations   212
9.8. Distribution of greatest haft height by level   213
9.9. Distribution of neck width by level   214
9.10. Stem-and-leaf display of greatest haft height and neck width data   215
9.11. EaOd-1 projectile point class distribution   216
9.12. Percentage stratigraphy of projectile point classes   217
10.1. Late prehistoric and historic peoples and archaeological complexes in the southern Great Plains   226
10.2. Late prehistoric Wichita simple-stamped vessel   230
10.3. Simple-stamped vessel from the Dismal River aspect type site   230
10.4. Smooth-surfaced vessel from the Dismal River aspect type site   231
10.5. Apache vessel from Otero Mesa, Fort Bliss, Texas   231
10.6. Vessel attributed to the Garza complex   233
10.7. Rim sherds from Ancestral Pueblo cooking jars   233
15.1. Proposed origin of the Navajo-Apache from Chipewyan ca. AD 800   304
15.2. Proposed Dene movement to become Sarsi ca. AD 1650   305
15.3. Chipewyan tools: arrowheads, scraper, and chithos   316
15.4. Archaeological sites suggesting the route of the ancestral Subarctic Chipewyan   323
16.1. Location of Athapaskan groups in British Columbia, Alberta, Yukon, and Alaska   357
16.2. Distribution of Athapaskan-speakers in North America   358
16.3. Athapaskan migration scenario, 500 BC–AD 1800   360
16.4. Hypothesized movement of Athapaskans to the Southwest and the U.S. Pacific Coast   361
16.5. Two generational scenarios for Athapaskan migration   363
16.6. Generational model concepts integrated with group alliance and group growth models of site formation   365
16.7. Eagle Lake Athapaskan and Plateau Pithouse Tradition lithic and faunal assemblage structures   366
16.8. Biogeographic zones within which Athapaskan migrational events could be explored   370
16.9. Punctuated point-and-arrow model for Athapaskan migration   372
17.1. Movements within a known range   379
17.2. Big trips   379
17.3. Temporary long-distance movement into new territories   380
17.4. Gradual encompassment of new territory   383
17.5. Alternate favored locales   385
17.6. Model of historic Chiricahua movements   399
18.1. Multidimensional scaling of Athapaskan and Plateau Pithouse Tradition small side-notched points   414

Tables

3.1. Dated western Dismal River sites in Colorado and Wyoming   47
4.1. Roster of Tierra Blanca complex sites   80
5.1. Correlate grid example   96
6.1. Comparisons of words for "man" and "water"   128
6.2. Words for "dog" and "horse" in Apachean and Northern Athapaskan languages   129
6.3. Comparison of Hopi and Navajo clan-phratry organization   131
9.1. Gull Lake projectile point class paradigm   216
9.2. Gull Lake site percentage stratigraphy   217
9.3. Basal edge shape contingency   220
11.1. Genetic variants of Athapaskans   245
12.1. Cognates in several Dene languages   251
12.2. Order of prefixes in the verb of Dene languages   252
12.3. Dene classificatory verb stems meaning "object is located"   253
12.4. Dene irregular verb stems   253
12.5. Dene place names compared   254
12.6. Apachean words for "corn"   258
12.7. Words for "corn" in northern and Pacific Coast Dene languages   258
12.8. Noncognate Apachean words   259
12.9. Distribution of the object pronoun *y-* in Navajo   259
12.10. Distribution of the object pronoun *y-* in Jicarilla Apache   259
12.11. Distribution of the object pronoun *y-* in Tsuut'ina   260
12.12. Incorporated noun in Tsuut'ina   260
12.13. Incorporated noun in Dëne Sųłiné   260
12.14. Numbers in Tsuut'ina and some Apachean languages   261
12.15. Time divergences for Apachean languages   263
12.16. Time divergences for Apachean, Dëne Sųłiné, and Tsuut'ina   263
12.17. Percentages of shared cognates in Apachean languages   264
13.1. Apache names containing the element *Jasque-* or *Jasquie-*   275
13.2. Cordero's 1796 list of Apache tribe names   279
14.1. Division based on /t/ → /k/ split   287
14.2. Divergence times based on cognates   288
14.3. Quotative evidentials used in Southern Athapaskan languages   289
14.4. East/west split based on discursive typology   291
14.5. Quotative evidentials in selected Athapaskan languages   293

14.6. Southwestern quotative evidentials (non-Apachean)   294
14.7. Comparison of selected languages and quotative evidentials   296
15.1. Comparative wordlist of Apache, Chipewyan, and Navajo   307
15.2. Northern and Southern Dene language divergence   313
15.3. North and South Dene ^{14}C dates   330

CHAPTER 1

Athapaskan Migrations, Mobility, and Ethnogenesis

An Introduction

DENI J. SEYMOUR

Child-of-the-Water was born to White-Painted Woman, and Killer-of-Enemies was his uncle. Yusn told them to separate. Yusn told Killer-of-Enemies, "You go out this way and take one grain of corn and put it in the ground. You will live from that." So they gave this corn to Killer-of-Enemies and Yusn said, "You shall live happily on this grain of corn." Child-of-the-Water and White-Painted Woman were on the side of the Chiricahua. Yusn told them, "You must live on yucca fruit, piñon nuts, and all the other wild plants."

| Morris Opler (1942:14) |

We were made in a Land of Ever Winter, a House of Ice and Winter, which we call in Apache, Kugha'bikine, House of Winter or House of Ice—Home, not House, on the shores of a big lake called Tuduubits'alidaa, Water That You Cannot See Over.... We looked around. But that there was always something to the south, that drew us. And we started drifting in that way. And, as we left our birthplace as a people, our Spirit Brother Warriors told us: "Go forth as a people."

| Elder Bernard Second of Mescalero (Farrer 1991:15, 21) |

As the accounts in these epigraphs suggest, Athapaskan-speakers split into distinctive tribes and bands and moved south from the Subarctic. Many of these migrants found their way to the American Southwest, others to the Pacific Coast. This act of migration is not disputed among scholars, for as Opler (1938: 381) noted, "Apachean specialists agree that the Apacheans came from the north, from the great hive of Athapaskan speakers in the Mackenzie Basin of

Canada (Sapir 1936)," or as some Mescalero say, from "the Land of Ever Winter" (Carmichael and Farrer, Chapter 8).[1] There is, however, no consensus on the route, the timing, or the nature of the evidence. Moreover, there is a sizable unaccounted-for geographic gap between the Southwest and Canada, where, until recently, Athapaskan evidence has not been specifically sought and therefore not identified. Thus it is just now that we can look forward to the possibility of joining these two regions through material evidence of their presence and routes.

Deficiencies in data and understandings are surprising given the amount of scholarly thought devoted to these groups, and the historic Apache and Navajo in particular. Among the many questions remaining are when the migration was initiated and when and by which routes the first groups arrived in the southern latitudes (Gunnerson 2006:5; Opler 1983). As Lockwood (1938:1–2) noted in the early twentieth century, "The fact is, no scholar has been able to... say just when they [Apache] made their appearance in the Southwest as a distinct nation." Schroeder (1954:597) reiterated this deficiency, noting, "The date of entry of the Athabascan [in the Southwest] stands out as one of today's most controversial problems." Today this remains a basic question in Southwestern research, just as the circumstances and timing of departure are in the north. Opler (1983:381) noted: "Because the Apacheans were basically mobile hunters and gatherers, especially during prehistoric and protohistoric times, archeological evidence concerning them is meager. Almost all firm Apachean archeological data pertain to the Navajo, who built sturdier homes than their linguistic congeners."

Yet much has changed in the thirty years since that last statement was made. Increasingly abundant archaeological data are available and substantive theoretical and methodological advances have been made to begin to address these questions, the most pertinent of which are summarized in this book. But the content is not limited to archaeology or to this specific problem. The book goes beyond Athapaskan studies to examine mobility (especially long-distance mobility), the role of genetics in the examination of prehistory, how culture change and assimilation influence our ability to recognize material evidence, and how ethnogenesis and political sensitivities affect the way we discuss these issues. The book summons data from specialists in multiple fields of investigation to address common interests for anthropological research.

This book represents a fundamental paradigm shift, as new directions of inquiry begin to take hold. The focus shifts from an ethnohistoric- or linguistics-dominated perspective, in which a late arrival via the Plains holds sway, to one in which actual archaeological and genetics data are presented that support an early pre-Spanish arrival by small groups using various routes, including through the mountains, where the earliest and most abundant evidence has been found. Such changes in paradigm can be threatening to existing canons, and sometimes the significance of this new research is not immediately realized.

It is only in the past decade that archaeological data have been able to hold their own with respect to other forms of evidence, as applied to addressing these questions of migrations, culture change, and ethnogenesis. Acquisition of new data in a matrix of newly developed method and theory provides confidence in these new directions. Now researchers in other fields must begin to incorporate archaeological data from both the Subarctic and the Southwest, and this book is the first substantive attempt to do so. Archaeological data must be incorporated into a coherent scenario that includes genetics, linguistics, and historical data, often requiring a revision or reconsideration of existing and well-entrenched views.

As Brugge (Chapter 6) notes, tracing the route or routes of migration must ultimately rely on archaeological evidence. This means considering what constitutes reasonable evidence and examining long-held methodological issues, such as how to distinguish in situ cultural developments from replacement through migration (Walde, Chapter 9), how to separate late assemblages on multicomponent sites (Seymour, Chapter 5), whether projectile points are truly diagnostic and whether flaked-stone artifacts traditionally considered nondiagnostic might in fact be diagnostic (Brunswig, Chapter 2; Gilmore and Larmore, Chapter 3; Seymour, Chapter 5; Walde, Chapter 9), whether pottery is a useful index of identity during this period (Gilmore and Larmore, Chapter 3; Seymour, Chapter 5; Hill, Chapter 10; Gordon, Chapter 15), and how to connect the material record with modern descendant populations in the face of substantial behavioral and material change (Brugge, Chapter 6; Seymour, Chapter 5).

The timing of the movement southward and arrival at various places along the way is also dependent on the use of dating methods that are innovative and focused on the problems of this period (see Brunswig, Chapter 2; Gilmore and Larmore, Chapter 3; Seymour, Chapter 5). Yet as Dykeman and Roebuck (Chapter 7) remind us, traditional origin stories often provide information on how specific groups migrated to their homeland as well as how they gathered members from different directions and incorporated different peoples into their own. This type of information is not supplied by chronometric or other types of empirical data, though it is suggested by genetics (Malhi, Chapter 11). In this regard, Carmichael and Farrer's contribution (Chapter 8) emphasizes the route specific to the (or a portion of the) Mescalero and suggests they were the last of the Apache groups to migrate south. Critics might argue that because oral information changes to accommodate modern conditions, these accounts are not reliable. Still, when such accounts are seriated with respect to when they were collected and checked against an archaeological record, they provide a way to trace group-specific perceptions as to their origins and arrival.

Webster (Chapter 14), on the other hand, compares the use of an independent verb of speaking with dependent enclitic markings for quotative evidentials to suggest that there was only one migration into the Southwest, in contrast to other data. This contradiction between inferences derived from different data sources emphasizes the need to be cognizant of the problem of "readback"—the process in which scholarly writing is transformed into traditional knowledge (e.g., McGhee 2008:589) when one is analyzing and incorporating the content of traditional stories. Webster, however, proposes a division that may be explained by two possible hypotheses: (1) an earlier arrival and more prolonged process of entry of Southern Athapaskan–speakers into the Southwest and/or (2) a more intensive interactional relation between an Eastern discursive Apachean subgroup and non-Apachean peoples. Significantly, as Walde (Chapter 9) points out, discussions of ethnicity and migrations are now part of wider social and legal debates, so it is important that archaeologists make the strengths and weaknesses of their interpretations clear. He also clarifies the role of explicit archaeological theory in tackling these very difficult problems, something that both Magne (Chapter 16) and Seymour (Chapter 17) advocate with regard to how mobile people, and specifically the ancestral Athapaskans, migrate.

This book seeks to bring together in one source the diversity of current views on many of these points. One primary goal has been to sustain the dialogue between leading scholars that began before the Society for American Archaeology symposium from which this book arose. In that session we heard a diversity of views on Athapaskan migrations from Canada to the Southwest, reminding us of the need to continue reaching across disciplinary lines and political boundaries, remaining open to nonconventional and opposing perspectives on these issues. As Rice (Chapter 12) says, the lack of a match between the linguistic evidence and the archaeological evidence reported herein shows how much more we have to learn. The authors collectively see this as constructive because it means we can ask fresh questions.

The contributing authors discuss a variety of issues, including migration, movement among the mobile, ethnogenesis, and culture change. All these topics are relevant to the general theme, and they affect the way different interest groups understand and recognize the questions of arrival, emergence, identity formation, and culture change. This informal consortium of researchers is committed to working out the problems by seeking new techniques and innovative methodologies, scrutinizing the data, and striving to remain open-minded as we attempt to close the geographical and conceptual gaps between us.

As noted, we do not all agree, and many contrasting and conflicting points of view are included in this book. Yet one of the strengths of this book is this diversity of views, as well as the depth of data control and the sophistication with which topics are addressed. If nothing more, each author's position and basis is presented clearly so that an evaluation can be made. It is too early to thoroughly sort the chaff from the substance, but we recognize that both elements are essential at the beginning of the long-term intellectual process of amassing cumulative knowledge. Even so, there is a remarkable similarity in many of the themes we share. What does seem clear is that one's conceptual framework is key in how one approaches the problem, how one frames the questions, and which types of data one looks for and recognizes as valid.

One of our goals is to erect bridges between what have previously been perceived as barriers between the subdisciplines that make up anthropology. Most treatments of Athapaskans, Apaches, and the migration of these groups emphasize one aspect, generally linguistics or ethnohistory. Archaeological data are incorporated as little more than accessories. These dominant perspectives sometimes rigidly determine the direction of research and preselect acceptable conclusions, exerting considerable peer pressure to stay focused on existing scenarios. This book incorporates a four-field approach, which will appeal to many anthropologists, historians, geneticists, linguists, and Native American scholars. Rather than focus on one field, the authors bring varied evidence and a wide range of specialties to bear on these questions. The authors incorporate new data with existing data to arrive at a revised scenario of Athapaskan migrations. This alone makes the book a milestone and a critical advance in knowledge building.

Long-standing and newly conceptualized problems can be approached from a variety of perspectives, as is shown by each of the viewpoints included in this book. These varied approaches include genetics (Malhi, Chapter 11), linguistics (Brugge, Chapter 6; Rice, Chapter 12; de Reuse, Chapter 13; Webster, Chapter 14; Gordon, Chapter 15), and ethnography (Brugge, Chapter 6; Dykeman and Roebuck, Chapter 7; Carmichael and Farrer, Chapter 8), as well as archaeology and oral history, considered by the majority of the contributions. Still, even those originating in the same discipline may disagree owing to differences in training, theoretical background, perceptions of evidentiary strength, and the historical and theoretical matrices in which data are evaluated. While most of the authors tackle only one region or culture group, Gordon (Chapter 15) uses a variety of lines of evidence in an effort to synthesize many of the complex issues involved and the entire route, and Carmichael and Farrer (Chapter 8) discuss the Mescalero Apache's traditional perspective on a large portion of their route south. Each study clarifies the complexity of these problems, highlighting the necessity for researchers in related subfields to work together in attempting to solve these problems and the need for sound, though innovative, and explicit methodologies. Even the theory discussed by Magne (Chapter 16) and Seymour (Chapter 17) requires a grasp of the long history of research on this topic and the intricacies of the archaeological record in each area.

Efforts in this regard to address basic questions must reconcile historical and archaeological perspectives with those based on the varied oral traditional information of Athapaskan-speaking groups. Some Southwestern Athapaskans consider the migration story a myth and believe that they have always been in the Southwest. On the other hand, some Chiricahua oral histories refer to the migration south along the forested flanks of the Rocky Mountains, "between the treeless heights and the treeless plains" (Cole 1981, 1988), which is consistent with the placement on the landscape of the earliest known proto-Apachean evidence in Colorado (Brunswig, Chapter 2; Gilmore and Larmore, Chapter 3) and with the mountain-based occurrence of the earliest ancestral Apache evidence (Cerro Rojo) in southern New Mexico and Arizona (Seymour, Chapter 5). As

Carmichael and Farrer (Chapter 8) note, their version of a traditional Mescalero Apache migration story conveys the general route and approximate timeline for their migration from the "Land of Ever Winter." It is expected, however, that different groups and bands, as well as local groups within larger entities, traveled south by different routes and at different rates (Seymour, Chapter 17).

Clearly, the expectation for the presentation of a single cohesive perspective on this issue is a feature of modern politics, because in reality there are within-tribe variations in oral historical accounts. Too often researchers present the dominant faction's perspective, failing to assess whether or not it is representative of all the knowledge held within a tribe and consistent with other forms of evidence and with earlier versions. Each of around sixty Navajo clans has its own origin story because each clan experienced aspects distinct to its own origin and has reproduced these accounts in different historical contexts. As Dykeman and Roebuck (Chapter 7) note, one scholar presented 23 different versions of the origin stories set down since 1895, although the general outline of these accounts is consistent, providing the basic elements of the Navajo worldview, which is celebrated, re-created, and renewed in ceremonies, healing practices, and other oral traditions. Western Apache clans also show considerable variability with regard to statements of origin because of how each came to be Western Apache, ended up in historical Western Apache territory, and incorporated elders' stories into their modern understandings. Some Chiricahua land-claims interviews from the 1950s under the Indian Claims Commission Act tell of origins in Mexico (see Seymour, Chapter 17). Here interaction with the Tarahumara, Yaqui, Ópata, and others meant that people of diverse backgrounds were incorporated into and ultimately became Apache, sometimes situated to the south of their points of initial origin. At times the Western Apache incorporated O'odham and Yavapai through various means, just as some Navajo clans recognize Apachean origins among the neighboring Puebloans or O'odham. In still other instances, notions of origins and migrations have been catapulted into the political and economic arenas, where modern sensibilities influence their interpretation.

Warburton and Begay (2005:552) stress the diverse origins of early Navajo traits, stating that "Navajo culture and identity, like all culture and identity, is an evolutionary process." This latter point is of considerable importance and gains merit when evaluated in the context of archaeological data. Archaeological data support the notion that the Navajo, as the Dinetah archaeological complex, did not come together until AD 1541, with its hogans and Dinetah Gray pottery (Seymour 2009; Dykeman and Roebuck, Chapter 7; Opler 1983), but this does not mean that the area lacked an earlier Athapaskan presence. For example, Opler (1983:381) comments:

> It is unrealistic to suppose that the oldest hogans that were built have resisted the ravages of time or even that the very oldest have been discovered.

Since most Apacheans are known to have lived in dwellings less substantial than the Navajo hogan, there is no certainty that this was the earliest Apachean house type of the area; on comparative groups it is possible to argue that the forked-stick hogan was a specialization developed after the Navajo had lived for some time in their traditional homeland.

Becoming Navajo or any of the other currently recognized Athapaskan tribes involved what was likely a protracted process of differentiating from other Athapaskan groups (also see Opler 1983:381), although Dykeman and Roebuck (Chapter 7) argue that the Navajo emergence was abrupt as the group incorporated attributes from neighbors. Each group emerged as distinct at different times, although Opler (1983:384) notes that "once the Apacheans reached the Southwest, their linguistic and political differentiation proceeded rather rapidly and that by the beginning of the eighteenth century they were distinct tribes, each occupying what it had come to consider to be its traditional territory." This, however, likely originates in the assumption of a relatively late arrival of these groups. As Brugge (Chapter 6) suggests, this question of how the migrants differentiated into separate peoples has been one of the most interesting. Many of us would consider that this process, which began early, had sufficiently progressed when by 1541 the Navajo had emerged as a separate tribe with its distinct constellation of traits. As Dykeman and Roebuck (Chapter 7) note, specific stories and symbols tying the Navajo people to a particular place, Dinétah, were critical to the emergence of Navajo cultural identity, as were the social practices of the people who shared those stories. Foreign ideas and practices were incorporated into Navajo culture, but they were symbolically Navajo-ized as part of the Navajo tendency to change to preserve tradition.

Most understand a similar process in the way a number of other Apachean groups emerged to become the modern divisions. De Reuse (Chapter 13), however, documents possible evidence of Gileño and Mimbreño Apache who eventually lost their identity as distinct groups.[2] The linguistic evidence suggests that these Athapaskan-speakers were neither Western Apache– nor Chiricahua-speakers but spoke a dialect variety linguistically intermediate between the recorded Western Apache and Chiricahua languages. This suggests that some Apache groups disappeared from history, leaving little but a linguistic trace. Such a process could have occurred by a variety of means, including intermixing with other Apachean and non-Apachean groups, as has been historically documented.

This, of course, is the distinction between biological heredity and cultural identity, which is also discussed with reference to the Mescalero by Carmichael and Farrer (Chapter 8). This distinction is recognized by most modern scholars, who agree that influences from and intermixing with neighboring groups resulted in the transformation of early Athapaskans into the groups now recognized in the American Southwest, affecting many aspects of their culture, including language (Goss 1968; Hester 1962; Brugge, Chapter 6; Hill, Chapter 10; Seymour, Chapter 17; Webster, Chapter 14). This explains why the Dismal River cultural and technological pattern seen on the Front Range of the Rocky Mountains (Brunswig, Chapter 2; Gilmore and Larmore, Chapter 3) looks different in some ways from that in the mountainous portions of the southern Southwest (Seymour, Chapter 5), despite an underlying similarity in other aspects of the material culture and land-use patterns. It also explains why some manifestations, such as Dismal River, Cerro Rojo (Seymour, Chapter 5), and Tierra Blanca (Hughes, Chapter 4), remain controversial with respect to their identification as Athapaskan assemblages.

Part of the Apachean way of life involved recruitment by a variety of means and the borrowing of technologies from neighbors. These practices resulted in elements of material culture diverging independently from that held in common, making cultural affiliation associations especially complex. Discussing this issue in relation to pottery technology the Apacheans borrowed from surrounding groups, Hill (Chapter 10) explores the mechanisms of where and how ceramic technology was transferred to Athapaskan groups before or after their arrival in the Greater Southwest (also see Opler 1971a:32; Seymour 2008a). As Dykeman and Roebuck (Chapter 7) note, the Navajo incorporated select Puebloan ideas and elements of material culture but modified them and made them their own.

Definition of early Athapaskan material culture is contentious, and several contributors address this problem, providing the outline of the argument while pointing the reader to in-depth work for further discussion of the issue, which could fill an entire volume in and of itself. Rather than redefine the archaeological complex in the southern Southwest, Seymour (Chapter 5) offers a methodological discussion of some of the ways in which we infer the evidence is actually ancestral Apache.

Central to this issue is that there are fundamental differences of opinion on how pottery is used to identify Athapaskans. While some may find the pottery data presented by the Colorado archaeologists (Brunswig; Gilmore and Larmore) convincing, the Colorado authors are presented with much less variation than in the southern Southwest. Hill's (Chapter 10) criticism of pottery as an ethnic identifier must be taken seriously before these traditional sources of cultural affiliation can be applied. In the southern Southwest we often see non-Athapaskan pottery on Athapaskan sites, pottery that was obtained through raiding, trading, scavenging, and so on, as I have discussed (Seymour 2008a). Therefore, Southwesternists question whether pottery found on early Athapaskan sites was made by them or obtained by other means. It is also unclear whether early Athapaskans were making pottery or obtaining it from others on a routine basis and the degree to which recruitment practices affected pottery characteristics and use (e.g., adoption of women potters from different tribes). Most agree that Athapaskans learned technology from neighbors after their arrival in the Southwest, and it is thus one of the most variable aspects of the assemblage. This raises the question whether and how it is diagnostic; it is quite variable, and therefore the basis for this variability must be understood before it can become a useful index of cultural affiliation. Moreover, it is not routinely present, so sites must be identifiable by other means or only a small subset will be distinguished (Seymour 2002). This entire argument exemplifies the contentious and difficult nature of ancestral Apachean studies, in which different criteria are applied and different kinds of evidence are given greater or lesser weight.

Most anthropologists accept that regardless of biological derivation, one becomes Apachean (or part of any other group) by virtue of adopting the cultural identity of the dominant group—by practicing the Apachean way of life. This transformation is especially pronounced when groups are isolated by their distinctive lifeways, separate territories, and opposing economic pursuits. Brugge (Chapter 6), however, departs from others and suggests that the early Navajo were not initially Athapaskan-speakers but instead originated with the hunting-and-gathering cultures already in the Southwest. This is not so different from what others are suggesting, that is, that the migrating Athapaskans intermixed with groups already present. It differs, however, in its emphasis and departure from paradigmatic anthropological theory regarding cultural identity in suggesting that language and practice do not establish a group's socio-political identity. The argument is that Athapaskan culture and language were overlaid on an existing set of socio-political relationships. This seems to be an attempt to reconcile modern perceptions of place, alluded to by Carmichael and Farrer, regarding notions that Athapaskans have always been here in the Southwest. The political ties established and extended through connections with established groups is consistent with the concept conveyed by a Warm Springs Apache, whom I cite in Chapter 17, that the migrants "knew the people whose land they crossed." Brugge's politically accommodating twist in conventional archaeological logic seems evident in the way he phrases his perspective, stating that the earliest Navajo may not have been Athapaskan-speakers but were hunter-gatherers indigenous to the Southwest and descended from the Archaic populations that later incorporated Athapaskan migrants. A more customary approach would be to acknowledge that the dominant surviving culture (e.g., Navajo) incorporated other peoples who then became Navajo. This rendition would be more in line with anthropological theory of identity formation. Most extant cultures incorporated others into their social and biological communities. In fact, this pluralism is a defining characteristic of the historic period in the Americas.

Acknowledgment of the probability of this process of change has resulted in the phrase "pre-differentiation Athapaskans" to distinguish the earliest Athapaskan arrivals, which have been assumed to be alternatively a homogenous or a diverse group. How researchers think about this issue and approach identifying the archaeological signature rests on whether it is hypothesized that at some point ancestral Chiricahua and ancestral Dinétah, for example, arrived in the

Southwest (or left the Subarctic) during a single migration and were of one stock, or whether they emerged from different sources and from many distinct migrations (although the actual past is probably far more complex) (Opler 1983:381). This, of course, also has implications for whether aspects of culture can be identified that were present before initial Athapaskan dispersal from the Subarctic (e.g., Perry 1983) and in what ways these remained bundled until the migrants reached the Southwest or whether and in what ways they were altered along the way. The active role of environment and social interactions in transforming culture are of course relevant here. A related question is at what point a new calibration of an Athapaskan cultural base or series of bases can be identified for the Southwest (and elsewhere along the route, for example at Promontory Point; Grayson 2011:333). A basic assumption is that groups with a common heritage should share many aspects of material culture but that environment and many other factors affect groups as they separate, creating tangible differences.

Pre-differentiation Athapaskans are distinguished from those who are later represented by (a) the early Dinétah and other proto-Apachean signatures, (b) their historically referenced nineteenth-century counterparts, and (c) their modern descendants. It is recognized that substantial social, cultural, and behavioral change has occurred through time which has had substantive material and spatial consequences. This recognition is the basis for not taking documentary sources or oral historic and oral traditional accounts at face value and not assuming there is continuity in material and spatial manifestations from the beginning to the present. That is why many archaeologists tend not to use the direct historical approach in attempting to solve these problems for highly mobile groups. Sharing a common heritage, these southward-moving Athapaskan-speaking groups were "transformed and modified in a variety of ways as the Athapaskan-speaking population segmented over centuries to produce the many historic divisions" (Perry 1983:715). We are only now beginning to see the consequences of these processes in the archaeological record. Much debate centers on the material consequences of these processes, necessitating that the ramifications be explicitly considered.

As early Athapaskans were influenced by surrounding groups, took on new technologies, and practiced new ways of life, they began to change in fundamental ways from one another. From a practical standpoint, this means not only that pre-Dinétah manifestations are expected to be different from Dinétah, but that pre-differentiation Dinétah is expected to be different from pre-differentiation Chiricahua, for example, and that both (all) may merge at some point in the distant past with a common ancestor and common ancestral material culture complex. This is similar to the logic discussed by Perry (1983) in his ethnographic efforts to define an earlier culture stratum or common base. Such a rendering of the past allows us to understand the types of data that may accompany these changes and, importantly, provides a basis to prove this suggested scenario wrong.

It is currently widely agreed that ancestral or pre-differentiation Athapaskans arrived in the Southwest in pre-Spanish times. Some researchers continue to argue for a late arrival owing to their almost singular reliance on European documentary sources (and equally vehement rejection of oral historic evidence), which when taken at face value seem to indicate a post–Pueblo Revolt arrival in the southernmost portions of the Southwest. These thirty-year-old arguments (Schaafsma 1981; Wilcox 1981), proposed when archaeological data were scarce, are now at considerable odds with the increasingly abundant archaeological record, which, in turn, suggests new interpretations of the documentary record. Archaeological evidence of early Apacheans from Colorado, New Mexico, Arizona, and West Texas precedes mention of these migrants in documentary accounts by at least 200 to 300 years (see Brunswig, Chapter 2; Gilmore and Larmore, Chapter 3; Seymour, Chapter 5).

Current research presented in various chapters in this book (and drawn from much more in-depth treatments) provides a viable basis for arguing for a potential pre-fifteenth-century arrival and alternative interpretations of seemingly straightforward documentary sources. This makes Athapaskans contemporaneous with many of the prehistoric Southwestern groups. Many early archaeologists, of course, had argued that Athapaskans had arrived sometime between AD 800 and 1000, suggesting that they were the basis for population aggregation, the downfall of the Pueblos, and the defensive posture of many sites (Forbes 1960:xiv–xxiii; Gladwin 1957; Hall 1944; Jennings 1940; Underhill 1956:15–17). The difference is that we now have Athapaskan data to address these questions directly, including suites of chronometric dates derived directly from or directly associated with distinctly Athapaskan material culture from a number of different sites (see Brunswig, Chapter 2; Gilmore and Larmore, Chapter 3; Seymour, Chapter 5).

These last points are important, and so I reiterate: (a) *suites of chronometric dates* (b) that have been *derived directly from or are directly associated with distinctly Athapaskan material culture* (c) have been *obtained from a number of different sites*. When the types of data indicated in these three points are lacking, they often serve as the basis for criticism of chronometric results, and the authors in this book have made concerted efforts to ensure that their dating methods are sound and conclusions sufficiently supported as a basis for their hypotheses and inferences. These points are emphasized because a common initial refrain from status-quo-protecting skeptics is "it's poorly dated." The intent is usually to question the quality, reliability, or context of chronometric dates. Such disparaging comments tend to receive ready and widespread acceptance without reasonable assessment of the details of the selection and analysis process, and are irresponsible when used simply as a tactic to discredit. Comments like these can effectively derail an argument owing to the generally poor understanding of chronometric dating among archaeologists. Very specific information needs to be provided as to why the dating results are not reliable. Critics have a responsibility to state precisely what is wrong with a specific date or dating methodology; what seems poor to one may be based on a rigorous and systematic dating program with multiple quality dates. In the Southwest some scholars consider any technique other than tree-ring dating to be suspect and the context poorly dated. This is an unreasonable standard in regions where tree-ring dating is not viable, as in many parts of the Southwest.

Suggesting that processes of change can best be understood against the backdrop of what was and is being changed, Perry (1983) has proposed a description of the proto-Athapaskan culture base in southern Alaska more than 2,000 years ago. Drawing on archaeological, linguistic, ecological, and comparative ethnographic evidence, he characterizes the common heritage of Athapaskan-speaking groups:

> Utilizing a variety of food sources in a multifaceted environment, population aggregates were large enough to maintain a tendency toward local endogamy, with intermarrying matrilineages and matrilocal residence involving bride service and family-arranged marriages. These population aggregates were also small enough to subsist through a combination of hunting, gathering, and fishing without food production. They probably had local home or base villages, or other areas to which they returned often, but retained a high capacity for mobility, ad hoc exploitation of food sources, and the ability to coalesce into larger groups for certain purposes.
>
> Proto-Athapaskan concepts of reality entailed recognition of a powerful essence, potentially harmful and beneficial, in all objects. They coped with the dangers they associated with femaleness through menstrual seclusion and other measures of avoidance. They conceived of the human soul in two parts, one of which was manifest in the breath associated with life, the other with the shadow. To widen the gap between death and the living, they rid themselves of the property, the dwelling, and the name of the deceased. They believed that the owl could speak to them in their language and that malevolent beings whistled in the forest. They perceived a power in the human gaze. They took sweat baths to cleanse themselves and restore their health, held the bear in awe but did not conduct ceremonies for it, and used a bull roarer and a small, shallow one-sided drum.
>
> These features persisted through the following millennia and radiated through a variety of environmental settings remote from the Proto-Athapaskan core habitat. (Perry 1983:729)

These descriptive attributes, which have material culture consequences, are consistent with the earliest (pre-differentiation) Athapaskan manifestations in the Southwest, which are found in New Mexico and in southeastern Arizona. These are characterized by use of brush huts or wickiups, semi-subterranean structures in colder, more northern latitudes, and reuse of prehistoric features

(Brown 1991, 1996, 1998; Brown and Hancock 1992; Seymour 2002, 2003, 2004a, 2004b). Remnants of these shelters are found in small and large sites — the latter were where residents would coalesce into larger groups for certain purposes. Their flaked-stone assemblage is suggestive of a hunting and butchering complex, supplemented with plant-food exploitation, and is relatively widespread, described as the Cerro Rojo complex (Seymour, Chapter 5). The character of this complex conveys adherence to a general adaption that was expressed in distinctive stylistic variants and in the way the landscape was used and terrain selected. These materials are consistent with those predicted by Opler (1983:381), who suggested that "because the Apacheans were basically mobile hunters and gatherers, especially during prehistoric and protohistoric times, archaeological evidence concerning them is meager"; they are "known to have lived in dwellings less substantial than the Navajo hogan."

A mobile way of life, sustained by hunting and gathering (and perhaps even raiding quite early), brought these groups south, seemingly by both mountain and plains routes, potentially using both environments as they moved south or splitting in the far north and coming down separately (Brunswig, Chapter 2; Haskell 1987; Seymour 2008b), although this is not altogether resolved and remains a research question. As Opler (1983:381–383) has outlined, arguments have been proposed for the routes of arrival of Apachean people by way of the western High Plains (e.g., Gunnerson 1960; Gunnerson and Gunnerson 1971; Hester 1962; Keur 1941:5; Schaafsma 1996, 2002; Wedel 1940; Wilcox 1981), or specifically along Colorado's Front Range and western Plains margin (Gilmore and Larmore, Chapter 3), while others have argued for movement through the intermountain region, including Gordon in this book (Chapter 15), who suggests migrants turned south on the Green River before reaching Utah, moving along the Colorado River of western Colorado's Uncompahgre Plateau, reaching the San Juan River and the Four Corners. Brugge and others have also argued they may have gone through the Great Basin and western slopes of the Rockies (Brugge 1993 and Chapter 6; Butler 1986; Huscher and Huscher 1942, 1943; Riley 1954; Spencer 1947:27; Steward 1936:63; Underhill 1956:22–23, 25–26; Van Valkenburg 1938; Wilmeth 1977) or the Rocky Mountains (Opler 1971b, 1975; Perry 1980; Wright 1984). Proponents of the plains route propose that Dismal River is an Apachean manifestation, as argued in this book by both Brunswig (Chapter 2) and Gilmore and Larmore (Chapter 3). Opler (1983:383–384) is one of many to argue against this interpretation of Dismal River as ancestral Apachean. Tierra Blanca has been proposed as a Plains Apache complex, but others, such as Hughes (Chapter 4), dispute the Athapaskan affiliation of Tierra Blanca, although usually the critiques are vague and do not propose a viable method of distinguishing groups or disproving this inference of cultural affiliation.

Some still argue for a southern plains-to-the-mountains route for the Southwestern Apachean groups, but Seymour's (2002, 2003, 2004b, 2008b, 2009) data indicate that the earliest chronometric evidence on directly dated pottery (luminescence) and features (radiocarbon) that represent distinctive Athapaskan material culture are in southern New Mexico and southern Arizona rather than on the plains. Only time will tell if this is a function of sample or an accurate reflection of a sequence of events. These earliest dates place the arrival before the fifteenth century, perhaps as early as the late 1200s, allowing us to possibly explain many of the processes under way at the time. Authors in this book acknowledge that archaeologists seek empirical data on the timing but they equally value the historical and oral historical data to explain the social processes behind the many transformations seen in the material record.

These and many other issues are implicit in and explicitly discussed in the following chapters. The contributors focus on widely divergent geographic areas and bring their unique perspectives to the table. The final chapter was prepared by a scholar who was asked to evaluate the other contributions. Drawing from his personal research, Carlson re-centers the book on the topic of migration from the Subarctic to the Southwest, at the same time highlighting weaknesses, strengths, and new directions of the contributions, the book as a whole, and the endeavor of researching long-distance Athapaskan migrations and ethnogenesis.

As editor, I have attempted to include as many viewpoints as possible so that no matter the perspective, the content is of interest to a wide readership. Readers can dispute or extol the use of indigenous elder knowledge, or, on the opposite extreme, they can ponder the significance of empirical data, such as new DNA evidence or archaeological evidence of Apacheans in the southern Southwest in the 1300s. Methodological contributions and migration theory add to the breadth of the book, as does the extensive geographic coverage from Texas, New Mexico, Colorado, and Arizona, and then all the way to the Subarctic.

Many people believe that edited volumes should contain chapters that are in general agreement. I have not made that a requirement in this book; rather, I intend to show how varied the perspectives are with respect to approach chosen, theory applied, methods used, data brought to bear, and conclusions drawn. In essence, this is a reflection of the current pluralistic nature of our discipline, where questions revolve as much around how we justify knowledge claims and how we convey what we think we know as around the content of the issues being raised. Athapaskan studies, and studies of migration, culture change, and ethnogenesis, take many forms, and each has an important perspective to add to the very complex suite of problems. Not all problems are solved in this volume; rather, new approaches and fresh perspectives are presented and a host of new questions and possibilities are raised that set a new direction for Athapaskan studies and research into ethnogenesis and mobile group migration. This book can be viewed as a platform for learning and for acquiring new knowledge.

The content of this book provides a basis from which to embark on future research. Together these chapters move Athapaskan studies from a time when few archaeological data were available to the present, when data of a variety of types are appearing and converging and clashing at ever increasing rates, establishing a new baseline from which to work. This is important because many students are still taught that Athapaskans were not in the Southwest until the mid-1500s or later. Ethnohistorians—reliant on the written historic record—think Apacheans were not in the Southwest until after the 1680s. Students are unaware that many different signatures of Athapaskans have been defined. Cultural resource managers are largely unaware of these new findings and their identifiable signatures, which means sites are being missed and misidentified and their significance ineffectively evaluated. Many practitioners are unfamiliar with the notion that unlike more stationary groups, mobile groups with a common origin are likely to manifest in distinctive ways throughout the expansive geographic areas they inhabit and across the varied social landscapes they encounter. It is hoped that this book will instigate new debates and move research forward at an increased rate and with heightened precision.

Acknowledgments

I thank Reba Rauch for providing additional comments on my chapters. I am grateful to the volume reviewers for their candid comments, which on the whole improved the content, and to Keren Rice who oversaw the use of Athapaskan fonts. Most importantly, I want to express appreciation to all the contributing authors, whose chapters made this book possible.

Notes

1. As Carlson has pointed out, the Subarctic is not really a land of "ever winter" and neither is the Arctic or Siberia, for that matter. Even during the Pleistocene the summers warmed up considerably. Carlson (personal communication 2009) suggests that "the land of ever winter" is derived from an Athapaskan myth but does not reflect reality at the time of the Athapaskan migrations considered in this book. It likely survived in traditional stories because of its "rich descriptive imagery," consistent with places of importance being given "handsomely drafted names—bold, visual, evocative" (see Basso 1996:23). In some ways it illustrates a point I make in Chapter 17 about place names, remembrances of the landscape, and the ability to transfer these memories to new locations.
2. Many, including myself and Brugge (personal communication 2009), believe Gileño was an overarching label applied by the Spanish to a number of different Apachean groups that resided north of the Gila River, although I think de Reuse's linguistic data are intriguing.

References

Basso, Keith H.
1996 *Wisdom Sits in Places: Landscape and Language among the Western Apache*. Albuquerque: University of New Mexico Press.
Brown, Gary M.
1991 *Archaeological Data Recovery at San Juan Coal Company's La Plata Mine, San Juan County, New Mexico*. Technical Report No. 355. Albuquerque: Mariah Associates.

1996   The Protohistoric Transition in the Northern San Juan Region. In *The Archaeology of Navajo Origins*, edited by Ronald H. Towner, pp. 47–69. Salt Lake City: University of Utah Press.

1998   The Transition from Prehistory to History in the Mimbres Region. Paper presented at the conference "The Transition from Prehistory to History in the Southwest,", Albuquerque, New Mexico.

Brown Gary M., and Pat M. Hancock

1992   The Dinetah Phase in the La Plata Valley. In *Cultural Diversity and Adaptation: The Archaic, Anasazi, and Navajo Occupation of the Upper San Juan Basin*, edited by Lori S. Reed and Paul F. Reed, pp. 69–90. Cultural Resources Series No. 9. Santa Fe: New Mexico Bureau of Land Management.

Brugge, David M.

1993   Thoughts on the Significance of Navajo Traditions in View of the Newly Discovered Early Athabaskan Archaeology North of the San Juan River. In *Why Museums Collect: Papers in Honor of Joe Ben Wheat*, edited by Meliha S. Duran and David Kirkpatrick, pp. 31–38. Papers No. 19. Albuquerque: Archaeological Society of New Mexico.

Butler, Robert B.

1986   Prehistory of the Snake and Salmon River Area. In *Great Basin*, edited by Warren L. d'Azevedo, pp. 127–134. Handbook of North American Indians, Vol. 11, William C. Sturtevant, general editor. Washington, D.C.: Smithsonian Institution.

Cole, Donald C.

1981   An Ethnohistory of the Chiricahua Apache Indian Reservation, 1872–1876. Unpublished Ph.D. dissertation, University of New Mexico, Albuquerque.

1988   *The Chiricahua Apache: From War to Reservation, 1846–1876*. Albuquerque: University of New Mexico Press.

Farrer, Claire R.

1991   *Living Life's Circle: Mescalero Apache Cosmovision*. Albuquerque: University of New Mexico Press.

Forbes, Jack D.

1960   *Apache, Navaho, and Spaniard*. Norman: University of Oklahoma Press.

Gladwin, Harold S.

1957   *A History of the Ancient Southwest*. Portland, Maine: Bond Wheelwright Co.

Goss, James A.

1968   Culture-Historical Inference from Utaztekan Linguistic Evidence. In *Utaztekan Prehistory*, edited by Earl H. Swanson Jr., pp. 1–42. Occasional Papers No. 22. Pocatello: Idaho State University Museum.

Grayson, Donald K.

2011   *The Great Basin: A Natural Prehistory*. Berkeley and Los Angeles: University of California Press.

Gunnerson, Dolores A.

2006   *Apache History and Jicarilla Origins, 1525–1801*. Reprinted. Lincoln, Nebraska: J&L Lee Co.

Gunnerson, James H.

1960   *An Introduction to Plains Apache Archeology—The Dismal River Aspect*. Anthropological Papers No. 58, Bureau of American Ethnology Bulletin No. 173, pp. 131–260. Washington, D.C.: Smithsonian Institution.

Gunnerson, James H., and Dolores A. Gunnerson

1971   Apachean Culture: A Study in Unity and Diversity. In *Apachean Culture History and Ethnology*, edited by Keith H. Basso and Morris E. Opler, pp. 7–28. Anthropological Papers of the University of Arizona No. 21. Tucson: University of Arizona Press.

Hall, Edward T., Jr.
1944   Recent Clues to Athapascan Prehistory in the Southwest. *American Anthropologist* 46(1):98–105.

Haskell, J. Loring
1987   *Southern Athapaskan Migration, AD 200–1750*. Tsaile, Arizona: Navajo Community College Press.

Hester, James J.
1962   *Early Navajo Migrations and Acculturation in the Southwest*. Museum of New Mexico Papers in Anthropology No. 6. Santa Fe: Museum of New Mexico Press.

Huscher, Betty H., and Harold A. Huscher
1942   Athapascan Migration via the Intermountain Region. *American Antiquity* 8(1):80–88.
1943   The Hogan Builders of Colorado. *Southwestern Lore* 9(2):21–25.

Jennings, Jesse D.
1940   A Variation of Southwestern Pueblo Culture. *Laboratory of Anthropology, Technical Series* 10:1–11.

Keur, Dorothy L.
1941   *Big Bead Mesa: An Archaeological Study of Navaho Acculturation, 1745–1812*. Memoirs No. 1. Menasha, Wisconsin: Society for American Archaeology.

Lockwood, Frank C.
1938   *The Apache Indians*. New York: Macmillan.

McGhee, Robert
2008   Aboriginalism and the Problems of Indigenous Archaeology. *American Antiquity* 73(4):579–597.

Opler, Morris E.
1938   *Myths and Tales of the Jicarilla Apache Culture*. Memoirs No. 31. New York: American Folklore Society.
1942   *Myths and Tales of the Chiricahua Apache Indians*. Memoirs No. 37. New York: American Folklore Society.
1971a Pots, Apaches, and the Dismal River Culture Aspect. In *Apachean Culture History and Ethnology*, edited by Keith H. Basso and Morris E. Opler, pp. 29–33. Anthropological Papers of the University of Arizona No. 21. Tucson: University of Arizona Press.
1971b Jicarilla Apache Territory, Economy, and Society in 1850. *Southwestern Journal of Anthropology* 27(4):309–329.
1975   Review of "The Jicarilla Apaches: A Study in Survival," by Dolores H. Gunnerson. *Plains Anthropologist* 20(68):150–157.
1983   The Apachean Culture Pattern and Its Origins. In *Southwest*, edited by Alfonso Ortiz, pp. 368–392. Handbook of North American Indians, Vol. 10, William C. Sturtevant, general editor. Washington, D.C.: Smithsonian Institution.

Perry, Richard J.
1980   The Apachean Transition from the Subarctic to the Southwest. *Plains Anthropologist* 25 (90):279–296.
1983   Proto-Athapaskan Culture: The Use of Ethnographic Reconstruction. *American Ethnologist* 10(4):715–733.

Riley, Carroll L.
1954   Survey of Navajo Archaeology. *University of Colorado Studies in Anthropology, No. 4*, pp. 45–60.

Sapir, Edward
1936   Linguistic Evidence Suggestive of the Northern Origin of the Navaho. *American Anthropologist* 38(2):224–235.

Schaafsma, Curtis F.
1981   Early Apacheans in the Southwest: A Review. In *The Protohistoric Period in the North American Southwest, AD 1450–1700*, edited by David R. Wilcox and W. Bruce Masse, pp. 291–320. Anthropological Research Papers No. 24. Tempe: Arizona State University.

1996   Ethnic Identity and Protohistoric Archaeological Sites in Northwestern New Mexico: Implications for Reconstructions of Navajo and Ute History. In *The Archaeology of Navajo Origins*, edited by Ronald H. Towner, pp. 19–46. Salt Lake City: University of Utah Press.

2002   *Apaches de Navajo: Seventeenth-Century Navajos in the Chama Valley of New Mexico*. Salt Lake City: University of Utah Press.

Schroeder, Albert H.
1954   Transition to History in the Pueblo Southwest: Comments. *American Anthropologist* 56(4):597–599.

Seymour, Deni J.
2002   *Conquest and Concealment: After the El Paso Phase on Fort Bliss; An Archaeological Study of the Manso, Suma, and Early Apache*. With contributions by Mark E. Harlan and David V. Hill. Lone Mountain Report 525/528. Conservation Division, Directorate of the Environment, United States Army Air Defense, Artillery Center, Fort Bliss, Texas. Qualified researchers may obtain this document by contacting martha.yduarte@us.army.mil.

2003   *Protohistoric and Early Historic Temporal Resolution*. Conservation Division, Directorate of Environment, Fort Bliss. Lone Mountain Report 560-003. Qualified researchers may obtain this document by contacting martha.yduarte@us.army.mil.

2004a A Ranchería in the Gran Apachería: Evidence of Intercultural Interaction at the Cerro Rojo Site. *Plains Anthropologist* 49(190):153–192.

2004b Before the Spanish Chronicles: Early Apache in the Southern Southwest. In *Ancient and Historic Lifeways in North America's Rocky Mountains: Proceedings of the 2003 Rocky Mountain Anthropological Conference, Estes Park, Colorado*, edited by Robert H. Brunswig and William B. Butler, pp. 120–142. Greeley: Department of Anthropology, University of Northern Colorado.

2008a Apache Plain and Other Plainwares on Apache Sites in the Southern Southwest. In *Serendipity: Papers in Honor of Frances Joan Mathien*, edited by R. N. Wiseman, T. C. O'Laughlin, C. T. Snow, and C. Travis, pp. 163–186. Papers No. 34. Albuquerque: Archaeological Society of New Mexico.

2008b Despoblado or Athapaskan Heartland: A Methodological Perspective on Ancestral Apache Landscape Use in the Safford Area. In *Crossroads of the Southwest: Culture, Ethnicity, and Migration in Arizona's Safford Basin*, edited by David E. Purcell, pp. 121–162. New York: Cambridge Scholars Press.

2009   Comments on Genetic Data Relating to Athapaskan Migrations: Implications of the Malhi et al. Study for the Apache and Navajo. *American Journal of Physical Anthropology* 139(3):281–283.

Spencer, Katherine
1947   *Reflection of Social Life in the Navajo Origin Myth*. University of New Mexico Publications in Anthropology No. 3. Albuquerque: University of New Mexico Press.

Steward, Julian H.
1936   Pueblo Material Culture in Western Utah. *University of New Mexico Bulletin* 287, Anthropological Series, 1(3):1–64.

Underhill, Ruth M.
1956   *The Navajos*. Norman: University of Oklahoma Press.

Van Valkenburg, Richard F.
1938   *A Short History of the Navajo People*. U.S. Department of Interior. Window Rock, Arizona: Navajo Service.

Warburton, Miranda, and Richard M. Begay
2005   An Exploration of Navajo-Anasazi Relationships. *Ethnohistory* 52(3):533–561.

Wedel, Waldo R.
1940   Culture Sequences in the Central Great Plains. In *Essays in Historical Anthropology of North America*, edited by Julian Steward, pp. 291–352. Smithsonian Miscellaneous Collections Vol. 100. Washington, D.C.: Smithsonian Institution.

Wilcox, David R.
1981   The Entry of the Athabaskans into the American Southwest: The Problem Today. In *The Protohistoric Period in the American Southwest, AD 1450–1700*, edited by David R. Wilcox and W. Bruce Masse. Anthropological Research Papers No. 24. Tempe: Arizona State University.

Wilmeth, Roscoe
1977   Chilcotin Archaeology: The Direct Historical Approach. In *Problems in the Prehistory of the North American Subarctic: The Athapaskan Question*, edited by J. W. Helmes, S. Van Dyke, and F. J. Kense, pp. 97–101. Calgary, Alberta: University of Calgary Archaeological Association.

Wright, Gary A.
1984   *People of the High Country: Jackson Hole before the Settlers*. New York: Peter Lang.

CHAPTER 2

Apachean Archaeology of Rocky Mountain National Park, Colorado, and the Colorado Front Range

ROBERT H. BRUNSWIG

Plains Apaches (of the Athapaskan language family) are documented through ethnohistoric records as present in the eastern High Plains, western Great Plains, Southern Plains, and eastern periphery of the Southern Rocky Mountains from ca. AD 1650 to 1750 (see Brunswig 1995; Clark 1999; Gilmore and Larmore 2005; Gunnerson 1960, 1969, 1987; Kalasz et al. 1999; Scheiber 2006:141–148; Tucker et al. 2005; and Gilmore and Larmore, this volume). During that period the Apache shared eastern plains, foothills, and Front Range mountain landscapes with other protohistoric and early historic groups, predominantly eastern bands of the Ute tribe that had established long-term residence in the intermontane Colorado Rockies from as early as AD 1000 (see Brunswig 2005:86–94, 130–131; Brunswig, Diggs, and Montgomery 2009; Brunswig, McBeth, and Elinoff 2009; Brunswig and Sellet 2008a, 2008b, 2011). Apachean ceramics, primarily in the form of Dismal River and Ocate Micaceous types, including a western variant of Dismal River Lovitt Simple Stamped and Lovitt Plain subtypes (Brunswig 1995; see also Gilmore and Larmore 2005:7–9, 46–48 and this volume), have been identified at several sites within and along the eastern periphery of Colorado's Southern Rocky Mountains, including high-altitude camps (Lawn Lake/5LR318) in Rocky Mountain National Park and the Devil's Thumb Site (5BL6904) in the Indian Peaks Wilderness west of Boulder (see Brunswig 2001a; Kindig 2000).

Earliest historic references to Athapaskan-speaking, Apachean peoples in the eastern High Plains and mountains of Colorado date to the seventeenth and eighteenth centuries. Archaeological evidence suggests that Apachean groups arrived in Colorado's Front Range mountains and foothills two to three centuries earlier (Gilmore 2004; Kindig 2000:106). A currently well-accepted scenario for the ultimate presence of Athapaskan-speaking peoples in the American West and Southwest (ancestors of the historic Apache and Navajo) is that they arrived after a period of long-term migration of ancestral groups from western Canadian homelands starting between 800 and 1,000 years ago (Brunswig 1995; Magne and Matson 2004; Perry 1980; Seymour 2008 and Chapter 1, this volume).

Protohistoric Apachean sites in Colorado's High Plains and mountains have been, and continue to be, most frequently identified as culturally and technologically affiliated with the Dismal River culture by Colorado archaeologists, Dismal River having been initially defined at protohistoric sites in southwestern Nebraska (Brunswig 1995; Gilmore and Larmore 2005:4–9; Gunnerson 1987:114–115; Kindig 2000:106–107; Tucker et al. 2005). That affiliation, while questioned in some quarters (cf. Gulley 2000), remains the most logical link between sites in Colorado and the southern Great Plains believed associated with historic Apachean populations. However, scientifically affirming the connection will require a sustained research effort. Even earlier manifestations of Apachean groups in the western Great Plains, central Rockies, and southwestern Canada are believed by some archaeologists to be represented by the preceramic Avonlea culture (Brunswig 1995:172–173; Gilmore 2004; Gilmore and Larmore, this volume; Kehoe 1966:839; Wilcox 1988:273). For the most part, Apachean material culture, except for ceramics in northern Colorado, is difficult to distinguish from that of Ute and other contemporary cultural assemblages, all usually containing triangular side-notched and unnotched projectile point types and nondiagnostic lithic processing tools. Its chief distinguishing trait in northern Colorado, lacking other diagnostic criteria and given a relative lack of current efforts to establish additional archaeological criteria, is pottery (e.g., Lovitt Plain [western and eastern variants] and Lovitt Stamped types), first identified at Dismal River aspect sites in southwestern Nebraska (see Baugh and Eddy 1987; Brunswig 1995:176–188; Ellwood 2002:57–60; Gunnerson 1987: 114–115). Seymour (2004, 2009) has suggested a more holistic approach to archaeologically defining past cultural groups that uses landscape utilization patterns, lithic debitage patterning, and so on. However, that approach is still in the early stages of development in Colorado. In the northern portion of the Southern High Plains, pottery associated with historic Apache groups technologically influenced by close contact with late Pueblo populations in northeastern New Mexico includes Ocate Micaceous (early) and Cimarron Micaceous (late) types (Baugh and Eddy 1987:797; Brunswig 1995:180, 188–190; Ellwood 2002:60–65; Gunnerson 1969:26–27).

By the mid to late eighteenth century, Apache bands resident in the Great and Central Plains and Rocky Mountains were being pushed southward into the Southern High Plains and eastern Southwest by the expansion of Numic Comanche and Ute bands from the Northwest Plains (Comanche) and southern Rocky Mountains (Utes) (Brunswig 1995:175–176; Buckles 1968:56; Cassells 1997:239–240; Clark 1999:310). It is likely that northeastern Colorado Apache bands joined other Apache groups, members of the archaeologically defined Sangre de Cristo culture, who lived in the southern plains and river valleys of western Oklahoma, extreme southeastern Colorado, and northeastern New Mexico during and shortly after abandonment of Dismal River sites in southwest Nebraska and northeastern Colorado (Brunswig 1995:180; Kalasz et al. 1999:250–256). However, ethnohistoric evidence shows that Apache hunting and raiding parties continued to visit the Rocky Mountain National Park area from southern Colorado and northern New Mexico as late as the mid-nineteenth century, a fact documented by former Arapaho inhabitants who, on a visit to the park in 1914, described a running battle between Arapaho warriors and an Apache raiding party in 1845 (Toll 1962:17–18).

APACHEAN ARCHAEOLOGY IN ROCKY MOUNTAIN NATIONAL PARK

This chapter describes archaeological evidence for Apache occupations in Rocky Mountain National Park (RMNP). Before 1998, evidence of park Apachean occupations remained unidentified in museum collections and buried in unpublished archaeology records. However, a five-year (1998–2002) archaeological inventory and research project—a National Park Service–funded Systemwide Archeological Inventory Program (SAIP) project directed by the author (see Brunswig 2005)—provided the means to assess preexisting evidence and generate new field data on Apache occupations in the park. During SAIP, more than 30,000 acres were surveyed in all park environmental-ecological zones and more than a dozen sites of different cultural periods were excavated. The Apache, along with ancestors of the modern Ute tribe, were among the earliest historically and archaeologically documented Native American groups in the north-central Colorado Rocky Mountains. During the RMNP SAIP project, only a single site with new evidence of Apachean cultural affiliation, Lawn Lake/5LR318, was uncovered. Lawn Lake contained ceramics in stratified contexts whose typological and physical traits were consistent with ones that I previously proposed as a western Dismal River variant type (Brunswig 1995:182–188). Further, my research in the RMNP museum documented the existence of five previously known and surface-collected sites with undoubted eastern Dismal River pottery, indicative of late prehistoric through early historic Apachean cultural components or, minimally, evidence of contact with Apachean populations: 5LR2 (Forest Canyon Pass), 5LR4 (Mummy Pass), 5LR6 (Flattop Game Drive), 5LR12 (Old Man Mountain), and 5LR90. Locations of those sites, along with other temporally associated (contemporary) protohistoric/early historic cultural affiliation components (e.g., Ute and Puebloan), are shown in Figure 2.1.

The Lawn Lake Site

Lawn Lake (5LR318), Rocky Mountain National Park's only excavated site with a stratified Apachean occupation, is situated on the east bank of Roaring River immediately below its headwater outlet from Lawn Lake, a glacial cirque lake (see Figure 2.1). Lawn Lake lies within the subalpine forest zone with easy access to nearby alpine tundra grassland used by seasonally migrating game (e.g., elk,

FIGURE 2.1. Sites in Rocky Mountain National Park with latest late prehistoric, protohistoric, and early historic components (as defined by ceramic types) associated with historically documented tribes. Image by Robert Brunswig.

bighorn sheep) (Brunswig 2001a). The Lawn Lake Site, excavated by the University of North Colorado (UNC) during SAIP, was found to contain stratified Paleoindian, early archaic, middle archaic, early ceramic, and terminal late prehistoric/protohistoric occupations, each representing short-term hunting camp visits over 9,000 years. Before UNC's excavation, evidence of a Ute cultural component, identified by Ute Uncompahgre Brownware pottery, was recovered from the site's surface during an early reconnaissance survey.

Lawn Lake's Apachean camp component, believed to represent a summer high-altitude hunting camp, included 18 potsherds that I identified through physical and microscopic analysis as a western variant of the Dismal River Lovitt Plain type (Brunswig 1995:182–188). Lawn Lake's Apachean ceramics included several rim sherds from open-mouth, semi-globular vessels with excurvate rims and rounded to subrounded lips (see Figure 2.2). Exterior surfaces of the Lawn Lake sherds and Apachean sherds analyzed from other park sites nearly always exhibit scraping tool marks with evidence of smoothing associated with vessel thinning. Light fingertip indentations from molding the wet clay are often visible on interior surfaces. Paste temper of Lawn Lake and other park sites' Dismal River sherds universally consisted of medium to fine quartz sand with small to medium amounts of fine to medium-size muscovite mica flecks.

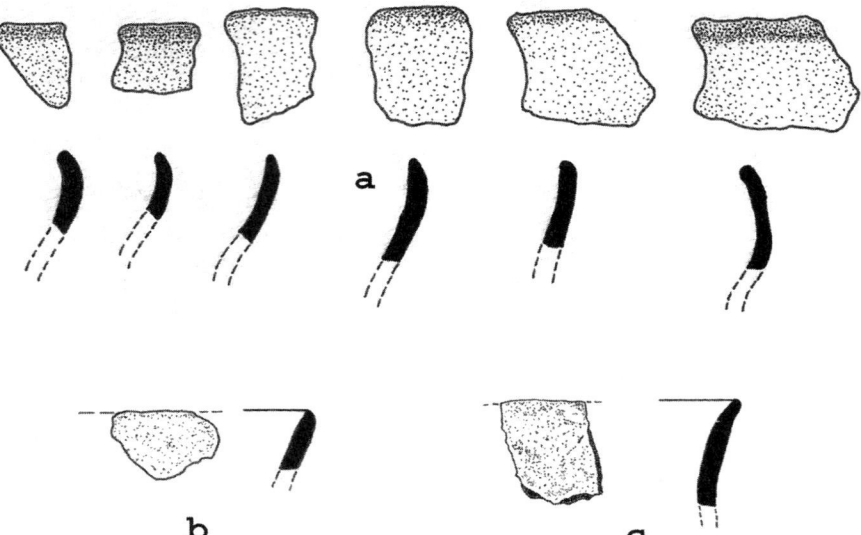

FIGURE 2.2. Dismal River (Apachean) and Uncompahgre Brown (Ute) rim sherd illustrations from sites 5LR318 (a), 5LR9826 (b), and 5LR10,216 (c), Rocky Mountain National Park, Colorado. Image by Robert Brunswig.

At this point, it should be noted that misidentification of pottery from the region's other contemporary, ceramic-using cultural tradition, the Ute, as Apachean pottery is unlikely. I have worked with and analyzed Ute pottery, known as Uncompahgre Brownware, for more than a decade, and from 2007 to 2010 I was engaged in excavation of a late prehistoric/protohistoric hunting camp with Uncompahgre Brown ceramics in North Park Valley, northwest of Rocky Mountain National Park. Although Dismal River and Ute vessels are morphologically similar (open-mouth jars with slightly pointed to rounded bases), their technical and manufacturing traits are significantly different (Brunswig 1995; Brunswig and Sellet 2011; Reed 2003; Reed and Carpenter 2010). Ute pottery is coil-built with coil lines pinched closed with fingertip and fingernail (and sometimes blunt tool) indentation; then exterior and interior surfaces were partially obliterated by wiping. Apachean pottery is nearly always built through molding and accretion, sometimes by adding clay slabs, then thinning and shaping with a wood or bone paddle and scraping. Temper inclusions are noticeably different in the two traditions. Ute pottery temper is typically sand with smaller amounts of granite and/or biotite and, in the case of the North Park examples, small amounts of local shale. Mica temper, whether natural or intentionally added, is a common Apachean ceramic trait but absent in Ute pottery.

Charcoal residue embedded in the exterior pores of one of the Lawn Lake sherds was extracted and radiocarbon-dated to 540 ± 50 rcybp (uncalibrated) (AD 1310–1510) (Beta-144870, 2σ), an early date for either the Lovitt Stamped or Plain ceramic subtype, given that most Southwest Nebraska Dismal River site chronologies, based primarily on tree-ring dating of pit house post timbers, place their time ranges between AD 1525 and 1725 (Brunswig 1995:177; 2001a:80–83; Gunnerson 1960; O'Brien 1984).

Other information from the Lawn Lake Apache occupation comes from source analysis of its lithic assemblage. That analysis revealed not only that its tools and waste flakes (debitage) showed evidence of extensive retooling of weapons and game-processing tools, but that three-quarters of its tool and waste-flake materials were locally obtained from adjacent, western interior montane valleys of North Park and Middle Park to the west (Brunswig 2001a:76). Seventy-four percent of lithic materials were regionally local Kremmling chert (41 percent) and Table Mountain jasper (23 percent). Thirteen percent came from unidentified sources (possibly the Colorado Front Range foothills and eastern plains) while the final 6 percent was from south-central Wyoming (Hartville chert and Spanish Diggings chert and quartzite). Heavy emphasis on interior mountain basin sources suggests Lawn Lake Apache bands either traveled west for their tool materials or, alternatively, traded with contemporary Ute bands that occupied North Park and Middle Park to the west and northwest and even today consider those areas traditional lands (Brunswig, McBeth, and Elinoff 2009; Brunswig, Diggs, and Montgomery 2009; Brunswig 2011; Brunswig and Sellet 2011).

Forest Canyon Pass, Old Man Mountain, Flattop Game Drive, and 5LR612 Sites

The Forest Canyon Pass site (5LR2) is a series of closely spaced camps in upper subalpine forest and subalpine-alpine ecotone. It is located on either side of the Ute Trail, which, as we know from associated archaeological finds, has been used by Native Americans to cross the Continental Divide for more than 9,000 years (Brunswig 2001b:49–50; Brunswig, Doerner et al. 2009; Mayer 1989). Hundreds of artifacts, including ceramics, have been collected from the site, representing Paleoindian through early historic cultural components. Ceramics from Forest Canyon Pass, curated in the park museum, include one Lovitt Stamped and four Lovitt Plain body sherds, evidence that early Apache were present on the pass and trail. Analysis of the Apache pottery showed that it had traits identical to Lovitt Stamped and Lovitt Plain sherds I have examined from Nebraska Dismal River sites, including the White Cat Village (25HN37) type site. Its presence in the park suggests visits of *eastern* Apachean groups to the area or may reflect the possibility that the pottery was acquired through trade between eastern Dismal River populations and locally indigenous Apachean bands or even regionally resident non-Apachean groups such as the Ute, now known to have inhabited the Southern Rockies at the same time (Brunswig, Diggs, and Montgomery 2009; Brunswig, McBeth, and Elinoff 2009; on early Ute habitation in the Southern Rockies, see Brunswig and Sellet 2008a, 2008b). The possibility of "imported" Apachean ceramics, if they were not locally produced, deriving from trade with local Colorado Front Range non-Apachean groups is considered less likely since the primary locally resident cultural group, the Ute, as noted above, produced its own ceramics and Apachean and Ute ceramics have not (yet) been documented together. That fact, while not ruling out trade, does, in my estimation, mitigate the trade origin hypothesis pending new discoveries. Analysis of six Forest Canyon Pass body sherds and one rim sherd curated in the park museum confirmed that they belonged to the Apachean Ocate Micaceous type, common to the south-central High Plains and northeastern New Mexico. The presence of Ocate Micaceous ceramics in the park shows a cultural connection to southern Colorado and northern New Mexico, possibly via trade with plains- and foothills-dwelling Dismal River Apache bands.

Old Man Mountain (5LR12) is located in a protected cleft and rock overhang on a granite massif outcrop in montane forest on the park's eastern boundary, immediately west of Estes Park (see Figure 2.1). Over several decades, the site has produced surface finds of several ceramic types, including Dismal River (Lovitt Plain) pottery (Benedict 1985:16–22), a fact supported by my physical and microscopic analysis of park museum specimens (Brunswig 2005:132, 212–213). Old Man Mountain served as a prehistoric through historic period camp since at least early archaic times (ca. 6,000 rcybp) and as a sacred site and landmark (for vision quest) since the early historic period (Benedict 1985: 32–33).

Flattop Game Drive (5LR6) is a large alpine mountain ridge flanked by steep canyons or steeply plunging mountain slopes on its southern and northern sides (see Figure 2.1 for its location in the park). A prehistoric trail passes through the site from lower-elevation camps on its lower northern slope, and after crossing the site from east to west, it traverses the Continental Divide into the park's western Kawunechee Valley. While most of 5LR6 lies in alpine tundra, its eastern end, which includes a small game-processing camp area, is located in tundra-subalpine ecotone. Several game drive lines (e.g., rock cairn lines and rock-walled game blinds) dated by lichenometry and radiocarbon dating over several thousand years have been mapped on more open areas of the mountain, and some game blinds are located in boulder fields, which served as natural hunting trap localities. Projectile points and ceramics recovered from 5LR6 over several decades show that it served as a hunting territory and hosted a section of a cross-continental major trail network used from late Paleoindian through early historic times (Benedict 1996:21–75; Brunswig 2005:280–287; Doerner and Brunswig 2008). Mica-tempered sherds recovered from the site by University of Denver graduate student Mary Yelm in the 1930s were described as having traits now known to be consistent with Dismal River ceramic types (see Benedict 1996:56–57; Brunswig 2005:196; Yelm 1935:94, 96–97, Table 8-D). Unfortunately, although catalogued information on Yelm's sherd collection from the site was absent from the park museum files, my examination of pottery curated in the museum and individually tagged as having come from Flattop Mountain's mid-northern slope, and possibly Yelm's "missing" pottery, led to their identification as western Dismal River Lovitt Plain ceramics. It is important to note that Ute pottery sherds (Uncompahgre Brownware), chronologically contemporary with Apachean park ceramics, were also found in the museum's Flattop Game Drive artifact collection.

Two other RMNP sites, 5LR4 (Mummy Pass) and 5LR90 (Specimen Mountain) (see Figure 2.1), also yielded Dismal River Lovitt Plain body sherds from park museum collections. Mummy Pass, located in alpine tundra in the park's extreme north, is situated on a major Native American trail and pass associated with several well-documented high-altitude hunting camps dating from late Paleoindian through early historic times (Benedict 1996:56–57; Brunswig 2005:196; Yelm 1935:94, 96–97). Ute ceramics recovered from a rockshelter (5LR10216) 1 km north of 5LR4 provided a carbon-residue AMS radiocarbon date of 200 ± 40 rcybp (AD 1670–1830, 2σ) (Beta-10216) (Brunswig 2002:56–57, 2005:216).

OTHER RECENTLY DISCOVERED APACHE SITES IN THE COLORADO FRONT RANGE

Recent research in the Colorado Front Range has identified four other sites with western Dismal River pottery belonging to the Lovitt type series (Lovitt Plain and Lovitt Stamped) and with chronometric dates equally as early as that provided by the abovementioned Lawn Lake sherd (see Gilmore and Larmore 2005; Kindig 2000, 2003; Tucker et al. 2003, 2005:18–19).

Devil's Thumb Trail

In the late 1990s, surveys led by Jim Benedict of the Center for Mountain Archeology (Ward, Colorado) documented an Apache occupation at the Devil's Thumb Trail site (5BL6904) in the Indian Peak's Wilderness, south of Rocky Mountain National Park (Figure 2.3). Test excavations at Devil's Thumb Trail, located in the upper subalpine environmental zone, produced tool-marked rim sherds of the Lovitt Plain type. AMS radiocarbon-dating of hearth wood charcoal associated with the pottery yielded a date of 350 ± 50 rcybp (AD 1500–1700, 2σ) (AA-22853) (Kindig 2000:99–107).

At this point, it should be noted that wood charcoal–based radiocarbon dates associated with high mountain camps such as the Devil's Thumb site, and those described below, *may* reflect unduly old dates based in what is referred to as the "old wood" problem (e.g., the burning of dried wood left lying on the surface for decades if not centuries) (see Baker et al. 2007; Schiffer 1986). However, I contend that "old wood" is less of an issue in Colorado's Rocky Mountains than in the lower-elevation, lower-moisture, more arid climatic conditions of the American Southwest, where "old wood" is considered particularly troublesome. In my experience in survey and excavation in the Colorado Rockies, I have observed highly limited and relatively short-term preservation of wood due to exposure to extreme mountain elements, in which freeze-thaw conditions, water saturation of wood from burial in winter snowbanks, frequent fires, and exposure to high solar radiation rapidly destroy most surface wood.

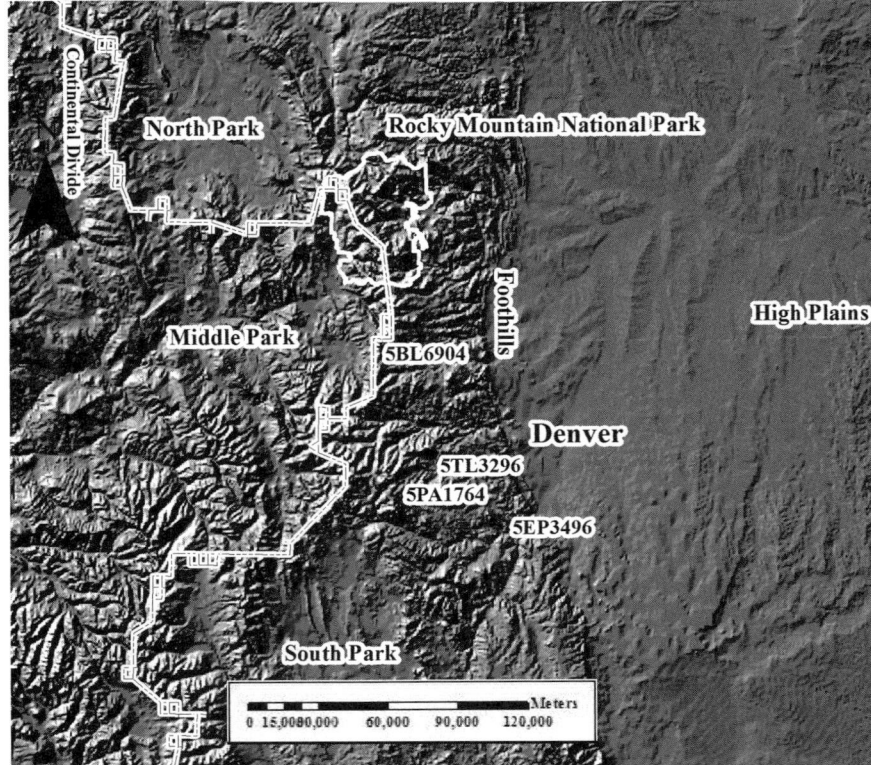

FIGURE 2.3. Locations of recently documented Apachean occupation sites with Dismal River ceramics south of Rocky Mountain National Park. Image by Robert Brunswig.

Eureka Ridge and Pinnacle Sites

Farther south in the lower montane zone, between the great interior basin valley of South Park and the Front Range foothills southwest of Denver, are two small campsites with Dismal River ceramics, discovered between 2002 and 2004 (see Figure 2.3). Pottery recovered from one site, Eureka Ridge (5TL3296), ~500 sherds, was identified as belonging to Dismal River Lovitt Plain and Lovitt Stamped types (Gilmore and Larmore 2005 and this volume). Organic (wood charcoal) residue from three pulverized Lovitt Plain and Lovitt Stamped sherds was extracted and AMS radiocarbon-dated at 305 ± 30 rcybp (AD 1585–1705) (Beta-AA-60679, 2σ), 410 ± 30 rcybp (AD 1480–1600) (Beta-187965, 2σ), and 460 ± 40 rcybp (AD 1430–1550) (Beta-187966, 2σ) (Gilmore and Larmore 2005: 8, 39–49, Table 2). Much of the site's lithic assemblage was sourced to known quarry and geological outcrops in nearby South Park (Trout Creek jasper and silicified wood). However, material identified as Kremmling chert could have come from as far away as North Park and South Park, although Kremmling chert-like materials have also been identified in natural cobbles and partial cores occurring on South Park sites (see Lincoln et al. 2003). Long-distance transport or trade of obsidian found at the site is indicated by the presence of obsidian geochemically (XRF) sourced to the Jemez Mountains of north-central New Mexico, 150 miles to the south.

The recently excavated Pinnacle site (5PA1764) is located in the Front Range mountains west of Denver, less than 20 miles from the Eureka Ridge site (Tucker et al. 2003, 2005). Pinnacle is a small open camp with multiple hearths and more than 20 sherds identified as belonging to the Western Dismal River Lovitt Plains subtype (Ellwood 2003; Tucker et al. 2005:14).

Radiocarbon and thermoluminescence analyses of hearth charcoal and fired hearth rock at Pinnacle resulted in early Apachean era occupation dates. Wood charcoal from one feature (No. 2) returned an AMS date of 470 ± 60 rcybp (AD 1400–1560) (Beta-172328, 2σ) (Tucker et al. 2003:43–44, Appendix B; Tucker et al. 2005). Blue-light optically stimulated luminescence (Blue OSL) dating of quartz heated in a second hearth (No. 1) containing 12 Dismal River sherds resulted in an interpreted date range of AD 1354–1496 (central date of AD 1425) (Tucker et al. 2005:14). Lithic materials from Pinnacle, like those at Eureka Ridge, came from largely local sources, primarily from South Park (Trout Creek jasper, silicified chert) and the Front Range foothills (Dakota quartzite). Recovery of obsidian sourced to Obsidian Cliff (Yellowstone National Park, Wyoming), 500 miles to the northwest, however, denotes yet another case of Apache-associated long-distance trade contacts, possibly through intermontane tribal intermediaries such as the Ute, in this case with more westerly, interior central Rocky Mountain populations. Alternatively, the presence of Yellowstone obsidian at Pinnacle could be interpreted as suggesting the site was more directly associated with another regional interior population, the Ute, who traded it to the Apache for other products. Yellowstone obsidian is documented in prehistoric Ute occupation levels at the earlier-noted North Park Valley site 5JA421, a site that contains Ute pottery with possible Southwest or even eastern Great Basin ceramic traits in the form of braided handles (see Brunswig and Sellet 2008a, 2008b, 2011).

The Borman–Pikes Peak Vessel

A final example of a recent Apachean find comes not from archaeological site documentation but from the discovery of a complete Dismal River (western variant) pot (5EP3496) by a nonarchaeologist (Sheila Borman) on the slopes of Pikes Peak, west of Colorado Springs (Figure 2.3). Existence of the vessel, identified as a Western Dismal River type variant (e.g., western Lovitt Plain), was reported by archaeological ceramicist Priscilla Ellwood (see Ellwood 2006, 2010; Gilmore and Larmore 2005:Table 2; Tucker et al. 2005:19, Table 1). Significance of the Pikes Peak vessel lies less in its technical traits and more in the fact that AMS dating of its surface embedded-carbon residue provides another early Dismal River ceramic radiocarbon date of 470 ± 40 rcybp (AD 1400–1560) (Beta-155784, 2σ).

Conclusion

A growing body of evidence suggests that Apachean occupations in Colorado's Front Range mountains and foothills were more common and earlier in date than previously believed. The greatest known "concentration" of latest late prehistoric and protohistoric Apachean sites, although still small in number, occurs in Rocky Mountain National Park in the form of small campsites focused on hunting and transit (trails and passes) and ranging from lower montane to upper subalpine environmental zones. Chronometric dates, mainly from ceramic wood carbon residues, vary from as early as 540 rcybp (AD 1410) to as late as 350 rcybp (AD 1600). As noted by Gilmore and Larmore (2005:54–58; this volume) and Kindig (2000:107), Colorado's Apachean chronology appears as much as two centuries earlier than Dismal River sites along the more easterly boundary of the High Plains and Great Plains in Nebraska. Gilmore and Larmore (2005: 54–58; this volume) have posited that ceramic-using Apachean populations may in fact be proto-Apache/proto–Dismal River in nature and progenitors of the later village-based Dismal River communities of southwest Nebraska.

In 1995 I suggested that "there is very limited and largely circumstantial evidence of a Late Prehistoric, ca. AD 1300–1550, aceramic and ceramic Apachean presence in Colorado Eastern Plains and foothills" (Brunswig 1995:175). What I did not anticipate was that new evidence for those earliest occupations would come first and foremost from Colorado's Front Range mountains, including high-altitude localities in excess of 10,000 feet. It is significant that emerging archaeological evidence for these early Colorado Apache hunter-gatherers frequently occurs along important trail and pass corridors and is associated with what are interpreted as seasonal (summer) hunting camps, occupied as part of seasonal migratory visits to the mountain areas where they are found. It is also suggested that seasonal (?) Apache visitors to Front Range hunting territories regularly interacted (peacefully or in competition) with other tribal groups, most importantly with the Ute, who consider the region's mountains one of their traditional homelands. Recent fieldwork in both Rocky Mountain National Park and the adjacent interior North Park basin valley supports the presence of prehistoric Ute bands that practiced a seasonal transhumant subsistence pattern associated with high summer hunting in park alpine areas and early spring, late summer, fall, and winter occupation of basin valley sites starting as early as AD 1100 (Brunswig, McBeth, and Elinoff 2009; Brunswig, Diggs, and Montgomery 2009; Brunswig 2011; Brunswig and Sellet 2011).

Prehistoric Ute bands now appear to have been preceramic until ca. AD 1250 to 1350, when Uncompahgre Brownware pottery appears at both high mountain summer camps and lower-elevation interior mountain valley sites. At present, we have no evidence of Apachean (Dismal River or other micaceous wares) west of the Continental Divide in the north-central Colorado Rockies, only east of, and along, the divide. With emerging evidence of Apachean ceramics in the Colorado Front Range between AD 1400 and 1500, it is proposed that Ute and

Apache ancestral bands maintained a wary but functional relationship for seasonally exploiting high-altitude animal and plant resources during summer months in Rocky Mountain National Park but largely restricted their respective cool-season residences to western (Ute) and eastern (Apache) slopes of the Continental Divide.

It was only after ca. AD 1725, with the southeastward migration of another Ute-related Numic group, the Shoshonean Comanche, that the Apache-Ute balance was broken and Apache hunting bands were forced out of the mountains and into the southern plains by an expanding Ute-Comanche coalition (Clark 1999:310). This scenario is similar to Gilmore and Larmore's statement (this volume) that the Apache were probably forced out of the highlands by the encroaching Numic-speaking groups ca. 1500 (see Figure 3.20), and then again off the Central Plains ca. 1725 (Figure 3.21) by continued encroachment by Numic speakers. What is less evident are the types of interactions that occurred between the two cultural populations. Almost certainly trade happened to some degree. Archaeological research in North Park has provided abundant evidence of obsidian from nearly every known source in the western United States (New Mexico, Idaho, Utah, Wyoming) in our late prehistoric/early protohistoric Ute site. Unfortunately, we know very little about the presence or sources of obsidian from known Colorado Apachean sites. We do know that obsidian sourced to Cerro del Medio (northern New Mexico) was recovered from the Eureka Ridge site (South Park) discussed earlier and in Gilmore and Larmore (this volume). Obsidian from Yellowstone's Obsidian Cliff is found at our North Park Ute site and has been identified at Dismal River sites in southeast Wyoming (Reher and Kunselman 1990; Scheiber 2006:148). What is unclear is whether obsidian from a recently discovered source in Rocky Mountain National Park (La Poudre Pass) was known to the Apache or, if not, was traded to them by North Park Utes, who were well aware of its existence (Brunswig and Sellet 2011). We are also unclear about other forms of interaction that may have taken place between the two groups, such as technological and stylistic transfer and co-influence related to late prehistoric/protohistoric Apache and Ute ceramic types. Hill (this volume) has suggested that Apachean affiliation of ceramic types such as Dismal River or the southern micaceous wares was less than certain, given variability in raw materials available to mobile hunter-gatherer populations (i.e., the western early Apache [Dismal River]), the technological and stylistic influence of associated Formative cultures (the Plains Caddo and Ancestral Pueblo), and the acquisition of pottery through trade. Historic Apache affiliation with earlier Dismal River and southern micaceous types is based on a reasonable body of archaeological and ethnohistoric evidence but is not yet fully definitive.

Over time, we need to systematically expand efforts to untangle the complex web of different Front Range Native American populations in the latest prehistoric and historic periods and better understand their dynamics and histories of cultural interaction. A first step should be increased emphasis on ceramic analysis, including petrographic and chemical source analysis of clays and temper inclusions, to better determine the geographic origins of pottery types we associate with early Athapaskan populations of the Colorado Rockies, foothills, and plains. This book, with its varied new data sets and working models of Athapaskan migration, archaeological and cultural inventories (artifacts, features, architecture), and ecological-behavioral systems, is part of a solid foundation for future research.

References

Baker, Steven G., Jeffrey S. Dean, and Ronald H. Towner
2007 Rewriting the Prehistory of Western Colorado? The Old Wood Calibration Project. Draft of a progress report prepared for the 2007 Annual Meeting of the Colorado Council of Professional Archaeologists, Glenwood Springs, Colorado.

Baugh, Timothy, and F. W. Eddy
1987 Rethinking Apachean Ceramics: The 1985 Southern Athapaskan Ceramics Conference. *American Antiquity* 52(4):793–799.

Benedict, James B.
1985 *Old Man Mountain: A Vision Quest Site in the Colorado High Country*. Research Report No. 4. Ward, Colorado: Center for Mountain Archeology.
1996 *The Game Drives of Rocky Mountain National Park*. Research Report No. 7. Ward, Colorado: Center for Mountain Archeology.

Brunswig, Robert H., Jr.
1995 Apachean Ceramics East of Colorado's Continental Divide: Current Data and New Directions. In *Archaeological Pottery of Colorado: Ceramic Clues to the Prehistoric and Protohistoric Lives of the State's Native Peoples*, edited by Robert H. Brunswig, B. Bradley, and S. M. Chandler, pp. 172–207. Occasional Papers No. 2. Denver: Colorado Council of Professional Archaeologists.
2001a *Lawn Lake (5LR318): Results of an Archeological Mitigation Research Project at a High Altitude Prehistoric Site in Rocky Mountain National Park*. Report to Rocky Mountain National Park, National Park Service, Estes Park. Greeley: Department of Anthropology, University of Northern Colorado.
2001b *Report on 2000 Archaeological Surveys in Rocky Mountain National Park by the University of Northern Colorado*. SAIP Report to Rocky Mountain National Park, National Park Service, Estes Park. Greeley: Department of Anthropology, University of Northern Colorado.
2002 *Report on 2001 Field Investigations of the University of Northern Colorado to the State Archaeologist, Colorado State Historic Preservation Office*. SAIP Report to Rocky Mountain National Park, National Park Service, Estes Park. Greeley: Department of Anthropology, University of Northern Colorado.
2005 *Prehistoric, Protohistoric, and Early Historic Native American Archeology of Rocky Mountain National Park: Final Report of Systemwide Archeological Inventory Program Investigations by the University of Northern Colorado (1998–2002)*. Greeley: Department of Anthropology, University of Northern Colorado.
2011 The Numic Expansion and Colorado's Southern Rockies: The View from North Park Valley and Rocky Mountain National Park. Paper presented at the 76th Annual Meeting of the Society for American Archaeology, Sacramento.

Brunswig, Robert H., Jr., Bruce Bradley, and Susan M. Chandler
1995 *Archaeological Pottery of Colorado: Ceramic Clues to the Prehistoric and Protohistoric Lives of the State's Native Peoples.* Occasional Papers No. 2. Denver: Colorado Council of Professional Archaeologists.

Brunswig, Robert H., D. Diggs, and C. Montgomery
2009 *Native American Lives and Sacred Landscapes in Rocky Mountain National Park: Report to Rocky Mountain National Park, National Park Service.* Greeley: Anthropology Program, University of Northern Colorado.

Brunswig, Robert H., J. Doerner, D. Diggs, J. Connor, L. Benton, and K. Edwards
2009 *Report on a Pilot Study for Investigations into Cultural-Natural Landscapes and Ecological Patch Islands in Forest Canyon Pass, Rocky Mountain National Park.* Report to the National Park Service. Greeley: Anthropology Program, University of Northern Colorado.

Brunswig, Robert H., S. McBeth, and L. Elinoff
2009 Re-enfranchising Native Peoples in the Southern Rocky Mountains: Integrated Contributions of Archaeological and Ethnographic Studies on Federal Lands. In *Post-colonial Perspectives in Archaeology*, edited by Peter Bikoulis, D. Lacroix, and M. Pueramaki-Brown, pp. 55–69. Calgary, Alberta: Chacmool Archaeological Association.

Brunswig, Robert H., and F. Sellet
2008a *2007 Archaeological Investigations at 5JA421, 5JA1475 (Pederson Ridge), 5JA1804, and 5JA1805 in North Park, Colorado: Report to the Bureau of Land Management, Kremmling Field Office.* Greeley: Anthropology Program, University of Northern Colorado.
2008b *Preliminary Report on 2008 Archaeological Research at 5JA421, 5JA1183, 5JA1808 (Ballinger Draw Fen) and 5JA1805 in North Park, Colorado: Report to the Colorado State Historical Fund and Bureau of Land Management, Kremmling Field Office.* Greeley: Anthropology Program, University of Northern Colorado.
2011 *Final Report on 2009 Archaeological and Supporting Studies Research at 5JA421 and the Upper Ballinger Draw Valley, North Park, Colorado: Report to the Colorado State Historical Fund and the Bureau of Land Management, Kremmling District.* Greeley: Department of Anthropology, University of Northern Colorado.

Buckles, William G.
1968 Archaeology in Colorado: Historic Tribes. *Southwestern Lore* 34(3):53–67.

Cassells, E. Steve
1997 *The Archaeology of Colorado.* Boulder, Colorado: Johnson Books.

Clague, John, S. G. Evans, V. N. Rampton, and G. J. Woodsworth
1995 Improved Age Estimates for the White River and Bridge River Tephras, Western Canada. *Canadian Journal of Earth Sciences* 32:1172–1179.

Clark, Bonnie
1999 The Protohistoric Period. In *Colorado Prehistory: A Context for the Platte River Basin*, edited by Kevin P. Gilmore, Marcia Tate, Mark L. Chenault, Bonnie Clark, Terri McBride, and Margaret Wood, pp. 309–335. Denver: Colorado Council of Professional Archaeologists, Colorado Historical Society.

Doerner, James, and R. H. Brunswig
2008 *Modeling Paleoenvironmental and Archeological Landscapes on Ancient Game Drive Systems in Rocky Mountain National Park, North Central Colorado.* Greeley: Geography and Anthropology Programs, University of Northern Colorado.

Ellwood, Priscilla B.
2002 *Native American Ceramics of Eastern Colorado*. Natural History Inventory of Colorado No. 21. Boulder: University of Colorado Museum.
2003 Ceramic Analysis, Appendix B. In *The Pinnacle Site (5PA1764): Data Recovery Investigations at an Open Prehistoric Camp near Eleven Mile Canyon Reservoir, Park County, Colorado*, by Gordon C. Tucker Jr., M.J. Tate, and J.J. Fariello. Aurora, Colorado: Tate and Associates.
2006 Analysis of, and Investigations into, the Borman–Pikes Peak Whole Vessel (5EP 3496), El Paso County, Colorado. Document EP.CU.R4, on file at the Colorado State Archaeologist's Office, Denver. Boulder: University of Colorado Museum.
2010 Analysis of and Investigations into the Borman–Pikes Peak Whole Vessel (5EP3496), El Paso County, Colorado. *Southwestern Lore* 76(2):1–31.

Gilmore, Kevin P.
2004 Way Down upon the South Platte River: Southern Avonlea Manifestations in Colorado and a Population-Based Scenario for Athapaskan Migration. In *Ancient and Historic Lifeways in North America's Rocky Mountains: Proceedings of the 2003 Rocky Mountain Anthropological Conference, Estes Park, Colorado*, edited by Robert H. Brunswig and William B. Butler, pp. 146–167. Greeley: Department of Anthropology, University of Northern Colorado.

Gilmore, Kevin P., and Sean Larmore
2005 *Archaeology of the Eureka Ridge Site (5TL3296), Teller County, Colorado*. Submitted by RMC Consultants to the USDA Forest Service, Pike National Forest, Pueblo. On file at the Office of Archaeology and Historic Preservation, Denver, and the USDA Forest Service, Pueblo, Colorado. Lakewood, Colorado: RMC Consultants.

Gulley, Cara C.
2000 A Reanalysis of Dismal River Archaeology and Ceramic Typology. Unpublished Master's thesis, Department of Anthropology, University of Colorado, Boulder.

Gunnerson, James H.
1960 *An Introduction to Plains Apache Archeology—The Dismal River Aspect*. Anthropological Papers No. 58, Bureau of American Ethnology Bulletin No. 173, pp. 131–260. Washington D.C.: Smithsonian Institution.
1969 Apache Archaeology in Northeastern New Mexico. *American Antiquity* 34(1): 23–39.
1987 *Archaeology of the High Plains*. Cultural Resource Series No. 19. Denver: Colorado State Office, U.S. Bureau of Land Management.

Kalasz, Stephen M., Mark Mitchell, and Christian J. Zier
1999 Late Prehistoric Stage. In *Colorado Prehistory: A Context for the Arkansas River Basin*, by Christian J. Zier and Stephen M. Kalasz, pp. 141–263. Denver: Colorado Council of Professional Archaeologists, Colorado Historical Society.

Kehoe, Thomas F.
1966 The Small Side-Notched Point System of the Northern Plains. *American Antiquity* 31(6):827–841.

Kindig, Jean Matthews
2000 Two Ceramic Sites in the Devil's Thumb Valley. In *This Land of Shining Mountains: Archeological Studies in Colorado's Indian Peaks Wilderness Area*, edited by E. Steve Cassells, pp. 95–123. Research Report No. 8. Ward, Colorado: Center for Mountain Archeology.

2003   Dendrochronological and Radiocarbon Dates for the Dismal River Aspect. Poster presented at the 6th Biennial Rocky Mountain Anthropological Conference, September 18–19, Estes Park, Colorado.

Lincoln, Thomas, E. Friedman, R. Brunswig, S. Bender, J. Della Salla, and J. Klawon
2003   *South Park Archaeology Project: Final Report of Archaeological Investigations Conducted in 2001 and 2002, South Park, Colorado, Report to the Colorado State Historic Fund.* Greeley: Department of Anthropology, University of Northern Colorado.

Magne, Martin, and R. G. Matson
2004   A New Look at the Intermontane Model of Athapaskan Migration. In *Ancient and Historic Lifeways of North America's Rocky Mountains: Proceedings of the 2003 Rocky Mountain Anthropological Conference*, edited by Robert H. Brunswig and W. B. Butler, pp. 38–64. Greeley: Department of Anthropology, University of Northern Colorado.

Mayer, Marie
1989   *Forest Canyon Pass, Rocky Mountain National Park, Larimer County, Colorado: A High Altitude Survey.* Denver: Colorado Archaeological Society.

O'Brien, Patricia J.
1984   *Archeology in Kansas.* Museum of Natural History Public Education Series No. 9. Lawrence: University Press of Kansas.

Perry, Richard J.
1980   The Apachean Transition from the Subarctic to the Southwest. *Plains Anthropologist* 25(90):279–296.

Reed, Lori Stephens
2003   *Ceramic Analysis Report on Prehistoric Pottery from Rocky Mountain National Park.* Farmington, New Mexico: Animas Ceramic Consulting.

Reed, Lori Stephens, and A. Carpenter
2010   *5JA421 Ceramic Analysis.* Farmington, New Mexico: Animas Ceramic Consulting.

Reher, Charles A., and Raymond Kunselman
1990   Obsidian Source Use in the High Plains of Southeastern Wyoming. Paper presented at the 48th Annual Plains Anthropological Conference, Oklahoma City.

Scheiber, Laura L.
2006   The Late Prehistoric on the High Plains of Western Kansas: High Plains Upper Republican and Dismal River. In *Kansas Archaeology*, edited by Robert J. Hoard and William E. Banks, pp. 133–150. Lawrence: University Press of Kansas.

Schiffer, Michael B.
1986   Radiocarbon Dating and the "Old Wood" Problem: The Case of the Hohokam Chronology. *Journal of Archaeological Science* 13(1):13–30.

Seymour, Deni J.
2004   A Ranchería in the Gran Apachería: Evidence of Intercultural Interaction at the Cerro Rojo Site. *Plains Anthropologist* 49(190):153–192.
2008   Despoblado or Athapaskan Heartland: A Methodological Perspective on Ancestral Apache Landscape Use in the Safford Area. In *Crossroads of the Southwest: Culture, Ethnicity, and Migration in Arizona's Safford Basin*, edited by David E. Purcell, pp. 121–162. New York: Cambridge Scholars Press.
2009   Distinctive Places, Suitable Spaces: Conceptualizing Mobile Group Occupational Duration and Landscape Use. *International Journal of Historical Archaeology* 13(3):255–281.

Toll, Oliver
1962   *Arapaho Names and Trails: A Report of a 1914 Pack Trip*. Privately printed. Reprinted. Estes Park, Colorado: Rocky Mountain Nature Association, 2003.

Tucker, Gordon C., Jr., Marcia J. Tate, Bill Tate, and Juston J. Fariello
2003   *The Pinnacle Site (5PA1764): Data Recovery Investigations at an Open Prehistoric Camp near Eleven Mile Canyon Reservoir, Park County, Colorado*. Aurora, Colorado: Tate and Associates.
2005   The Dismal River Complex in Eastern Colorado: A View from the Pinnacle Site (5PA1764). *Southwestern Lore* 71(2):1–31.

Wilcox, David R.
1988   Avonlea and Southern Athapascan Migrations. In *Avonlea Today: Archaeology and Prehistory*, edited by L. B. Davis, pp. 273–280. Saskatoon: Saskatchewan Archaeological Society.

Yelm, Mary
1935   Archaeological Survey of Rocky Mountain National Park–Eastern Foothill Districts. Master's thesis, Department of Anthropology, University of Denver, Denver, Colorado.

CHAPTER 3

Looking for Lovitt in All the Wrong Places

Migration Models and the Athapaskan Diaspora as Viewed from Eastern Colorado

KEVIN P. GILMORE AND SEAN LARMORE

The entry of Athapaskans into the American Southwest and Southern Plains is one of the few cases of undisputed migration in American archaeology (Wilcox 1981:213). The modern Navajo and Apache are descendants of people who began a series of migrations sometime before AD 1000 and eventually arrived in their modern homelands before AD 1550 (Brown 1996; Reed and Horn 1988, 1990). Abundant data support an Athapaskan diaspora, primarily the linguistic similarities between Southwest Apachean-speakers and Athapaskan-speakers from west-central Canada (Hoijer 1956). When and why Athapaskan people left their homeland in what is now northern Canada and interior Alaska, and what path they took on their journey south, has long been debated (Huscher and Huscher 1942; Opler 1983; Perry 1991; Schaafsma 1996; Schlesier 1994; Tweedie 1968; Wilcox 1988; Gordon, this volume). Athapaskan migration is incompletely understood because the physical evidence for it in the archaeological record appears to be minimal. However, recent discoveries at archaeological sites in the Southern Rocky Mountains and western High Plains of Colorado and Wyoming demonstrate a fourteenth- to fifteenth-century Athapaskan presence in this region; these sites reflect the traditional northern Athapaskan subsistence strategy of utilizing resources available in a broad range of elevation zones (Holmes 1975:101; Perry 1980). In this chapter we provide a brief overview of these new data in order to set the stage for a discussion of early migration patterns along Colorado's Front Range. (The context and material culture of these sites are explored in greater detail in Gilmore and Larmore 2005.)

Researchers have focused on three potential routes for Athapaskan migration through the western United States: an Intermountain route south through Colorado's Western Slope and Rocky Mountains (e.g., Brugge 1983; Huscher and Huscher 1942, 1943; Perry 1991; Steward 1937, 1940; Taylor 2004; Gordon, this volume); a route through the western High Plains (e.g., Dittert et al. 1961;

Gunnerson 1960; Gunnerson and Gunnerson 1971; Hester 1962; Keur 1941; Schaafsma 1996, 2002; Wedel 1940; Wilcox 1981); and a combination of both, arising from an early split into eastern and western proto-Apache north of Colorado (Haskell 1987). Gunnerson and Gunnerson (1971) suggested further that early Athapaskans diverted west into the San Luis Valley and then into northern New Mexico by way of the Rio Grande. Although the routes themselves have important archaeological implications, they are also associated with particular time frames. Supporters of an intermountain route generally advocate a pre–AD 1500 entry into the Southwest (Brugge 1984; Hogan 1989), based on the increasingly early dates obtained from the Dinetah region of north-central New Mexico and the presence by that time of material culture already well adapted to the Southwest (e.g., Brown and Hancock 1992; Reed and Horn 1988, 1990). Supporters of a High Plains route have advocated an entry into northeast New Mexico ca. AD 1540 and then west across the Continental Divide after ca. AD 1680 (e.g., Schaafsma 1996, 2002). We propose that a significant number of Athapaskans migrated along Colorado's Front Range and western Plains margin (Figure 3.1), a route that geographically splits the difference between the two previously proposed routes and also suggests a much earlier entry of Athapaskans into the Southwest.

Migration is rarely simple and unidirectional, and we believe that the migration of the proto-Apache was no different. To support our contention, we examine the existing archaeological record for clues regarding push and pull factors affecting proto-Apache migration, as well as what structure the migration might have taken. Our discussion of this migration follows the lead of Anthony (1990, 1992), who advocates the application of geographic and demographic models derived from the study of modern human population movement to the past (although there are differences in opinion in how appropriate it is to apply these models to highly mobile groups—see Seymour, Chapter 17 in this volume, for a contrasting view). He assumes that the behavioral processes that make up migration were the same in the past as they are in the present, and that migration can be understood as the movement of defined subgroups (often kin based) having specific goals, targeting known destinations, and likely using familiar routes (Anthony 1990:895–896). Anthony (1990) distinguishes between long-distance migration and the more common short-distance movements of individuals and small social groups within a local area, and he classifies different migration structures that should be identifiable through archaeological data. Using the terminology of his examples, we believe that evidence from Colorado's Front Range (above 8,000 ft, or 2,440 m, in elevation) supports chain migration, leapfrogging, and return migration.

To put Athapaskan migration in context, we examine the cultural, temporal, demographic, and environmental circumstances in which it took place. First, and most important, we need to identify Athapaskans in the archaeological record.

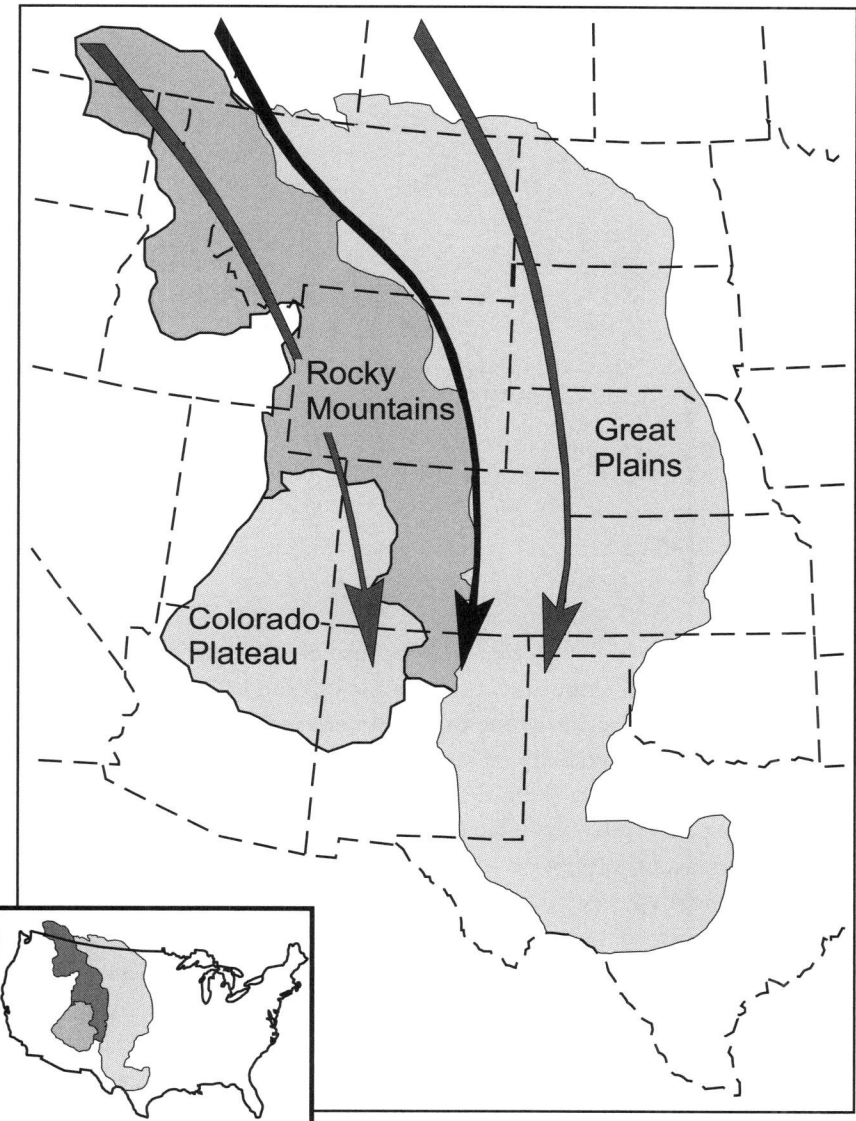

FIGURE 3.1. Generalized Athapaskan migration routes. Hypothesized routes through the Intermountain and Great Plains regions are in gray, and the Plains margin corridor hypothesized in this chapter is in black (*center*). Image by Kevin Gilmore.

CULTURAL CONTEXT

Several archaeological complexes are identified as possibly representing the archaeological manifestation of Athapaskans on the Plains. In past decades the Avonlea phase (AD 200–750) of the Northern Plains has been attributed to early Athapaskans (Davis 1988; Gilmore 2004a; Haskell 1987), although this interpretation has fallen out of favor in recent years (Reeves 2003; Walde 2003, this volume). Another archaeological culture assigned an Athapaskan ethnic affiliation is the Dismal River aspect of the Central Plains of Nebraska, Kansas, and eastern Colorado. This archaeological unit was assigned a proto-Apache ethnic affiliation by James Gunnerson in his 1960 synthesis, based on both

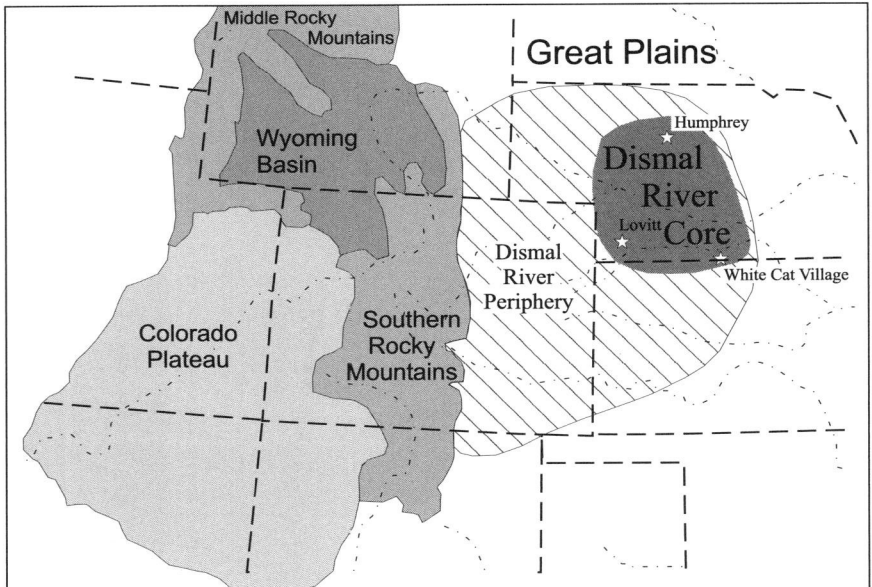

FIGURE 3.2. Core and periphery of the Dismal River culture. White stars indicate the location of the excavated larger villages or hamlets. Based on Gunnerson (1960). Image by Kevin Gilmore.

archaeological and ethnohistoric data. The Dismal River aspect has been dated through dendrochronology between circa AD 1625 and 1750 (Brunswig 1995; Gunnerson 1960). Associating the Dismal River aspect with the proto-Apache has depended almost entirely on seventeenth-century accounts of sixteenth-century Spanish incursions into the Central Plains (Champe 1949; Gunnerson and Gunnerson 1971; D. Gunnerson 1974; Hammond and Rey 1940). Although equating the eastern Dismal River aspect with the proto-Apache has been critically reexamined (Gulley 2000), Dorothy Gunnerson's primary research (1974) has largely withstood the test of time. As we discuss below, if the eastern Dismal River aspect were not proto-Apache, who in fact were they? No plausible alternative explanation has been proffered except Gulley's (2000) assertion that the Dismal River aspect represents a generalized Plains lifeway that combines traits from many different groups. However, it is precisely this amalgamation of traits that has come to define Athapaskan adaptation (Eiselt 2006).

DIAGNOSTIC MATERIAL CULTURE

As described by J. Gunnerson (1960), the core of the Dismal River aspect was located in western Nebraska and northwest Kansas (Figure 3.2), where people lived in small villages or isolated habitation structures, relied in part on corn horticulture, and made small side-notched and unnotched projectile points and culturally diagnostic bipointed bifaces with central lugs (Gunnerson 1960, 1968, 1979). Ceramics associated with these sites were Lovitt Plain and Simple Stamped types (Gunnerson 1960; Hill and Metcalf 1941). These vessels were constructed by accretion (with rare coiled examples), finished by grooved or thong-wrapped paddle and anvil, and then smoothed or, in some cases, burnished or

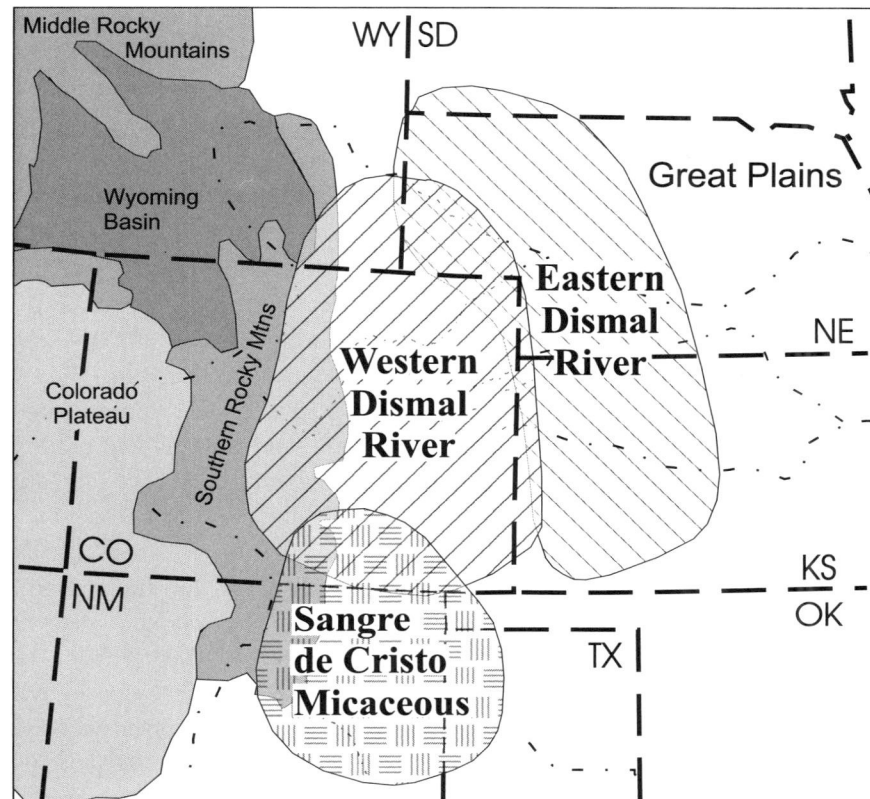

FIGURE 3.3. Distribution of prehistoric Athapaskans based on ceramic wares. Based on discussion in Baugh and Eddy (1987) and Brunswig (1995). Image by Kevin Gilmore.

scraped (Brunswig 1995; Gulley 2000). Since Gunnerson's synthesis, the Dismal River aspect has been understood to be divided (based on ceramic and other criteria) into three variants (Figure 3.3). The eastern variant consists of the originally defined Dismal River aspect found on the Central Plains of Kansas and Nebraska. Sites of the western variant are found on the High Plains and in the Southern Rocky Mountains of Colorado and Wyoming, and sites of the southern variant (Sangre de Cristo Micaceous) are found in southern Colorado and northeast New Mexico (Brunswig 1995, this volume; Gunnerson 1968).

Unlike the more sedentary eastern Dismal River people of the Central Plains, western Dismal River people employed a hunting-gathering economy with scant evidence of earthlodge architecture, such as that found in eastern Dismal River sites, and little evidence of corn horticulture. What little evidence for earthlodge architecture there is for the western Dismal River comes from the Cedar Point Village site (5EL8) on the High Plains, 60 miles east of the Front Range. The seven shallow pit structures at this site were assigned a possible Dismal River affiliation, but this association is not given much credence as the structures do not resemble the habitation structures in Dismal River sites to the east, and the associated material culture, including the pottery, was ambiguous in its cultural association and considered to have little diagnostic value (Wood 1971).

There are no chronometric dates from Cedar Point Village. There is, however, recent documentation of small temporary structures in Colorado at both Eureka Ridge (Gilmore and Larmore 2005) and the Pinnacle site (Tucker et al. 2005). At Eureka Ridge a circular alignment of postholes 2.4 m in diameter was interpreted as evidence for a hide lodge that was removed at the end of the occupation, and a stone circle at the Pinnacle site was interpreted as the anchor stones for a habitation structure. Early dates from tipi ring sites in southeast Colorado have also been offered as proto-Apache (Nowak and Kingsbury 1979; Lintz and Anderson 1989; Kalasz et al. 1999). The earliest Dinetah structures from northeast New Mexico were forked-stick wickiups (Brown and Hancock 1992), whose archaeological signature is very similar to the structure at Eureka Ridge.

Apparently, both eastern and western Dismal River people manufactured Lovitt Plain and Lovitt Simple-stamped grayware, and cord-marked pottery also occurred at sites of the western variant. People of the distinct southern Dismal River variant relied on both semi-sedentary and nomadic hunting-and-gathering economies, constructed small adobe and infrequently masonry habitation structures (Gunnerson 1979; see Hughes, this volume, for similar Tierra Blanca structures), and manufactured micaceous plainware ceramics distinct from Lovitt types (see Hughes, this volume, and Habicht-Mauche 1988 for a description of the very similar Perdido Plain type). Southern micaceous ware is designated Sangre de Cristo, with temporally sequential Ocate Micaceous and Cimarron Micaceous types, the latter closely resembling both historic Jicarilla (Eiselt 2005; Gunnerson 1979:167–168) and eastern Pueblo ceramics (Habicht-Mauche 1988, 1991).

Eiselt (2005) notes that very little progress has been made since Gunnerson's initial publication on the Dismal River aspect (1960) to increase our understanding of the micaceous pottery tradition. Indeed, it is nearly impossible to reconcile the relationship between the myriad plain and micaceous wares attributed to Athapaskans on the Central and Southern Plains and throughout the greater Southwest.

Conventional wisdom attributes the origin of Apachean micaceous pottery to the northern Rio Grande Pueblos (Brugge 1982). Brugge also asserts that the earliest Apachean adoption of micaceous pottery occurred by 1640 among the Cuartelejo as a result of their association with Puebloan groups, and was fully adopted by all Apache groups by the time of the Pueblo Revolt in 1680. Participants in the 1985 Southern Athapaskan Ceramic Conference (Baugh and Eddy 1987) estimated the adoption of micaceous ceramic technology by the Apache no earlier than 1625. Conference participants were also unable to arrive at a consensus to refute the concept that micaceous ceramics originated with the northern Rio Grande Pueblos and subsequently diffused to Athapaskan potters (although Plains Caddoans were also identified as a possible source for the technology). This was due to the inability of the participants to consistently distinguish among Tierra Blanca Plain, Perdido Plain (sequential Southern Plains micaceous wares attributed to the Faraon Apache), and Pecos Faint-striated on the Southern Plains, or between the types included under Sangre de Cristo Micaceous (Ocate and Cimarron) and Taos and Picuris micaceous wares in the eastern Southwest. Warren (1981) discounted any attempt to discern these types without the aid of petrographic analysis, and after her investigations, Habicht-Mauche (1988) applied petrographic analysis in an attempt to separate Perdido, Tierra Blanca, and Pecos Faint-striated. Her conclusions affirmed Warren's (1981) assertion that the identification of different types cannot be accomplished through the use of macroscopic qualities alone. Habicht-Mauche (1988) also concluded that Perdido Plain, Tierra Blanca Plain, and Pecos Faint-striated constitute a shared ceramic tradition, and that Pecos Faint-striated (subsumed under her newly defined Rio Grande Striated Ware) was the inspiration for some Apachean Llano Estacado wares (which subsumed Perdido Plain and Tierra Blanca Plain). In addition, she observed that Southwestern-style culinary wares were being produced by nomadic hunter-gatherers of the southern Plains (see Boyd et al. 2002 for an alternative viewpoint). Finally, she suggested that rather than arriving in the Southwest with a Caddoan-derived micaceous tradition, southern Apaches acquired pottery-making skills from the northern Rio Grande Pueblos.

Conversely, Gunnerson and Gunnerson (1971) suggest that the Apache acquired their ceramic technology from multiple sources, essentially creating a hybridized ceramic technology. In other words, the micaceous plainwares attributed to the proto-Apache are a combination of construction methods (paddle/anvil and coil/scrape) and pastes that originated from many different sources, reflecting the nomadic settlement patterns of the proto-Apache and their contacts with many other cultures. More recently, Reed (2008) has suggested that the Taos and Picuris pueblos may have acquired the tradition of micaceous clay use from the Apache, and Eiselt (2005) presents compelling evidence in support. The ubiquity and provincial variability of micaceous pottery from the latest prehistoric period through the historic period, coupled with a relative lack of chronometric control, has stymied efforts to convincingly establish the cultural-historical origins of the micaceous tradition (e.g., Habicht-Mauche 1988; Warren 1981). However, it is precisely this hybridized nature of ceramic technology that should characterize and serve to identify proto-Apache pottery in the archaeological record (also see Seymour 2008a, this volume).

Until recently, there were no examples of micaceous pottery dated before about AD 1550, which gave credence to the hypothesis that the technology was transmitted from the Puebloans to the proto-Apache. As a result, the distribution of micaceous pottery outside Puebloan archaeological contexts was thought to reflect the ethnohistoric distribution of Apache tribes such as the Cuartelejo, Paloma, Carlana, Querecho, Vaquero, Faraon, and Jicarilla. By about 1700 the Cuartelejo, Carlana, Paloma, and Dismal River had coalesced into the Jicarilla Apache (Eiselt 2006).

Differentiating Apache micaceous pottery (Ocate and Cimarron) from Taos and Picuris pottery is complicated by the fact that all these types are visually similar and contain mica as their primary paste constituent (Eiselt 2005). Furthermore, Apache, Pueblo, and Hispanic potters used many of the same clay sources (Eiselt 2005; Hill, this volume). Eiselt (2005) provides a useful summary of the temporal trajectory of micaceous pottery manufacture by the northern Rio Grande Pueblos. She notes that the earliest Puebloan micaceous pottery type is Taos Micaceous, which was thought to have been produced as early as AD 1550 (Ellis and Brody 1964). A reevaluation of the Taos Pueblo excavations by Olinger and Woosley (1989) indicates that Taos Micaceous was not produced until the 1700s, much later than Ocate Micaceous. Interestingly, the Jicarilla Apache did not settle near Taos until the 1700s, coincident with the initial production of Taos Micaceous.

The temporal placement of Penasco Micaceous is also ambiguous. Dick (1990) originally placed its manufacture around AD 1500 but revised his interpretation to coincide with the Pueblo Revolt and the return of the Picuris from El Cuartelejo in 1706. Recent reinterpretation posits that for both Taos and Picuris, the initial manufacture of micaceous ware followed sustained contact with the Apache. Eiselt (2005) recognizes this, and notes that the ceramic sequences at Picuris Pueblo and Taos Refuse Mound III call into question the accepted sequence in the origin of historic micaceous ceramic traditions; these sequences leave open the possibility that the Jicarilla may have played a major role in its development. Dates associated with other micaceous wares attributed to the proto-Apache that significantly predate the acquisition of micaceous pottery by the Puebloans, such as Tierra Blanca Plain, with a beginning date of AD 1450 (Habicht-Mauche 1988), also suggest that transmission of this technology is best explained as flowing from the proto-Apache to the Pueblos.

The early dates for Dismal River micaceous ware found at sites along the Front Range that we summarize here and elsewhere (Gilmore and Larmore 2005) require a revision of the origins of the micaceous tradition. The suite of sites containing micaceous ceramics (or at least the use of clays with a mica component) dated to the early 1400s indicates that the proto-Apache were using micaceous clays by this time. Some examples of Early Ceramic Woodland cord-marked ceramics are known to contain residual micaceous clays, and thus the adoption of micaceous clay may have originated through contact with Central Plains groups and may have been one attribute among several that was borrowed from resident Plains groups the proto-Apache encountered during their migration south.

The AD 1435 date from an Ocate Micaceous vessel from north of the Great Sand Dunes in the San Luis Valley of Colorado provides the earliest known direct date for this type (Larmore 2008; Reed 2008). The San Luis Valley is also one of the suggested migration routes for Athapaskans (Gunnerson and Gunnerson 1971; Huscher and Huscher 1942). The similarity of Ocate Micaceous and

Dismal River wares suggests common origins (Brunswig 1995; Eiselt 2005; Gunnerson 1968), and the increasingly early dates reported for Apache pottery further suggest that the ultimate origin of the micaceous pottery tradition may actually have been during the occupation of the west-central Plains by the proto-Apache. Given both new data and reevaluated older data, Habicht-Mauche's (1988) assertion that Tierra Blanca Plain is derived from Pecos Pueblo may be in need of reevaluation as well (Dick 1990; Eiselt 2005; Olinger and Woosley 1989).

In other words, all three Pueblos (Taos, Picuris, and Pecos) that manufactured micaceous pottery during the historic period developed the technology after the arrival of the Apache in northeast New Mexico. Thus the preponderance of evidence suggests that the Apache introduced the micaceous ceramic tradition to the Pueblos and not vice versa. This lends credence to the concept that western Dismal River pottery is the precursor to the protohistoric micaceous ceramic tradition.

Although some have questioned the uncritical equating of *all* Dismal River manifestations with proto-Apache groups (Gulley 2000; Opler 1983), several lines of evidence, besides the similarities between older western Dismal River ceramics and more recent eastern Dismal River ceramics, suggest that the proto-Apache were part of the Dismal River cultural pattern. Not the least of these is that the geographic location, temporal span, and ethnohistoric accounts all corroborate this assertion. One of the primary lines of evidence to attribute the eastern Dismal River aspect to the proto-Apache is the ethnohistoric accounts of the Spanish and the interpretation of these accounts by scholars (D. Gunnerson 1974; J. Gunnerson 1960; Hammond and Rey 1940). Gulley (2000) questions the accuracy of the Spanish in regarding the Querecho and Teya as Apache. But if the Querecho and Teya were not proto-Apache, then who, in fact, were they? Considering the timing of the Spanish accounts (late sixteenth century) and the increasing evidence for an early Athapaskan entry into the Southwest, the preponderance of the evidence suggests that these groups were proto-Apache. However, we acknowledge the seeming contradictions between the subsistence strategies and decreased mobility exhibited by the eastern Dismal River aspect in light of the highly mobile adaptations of the Apache both historically and prehistorically. Horticulture and substantial dwellings do not fit the classic profile of Athapaskans, but if one considers the amalgamation of Plains traits that were adopted by the proto-Apache, it is not outside the realm of possibility that one segment of the proto-Apache population would have adopted horticulture and a semi-sedentary lifeway characterized by semi-subterranean structures—especially during what may have been an environmentally and demographically turbulent time.

If we accept the Dismal River aspect as an archaeological phenomenon that represents, at least in part, proto-Apachean occupation of the Central Plains, we have to ask a question: since the eastern Dismal River aspect is a postcontact phenomenon, what were the Athapaskans doing for the 400 years between

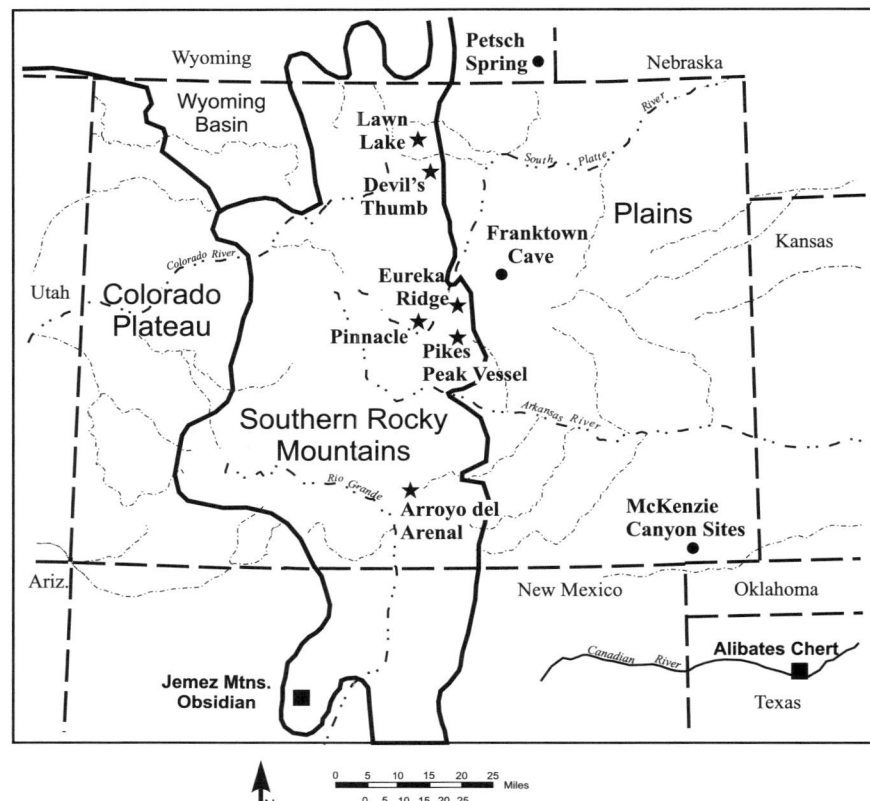

FIGURE 3.4. Location of dated western Dismal River sites in Colorado and Wyoming discussed in the text. Stars indicate high-elevation sites (>2,500 m), and circles indicate low-elevation camps (<1,900 m). Squares indicate sources of exotic lithic material found at the Eureka Ridge site. Image by Kevin Gilmore.

entering the northern Rocky Mountains ca. AD 1200 and their hypothesized appearance as the eastern Dismal River aspect on the Central Plains ca. AD 1625? The answer to this question may lie in evidence from recent investigations at sites found along Colorado's Front Range.

Proto-Apache Sites in the Colorado High Country

Although Dismal River pottery has been identified in eastern and southeastern Colorado and Wyoming in dozens of undated surface artifact scatters over the past five decades (Gunnerson 1987; Kalasz et al. 1999; Lintz and Anderson 1989), it is only within the last decade that archaeologists have obtained a significant number of chronometric dates and substantial information from excavated contexts (Figure 3.4; Table 3.1). Materials from nine sites provide data from which to identify and reconstruct early Athapaskan migration along Colorado's Front Range (Gilmore and Larmore 2005). These sites provide a remarkably tight cluster of dates with an associated two-sigma calibrated date range of AD 1300–1650, which encompasses the transition between the middle ceramic and protohistoric periods (Clark 1999; Gilmore 1999). Significantly, most of these sites are found in the High Country between 8,000 ft and 11,300 ft (2,440–3,440 m), and most are situated in relatively isolated areas of low site density and what is perceived by the modern eye to be limited resources. Col-

TABLE 3.1. Dated Western Dismal River Sites in Colorado and Wyoming.

Site	Site Name	Lab #	Dating Method	Radiocarbon Age and 2-sigma age range	Reference
5BL6904	Devil's Thumb Trail	AA-22853	¹⁴C	350 ± 50 BP (AD 1450–1640)	Kindig 2000
5LR318	Lawn Lake	Beta 144870	AMS Carbon residue	540 ± 50 BP (AD 1300–1445)	Brunswig 2001
5PA1764	Pinnacle	Beta 172328	AMS	470 ± 60 BP (AD 1310–1630)	Tucker et al. 2005
5PA1764	Pinnacle	—	TL on soil Blue OSL	AD 1354–1496	Tucker et al. 2005
5PA1764	Pinnacle	—	TL on soil IRSL	AD 1134–1226*	Tucker et al. 2005
5EP3496	Pikes Peak Vessel	Beta 155784	AMS Carbon residue	470 ± 40 BP (AD 1330–1610)	Ellwood 2006
5TL3296	Eureka Ridge	Beta 187965	AMS Crushed sherd	410 ± 30 BP (AD 1430–1620)	Gilmore and Larmore 2005
5TL3296	Eureka Ridge	Beta 187966	AMS Crushed sherd	460 ± 40 (AD 1400–1615)	Gilmore and Larmore 2005
5TL3296	Eureka Ridge	AA-60679	AMS Crushed sherd	305 ± 30 (AD 1490–1650)	Gilmore and Larmore 2005
5DA272	Franktown Cave	AA-60690	AMS Crushed sherd	643 ± 48 (AD 1280–1400)	Gilmore 2005
5DA272	Franktown Cave	AA-60694	AMS Corn	380 ± 34 (AD 1440–1630)	Gilmore 2005
5DA272	Franktown Cave	AA-60695	AMS Corn	293 ± 36 (AD 1485–1660)	Gilmore 2005
5SH2373	Arroyo del Arenal	Beta-209450	AMS Crushed sherd	380 ± 50 (AD 1430–1640)	Larmore 2008
5LA1052	McKenzie Canyon	DIC-322	¹⁴C date Bone	600 ± 55 (AD 1290–1420)	Nowak and Kingsbury 1979
48LA303	Petsch Springs	Beta 28869	¹⁴C date Soil	420 ± 220 (AD 1240–1954)	Reher 1971, 1989
48LA303	Petsch Springs	Beta 28870	¹⁴C date Soil	380 ± 80 (AD 1410–1660)	Reher 1971, 1989

Note: * indicates date rejected by authors.

lectively, these sites contain material culture very similar to that of the eastern Dismal River aspect and provide the evidence for early Athapaskans and their movement along the Front Range.

The complete projectile points from these sites are stylistically similar to other small side- and tri-notched points that are ubiquitous on the western High Plains during the latter part of the late prehistoric and protohistoric periods

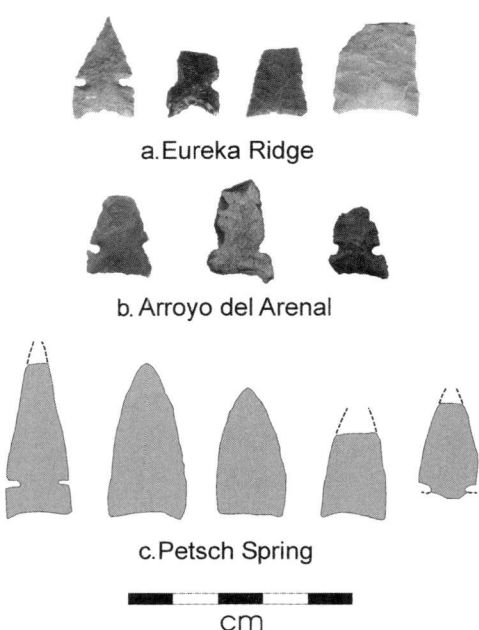

FIGURE 3.5. Projectile points from western Dismal River sites. (a) Eureka Ridge site, 5TL3296 (Gilmore and Larmore 2008); (b) Arroyo del Arenal site, 5SH2373 (Larmore 2005); (c) Petsch Spring site, 48LA303 (drawing adapted from Reher 1971). Image by Kevin Gilmore.

(Figures 3.5 and 3.6). Some of these points have distinct single spurs on the base (Figures 3.5a, 3.6a–e, and 3.6h), a stylistic element found on some protohistoric points in western Canada that has been cited by some as being diagnostic of Athapaskan technology (Omerod 2004:82). Artifact assemblages from two of the Colorado sites, Eureka Ridge (Gilmore and Larmore 2005) and Arroyo del Arenal (Larmore 2008), also contain double-bitted bifaces similar to those Gunnerson (1960, 1969, 1979) considered diagnostic of Dismal River material culture (Figure 3.7). Seymour (2002, 2004a, and Chapter 5, this volume) reported similar artifacts from contemporary Cerro Rojo complex sites in south-central New Mexico.

The lithic raw materials found at Eureka Ridge are diverse and represent half a dozen sources within a 50-km radius. The range of exploited lithic raw material represents a mature knowledge of the region and its resources, which suggest that the residents of Eureka Ridge (and perhaps their immediate ancestors) were not newcomers to the region (cf. Baugh 1984; Hughes, this volume; Speilmann 1991). Exotic materials from sources up to 250 km away, such as obsidian from the Jemez Mountains and Alibates chert, represent long-distance transport or acquisition through trade (see Figure 3.4).

The most compelling evidence for a cultural association between the three Dismal River variants is found in the ceramics (see Hill, this volume, for a cautionary perspective). Utilitarian ceramics (among other classes of technological/functional material culture such as domestic architecture) are thought to be an ideal medium for examining migration because these aspects of material culture are less susceptible to conscious or unconscious manipulation than are media or cultural practices that contain more symbolic content, and

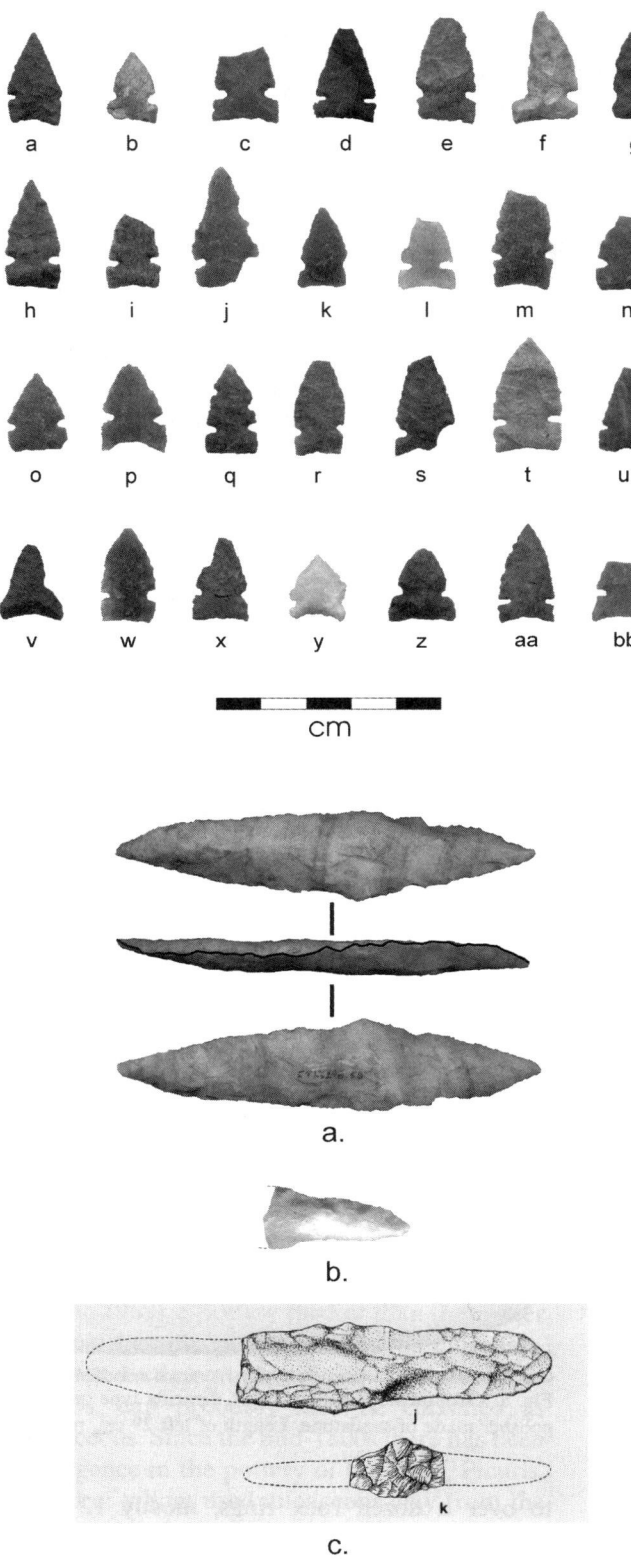

FIGURE 3.6. Small side-notched projectile points from the Franktown Cave site, 5DA272. From Gilmore (2005).

FIGURE 3.7. Diagnostic proto-Apache bipointed bifaces. These artifacts exhibit central lugs and are also called "double bitted drills" in the literature. (a) Eureka Ridge site (5TL3296); (b) Arroyo del Arenal site (5SH23730); (c) drawings of examples of this artifact type from the Glasscock site, 29MO20 (j), and the Sammis site, 29CX68 (k), in northeastern New Mexico (adapted from Gunnerson 1979:Figure 4). Both New Mexico sites are cross-dated to the early 1700s (Gunnerson 1968).

are therefore more resistant to change (Cameron 1995; Burmeister 2000; Stark et al. 1995). Theoretically, this is in part related to the techniques used to form ceramics. Manufacturing techniques strongly influence the shape of vessels, and these techniques are the result of learned "motor habit patterns" that are mostly unconscious and therefore less susceptible to change during transmission from generation to generation (Arnold 1985).

Most of the fragmentary vessels recovered at Eureka Ridge were manufactured by patch accretion, with some inconclusive evidence that a few were constructed by coiling. The vessel walls are relatively thin, and the interior and exterior surfaces were finished by different methods, including wiping, scraping, and shaping with a thong or cord-wrapped paddle and anvil (Figure 3.8). Some of the rims were burnished when leather hard, as indicated by the sheen visible on the edge of the rim in Figure 3.8b. Many of the Eureka Ridge sherds exhibit almost completely obliterated parallel vertical lineations, suggesting simple stamping, which is a defining trait of Lovitt Simple Stamped (Gunnerson 1960; Hill and Metcalf 1941). A small number of the sherds at Eureka Ridge exhibit partially obliterated fine cord marks, although they are otherwise technologically indistinguishable from the other sherds. Decorative elements in the form of parallel diagonal tool impressions were found on the rims of vessels from Eureka Ridge and the Devil's Thumb Trail site (Kindig 2000). A micaceous plainware rim sherd from the Franktown Cave site south of Denver is also technologically and morphologically indistinguishable from those at Eureka Ridge (Figure 3.9). A direct accelerator mass spectroscopy (AMS) date from this sherd of 640 BP (AD 1280–1400, two-sigma calibrated range) was initially thought to be too old (Gilmore 2005). However, given the dates of comparable antiquity associated with western Dismal River occupations such as that from Rocky Mountain National Park (Brunswig, this volume) and from the McKenzie Canyon locality in southeastern Colorado (Nowak and Kingsbury 1979), the Franktown Cave date is likely accurate and dates the manufacture of this vessel. As such, it represents one of the oldest dates associated with the western Dismal River culture (Brunswig, this volume; Gilmore and Larmore 2005). Recently, an Ocate Micaceous vessel that had been finished by wiping both the interior and exterior surfaces was recovered from Arroyo del Arenal (Larmore 2005, 2008; Reed 2008), located in the San Luis Valley of Colorado (Figure 3.10). As mentioned above, a direct AMS date from a crushed sherd from this vessel of 380 BP (AD 1430–1640, two-sigma calibrated range) is the earliest established date for the Ocate Micaceous type.

Crucial to evaluating the timing for early Athapaskan migration are the associated AMS and radiocarbon dates. The vast majority of chronometric dates associated with sites representing the Athapaskan migration and occupation of the Rocky Mountain and Plains margin have been generated during the past 10 years, and almost all are direct dates on diagnostic ceramics and their residues (see Table 3.1).

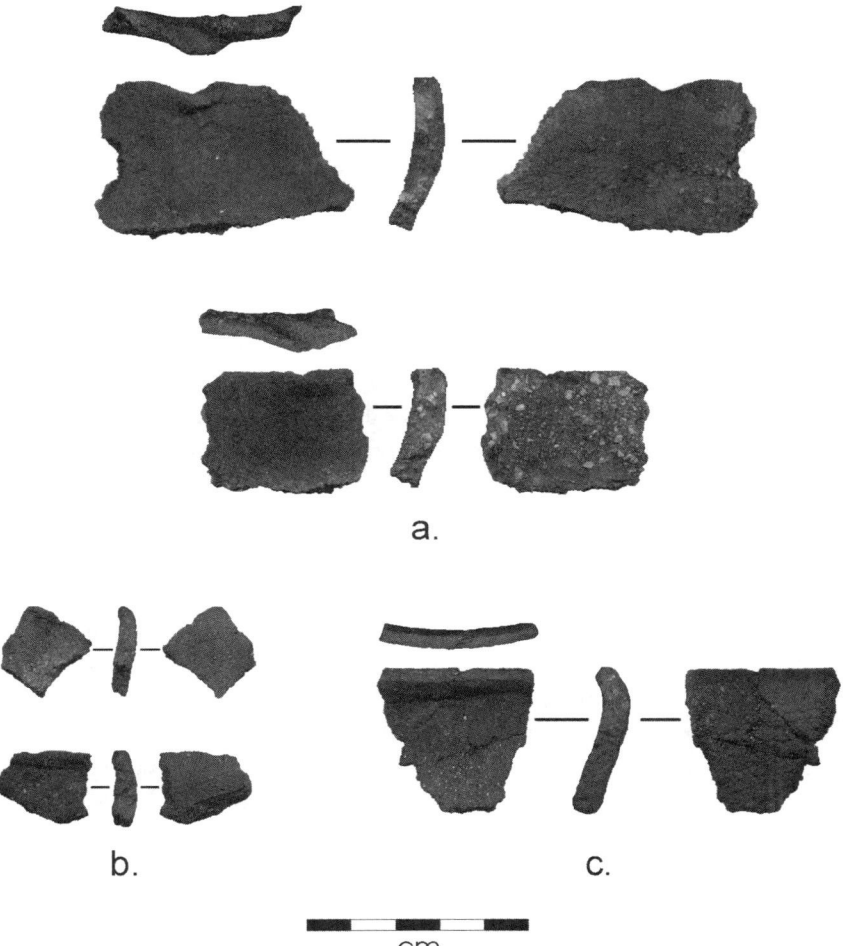

FIGURE 3.8. Sherds from the Eureka Ridge site. (a) Artifact concentration 1; (b) artifact concentration 5; (c) artifact Concentration 3. Note the diagonal tool impressions on the rim of *a* and the burnished facet on the lip of *c*. The brightness and contrast of the original images have been increased to accentuate detail. Image by Kevin Gilmore.

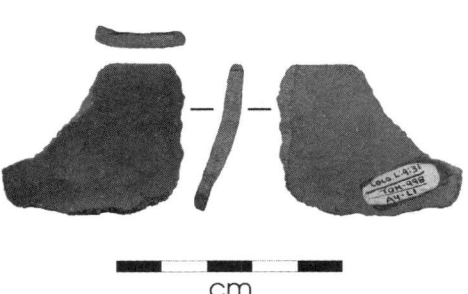

FIGURE 3.9. Ceramic sherd from Franktown Cave. This sherd has an AMS date of 643 ± 48, two-sigma calibrated range of AD 1280–1400. The brightness and contrast of the original image have been increased to accentuate detail.

FIGURE 3.10. Micaceous sherd from the Arroyo del Arenal site. Exterior is to the left.

Temporal Context

Before the development of AMS dating methods, which allow dating of small amounts of organic material, few dates were available from the relatively recent and often shallowly buried archaeological sites associated with the Athapaskan diaspora. Suspected Athapaskan sites are often found as surface scatters on stable surfaces, and so they lack the intact features in undisturbed stratigraphic contexts that often contain sufficient charcoal for standard radiocarbon dating (also see Seymour 2010). Direct dating of cooking residues on ceramics, and dates from the organic material remaining within the paste from the manufacturing process itself—derived from crushed ceramic sherds—represent a small but powerful data set. We believe these dates derived from crushed sherds recovered from Eureka Ridge (Gilmore and Larmore 2005), Arroyo del Arenal (Larmore 2008; Reed 2008), Lawn Lake (Brunswig 2001), and Franktown Cave (Gilmore 2005) reflect the manufacture and use of these pots; however, older organic material in the clays used to manufacture these pots could possibly result in dates that are actually older than the manufacture. Hill (2004) states that the paste used to manufacture the ceramics from Eureka Ridge was derived from weathered granite, a source that has much less potential to contain old carbon than do alluvial clays, for example.

The summed probability of 13 of the 14 AMS and standard radiocarbon dates associated with nine western Dismal River Aspect sites and other sites attributed to Athapaskans gives us a good idea of when Athapaskan groups occupied the region. Athapaskans were apparently in the mountains and on the plains margin by AD 1400 (possibly much earlier) and had apparently left the area by AD 1650 (Figure 3.11). What is perhaps most interesting is that this occupation predates the eastern Dismal River occupation of the plains by more than 200 years. So how is it that proto-Apache people found themselves in Colorado's Front Range by the fifteenth century? What is the relationship between the proto-Apache people and the people of the later eastern and southern Dismal River variants?

We believe that the answers to these questions lie in the coincidence of several factors. Beginning in the twelfth century, a convergence of population, cultural, and environmental forces created the ideal situation for small groups to move into and through the mountain-plains margin from the north.

Population Context

Several factors, including traditional northern Athapaskan subsistence strategies (utilizing resources available in a broad range of elevation zones), regional population dynamics, and paleoenvironmental conditions, would have facilitated Athapaskan movement to the south. Proxy indicators of hunter-gatherer populations, represented by the summed probability distribution of calibrated archaeological radiocarbon dates (Reimer et al. 2004), suggest that the resident human population in eastern Colorado began to precipitously decline around

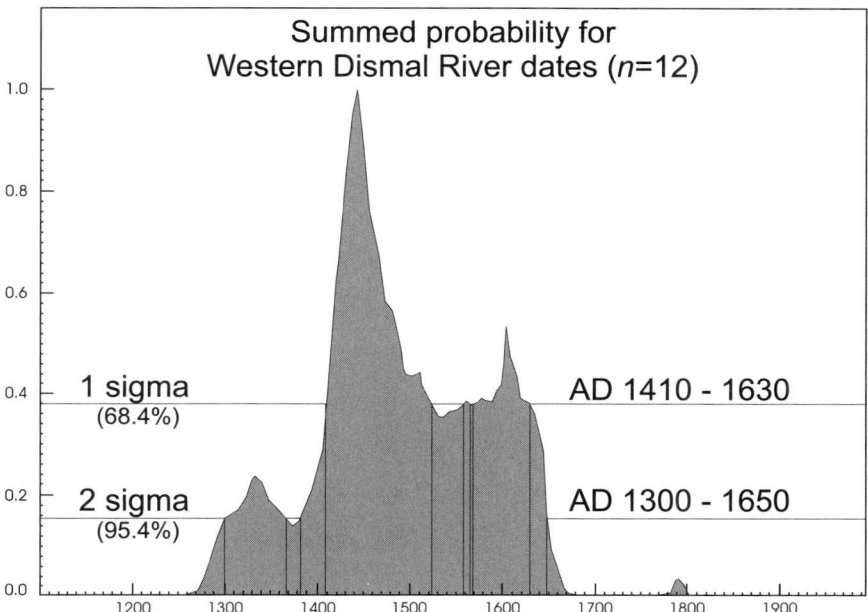

FIGURE 3.11. Summed probability distribution for radiometric dates from western Dismal River sites in Colorado and Wyoming. This includes 13 of the 14 AMS and standard radiocarbon dates associated with these sites; one date from the Petsch Spring site with large standard deviation (420 ± 220) (AD 1240–1954) was not included in this analysis. Image by Kevin Gilmore.

AD 1150. Three hundred years later the population was as small as it had been during the late archaic, 1,500 years earlier (Gilmore 2004b, 2008b) (Figure 3.12). Archaeological evidence suggests that both the Upper Republican people of northeastern Colorado and the Apishapa of southeastern Colorado had abandoned the eastern part of the state between ca. AD 1300 and 1350 (Baugh 1994; Gilmore 1999; Kalasz et al. 1999; Scheiber 2005; Scheiber and Reher 2007). Consequently, the hypothesized entry of small bands of Athapaskans into eastern Colorado between AD 1300 and 1350 was probably uncontested (i.e., Gunnerson's [1960] concept of the "open niche"). Rapid, uncontested migration and subsequent residence in the area by small, highly mobile groups would explain the relative paucity of archaeological evidence for Athapaskans along this migration route, not to mention the difficulties of determining how Athapaskans might appear in the archaeological record (Magne and Matson 2004:54). Moreover, our inability to make this determination could help explain why the evidence for Athapaskan migration has been slow to materialize (see also Perry 1991:10–12).

Paleoenvironmental Context

While the low resident population in the foothills and along the plains margin would have been an important pull factor that influenced the timing and location of migration, environmental conditions were also favorable for the migration of Athapaskans. Between the thirteenth and fifteenth centuries, paleoenvironmental records throughout the West document a period of transition between the Medieval Climate Anomaly (MCA) and the Little Ice Age (LIA)

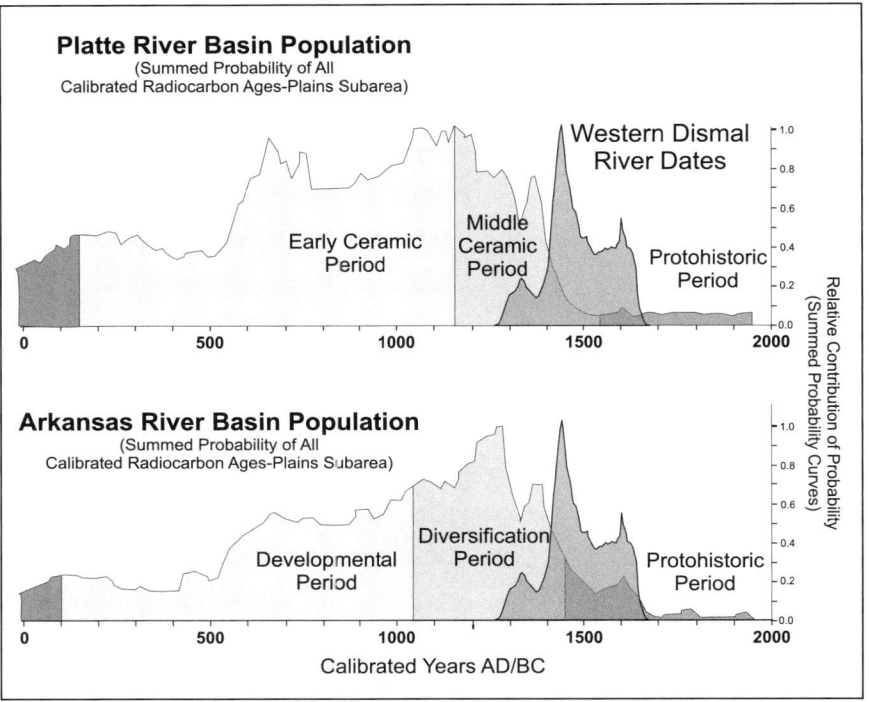

FIGURE 3.12. Comparison of summed probability distributions of all archaeological radiocarbon dates for eastern Colorado with dates associated with western Dismal River sites. This pattern suggests that Athapaskan populations entered eastern Colorado at a time when resident population numbers were in steep decline.

(Benedict 1973, 1985; Bradley 2000; Broecker 2001; Cook et al. 1999; Cook et al. 2004; Laird et al. 1996; Laird et al. 1998; Mann and Jones 2003; Woodhouse et al. 2002; Woodhouse and Overpeck 1998). Aggregated records of paleoenvironment, derived from eolian activity, Northern Plains lake sediments, and tree rings on the Northern and Central Plains, characterize the MCA (ca. AD 950–1450) as generally dry conditions, an increased frequency of drought, and greater interdecadal variability in climate. During episodes of high variability in climate, the number and distribution of certain critical economic plants and animals fluctuate in ways that may be difficult or impossible to predict, possibly resulting in cultural instability (Gilmore 2008a; Gilmore and Sullivan 2010). In contrast, the LIA (ca. AD 1450–1850) was a period of cooling temperatures, increased effective moisture, and, from the mid-1500s to the mid-1700s, decreased interdecadal variability of climate.

Based on tree-ring records, the reconstructed Palmer Drought Severity Index (PDSI) for areas that cover portions of the Southern Rockies and High Plains of Colorado indicates an episode of increased drought frequency and severity from AD 900 to 1500 that appears to correlate with the MCA and the early part of the LIA (Cook et al. 2004; Cook et al. 2007) (Figure 3.13). The MCA on the western High Plains is characterized as a period of widespread mobilization of eolian sand and the reactivation of dunes from Canada to New Mexico, starting at AD 950 and ending by AD 1450 (950–500 cal. BP) (Forman et al. 2001; Gilmore 2008a). Records of increased frequency and severity of drought,

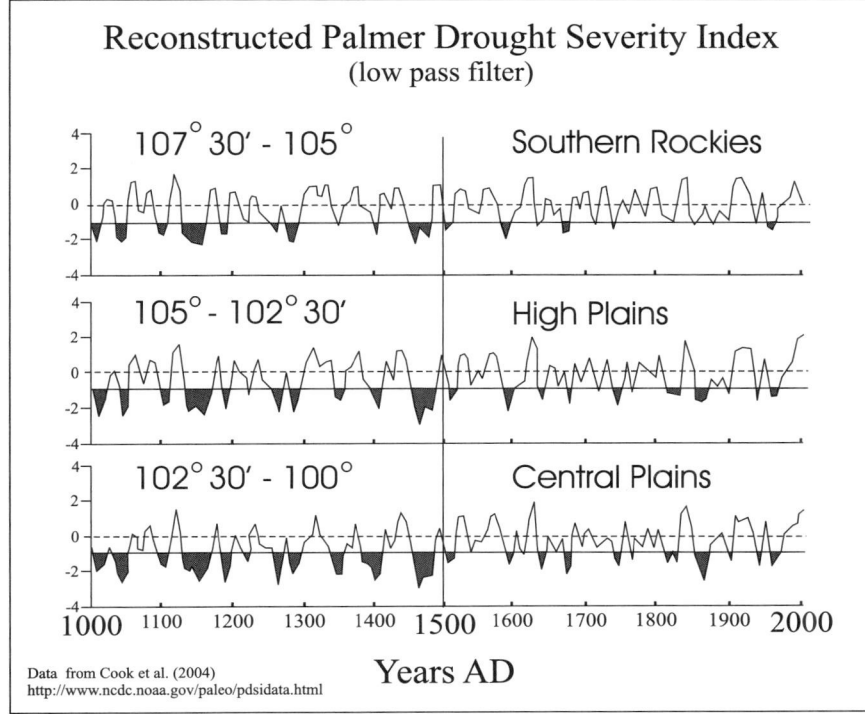

FIGURE 3.13. Reconstructed Palmer Drought Severity Index for areas in the western United States. PDSI values less than −1.0 (*dark gray*) in the smoothed curve indicate periods of drought. Data from Cook et al. 2004; http://www.ncdc.noaa.gov/paleo/pdsidata.html. Image by Kevin Gilmore.

coupled with greater variability in climate, are found in sediments from small fens and marshes in eastern Colorado (Gilmore 2008a; Gilmore and Sullivan 2010). These drier conditions would have made the mountains, which were less affected by drought than the lower elevations, an attractive refuge from harsher conditions on the plains. Collectively, these environmental factors set the stage for Athapaskan entry into the area.

During the latter portion of the MCA, between AD 1250 and 1450, conditions were cool and relatively dry and climate variability was high. After AD 1500 most paleoenvironmental records indicate an increase in effective moisture along the western plains/mountains margin and High Plains of eastern Colorado, coupled with a decrease in the variability of climate (Gilmore 2008a). Greater variability in climate makes resources less predictable on a year-to-year or season-to-season basis, which effectively lowers human carrying capacity.

The transition from the warm and dry but relatively unstable climate of the MCA to the cooler, wetter, and somewhat more stable climate of the LIA may have been a push factor for the abandonment of eastern Colorado by plains-adapted Upper Republican and Apishapa peoples. This abandonment, in combination with the transition to cooler temperatures, could also have provided the impetus for movement of Athapaskans (who were already adapted to high-latitude and high-altitude environments) from the Northern Rockies and Northwest Plains south into eastern Colorado (Figure 3.14).

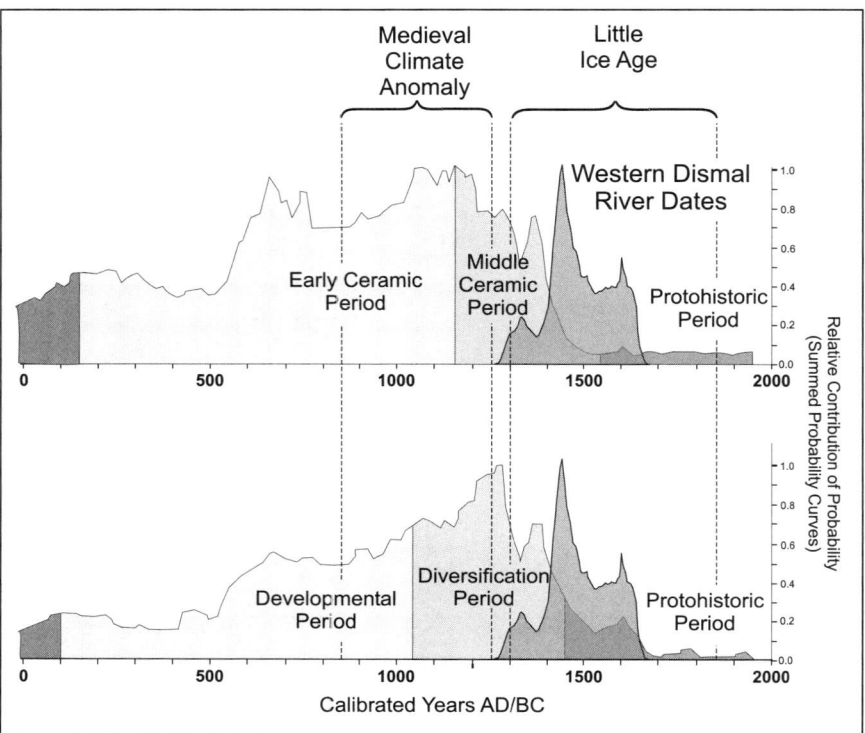

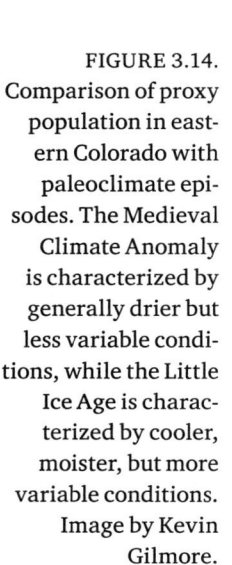

FIGURE 3.14. Comparison of proxy population in eastern Colorado with paleoclimate episodes. The Medieval Climate Anomaly is characterized by generally drier but less variable conditions, while the Little Ice Age is characterized by cooler, moister, but more variable conditions. Image by Kevin Gilmore.

A Scenario for Athapaskan Migration

The following scenario considers evidence of population movements ancestral to the eastern Apache and does not consider the proto-Navajo or Dinétah, who appear in the archaeological record of northwest New Mexico by the early 1500s (Towner and Dean 1996) and perhaps even earlier (e.g., Reed and Horn 1990), or the Cerro Rojo complex defined by Seymour (2002, 2004a), a proto-Apache manifestation from the southern Southwest. A third scenario not evaluated, but deserving of consideration at some point, is that the Promontory phase of north-central Utah (ca. AD 1350–1600) is related to both Plains and Northwest cultures, based on similarities in material culture (Aikens 1966; Gunnerson 1956; Janetski 1994). Linguistic evidence suggests that the migration of the people ancestral to the Navajo, San Carlos, Chiricahua, and Mescalero occurred earlier than that of the Jicarilla and the Lipan, although these groups maintained some contact (Hoijer 1971b). Separation during migration is likely to have been geographic as well as temporal, with the ancestors of these different groups taking different migration routes south (i.e., a potential Intermountain route).

As mentioned before, evidence for the movement of several other groups, in addition to the Athapaskans, appears in the archaeological record of the twelfth and thirteenth centuries. During the twelfth century Numic people expanded out of the Great Basin and into eastern Utah and western Colorado (Reed 1994); the Ancestral Puebloans were well established throughout the Four Corners

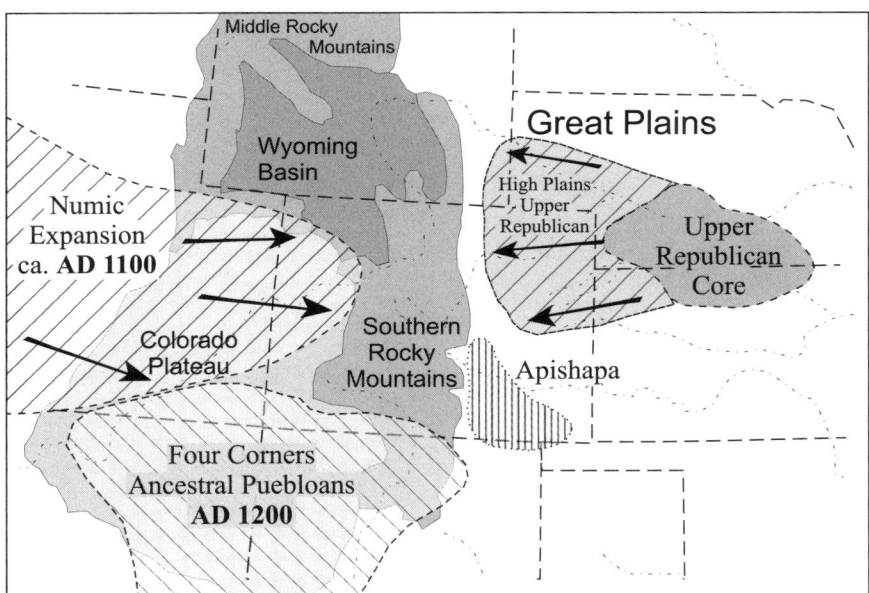

FIGURE 3.15. Geographic distribution of cultures recognized in the archaeological record in the Plains and Rocky Mountains during the twelfth century AD. Image by Kevin Gilmore.

area, and populations were increasing (Lipe and Varien 1999) (Figure 3.15). Although the resident population east of the Rocky Mountains was apparently declining by the mid-twelfth century (Gilmore 2004b, 2008b), it was still relatively high, and in fact Upper Republican people had expanded west from their core area in Nebraska and Kansas into northeastern Colorado (Gilmore 1999; Scheiber 2005; Wood 1971). By the twelfth century the Apishapa had been well established in small hamlets along the tributaries of the Arkansas River in southeastern Colorado for several hundred years, and Sopris phase people were living in small hamlets along the upper Purgatoire River (Kalasz et al. 1999).

During the thirteenth century Numic people continued to expand into the Wyoming Basin and up to the Continental Divide in northwestern Colorado (Reed 1994) (Figure 3.16). Toward the end of the thirteenth century the Ancestral Puebloans abandoned the area north of the San Juan River and traded a relatively dispersed settlement pattern for one consisting of large aggregated villages in the Rio Grande Valley (Cordell 1995). The dispersed Upper Republican settlements of the High Plains of Colorado were also abandoned; presumably, these people returned to the Upper Republican core area on the Central Plains. The Apishapa remained in the Arkansas River Valley, but they too were moving from smaller dispersed hamlets into larger aggregated settlements (Kalasz et al. 1999).

By the middle of the fourteenth century the Upper Republican people had abandoned their core area. They may have moved east and participated in the development of the proto-Pawnee Loup River/Itskari phase, or possibly they moved to the northeast into the Missouri River Valley as part of the Initial Coalescent tradition (although where these people actually ended up is unclear)

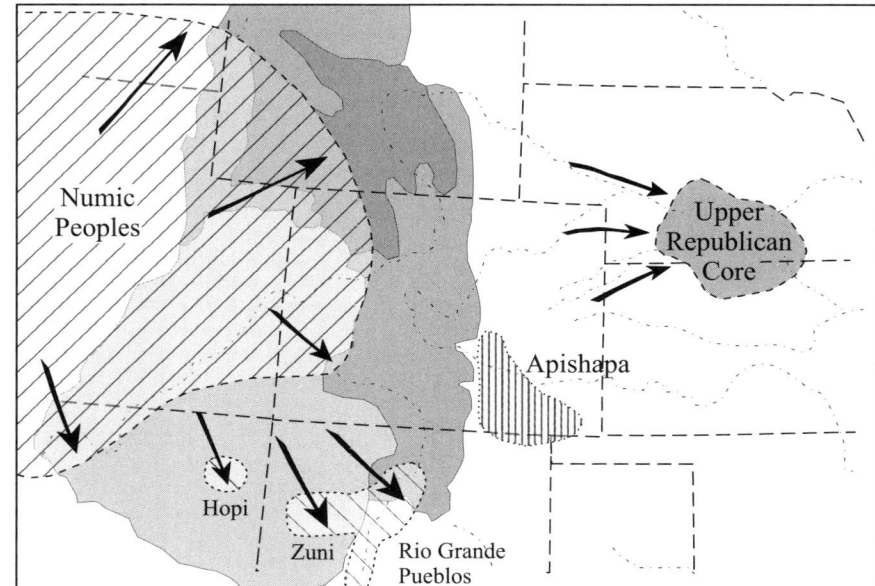

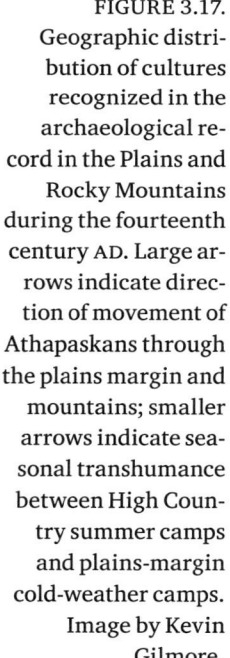

FIGURE 3.16. Geographic distribution of cultures recognized in the archaeological record in the Plains and Rocky Mountains during the thirteenth century AD. Image by Kevin Gilmore.

FIGURE 3.17. Geographic distribution of cultures recognized in the archaeological record in the Plains and Rocky Mountains during the fourteenth century AD. Large arrows indicate direction of movement of Athapaskans through the plains margin and mountains; smaller arrows indicate seasonal transhumance between High Country summer camps and plains-margin cold-weather camps. Image by Kevin Gilmore.

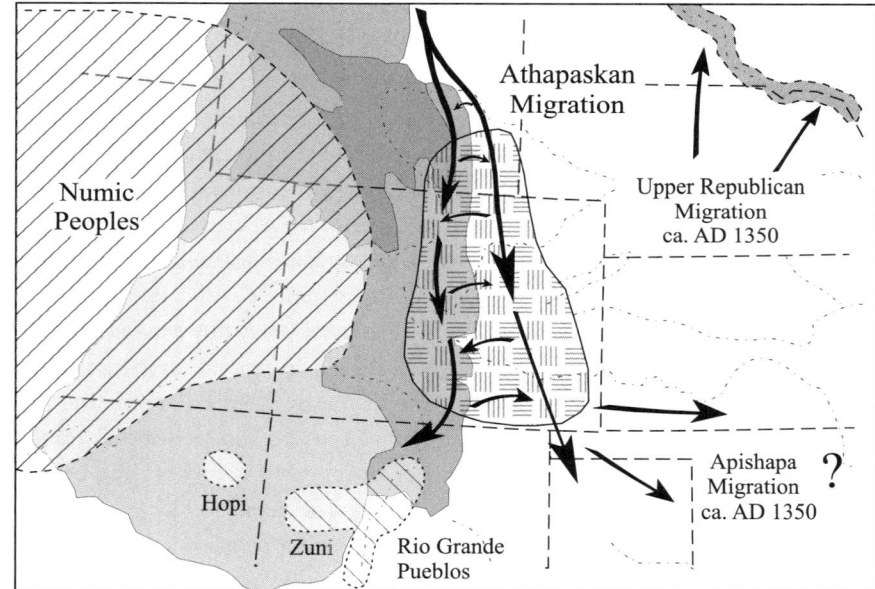

(Steinacher and Carlson 1998). The Apishapa disappeared from the Arkansas Basin, possibly being absorbed into Caddoan groups to the south and east (Gunnerson 1989; Kalasz et al. 1999) (Figure 3.17). As resident populations in eastern Colorado declined or emigrated, Athapaskans moved into the area from the north. These small groups presumably moved down the base of the Rockies using a system of seasonal transhumance, which took advantage of the high-altitude resources most similar to the high-latitude resources of their ancestral homeland and less affected by the drier climate on the plains at this time. The

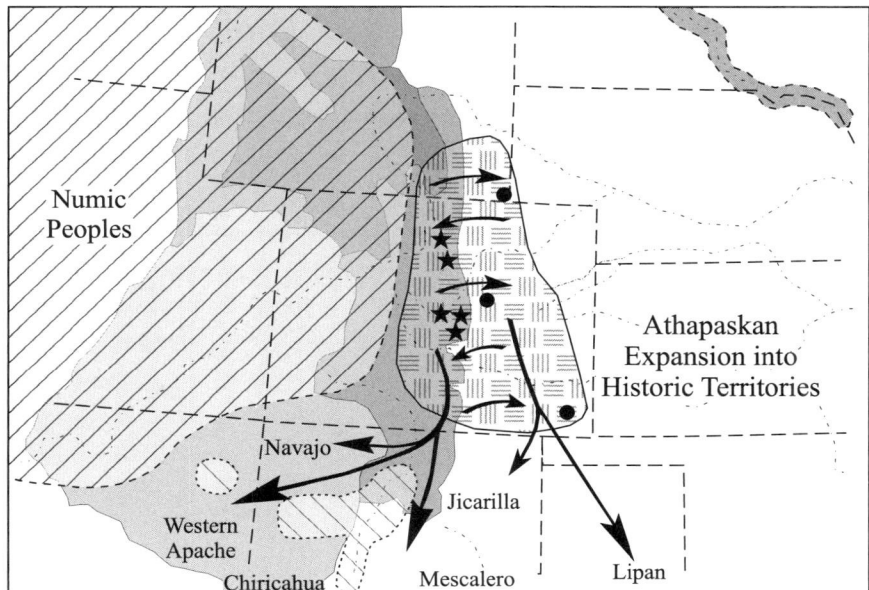

FIGURE 3.18. Geographic distribution of cultures recognized in the archaeological record in the Plains and Rocky Mountains during the fifteenth century AD. Stars designate high-elevation Athapaskan sites; circles designate lower-elevation cold-season camps. Arrows indicate movement of Southern Athapaskans into historic geographic distribution. Image by Kevin Gilmore.

proto-Apache had little competition from the highly dispersed groups that remained at lower elevations, and no competition at all for the upland resources east of the Continental Divide.

Between AD 1400 and 1500 Athapaskans moved into the Southern Plains and began to participate in the Southern Plains Macroeconomy (Baugh 1984), a trading sphere that eventually included the Apache, the Plains Caddoan, and the eastern Pueblos (see Spielmann 1991). The proto-Apache are recognized in the Southern Plains as the Tierra Blanca complex (Hughes, this volume). Habicht-Mauche (1988) surmised that the Apache quickly dominated the trade network between the Southern Plains and the eastern Pueblos, developing a shared ceramic tradition with Pecos Pueblo in particular (e.g., Pecos Faint-striated), while acquiring other material goods such as obsidian (Baugh 1984, 1986; Habicht-Mauche 1987, 1991, 2005; Spielmann 1983). By AD 1700 the proto-Apache had most likely moved into their historic territories, although presumably the boundaries between what would become the historic Athapaskan groups remained fluid. As the populations of these Athapaskan groups expanded and they occupied the Southern Plains and Southwest, proto-Apache groups continued to reside in the mountains and plains of eastern Colorado for the next 150 to 250 years. These northern Athapaskans are recognized archaeologically as the Western Dismal River culture, exemplified by Eureka Ridge and the other dated High Country sites indicated in Figure 3.18. The presence of exotic materials at many Western Dismal River sites, such as obsidian from Obsidian Cliff in the Yellowstone area of Wyoming and Montana and from the Jemez Mountains of north-central New Mexico, as well as Alibates chert from the Texas Panhandle, speaks to the continued movement of individuals, groups, and materials both north and south along the original migration corridor (Figure 3.19). The

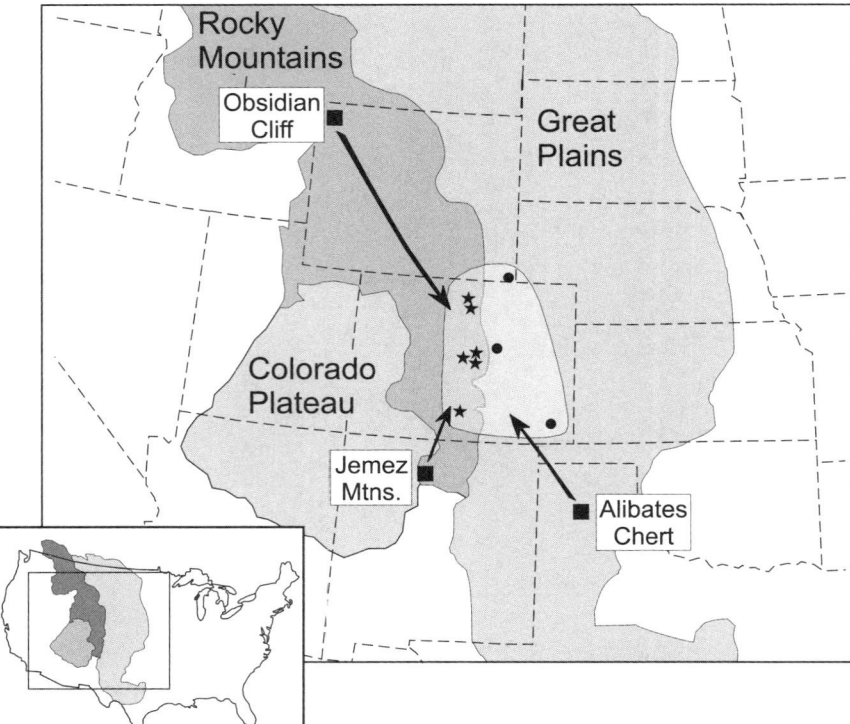

FIGURE 3.19. Geographic distribution of source areas of exotic lithic materials found at western Dismal River sites in Colorado. Image by Kevin Gilmore.

presence of exotic materials is best explained by intragroup contact and not trade between different ethnic groups, due to the probable lack of any other groups besides Athapaskans on the western High Plains after about AD 1350. However, beginning about AD 1450, Plains-Pueblo interaction increases significantly, as evidenced by the amount of exchanged goods in the archaeological record (Baugh 1984, 1986; Habicht-Mauche 1988, 1991; Spielmann 1983). Before 1350 the movement of exotic goods northward was probably the result of exchange, so that by 1450 Athapaskans were actively participating and perhaps even facilitating the Southern Plains Macroeconomy (Baugh 1984, 1991). As Spielmann notes, "the increasing intensity of Plains/Pueblo interaction beginning in the mid-1400s suggests an earlier date for the Athabascan entry onto the Southern Plains than is currently accepted" (1983:269).

More important than the movement of material was the transmission of information and ideas. Evidence for the continued exchange of information and ideas between people living in different areas is found in the ceramics recovered from these sites, which reflect the influence of potters from areas as diverse as the western High Plains (Ellwood 2002) and the eastern Pueblos (Eiselt 2005, 2006; Habicht-Mauche 1988, 1991). The transmission of ideas may have even moved north to south, judging by the recent suggestion that Athapaskans may have introduced micaceous culinary ware to the eastern Pueblos instead of the reverse (Reed 2007; see Eiselt 2005, 2006 for a discussion). As noted in detail earlier in this chapter, the development of eastern Pueblo micaceous pottery did not begin until after sustained contact with the Apache. Consistent with the above discussion, the presence of exotic Southwestern ceramic wares and other material goods in archaeological contexts on the Southern Plains ca. AD 1200–1350 could be attributed to an earlier entry of Athapaskan people into the area than had been previously thought. During this time corn became part of Athapaskan subsistence in eastern Colorado, as indicated by the dates from corn at Franktown Cave and the corn pollen associated with the Borman–Pikes Peak vessel (Ellwood 2006, and see Table 3.1). Whether corn was grown or acquired through trade (and whether this trade was with Plains or Southwest groups) remains unknown.

The diffusion of technology mirrors the even broader geographic distribution of new words coined for novel concepts introduced after European contact. For instance, Brugge (this volume) points out that the construction of the word for "horse" from the term for "dog" is common to the lexicons of Athapaskan groups from the south to the north, and it is thought to have spread from the point where the horse was first encountered by the southwestern Apacheans northward to the northern Athapaskans. This suggests that at least indirect contact was maintained between northern and southern groups from the time of the initial migration through the early contact period, which is consistent with glottochronological estimates of no more than 600 years of separation between the Northern and Southern Athapaskans (Hale and Harris 1979; Hoijer 1956).

Between AD 1550 and 1650 proto-Apachean groups left the mountains and High Plains of Colorado. Possible push factors are cooling temperatures in the mountains associated with the LIA and the expansion of Numic groups beyond the Continental Divide (Reed 1994) and onto the eastern slope of the Rocky Mountains. Possible factors that pulled the proto-Apache toward the plains were increasing effective moisture coupled with low population density (Gilmore 2008b) (Figure 3.20).

An increase in effective moisture after AD 1500 allowed highly mobile, mountain-adapted people, who had established trade relationships with horticulturalists and who perhaps had some experience growing corn, to move onto the plains. Once on the Central Plains, the proto-Apache adopted an economy much more reliant on food production, which naturally led to less mobility. Those who occupied the small hamlets and villages on the Central Plains of Nebraska and Kansas are identified in the archaeological record as the Eastern Dismal River aspect, dated to AD 1625–1725.

It is unclear what happened to the Dismal River culture after AD 1725, but there is some speculation that Athapaskans were driven off the Central Plains at this time by the movement of the Comanche to the south and east, by the movement of the Pawnee to the south and west, and by the increasing incursions into the region from the north by the French and from the south by the Spanish (Gunnerson 1979). After ca. AD 1725 Dismal River migrants may have moved

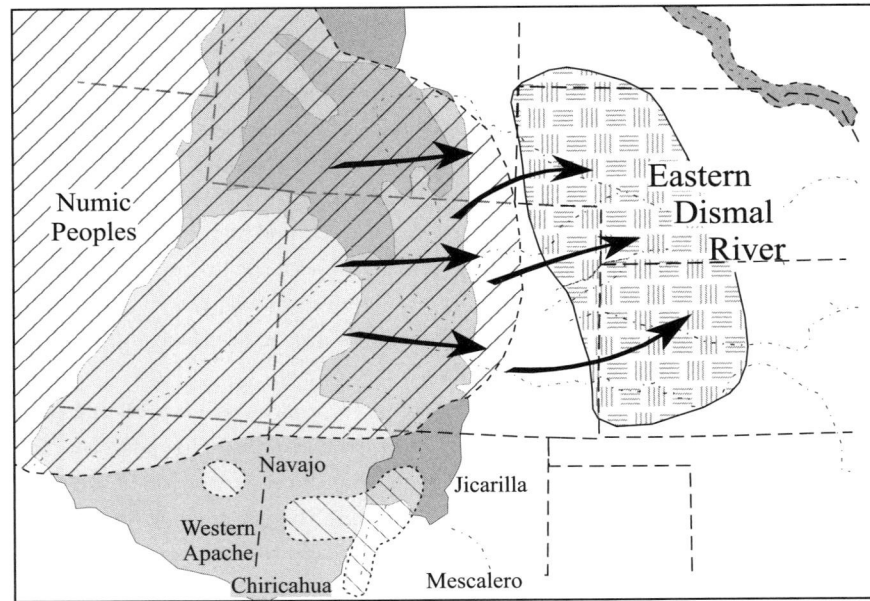

FIGURE 3.20. Geographic distribution of cultures recognized in the archaeological record in the Plains and Rocky Mountains during the sixteenth and seventeenth centuries AD. Western Athapaskans move from the western part of their territory to the Central Plains ca. AD 1500 due to both eastern expansion of Numic populations and amelioration of climate. Image by Kevin Gilmore.

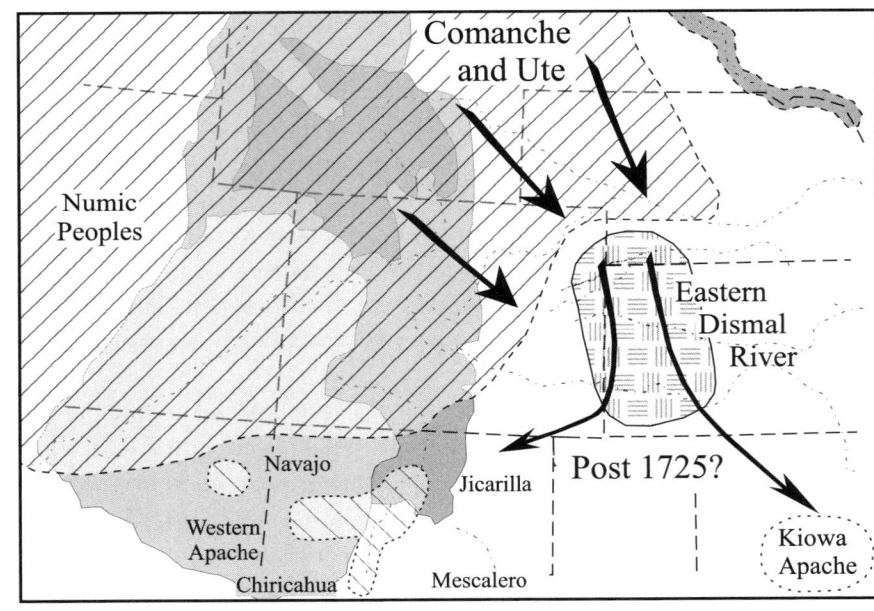

FIGURE 3.21. Geographic distribution of cultures recognized in the archaeological record in the Plains and Rocky Mountains during the eighteenth century AD. The Eastern Dismal River people abandon the Central Plains ca. AD 1725 due to continued eastern and southern expansion of Numic populations. These Athapaskans are absorbed into the Jicarilla as the Llanero band and/or become the band recognized historically as the Kiowa-Apache or Plains Apache. Image by Kevin Gilmore.

to the Southern Plains, where they were absorbed into the Jicarilla (Querecho/Vaquero) (Eiselt 2006; Gunnerson and Gunnerson 1971; D. Gunnerson 1974), possibly the Llanero band of the Jicarilla, while others could have become part of the Lipan (J. Gunnerson 1979:163) or Mescalero (Seymour 2004b). It is also during this time (after AD 1700) that the Navajo coalesced into the Dinétah region (Wilshusen and Towner 1999) (Figure 3.21).

THE STRUCTURE OF MIGRATION

A permanent change of residence, migration is usually a response to a number of push and pull factors (also see Magne, this volume). Migration is the end result of a conscious analysis of the associated costs and benefits by the migrants. People do not move to a place at random; they move to places where there is opportunity and about which they already have information. Paraphrasing Anthony (1990), Magne (2001, this volume) points out that migrants never go where they haven't been before. They also migrate following identifiable patterns, and the structure of the migration into Colorado from the north is suggested by the nature and location of Western Dismal River sites. Perry (1991:9) has characterized Athapaskan migration as a "radiation model," in which populations expand continuously outward into a variety of niches located at the margins of their range. Although Perry's term is metaphorical, we believe that it is a useful model for explaining Athapaskan segmentation.

Long-distance migration is dependent on the long-distance transmission of information. We suggest that during the initial migration of Athapaskans into eastern Colorado before ca. AD 1400, the first information about this new area was gathered by scouts, presumably male (Anthony 1990). These highly mobile, small groups of males would have left ephemeral traces of their passage in the archaeological record of the region. The archaeological sites representing these groups during this period would be small, low-density lithic scatters with a paucity of diagnostic ceramic artifacts, which makes both temporal and ethnic assignment difficult if not impossible. Thus the nature and structure of scouting parties would make them relatively invisible archaeologically. Information gathered by scouts during this period regarding potential migration destinations was communicated back to their point of origin. The groups that followed the scouts would have been more demographically complex, although still composed almost exclusively of young adults. Archaeological sites representing these groups would have a higher density and diversity of cultural material.

In contrast, sites such as Eureka Ridge, with more complex assemblages representing repeated use by larger, more demographically diverse groups, may be evidence for chain migration or leap-frogging (Anthony 1990). Both of these modes of migration involve the movement of people, usually young adults and some young families, from the point of origin to a known point already determined by scouts. These groups are usually followed by additional migrants, often relatives or those possessing other close social ties to the original migrants. The technological uniformity of the ceramic vessels from several of the occupations represented at Eureka Ridge suggests ties between the potters closer than simply a shared tradition, and perhaps represents potters from a single family lineage. As mentioned above, domestic pottery, originating in household production, is possibly the most reliable indicator of ethnic and even family affiliation (Cameron 1995; Burmeister 2000; Stark et al. 1995). The production technology and vessel shape (Hill, this volume) are more important than formal traits, and if production techniques are handed down within family lines (as they overwhelmingly are, based on ethnographic information), then various production traditions of family groups should be discernible in the archaeological record (Arnold 1985; Burmeister 2000). Anthony (1990) suggests that the archaeological pattern produced by leap-frogging should resemble islands of settlement in desirable locations separated by significant expanses of unsettled, less desirable territory. This description fits Eureka Ridge, although, as mentioned above, the desirability of the location is not readily apparent to the modern eye.

In addition to materials, return migrants bring ideas. The diagnostic single-spurred projectile points found in early postcontact sites in central British Columbia may have their origin in older late prehistoric points from the Northern Plains, High Plains, and High Country sites in eastern Colorado.

Most migratory streams develop a counterstream that moves back to the migrants' place of origin. Although sometimes interpreted as long-distance trade, in fact transfers of materials may represent return migration. This may be the case in the previously mentioned exotic lithic materials from New Mexico and Texas found at Eureka Ridge and Arroyo del Arenal, which could be attributable to initial participation by Athapaskans in the Southern Plains Macroeconomy (Baugh 1984). To date, other than Arroyo del Arenal, no direct dates have been obtained from contexts with Ocate Micaceous ware. As more sites with early culinary ware (i.e., Ocate Micaceous/Tierra Blanca Plain) are dated in southeastern Colorado and northeastern New Mexico, more examples of return migration will likely be identified in the archaeological record of the region.

Conclusions

A growing body of evidence indicates that people possessing technologies similar to those found in both the Plains and Southwest were living in the Southern Rocky Mountains and Front Range–Plains ecotone of eastern Colorado and Wyoming by the early fifteenth century. Similarities in material culture with both Northern Athapaskans and the protohistoric Jicarilla suggest that these people were the ancestors of some, if not all, of the Southern Athapaskans. The geographic distribution and material content of the sites left by these people provide data that allow for a critical examination of the cultural and environmental context of their migration from their ancestral homeland to the Southwest and Southern Plains, as well as the structure of these migrations. The evidence suggests that the migration of small bands of Athapaskans was through the foothills-plains periphery along Colorado's Front Range and may have been facilitated by the decline of the relatively large resident populations of less mobile hunter-gatherers (i.e., Upper Republican, Apishapa, and Antelope Creek). Interpretations of the data from the Eureka Ridge site and others in the Front Range–Plains periphery of Colorado suggest that this migration was accomplished by small groups which were closely linked culturally, and quite likely related, and which reoccupied the same site multiple times over decades or possibly centuries. These data, coupled with the transfer of material both forward and back along the hypothesized migration corridor, suggest that these migrants followed a pattern of "leap-frogging" and return migration.

Given the dates from these sites, it is evident that the initial migration through Colorado's Front Range–Plains periphery occurred before AD 1400 (and possibly much earlier—Opler [1983] provides a divergence date between Western Apache and the Kiowa-Apache at AD 1300), during a period of increased frequency and severity of drought recorded throughout western North America. This episode of warmer, drier conditions is associated with the MCA. A warm, dry, and highly variable climate made the elevations of the foothills and mountains more hospitable. Since Athapaskans were already adapted to high-latitude environments, occupation of similar high-elevation environments during their migration would be expected, and so the distribution of sites associated with these people should show a bias toward higher elevations. Traditional knowledge of the Apache supports the use of the area "between the treeless heights and the treeless plains" as travel corridors (Cole 1981, 1988, cited in Seymour, Chapter 17, this volume), and using mountain chains or foothills for travel offers many advantages (Kelly 2003, cited by Magne, this volume; Seymour, Chapter 17, this volume).

The eastward expansion of Numic people may have forced the Western Dismal River Athapaskans east out of the Front Range territory they had occupied for the previous 200 to 250 years, but the amelioration of generalized drought conditions after AD 1500 allowed those remaining in eastern Colorado to move to the Central Plains and adopt a semi-sedentary horticultural economy recognized archaeologically as the Eastern Dismal River aspect.

If we accept the premise that the pottery from these early Western Dismal River aspect sites are indeed representative of proto-Apache, and if we accept further the technological similarity between Ocate Micaceous and Eastern Dismal River aspect pottery (Eiselt 2005; Gunnerson 1968), it suggests that Athapaskans entered the Southern Plains and Southwest earlier than previously thought and that these groups brought a micaceous clay ceramic tradition with them. Recently acquired early dates for micaceous clay pottery in eastern and southern Colorado indicate that the diffusion of this technology was north to south and adopted by eastern Rio Grande Pueblos no earlier than AD 1500 and more likely ca. AD 1700. Puebloan adoption of the micaceous pottery tradition did not begin in earnest until after the Pueblo Revolt of 1680, when profound changes took place in Puebloan society and the Jicarilla Apache took up permanent residence in the northern Rio Grande region. Testing this model requires a concerted effort to subject early Southwest culinary wares to petrographic and Instrumental Neutron Activation Analysis (INAA) (Hill, this volume). An early entry into the region is further supported by the established familiarity with the region and its resources (including utilization of a wide variety of local and exotic tool stone sources) by the fifteenth century. This suggests that early Athapaskans must have penetrated the Southern Plains and Southwest in the fourteenth century. Recognizing sites of the proto-Apache from this time will involve increasingly sophisticated applications of middle-range theory (Seymour, Chapter 5, this volume) and a renewed focus on plain and micaceous wares from the Central and Southern Plains and northern Southwest (e.g., Habicht-Mauche 1988).

Although this chapter does not deal specifically with ancestral Navajo and their proposed entry into northwest New Mexico, recent evidence suggests that the Front Range–Plains periphery was a primary migration corridor for at least some groups. We do not specifically reject an Intermountain route for Athapaskan migration, yet little evidence has emerged in support of this route since the earlier debates (i.e., Haskell 1987; Huscher and Huscher 1942; Wilcox 1981). However, we find it plausible that multiple migration routes were taken. We also suspect that, given the increasingly early dates for the Dinétah phase (see discussion in Brown 1996:51), relatively early sites will eventually be discovered in western Colorado (in keeping with the model that high elevations would have offered resources similar to those in the high-latitude Athapaskan homeland). Recent large-scale inventories in the San Luis Valley identified potential "Western Athapaskan" pottery as the precursor to Dinetah Gray (Reed 2007), but the association is tenuous and not well supported. It remains to be determined how these early protohistoric sites will be differentiated between Ute (Uncompahgre Brownware) and pre-Dinétah ceramic traditions (i.e., Brown 1996:49, 59, 63; Reed 2007; Schaafsma 1996). Brugge, in fact, has stated that pre-Dinétah ceramic technology would differ markedly from Dinétah phase plainware (Brugge 1996:258), and Reed (2007) has lately taken on the effort to identify what pre-Dinétah "Western Athapaskan" ceramic ware might look like. We must continue to keep in mind what VanStone stated nearly 40 years ago about "the importance of cultural flexibility as an Athapaskan adaptive strategy": "Indians moving into different environments in most cases readily borrowed techniques and technologies from the people already present and accommodated those techniques within Athapaskan culture" (VanStone 1974). The obliterated cord marks on sherds from Eureka Ridge may represent the acquisition of the paddle-and-anvil technique from resident Northern and Central Plains groups as Athapaskans passed through the plains. Acquisition of paddle-and-anvil ceramic technology from Central Plains groups may mark the beginning of the proto-Apache foray into ceramic manufacture. From this point forward, early Athapaskans increasingly developed a hybridized pottery tradition that now confounds archaeologists attempting to sort out protohistoric pottery. As we note above, it is precisely these amalgamated or hybridized pottery forms that we should expect and look for in order to identify early Athapaskan ceramics in the archaeological record (also see Seymour 2008a).

The early dates obtained from sites such as Eureka Ridge (Gilmore and Larmore 2005) and Arroyo del Arenal (Larmore 2008) have implications for the timing of Athapaskan entry into the Southern Plains and Southwest. Both these and other Colorado sites have yielded chronometric dates that indicate that Athapaskans were well established in eastern Colorado by the early fifteenth century. The presence of exotic raw material such as Jemez Mountain obsidian and Alibates chert at Eureka Ridge indicates that Athapaskan groups had already penetrated the northern Southwest and Southern Plains by this time. Whether the acquisition of exotic raw material was the result of direct exchange between proto-Apache groups or down-the-line trade with other groups is immaterial; the mere presence indicates that these trade relationships were in place by the mid-fifteenth century. In sum, the early dates associated with Athapaskan sites along Colorado's Front Range support a pre–AD 1400 entry of the proto-Apache into eastern Colorado and the Southern Plains and provide tantalizing evidence for a much earlier, perhaps fourteenth-century (or earlier) entry of Athapaskan people into the traditional Southern Athapaskan homelands.

Acknowledgments

The impetus for this research was the discovery of the Eureka Ridge site during a salvage timber inventory undertaken by RMC Consultants on behalf of the Pike–San Isabel National Forest. Eligibility testing took place under a Colorado Historical Society grant (2004-AS-010) with the support of Al Kane, retired Pike–San Isabel National Forest archaeologist. Data from the Arroyo del Arenal site was acquired through another Colorado Historical Society site assessment grant (2007-AS-001), which could not have been undertaken without the support of Adrienne Anderson of the National Park Service, staff from Great Sand Dunes National Park, and RMC Consultants. We especially thank Deni Seymour for inviting us to present a paper in the symposium "The Earliest Athapaskans in the Southern Southwest: Implications for Migration" at the 73rd Annual Meeting of the Society for American Archaeology. Kathy Corbett offered expert advice on how to improve this chapter, and Kay Wall at ERO Resources provided valuable technical editing support. Finally, we thank Sunday Eiselt for generously sharing her unpublished data.

References

Aikens, C. Melvin
1966 *Fremont-Promontory-Plains Relationships*. University of Utah Anthropological Paper No. 82. Salt Lake City: Department of Anthropology, University of Utah.
Anthony, David W.
1990 Migration in Archeology: The Baby and the Bathwater. *American Anthropologist* 92(4):895–914.
1992 The Bath Refilled: Migration in Archeology Again. *American Anthropologist* 94(1):174–176.
Arnold, Dean E.
1985 *Ceramic Theory and Cultural Process*. New York: Cambridge University Press.
Baugh, Timothy G.
1984 Southern Plains Societies and Eastern Frontier Pueblo Exchange during the

Protohistoric Period. *Papers of the Archaeological Society of New Mexico* 9:154–167.

1986 Culture History and Protohistoric Societies in the Southern Plains. In *Current Trends in Southern Plains Archaeology*, edited by Timothy G. Baugh, pp. 167–187. *Plains Anthropologist* 31(114), Part 2, Memoir 21.

1991 Ecology and Exchange: The Dynamics of Plains-Pueblo Interaction. In *Farmers, Hunters, and Colonists: Interaction between the Southwest and the Southern Plains*, edited by Katherine A. Spielmann, pp. 89–106. Tucson: University of Arizona Press.

1994 Holocene Adaptation in the Southern High Plains. In *Plains Indians, AD 500–1500: The Archaeological Past of Historic Groups*, edited by Karl Schlesier, pp. 264–289. Norman: University of Oklahoma Press.

Baugh, Timothy, and F. W. Eddy

1987 Rethinking Apachean Ceramics: The 1985 Southern Athapaskan Ceramics Conference. *American Antiquity* 52(4):793–799.

Benedict, James B.

1973 Chronology of Cirque Glaciation, Colorado Front Range. *Quaternary Research* 3(4):585–599.

1985 *Arapahoe Pass: Glacial Geology and Archaeology at the Crest of the Colorado Front Range*. Research Report No. 3. Ward, Colorado: Center for Mountain Archeology.

Boyd, Doug K., Kathryn Reese-Taylor, Hector Neff, and Michael D. Glascock

2002 Protohistoric Ceramics from the Texas Southern Plains: Documenting Plains-Pueblo Interaction. In *Ceramic Production and Circulation in the Greater Southwest: Source Determination by INAA and Complementary Mineralogical Investigations*, edited by Donna M. Glowacki and Hector Neff, pp. 14–151. Cotsen Institute of Archaeology Monograph No. 44. Los Angeles: University of California.

Bradley, Ray

2000 1000 Years of Climate Change. *Science* 288(5470):1353–1354.

Broecker, Wallace S.

2001 Was the Medieval Warm Period Global? *Science* 291(5508):1497–1499.

Brown, Gary M.

1996 The Protohistoric Transition in the Northern San Juan Region. In *The Archaeology of Navajo Origins*, edited by Ronald H. Towner, pp. 47–69. Salt Lake City: University of Utah Press.

Brown, Gary M., and Pat M. Hancock

1992 The Dinetah Phase in the La Plata Valley. In *Cultural Diversity and Adaptation: The Archaic, Anasazi, and Navajo Occupation of the Upper San Juan Basin*. Cultural Resources Series No. 9, edited by Lori S. Reed and Paul F. Reed, pp. 69–90. Santa Fe: New Mexico Bureau of Land Management.

Brugge, David M.

1982 Apache and Navajo Ceramics. In *Southwestern Ceramics: A Comparative Review*, edited by A. H. Schroeder, pp. 279–295. Arizona Archaeologist No. 15. Phoenix: Arizona Archaeological Society, Phoenix.

1983 Navajo Prehistory and History to 1850. In *Southwest*, edited by Alfonso Ortiz, pp. 489–501. Handbook of North American Indians, Vol. 10, William C. Sturtevant, general editor. Washington, D.C.: Smithsonian Institution.

1984 The Protohistoric among Non-Pueblo Groups of the Southwest. In *Collected Papers in Honor of Harry L. Hadlock*, edited by N. L. Fox, pp. 169–175. Papers No. 9. Albuquerque: Archaeological Society of New Mexico.

1996   Navajo Archaeology: A Promising Past. In *The Archaeology of Navajo Origins*, edited by Ronald H. Towner, pp. 255–271. Salt Lake City: University of Utah Press.
2008   Emergence of the Navajo People. Paper presented at the 73rd Annual Meeting of the Society for American Archaeology, Vancouver, British Columbia.

Brunswig, Robert H., Jr.
1995   Apachean Ceramics East of Colorado's Continental Divide: Current Data and New Directions. In *Archaeological Pottery of Colorado: Ceramic Clues to the Prehistoric and Protohistoric Lives of the State's Native Peoples*, edited by Robert H. Brunswig, B. Bradley, and S. M. Chandler, pp. 172–207. Occasional Papers No. 2. Denver: Colorado Council of Professional Archaeologists.
2001   *Lawn Lake (5LR318): Results of an Archeological Mitigation Research Project at a High Altitude Prehistoric Site in Rocky Mountain National Park*. Report to Rocky Mountain National Park, National Park Service, Estes Park. Greeley: Department of Anthropology, University of Northern Colorado.

Brunswig, Robert H., Jr., Bruce Bradley, and Susan M. Chandler (editors)
1995   *Archaeological Pottery of Colorado: Ceramic Clues to the Prehistoric and Protohistoric Lives of the State's Native Peoples*. Occasional Papers No. 2. Denver: Colorado Council of Professional Archaeologists.

Burmeister, Stefan
2000   Archaeology and Migration: Approaches to an Archaeological Proof of Migration. *Current Anthropology* 41(4):539–553.

Cameron, Catherine M.
1995   Migration and the Movement of Southwestern Peoples. *Journal of Anthropological Archaeology* 14:104–124.

Champe, John L.
1949   White Cat Village. *American Antiquity* 14(4):285–292.

Clark, Bonnie
1999   The Protohistoric Period. In *Colorado Prehistory: A Context for the Platte River Basin*, edited by Kevin P. Gilmore, Marcia Tate, Mark L. Chenault, Bonnie Clark, Terri McBride, and Margaret Wood, pp. 309–335. Denver: Colorado Council of Professional Archaeologists, Colorado Historical Society.

Cook, Edward R., D. M. Meko, David W. Stahle, and M. K. Cleaveland
1999   Drought Reconstructions for the Continental United States. *Journal of Climate* 12(4):1145–1162.

Cook, Edward R., Richard Seager, Mark A. Cane, and David W. Stahle
2007   North American Drought: Reconstructions, Causes, and Consequences. *Earth-Science Reviews* 81:93–134.

Cook, Edward R., Connie A. Woodhouse, C. M. Eakin, D. M. Meko, and David W. Stahle
2004   Long-Term Aridity Changes in the Western United States. *Science* 306(5698):1015–1018.

Cordell, Linda S.
1995   Tracing Migration Pathways from the Receiving End. *Journal of Anthropological Archaeology* 14(2):203–211.

Davis, Leslie B. (editor)
1988   *Avonlea Yesterday and Today: Archaeology and Prehistory*. Saskatoon: Saskatchewan Archaeological Society.

Dick, Herbert. W.
1990   Background Information for the Study of Micaceous Pottery. Handout at the

Euro-American Ceramics Workshop, New Mexico Archaeological Council, Santa Fe.

Dittert, Alfred E., Jr., James J. Hester, and Frank W. Eddy
1961 *An Archaeological Survey of the Navajo Reservoir District, Northwestern New Mexico*. Monographs of the School of American Research No. 23. Santa Fe: School of American Research and the Museum of New Mexico.

Eiselt, Bernice Sunday
2005 Eastern Apache Archaeology and Ceramics. Unpublished manuscript.
2006 The Emergence of Jicarilla Apache Enclave Economy during the Nineteenth Century in Northern New Mexico. Unpublished Ph.D. dissertation, University of Michigan, Ann Arbor.

Ellis, Florence H., and J.J. Brody
1964 Ceramic Stratigraphy and Tribal History at Taos Pueblo. *American Antiquity* 29(3):316–327.

Ellwood, Priscilla B.
2002 *Native American Ceramics of Eastern Colorado*. Natural History Inventory of Colorado No. 21. Boulder: University of Colorado Museum.
2006 Analysis of, and Investigations into, the Borman–Pikes Peak Whole Vessel (5EP3496), El Paso County, Colorado. Document EP.CU.R4, on file at the Colorado State Archaeologist's Office, Denver. Boulder: University of Colorado Museum.

Forman, S. L., R. Oglesby, and R. S. Webb
2001 Temporal and Spatial Patterns of Holocene Dune Activity on the Great Plains of North America: Megadroughts and Climate Links. *Global and Planetary Change* 29:1–29.

Gilmore, Kevin P.
1999 Late Prehistoric Stage (AD 150–1540). In *Colorado Prehistory: A Context for the Platte River Basin*, edited by Kevin P. Gilmore, Marcia Tate, Mark L. Chenault, Bonnie Clark, Terri McBride, and Margaret Wood, pp. 175–307. Denver: Colorado Council of Professional Archaeologists.
2004a Way Down upon the South Platte River: Southern Avonlea Manifestations in Colorado and a Population-Based Scenario for Athapaskan Migration. In *Ancient and Historic Lifeways in North America's Rocky Mountains: Proceedings of the 2003 Rocky Mountain Anthropological Conference, Estes Park, Colorado*, edited by Robert H. Brunswig and William B. Butler, pp. 146–167. Greeley: Department of Anthropology, University of Northern Colorado.
2004b Analysis of the Artifact Collection from the Jarre Creek Site (5DA541): A Terminal Early Ceramic Period Occupation on the Palmer Divide, Colorado. *Southwestern Lore* 70(2):1–32.
2005 National Register of Historic Places Registration Form for the Franktown Cave Site (5DA272). On file at the Office of Archaeology and Historic Preservation, Denver, Colorado.
2006 And Miles to Go Before I Sleep: A Model for Prehistoric Athapaskan Migration along the Western High Plains Margin. Paper presented at the 71st Annual Meeting of the Society for American Archaeology, San Juan, Puerto Rico.
2008a The Context of Culture Change: Environment, Population and Prehistory in Eastern Colorado, 1000 BC–AD 1540. Unpublished Ph.D. dissertation, Department of Geography, University of Denver, Denver, Colorado.
2008b Ritual Landscapes, Population and Changing Sense of Place during the Late Prehistoric Transition in Eastern Colorado. In *Archaeological Landscapes on the High*

Plains, edited by Laura L. Scheiber and Bonnie Clark, pp. 71–114. Boulder: University Press of Colorado.

Gilmore, Kevin P., and Sean Larmore
2005 *Archaeology of the Eureka Ridge Site (5TL3296), Teller County, Colorado.* Submitted by RMC Consultants to the USDA Forest Service, Pike National Forest, Pueblo. On file at the Office of Archaeology and Historic Preservation, Denver, and the USDA Forest Service, Pueblo, Colorado. Lakewood, Colorado: RMC Consultants.

Gilmore, Kevin P., and Donald G. Sullivan
2006 Of Humic Bondage: Evidence of Late Holocene Climate Change from Peat Humification Analysis of Cores from Small-Scale Fens in Eastern Colorado. Paper presented at the 102nd Annual Meeting of the Association of American Geographers, Chicago.
2010 Paleoenvironment and "Pocket Fen" Development on the High Plains. *Geographical Review* 100(3):413–429.

Gulley, Cara C.
2000 A Reanalysis of Dismal River Archaeology and Ceramic Typology. Unpublished Master's thesis, Department of Anthropology, University of Colorado, Boulder.

Gunnerson, Dolores A.
1974 *The Jicarilla Apache: A Study in Survival.* DeKalb: Northern Illinois University Press.

Gunnerson, James H.
1956 Plains-Promontory Relationships. *American Antiquity* 22(1):69–72.
1960 *An Introduction to Plains Apache Archeology—The Dismal River Aspect.* Anthropological Papers No. 58, Bureau of American Ethnology Bulletin No. 173, pp. 131–260. Washington, D.C.: Smithsonian Institution.
1968 Plains Apache Archaeology: A Review. *Plains Anthropologist* 13(41):167–189.
1969 Apache Archaeology in Northeastern New Mexico. *American Antiquity* 34(1):23–39.
1979 Southern Athapaskan Archaeology. In *Southwest*, edited by Alfonso Ortiz, pp. 162–169. Handbook of North American Indians, Vol. 9, William C. Sturtevant, general editor. Washington, D.C.: Smithsonian Institution.
1987 *Archaeology of the High Plains.* Cultural Resource Series No. 19. Denver: Colorado State Office, U.S. Bureau of Land Management.
1989 *Apishapa Canyon Archaeology: Excavations at the Snake Blakeslee and Nearby Sites.* Reprints in Anthropology, Vol. 41. Lincoln, Nebraska: J and L Reprint Co.

Gunnerson, James H., and Dolores A. Gunnerson
1971 Apachean Culture: A Study in Unity and Diversity. In *Apachean Culture History and Ethnology*, edited by Keith H. Basso and Morris E. Opler, pp. 7–28. Anthropological Papers of the University of Arizona No. 21. Tucson: University of Arizona Press.

Habicht-Mauche, Judith A.
1987 Southwestern-Style Culinary Ceramics on the Southern Plains: A Case Study of Technological Innovation and Cross-Cultural Interaction. *Plains Anthropologist* 32(116):175–191.
1988 An Analysis of Southwestern Style Ceramics from the Southern Plains in the Context of Plains-Pueblo Interaction. Unpublished Ph.D. dissertation, Department of Anthropology, Harvard University, Cambridge, Massachusetts.
1991 Evidence for the Manufacture of Southwestern-Style Culinary Ceramics on the Southern Plains. In *Farmers, Hunters, and Colonists: Interaction between the*

Southwest and the Southern Plains, edited by Katherine A. Spielmann, pp. 89–106. Tucson: University of Arizona Press.

1992 Coronado's Querechos and Teyas in the Archaeological Record of the Texas Panhandle. *Plains Anthropologist* 37(140):247–259.

2005 The Shifting Role of Women and Women's Labor on the Southern High Plains. In *Gender and Hide Production*, edited by Lisa Frink and Kathryn Weedman, pp. 37–56. Walnut Creek, California: AltaMira Press.

Hale, Kenneth, and David Harris

1979 Historical Linguistics and Archeology. In *Southwest*, edited by Alfonso Ortiz, pp. 170–177. Handbook of North American Indians, Vol. 9, William C. Sturtevant, general editor. Washington, D.C.: Smithsonian Institution.

Hammond, George P., and Agapito Rey (editors and translators)

1940 *Narratives of the Coronado Expedition, 1580–1594*. Coronado Historical Series Vol. 2. Albuquerque: University of New Mexico Press.

Haskell, J. Loring

1987 *Southern Athapaskan Migration: AD 200–1750*. Tsaile, Arizona: Navajo Community College Press.

Hester, James J.

1962 *Early Navajo Migrations and Acculturation in the Southwest*. Museum of New Mexico Papers in Anthropology No. 6. Santa Fe: Museum of New Mexico Press.

Hill, Asa T., and George Metcalf

1941 A Site of the Dismal River Aspect in Chase County, Nebraska. *Nebraska History Magazine* 22(2):158–226.

Hill, David V.

2004 Petrographic Analysis of Three Sherds from Eureka Ridge, 5TL3296. Prepared for RMC Consultants, Denver.

Hogan, Patrick F.

1989 Dinetah: A Reevaluation of Pre-revolt Navajo Occupation in Northwestern New Mexico. *Journal of Anthropological Research* 45(1):53–56.

Hogan, Patrick, and B. Munford

1988 Excavations at LA 16151. In *Anasazi and Navajo Occupation of the San Juan Breaks: Data Recovery on the Bolack Exchange Lands, Phase I*, edited by P. Hogan and L. Sebastian. Albuquerque: Office of Contract Archaeology, University of New Mexico.

Hoijer, Harry

1956 Athapaskan Kinship Systems. *American Anthropologist* 58(2):309–333.

1971a Athapaskan Morphology. In *Studies in American Indian Languages*, edited by Jesse Sawyer, pp. 113–148. University of California Studies in Linguistics Vol. 65. Berkeley: University of California Press.

1971b The Position of the Apachean Languages in the Athapaskan Stock. In *Apachean Culture History and Ethnology*, edited by Keith H. Basso and Morris E. Opler, pp. 3–6. Anthropological Papers of the University of Arizona No. 21. Tucson: University of Arizona Press.

Holmes, Charles E.

1975 A Northern Athapaskan Environmental System in Diachronic Perspective. *Western Canadian Journal of Anthropology* 5(3–4): 92–124.

Huscher, Betty H., and Harold A. Huscher

1942 Athapascan Migration via the Intermountain Region. *American Antiquity* 8(1): 80–88.

1943   The Hogan Builders of Colorado. *Southwestern Lore* 9(2):21–25.
Janetski, Joel C.
1994   Recent Transitions in the Eastern Great Basin. In *Across the West: Human Population Movement and the Expansion of the Numa*, edited by David Rhode and David B. Madsen, pp. 157–178. Salt Lake City: University of Utah Press.
Kalasz, Stephen M., Mark Mitchell, and Christian J. Zier
1999   Late Prehistoric Stage. In *Colorado Prehistory: A Context for the Arkansas River Basin*, by Christian J. Zier and Stephen M. Kalasz, pp. 141–263. Denver: Colorado Council of Professional Archaeologists, Colorado Historical Society.
Keur, Dorothy L.
1941   *Big Bead Mesa: An Archaeological Study of Navaho Acculturation, 1745–1812*. Memoirs No. 1. Menasha, Wisconsin: Society for American Archaeology.
Kindig, Jean Matthews
2000   Two Ceramic Sites in the Devil's Thumb Valley. In *This Land of Shining Mountains: Archeological Studies in Colorado's Indian Peaks Wilderness Area*, edited by E. Steve Cassells. pp. 95–123. Research Report No. 8. Ward, Colorado: Center for Mountain Archeology.
Laird, Kathleen R., Sherilyn C. Fritz, and Brian F. Cumming
1998   A Diatom-Based Reconstruction of Drought Intensity, Duration, and Frequency from Moon Lake, North Dakota: A Sub-decadal Record of the Last 2300 Years. *Journal of Paleolimnology* 19(2):161–179.
Laird, Kathleen R., Sherilyn C. Fritz, Kirk A. Maasch, and Brian F. Cumming
1996   Greater Drought Intensity and Frequency before AD 1200 in the Northern Great Plains, USA. *Nature* 384:552–554.
Larmore, Sean
2005   Preliminary Investigations at Site 5SH2373, Great Sand Dunes National Park. Paper presented at the Colorado Archaeological Society Great Sand Dunes Research Symposium, Alamosa, Colorado.
2008   *Archaeological Investigations at the Arroyo del Arenal Site (5SH2373), Great Sand Dunes National Park and Preserve, Saguache County, Colorado*. Prepared for the Friends of the Dunes by ERO Resources Corporation, Denver, and the Colorado State Historic Fund (2007-AS-001). On file at the Colorado Historical Society, Office for Archaeology and Historic Preservation.
Lintz, Christopher
1991   Texas Panhandle–Pueblo Interactions from the Thirteenth through the Sixteenth Century. In *Farmers, Hunters, and Colonists: Interaction between the Southwest and the Southern Plains*, edited by Katherine A. Spielmann, pp. 89–106. Tucson: University of Arizona Press.
Lintz, Christopher, and Jane L. Anderson
1989   *Temporal Assessment of Diagnostic Materials from the Pinon Canyon Maneuver Site*. Memoirs No. 4. Denver: Colorado Archaeological Society.
Lipe, William D., and Mark D. Varien
1999   Pueblo III (AD 1150–1300). In *Colorado Prehistory: A Context for the Southern Colorado River Basin*, edited by William D. Lipe, Mark D. Varien, and Richard H. Wilshusen, pp. 290–352. Denver: Colorado Historical Society.
Magne, Martin P. R.
2001   Plateau and Plains Athapaskan Movements in Late Prehistoric and Early Historic Periods. Paper presented at the 66th Annual Meeting of the Society for American Archaeology, New Orleans.

Magne, Martin, and R. G. Matson
2004 A New Look at the Intermontane Model of Athapaskan Migration. In *Ancient and Historic Lifeways of North America's Rocky Mountains: Proceedings of the 2003 Rocky Mountain Anthropological Conference*, edited by Robert H. Brunswig and W. B. Butler, pp. 38–64. Greeley: Department of Anthropology, University of Northern Colorado.

Mann, Michael E., and Phillip D. Jones
2003 Global Surface Temperatures over the Past Two Millennia. *Geophysical Research Letters* 30(15):1–4.

Nowak, Michael, and Lawrence A. Kingsbury
1979 *Archaeological Investigations on Carrizo Ranches, Inc., Las Animas County, Colorado*. Publications in Archaeology No. 1. Colorado Springs: Department of Anthropology, Colorado College.

Olinger, B., and A. I. Woosley
1989 Pottery Studies Using X-Ray Fluorescence, Part 4: The Pottery of Taos Pueblo. *Pottery Southwest* 16(1):1–8.

Omerod, Patricia
2004 Athapaskan Lithics at Eagle Lake, B.C., Compared to Southwest Athapaskan Apachean and Navajo Lithics. In *Proceedings of the 6th Biennial Rocky Mountain Anthropological Conference*, edited by Robert H. Brunswig Jr. and William B. Butler, pp. 81–93. Greeley: University of Northern Colorado.

Opler, Morris E.
1983 The Apachean Culture Pattern and Its Origins. In *Southwest*, edited by Alfonso Ortiz, pp. 368–392. Handbook of North American Indians, Vol. 10, William C. Sturtevant, general editor. Washington, D.C.: Smithsonian Institution.

Perry, Richard J.
1980 The Apachean Transition from the Subarctic to the Southwest. *Plains Anthropologist* 25(90):279–296.
1991 *Western Apache Heritage: People of the Mountain Corridor*. Austin: University of Texas Press.

Reed, Alan D.
1994 The Numic Occupation of Western Colorado and Eastern Utah during the Prehistoric and Protohistoric Periods. In *Across the West: Human Population Movement and the Expansion of the Numa*, edited by David B. Madsen and David Rhode, pp. 188–199. Salt Lake City: University of Utah Press.

Reed, Alan D., and Jonathan C. Horn
1988 *Archaeological Investigations of Kin 'Atsa' (LA 49498): A Late Archaic-Basketmaker Transition, Basketmaker II and Dinetah Phase Navajo Habitation Site in San Juan County, New Mexico*. Montrose, Colorado: Nickens and Associates.
1990 Early Navajo Occupation of the American Southwest: Reexamination of the Dinetah Phase. *Kiva* 55(5):283–300.

Reed, Lori Stephens
2007 Ceramic Analysis. In *Final Report on the Archaeological Inventory and National Register Evaluation of the Baca Land Exchange BLM Parcels, Biedell Creek Project Area, Saguache County, Colorado, Volume II: Appendices*. Prepared for the National Park Service, Denver, and the Bureau of Land Management and the U.S. Fish and Wildlife Service, Lakewood, Colorado.
2008 Ceramic Analysis. In *Archaeological Investigations at the Arroyo del Arenal Site (5SH2373), Great Sand Dunes National Park and Preserve, Saguache County,*

Colorado. Prepared for the Friends of the Dunes by ERO Resources Corporation, Denver, and the Colorado State Historic Fund (2007-AS-001). On file at the Colorado Historical Society, Office for Archaeology and Historic Preservation.

Reeves, Brian O. K.
2003 Ancestral Plains Apachean Eastern Slope Migrations from the Western Boreal Forest to the Greater Yellowstone. Paper presented at the 5th Biennial Rocky Mountain Anthropological Conference, Estes Park, Colorado.

Reher, Charles A.
1971 A Survey of Ceramic Sites in Southeastern Wyoming. Unpublished Master's thesis, Department of Anthropology, University of Wyoming, Laramie.
1989 The High Plains Archaeology Project: Interim Report. *Wyoming Archaeologist* 32: xviii–xxvi.

Reimer, P. J., M. G. L. Baillie, E. Bard, A. Bayliss, J. W. Beck, C. Bertrand, P. G. Blackwell, C. E. Buck, G. Burr, K. B. Cutler, P. E. Damon, R. L. Edwards, R. G. Fairbanks, M. Friedrich, T. P. Guilderson, K. A. Hughen, B. Kromer, F. G. McCormac, S. Manning, C. Bronk Ramsey, R. W. Reimer, S. Remmele, J. R. Southon, M. Stuiver, S. Talamo, F. W. Taylor, J. van der Plicht, and C. E. Weyhenmeyer
2004 The IntCal04 Terrestrial Radiocarbon Age Calibration, 0–26 cal kry BP. *Radiocarbon* 46(3):1029–1058.

Schaafsma, Curtis F.
1996 Ethnic Identity and Protohistoric Archaeological Sites in Northwestern New Mexico: Implications for Reconstructions of Navajo and Ute History. In *The Archaeology of Navajo Origins*, edited by Ronald H. Towner, pp. 19–46. Salt Lake City: University of Utah Press.
2002 *Apaches de Navajo: Seventeenth-Century Navajos in the Chama Valley of New Mexico*. Salt Lake City: University of Utah Press.

Scheiber, Laura L.
2005 Late Prehistoric Bison Hide Production and Hunter-Gatherer Identities on the North American Plains. In *Gender and Hide Working*, edited by Lisa Frink and Kathryn Weedman, pp. 57–76. Walnut Creek, California: AltaMira Press.

Scheiber, Laura L., and Charles A. Reher
2007 The Donovan Site (5LO204): An Upper Republican Animal Processing Camp on the High Plains. *Plains Anthropologist* 52(203):337–364.

Schlesier, Karl H.
1994 Commentary: A History of Ethnic Groups in the Great Plains, AD 150–1550. In *Plains Indians, AD 500–1500: The Archaeological Past of Historic Groups*, edited by K. H. Schlesier, pp. 308–381. Norman: University of Oklahoma Press.

Seymour, Deni J.
2002 *Conquest and Concealment: After the El Paso Phase on Fort Bliss; An Archaeological Study of the Manso, Suma, and Early Apache*. With contributions by Mark E. Harlan and David V. Hill. Lone Mountain Report 525/528. Conservation Division, Directorate of the Environment, United States Army Air Defense, Artillery Center, Fort Bliss, Texas. Qualified researchers may obtain this document by contacting martha.yduarte@us.army.mil.
2004a A Ranchería in the Gran Apachería: Evidence of Intercultural Interaction at the Cerro Rojo Site. *Plains Anthropologist* 49(190):153–192.
2004b Before the Spanish Chronicles: Early Apache in the Southern Southwest. In *Ancient and Historic Lifeways in North America's Rocky Mountains: Proceedings of the 2003 Rocky Mountain Anthropological Conference, Estes Park, Colorado*, edited by

Robert H. Brunswig and William B. Butler, pp. 120–142. Greeley: Department of Anthropology, University of Northern Colorado.

2008 Despoblado or Athapaskan Heartland: A Methodological Perspective on Ancestral Apache Landscape Use in the Safford Area. In *Crossroads of the Southwest: Culture, Ethnicity, and Migration in Arizona's Safford Basin*, edited by David E. Purcell, pp. 121–162. New York: Cambridge Scholars Press.

2010 Contextual Incongruities, Statistical Outliers, and Anomalies: Targeting Inconspicuous Occupational Events. *American Antiquity* 75(1):158–176.

Spielmann, Katherine

1983 Late Prehistoric Exchange between the Southwest and Southern Plains. *Plains Anthropologist* 28(102):257–272.

Spielmann, Katherine (editor)

1991 *Farmers, Hunters, and Colonists: Interaction between the Southwest and the Southern Plains*. Tucson: University of Arizona Press.

Stark, Miriam T., Jeffery J. Clark, and Mark D. Elson

1995 Causes and Consequences of Migration in the 13th Century. *Journal of Anthropological Archaeology* 14(2):212–246.

Steinacher, Terry L., and Gayle F. Carlson

1998 The Central Plains Tradition. In *Archaeology on the Great Plains*, edited by Raymond Wood, pp. 235–268. Lawrence: University Press of Kansas.

Steward, Julian H.

1937 Ecological Aspects of Southwestern Society. *Anthropos* 32(1):87–104.

1940 Native Cultures of the Intermontane (Great Basin) Area. In *Essays in Historical Anthropology of North America*, edited by Omer C. Stewart, pp. 445–502. Smithsonian Miscellaneous Collections No. 100. Washington, D.C.: Smithsonian Institution.

Taylor, Allan Ross

2004 An Instructive Subject of Study: The When and How of the Arrival of the Ancestral Navajos in the Southwest. Unpublished Master's thesis, Department of Anthropology, University of Colorado, Boulder.

Towner, Ronald H., and Jeffrey S. Dean

1996 Questions and Problems in Pre–Fort Sumner Navajo Archaeology. In *The Archaeology of Navajo Origins*, edited by Ronald H. Towner, pp. 3–18. Salt Lake City: University of Utah Press.

Tucker, Gordon C., Jr., Marcia J. Tate, Bill Tate, and Juston J. Fariello

2005 The Dismal River Complex in Eastern Colorado: A View from the Pinnacle Site (5PA1764). *Southwestern Lore* 71(2):1–31.

Tweedie, M. Jean

1968 Notes on the History and Adaptation of the Apache Tribes. *American Anthropologist* 70(6):1132–1142.

VanStone, James W.

1974 *Athapaskan Adaptations: Hunters and Fishermen of the Subarctic Forests*. Chicago: Aldine.

Walde, Dale

2003 Points Are Not People: Avonlea and Athabaskan Migrations. Paper presented at the 5th Biennial Rocky Mountain Anthropological Conference, Estes Park, Colorado.

Warren, Helene

1981 The Micaceous Pottery of the Rio Grande. In *Collected Papers in Honor of Erik*

Kellerman Reed, edited by Albert H. Schroeder, pp. 149–165. Papers No. 6. Albuquerque: Archaeological Society of New Mexico.

Wedel, Waldo R.
1940   Culture Sequences in the Central Great Plains. In *Essays in Historical Anthropology of North America*, edited by Frances Sellman Gaither Nichols, pp. 291–352. Smithsonian Miscellaneous Collections No. 100. Washington, D.C.: Smithsonian Institution.

Wilcox, David R.
1981   The Entry of the Athabaskans into the American Southwest: The Problem Today. In *The Protohistoric Period in the American Southwest, AD 1450–1700*, edited by David R. Wilcox and W. Bruce Masse. Anthropological Research Papers no. 24. Tempe: Arizona State University.
1988   Avonlea and Southern Athapascan Migrations. In *Avonlea Today: Archaeology and Prehistory*, edited by L. B. Davis, pp. 273–280. Saskatoon: Saskatchewan Archaeological Society.

Wilshusen, Richard H., and Ronald H. Towner
1999   Post-Puebloan Occupation (AD 1300–1840). In *Colorado Prehistory: A Context for the Southern Colorado River Basin*, edited by William D. Lipe, Mark D. Varien, and Richard H. Wilshusen, pp. 353–369. Denver: Colorado Council of Professional Archaeologists.

Wood, W. Raymond
1971   Pottery Sites near Limon, Colorado. *Southwestern Lore* 37(3):53–85.

Woodhouse, Connie, J. J. Lukas, and P. M. Brown
2002   *Eastern Colorado Palmer Drought Severity Index Reconstruction*. International Tree-Ring Data Bank. IGBP PAGES/World Data Center for Paleoclimatology Data Contribution Series No. 2002-083. Boulder, Colorado: NOAA/NGDC Paleoclimatology Program.

Woodhouse, Connie A., and Jonathan T. Overpeck
1998   2000 Years of Drought Variability in the Central United States. *Bulletin of the American Meteorological Society* 79(10):2693–2714.

CHAPTER 4

Tierra Blanca

A Complex Issue

DAVID T. HUGHES

Tierra Blanca complex is the nebulous term used to indicate archaeological sites on and adjacent to the Llano Estacado of the central Texas Panhandle, sites that have some resemblance to the final occupation of the Tierra Blanca site. Connection between Tierra Blanca site components and the American Southwest were noted by Holden in 1931 and reiterated by Jack Hughes in the 1950s when he began studying Texas Panhandle archaeology. A summary of the Tierra Blanca complex was presented by Hughes (1991) following partial reviews of excavated components by Spielmann (1982) and Habicht-Mauche (1987). A comprehensive review of prior literature, some unpublished manuscripts, and collections at the Panhandle-Plains Historical Museum was prepared by Boyd (1997). Most of the studies of Tierra Blanca–like materials emphasize the economy, especially interregional exchange, and offer only limited interpretations about culture history or the place of Tierra Blanca in Texas Panhandle prehistory.

TIERRA BLANCA ARCHAEOLOGY

Key traits used to define the Tierra Blanca complex include Southwestern glazed pottery, gray or black plainware tempered with micaceous sand, a substantial presence of obsidian, and triangular side-notched arrow points such as the Harrell and Washita, as well as unnotched Fresno-like points and a constricted base point identified as Talco-like. Tierra Blanca settlement types may include both base camps and hunting camps (Hughes 1991:35; Boyd 1997), and occupation is centered on the northern forks of the Red River, extending at least to the southern valley margin of the Canadian River and possibly to the southern divide of the Beaver River in Oklahoma (Figure 4.1). Features on the sites may include racks and stands (presumably for drying meat or hides), stone tipi rings, slab-lined jacal structures, and roasting pits. Boyd rightly points out that "there is no diagnostic artifact that is exclusive to the Tierra Blanca complex" (Boyd 1997: 369). This usage seems to refer to discrete artifact styles that are in themselves

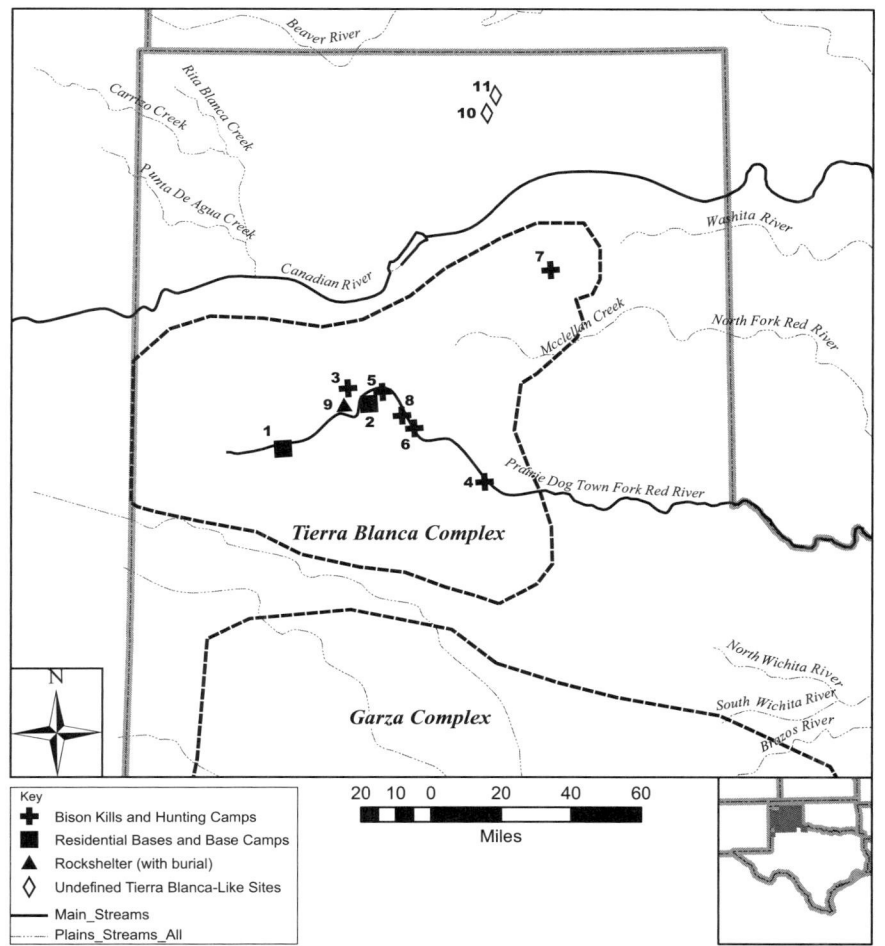

FIGURE 4.1. Distribution of Tierra Blanca and related archeological sites in the Texas Panhandle. Adapted from Boyd (1997:Figure 98).

unique to the Tierra Blanca complex. The lack of uniquely characteristic artifacts makes application of the taxon to new components uncertain. Confusion about diagnostics is pervasive in that all the artifacts and features seen as diagnostic for Tierra Blanca are incorporated in the list of characteristic traits for other taxa, including Garza, Wheeler, and other undefined protohistoric components. Despite the lack of artifact types, styles, or traits that are in and of themselves uniquely linked to the Tierra Blanca complex, we can recognize a larger assemblage that, taken as a collective set of traits, may be indicative of a unique cultural pattern: the Tierra Blanca complex. Correlate grids, as Seymour uses for Cerro Rojo (Chapter 5, this volume), may offer a methodological framework that can overcome these limits of traditional typological analysis.

This assemblage of traits, together with the historical occurrence of Tierra Blanca after the predominant Antelope Creek phase and other Plains Village components, has led to a prima facie assumption that the Tierra Blanca complex represents an early manifestation of the Southern Plains Athapaskans. This

TABLE 4.1. Roster of Tierra Blanca Complex Sites.

MAP REF	SITE NAME	SITE NUMBER	PUBLICATION
Residential & Base Camps			
1	Tierra Blanca	41DF3	Holden 1931; Spielmann 1982, 1983
2	Blackburn	41RD20	Spielmann 1982, 1983
Bison Kills & Hunting Camps			
3	Fifth Green	A1363	Kalokowski 1986
4	Tule Mouth Sites	41B173, 81, 83	Katz and Katz 1976
5	Palisades (Hughes Rockshelter)	A530	Unpublished
6	Cita Mouth	A288	Unpublished
7	Fatheree	41GY32	Hughes et al. 1978
8	Water Crossing #2	A148	Unpublished
Rockshelter with Burial			
9	Canyon City Club Cave	A251	Hughes 2011
Tierra Blanca–Like Sites			
10	Broken Jaw	41HF8	Quigg et al. 1993
11	Unnamed shelter	41HF86	Quigg et al. 1993

Note: Data from Boyd (1997:371, Table 85).

assumption is most often reflected in informal conversations but can be seen in the writings of Jack Hughes (1978, 1991).

That there is a ceramic-bearing archaeological assemblage that follows the Antelope Creek phase is not in doubt, but its association with the ancestral Apache is open to debate. Since Tierra Blanca is used to the point of synonymy to refer to early Panhandle Apache, indiscriminate application of the complex term in this setting could further cloud the issue. This is the logic behind avoiding it in this particular context.

Numerous sites have been found from the Red River drainage north in the Texas Panhandle that produce Southwestern glaze ceramics, striated gray or black pottery, notched and unnotched triangular arrow points, and other lithic artifacts characteristic of the late prehistoric Plains cultures of the region (see Figure 4.1). This assemblage has produced radiocarbon dates that range from the late thirteenth century through the fifteenth century (see Boyd 1997:372, Table 86). The meaning of the radiocarbon dates is difficult to evaluate since no archaeological sites that have substantial Tierra Blanca materials have been thoroughly described and reported (see Boyd 1997:368–369). The basic problem is that few dates exist, and these have little contextual meaning because so few contexts have been published. Hughes (1991:35) names the Tierra Blanca ruin of Deaf Smith County and the Fifth Green site in Randall County the type sites for Tierra Blanca base camps and hunting camps, respectively (see Table 4.1).

During the summer of 1930, W. C. Holden spent some time working in northeast New Mexico and the western Panhandle seeking information about the possible relationship between what was then thought of as the Canadian River ruins and the Pueblos. He spent four days excavating at Tierra Blanca in the summer of 1930 because "decorated pottery of true Pueblo type was found in typical slab-stone ruins" (Holden 1931:50). Because of the presence of Puebloan pottery and obsidian at Tierra Blanca, Holden hoped that "these ruins might prove to be the 'key' that we have been searching for to show the real relationship of the Panhandle culture to the Pueblo culture" (Holden 1931:50).

The site contained about a dozen more-or-less circular ruins. Each varied from 6 to 30 ft (1.85 m to 9.2 m) in diameter. The entire site covered about 4 acres (1.6 ha). Holden focused on a single ruin that was 23 ft (7.1m) north to south and 27 ft (8.3 m) east to west. The house floor was 18 inches (about 45 cm) below the ground surface. Holden recovered 29 sherds from his excavations, divided by three 6-inch (15-cm) levels. These sherds included 17 glazed polychrome, 1 grayware, 7 red and white polychrome, and 3 "plain, crude grey of the Canadian type" (Holden 1931:51), presumably what we would now call Borger cord-marked. Holden identified Glazes II, IV, and V in the collection (Holden 1931:51). Notably, the glazewares were found in the upper 12 inches of the deposits (Levels I and II) and the polychromes and "plain, crude grey" pottery were found in the lower 12 inches of the deposits (Levels II and III), hinting at a stratigraphic separation of two components on the site. Holden recognized the multicomponent potential of the Tierra Blanca site when he concluded that "Pueblo Indians much later made temporary camps at these old slab-stone ruins on the Tierra Blanca for the purpose of hunting buffalo" (Holden 1931:53).

During 1979 and 1980 Spielmann conducted additional excavations at the Tierra Blanca site in order to secure information for her study of Plains-Pueblo interaction (Spielmann 1982). Flotation produced one corncob tip of 12-rowed corn, a few cupule fragments, and some corn pollen (Spielmann 1982:296), and Spielmann concludes that the lack of cobs showed that corn from Tierra Blanca was not grown there (Spielmann 1982:296). Spielmann reports three structures from Tierra Blanca, including a tipi ring (Figure 4.2) with a central saucer-shaped hearth (Spielmann 1982:283, Figure 13b); a circular slab-lined stone feature with central hearth (Figure 4.3), Structure 2, which may have been the base or foundation of a jacal structure (Spielmann 1982:283, Figure 13a); an impermanent structure, Structure 1, marked by a hard-packed sand/clay floor "ringed on the windward side by a scatter of small boulders" (Spielmann 1982: 282); and a roasting pit. Radiocarbon dates for Structure 2 and the roasting pit suggest a time span of AD 1200 to 1400 (Spielmann 1982:286). One radiocarbon sample from the tipi ring provided a date of AD 1425–1525 (Spielmann 1982:

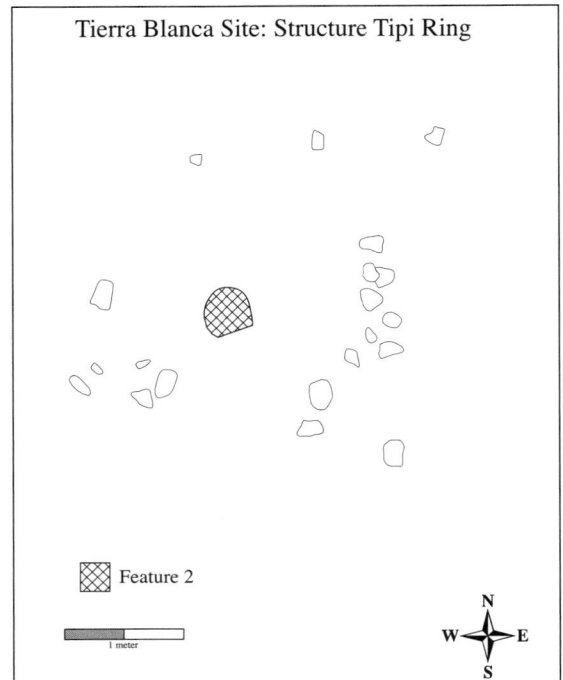

FIGURE 4.2. Tierra Blanca site tipi ring structure. Modified after Spielmann (1991:204, Figure 13b).

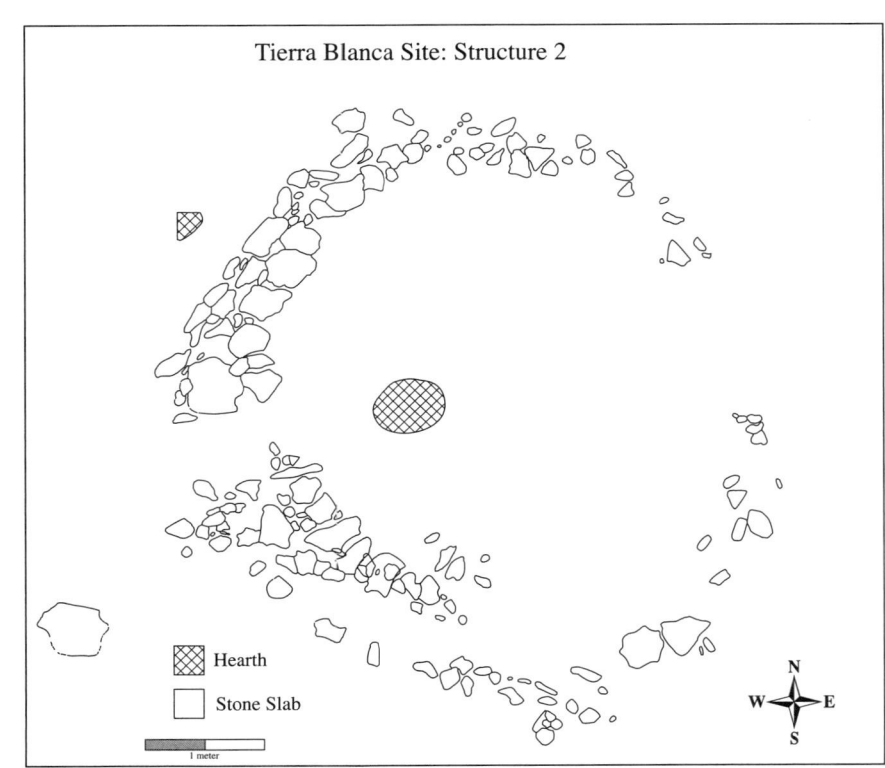

FIGURE 4.3. Tierra Blanca site, Structure 2. Modified after Spielmann (1991:204, Figure 13a).

286). Many pieces of obsidian, possibly from the Valles Caldera, were found (Spielmann 1982:310), but no frequency comparison to other lithic material types is offered, so the "many" is difficult to evaluate. The obsidian is represented by small unretouched flakes. The upper component at the Tierra Blanca site, which is the likely Tierra Blanca complex occupation, produced glazes C through early E with glazes C and D dominant, supporting a date of AD 1425–1525. However, the presence of faint-striated sherds at Tierra Blanca was used to infer a later, seventeenth-century, occupation (Spielmann 1982:323), which is corroborated by the presence of a metal projectile point on the surface of the site.

The Fifth Green site, attributed by Jack Hughes (1991) as typical of Tierra Blanca complex hunting campsites, was dug by Hughes in 1976. An unpublished manuscript (Kalokowski 1986) presents the basic data from the excavation. Artifacts from the site included Harrell and Fresno arrow points, one Talco point made of Edwards Plateau chert, and a possible metal awl pointed on both ends with a slight center arch (Kalokowski 1986:44[1]). Substantial bison bone on the site led to the inference that the site may have been a hunting and processing camp. The principal characteristics of the site are a large fire basin, a scatter of caliche rocks that may indicate a tipi ring, and a cluster of bison limb bones stuck vertically into the ground as if used for bracing posts (see Figure 4.4 for the location of these features). This last feature is interpreted as evidence of drying racks for hide or meat (Kalokowski 1986:63). In addition to the lithics and faunal materials, the site produced a gray-to-black pottery with micaceous temper, similar to Perdido Plain. No radiocarbon dates were obtained for the Fifth Green site, and no comparison was made to Tierra Blanca or related sites. The report concludes that the site represents a single-component, short-term occupation by Faraon Apaches (Kalokowski 1986:65).

In 1956 Jack Hughes, then with the Panhandle-Plains Historical Museum of Canyon, Texas, conducted salvage excavations at the Canyon City Club Cave in Randall County, Texas. Although never published, the manuscript of that effort (Hughes 1971) concludes that "Level 1 represents a brief occupation by a terminal prehistoric group with a nondescript trait inventory—probably Apache" (Hughes 1971:148). The "nondescript trait inventory" includes small surface fireplaces and possibly a single flexed burial. No ceramics or diagnostic lithic artifacts were linked with Level 1 of the Canyon City Club Cave. The Cologne Radiocarbon Calibration and Climate Research Package (CalPAL) correction of the two Level 1 radiocarbon dates provides calendric ages of cal AD 1525 ± 75 and cal AD 1570 ± 62. The term "Tierra Blanca complex" was not used in that analysis.

Several other archaeological sites that postdate AD 1450 and that could be attributed to the Tierra Blanca complex have been partially excavated. These include the Blackburn site in Randall County (Spielmann 1982, summarized by Boyd 1997), which may represent a severely deflated base camp. Bison hunting

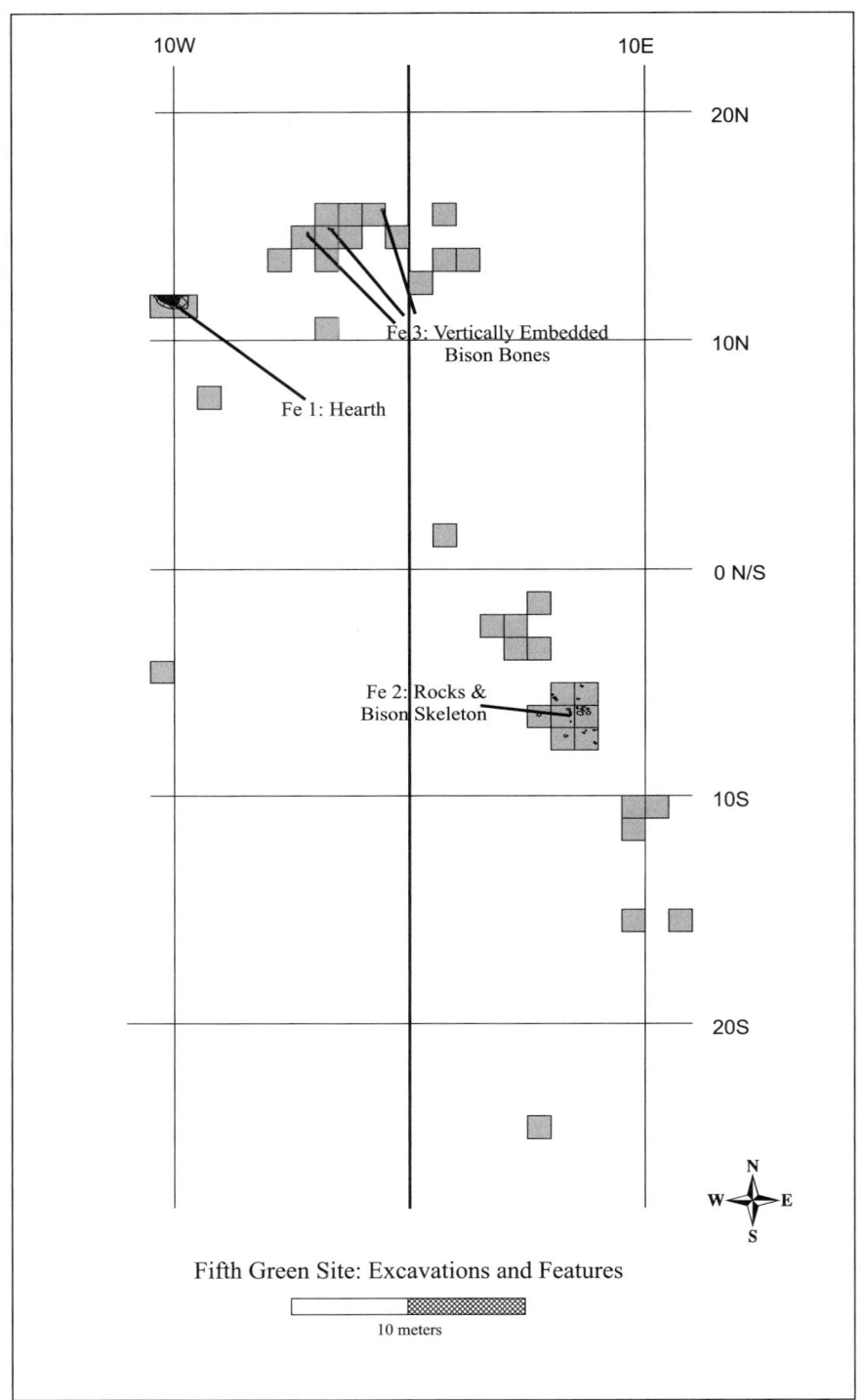

FIGURE 4.4. Fifth Green site excavations and features. Created from original drawings and notes by Kalokowski (1986).

and processing sites include the Tule Mouth site (Katz and Katz 1976), the Fatheree Site (Hughes et al. 1978), unpublished work on the Palisades site (now Hughes Rockshelter), the Cita Mouth site, and Water Crossing No. 2 in Palo Duro Canyon (see Boyd 1997). These and two sites that are reputedly similar to Tierra Blanca from the extreme northern Texas Panhandle have been summarized by Boyd (1997:371–380).

The characteristics archaeologists have used to assign sites to the Tierra Blanca complex are a preponderance of late glaze polychrome ceramics from New Mexico; grayware faint-striated pottery, possibly with micaceous temper or inclusions not unlike Perdido Plain pottery or similar to Southwestern utility wares (Vehik 1998:839); stone-outlined tipi rings at base camps and possibly at hunting camps; possibly stone-slab-lined semi-permanent structures at base camps; and some means of estimating age of the site to indicate that it postdates AD 1450. There may be some minor differences in style and craftsmanship between the Washita and Harrell points of the Tierra Blanca complex and earlier Southern Plains Village occupations (see Blakeslee et al. 2003:170), but the specific differences are not detailed. The economy of the Tierra Blanca people definitely included bison hunting and may or may not have included horticulture (see Spielmann 1982:296 and Hughes 1991:35 for more information).

THE ATHAPASKAN CONNECTION

Most authors attribute the Tierra Blanca complex to terminal prehistoric or protohistoric Southern Plains Athapaskans because the complex postdates the Antelope Creek phase, which is regularly attributed to Plains Caddoans, and it immediately antedates the protohistoric Apache (Querecho) in the area where the latter are normally identified. Maestas (2003) suggests that the material culture of the Tierra Blanca complex "is comparable to the diversity of material culture documented for Apache de los Llanos in documents and archaeology between 1650 and 1800" (Maestas 2003:50). He is assuming, however (as have others), that other groups that might also have been present did not also have a similar range of material culture owing to a similar range of behaviors.

Hughes has routinely referred to the gray micaceous pottery found in the most recent archaeological components in the Texas Panhandle as "Apachean" (see Hughes 1971, 1978, 1991), primarily because of its similarity to Perdido Plain and to tradewares from the Rio Grande Valley and Sangre de Cristo Mountain area. Yet the range of variation or degree of similarity of this pottery to recognized types has not yet been shown. A conference on Apachean ceramics held in 1985 attempted to evaluate and standardize the nomenclature and identification of the different wares present in late prehistoric and historic Apachean sites (Baugh 1987). As a result of this conference, the grayware most often associated with Tierra Blanca sites was formally defined as Tierra Blanca Plain within the Llano Estacado Grayware (Baugh 1987:797). This would seem to support Hughes's inference.

A panel discussion was held in 2000 among Blakeslee, Boyd, Flint, Habicht-Mauche, Hickerson, Jack Hughes, and Riley to consider the archaeological and ethnographic evidence pertaining to the Querecho and Teya of the Coronado expedition (Flint and Flint 2003:164–186). The participants addressed the distribution of Tierra Blanca complex sites and the possible relationship between the Tierra Blanca and peoples assumed to be Athapaskan-speakers—specifically, the Querecho. Opinions varied within the group: some said firmly that Tierra Blanca represents the Querecho and is Apache; others expressed the real concern that data on Querecho material culture and characteristic traits of Tierra Blanca are so sparse as to render firm conclusions impractical. One reason for this hesitation is that a complex has been defined but researchers have not been explicit about connecting it to the historic record. Seymour's chapter does this explicitly, and as she points out, debate around Tierra Blanca is an excellent example of why it is important to focus on this methodological issue and be aware of the theory behind interpretations (Seymour, Chapter 5, this volume). Otherwise it is just one person's opinion against another's without tangible ways to make distinctions and evaluate interpretations.

Boyd suggests that the association between Tierra Blanca and Athapaskans be considered a working hypothesis, although he likes "the idea that Querecho equals Tierra Blanca and Teya equals Garza for their inherent simplicity and neatness" (Blakeslee et al. 2003:174). Evidence for the connection of Tierra Blanca with Athapaskans, primarily the Querecho, is based on the Tierra Blanca economy, which was dominated by bison hunting and possibly bison hide processing combined with trade for vegetal foodstuffs.

Because of the traditional connection of the Tierra Blanca complex with Southern Plains Athapaskans, regional archaeologists and ethnohistorians have looked to Tierra Blanca for information about the Athapaskan immigration into the Southern Plains. Most researchers accept AD 1450 as the likely early date of the Tierra Blanca complex and believe it extended into the middle of the seventeenth century. A point of concern for Plains Athapaskan origins is that by AD 1450 Tierra Blanca represented an established cultural presence with a developed adaptation to Plains bison hunting, possibly a dual settlement system that depended on the season, and well-developed established trading connections to the American Southwest. Such developments do not happen instantaneously, so the people represented by the Tierra Blanca complex must certainly have entered the area sometime before AD 1450, and this contradicts interpretations of ethnohistoric data, which tend to hold sway in Texas.

The difficulty with assessing the date of origin of Tierra Blanca lies with the paucity of well-reported and thoroughly analyzed components, the lack of ready distinctions for what we might think of as "proto–Tierra Blanca," and an understanding of the time required for adaptation to the local environment, given the assumption of a relatively late presence for Athapaskans on the Plains. Jack Hughes expressed his opinion that "the Tierra Blanca complex began in the

1300s and had quite an effect. [Its beginning produced] a lot more trade goods up in the Canadian breaks, in the big Caddoan-speaking villages" (Blakeslee et al. 2003:178).

Summary and Conclusions

The Tierra Blanca complex is not clearly defined on the basis of distinctive items of material culture, largely because much of the area in which it occurs is privately held. As a complex of associated traits within a definable region, it does appear to represent a material reality. The Tierra Blanca complex temporally follows the Plains Caddoan occupation of the Antelope Creek phase and related materials. Because the High Plains of the Texas Panhandle are the home of the Querecho, who are presumed to be early historic or protohistoric Apache, the equation of Tierra Blanca complex material culture with Apache people and culture seems a reasonable hypothesis.

I emphasize that the equation of Tierra Blanca with the Apache is a reasonable hypothesis, reiterating Boyd's comments (Blakeslee et al. 2003:174). If we accept for the moment that Tierra Blanca represents an early Athapaskan occupation, we must decide how reliable the established beginning dates for Tierra Blanca are. Could it be that the date of AD 1450 that people accept for Tierra Blanca is a *terminus ante quem* date for Athapaskans in the Texas Panhandle? If so, Hughes's comment about the Athapaskans arriving in the AD 1300s (Blakeslee et al. 2003:178) may be a real possibility.

The difficulty with evaluating the origin of the Tierra Blanca complex is the lack of reliable data from excavated post–Antelope Creek sites and distributional information about terminal prehistoric/protohistoric sites in the region. This lack can be addressed only by a concerted effort to identify archaeological sites that may immediately predate recognizable Tierra Blanca occupations, followed by an attempt to assess their relationship to the Tierra Blanca complex. Additionally, until such time as at least one site that represents the Tierra Blanca complex is fully reported, the minutiae of elements within the complex cannot be assessed. This is not a fault of prior research: Holden was looking for connections between the Panhandle and the Southwest, Spielmann was looking at trade relationships in the same connection, and their analyses were sufficient to respond to the questions they were asking. Only recently have we begun to ask questions about ethnogenesis in the culture-historical record in the Panhandle (and elsewhere), and these new, potentially more difficult questions require new answers from new research.

Notes

1. The manuscript of Kalokowski's report was provided by the Panhandle-Plains Historical Museum and is not paginated. Pagination was included for D. Hughes's reference purposes on the copy provided.

REFERENCES

Baugh, Timothy, and F. W. Eddy
1987 Rethinking Apachean Ceramics: The 1985 Southern Athapaskan Ceramics Conference. *American Antiquity* 52(4):793–799.

Blakeslee, Donald J., Douglas K. Boyd, Richard Flint, Judith Habicht-Mauche, Nancy P. Hickerson, Jack T. Hughes, and Carroll L. Riley
2003 Bison Hunters of the Llano in 1541: A Panel Discussion. In *The Coronado Expedition from the Distance of 460 years*, edited by Richard Flint and Shirley Cushing Flint, pp. 164–186. Albuquerque: University of New Mexico Press.

Boyd, Douglas K.
1997 *Caprock Canyonlands Archaeology: A Synthesis of the Late Prehistory and History of Lake Alan Henry and the Texas Panhandle-Plains*. Reports of Investigations No. 110, 2:337–486. Austin, Texas: Prewitt and Associates.

Flint, Richard, and Shirley C. Flint (editors)
2003 *The Coronado Expedition from the Distance of 460*. Albuquerque: University of New Mexico Press.

Habicht-Mauche, Judith A.
1987 Southwestern-Style Culinary Ceramics on the Southern Plains: A Case Study of Technological Innovation and Cross-Cultural Interaction. *Plains Anthropologist* 32(116):175–191.

Holden, William C.
1931 Texas Tech Archeological Expedition, Summer 1930. *Bulletin of the Texas Archeological and Paleontological Society* 3:43–52.

Holmes, Charles E.
1975 A Northern Athapaskan Environmental System in Diachronic Perspective. *Western Canadian Journal of Anthropology* 5(3–4): 92–124.
2007 The East Beringian Tradition and the Transitional Period: New Data from Swan Point. Paper presented at the annual meeting of the Alaska Anthropological Association, Fairbanks.

Honigman, John J.
1981 Expressive Aspects of Subarctic Indian Culture. In *Subarctic*, edited by June Helm, pp. 718–738. Handbook of North American Indians, Vol. 6, William C. Sturtevant, general editor. Washington, D.C.: Smithsonian Institution.

Hoopes, John W., and William K. Barnett
1995 The Shape of Early Pottery Studies. In *The Emergence of Pottery: Technology and Innovation in Ancient Societies*, edited by William K. Barnett and John W. Hoopes, pp. 1–7. Washington, D.C.: Smithsonian Institution.

Hopi Dictionary Project
1998 *Hopi Dictionary/Hopìikwa Lavàytutuveni: A Hopi-English Dictionary of the Third Mesa Dialect*. Tucson: University of Arizona Press.

Hovezak, Timothy D., and Leslie M. Sesler
2002 *Archaeological Investigations in the Fruitland Project Area: Late Archaic, Basketmaker, Pueblo I, and Navajo Sites in Northwestern New Mexico*. Research Papers No. 4. Dolores, Colorado: La Plata Archaeological Consultants.

Huebner, Jeffery A.
1991 Late Prehistoric Bison Populations in Central and Southern Texas. *Plains Anthropologist* 36(137):343–356.

Hughes, David
1989 Terminal Archaic Bison Kills in the Texas Panhandle. In *The Light of Past Experi-

ence: Essays in Honor of Jack T. Hughes, edited by Beryl C. Roper, pp. 183–204. Publication No. 5. Amarillo, Texas: Panhandle Archaeological Society.

Hughes, Jack T.
1971 The Canyon City Club Cave in the Panhandle of Texas. Ms. on file, Texas Historical Commission, Austin.
1978 Archeology of Palo Duro Canyon. *Panhandle-Plains Historical Review* 51:35–58.
1991 Prehistoric Cultural Development on the Texas High Plains. *Bulletin of the Texas Archeological Society* 60:1–55.
2011 *The Canyon City Club Cave in the Panhandle of Texas*. Edited by Christopher R. Lintz. Hughes/Tunnell Memorial Volume, Publication No. 10. Amarillo, Texas: Panhandle Archeological Society.

Hughes, Jack T., H. Charles Hood, and Billy Pat Newman
1978 *Archeological Testing in the Red Deer Creek Watershed in Gray, Roberts, and Hemphill Counties, Texas*. Archeological Research Laboratory, Killgore Research Center. Canyon: West Texas State University.

Kalokowski, H. Paul, Jr.
1986 Archeological Testing of the Fifth Green Site (A1363), Randall County, Texas. Archeological Research Laboratory, Killgore Research Center, West Texas State University. Ms. on file, Panhandle-Plains Historical Museum.

Katz, Susana R., and Paul Katz
1976 *Archeological Investigations in Lower Tule Canyon, Briscoe County, Texas*. Office of the State Archeologist Survey Report No. 16. Austin: Texas Archeological Commission.

Maestas, Enrique Gilbert-Michael
2003 Culture and History of Native American Peoples of South Texas. Unpublished Ph.D. dissertation, University of Texas, Austin.

Quigg, J. M., C. Lintz, F. M. Oglesby, A. C. Earls, C. D. Frederick, W. N. Trierweiler, D. Owsley, and K. W. Kibler
1993 *Historic and Prehistoric Data Recovery at Palo Duro Reservoir, Hansford County, Texas*. Technical Report No. 485. Austin: Mariah and Associates.

Spielmann, Katherine
1982 Inter-societal Food Acquisition among Egalitarian Societies: An Ecological Study of Plains/Pueblo Interaction in the American Southwest, Volume 1. Unpublished Ph.D. dissertation, Department of Anthropology, University of Michigan, Ann Arbor.
1983 Late Prehistoric Exchange between the Southwest and Southern Plains. *Plains Anthropologist* 28(102):257–272.

Spielmann, Katherine (editor)
1991 *Farmers, Hunters, and Colonists: Interaction between the Southwest and the Southern Plains*. Tucson: University of Arizona Press.

Vehik, Susan C.
1998 Tierra Blanca Complex. In *Archaeology of Prehistoric Native America: An Encyclopedia*, edited by Guy E. Gibbon and Kenneth M. Ames, p. 839. Oxford: Taylor and Francis.

CHAPTER 5

Isolating a Pre-differentiation Athapaskan Assemblage in the Southern Southwest

The Cerro Rojo Complex

DENI J. SEYMOUR

One reason Athapaskan migration southward out of Canada remains an unresolved problem is because archaeologists have not known when these distinctive groups arrived in the Southwest or what their material culture looked like during this initial colonization. Linguistic studies have provided hints, as have other sources, but archaeological evidence has largely eluded researchers. Because a mirror image of the Subarctic assemblage is not present in the Southwest, we assume that fundamental changes occurred along the way as early Athapaskan people adapted to new environments and borrowed from neighbors. This pattern of cultural flexibility as an Athapaskan adaptive strategy is consistent with ethnographic understandings of Athapaskans (e.g., Kluckhohn and Leighton 1962; VanStone 1974) and so is easily accommodated conceptually. This means that the constellation of traits representing the earliest Athapaskans must be defined independently in the Southwest near the southern end of their migration tack.

The descendants of these migrants still occupy the region, and so one might legitimately suggest that researchers simply use the direct historical approach, examining modern ethnographic or historic characteristics to extrapolate back in time. The problem with this approach is that a pervasive continuity cannot be readily identified between nineteenth-century traits and those occurring much earlier in time.[1] This is because by the late historic and ethnographic periods fundamental changes had already occurred in the material culture of the Chiricahua and Mescalero Apache. The ancestors of these groups resided in the southern portion of the American Southwest, where the earliest Athapaskan evidence has been found in the fourteenth century.

As an example of the substantial nature of these changes, archaeological evidence documents a shift to lower elevations for residential sites and thermal features in the late historic period that seems to relate directly to pressure from enemies and neighbors. Thick vegetation and canyon walls helped to dissipate smoke, dissolve noise, and hide inhabitants; this shift also accommodated the terrain requirements and greater visibility of skin tipis and canvas-covered wickiups, which gradually became more important through time (Seymour 2009a, 2010a, 2012). This pattern is confirmed and explained by ethnographic information (Ball 1988:102) and also by Chiricahua Land Claims interviews in which, with reference to a late historic site in Mexico, Robert Geronimo (Henderson 1957:404) noted that the "main camp [was] down in [a] big canyon where they could hide their fire. Of course in old time[s], [they] had fires in high elevations." Thus the problem has become one of discerning which attributes can be established as having ancient roots and which are more recent additions and alterations, as well as identifying those traits and practices that fell away or were relevant to only a subset of bands or local groups.

The consensus among researchers has been that Apache sites can only rarely be identified in the absence of European artifacts. Historian John Wilson (1975: 15) noted, "The perishable dwellings would make Apache camps difficult to find and even then an ethnic or temporal identification might be impossible." One study directed at isolating the indigenous Apache artifact assemblage at three sites was unable to substantiate or refute an Apache presence based on an examination of flaked-stone artifacts (Beidl 1990). Another study led to a similar conclusion, suggesting that the problem of distinguishing the Apache assemblage from the multitude of flaked-stone scatters is far from being solved (Adams et al. 2000:5). Further complicating the problem is that these sites and their artifacts are often confused with prehistoric manifestations. Researchers mistake historic materials for prehistoric (see examples in Seymour 2002, 2008a, 2008b, 2009a, 2009c, 2010b; Seymour and Church 2007), identify prehistoric material as historic, or confound material culture from other groups with Apache. An example of the last kind of error is provided by Ferg's (2004) Chiricahua and Mescalero Apache pottery study, in which at least a third of the whole vessels illustrated as Apache are actually non-Apache pots identifiable as Ancestral Pueblo or O'odham. As a result of these kinds of problems, the commonly understood view is that efforts to identify ancestral Apache sites will be unsuccessful when artifact attributes and other characteristics of indigenous material culture are used. This is one reason so much effort has focused on the investigation of battle sites and the latest of historic Apache sites, which have clear modern analogues or a basis in the historic documentary, oral historic, or ethnographic records.

In this chapter I present my methodology and the results of my work to isolate terminal prehistoric and historic period early Athapaskan culture groups (the ancestral Chiricahua and Mescalero among them) through their archaeology. The goal has been to distinguish a set of material culture and landscape-use attributes that together characterize ancestral Apache habitation sites in the absence of European material culture. I have focused on establishing a temporal

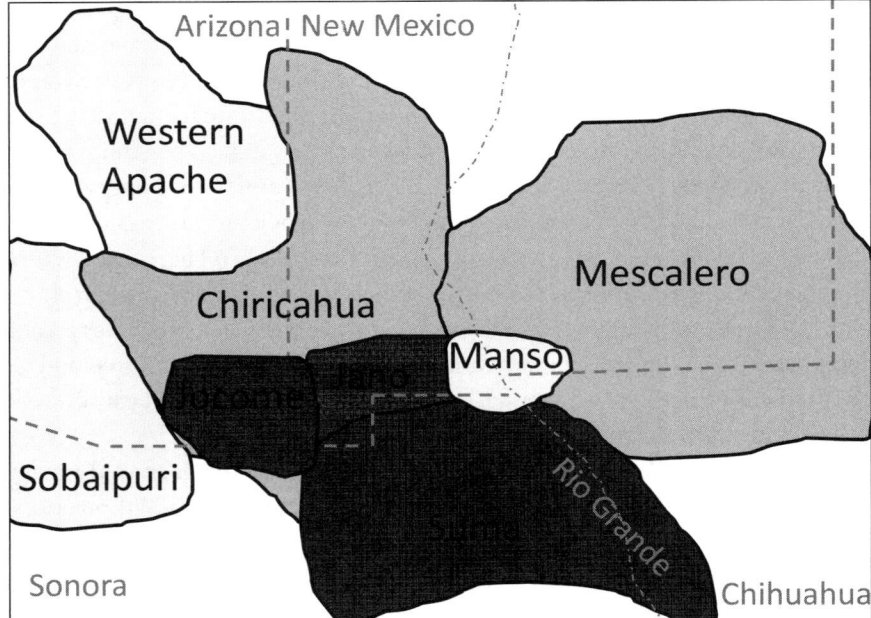

FIGURE 5.1. Idealized distribution of mobile groups in the southern Southwest. The area used by each was much larger than the core territories shown here and overlapped considerably. Image by Deni Seymour.

and material framework for identification of these sites and devising approaches for inference verification.

The Cerro Rojo complex, found in the basin-and-range portion of the southernmost American Southwest, has been the most thoroughly defined of the new mobile group complexes. This and contemporaneous non-Athapaskan complexes thought to represent a series of contemporaneous mobile groups (Figure 5.1) have been characterized on the basis of indigenous features and artifacts and autochthonous aspects of terrain selection and landscape use (Seymour 2002, 2003, 2004a; 2009c).[2] The method used to distinguish this ancestral Apachean complex is a combination of existing culture area definitional procedures and new approaches that are more appropriate to modern practices and specifically to the characterization of mobile groups. The development and application of new methodologies has been necessitated by the fact that these mobile culture groups were not initially defined during the culture history era precisely because they were more difficult to pin down than more stationary groups. Moreover, assumptions regarding applicable principles pertaining to culture area character and trait transmission have had to be revised owing to differences between stationary farming and highly mobile groups in the ways they use the landscape. Explicit presentation of the methodology used and a description of the salient elements of the complex provide justification for knowledge claims about the identification of pre-differentiation early Athapaskans in the southern portion of the American Southwest. Development of appropriate theory addresses the common problem of underinterpretation that too often results in mere description, acceptance of documentary sources at face value, and uncritical reliance on direct historical analogues. Original technical reports and journal articles regarding the definition of the Cerro Rojo complex may be consulted for more detailed information (Seymour 2002, 2003, 2004a, 2004b, 2008a, 2008b, 2008c, 2009a, 2009b, 2009c, 2009e, 2010a, 2010b, 2011a).

CONNECTING THE DOCUMENTS AND ARCHAEOLOGICAL RECORDS: HISTORICALLY REFERENCED GROUPS

Traditional culture area definition methodologies have been less effective for Athapaskans than for many Southwestern groups, which is a primary reason these and other mobile groups were not defined along with the other great Southwestern cultures (e.g., Rouse 1975:42; Seymour 2009c). Thus a practical issue facing the archaeologist is how to isolate new material culture signatures, especially when these signatures were too obscure and difficult for the initial culture-area-focused archaeologists to identify. Fortunately, descendant groups and the documentary record provide evidence that there are archaeological culture groups that remain to be identified, justifying the considerable effort and ingenuity required to isolate them.

Documentary and ethnographic sources also establish expectations of what may be found in the archaeological record at particular points in time. By extracting relevant information from these sources, we can often connect narrative documentary and ethnographic statements to what is expected in the archaeological record using middle-range theory. From an archaeological perspective, relevant information that is focused on defining historically referenced peoples or places means selecting those aspects of the documentary record that have material or spatial relevance that can be identified in the archaeological record at specific places during specific times. This is a practical matter of appropriately matching documentary information to the archaeological question (e.g., Little 1992:4). While other aspects of the documentary record may be of value for other purposes, this approach acknowledges the limitations of the archaeological record and accepts that only certain types of data can potentially distinguish past people and places (Seymour 2011b).[3] Plainly stated, only a portion of the textual information has material and spatial correlates or can be connected to tangible remains through theory. This approach also recognizes the shortcomings of the narrative form of textual data (e.g., Galloway 2005); at the same time, it accepts that these are the types of documents that tend to have greatest relevance to early Athapaskan and non-Athapaskan mobile groups in this region.

Accepting that each data source (archaeological, ethnographic, and documentary) is an independent line of evidence, Leone and Potter (1988:13–14; see also Binford 1987) have suggested that one can establish "descriptive grids," which are "based on insights from the documentary [and ethnographic] records, against which to array the archaeological record." In this methodology "one creates a framework and then derives from it expectations of the archaeological record." It is important to acknowledge, however, that relevant information contained in the documents is rarely actually descriptive, and that even seemingly descriptive elements may incorrectly characterize past systems, places, people, or geographic referents. For this reason, what have been referred to as "descriptive grids" may be more effectively conceptualized as material and spatial *correlate grids*. Even when "descriptive" elements are seemingly direct and straightforward (e.g., a group lived on a hill), they involve interpretive and relational statements that require verification and analysis through independent means.

Correlate grids, established from careful and deliberate analysis of documentary sources and construction of behavioral models that link these correlates, have served as the basis for distinguishing two classes of protohistoric mobile groups in the southern Southwest at the time of first contact forward to the late historic period (Seymour 2002, 2003, 2004a). During this effort the operative questions were how to establish expectations that could distinguish the ancestral Apache from contemporaneous mobile groups (Jano, Jocome, Manso, and Suma, to name a few), how to distinguish Apache from preceding groups, and how to distinguish different Apachean groups from one another. While there are several ways to handle this problem, it is the historical point of view that distinguishes this effort from other culture area definitional problems of the prehistoric period. Cultural identity in the historic period takes on many dimensions, beyond archaeologically definable "culture groups." Historical documentation allows us to establish the presence of "historically referenced groups" and provides an independent data source from which to work. The task is complicated by the fact that attributes other than those traceable by material evidence were often used by historical Europeans to distinguish these groups.

Because the Apache and various other mobile groups were described in historical and ethnographic records, an interpretive dimension is added that allows us to "work back and forth, from one to the other, using each to extend the meaning of the other" (Leone and Potter 1988:14). Information that has material and spatial correlates can be extracted from the ethnographic and documentary records to establish expectations of what to look for in the archaeological context. Sometimes these textual and graphic elements are ostensibly direct and straightforward (e.g., they lived on a hill; they lived in grass huts); at other times they may be derived from evaluative or interpretive statements, even misunderstandings, but may be useful as long as the historical context of the statements is critically assessed (Seymour 2009d:405–406).

While the historically referenced and ethnographically documented groups in the southern Southwest share some common traits—such as being mobile, living in small groups, and hunting and gathering—there are also important points of difference that allow distinctions to be suggested. For example, one class of mobile group tended to reside near rivers, marshes, and playas and to engage in net fishing, catching waterfowl and small game, and cutting raw meat with their [apparently notable] flint knives, and also lived on hills (rather than or in addition to living in the mountains; i.e., the Canutillo complex). The other class was inclined to be in and near the mountains, tended to avoid eating fish and things that swam under the water, and were apt to hunt larger game (e.g., Opler 1941:330–332, 1983b:431; i.e., the Cerro Rojo complex). These and many other indices of social and behavioral practices provide an empirical basis, along with the use of middle-range theory, for distinguishing archaeological culture groups and building inferences as to which ones might be representative of specific historically referenced groups.[4]

By constructing a correlate grid, as shown in Table 5.1, we can advance expectations that can (a) help discover new archaeological manifestations and (b) connect groups identified in the documentary record or discussed in the ethnographic record to those identified archaeologically.[5] When we encounter a lack of correspondence between sources, our opportunities are heightened for extending our knowledge of the past (e.g., Leone and Potter 1988:14, 16), or more accurately, when we encounter a lack of correspondence between correlates (or interpretations) derived from sources, our opportunities are heightened for extending our knowledge of the past and refining our theories.

Searching within the Archaeological Record

Unique archaeological signatures can be extracted from the archaeological record even without assistance from documentary sources, although the task is made easier and more effectively interpretable by documentary content. Because the expected ancestral Apachean signatures are time specific—that is, early Athapaskans did not appear until late in the prehistoric period and persisted into the historic period—a temporal period can be bracketed. By AD 1450 the postulated end of the prehistoric pattern and the initiation of new ones are indicated throughout much of the Southwest. Thus sites that have produced dates after this temporal threshold are of potential interest for an initial examination that can test the models derived from documentary and ethnographic sources.

This effort to isolate historic mobile groups in the southern Southwest was initially aided by the fact that a number of previously recorded sites had produced chronometric dates (largely radiocarbon) falling within the target period (AD 1450–1700). These sites were mostly multiple component, and the dates were generally obtained during work focused on prehistoric resources and research themes.[6] The late-occurring assemblages were separated from the prehistoric ones by means of a comparison of assemblages across a number of the sites with late-dating components. Systematic comparisons of the surface assemblages or museum-curated collections on each site dating to this target period established a set of assemblage elements that were shared by each.[7] The commonalities of their artifact and feature assemblages were analyzed, along with their terrain attributes and landscape placement within specific geographic areas. For example, as the flaked-stone assemblages[8] were analyzed on these

TABLE 5.1. Correlate Grid Example in Which Expectations Drawn from Text Passages Are Made Explicit through Inferences and Material and Spatial Correlates.

TEXT PASSAGE OR MAP DATA	RESULTING MATERIAL OR SPATIAL CORRELATES AND INTERMEDIATE INFERENCES
"Now we are seeing the Apaches enter that camp. They have come in two or three times, pretending to be peaceful, to sell their buckskin and later steal the horses." —Don Diego de Vargas, 1691 (Kessell and Hendricks 1992:66)	Archaeological evidence of Apachean groups in this region should be lacking before 1691 if the following interpretation is correct: 1. "As of April 1691 the Apaches were just starting to show up at Janos [presidio]" (Curtis Schaafsma, personal communication 2010), with the implication that they had just migrated this far south. Archaeological evidence of Apachean groups in this region should be present before 1691 if the one of following interpretations is correct: 2. The Apache had just allied or associated themselves with non-Apache groups in this specific area and so are first introduced to their allies. 3. The Apache moved into or began raiding in this subregion from an adjacent one where they had been since pre-Spanish times. 4. They just recognized the value of begging from the Spanish at this time.
"They live in rancherías, without permanent habitations. They live by hunting." —Castañeda de Nájera, 1540–1541 (Flint and Flint 2005:417)	Mobile hunter-gatherers Curvilinear surface structures or tipi rings, impromptu Dispersed housing, not compact Housing layout is unplanned Paucity of material culture
His sons "live separately and wander about subsisting by hunting and gathering mescal through the sierras…and the other intervening hills and rugged mountains." —Lafora, 1766–1768 (Kinnaird 1958:78)	Situated on raised topographic features, specifically hills and mountains Mobile hunter-gatherers Frequent areas where mescal/agave grows Inhabit small residential sites in individual families

late-dating sites, similarities in tool forms, stylistic attributes, and technological aspects of their production emerged (Figure 5.2). This led to the identification of a series of assemblage characteristics that differed from those of the preceding Jornada Mogollon, Hohokam, Mimbres, Archaic, and Paleoindian assemblages. Ultimately, through this extractive method, two clearly discrete, late-dating archaeological assemblages were isolated, one of which was eventually inferred to be Athapaskan.

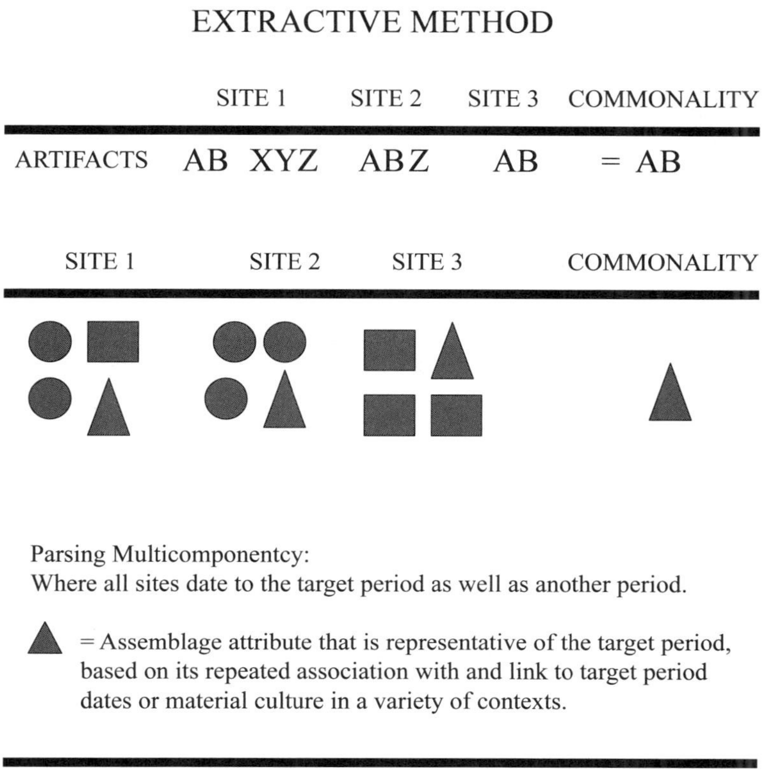

EXTRACTIVE METHOD

	SITE 1	SITE 2	SITE 3	COMMONALITY
ARTIFACTS	AB XYZ	AB Z	AB	= AB

SITE 1	SITE 2	SITE 3	COMMONALITY
●■ ●▲	●● ●▲	■▲ ■■	▲

Parsing Multicomponentcy:
Where all sites date to the target period as well as another period.

 = Assemblage attribute that is representative of the target period, based on its repeated association with and link to target period dates or material culture in a variety of contexts.

FIGURE 5.2. Simplified model of the extractive method, in which elements relating to unique culture groups can be distinguished within a specific target temporal period. Late-dating assemblages can be sorted in multicomponent sites through the use of commonalities found on a subset of sites. Attributes isolated may be stylistic traits, tool forms, material types, technological aspects of their production, or freshness of flaking debris. Nature of and investment in features as well as characteristics of landscape use are also helpful indices.

This extractive method involves comparison across a number of sites that all share late-dating components but that also are usually characterized by earlier (and sometimes later) components. Single-component sites are rare, and most work has been conducted on sites that also date to earlier periods (Seymour 2010b). The attributes potentially representative of the target component become clear when we establish which attributes are common to all sites even though these sites also possess dissimilar components associated with the preceding Mogollon, Archaic, and Paleoindian cultures (see Figure 5.2).[9] Such late-dating components are indicated and expected on most examined sites because of their late chronometric dates. This late-dating component should be the only distinctive characteristic these sites share.[10] For example, all Jornada Mogollon sites should differ from Archaic sites but would possess similarities in the late-dating target assemblage. In this way we can identify the targeted component by isolating the series of attributes common to all the sites regardless of and distinctive from other components present.

The observed rudimentary pattern must then be expanded, refined, and confirmed through the examination of the occurrence of other late-dating components in new contexts, across different environmental and landscape zones, at different times, and in different historic tribal territories. The ability to predict the location and nature of new residential or other types of sites provides compelling evidence that the signature is appropriate, especially when chronometric dates confirm their use during the target period and when Apache-specific symbolic representations (such as rock art) are encountered. The tentative pattern extracted from the data is evaluated by investigation of areas that do not conform to the pattern as well, thereby establishing boundary conditions for inference building. Similarities between components on sites allow the isolation of a complex that is ultimately assigned a tentative cultural affiliation. The identification of key attributes and the cultural assignment are repeatedly checked by comparison to sites assigned to the ancestral Apache in other regions and sites of affirmed historically documented Apachean affiliation.

HISTORICAL-ETHNOGRAPHIC ANALOGUES AND CHANGE

The preceding methodology is useful for isolating archaeological culture groups with or without reference to ethnographic populations.[11] On the other hand, some material and spatial attributes isolated in the archaeological record can be understood more thoroughly by reference to patterns found among descendant populations. Such ethnographic analogues can be useful for interpreting results and relating such groups to historically documented ones, providing a systematic procedure for doing so. These analogues can be effective if comparison is done in a way that does not a priori assume that continuity exists or that cultural elements are transmitted as a coherent package. Continuity must be demonstrated, and it must be recognized that not all elements of material culture change at the same rate. Housing type or pottery may change when flaked-stone technology and style stay constant because of the dissimilarity of the operative factors behind their character.[12] This is important to understand because culture historians often assume that a set of attributes varied and coalesced in concert with one another, forming a cohesive whole (a constellation of traits) that remained relatively stable (within periods) across time and space, but this is not the case with mobile groups of the terminal prehistoric and historic periods in the area studied. Each material culture element must be considered in its own way and then evaluated in relation to other relevant elements. Housing type is explained in one way, stone tool use in another, and variations in pottery in still another. The principles describing each are multiple and varied and only loosely coupled, although they may be related logically and cohere substantively (see Schiffer's 1988 discussion of middle-range theory).

Because adoption and alteration of various material culture elements are not necessarily in sync with one another, it is especially productive to examine each at its critical time of transformation. For example, during the reservation period, as Cerro Rojo transforms into the Cerro Alto complex, there is an overlap in the use of glass and stone tool forms in some identified Mescalero contexts. Specifically, tool forms such as end scrapers, perforators, gravers, spokeshaves, and fleshers share stylistic attributes in each medium. There is also an overlap in wickiup and tipi use. This short period of overlap and convergence of forms in two media (wickiups and tipis in mountain contexts) or materials (stone and glass) allows the archaeologist to see traditional technologies changing to their historic and modern forms. It is assumed that similar transformations occurred throughout Athapaskan prehistory, both during migration to and once the migrants had arrived in the Southwest. The stylistic similarities of tool forms in both materials (stone and glass) and the co-occurrence of certain forms in glass with different forms in stone give us confidence in the identification of these forms and technologies as Apachean and allow this confidence to be extended to earlier periods when only the stone forms and technologies are present. The co-occurrence of tipis and wickiups in a few contexts provides confirmation of the signatures of both of these shelter forms, so that in the absence of the better-recognized tipi outlines the more unobtrusive wickiup outline can be identified with confidence. The overlap in some instances provides hints as to portions of the landscape used by the Apache and documents the changes in terrain sectors selected for use, based on housing type, and in geographic setting, based on subsistence strategy (farming versus hunting-gathering-raiding) or changing neighbor relations.

Some of the most effective and convincing confirmation continues to be provided by historically documented contexts for which documentary data exist, such as historic photographs and journal entries. The noted patterns at some sites could be verified or refined based on the similarities and differences found in these more conclusive situations. For example, several C. S. Fly photographs were taken of the Cañon de los Embudos site, where in the spring of 1886 Geronimo almost surrendered. The terrain characteristics are sufficiently distinctive that the location could be identified with certainty (Hayes and Hayes 1991; Van Orden 1991). Comparisons of housing types in the photographs with current on-the-ground archaeological signatures show the range of contemporaneous housing types used by a single group, the varied and often nondescript nature of their archaeological signature, their placement on the terrain, and use of the larger landscape (Seymour 2009e). Other aspects of material culture, including flaked stone, groundstone, flaked glass, and pottery artifacts, provide conclusive evidence of the nature of the Apachean material culture signature at one point in time by a specific historically known group. Similar studies that compare archaeological with documentary evidence have been carried out for the Cochise-Howard Treaty site, whose specific location is identified in documents and photographs (Seymour and Robertson 2008).

Convoluted Continuity in Descendant Populations and the Iterative Approach

Convoluted Continuity

Some attributes have been retained by descendant populations because those aspects are still functional and are part of underlying structural-organizational aspects of culture. Symbolic representations of belief systems found in rock art provide a notable example, although they are found on only a select few Apache

FIGURE 5.3. Charcoal-drawn mountain spirit images at a large Peloncillo Mountain Apache site (The Hormiguero site; AZ CC:12:58, ASM) date to the 1600s or early 1700s. This *gaʔhe* is the most complete. Photograph and image by Deni Seymour.

sites. Representations that are distinctive and have been retained by Athapaskan groups leave little question as to the affiliation and time depth of these symbols.

Still, modern understandings of these depictions may be at odds with archaeological evidence. When this occurs, explanations must be sought that acknowledge culture change and the convoluted nature of continuity. For example, according to Carmichael and Farrer (this volume), some cultural specialists at Mescalero indicate that mountain spirit (*gaʔhe*) depictions were not used until the late nineteenth century. On the other hand, charcoal-drawn mountain spirit images at a large Peloncillo Mountain Apache site (the Hormiguero site; AZ CC:12:58, ASM) suggest a greater time depth of usage for the Chiricahua, many of whom now also reside at Mescalero (Figure 5.3). These illustrations were sketched on the back wall of a rockshelter that also contains a storage platform and a probable fragment from a mountain spirit headdress or wand (other rockshelters portray wasp-waisted red men, the former also considered an attribute of Apachean rock art). A date from this platform and five other luminescence and radiocarbon dates from Apache brownware pottery and storage platforms, respectively, at this site suggest a series of short-term occupations in the 1600s to early 1700s. This context and association indicate use of mountain spirit symbolism among the Chiricahua (and perhaps groups speaking a dialectal variety intermediate between modern Chiricahua and Western Apache; see de Reuse, this volume) much earlier than among the Mescalero.[13]

Investigation of inferred Apachean rock art representations throughout the southern Southwest indicate that ancestral people occupying the Mescalero

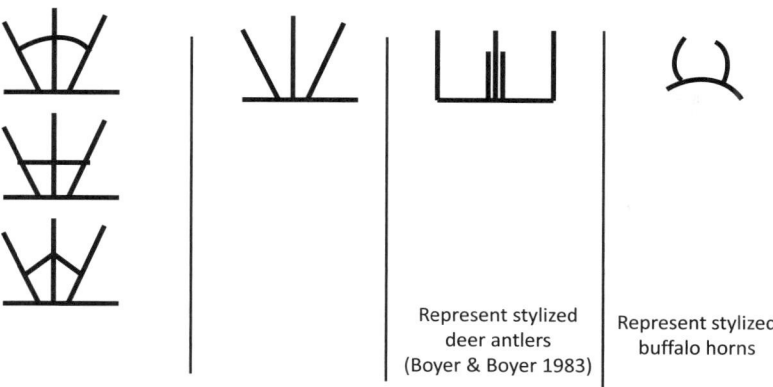

FIGURE 5.4. Ceremonial headdresses vary between Apache regions within the Southwest consistent with rock art distributions. Plains-oriented groups exhibit wind god and buffalo-horned images while mountain-oriented groups depict mountain spirit images, referenced as *gq'he* among these southern Apachean groups. They also seem to vary through time. This figure shows known Western Apache headdress styles on the far left (ethnographic examples), then a potential early Chiricahua style (archaeological example), followed by a late Chiricahua style (archaeological and ethnographic examples), and on the far right, a plains-style headdress (archaeological and ethnographic examples). Image by Deni Seymour.

and Lipan areas depicted wind gods and buffalo-horned images (see Bilbo 1988; Unglaub 2010), consistent with their plains orientation.[14] Those in the mountains to the west of the Rio Grande, including in Arizona, portrayed mountain spirits.[15] Yet, through time, because of overlapping territories and travel routes, and owing to historical factors including the geographic reshuffling of groups, overlap in depicted symbolism occurred in the center of the area, on both sides of the Rio Grande (Figures 5.4 through 5.6a and b).

To complicate matters further, a temporal change seems apparent in the way mountain spirit headdresses are depicted. Initially, it seems, headdresses were fan-shaped, and while the Western Apache retained this style or a variation thereof, the Chiricahua shifted to the antler-like rectilinear form seen in photographs of Chiricahua ceremonies (Figures 5.7 and 5.8) and found archaeologically far to the west, including in the Dragoon Mountains of southern Arizona. Chiricahua residents living at Mescalero may have transferred this antler-like style to Mescalero or vice versa when the Chiricahua returned from captivity, so that in the reservation period, and currently, when mountain spirits are depicted, they are this rectilinear form (but see Chapter 8). Wind gods, buffalo-horned images, and mountain spirits are maintained in late historic and modern rock art found in the intermediate zone.

If new data continue to support these suggested temporal and geographic distributions, rock art will be a useful relative dating technique as well as a way to connect specific aspects of material culture to early Athapaskans. This

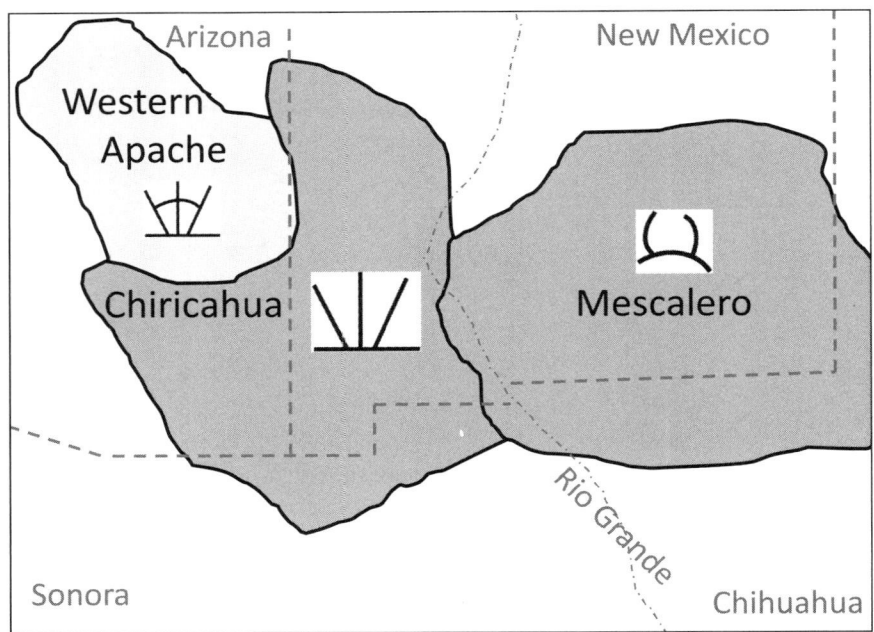

FIGURE 5.5. Early rock art depictions suggest a relatively simple distinction between mountains and plains Apaches. Wind god and buffalo-horned images characterize those to the east while mountain spirit depictions are typical of those to the west. Image by Deni Seymour.

FIGURE 5.6A. The wind god image with horns is from Alamo Mountain, New Mexico. Zigzag lines here and elsewhere seemingly represent both lightning and snakes. Photograph by LeRoy Unglaub.

inferred rock art sequence provides an important example of how symbolic representations may change through time but can still be useful tools for assigning cultural affiliation, especially when intermediate periods of change are captured in the archaeological record. Of course, other rock art images thought to be indicative of Apachean groups must also be incorporated when we consider changes through time, as in the work of Loendorf (2004).

FIGURE 5.6B. The buffalo-horned image is from the Uves Range, New Mexico, and represents a case of overlapping styles seen on either side of the Rio Grande in the later historic period. The wasp waist and arms bent at the elbows are also considered characteristic of Apachean rock art. Photograph by Deni Seymour.

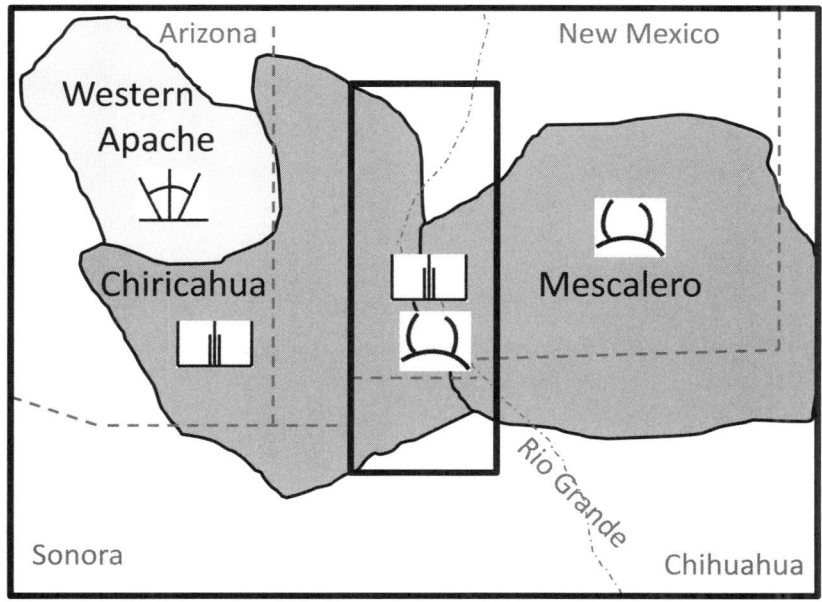

FIGURE 5.7. As Apachean groups moved around, intermixed, changed lifeways, and encountered new challenges, they altered some of their symbolic representations. Rather than the simple east-west distinction of earlier times, there seems to be an overlap in symbolism in the intermediate area on either side of the Rio Grande. There is also a change in stylistic representation of the mountain spirit headdress as it is adopted by Mescalero. Image by Deni Seymour.

FIGURE 5.8A. The antler-like rectilinear form of mountain spirit headdress, depicted here in rock art in the Florida Mountains, New Mexico, seems to be a late addition and is characteristic of the late historic period Mescalero and Chiricahua. Photograph by LeRoy Unglaub.

FIGURE 5.8B. This Edward Curtis image (cropped) housed in the Library of Congress shows a seemingly intermediate headdress form that incorporates the fan-like structure with the rectilinear frame. (Library of Congress database says 1906 but x1924-06 is written on the image; LC-USZ62-112201 [b&w film copy neg.]; Call Number: LOT 12310-A <item> [P&P] [P&P]; Edward S. Curtis Collection; Curtis no. 1924-06.)

The Iterative Approach

These complications of convoluted continuity mean that even distinctly Athapaskan symbolic representations cannot be taken at face value. If we understand their intricacies of use and change, however, these distinct symbolic representations can be helpful for advancing hypotheses of ancestral Apachean affiliation for other forms of material culture when found in direct association (acknowledging the prevalence of multicomponentcy). When these other forms of material culture are found with Athapaskan rock art in other geographically dispersed contexts, the hypothesis that they are ancestral Apachean can be tested using the extractive methodology to separate out components, as discussed above. The association of a material culture item (e.g., storage platform) with a definitive Athapaskan cultural element (e.g., rock art) suggests an Apachean cultural association for the former as well. When storage platforms are found in association with Athapaskan rock art in another site, the association is strengthened. Repeated occurrences along with late dates strengthen the association further. This seems to be the basic methodology used by our cultural historical forefathers as well.

This direct relationship, however, is not usually found in archaeological contexts where material culture is scant. Unlike for stationary farming communities, the material culture package or constellation of traits associated with specific mobile groups, such as the ancestral Chiricahua and Mescalero Apache, will be found in many spatially separated and diverse types of contexts. Evidence is expected to be spread across many different sites because people were not staying in one place for long; consequently, tools were deposited at several sites occupied sequentially rather than deposited in one location occupied over the long term. Repeated visits to one site may leave a similar set of debris if a similarly limited range of activities was conducted there during each visit, although the frequency of material may increase. Repeated visits may result in the accumulation of a diversity of materials if the location was reused by the same culture group for a more diverse range of activities. A more diverse set of artifacts may occur during a single visit if the duration of occupation is sufficiently long to capture a greater range of activities.

Because of these limiting factors, it is common to find a storage platform in direct association with Apachean rock art at one site but in loose association with house rings at another site. At still another site these houses may be found with pottery or flaked stone. Additional associational iterations of various types may establish links between specific material culture signatures in different sites that in aggregate characterize a representative complement of the early ancestral Apachean assemblage. These are then repeatedly checked as new sites are encountered in an iterative approach that links attributes found in different contexts. This effort is necessitated by and carried out with the same justification that geneticists frequently use to enlarge a fractional sample of DNA.

Similarly, directly dated feature elements (AMS radiocarbon dating of grass or leaves on the platforms; luminescence dating of burned caliche or rocks in thermal features) and artifacts (luminescence dating of pottery or burned flakes) place a subset of the features and artifacts in the target period, linking them in the temporal dimension to sites that do not have datable materials. Given that only certain culture groups survived from terminal prehistoric into late historic times, the persistence of specific attributes and material culture sets throughout this period can be part of an effective argument for their association with one or more of these late groups.[16] The wide geographic distribution of certain linked cultural elements tends to argue for an association with the ancestral Apache because few other groups occupied such an expansive geographic range. The direct association of certain elements with distinctly Apachean evidence in a subset of contexts reinforces this link. Persistence of the pattern into the late historic period when few other groups survived strengthens it even further.

These types of multidirectional and multifaceted extractive and iterative approaches of linking attributes found in different contexts are required for ancestral Apache sites because of Apacheans' high mobility and use of zones many hundreds of miles from their home bases or centers of occupation. This meant that their encampments were not restricted to an easily definable culture area bounded by the distribution of diagnostic artifacts, such as pottery. Diagnostic pottery and rock art are rare on ancestral Apachean residential sites, and their character changes through time and differs between geographic areas.

Moreover, the Apacheans' raiding adaptation, their involvement in trade, their proclivity to scavenge, and their recruitment of non-Apachean people meant that items obtained from other groups frequently outshine the impoverished character of their own assemblages (Seymour 2010b). Moreover, the pottery found among the various archaeological complexes defined as proto-Apachean is not consistent in character. This is because (a) pottery was not as important to mobile groups as it was to many stationary farmers or used in as wide a variety of circumstances, (b) pottery is one artifact class that was sometimes borrowed from other groups, and (c) substitute types of containers were much more practical for mobile people because they did not break as easily when moved around and they could be easily replaced. Also, although ceramic vessels (jars) were often used as storage containers by more stationary groups, mobile groups sometimes stored in different ways and with different vessel materials. They also sometimes stored in different contexts than more stationary groups, which farmed and reserved seed and stores for future use. Foodways (how food is prepared; what food is eaten; what facilities, utensils, and containers are needed), like caching or storage behavior, differ between mobile and stationary peoples as well.

Some pottery found on Apache sites shows probable indications of the borrowing of technologies from neighboring groups, as is consistent with what is known about Athapaskan borrowing and member recruitment behavior (also see Opler 1971a:32). Ethnographic and documentary data indicate that raiding, trading, and scavenging occurred and that women from neighboring groups, many of whom were potters, were adopted into the tribe (Seymour 2008a). These processes explain the variability found on Athapaskan sites and changes through time, as does the nature of clays, as discussed by Hill (this volume). The lack of investment in durable material culture development in general also explains the absence of standardization. This lack of investment relates to the unplanned abandonment of possessions and residences owing to surprise attacks and because the people simply carried fewer materials with them as they moved across the landscape.

All these factors mean that diversity in pottery found on Apachean sites is expected. The question remains as to whether there is one ceramic type in each Apachean subregion that can effectively define the presence of Apache at any specific time or whether it is the diversity itself that is the distinctive marker (Seymour 2008a). Another open question is whether ancestral Apacheans arrived with a single ceramic technology or whether they adopted it/them once in the Southwest (also see Gilmore and Larmore, this volume; Gordon, this volume). Comparison of the pottery associated with the Dismal River aspect in Colorado (see Brunswig, this volume; Gilmore and Larmore, this volume) with the earliest types found on ancestral Apachean sites in the southern Southwest suggests that each Apachean group developed pottery that was most like that used by neighboring groups or borrowed/obtained it from those groups or were influenced by these surrounding groups in its adoption. At a minimum they shared clay resources with adjacent peoples (see Hill, this volume).

Fundamental to the culture-area concept is the ability to bound distributions spatially and temporally and to accentuate differences between neighboring groups. Because many of the attributes adopted by the ancestral Apache came from their closest neighbors, their material culture signature (such as pottery) is not always sharply distinctive from that of their neighbors.

Also, because of the customary habit of borrowing useful technology from or intermarrying with others, one Athapaskan group might appear very different from the next with respect to constituents of the material culture assemblage. It is unwise to generalize from one Apachean group to another without specific and widespread archaeological data to support such statements. This is especially important because the documentary and ethnographic records are often inaccurate with respect to on-the-ground patterns, especially in the early periods.

Retention of Lifeway Attributes by Descendant Populations

In reality, symbolic announcements of Apachean ancestry rarely arise. Many attributes were retained in descendant populations because they derive primarily from the practice of a generalized lifeway rather than being specifically related to heritage. An example can be seen in the effect of mobility on shelter types. Cross-cultural studies and middle-range theory indicate that factors other than ethnicity motivate the construction of insubstantial housing types in the preferred terrain sectors (Seymour 2008b, 2009a, 2009b, 2009e, 2010a, 2010b).

The rudimentary housing types referred to as huts and recognized archaeologically by various rock outlines and clearings were also constructed by other groups with few elaborations that might distinguish between them. Also, more than one structure type was present among various Athapaskan groups, suggesting again that in the case of the Apache, heritage was not the operative factor in housing form. Studies at Cañon de los Embudos show that many different ethnographic and archaeological housing forms may occur at a single site that was occupied by the same people at the same time. Rather, housing type seems correlated with mobility, climate, terrain variability, resource availability, historical contacts, and a number of other factors (Seymour 2008b, 2009b, 2009e, 2010a, 2010b). Current data indicate that mobile group housing is not necessarily an ethnic identifier but an attribute that when present signals a specific adaptation of which the Apache took part. Other aspects of material, spatial, and landscape evidence must be used to extend inferences with respect to cultural identity.

Interregional Comparisons

Researchers working in other culture areas have constructed important arguments relating archaeological complexes to historically referenced groups, including the ancestral Apache. Many of the inferences regarding identity are still disputed, but similarities beyond the Southwest suggest either (1) that all are ancestral Apachean owing to the fact that Apachean groups were the only ones to have occupied all these expansive geographic areas or (2) that the resulting commonalities are related to some other factor, such as tool forms and styles typical of hunter-gatherer groups in general owing to similar tasks, constraints, and lifeways.

The distinctive tool forms identified in the Cerro Rojo complex were examined with reference to comparable assemblages obtained from known or suspected ancestral Apache sites in other areas. Diagnostic artifacts, assemblages, and features were identified and compared between regions. These comparisons included a subset of Dismal River aspect sites described by Gunnerson (1960) from Nebraska (and now also by Brunswig and by Gilmore and Larmore in this volume), Tierra Blanca assemblages from West Texas thought to be Apache (Hughes 1978, 1989; Spielmann 1982; but see Hughes, this volume), and Lipan assemblages from the eighteenth-century mission site of San Lorenzo de la Santa Cruz in south-central Texas known to be Apache (Tunnell and Newcomb 1969). The likeness of fundamental attributes of these various assemblages provided one line of evidence to suggest that the Cerro Rojo complex might be ancestral Apachean (Figures 5.9 through 5.11).[17]

Furthermore, dating of contemporaneous potential Apachean complexes in these other areas has strengthened the arguments that link them to ancestral Apaches. These comparisons have also shown the considerable variation

FIGURE 5.9. Side-notched arrow points from the Cerro Rojo site on Fort Bliss. Simple unnotched or basally indented triangular points also commonly supplement the assemblage but vary throughout the region. Photograph by Deni Seymour.

FIGURE 5.10. Cerro Rojo complex flaked-stone tools. (The full range of flaked-stone tool forms, not shown, includes fleshers and drills.) Photograph by Deni Seymour of artifacts collected on Fort Bliss, New Mexico.

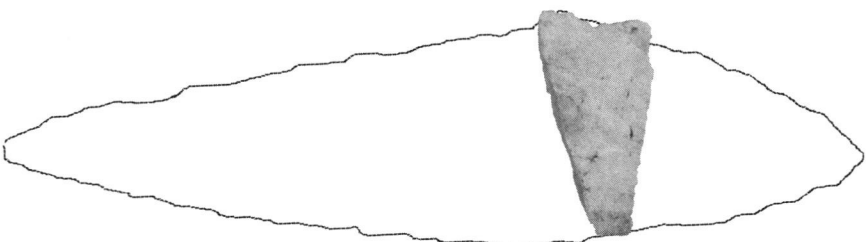

FIGURE 5.11. Bifacial knives represent a subset of the Cerro Rojo complex flaked-stone assemblage, but usually only fragments are found, and these are often reworked, as in this example. This knife has been reconstructed based on knife examples in surrounding areas. Photograph by Deni Seymour of artifacts collected on Fort Bliss, New Mexico.

between geographic areas in certain aspects, such as ceramics, while highlighting the similarities in others, such as flaked stone. Work in all these areas is continuing to reinforce the notion that Apacheans were present in these regions centuries earlier than the first documentary mention (also see Brunswig, this volume).

I have undertaken additional studies throughout other areas also occupied by distinct Apachean groups. These areas include along the border between the mountainous Southwest and the Llano Estacado, where the Llano Estacado–based Apachean Pecos complex is being defined in the Carlsbad-Roswell areas of New Mexico, which historically included but were not limited to the Siete Rios, Mescalero, and Lipan Apache. Investigations into the mobile group components at and near the Salinas and Galisteo Basin pueblos provide another perspective on these already defined complexes. Further comparisons with Western Apache, Jicarilla, Dinétah, and pre-Dinétah assemblages as well as ancestral Chiricahua assemblages (which may become distinguishable as the Gileño complex later in time) provide perspectives on the commonalities among and distinctions between widely dispersed ancestral Apachean groups at various points in time. To date, I have discovered or visited hundreds of ancestral Apachean sites throughout each of these regions, providing a basis for comparison and grounds for generalization.

DESCRIPTION OF THE CERRO ROJO COMPLEX

The methodology described in the preceding pages resulted in the identification of the Cerro Rojo archaeological complex in the southern Southwest. Owing to its character, dates, and associations, this complex has been attributed to the ancestral Apache or pre-differentiation Athapaskans; it has been described in detail elsewhere (Seymour 2002, 2003, 2004a, 2004b; Seymour and Church 2007).[18]

The Cerro Rojo complex has been chronometrically dated between ca. AD 1300 and 1850 (Seymour 2002, 2003, 2004a, 2008b, 2008c). Elsewhere (Seymour 2008c) I have presented a summary of the earliest ancestral Apache dates (associated with Cerro Rojo material culture), which also includes later Apachean dates from the same sites to show how reuse of locations through time can obscure identification of these earliest components. During this time most Southwestern farming culture groups show local and regional changes in community composition, formation of more numerous and more consolidated ethnic alliances, a change in the organization of production and exchange, and population increase and aggregation in certain areas (Cordell 1995; Habicht-Mauche 1995). These social organizational changes are inferred to reflect an in-migration of people from the San Juan/Mesa Verde areas (Habicht-Mauche 1995), just as one would expect as "predatory" mobile populations moved south.

These ancestral Apachean people moved across the landscape, residing in distinct centers of occupation (see Seymour, Chapter 17, this volume), venturing out into other areas, and focusing on hunting and gathering along with raiding and trading. They used the mountains and foothills for habitation and moved to specific resource areas. This is similar to what Opler (1971b) documented for the Jicarilla, though unlike the Chiricahua and Mescalero, the Jicarilla also farmed. The Jicarilla farmed on the plains, he noted, but otherwise they stayed "near the mountains and slept in the protection of the brush in the foothills every night" (Opler 1971b:321). From here ancestral Apachean groups in general ventured onto the plains and river margins to exploit a range of resources, perhaps camping over when in areas not used by other groups that might contest their presence.

The Cerro Rojo complex is present throughout southeastern Arizona, southern New Mexico, portions of southwest Texas, and into the northern portions of Chihuahua and Sonora. The hundreds of residential sites now known consist of isolated hut rings (such as at various sites in the Dragoon Mountains) and paired structures (as in the Whitlock and Hueco Mountains) as well as variably sized encampments from a few hut rings to 40 or 50 structures (Castner 1/FB 16710 in the Franklin Mountains; the Hormiguero site in the Peloncillo Mountains; LA 135276 in the Florida Mountains), the larger ones containing more than 200 hut rings (Cerro Rojo site; FB 9609/LA 37188 in the Hueco Mountains). These larger sites are the archaeological representation of what Basehart (1960:60–61, 110) referred to as "nuclear centers" and other ethnologists have described as where people coalesced for certain purposes, such as to prepare for specialized hunting events or for ceremonies or to organize raids and other offensives (John 1989; Perry 1983:722, 729). The residential areas of these larger encampments, however, are arranged in different ways throughout the region. These include single structures that are widely spaced but nonetheless part of a single contemporaneous encampment (East Stronghold of the Dragoon Mountains), small clusters of structures and rockshelters widely separated from one another (Hormiguero site in the Peloncillo Mountains), and dense clusters of structures that are spatially discrete (Cerro Rojo site). These types of sites are distinct from those that seem to have resulted from visits by small groups using one or two structures that are temporally and spatially separated from others and are focused not with reference to one another but rather on a physiographic attribute, such as a spring (Whitlock Mountains). Many nonresidential site types have been documented as well, but this treatment focuses on habitation sites.

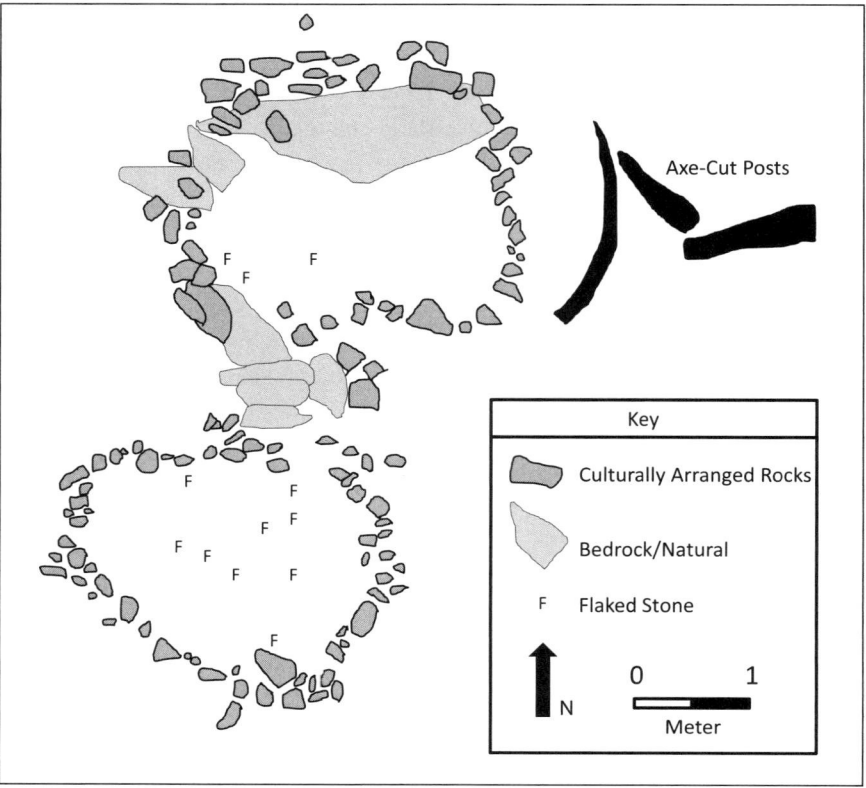

FIGURE 5.12. Two adjacent wickiup ring outlines on the Hormiguero site (AZ CC:12:58, ASM) in the Peloncillo Mountains of southern Arizona. This is one of many types of housing features found on Cerro Rojo complex sites, which are inferred to be ancestral Apachean. Image by Deni Seymour.

Shelter types include use of natural rockshelters with or without modification in the form of wall additions, as well as lean-tos and wickiups. Hut outlines may include single rings of rocks, clearings in a rocky surface with gravel and rocks pushed around the perimeter, boulder-rimmed circles with cobbles added to the intervening spaces, and slab-ringed circles, presumably used to hold hides in place in winter (Figure 5.12). These tend to be situated on the tops, slopes, or saddles of mountains and in rocky outcrops. Reuse of prehistoric pueblos and rooms has been repeatedly documented throughout the region as well, especially on the basin floors, where building material might be scarce and where abandoned ruins provided trouble-free shelter.

Relatively large rock circles consisting of a few large cobbles or boulders form what are inferred to be tipi rings, which seem to have been used relatively late in these mountain zones (Seymour 2002, 2008b, 2009a, 2009e, 2010a). They tend to be found on flat ridges, in the low-lying areas at the base of slopes, on benches, or on the lower portions of gentle slopes where they would be protected from the wind and out of view.

Other feature forms include cairns, storage platforms and other types of caches, water catchment features, ramparts, defensive walls, potential gaming features, trail markers, and rock art—petroglyphs and also pictographs, often in charcoal and black, red, white, yellow, and blue paint. Thermal features are variable and include many inconspicuous small ash and charcoal stains, scatters of fire-cracked rock and ash that are flush with the ground surface, and large roasting features such as ring middens and burned rock middens that may be mounded a meter or more above the modern ground surface owing to multiple reuses.

These ancestral Apachean groups used points that fall within the general class of Desert side-notched projectile points along with basally indented types (see Figure 5.9). The most distinctive forms are small and thin and have affinities to Harrell and Washita as well as other previously defined styles (though often thinner and narrower), but point attributes vary substantially between regions and through time. For example, point blades seem to be much narrower in southern Arizona than in the Mescalero area. These projectile point styles as a general type were not limited to Athapaskans, and there is considerable variability throughout the Southwest even among Athapaskan groups. Thus projectile point attributes alone, as classically measured, are not especially useful for isolating the signature. Their presence and distinctive stylistic attributes may contribute to the recognition of an Apachean assemblage, but by themselves projectile points are generally not sufficient for the assignment of cultural identity. The salient attributes that distinguish the basally indented forms used by ancestral Apacheans as opposed to contemporaneous groups have not yet been definitively discerned.

Another tool form includes finely retouched bifacial knives. Only fragments have been identified in the Cerro Rojo complex, and these specimens usually show evidence of reuse even in their fragmentary state, suggesting that the tool stone was recycled by refashioning other tool types. Recovered specimens suggest that they were of the size and shape illustrated for Dismal River in Colorado (Gilmore and Larmore, this volume). Most protohistoric groups have finely crafted bifacial knives (e.g., Shoshonian knives among the Navajo, Harahey-like knives in the Canutillo complex and among Toyah phase and other complexes of the plains, hill country, and coastal regions of Texas), suggesting that they were an important component of regional and supraregional tool kits during this period. Images of these and other Cerro Rojo complex artifacts and those of the contemporary Canutillo complex are available in other sources (Seymour 2002, 2004a; also see Figures 5.9 through 5.11).

There are also a host of tools that are stylistically distinctive but fall outside the range of tool forms usually thought of as diagnostics, suggesting a need to expand this concept to a wider range of tool forms and attributes (see Figure 5.10). These include perforators, which are often made on burinated flakes; gravers; spokeshaves; informal knives consisting of a large, often backed, cortical flake with a naturally sharp edge; agave knives, which are wedge-shaped with sawtooth-like edges crafted on coarse durable materials; unifacially retouched side and end scrapers that consist of forms that were both hafted and hand held; fleshers; burins; denticulates; and choppers that may be akin to the

Subarctic chithos but are so widespread among most of the Southwestern regional culture groups that they are probably not specifically diagnostic, in contrast to Gordon's (this volume) view. Groundstone includes expedient forms such as handstones, grinding slicks, mortar cups, boulder slab metates, and reuse of prehistoric one-hand manos and basin metates. Pecked stones, pounders, and shaft straighteners are also present.

Ceramics are not always found on sites and are, in fact, rare. When they are present, they represent (a) brownware pottery presumably made by the Apache, (b) pottery obtained from neighboring groups through trading, raiding, gifting, and scavenging, or (c) pottery left by previous occupants (Seymour 2002, 2008a, 2010b). Ceramic vessels made by these southern Apache were seemingly constructed by paddle and anvil of self-tempered brown clay that while not micaceous or organically tempered may fortuitously contain small amounts of either material in the paste (as do many other ceramics in the area). The exterior surfaces of thin vessel walls were smoothed to form a matte surface or lightly wiped, but not incised, as often found in Western Apache and Yavapai ceramics (Seymour 2002, 2008a).

This brief overview of the range of material culture is provided only as a summary. More in-depth treatments including illustrations can be found elsewhere, as cited above. As was alluded to in the preceding pages, any specific artifact type might be absent on a specific site, but in aggregate several sites tend to produce a wider range of the nonperishable material culture associated with the pre-differentiation Athapaskans in the southern Southwest. Analysis of the presence of several attribute classes (flaked stone, pottery, housing, nonstructural features, landscape, terrain, and chronometric dates) together strengthens the case that the site is ancestral Apachean. Also, understanding the basis for the behavior behind the patterns helps distinguish whether a site is Apachean with the material culture of another group rather than a "limited-use" site of that other group. Structures may be found that are indicative of a mobile lifeway and short-term use, while the artifacts present will provide more specific information on cultural identity. Landscape use and terrain selection are also informative about cultural identity but vary among ancestral Apachean groups, depending on relations with neighbors, housing type, duration of stay, and other factors.

Conclusion

The cultural associations of archaeological complexes that have been argued to relate to early Athapaskans (Dismal River, Tierra Blanca, Cerro Rojo) are often questioned. This is largely because archaeologists do not agree on the types of data needed to construct identity arguments, do not always consider how assemblages change through time or across geographic space, and do not typically consider how culture group boundaries among mobile groups might require different approaches than those used for relatively more stationary groups. Many ethnohistorians in this region believe that the documentary record provides the key, and they do not accept or understand the critical role played by archaeological data, the intricate ways in which archaeological and documentary data interface, and the need for the application of sound archaeological practice attuned to the material record. Moreover, and central to this chapter, rarely is the methodological basis for constructing cultural identity discussed in an explicit manner. Many researchers have also not used an explicit methodology to connect on-the-ground data and defined complexes to the documentary record. This is especially pertinent when alternative viewpoints are expressed, many of which lack the linking arguments that would justify claims; rather, they leap from description to conclusion or languish in description for lack of knowledge of how to link data to interpretations. Methodology is of considerable importance in assessments as to whether the archaeologist has adhered to the standard rules of evidence and applied procedural strategies appropriate for the data sets available and questions being asked. Adequate control of method and theory and intimate knowledge of local and regional archaeological signatures also allow the archaeologist to know when it is necessary to implement new methods and techniques. The tasks involved are complicated and demanding. If they were less challenging, archaeological definition of these groups would have been accomplished some time ago. This does not mean that the task is impossible or that we are justified in abandoning rigorous research practice.

Understanding the behavior behind material and spatial evidence is of primary concern when we attempt to isolate the signature of mobile Athapaskan peoples because operative factors changed through time. This type of middle-range theory has the potential to transform speculation into interpretation by making the linking arguments explicit. It is not reasonable to expect that early pre-differentiation Athapaskan signatures will mimic those of the late historic period in all respects. This is because so many of the factors influencing tool manufacture, site location selection, intergroup relations, housing types, and so on changed in the several hundred years between the Athapaskans' initial entry and their final disposition in the historical annals of Southwestern history and ethnography.

Because these issues are so complex, it is important to clarify how links are made between each of the data sources: documentary, ethnographic, and archaeological. When correlate grids are established, it is possible to see which attributes are being emphasized, how inferences are being drawn from them, and how these are being used for higher-level inferences, including understanding cultural identity. When relevant data and inferences deriving from them are explicitly presented, it is possible to proceed with research, incorporate new findings, and then revise the correlate grid once new information from other sources (such as archaeology) is put into the equation. These alterations indicate when new knowledge has been acquired, and they mark a change in conceptualization, signaling to other researchers the reason for the change and the onset of alternative interpretations of original sources. This means that if one correlate is incorrect or requires reinterpretation, that correlate can be interchanged with another or given less weight. If the inferences drawn from the correlate are faulty, that specific portion of the equation can be eliminated or altered while the remainder of the construction is retained.

Here and elsewhere I have presented testable hypotheses about these patterns of material culture which are inferred to characterize the proto-Apache and which embody changes through time in these portions of the Southwest. Tests of these predictions over time will add to our knowledge base and move the field forward. There is considerable unrealized value in anticipating future research and laying out a basis for new conceptualizations through testable hypotheses. This is evident in the new perspectives brought to Athapaskan research over the last decade. It is also useful to consider the stages of knowledge construction, the ways in which knowledge accumulates, and how initial hypotheses are verified. While the tendency is to cling to long-held notions, consideration of these new data and systematic pursuit of increasingly more rigorous results through a variety of discipline-specific means will be the most productive work in the next stage of information gathering. As Carlson (this volume) suggests, it is useful to explicate the theoretical principles that underlie the comparative method as it is applied to material objects and their distributions in time and space. Our predecessors invested a considerable amount of thought in these issues, so it is appropriate for us to incorporate their approaches. It is also necessary to consider how certain of the attendant assumptions are not applicable to mobile people, but this work requires explicit awareness and testing of these principles.

Unquestioned adherence to methodologies devised for stationary farming groups and the most robust culture group signatures often results in solidification and polarization of positions. Stubborn adherence to extant practice with the reasoning that "this is the way it has always been done" ignores the fact that numerous culture groups have defied identification by extant practice. Rather, knowledge will be advanced through exploration of alternatives and consideration of fine distinctions that can make all the difference in interpretations.

The compartmentalized type of investigation inherent in the explicit use of correlate grids recognizes the multifaceted nature of research, the diverse sources from which inferences arise, and the many ways in which each bit of data can be used and interpreted. It also acknowledges that one new find (a new document or a new archaeological discovery) can substantially alter the way various aspects of the past are perceived. New finds have the potential to modify the direction of future research because they change the way these correlates are perceived and provide alternate conceptualizations of a seemingly basic or descriptive fact. This is important because usually one or a few descriptions and correlates assume the greatest weight in our distinguishing between people or places. It is critical to identify these turning points or critical bits of data on which key conceptualizations hinge and to understand how dominant strings of logic are sometimes linked to them. This allows logical flows to be modified, and these correctives ensure that logical strings are made to work as tools rather than linger as blinders. So much of the work done in the past is fundamentally on the correct course but suffers from one or more turns in the wrong direction at some point in the argument. These often take future research down paths that in hindsight can be seen as inappropriate. By identifying these turning points, we can salvage the initial portion of the argument while augmenting it with new findings and directions of consideration. This course allows researchers the room (and a structured framework by which) to revise and advance their findings. It also acknowledges the cumulative nature of research—that we are always building on the shoulders and careful work of earlier scholars and responding to the good graces of our colleagues.

NOTES

1. A fundamental change also occurs in 1541 for Navajo material culture.
2. My research focuses on areas north of the international border because I hold permits to conduct work in the U.S. portion of the Greater Southwest. Moreover, this work requires an intimate familiarity with specific mountain ranges as well as the broad perspective afforded by interregional comparisons. These requirements must be balanced between focusing on one area and not being stretched too thin while investigating differences between regions and specific sites.
3. Selective use of source content is viewed with skepticism. Though not often articulated, this unease arises because of a concern that only certain agreeable aspects of the record will be chosen. I am not advocating this. Archaeologists, historians, and ethnohistorians all selectively draw material from the documentary record. Rarely, however, do they do so in an explicit manner or in a way that can be scrutinized by others or rationalized by considered method and theory. I am suggesting that researchers must have a selection process when culling data and that this process must be clear, theoretically justifiable, and methodologically sound. For the archaeologist seeking material and spatial correlates, this process must involve careful consideration of those aspects of the documentary and oral historic records that have relevance to tangible forms of evidence so they are accessible to the archaeologist.
4. In this sense I am referring to the middle-range theory proffered by Schiffer (1988) rather than Binford (1977).
5. This distinction between using riverine sources and living in the hills, on the one hand, and avoiding riverine sources and living in the mountains, on the other, was the primary criterion used to suggest which of the two mobile groups encountered by the Coronado expedition along the Rio Nexpa and at Chichilticali was ancestral Apachean (see Seymour 2008c, 2009d).
6. Such fortuitous chronometric results can be useful for demonstrating a late presence at a particular place but do little to elucidate the nature of that occupation unless associated with separable material culture that can be definitively attributed to the period.
7. Many constituents of the ancestral Apachean assemblage are plain and simple, and thus evidence becomes lost in the ubiquity of the prehistoric background scatter, a problem that is especially pronounced when previously occupied sites were reused.

These sometimes unobtrusive distinctions are most visible to those familiar with the background scatter—the signature of prehistoric culture groups—and with the fundamental distinctions between technological organizations. Such knowledge allows those earlier sites and components to be eliminated from consideration and provides a basis for sorting mixed assemblages. It is important to know firsthand what specifically is *not* being sought so that certain prehistoric signatures can be eliminated or better-known historic signatures can be distinguished. Fundamental distinctions in approaches to tool and container production provide one level of distinction. It is also important to understand the basic differences between core-reduction and biface-reduction technologies, as these are two distinct ways of approaching tool production. Additionally, it is useful to understand material culture attributes sufficiently to distinguish seemingly minor differences such as plainware pottery finishing techniques (polished, wiped, scored, matte surface treatment) and compositional differences (e.g., mica vs. feldspar).

8. Most sites were flaked-stone scatters, which reflects the propensity of sites throughout this region.
9. Some attributes common to late-dating sites (such as burned rock scatters representing small thermal features) will not necessarily be indicative of the target period but are so ubiquitous that they are commonly found, regardless of period.
10. Instances of multiple componentcy by a number of different culture groups on one site is common and complicates the separation of components, but the same principles apply. Figure 5.1 is a simplified version of this concept.
11. This procedure is effective for isolating task-specific tool kits as well. The initial definition of the Cerro Rojo complex probably segregated a task-specific tool kit on nonresidential sites. Expansion of the sample of sites and incorporation of components from residential sites used for variable durations provided a more encompassing artifact and feature assemblage.
12. Cordell (1995:207) discusses a similar issue in which certain elements change, precluding a site unit intrusion.
13. As de Reuse (this volume) points out, "Opler (1941, 1983a) started using the cover term 'Chiricahua' for Chiricahuas proper, Gileños, and Mimbreños because they are now so close culturally." Intermediate headdress forms (fan-shaped without crossbars) may be an indication of an Apache group that disappeared from history without leaving a clear linguistic trace but left interpretable evidence in the material record, if only it is recognized as an identity index.
14. Here I acknowledge the work of rock art enthusiast LeRoy Unglaub, who has spent considerable time locating and documenting these distributions in New Mexico and correlating them with documentary and ethnographic evidence to make their connection to Apacheans. He graciously brought me to many of the wind god and buffalo-horned image panels.
15. This of course relates to the realities of their environments but may also have implications for the distinctive origins and migration routes of these groups.
16. For example, the Jano and Jocome had disappeared as distinct groups sometime in the 1700s because their populations were low and they were ultimately absorbed into surrounding groups, including the Apache. This means that mobile groups found in certain areas after this threshold transformation have a higher likelihood of being Apache. If a pattern is found in one area, such as near El Paso, and it is also found in southeastern Arizona, the likelihood is increased that the designated pattern is Apachean because other surviving groups did not inhabit both of these widely dispersed

areas in the late 1700s. By this time the Jano and Jocome had become Apache, seemingly adopting many of their ways of life, including ways of using the landscape and selecting terrain. Incorporation of these other groups changed the basic Apachean material culture signature, as is discussed elsewhere in this volume.

17. All indications are that Tierra Blanca is ancestral Apachean. One reason some researchers hesitate to regard Tierra Blanca as Apache is that an archaeological complex has been defined but researchers have not always been explicit about connecting this complex to the historic record. Debate around Tierra Blanca is an excellent example of why it is important to focus on this methodological issue and be aware of the theory behind interpretations. Otherwise opinions cannot be rigorously evaluated and there are no effective ways to make distinctions and evaluate interpretations.

18. The Pecos complex is still being defined on the margin between the Llano Estacado and the mountainous Southwest and relates at least to the Siete Rios and perhaps the Lipan Apaches; the Gileño complex is found west of the Rio Grande in ancestral Chiricahua territory. The Cerro Rojo complex may predate these other complexes and therefore has the potential to represent a widespread and perhaps the earliest pre-differentiation Athapaskan complex.

References

Adams, Christopher, Diane E. White, and David M. Johnson
2000 *Last Chance Canyon, 1869 Apache/Cavalry Battle Site.* Alamogordo, New Mexico: Lincoln National Forest.

Ball, Eve
1988 *Indeh, an Apache Odyssey.* Norman: University of Oklahoma Press.

Basehart, Harry W.
1960 *Mescalero Apache Subsistence Patterns and Socio-Political Organization: Sections I and II.* Report of the Mescalero-Chiricahua Land Claims Project. Albuquerque: University of New Mexico.

Beidl, Jacqueline
1990 Analyses of Artifacts from Three Potential Apache Sites in the Mountains of Southcentral New Mexico. Unpublished Master's thesis, Department of Anthropology, New Mexico State University, Las Cruces.

Bilbo, Michael
1988 The Apache Wind God at Alamo Mountain. *Artifact* 26(2):89–112. El Paso Archaeological Society, El Paso, Texas.

Binford, Lewis R.
1977 General Introduction. In *For Theory Building in Archaeology: Essays on Faunal Remains, Aquatic Resources, Spatial Analysis, and Systemic Modeling*, edited by L. R. Binford, pp. 1–10. New York: Academic Press.
1987 Researching Ambiguity: Frames of References and Site Structure. In *Method and Theory for Activity Area Research: An Ethnoarchaeological Approach*, edited by Susan Kent, pp. 449–512. New York: Columbia University Press.

Boyer, L. Bryce, and Ruth M. Boyer
1983 The Sacred Clown of the Chiricahua and Mescalero Apaches: Additional Data. *Western Folklore* 42(1):46–54.

Cordell, Linda S.
1995 Tracing Migration Pathways from the Receiving End. *Journal of Anthropological Archaeology* 14(2):203–211.

Ferg, Alan
2004   An Introduction to Chiricahua and Mescalero Apache Pottery. Arizona Archaeologist No. 35. Phoenix: Arizona Archaeological Society.

Flint, Richard, and Shirley Cushing Flint
2005   *Documents of the Coronado Expedition, 1539–1541: "They Were Not Familiar with His Majesty nor Did They Wish to Be His Subjects."* Dallas, Texas: Southern Methodist University Press.

Galloway, Patricia
2005   Conjoncture and Longue Durée: History, Anthropology, and the Hernando de Soto Expedition. In *The Hernando de Soto Expedition: History, Historiography, and "Discovery" in the Southeast*, edited by Patricia Galloway, pp. 283–294. Lincoln: University of Nebraska Press. Originally published in 1997.

Gunnerson, James H.
1960   *An Introduction to Plains Apache Archeology—The Dismal River Aspect.* Anthropological Papers No. 58, Bureau of American Ethnology Bulletin No. 173, pp. 131–260. Washington, D.C.: Smithsonian Institution.

Habicht-Mauche, Judith A.
1995   Changing Patterns of Pottery Manufacture and Trade in the Northern Rio Grande Region. In *Ceramic Production in the American Southwest*, edited by Barbara Mills and Patricia Crown, pp. 167–199. Tucson: University of Arizona Press.

Hayes, A. C., and K. Hayes
1991   Sierra Madre Revisited. *Journal of Arizona History* 32(1):125–152.

Henderson, Richard N.
1957   Field notes of Mescalero-Chiricahua Land Claims interviews with various Chiricahua tribal members. Papers on file with Deni J. Seymour.

Hughes, Jack T.
1978   Archeology of Palo Duro Canyon. *Panhandle-Plains Historical Review* 51:35–58.
1989   Prehistoric Cultural Developments on the Texas High Plains. *Bulletin of the Texas Archeological Society* 60:1–55.

John, Elizabeth A. H. (editor)
1989   *Views from the Apache Frontier: Report on the Northern Provinces of New Spain.* By José Cortés. Translated by John Wheat. Norman: University of Oklahoma Press.

Kessell, John L., and Rick Hendricks (editors)
1992   *By Force of Arms: The Journals of Don Diego de Vargas, New Mexico, 1691–93.* Albuquerque: University of New Mexico Press.

Kinnaird, Lawrence (editor)
1958   *The Frontiers of New Spain: Nicolás de Lafora's Description, 1766–1768.* Publications Vol. 13. Berkeley, California: Quivira Society.

Kluckhohn, Clyde, and Dorothea Leighton
1962   *The Navajo.* Natural History Library. Garden City: Anchor Books, Doubleday.

Leone, Mark P., and Parker B. Potter
1988   Introduction: Issues in Historical Archaeology. In *The Recovery of Meaning: Historical Archaeology in the Eastern United States*, edited by Mark P. Leone and Parker B. Potter, pp. 1–22. Washington, D.C.: Smithsonian Institution Press.

Little, Barbara
1992   Text-Aided Archaeology. In *Text-Aided Archaeology*, edited by Barbara Little, pp. 1–6. Boca Raton, Florida: CRC Press.

Loendorf, Lawrence
2004   Rock Art and Southward Moving Athapaskans. In *Proceedings of the 2003 Rocky*

Mountain Anthropological Conference, Estes Park, Colorado, edited by Robert H. Brunswig and William B. Butler. Greeley: University of Northern Colorado.

Opler, Morris E.
1941 *An Apache Life-Way: The Economic, Social, and Religious Institutions of the Chiricahua Indians.* Chicago: University of Chicago Press. Reprinted. Lincoln: University of Nebraska Press, 1996.
1971a Pots, Apaches, and the Dismal River Culture Aspect. In *Apachean Culture History and Ethnology*, edited by Keith H. Basso and Morris E. Opler, pp. 29–33. Anthropological Papers of the University of Arizona No. 21. Tucson: University of Arizona Press.
1971b Jicarilla Apache Territory, Economy, and Society in 1850. *Southwestern Journal of Anthropology* 27(4):309–329.
1983a Chiricahua Apache. In *Southwest*, edited by Alfonso Ortiz, pp. 401–418. Handbook of North American Indians, Vol. 10, William C. Sturtevant, general editor. Washington, D.C.: Smithsonian Institution.
1983b Mescalero Apache. In *Southwest*, edited by Alfonso Ortiz, pp. 419–439. Handbook of North American Indians, Vol. 10, William C. Sturtevant, general editor. Washington, D.C.: Smithsonian Institution.

Perry, Richard J.
1983 Proto-Athapaskan Culture: The Use of Ethnographic Reconstruction. *American Ethnologist* 10(4):715–733.

Rouse, Irving
1975 *Southwestern Archaeology Today.* New Haven: Yale University Press.

Schiffer, Michael B.
1988 The Structure of Archaeological Theory. *American Antiquity* 53(3):461–485.

Seymour, Deni J.
2002 *Conquest and Concealment: After the El Paso Phase on Fort Bliss; An Archaeological Study of the Manso, Suma, and Early Apache.* With contributions by Mark E. Harlan and David V. Hill. Lone Mountain Report 525/528. Conservation Division, Directorate of the Environment, United States Army Air Defense, Artillery Center, Fort Bliss, Texas. El Paso, Texas: Lone Mountain Archaeological Services. Qualified researchers may obtain this document by contacting martha.yduarte@us.army.mil.
2003 *Protohistoric and Early Historic Temporal Resolution.* Lone Mountain Report 560-003. Conservation Division, Directorate of the Environment, Fort Bliss. El Paso, Texas: Lone Mountain Archaeological Services. Qualified researchers may obtain this document by contacting martha.yduarte@us.army.mil.
2004a A Ranchería in the Gran Apachería: Evidence of Intercultural Interaction at the Cerro Rojo Site. *Plains Anthropologist* 49(190):153–192.
2004b Before the Spanish Chronicles: Early Apache in the Southern Southwest. In *Ancient and Historic Lifeways in North America's Rocky Mountains: Proceedings of the 2003 Rocky Mountain Anthropological Conference, Estes Park, Colorado*, edited by Robert H. Brunswig and William B. Butler, pp. 120–142. Greeley: Department of Anthropology, University of Northern Colorado.
2008a Apache Plain and Other Plainwares on Apache Sites in the Southern Southwest. In *Serendipity: Papers in Honor of Frances Joan Mathien*, edited by R. N. Wiseman, T. C. O'Laughlin, C. T. Snow, and C. Travis, pp. 163–186. Papers No. 34. Albuquerque: Archaeological Society of New Mexico.
2008b Surfing behind the Wave: A Counterpoint Discussion Relating to "A Ranchería in the Gran Apachería." *Plains Anthropologist* 53(206):241–262.

2008c Despoblado or Athapaskan Heartland: A Methodological Perspective on Ancestral Apache Landscape Use in the Safford Area. In *Crossroads of the Southwest: Culture, Ethnicity, and Migration in Arizona's Safford Basin*, edited by David E. Purcell, pp. 121–162. New York: Cambridge Scholars Press.

2009a Manso Tipis and Other Non Sequiturs Relating to the Protohistoric Southwest. In *Proceedings of the 2007 Jornada Mogollon Conference*. El Paso, Texas.

2009b Distinctive Places, Suitable Spaces: Conceptualizing Mobile Group Occupational Duration and Landscape Use. *International Journal of Historical Archaeology* 13(3):255–281.

2009c The Canutillo Complex: Evidence of Protohistoric Mobile Occupants in the Southern Southwest. *Kiva* 74(4):421–446.

2009d Evaluating Eyewitness Accounts of Native Peoples along the Coronado Trail from the International Border to Cibola. *New Mexico Historical Review* 84(3):399–435.

2009e Nineteenth-Century Apache Wickiups: Historically Documented Models for Archaeological Signatures of the Dwellings of Mobile People. *Antiquity* 83(319):157–164.

2010a Cycles of Renewal, Transportable Assets: Aspects of Ancestral Apache Housing. *Plains Anthropologist* 55(214):133–152.

2010b Contextual Incongruities, Statistical Outliers, and Anomalies: Targeting Inconspicuous Occupational Events. *American Antiquity* 75(1):158–176.

2011a *Where the Earth and Sky Are Sewn Together: Sobaipuri-O'odham Contexts of Contact and Colonialism*. Salt Lake City: University of Utah Press.

2011b Mats, Multiple Stories, and Terraces: Earliest Documentary Accounts of Indigenous Sonorans. In *The Latest Word from 1540: People, Places, and Portrayals of the Coronado Expedition*, edited by Richard Flint and Shirley Cushing Flint, pp. 154–193. Albuquerque: University of New Mexico Press.

2012 When Data Speak Back: Resolving Source Conflict in Apache Residential and Fire-Making Behavior. *International Journal of Historical Archaeology*.

Seymour, Deni J., and Tim Church

2007 *Apache, Spanish, and Protohistoric Archaeology on Fort Bliss*. Conservation Division, Directorate of the Environment, Fort Bliss. Lone Mountain Report 560-005. El Paso, Texas: Lone Mountain Archaeological Services. Qualified researchers may obtain this document by contacting martha.yduarte@us.army.mil.

Seymour, Deni J., and George Robertson

2008 A Pledge of Peace: Evidence of the Cochise-Howard Treaty Campsite. *Historical Archaeology* 42(4):154–179.

Spielmann, Katherine

1982 Inter-societal Food Acquisition among Egalitarian Societies: An Ecological Study of Plains/Pueblo Interaction in the American Southwest, Volume 1. Unpublished Ph.D. dissertation, Department of Anthropology, University of Michigan, Ann Arbor.

Tunnell, Curtis D., and W. W. Newcomb Jr.

1969 *A Lipan Apache Mission: San Lorenzo de la Santa Cruz, 1762–1771*. Bulletin No. 14. Austin: Texas Memorial Museum.

Unglaub, LeRoy

2010 Identification of Apache Iconography in Southern New Mexico and Far West Texas. Paper presented at the 2010 New Mexico Archaeological Council Fall Conference, Albuquerque.

Van Orden, Jay
1991 *Geronimo's Surrender: The 1886 C. S. Fly Photographs*. Monograph No. 8. Tucson: Arizona Historical Society.

VanStone, James W.
1974 *Athapaskan Adaptations: Hunters and Fishermen of the Subarctic Forests*. Chicago: Aldine.

Wilson, John P.
1975 *Historical Profile of Southwestern New Mexico*. Prepared for the U.S. Department of the Interior, Bureau of Land Management, Cultural Resources Management Division. Las Cruces: Department of Sociology and Anthropology, New Mexico State University.

CHAPTER 6

Emergence of the Navajo People

DAVID M. BRUGGE

One of the classic problems of Southwestern culture history is that of the migration of Athapaskan-speaking peoples from the distant Subarctic region. In the American Southwest today they are represented by several tribal entities: the Jicarilla Apache, the Lipan Apache, the Mescalero Apache, the Chiricahua Apache, the Western Apache, and the Navajo. In Spanish colonial times many other names were in use. The earliest inclusive designation was *Querecho* or *Corecho* (Bancroft 1962:60–61, 86n18; Brugge 2006:46–47), but *Apache* became the standard after a colony was established (1598). In some contexts, soon after the arrival of the first settlers, the name *Querecho* seems to have been applied to those of the Southwest proper and *Vaquero* to those of the High Plains (Hammond and Rey 1953:8, 415). The terms used for local groups—sometimes tribes, at other times bands, and some perhaps no more than large extended families—increased as the colonists gained greater familiarity with neighboring peoples, with as many as 24 names appearing in Elizabeth John's (1975) index.

After the relationship of this language group to the Northern Athapaskan languages was discovered about a century and a half ago—first reported by William W. Turner in 1852 (Goddard 1996:294)—the fact of migration from the north was soon assumed. The date of the migration, the route or routes taken, and the cultural changes and adaptations that led to the separate Apachean tribes have been matters of speculation, investigation, and contention. How the migrants differentiated into separate peoples has been perhaps one of the most interesting questions.

The Navajo have long been recognized as the most distinctly different, so much so that their name is the only one today that is almost consistently used without identification as Apachean. In early Spanish-language documents the routinization of this usage is progressive through the centuries from sometime in the 1600s. Recognition of the Navajo connection to the other Apache tribes was not lost, and as a result it is not always clear whether or not, when *Apache* is used in a more general sense, the Navajo are to be included. Even when *Apache* is used in a more restricted sense, it is often uncertain as to whether in specific contexts it is the Navajo who are the subject.

The Navajo differences are pervasive, appearing in genetics, language, social structure, economy, material culture, and religion, but vary in comparison with the other tribes. The Navajo share clans with the Western Apache and certain religious beliefs with the Jicarilla, but in each case with no other Apacheans. This chapter presents evidence as to how the Navajo came to develop what is now considered their traditional way of life. It is argued that the earliest Navajo may not have been Athapaskan-speakers but were hunter-gatherers indigenous to the Southwest and descended from the Archaic populations that later incorporated Athapaskan migrants. It is also argued that more than one route of migration likely occurred, possibly including through the Great Basin.

Genetics

In terms of genetics, the Navajo show the greatest evidence of Southwestern ancestry in their maternal line, especially with the Puebloans, through their mitochondrial DNA (mtDNA), but not in their paternal ancestry. It is unfortunate that the genetic data available fail to distinguish clearly among the other Apachean peoples, but on the whole the Navajo retain far stronger ties with older Southwest populations (Brugge 2003; Romero 1998; Malhi et al. 2008; Malhi, this volume).

Among the Northern Athapaskans, the mtDNA haplogroup A is most common by far, to the degree of being the only haplogroup reported by most studies. Among the Apacheans, three haplogroups (B, C, and D) are present in small proportions, but in all cases well below 20 percent, except among the Navajo, where haplogroup B has been found to be present at up to 50 percent. It is haplogroup B that is most distinctive of the Puebloan peoples, in various studies appearing as high as 56 percent for prehistoric Puebloans in Arizona, 55–64 percent at Zuni, 73 percent for prehistoric Fremont of Utah, and 86 percent for the Tanoan (Brugge 2003:50–53; Malhi, this volume).

A study of nuclear DNA on seven chromosomes suggests a similar gradation in which Navajo most resembled the Puebloans and least resembled the Northern Athapaskans, with the other Apaches falling between the two extremes (Romero 1998; Brugge 2003:53–54). While there are problems with adequacy of some of the samples in the mtDNA studies and with the identity of some tribes included under general cultural and linguistic headings, the overall trend is clear. The Navajo, along with the Western Apache, have significantly greater old Southwestern ancestry in the female line than do the other Apacheans, one that connects best with the Tanoan and the Fremont (Brugge 2003; Malhi, this volume).

Comparisons of haplotypes in mtDNA and haplogroups in Y chromosome DNA suggest that the early separation of the Apachean ancestors was composed of a relatively small group of people (Malhi et al. 2008:9; Malhi, this volume). This does not, however, imply the rate of growth of the ancestral group or how it might have divided during migration. Moreover, the genetic data have not been sufficiently fine-grained to allow us to pinpoint relationships between specific Apachean and Northern Athapaskan tribes. The amalgamation of Athapaskan-speakers with others must account for a significant portion of Navajo population growth.

Linguistic Data

The linguistic data have received considerably more attention. It is possible to specify connections in somewhat greater detail, and it is clear that the overall Southwestern connection is with the southernmost Subarctic Athapaskans and with peoples who historically resided east of the Continental Divide. Nevertheless, it must be kept in mind that their location at the time of the split may well have been farther west and that the tribes involved may still not have differentiated. In view of the possibility that the Navajo Nation may have more than one ancestral Athapaskan connection, the possibility of more than one division on the way south must be considered. There is intratribal linguistic variation that cannot be considered in any detail here (Kari 1976; Saville-Troike 1974; Webster, this volume).[1]

The t-k isogloss among the Apacheans of stem-initial t- on the west and stem-initial k- on the east, generally separating more fully Southwestern tribes from tribes of the High Plains, extends also into the north. In the north, stem-initial k- appears in some Chipewyan communities and is considered of recent origin (Young 1983:394–395; Krauss and Golla 1981:80; Webster, this volume). For the Apacheans, the original t- has been retained in all or most Navajo dialects, Western Apache, Chiricahua, and Mescalero, while it has been replaced by k- in Lipan, Jicarilla, and Kiowa Apache and possibly in a former Navajo dialect.[2] Sarsi (Sarcee) retains the t-. There is a clear east-west or Southwest-Plains distinction in the surviving Apachean dialects, but merely a suggestion of a similar distribution in the north. This leaves us with some uncertainty as to just when and where this difference arose, but it probably indicates a relatively early division shortly before or early in the course of the Apachean migration. Should the change in some Chipewyan dialects be old, a similar east-west division there would indicate that the separation between the two Apachean clusters predates their leaving the north, but this is a tenuous inference as far as present knowledge is concerned.

Robert Young (personal communication 2000) considers Beaver the closest Subarctic Athapaskan speech community to Navajo and believes Sarsi to be next closest. This is, of course, a subjective judgment by a man intimately familiar with the Navajo language but with limited experience with the northern languages. Lexico-statistical data (see, for instance, Hoijer 1956) suggest that Chipewyan is the closest to all the Apachean languages, but the method has been criticized as not corresponding well to other ways of comparing the Athapaskan languages (Jorgensen 1980:73; Foster 1996:75–76).

The word for "man" or "person," in the sense of "person of our tribe," for the people of one's own tribe, has undergone interesting changes that relate to this east-west division (see Table 6.1). In the various northern languages that are closest to Apachean languages, "man" or "person" is in forms such as *denae*, *dəna*, and *dene*. Navajo retains this as *diné*.

The other t- Apacheans have all dropped the initial *di-/də-* and use variants of *ndee*. Jicarilla retains the first syllable, and changes the *n-* to *nd* by a regular process, resulting in *dìⁿdé*. Lipan usage has been variously reported as *dìⁿdí*, *dìdí*, and *dìní*. Kiowa Apache apparently retains the first syllable and changes the *n* to *d*; it is also reported as *diideⁿ* and adds a word-final *n*. This shift is unique to Kiowa Apache and apparently took place when it was somewhat separated from the other Apachean languages (Hoijer 1975:5–6; Britten 2009:xiv; Young 1983: 395–396, 298; 1958:201).

This raises the question of just what constitutes linguistic separation. Among the Northern Athapaskans, no good tree-and-branch pattern emerges from comparisons of the languages and dialects (Krauss and Golla 1981:68–69). Near intelligibility across most tribal lines ensured easy acceptance of linguistic innovations.

In earlier times the threat of famine or other disasters was such that the possibility of needing help from neighbors required an openness to extending hospitality or even sometimes acceptance as members despite social differences (VanStone 1974:27, 31–32; Gillespie 1981:15, 17–18; Rogers and Smith 1981:135). It might be noted, of course, that this customary attitude must be one source of the well-recognized tendencies to incorporate members of other ethnic backgrounds as well as to affiliate with more populous tribes, as did the Sarsi with the Blackfeet, and the Kiowa Apache[3] with the Kiowa. It is significant that Navajo clan origin stories about modern Pueblo usually give starvation, the proximate cause, as the reason for accepting refugees, rather than escape from a common enemy.

That a newly coined term might diffuse widely is another aspect of this phenomenon, a fact that tends to confound use of the distribution of such terms in order to infer previous social unities. Perhaps the most dramatic and readily recognized instances of such a distribution is the application of the word for "dog" to "horse" and the subsequent designation of dogs as "horse excrement" (see Table 6.2). The usage perhaps spread from the Southwestern Apacheans all the way north to the Sarsi and Beaver (Young 1958:200; Bray 1998), although the words for "dog" in the Apachean languages, Sarsi, and Beaver are not exact cognates, and the Beaver word for "horse" literally means "big dog." This suggests that there may have been regular, if perhaps indirect, communication between the western Apacheans plus Kiowa Apache and the Northern Athapaskans as late as early contact with Europeans, and perhaps not until the adoption of the horse by at least one of the southern tribes. Although the Lipan and Jicarilla were closer geographically to the Navajo and Western Apache, their languages

TABLE 6.1. Comparisons of Words for (1) Man and (2) Water.

	STEM-INITIAL T-		STEM-INITIAL K-
TRIBE	NORTHERN	WESTERN	EASTERN
Koyukon	1. denaa 2. too		
Ahtna	1. denae 2. tuu		
Tsekani	1. dəne 2. tuu		
Carrier	1. dəne 2. tuu		
Beaver	1. dəne 2. tuu		
Sarsi	1. dīná 2. tu		
Chipewyan	1. dëne 2. tuu		2. kuu
Navajo		1. diné 2. tó	
W. Apache		1. ṅⁿdé 2. tóo	
Chiricahua		1. nⁿdé 2. tó	
Mescalero		1. (ṅ)ⁿdéⁿ 2. tó	
Kiowa Apache			1. dį̇ⁿdé 2. kó
Jicarilla			1. dìⁿdé 2. kó
Lipan			1. diⁿdí 2. kó
Proto-Athapaskan	1. *də-ne' 2. *tu		

Sources: Bray 1998; Goddard 1996; Hoijer 1938, 1975:5–6, 8; Jetté and Jones 2000; Kari 1990; McClellan 1975; Morice 1932; Phone et al. 2007; Young 1958, personal communication 2000; Young and Morgan 1992.

do not fit the pattern that includes Kiowa Apache, who were at a much greater distance to the north from the Navajo. The Jicarilla term *chíníí* for modification of *łii'* may be semantically related to the Navajo despite the morphological difference. This seems to indicate that the northward spread of horses proceeded first from the Navajo or perhaps the poorly documented Apache de Quinía. It also seems unlikely that this usage would appear before horses began to displace

TABLE 6.2. Words for "Dog" and "Horse" in Five Apachean Languages and Nine Northern Athapaskan Languages.

Tribe	Dog	Horse
Lipan	nii'łi	łį'
Jicarilla	chíníí	łįį'
Western Apache	łichánee	łįį'
Navajo	łeéchąą'i	łįį'
Kiowa Apache	łiicheeh	łįį'
Sarsi	tłí, tłích'āh	istłí
Beaver	tłíízáá ("dog-genuine")	tłínchog ("dog-big")
Tsekani	tłįį	tłįchoo
Chipewyan	łį	łįchogh
Carrier	łii; łi	yeeztłii ("elk-dog")
Tagish	tłin	
Tutchone	łin'; tłin	
Ahtna	łic'ae	gan', gon (from Russian), xos (from English)
Koyukon	łeek	loset (from Russia)
Proto-Athapaskan	*łəŋʸ	

Note: Orthographics have been standardized to be consistent with Navajo usage.
Sources: Bray 1998; Britten 2009:xiv; Goddard 2001; Hoijer 1938, 1975:8; Jetté and Jones 2000; Kari 1990; McClellan 1975; Morice 1932; Phone et al. 2007; Young 1958, personal communication 2000; Young and Morgan 1992.

dogs as beasts of burden. It should be noted that the Spanish introduction of the equestrian complex, however inadvertent in its spread to Native Americans, became a powerful engine carrying many Southwestern traits to the north, especially on the High Plains.[4]

Cultural Evidence

Cultural interrelationships have become remarkably complex and difficult to interpret, but tracing the route or routes of migration must rely ultimately on archaeological evidence. This is because subsequent movements of peoples have obscured the traces of Athapaskan presence between the Subarctic boreal forest and the Southwestern deserts. On the other hand, ethnographic data can suggest beginning and end points and hint at routes in much the same way as do linguistic data.

Perry (1991) did a detailed comparison for the Western Apache and the other Athapaskan peoples, plus the Eyak, but placed emphasis on nonmaterial complexes. I did a similar comparison of mortuary customs (Brugge 1978) that included the Na-Dene stock generally as well as the Puebloans, but without a focus on the question of the dates and route of migration. Unfortunately, most ethnographic studies of the Navajo have dealt with their religion, where Puebloan influence is overwhelming, especially in ritual. Some of the Athapaskan themes that Perry identifies are present as underlying validations in Navajo thought. The intricate admixture of Athapaskan, Puebloan, and even some Mexican/Hispanic features in traditional Navajo culture presents both hurdles and opportunities for deeper insights.

Social Structure

In terms of social structure, the most prominent single complex is the clan system. I have regularly asserted that the Navajo clan system seems to derive from the Western Pueblo of the Southwest, while Aberle (1985; Dyen and Aberle 1974) and others have maintained that it came from the north or was developed independently in the Southwest through the interaction of the northern tradition and the way of life that came into being with the adoption of agriculture (Levy et al. 1989:353). While the Navajo clan/phratry system is different in some ways from the Hopi system, it shares basic similarities as well (see Table 6.3), and the influence, at least, of the Hopi or another Western Pueblo system is clear. The fact that of the Apacheans only the Navajo and the Western Apache have clans (Kaut 1957:11–15) indicates either that all the other Apacheans lost any hint of a clan structure or that they left the north without one. The tribes from which they may have diverged lack clans today, but it is possible that they may have once possessed them.

In the north, only those Athapaskans who lived where salmon came up the rivers (i.e., those flowing into the Pacific) clearly had clans, but considerable uncertainty exists regarding precontact times. Social organization of the groups closest to the coastal tribes resembled that of their more populous and culturally complex neighbors. For instance, that of the southern Carrier resembled that of the Bella Coola, and that of the northern Carrier resembled that of the Gitksan, while farther north the Tahltan had a clan-moiety system similar to that of the Tlingit. This led to speculation that clans among the Northern Athapaskans may be a late adaptation as a result of coastal influences (VanStone 1974:51–53, 57–58; Tobey 1981:418–420; MacLachlan 1981:461). If the ancestral or proto-Athapaskan people lived close to the coastal tribes, their kinship system may well be the basis of the conclusion by Dyen and Aberle (1974) that the more inland peoples once had a similar system, one that broke down as their ancestors expanded into different environments.

This matter is of consequence with regard to the ancestors of the Navajo and their route or routes to the American Southwest. They, or some of them, may have migrated from west of the Rocky Mountains, as has been previously suggested (Steward 1937; Ives and Billinger 2004). The times when a clan system, if any, arose and was lost by various tribes is, however, critical to this question, and these dates are not known. If there were Athapaskans who arrived in

TABLE 6.3. Comparison of Hopi and Navajo Clan-Phratry Organization.

Hopi	Navajo
1. Named matrilineal exogamous clans with matrilocal residence	1. Named matrilineal exogamous clans with matrilocal residence
a. Names of life forms—animals, plants, supernatural beings	a. Place names, events, ethnic origins, foreign clan names
b. Clans corporate	b. Clans not corporate
c. Clans owned land and rituals	c. Clans did not own land and ritual but were often spoken of as if they did
d. Clan house depository of ritual items	d. No clan houses, but medicine bundles sometimes asserted to belong to a clan
e. Clans duplicated in several villages	e. Clans not localized, present in many communities
f. Clan origins centripetal, migration stories	f. Clan origins centripetal with migration stories, but some split from existing clans
2. Unnamed exogamous phratries	2. Unnamed exogamous clan groups, essentially phratries
a. Members of clans within a phratry used kin terms to members of other clans in the phratry	a. Members of clans within a clan group used kin terms to members of other clans in the group

Note: Source for Hopi data is Rushforth and Upham 1992; for Navajo data, Reichard 1928.

the Southwest via the Great Basin, they probably crossed the mountains following the bison that spread through the mountains from the High Plains, a possibility supported by some Navajo tradition (Zolbrod 1984:276; Reichard 1977 [1939]:69–73).

Religious Beliefs and Practices

Religious beliefs and practices of the Navajo are a thorough and complex mixture of Northern and Southwestern traits and lore, for which adequate space is lacking for any in-depth treatment here. It is not possible to trace unique Northern aspects of ceremonialism directly back to specific Northern Athapaskan tribes, but a few suggestive hints exist. In terms of ritual paraphernalia and costume, the Eskimo technique of rod frames to create halos and feather supports around masks appears among the Navajo in interesting and unexpected ways. They occur as halos around gourd rattles (Figures 6.1 and 6.2) of otherwise strictly southern origin and for feather support to imitate Puebloan *tablita* headdresses (Figure 6.3), as well as the foundation for headdresses that strongly

FIGURE 6.1. Rod-frame halo on a gourd rattle found in a cache of ceremonial items in Palluche Canyon, New Mexico. This specimen probably dates from the mid-1700s. Photograph by Robert la Plante.

resemble those worn by Hispanic and Mexican *Matachina* dancers. A third style of headdress seems to have been a Navajo innovation (Figures 6.4 and 6.5) (Brugge 1994a, 1996).

The ethnographic record mentions this technique as usual among the Northern Athapaskans only for the Ingalik, a people strongly influenced by neighboring Eskimos (Honigman 1981:729, Figure 12; Fitzhugh and Croswell 1988:257, Figure 348). While it seems unlikely that the Athapaskans in contact with the elaborate art of the Northwest Coast would adopt this technique, the Arctic frugal use of material may well have appealed to the inland tribes to such a degree that its use was once much more widespread. Only the fortuitous preservation in one small dry cavity in the Navajo country and depictions in Navajo rock art in both the Dinétah and Canyon del Muerto provide evidence of its former popularity in early Navajo culture (Figure 6.6) (Brugge 1994a, 1996).

Another comparison is amenable to archaeological investigation only in an indirect way among the Navajo. This is the public display of supernatural power by religious practitioners. In the Dark-Circle-of-Branches ritual, which appears in some of the full nine-night performances of Mountainway and certain other ceremonies, some singers engage in dramatic presentations of such magic, including making a feather stand erect in a basket and "dance" in time with the

FIGURE 6.2. Pictograph of the Fringe Mouth God with a rattle and a rod-frame halo supporting feathers at the Blue Bull site, Canyon del Muerto, Canyon de Chelly National Monument, Arizona. Photograph by David Brugge.

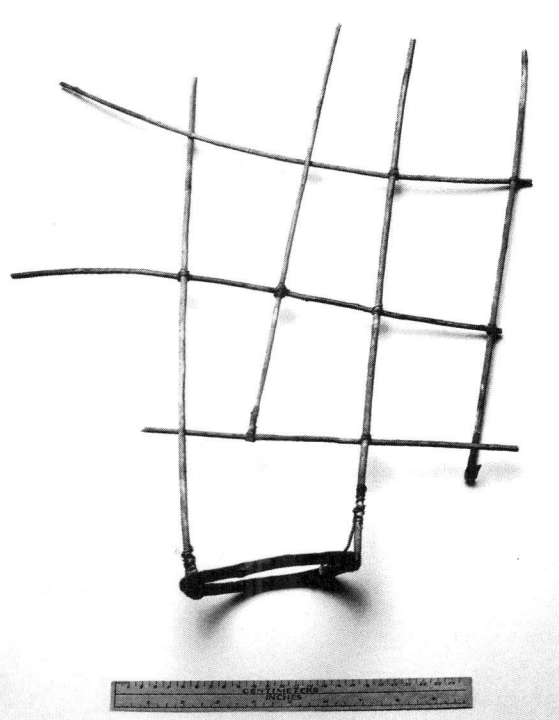

FIGURE 6.3. *Tablita*-like rod frame, missing one upright, from the Palluche Canyon Cache, New Mexico, which would have supported five vertical rows of features in three ranks. Photograph by Robert la Plante.

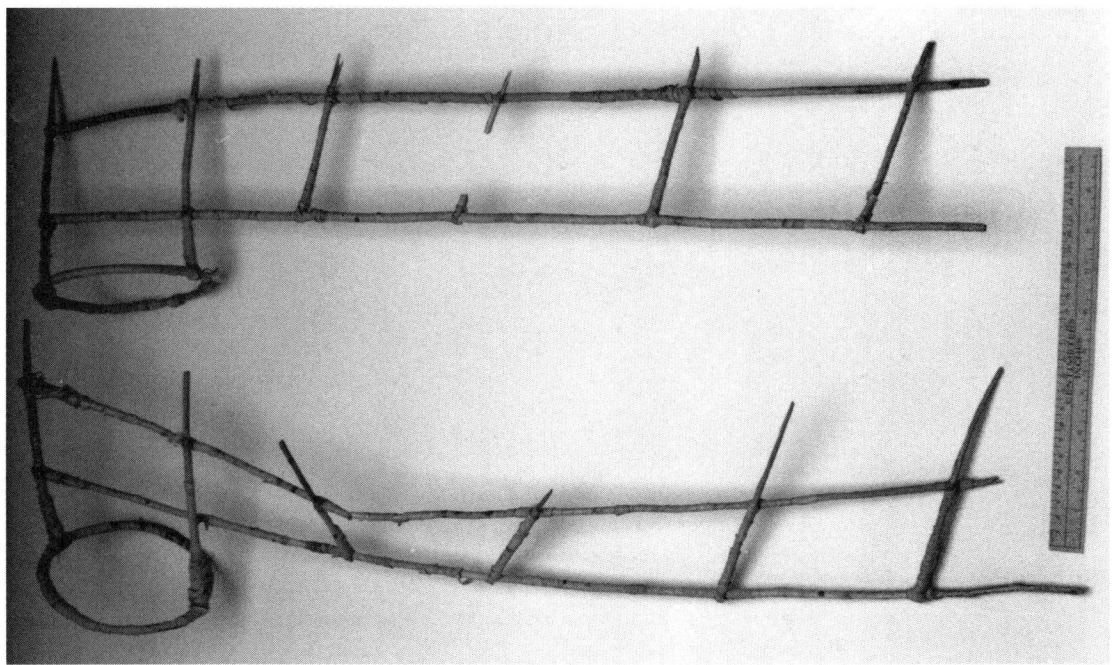

FIGURE 6.4. Ladder-like rod frames to support features for headdresses for performers. Found in a cache in Palluche Canyon, northwestern New Mexico. Photograph by Robert la Plante.

FIGURE 6.5. Pictograph of female Ye'ii performer, Sun Shield site, La Jara Canyon, New Mexico. Before about 1750. Photograph by David Brugge.

FIGURE 6.6. Dancers: female Ye'ii, Hunchback God, and deity resembling the Fringe Mouth God, Upper San Juan region, New Mexico. The two flanking figures wear feather headdresses supported by ladder-like rod frames. The right image also carries a rattle with a rod-frame halo. The feathers on the central figure's hump are also supported on a rod-frame foundation. This pictograph dates before about 1750. Photograph by David Brugge.

chant, or causing a broadleaf yucca to bloom and bear fruit (Matthews 1997 [1897]:47–48, facing 54, 61; Reichard 1950:547; Brugge 1978, 1996).

Among the Tutchone (Tutchone and Tagish are Northern Athapaskans), shamans "held séances to show off their great ability." Similar séances were held by Tagish shamans (McClellan 1981a:490, 1981b:502). This custom was apparently widespread among the Northern Athapaskans (VanStone 1974:68–69).

A related practice of supernatural dueling is reported for the Tutchone and the Ahtna of Alaska in which a prevailing shaman would kill his opponent (McClellan 1981b:502; de Laguna and McClellan 1981:661). I have heard a story of a similar competitive test of power between two Navajo singers who were rivals, each accused of killing the other's relatives until one made mistakes in his ritual and fell victim to the other's power (Zhunie Yellowhair, personal communication 1950).

Only the first sort of display of power among the Navajo might yield evidence through the remains of the Dark-Circle-of-Branches corral. Sites of this sort are distinctive in that at the finish of its use, the corral, which has an entryway on the east, is broken open to the other three directions. At older sites of this sort there are numerous brush shelters scattered about the exterior (from perhaps 20 to 50 m distant) but within easy walking distance. The corral is built not only for the display of power, however, but for curing sickness and I believe has roots unrelated to either function (Matthews 1997:36, facing 38 and 39, 47–50, facing 59).

Evidence of Food Quest

An example of an object relating to the food quest is the harpoon-like tip on Navajo arrows now employed in hunting prairie dogs; unfortunately, no good images are available. Descriptions of points of this sort obtained in the early to mid twentieth century consistently specified a point with one barb on the side on an unfletched shaft that was somewhat longer than other arrows. The point caught the prairie dog so that it could be pulled from its burrow (Kluckhohn et al. 1971: 34, 38, 40, 42).[5]

Forked-Pole Hogan

The conical Navajo dwelling called a forked-pole (or forked-stick) hogan is traditionally considered the oldest hogan type by both Navajos and archaeologists (Figure 6.7). The main support consists of three long straight poles with forked upper ends. Two of these are placed on the north and south, leaning inward with the forks interlocked. They are then tipped to the west into the fork of the third pole, providing a stable tripod frame with the strength to support log walls covered with earth. This construction technique contrasts with the straight poles leaned together and lashed in position in the Plains tipi and many of the other conical structures from the Southwest to Siberia. The forked-pole hogan was long considered unique to the Navajo, although a few neighboring tribes

FIGURE 6.7. A traditional Navajo dwelling from the 1930s. Hostee Bikini's wife and two of his children stand outside his winter hogan. Photograph by Milton Snow.

had copied this design for occasional use. It differs strongly from the domed or hemispherical wickiup constructed with curved poles used by many of the southernmost Apache and other tribes.

A literature search by Jett and Spencer (1981:54–55, 242–243) revealed a wider distribution of this forked-pole concept with variations in the use of one to four forked poles, but usually with the walls covered with brush, bark, or hide rather than earth. The Beaver, however, also used three forks, which presents the possibility that it was they from whom the Navajo's ancestors split, but again there is less than persuasive proof. The possibility of reverse diffusion from the south cannot be easily eliminated.

While various of these similarities have been cited in the past simply to support the idea of a northern origin for the Navajo, they may also indicate more specific connections to the north, both farther west and farther north, than have been postulated. It is possible that at the time of the departure of the Navajo's ancestors from the north, the distributions of both cultural features and tribal groups differed considerably from what we know on the basis of the historical record and ethnographic data, even to such an extent that some present-day tribes had not yet differentiated from common ancestral groups.

Promontory Point Culture

The identity of virtually all evidence claimed to represent the passage of ancestral Apacheans between the boreal forest and their historic locations has been contested, but one group of sites remains an especially strong contender in representing Northern Athapaskans on their way south. The Promontory Point culture in Utah exhibits an unusually wide range of northern traits.

I examined the artifacts from the caves on Promontory Point in 1998 and was so favorably impressed by what I found that I was convinced they were the product of a people from the north and were probably evidence of an Athapaskan presence, but I did not believe I could make that conclusion with absolute confidence. I did conclude that there was Athapaskan "feel" to the collection, something too subtle perhaps to counter arguments against an Athapaskan hypothesis, but too pervasive to be ignored.

The moccasins in the collection, undeniably strong evidence of northern origins, had a very restrained use of decorative techniques. Only two pair had porcupine quill decoration, and on the others any decorative elaboration was restricted to the method of stitching to join the various pieces of bison hide. The fact that the moccasins had soft soles suggested little or no influence of the sandal tradition of more southerly cultures.

On the other hand, the pottery, which had been originally described as distinct from that of the local Fremont peoples (Steward 1937:42–44, 48–49), has been more recently asserted to be entirely within that tradition (Aikens 1970: 203–204). There is, however, a lack of painted types, and the use of various forms of surface manipulation in a rather restrained manner is present in only a small proportion of the sherds and is simple in character. Navajo ceramics from the Dinétah sites share many Puebloan features. Similarly, the Promontory ware somewhat resembles Fremont pottery. Aside from some surface treatments that are similar to various Navajo usages and the black color of both paste and surface, the pottery does not look like that of the Dinétah with its strongly Pueblo character. Vessel forms are predominantly jars, bowls being less common, which is also true of Dinétah Grayware (Janetski and Smith 2007:331–332). Promontory pottery remains sufficiently distinct that it is recognized when it appears in indisputable Fremont sites.

I found that the Promontory bone flesher with a serrated blade was smaller and more delicate than those known from the High Plains sites (Gunnerson 1956:70, 1960:173–174, 215, 241, 248). It was also poorly provenienced and is not mentioned in the report on the Promontory Point caves (Steward 1937:25–29, 105–106).

At some of the Bear River sites of the Levee phase there appear other attributes that differentiate the Promontory material from most Fremont sites in ways that could be seen as Athapaskan, including a suggestion of conical dwellings with informal hearths on basin-shaped floors and entryways that might indicate vestibules, as well as barbed harpoon points (Jennings 1978:163, 172, Figure 158). As a result of the ceramic differences and other traits, such as moccasin type, Jennings concluded that the Promontory Point material is apparently alien to Fremont and an interpretive problem that may indicate a Plains origin (Jennings 1978:173, 179). There is good evidence of at least partial contemporaneity of the Promontory and Levee phases, however (Fry and Dalley 1979).

Recent research in the north has done much to give me greater confidence in the thought that Promontory Point materials might represent a Subarctic element in the Great Basin. Le Blanc's (2007:Figure 7) illustration of a serrated flesher from the Klo-kut phase in the Yukon provides a very satisfactory connection of the Promontory Point specimen to an Athapaskan type. The identification of the chitho-style scraper in the Promontory Cave collections and convincing evidence that the moccasin style found in the Promontory culture is earlier in the north further increase confidence in a Subarctic connection (Ives 2007:Figure 5; Ives and Billinger 2004).

The accumulation of data, I believe, dramatically increases the weight of the evidence for an Athapaskan origin for the Promontory culture. That Promontory is simply an aspect of the Fremont culture, as Aikens asserts (1970:2024), does not seem correct. More so, it seems to be an intrusion of a foreign people who preserved their own ways in a Fremont environment but received significant cultural influence from their hosting society. I am particularly struck by the differences between the Promontory moccasins and those from Hogup Cave, the former virtually identical in construction to one style made by Athapaskans and the latter in a distinctly Fremont style. This comparison of local moccasin styles indicates that the Promontory moccasins are intrusive. The question remains as to whether this foreign group next migrated to the High Plains or directly south into Navajo country, a question that I do not believe present data can answer.

While I cannot claim that the Promontory people were the only ancestors of today's Navajo people, or even their only Athapaskan ancestors, I suspect that they constitute at least a portion of that ancestry. They may have brought with them to the Southwest a substantial part of the Great Basin cultural inventory that is an important segment of the Navajo ethnographic record, although Ute and Paiute contributions to that inventory are doubtless also present. Just how fully the Promontory people may have adapted to the Great Salt Lake region before their departure is not clear in the archaeological materials and sites known so far.

Navajo Traditional Accounts

Here I want to shift my focus to a different kind of evidence as it relates to the hypothesis that the early Navajo were not initially Athapaskan-speakers but instead originated with the hunting-and-gathering cultures already in the Southwest. The Navajo traditional account of their origin begins with the emergence of the immortals from the lower worlds onto the present earth surface at a place called Hajíínáí in the San Juan Mountains in Colorado.[6] It is said that it was here that the first Navajo were created. This is a version of the Southwestern creation story that is adapted to a Navajo view. In this Navajo version, the first clans came about as the people created at the place of emergence journeyed through a large portion of Navajo country, encountering other small groups that usually received their names from the places where they joined the wanderers. In time, all settled on or near the San Juan River, where they welcomed others also, giving them names reflecting their places of origin.

There was a second creation, however. The beneficent Changing Woman, perhaps the most important Navajo deity, at her home on an island in the Pacific

Ocean, created the ancestors of some four to six Navajo clans. These are often claimed to be the original clans, suggesting that the earlier groups were at first no more than local lineages but became incorporated into a clan system. The former, sometimes referred to as the Western Water Clans, were sent to join their relatives on the San Juan River. As they traveled, they met other local groups, many in the western part of Navajo country, who merged with the migrants as new clans, and in some cases other new clans budded off one or another of Western Water Clans. Eventually, they reached a tall building, a Chaco outlier, which may or may not have still been occupied by pueblo dwellers. Here a number of new clans joined, and some had the life-form names of Pueblo clans.[7] It is probable that Anasáází communities surrounding the Chacoan Great House were still present nearby. Ultimately, most of these peoples reached the others on the San Juan (Wyman 1970:331–332; Martin 2002:56).

As time went on, a great many peoples of various tribes and Pueblos joined the Navajo. Many of these named for modern pueblos were doubtless refugees and fugitives from the missions that the Spanish colonists established in New Mexico, some escaping the turmoil resulting from the original imposition of Spanish rule and a mission system, others fleeing Spanish vengeance following abortive revolts later in the seventeenth century or the Reconquest, which ended Pueblo freedom after the Pueblo Revolt of 1680. Some final groups of refugees escaped the destruction of the pueblo of Awatovi by the more westerly Hopi towns in 1700 or fled civil strife at Hopi later in the eighteenth century, and most of them brought the Pueblo life-form names for their clans with them (Brugge 1994b:9, 2005:17). Other clans of Pueblo origin were founded by captives, as were two clans descended from Hispanic captives. The additions from non-Puebloan tribes included both voluntary recruits and captives, several of whom founded new clans as late as the 1860s (Brugge 2005:17; Mitchell 1978:17).

The two creations suggest two creation stories from two different peoples that merged to form the Navajo Nation. The story of the emergence is typically Southwestern (Parsons 1996) and undoubtedly derives from peoples long resident in this region. It is probable that it began with peoples descended from the Archaic populations of pre-Puebloan times who continued a lifeway more dependent on hunting and gathering in the hinterlands of the developing Puebloan communities (Brugge 2006). The creation of the Western Water Clans is more of a mystery. Changing Woman, who is said to have created these clans, is conceptually connected to White Shell Woman, said by some to be another name of the deity herself and by others to be her sister. White Shell Woman appears in the traditions of some Pueblos, and a similar being called White Corn Woman is present in others (Parsons 1996 [1939]:212; Tedlock 1992:238; Ortiz 1969:13, 89–90, 165). Another is described by the Cochiti as a sister to the "mother to the Navajos" (Lange 1958:238). In none of the Pueblo traditions does she play a major role.

Among the Apacheans she has at least three names: Changing Woman, White Shell Woman, and White Painted Woman. She is an important figure largely due to the prominence of girls' coming-of-age ceremonies for these peoples (Basso 1966:167–170; Opler 1941:281–282, 1994 [1938]:48–50; Buskirk 1986:13, 108). Her significance goes beyond this for the Navajo through her central role in Blessingway in Navajo ritual and the various contexts in which Blessingway functions (Wyman 1983:539–540).[8] It is unclear whether her association with the Western Water Clans is somehow basic to their history or a later elaboration of her role.

The Navajo Kinaaldá, or girls' puberty ceremony, as well as those of other Southern Athapaskans, may relate somehow to the West Coast Athapaskans. While most descriptions I have found do not seem very similar, that of the Hupa has some correspondences (cf. descriptions in Goddard 1911:53–54, 56–57; Heizer 1978; Helm 1981; Ortiz 1983).

The descriptions of the cultures given for the early clans do not seem at all to be Subarctic in nature, but one clan, said to have come from the region of Santa Fe or perhaps the upper Chama drainage, and perhaps arriving before the Western Water Clans, introduced not only buckskin shirts (and presumably other tailored garments), stronger bows, and greater skill at hunting, but a language close to modern Navajo (Matthews 1997 [1887]:142–143; Klah 1942). The implication is that the language or languages of the earlier clans were substantially different from the present Navajo language.

This is the strongest evidence, perhaps, that the early Navajo were not speakers of an Athapaskan language at all. My own view is that they may well have been peoples who were in many ways still Archaic in culture who lived in the hinterland around and about the developing pueblos, probably trading the products of hunting and gathering to those engaged in farming as their major economic activity. It is also possible that these may have been remnants of Puebloan peoples dispersed by the Great Drought and wars that led to the abandonment of the San Juan drainage by 1300. They did not participate fully in the cultural changes leading to the modern Pueblo societies, and in addition to having a simpler way of life, they were poorer and not nearly as numerous as the Pueblo peoples. Still, they were perhaps related to the Pueblo, much as the desert-dwelling Tohono O'odham (Papago) were related to the Akimel O'odham (Riverine Pima and Sobaípuri), or the upland Yumans to the Yumans along the Gila and Colorado Rivers (Brugge 2005, 2006).

Sites producing mostly lithics and initially believed on survey to be Archaic sometimes produce much later dates than the Archaic occupation in the San Juan Basin, not infrequently post-1300, after the pueblo dwellers had moved elsewhere. Navajo sites dating back as early as AD 1500 have now been identified in this region (Hancock 1997; Brown 1996:66–68).[9] There is also a report of corn pollen in sediments dating between AD 1300 and 1700 along the Upper San Juan River, suggesting a sparse population for which occupation sites had not been found (Eddy 1966:507–508). These sites indicate that by the sixteenth century, Navajo were already producing pottery and practicing agriculture, and therefore these sites may not represent the earliest Navajo settlement in the Southwest (Dykeman and Roebuck, this volume). Until earlier sites are identified, however, these represent the earliest identifiably Navajo sites in the San Juan Basin. Whether the occupants were already speakers of ancestral Navajo is uncertain. We still lack sites securely dated in the fourteenth and fifteenth centuries and cannot know whether the few radiocarbon dates from lithic scatters in these centuries reliably date the use of the sites, nor are the data from such sites sufficiently detailed to allow us to hazard a guess as to who the occupants might have been.

I do not believe we can yet say with any confidence just when Athapaskan-speakers first occupied lands west of the High Plains in northern New Mexico or what languages were spoken by the clans the Navajo describe as their earliest ancestors. Nevertheless, I feel strongly that the roots of the Navajo Nation extend to earlier dates than we thus far can discern with any clarity.

Acknowledgments

I benefited from long discussions with David H. Snow, who also read a draft of this chapter and commented on it. Charlotte T. Frisbie gave me valuable suggestions. John W. (Jack) Ives graciously gave me permission to cite data from unpublished papers on Promontory Point and on moccasins. The Athapaskan Migration symposium held in Calgary in September 2009 substantially broadened my knowledge of the Athapaskan-speaking peoples outside the Southwest. I am especially indebted to Ives, Joel C. Janetski, Victor Golla, and Michelle Knoll. I also thank Deni Seymour for a critical reading. Fellow contributors to this volume, especially Douglas Dykeman, Bryan Gordon, Willem J. de Reuse, Anthony K. Webster, and Keren Rice, also offered valuable comments. And at the last minute, Carol Condie loaned me a hard-to-find reference that made a significant contribution to this chapter, for which I am exceedingly grateful. The staff at the Anderson Room in the Zimmerman Library was, as always, very helpful in locating sources. And Lauren Rimbert expertly typed text and set up tables. To all and any others I may have forgotten, my thanks. All errors are my own darn fault.

Notes

1. The idea that the Fremont, or at least some of them, were speakers of Kiowa-Tanoan languages is strongly suggested by the correspondence between the Pueblo Tanoan and the Plains Kiowa, a possibility that might resolve the question of how the two branches of this family reached their historic locations, the Kiowa migrating across the Rockies east of the Great Basin and the Tanoan moving to the southeast, both with migration traditions that might lead back to the eastern Great Basin. It might be noted that there was a tradition among the Jemez (who speak the Tanoan language Towa) of a place called Teguayo (probably pronounced Tewayó and most likely accented as shown here); this name appears in the one of the most detailed, but probably also a bit garbled, descriptions in the tradition. Information dating from the 1660s indicates that it began about 180 leagues, or close to 540 miles, northwest of Santa Fe and included a large lake (Tyler and Taylor 1958:303–305). Thus the name given for the "Kingdom called Teguayo" probably indicates the ancestral country of the Tewa, Towa, and Tiwa.

2. I must note here, based on my own long experience among the Navajo throughout Navajo country, that Saville-Troike's (1974:74–75) contention that the Navajo language today uses stem-initial k- east of the Lukachukais is incorrect.
3. Note that the current desire of the Kiowa Apache to use "Plains Apache" as their tribal name will create confusion on the east, but I avoid that here by continuing to use "Kiowa Apache." The Apache de Quinía appear in seventeenth-century writings, such as Benavides's memorials (Ayer 1965; Hodge et al. 1945), but are absent later. This group may have merged with the Navajo or be ancestral to the Ollera band of the Jicarilla.
4. Among other traits, these probably include feather headdresses, eagle wing bone whistles, color-directional symbolism, straight tobacco pipes, and dry painting (of California/local and Mesoamerican origins), and possibly self-flagellation from the Franciscan Penitente custom, all in addition to traits directly associated with horses. Bone flutes and whistles have a long prehistory in California and the Southwest but do not appear in Plains archaeology until the historic period.

    I believe that the Navajo Naach'id, or tribal assembly, and the Dark-Circle-of-Branches were temporary replicas of a plaza-oriented pueblo and a big kiva, respectively. If this is correct, the Plains camp circle may well be a diffusion of the pueblo plaza concept northward.
5. This point has also been designated a leister, but a leister has barbs on three prongs and does not match the ethnographic descriptions. A bone artifact in the collections of the Laboratory of Anthropology in Santa Fe that was recovered from a deposit containing Navajo materials of the Gobernador phase and possibly the Dinétah phase in a rockshelter on the Pine River just north of the San Juan River, LA 4055, has been suggested as an example of a leister barb (Eddy 1966:601; Kluckhohn et al. 1971:34, 38, 40, 42; McClellan 1975:102; Wilmeth 1978:123–134, 234–235). I have shown a photograph of this specimen (Cat. No. 44164/11, Accession No. 1958–3, Museum of Indian Arts and Culture, Museum of New Mexico, Santa Fe) to John Ives and Joel C. Janetski. They agree that it does not resemble any harpoon or leister barb with which they are familiar. The Fremont bone harpoons illustrated by Janetski (1990:Figure 6) do not resemble, as far as I can determine, the prairie dog harpoons described for the Navajo but could perhaps be a source for the Navajo types.
6. This summary description is based on a number of sources, including Matthews (1997) [1887]; Franciscan Fathers (1910); Reichard (1928); Coolidge and Coolidge (1930); O'Bryan (1956); Fishler (1953); Wheelwright (1942); Mitchell (1978); and Brugge (2005).
7. I have had second thoughts as to the reliability of my source for this.
8. Changing Woman/White Shell Woman/White Painted Woman is also associated with the acquisition of the horse and among the Navajo other livestock as well, but this may be a late addition to her story (Clark 1966:13, 23, 30, 34–36, 47–58, 190–193).
9. The Navajo identification of some of these sites is still contested by some authorities (Schaafsma 1996), but the ethnic connections of others are well substantiated.

References

Aberle, David F.
1985 Discussions at the seminar "Temporal Change and Regional Variability in Navajo Culture." Santa Fe, New Mexico: School of American Research.

Aikens, C. Melvin
1970   *Hogup Cave*. Anthropological Paper No. 93. Salt Lake City: Department of Anthropology, University of Utah.

Ayer, Mrs. Edward E. (translator)
1965   *The Memorial of Fray Alonso de Benavides*. Albuquerque, New Mexico: Horn and Wallace.

Bancroft, Herbert Howe
1962   *History of Arizona and New Mexico, 1530–1888*. Albuquerque, New Mexico: Horn and Wallace.

Bannister, Bryant, William J. Robinson, and Richard L. Warren
1970   *Tree-Ring Dates from New Mexico A, G–H: Shiprock—Zuni—Mt. Taylor Area*. Tucson: Laboratory of Tree-Ring Research, University of Arizona.

Basso, Keith H.
1966   *The Gift of Changing Woman*. Bureau of American Ethnology Anthropological Papers No. 76. Washington, D.C.: Smithsonian Institution.

Boyer, Ruth McDonald, and Narcissus Duffy Gayton
1992   *Apache Mothers and Daughters: Four Generations of a Family*. Norman: University of Oklahoma Press.

Bray, Dorothy (editor)
1998   *Western Apache–English Dictionary: A Community-Generated Bilingual Dictionary*. Tempe, Arizona: Bilingual Press.

Britten, Thomas A.
2009   *The Lipan Apaches: People of Wind and Lightning*. Albuquerque: University of New Mexico Press.

Brown, Gary M.
1996   The Protohistoric Transition in the Northern San Juan Region. In *The Archaeology of Navajo Origins*, edited by Ronald H. Towner, pp. 47–69. Salt Lake City: University of Utah Press.

Brugge, David M.
1972   *The Navajo Exodus*. Newsletter, Supplement No. 5. Santa Fe: Archaeological Society of New Mexico.
1978   A Comparative Study of Navajo Mortuary Practices. *American Indian Quarterly* 4(4):309–328.
1994a The Palluche Canyon Cache. Ms. on file, Laboratory of Anthropology/Museum of Indian Arts, Museum of New Mexico, Santa Fe.
1994b *The Navajo-Hopi Land Dispute: An American Tragedy*. Albuquerque: University of New Mexico Press.
1996   Navajo Caches of the Dinetah. In *La Jornada: Papers in Honor of William E. Turney*, edited by Meliha S. Duran and David T. Kirkpatrick, pp. 33–45. Papers No. 22. Las Cruces: Archaeological Society of New Mexico.
2003   DNA and Ancient Demography. In *Climbing the Rocks: Papers in Honor of Helen and Jay Crotty*, edited by Regge N. Wiseman, Thomas C. O'Laughlin, and Cordelia T. Snow, pp. 49–56. Papers No. 29. Albuquerque: Archaeological Society of New Mexico.
2005   Navajo Clan Origins. In *Inscriptions: Papers in Honor of Richard and Nathalie Woodbury*, edited by Regge N. Wiseman, Thomas C. O'Laughlin, and Cordelia C. Snow, pp. 15–31. Papers No. 31. Albuquerque: Archaeological Society of New Mexico.

2006 When Were the Navajos? In *Southwestern Interludes: Papers in Honor of Charlotte J. and Theodore R. Frisbie*, edited by Regge N. Wiseman, Thomas C. O'Laughlin, and Cordelia C. Snow, pp. 45–52. Papers No. 32. Albuquerque: Archaeological Society of New Mexico.

Buskirk, Winfred
1986 *The Western Apache: Living with the Land before 1950*. Norman: University of Oklahoma Press.

Clark, LaVerne Harrell
1966 *They Sang for Horses*. Tucson: University of Arizona Press.

Coolidge, Dane, and Mary Roberts Coolidge
1930 *The Navajo Indians*. Boston: Houghton Mifflin.

de Laguna, Frederica, and Catharine McClellan
1981 Ahtna. In *Subarctic*, edited by June Helm, pp. 641–663. Handbook of North American Indians, Vol. 6, William C. Sturtevant, general editor. Washington, D.C.: Smithsonian Institution.

Dyen, Isidore, and David F. Aberle
1974 *Lexical Reconstruction: The Case of the Proto-Athapaskan Kinship System*. New York: Cambridge University Press.

Eddy, Frank W.
1966 *Prehistory in the Navajo Reservoir District, Northwestern New Mexico*. Museum of New Mexico Papers in Anthropology No. 15. Santa Fe: Museum of New Mexico Press.

Fishler, Stanley A.
1953 *In the Beginning: A Navaho Creation Myth*. University of Utah Anthropological Paper No. 13. Salt Lake City: University of Utah Press.

Fitzhugh, William W., and Aron Crowell
1988 *Crossroads of Continents: Cultures of Siberia and Alaska*. Washington, D.C.: Smithsonian Institution.

Foster, Michael K.
1996 Language and the Culture History of North America. In *Languages*, edited by Ives Goddard, pp. 64–170. Handbook of North American Indians, Vol. 17, William C. Sturtevant, general editor. Washington, D.C.: Smithsonian Institution.

Franciscan Fathers
1910 *An Ethnologic Dictionary of the Navaho Language*. Saint Michaels, Arizona: St. Michaels Press.

Fry, Gary F., and Gardiner F. Dalley
1979 *The Levee Site and the Knoll Site*. University of Utah Anthropological Papers No. 100. Salt Lake City: University of Utah Press.

Gillespie, Beryl C.
1981 Major Fauna in the Traditional Economy. In *Subarctic*, edited by June Helm, pp. 15–18. Handbook of North American Indians, Vol. 6, William C. Sturtevant, general editor. Washington, D.C.: Smithsonian Institution.

Goddard, Ives
1996 The Classification of the Native Languages of North America. In *Languages*, edited by Ives Goddard, pp. 240–323. Handbook of North American Indians, Vol. 17, William C. Sturtevant, general editor. Washington, D.C.: Smithsonian Institution.
2001 The Languages of the Plains. In *Plains*, Part I, edited by Raymond J. DeMallie,

pp. 61–70. Handbook of North American Indians, Vol. 13, William C. Sturtevant, general editor. Washington, D.C.: Smithsonian Institution.

Goddard, Pliny Earle
1911 *Jicarilla Apache Texts*. Anthropological Papers Vol. 8. New York: American Museum of Natural History.

Gunnerson, James H.
1956 Plains-Promontory Relationships. *American Antiquity* 22(1):69–72.
1960 *An Introduction to Plains Apache Archeology—The Dismal River Aspect*. Anthropological Papers No. 58, Bureau of American Ethnology Bulletin No. 173, pp. 131–260. Washington, D.C.: Smithsonian Institution.

Hammond, George P., and Agapito Rey (editors)
1953 *Don Juan de Oñate, Colonizer of New Mexico, 1595–1628*. 2 vols. Albuquerque: University of New Mexico Press.

Hancock, Patricia M.
1997 Dendrochronological Dates from the Dinétah. Paper presented at the 1997 Pecos Conference, Chaco Canyon National Park, New Mexico. Farmington, New Mexico: Cultural Resource Management Consultants.

Heizer, Robert F. (editor)
1978 *California*. Handbook of North American Indians, Vol. 8, William C. Sturtevant, general editor. Washington, D.C.: Smithsonian Institution.

Helm, June (editor)
1981 *Subarctic*. Handbook of North American Indians, Vol. 6, William C. Sturtevant, general editor. Washington, D.C.: Smithsonian Institution.

Hodge, Frederick Webb, George P. Hammond, and Agapito Rey (editors and translators)
1945 *Fray Alonso de Benavides' Revised Memorial of 1634*. Albuquerque: University of New Mexico Press.

Hoijer, Harry
1938 The Southern Athapaskan Languages. *American Anthropologist*, new series, 40(1):75–87.
1956 The Chronology of the Athapaskan Languages. *International Journal of American Linguistics* 22(4):219–232.
1975 The History and Customs of the Lipan, as told by Augustina Zuazua. *Linguistics* 161:5–37.

Honigman, John J.
1981 Expressive Aspects of Subarctic Indian Culture. In *Subarctic*, edited by June Helm, pp. 718–738. Handbook of North American Indians, Vol. 6, William C. Sturtevant, general editor. Washington, D.C.: Smithsonian Institution.

Ives, John W.
2007 Insights into Apachean Transition from the Subarctic Using Ceramic and Food Terms Etymologies. Paper presented at the 72nd Annual Meeting of the Society for American Archaeology, Austin, Texas.

Ives, John W. ,and Michael Billinger
2004 Was Julian Steward Right about the Promontory Cave Moccasins? Ms. on file, Canadian Archaeological Association. Available at http://canadianarchaeology.com/caa/node/2922.

Janetski, Joel C.
1990 Wetlands in Utah Valley Prehistory. In *Wetland Adaptations in the Great Basin*, edited by Joel C. Janetski and David B. Madsen, pp. 233–257. Museum of Peoples and Cultures Occasional Papers No. 1. Provo, Utah: Brigham Young University.

Janetski, Joel C., and Grant C. Smith
2007 *Hunter-Gatherer Archaeology in the Utah Valley.* Museum of Peoples and Cultures Occasional Papers No. 12. Provo, Utah: Brigham Young University.

Jennings, Jesse D.
1978 *Prehistory of Utah and the Eastern Great Basin.* University of Utah Anthropological Papers No. 98. Salt Lake City: University of Utah Press.

Jett, Stephen C., and Virginia E. Spencer
1981 *Navajo Architecture: Forms, History, Distributions.* Tucson: University of Arizona Press.

Jetté, Jules, and Eliza Jones
2000 *Koyukon Athabaskan Dictionary.* Fairbanks: Alaska Native Language Center, University of Alaska.

John, Elizabeth A. H.
1975 *Storms Brewed in Other Men's Worlds: The Confrontation of Indians, Spanish, and French in the Southwest, 1540–1795.* College Station: Texas A&M University Press.

Jorgensen, Joseph G.
1980 *Western Indians.* San Francisco: W. H. Freeman.

Kari, James (compiler and editor)
1976 *Navajo Verb Prefix Phonology.* New York: Garland.
1990 *Ahtna Athabaskan Dictionary.* Fairbanks: Alaska Native Language Center, University of Alaska, and Ahtna, Inc.

Kaut, Charles R.
1957 *The Western Apache Clan System: Its Origin and Development.* Publications in Anthropology No. 9. Albuquerque: University of New Mexico.

Klah, Hasteen
1942 *Navajo Creation Myth: The Story of the Emergence.* Recorded by Mary C. Wheelwright. Navajo Religion Series No. 1. Santa Fe, New Mexico: Museum of Navajo Ceremonial Art.

Kluckhohn, Clyde, W. W. Hill, and Lucy Wales Kluckhohn
1971 *Navaho Material Culture.* Cambridge: Belknap Press of Harvard University Press.

Krauss, Michael E., and Victor K. Golla
1981 Northern Athapaskan Languages. In *Subarctic,* edited by June Helm, pp. 67–85. Handbook of North American Indians, Vol. 6, William C. Sturtevant, general editor. Washington, D.C.: Smithsonian Institution.

Lange, Charles H.
1958 [1959] *Cochiti: A New Mexico Pueblo, Past and Present.* Carbondale: Southern Illinois University Press; London: Fefler and Simons.

Le Blanc, Raymond
2007 Athapaskan Archaeology: A View from the Northern Yukon. In *Ancient and Historic Lifeways in North America's Rocky Mountains: Proceedings of the 2003 Rocky Mountain Anthropology Conference,* pp. 2–22, edited by Robert H. Brunswig and William B. Butler, pp. 146–167. Greeley: Department of Anthropology, University of Northern Colorado.

Levy, Jerrold E., Eric B. Henderson, and Tracy J. Andrews
1989 The Effects of Regional Variation and Temporal Change on Matrilineal Elements of Navajo Social Organization. *Journal of Anthropological Research* 45(4):351–388.

MacLachlan, Bruce B.
1981   Tahltan. In *Subarctic*, edited by June Helm, pp. 458–468. Handbook of North American Indians, Vol. 6, William C. Sturtevant, general editor. Washington, D.C.: Smithsonian Institution.

Malhi, Ripan Singh, Angelica Gonzales-Oliver, Kari Britt Schroeder, Brian M. Kemp, Jonathan A. Greenberg, Solomon Z. Dobrowski, David Glenn Smith, Andres Resendez, Tatiana Karafet, Michael Hammer, Stephen Zegura, and Tatiana Brouko
2008   Distribution of Y Chromosomes among Native North Americans: A Study of Athapaskan Population History. *American Journal of Physical Anthropology* 137(4):412–424.

Martin, Rena
2002   Two Navajo Clan Traditions: Our Mothers, Our Fathers, Our Connections. Unpublished Master's thesis, University of New Mexico, Albuquerque.

Matthews, Washington
1997   [1887] *The Mountain Chant: A Navajo Ceremony*. Salt Lake City: University of Utah Press.

McClellan, Catharine
1975   *My Old People Say: An Ethnographic Survey of Southern Yukon Territory, Part I*. National Museum of Man Publications in Ethnology No. 6(1). Ottawa, Ontario: National Museums of Canada.
1981a   Tagish. In *Subarctic*, edited by June Helm, pp. 481–492. Handbook of North American Indians, Vol. 6, William C. Sturtevant, general editor. Washington, D.C.: Smithsonian Institution.
1981b   Tutchone. In *Subarctic*, edited by June Helm, pp. 493–506. Handbook of North American Indians, Vol. 6, William C. Sturtevant, general editor. Washington, D.C.: Smithsonian Institution.

Mitchell, Frank
1978   *Navajo Blessingway Singer: The Autobiography of Frank Mitchell*. Edited by Charlotte J. Frisbie and David P. McAllester. Tucson: University of Arizona Press.

Morice, A. G.
1932   *The Carrier Language (Dene Family): A Grammar and Dictionary Combined*. St. Gabriel-Mödling, Austria: Anthropos.

Nelson, Richard K.
1973   *Hunters of the Northern Forest*. 2nd ed. Chicago: University of Chicago Press.

O'Bryan, Aileen
1956   *The Dîné: Origin Myths of the Navajo Indians*. Bureau of American Ethnology Bulletin No. 163. Washington, D.C.: Smithsonian Institution.

Opler, Morris Edward
1941   *An Apache Lifeway: The Economic, Social, and Religious Institutions of the Chiricahua Indians*. Chicago: University of Chicago Press.
1994   [1938] *Myths and Tales of the Jicarilla Apache Indians*. Lincoln: University of Nebraska Press.

Ortiz, Alfonso
1969   *The Tewa World: Space, Time, Being, and Becoming in a Pueblo Society*. Chicago: University of Chicago Press.

Ortiz, Alfonso (editor)
1983   *Southwest*. Handbook of North American Indians, Vol. 10, William C. Sturtevant, general editor. Washington, D.C.: Smithsonian Institution.

Parsons, Elsie Clews
1996 [1939] *Pueblo Indian Religion*. 2 vols. Lincoln: University of Nebraska Press.
Perry, Richard J.
1991 *Western Apache Heritage: People of the Mountain Corridor*. Austin: University of Texas Press.
Phone, Wilhelmina, Maureen Olson, and Matilda Martinez
2007 *Dictionary of Jicarilla Apache: Abáachi Mizaa Iłkee' Siijai*. Albuquerque: University of New Mexico Press.
Reichard, Gladys A.
1928 *Social Life of the Navajo Indians*. Columbia University Contributions to Anthropology No. 7. New York: Columbia University Press.
1950 *Navajo Religion: A Study in Symbolism*. 2 vols. Bollingen Series No. 18. New York: Pantheon Books.
1977 [1939] *Navajo Medicine Man Sandpaintings*. New York: Dover.
Rogers, Edward S., and James G. E. Smith
1981 Environment and Culture in the Shield and Mackenzie Borderlands. In *Subarctic*, edited by Jane Helm, pp. 130–45. Handbook of North American Indians, Vol. 6, William C. Sturtevant, general editor. Washington, D.C.: Smithsonian Institution.
Romero, Francine Christine
1998 A Population Genetic Study of Athabascan Speaking Populations in the American Southwest. Unpublished Ph.D. dissertation, Department of Anthropology, University of New Mexico, Albuquerque.
Rushforth, Scott, and Steadman Upham
1992 *A Hopi Social History: Anthropological Perspectives on Sociocultural Persistence and Change*. Austin: University of Texas Press.
Saville-Troike, Muriel
1974 Diversity in Southwestern Athabaskan: A Historical Perspective. *Navajo Language Review* 1(2):67–84.
Schaafsma, Curtis F.
1996 Ethnic Identity and Protohistoric Archaeological Sites in Northwestern New Mexico: Implications for Reconstructions of Navajo and Ute History. In *The Archaeology of Navajo Origins*, edited by Ronald H. Towner, pp. 19–46. Salt Lake City: University of Utah Press.
Steward, Julian H.
1937 *Ancient Caves of the Great Salt Lake Region*. Bureau of American Ethnology Bulletin No. 116. Washington, D.C.: Smithsonian Institution.
Tedlock, Barbara
1992 *The Beautiful and the Dangerous: Encounters with Zuni Indians*. New York: Viking.
Tobey, Margaret L.
1981 Carrier. In *Subarctic*, edited by June Helm, pp. 413–432. Handbook of North American Indians, Vol. 6, William C. Sturtevant, general editor. Washington, D.C.: Smithsonian Institution.
Tyler, S. Lyman, and H. Darrel Taylor
1958 The Report of Fray Alonso de Posada in Relation to Quivira and Teguayo. *New Mexico Historical Review* 33(4):258–314.
VanStone, James W.
1974 *Athapaskan Adaptations: Hunters and Fishermen of the Subarctic Forests*. Chicago: Aldine.

Wilmeth, Roscoe
1978   *Anahim Lake Archaeology and the Early Chilcotin Indians*. National Museum of Man Mercury Series, Archaeological Survey of Canada Paper No. 82. Ottawa, Ontario: Canadian Museum of Civilization.

Wyman, Leland C.
1970   *Blessingway*. Tucson: University of Arizona Press.
1983   Navajo Ceremonial System. In *Southwest*, edited by Alfonso Ortiz, pp. 536–557. Handbook of North American Indians, Vol. 10, William C. Sturtevant, general editor. Washington, D.C.: Smithsonian Institution.

Young, Robert W.
1958   *The Navajo Yearbook, Report No. VII, Fiscal Year 1958*. Window Rock, Arizona: Navajo Agency.
1961   *The Navajo Yearbook, Report No. VIII, 1951–1961: A Decade of Progress*. Window Rock, Arizona: Navajo Agency.
1983   Apachean Languages. In *Southwest*, edited by Alfonso Ortiz, pp. 303–400. Handbook of North American Indians, Vol. 10, William C. Sturtevant, general editor. Washington, D.C.: Smithsonian Institution.

Young, Robert W., and William Morgan Sr.
1954   *Navajo Historical Selections*. Phoenix, Arizona: Bureau of Indian Affairs.
1992   *Analytical Lexicon of Navajo*. With the assistance of Sally Midgette. Albuquerque: University of New Mexico Press.

Zolbrod, Paul
1984   *Diné bahane': The Navajo Creation Story*. Albuquerque: University of New Mexico Press.

CHAPTER 7

Navajo Emergence in Dinétah

Social Imaginary and Archaeology

Douglas D. Dykeman and Paul Roebuck

Many scholars speculate that Navajo culture arose as Athapaskan migrants gradually adopted Puebloan traits and maize agriculture following the Pueblo refugee period of the late 1600s. Recently published archaeological work in Dinétah, the traditional Navajo emergence place, reveals Navajo sites dating from AD 1541 to 1625, rich in artifacts, diverse economies, and robust maize agriculture. The prominence of maize in these earliest sites is consistent with its importance in the Navajo social imaginary expressed in traditional creation accounts and illustrated in rock art in Dinétah (Figure 7.1). Navajo tradition and archaeological work in Dinétah show that Navajo culture emerged quickly, distinct from Puebloan and other Athapaskan groups, at least 150 years before the Pueblo refugee period. This necessitates rethinking the gradualist hypotheses of culture evolution. Understanding Navajo worldviews helps focus archaeological investigations and sheds light on Navajo cultural emergence.

In the nineteenth, twentieth, and twenty-first centuries we have witnessed increasingly complex articulations between culture and place. Global processes have impacted the creation and maintenance of community and identity under circumstances of migration, dislocation, and diaspora. Though its scale may be greater today, this is not a unique situation. In the last millennium Northern New Mexico was the scene of ancestral Puebloan community abandonment and consolidation, the translocation of Athapaskan- and Numic-speaking peoples, and the creation of Apache and Navajo community and cultural identity under the cross-pressures of local, regional, and global processes.

In the early centuries of the last millennium ancestral Puebloans created, abandoned, relocated, and consolidated communities in the Four Corners region of Utah, Arizona, Colorado, and New Mexico. Around this time (precisely when is debatable) Southern Athapaskans, by then already separated linguistically from their Chipewyan and Sarsi ancestors in northern Canada for some time (Hoijer 1938, 1956, 1971; Krauss 1973; Smith 1981:271; Young 1983; Foster 1996; Campbell 1997; Rice, this volume; Gordon, this volume), entered

FIGURE 7.1. Crow Canyon petroglyphs in Dinétah. Photograph by Douglas Dykeman.

the region and occupied the hinterlands surrounding the sedentary ancestral Puebloan settlements.

Several lines of evidence indicate that strong trading relationships resulted in the exchange of ideas and a variety of goods between the Puebloans and Apacheans (Parsons 1939:2:1039–1064; Opler 1983:380; Baldwin 1997; Torres 1999, 2003; Dykeman 2003). Numic-speakers (including the ancestors of the Shoshone, Ute, and Comanche) from the west, north, and east also entered the Pueblo periphery, competing with the Athapaskans and possibly "indigenous" hunting-and-gathering peoples (see Brugge, this volume). There are fewer lines of evidence supporting trading and more indicating raiding/warfare relationships between the Numic peoples and the Puebloans and Athapaskans (Lange 1979:203; Washington Matthews in Halpern and McGreevy 1997:165). We infer from linguistic evidence that sometime before AD 1200 (possibly AD 800— see Rice, this volume) Southern Athapaskans were a single group or a number of very closely related groups but after that time became separated (Opler 1983: 381). Starting in the sixteenth century, Spanish explorers and colonizers, with their new technology and ideas and their Old World diseases, entered the region from the south. Climate fluctuations produced a variety of environmental stresses.

Out of these cross-pressures, separate Navajo and Apache cultural identities emerged among the Southern Athapaskans. The Navajo became less mobile, increased their use of ceramics, adopted more substantial architecture forms, adapted Pueblo agriculture, and tied their identity intimately to the landscape of the upper San Juan River Basin. The Western Apache also became more sedentary on a relative scale among mobile groups (Seymour 2005b:4), but other Apaches (e.g., the Chiricahua, Mescalero, Plains, and Lipan), perhaps more conservative and somewhat less willing to take on a sedentary lifestyle, focused less on agriculture and more on gathering, hunting, trading, and raiding, ranging over larger areas through much of the American Southwest and the Southern Plains.

Complicating our understanding of these emerging identities, as Brugge observes in this volume, are the ongoing interactions and mixing of Apachean, Tanoan Numic, Puebloan, and possibly other indigenous peoples in the region as well as potentially successive waves of Athapaskan in-migration. Genetic studies (see Malhi, this volume) indicate that the total number of immigrants was quite small, which would make the archaeological remains of their transit much more difficult to find.

Over the last four generations, in the absence of adequate empirical archaeological data on the earliest Navajo sites, archaeologists advanced two major theories of Navajo cultural emergence: the refugee hypothesis and the acculturation hypothesis. The refugee hypothesis (Kidder 1920; Keur 1941; Dittert et al. 1961; D. Gunnerson 1956; Schaafsma 1979, 1981) holds that Navajo culture emerged late—coinciding with Pueblo people seeking refuge from the Spanish reconquest of the upper Rio Grande Valley in 1696 and going to live among the proto-Navajo Athapaskan-speakers in the upper San Juan region. According to the hypothesis, the Puebloans taught their hosts about farming, herding, polychrome ceramics, and stone architecture and imparted various religious and social institutions. Out of this acculturation the Navajo culture came into existence. Refugee hypothesis adherents generally also hold that the proto-Navajo Athapaskans arrived in the American Southwest as late as the 1600s from the east via the Plains (e.g., Wilcox 1981:219–222).

The acculturation hypothesis (Hodge 1895; Huscher and Huscher 1942, 1943; Farmer 1942; Hall 1944; Hester 1962; Eddy 1966; Perry 1991; Carlson, this volume) holds that Athapaskan-speaking immigrants from the north, coming into contact with ancestral Puebloan peoples in the Southwest, were acculturated, gradually adopting Puebloan culture traits and slowly acquiring maize agriculture as they shed their northern Athapaskan hunting-and-gathering practices and material culture to become the Navajo. Some proponents of this theory propose an early arrival in the Southwest for the Athapaskan-speakers, anywhere from AD 700–850 (Hall 1944), to AD 1000 (Kluckhohn and Leighton 1962:33), to AD 1200–1300 (Riley 1954:45; Perry 1980:293; Brugge 1983:490), and some also strongly favor an intermountain route of migration (e.g., Huscher and Huscher 1942, 1943).

Archaeological investigations undertaken in the 1990s in the wake of oil and gas development in the vicinity of Gobernador, Pump, and Largo washes in northwestern New Mexico are filling in some of the gaps in our knowledge of

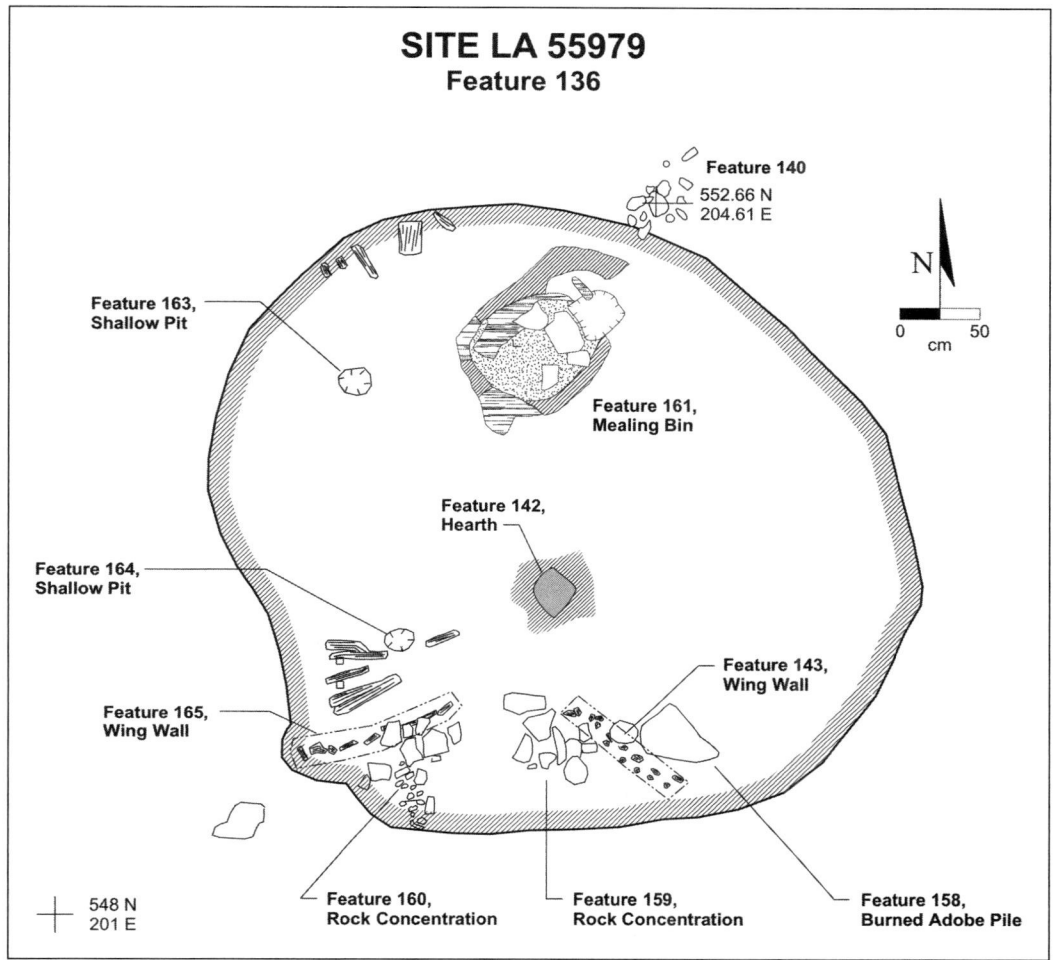

FIGURE 7.2. Feature 136: hogan from site LA 55979, tree-ring-dated to 1541. Photograph by Douglas Dykeman.

early Navajo culture. The new archaeological evidence reveals a starkly different developmental trajectory for the Navajo than has previously been theorized.

Navajo sites, distinguished by a combination of forked-stick hogans and sweat lodges, structured site layout, characteristic ceramic and lithic technology, maize agriculture, and distinctive grain storage methods, have been found in Dinétah in the upper San Juan Basin which date from the first half of the 1500s (Hall 1944; Dykeman 2000, 2003, 2004; Hovezak and Sesler 2002; Dykeman and Roebuck 2009a, 2009b). From the earliest Navajo sites yet discovered, such as LA 55979,[1] tree-ring-dated to AD 1541 (Dykeman 2000) (Figure 7.2), we find maize—maize pollen, cobs, kernels, cupules, or shanks—in every feature (Roebuck 2007; Dykeman and Roebuck 2009a). The Navajo maize varieties (identified from cob morphology and row counts) are similar to those from contemporary Pueblos of the early 1500s. Ethnobotanical and other empirical evidence at LA 55979 strongly support the idea that the Navajo grew maize and did not trade for it (Roebuck 2007).

Although it appears that the Navajo obtained maize and many elements of agricultural technology (including some rituals) from the Pueblo, aspects of grain storage were distinctly Navajoan, not Puebloan: grain storage on early Navajo sites was not for three years (as in Puebloan sites) but for a much shorter period, generally for one winter as measured by the volume of storage cists (Hill 1938:42–47; Brugge 1986:138; Sesler and Hovezak 2002:212). We infer that the Navajo economy was broader-based than the Puebloan and (later) Spanish economies in the region—it encompassed maize agriculture but did not give up exploitation, encouragement, and even cultivation of nondomesticated plants (Doolittle 2000; Doolittle and Mabry 2006) or hunting, trading, and raiding. This broad-spectrum economic strategy served the Navajo well in a natural (and social) environment subject to extremes and variable conditions, enabling them to quickly adapt to changing circumstances, shifting their activities as conditions warranted (Dykeman 2004).

Moreover, the early Navajos did not acquire all elements of the more complex and efficient ground-stone technology of the Pueblos. We attribute this to the maintenance of traditional Navajo food preparation methods (Dykeman 2004). The incorporation of cultural traits that occurred from the encounter of Puebloans and Athapaskans ran both ways. Pueblos adopted Athapaskan cultural elements, and Athapaskans adopted Puebloan elements. Baldwin (1997) suggests that sinew-backed bows, the mountain-lion-skin quiver and bow case, the bison-hide shield, the four-pointed star motif, and the heart-line motif in rock art and kiva art, which appear in Puebloan sites around 1400, were introduced by Apachean peoples. As early as AD 1520, Athapaskan hunting technology (including sinew-backed bows and arctic-style microblades) is found at Hopi, Unshagi (Jemez), and Pecos pueblos (Torres 1999; Dykeman 2003). Jemez Black-on-white and Rio Grande glazeware, along with high-quality Jemez obsidian and exotic Pedernal chert, appear on Navajo sites in Dinétah. Several Athapaskan groups adopted maize agriculture and elements of Pueblo philosophy and religion (Opler 1983).

Though Navajos adopted agriculture and became less mobile, they did not cease to be Athapaskans. They were not acculturated to become Puebloans. They did incorporate some select Pueblo ideas and elements of material culture, but they modified them and made them their own. From this mounting body of evidence from the earliest Navajo sites, several things are immediately apparent:

- Navajo culture did not emerge in the refugee period but at least 150 years earlier.
- The emergence of Navajo culture was not gradual but abrupt—the earliest known sites contain most of the distinctive Navajo cultural traits.
- Forked-stick hogans were a key element of the emerging culture.
- At the very beginning, farming maize figured strongly in the Navajo economy.

- Maize varieties were likely obtained from Puebloan people, but grain storage and aspects of planting and preparation were given a distinctly Navajo form.
- Incorporation is a better metaphor than acculturation for describing syncretic elements of Navajo cultural emergence.

The emphasis on maize in the early sites is consistent with the Navajo's own account of their origins. Most origin accounts (Matthews 1897; Stephen 1930; Goddard 1933; Spencer 1947; Fishler 1953; O'Bryan 1956; Wyman 1965; Zolbrod 1984) claim:
- Maize was present from the beginning.
- Many of the Navajo divinities are made from maize.
- Maize figures prominently in the creation of this world and the conditions for the flourishing of the earth-surface people in this world.
- The Navajo people themselves were created, in part, from maize.
- Aspects of maize agriculture were learned from/influenced by the Pueblo people.

The emphasis on maize is also consistent with the earliest Spanish historical accounts referring explicitly to the Navajo. In 1640, 100 years later than the earliest known Navajo sites, Fray Alonso de Benavides identified the *Apaches de Nabajo*—the "Apache of the wide fields" (Hewett 1906; Hodge et al. 1945). Brugge (1983) points out that the Spanish name for the Apache group may be a geographical place name rather than descriptions of their activities, but the place name itself does refer to farming.

Many archaeologists have used Spanish historical accounts to help them pinpoint the location of Navajo ethnogenesis in time and space, understand Navajo origins, and provide context for their hypotheses. Fewer have used the Navajo's own accounts of themselves or those of their neighbors. And some ignore all historical evidence, oral or written, and prefer to rely purely on empirical archaeological evidence.

For example, Jemez oral history (Sando 1979:418) records the Jemez origin in a lake south of Dulce, New Mexico, near the Continental Divide, and that while they resided in that region they "accepted a nomadic race identifiable as the Athapaskans who arrived in the Southwest probably after AD 950." The Jemez are clear that their relationship with the Athapaskans occurred well before their departure to the vicinity of their current location, which we can date to circa AD 1300. Some archaeologists ignore these oral accounts of Athapaskan presence because of insufficient corroborating empirical evidence from archaeological sites. Indeed, in the same volume in which Sando cites the Jemez oral history of relations with the Athapaskans, Gunnerson (1979:162) says unequivocally, "There is no evidence for the presence of Athapaskans in the Southwest before the 1500s."

That archaeologists have not had good *empirical* archaeological evidence of the beginning of the Southern Athapaskan occupation in the upper San Juan Basin may be an artifact of how we recognize and record sites in the region. Seymour (2005b) raises an interesting argument that archaeologists may miss low-visibility remains of highly mobile groups because of employing systems developed for studying more sedentary peoples. Highly mobile peoples leave very different traces than sedentary peoples. Raiders may not want their camps discovered; they may dismantle their wickiups and obscure their living areas. Roasting pits may have been located far from habitations. Mobile peoples made small fires of brushy materials on the surface of the ground and avoided reusing fire pits. Sites may have been located on saddles or other areas highly prone to erosion. The remains from such sites are far less visible than the substantial architecture of a pithouse, room block, or hogan. Given the cost of carbon dating, Seymour argues that modern archaeologists may unintentionally select larger chunks of charcoal to ensure good dates, thereby biasing their samples by avoiding sampling thin ashy thermal features formed from the combustion of brushy woods, and thus miss the presence of components left by more mobile peoples. We may have to change how we see the landscape before we recognize the remains of mobile peoples. This archaeological myopia may account for the lack of clear empirical evidence of early Athapaskan presence in the upper San Juan prior to the appearance of the Navajo.

The debate on when the Southern Athapaskans moved into the upper San Juan Basin and how long they occupied it before Navajo culture emerged is complex and has many partisans and differing explanations. It is clear that the discussion will continue until additional evidence comes to light from a variety of sources.

Unlike most of the other chapters in this book that focus on migration, our interest here is in the earliest emergence of distinctive *Navajo* culture and when, where, and how that emergence occurred, as well as what forms it took. The Navajo are generally acknowledged as the most sedentary of the Apachean peoples. However, their origin stories include many references to migration in the gathering of the clans and travel by the holy people who came before. But the emergence of Navajo culture—the Diné—occurred in a specific place, Dinétah. Significantly, the Navajo had left Dinétah and moved west and south by the time the first ethnographies were recorded. These were "advancing front"–style migrations (see Magne, this volume, and Rockman 2003) which took place in the 1700s. At the beginning of the eighteenth century the Navajo shifted their economic focus from corn agriculture to sheep herding. Areas to the west of Dinétah exerted a "pull" into landscapes more favorable for herding. As such, the environmental "learning" accompanying migration that Magne refers to in his migration model occurred before the migration out of Dinétah began.

The stories of Dinétah as a place are largely focused on an area where the Navajo no longer live and of which few Navajo have firsthand experience. Based on the tradewares found on early Navajo sites in Dinétah dating from AD 1541 to 1625, such as LA 55979, LA 78178, and LA 79469 (Dykeman and Roebuck 2009a), the Navajo's "big trips" (see Seymour, Chapter 17, this volume) might have involved moving from Dinétah to Jemez, Zuni, or Hopi—assuming those trade wares were acquired firsthand.

Social Imaginary

We believe ideas are an important source of cultural change, and we find Navajo origin accounts and other oral traditions essential sources of information for understanding the emergence of Navajo cultural identity. Understanding Navajo oral tradition has great utility for developing models that can be tested by archaeological information (Brugge 1981; Gill 1983; Roessel 1983; Dykeman 2003:32, 2004). The idea of *social imaginary* is a helpful concept for approaching Navajo oral tradition and bridging Navajo concepts with Spanish historical accounts and with modern archaeological theory.

Social imaginary, as used by Taylor (2004, 2007), is a term that describes the cultural milieu. The idea originated in the concept of public space discussed by, among others, Habermas (1989) and Warner (1990), and was further developed as social imaginary by Taylor and by Anderson (1991). Of "social imaginary," Taylor (2007:171–172) says:

> What I am trying to get at with this term is something much broader and deeper than the intellectual schemes people may entertain when they think about social reality in a disengaged mode. I am thinking rather of the ways in which they imagine their social existence, how they fit together with others, how things go on between them and their fellows, the expectations which are normally met, and the deeper normative notions and images which underlie these expectations.
>
> I want to speak of "social imaginary" here, rather than social theory, because there are important differences between the two. There are, in fact, several differences. I speak of "imaginary" (i) because I'm talking about the way ordinary people "imagine" their social surroundings, and this is often not expressed in theoretical terms, it is carried in images, stories, legends, etc. But it is also the case that (ii) theory is often the possession of a small minority, whereas what is interesting in the social imaginary is that it is shared by large groups of people, if not the whole society. Which leads to a third difference: (iii) the social imaginary is that common understanding which makes possible common practices, and a widely shared sense of legitimacy.

When we look at cultures, their social imaginary provides a context and rationale for understanding broad-based social, economic, and other behavioral practices and beliefs—the elements that set a group apart from their predecessors and their neighbors and mark them as a distinct cultural entity. We can begin to get at that social imaginary through images, stories, legends, and social practices, some of which leave evidence in the archaeological record.

Farella (1993:130), in examining the use of contemporary anthropological narratives, says:

> The stories provide a template, a standard, through which [people's] lives... can be ordered and understood. They describe the range of emotions and behaviors that are available to humans; they describe the range of the possible. Everyone in the world has stories like this, about the pattern of the universe. Anglo stories involve molecules, or stories about economic trends, or theories on developmental psychology. But all these stories describe the features of the world that matter, that are relevant and that must be paid attention to. We all try to describe and understand any particular instance in terms of the more general order described in our own stories.

For Paleo and Archaic peoples in the American Southwest, we have little access to the social imaginary. We do not know the oral histories, stories, legends, religion, and common beliefs of these peoples. With the Navajo we have a great deal of material—much of it from ritual contexts and much of it part of the creation accounts of prior worlds and the current world, gods and holy people, the adventures of culture heroes, and the preparation of this world for and the coming to be of the Navajo (see Matthews 1897; Stephen 1930; Goddard 1933; Spencer 1947; Fishler 1953; O'Bryan 1956; Wyman 1965; Zolbrod 1984), including the gathering of the clans (e.g., Matthews 1894; Reichard 1928; Spencer 1947).

We also have family accounts from Navajo people whose family histories extend back into the 1700s to a time when they lived in Dinétah (Benally et al. 1982; Cleveland et al. 1999). We have healing ceremonies centered on founding stories that are tied to specific places on the landscape: for example, Coyoteway (Luckert 1979), Male Red Antway (Wyman 1965), and Shootingway (Blue Eyes n.d.). Brugge (1993:33) cites a number of these, and he points out that many of them are concentrated at the old ancestral Puebloan centers: the Hopi Mesas, Canyon de Chelly, Mesa Verde, Mancos Canyon, Aztec Ruins, Chaco Canyon, and Chimney Rock. These places are mentioned in contexts of Navajo contact with living ancestral Pueblo people. There is, ostensibly, a large amount of information on Navajo use of lands in Colorado and Utah in oral history accounts held by the Navajo Nation (Martin 1997, cited by A. Taylor 2004; Benally et al. 1982). There are numerous Navajo ethnographies (e.g., Haile 1938; Klah 1942; Kluckhohn and Leighton 1946), as well as texts on Navajo philosophy (McNeley 1973, 1981; Witherspoon 1974; Reichard 1977 [1939]; Farella 1984), which give insight into Navajo thought and sense of place. All of these accounts taken together constitute the Navajo national historiography—the explanation of how they came to be and how their identity sets them apart from their neighbors as viewed from both the inside and the outside.

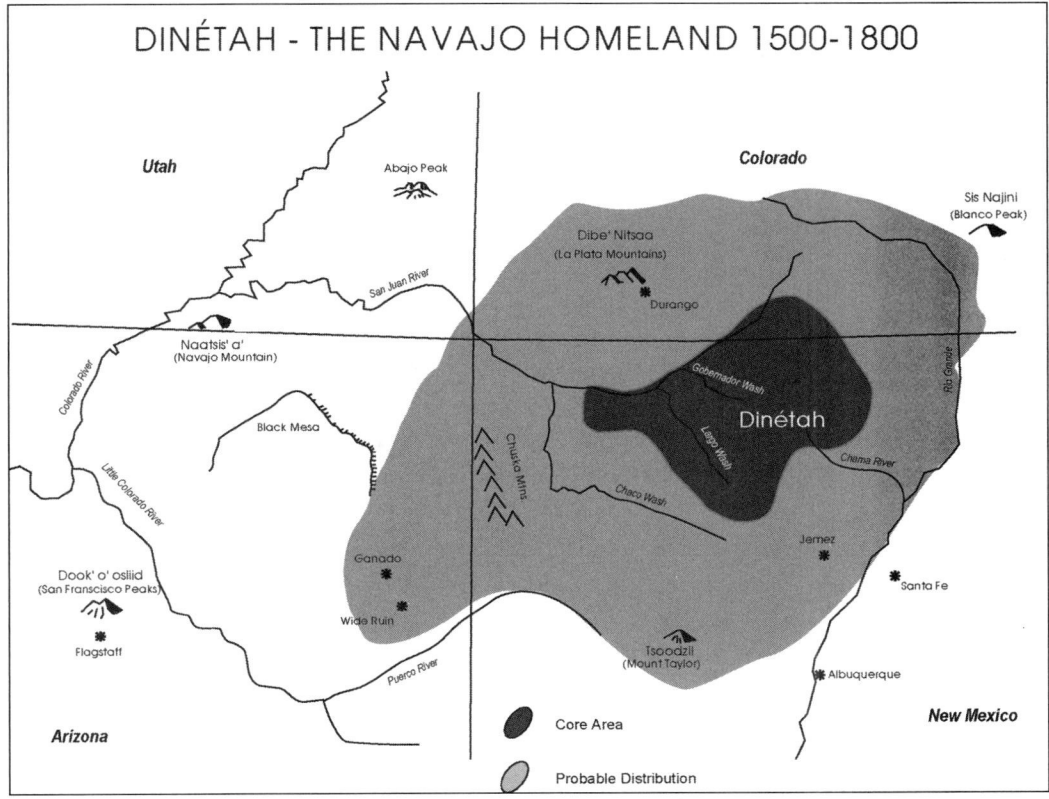

FIGURE 7.3. Map of the Dinétah region, the place of Navajo emergence. Photograph by Douglas Dykeman.

The Navajo greatly prize individualism (Farella 1984:195, 1993; Perry 1991: 138), and as one might expect for such a culture, they differ in their emphasis and interpretation of some of the details of this national history. For example, Spencer (1947) presents 23 different versions of the origin stories set down since 1895. However, the general outline of these accounts is consistent and provides a strong basis for understanding the basic elements of the Navajo social imaginary. The Navajo worldview is celebrated, re-created, and renewed in ceremonies, healing practices, and other oral traditions. And it has shaped how the Navajo have lived and adapted to their homeland in the Southwest (Figure 7.3).

If our theories are to adequately address complex social realities, we must avoid the temptation to reduce our explanations to a single variable (environmental, economic, evolutionary, or socio-biological determinism). Instead, we are looking for a variety of cross-pressures: cultural values, mores, and restrictions; marriage rules and kinship systems; food taboos; war and peace; drought and abundance; new technologies and old traditions; competition and cooperation; economic innovation; new religious movements; new trade arrangements; population dislocations; environmental limitations; and so forth. These are the explanatory factors in culture continuity and change. As archaeologists, we expect to see these ideas and practices reflected in architecture, the organization of public and private space, hunting technology, agricultural practices, ceramic manufacture, color symbolism and decorative arts, rock art, variations in wood use and thermal features, the location and abandonment of communities, shifting boundaries between different groups, and so forth. In other words, we expect to see them reflected in all aspects of material culture, which are, themselves, shaped, inspired, and tied to aesthetics, religious belief, ritual practice, and traditions, as well as the exigencies of earning a living and getting along with other groups—in short, the social imaginary.

Archaeologists can and should look to Navajo oral traditions and social imaginary for context for our models of Navajo culture emergence, continuity, and change. To understand Navajo thought, we look for paradigms, social norms, and organizing principles: the extended metaphor of the world built as a hogan, or life force moving in whorls/whirlwinds, the creative tension of male and female, or the power of thought and speech. We expect to see those paradigms reflected in the natural world (its geography: the movement of the sun, moon, stars, and seasons; the reproduction of life) and in social practice—in sunwise concentric circles and in finger-, hand-, and footprints in rock art (Figure 7.1); in star lore, the Navajo calendar, and agricultural fields planted in spirals or other ritualized patterns; in hogans and whole sites oriented to cardinal directions; in female and male activity areas in and around the hogan; in the uses of colors, shell, minerals, semi-precious stones, and herbs; in the power of ceremony to create and re-create the world; and in the subtle and not-so-subtle ways those beliefs and practices shape the social, cultural, and physical landscapes.

The origin stories tell us, among other things, where the Navajo emerged into this world—where Navajo culture was created; how the hogan serves as a microcosm of the universe; that maize was essential and important to Navajo identity from the very beginning of their existence; how the Navajo interacted with the Pueblo; how the Navajo migrated to their homeland by several different routes; and how they gathered the clans from different directions, at different times, and incorporated different peoples as they returned to Dinétah.

Also remarkable are the things left out of the accounts. The stories note the arrival of the Spanish (known as *Naakaiłbahí Nináádąą* to the Navajo) but do not consider the Pueblo Revolt or the Reconquista worth mentioning. They do not mark the Pueblo refugees coming to Dinétah as a significant event. They account for the arrival of Ute—known to the Navajo as the Arrow People (Washington Matthews in Halpern and McGreevy 1997:165)—but do not emphasize conflict with them. They emphasize agriculture and hunting but barely mention or do not mention at all herding or domestic animals. All of these omissions and inclusions strongly indicate that the stories' form and content were set well before the Pueblo Revolt and Spanish Reconquista at the end of the seventeenth century and before herding became an important economic practice and conflict with the Ute intensified in the eighteenth century. This is consistent with the new empirical archaeological evidence of Navajo sites dating from AD 1541 to 1625 from the Fruitland Coal Gas Development Area projects in Dinétah (Hogan et al. 1991).

We can compare oral histories in a manner analogous to lexico-statistics to help reveal how and when Navajo culture differentiated from other Apachean groups and how the Navajo distinguished themselves from their neighbors (see Webster's discussion of ethnopoetics, this volume). The Navajo, Western Apache, Jicarilla, and Lipan share a story of the beginning of agriculture that involves a man who travels down a river in a hollow log and is aided by his pet turkey. That story is not shared by the Chiricahua, Mescalero, or Kiowa Apache. The same four groups share with Puebloan peoples origin accounts that involve emergence from an underworld—other Apachean peoples do not. We can use the presence or absence of common concepts as evidence of shared public space where these ideas were shared and discussed. Shared stories and beliefs argue against the early separation of the Navajo and Western Apache from the Jicarilla and Lipan (Goodwin 1939; Matthews 1897; McAllister 1949; Opler 1938, 1940, 1942, 1983:369).

These comparisons are complicated, somewhat, as Brugge (this volume) points out, by "the possibility that the Navajo Nation may have more than one ancestral Athapaskan connection, the possibility of more than one division on the way south." In addition, ideas could have flowed both north and south and transformed the social imaginary across vast distances, as the Athapaskan-speakers were highly mobile. Language itself is important in understanding social imaginary. Witherspoon (1977:34) explains that in Navajo philosophy, knowledge, expressed in speech, transforms the world—reality as a mirror of language. He says: "The language of Navajo ritual is performative (Austin, 1962) not descriptive. Ritual language does not describe how things are; it determines how they will be. Ritual language is not impotent; it is powerful. It commands, compels, organizes, transforms, and restores. It disperses evil, reverses disorder, neutralizes pain, overcomes fear, eliminates illness, relieves anxiety, and restores order, health, and well-being" (Witherspoon 1977:34). It is not just ritual language, prayers, and songs, however, that have power. Everyday thought and speech matter. A common belief among Navajos is that if one thinks of good things and good fortune, good things will happen. If one thinks of bad things, bad fortune will occur. Witherspoon (1977:28) says: "In my first few years among the Navajo, I was constantly scolded for thinking about unhappy possibilities. As a product of another cultural world, I had learned to 'save something for a rainy day.' Among the Navajo I was told that planning for that 'rainy day' would bring about 'rainy days,' and that I had better forget about planning for 'rainy days' unless I wanted it to 'rain.'" This moral axis of Navajo social imaginary—that it is wrong to plan for a not-rainy day and save grain for a three-year drought—is consonant with practice observed in the archaeological record: we do not find the storage facilities (Dykeman and Roebuck 2009a).

This distinctly Navajo practice, different from that of the Pueblo and Spanish settlers, sets the Navajo economy apart and marks it as changeable and adaptable (see Dykeman 2004 for a model of Navajo culture change based on incorporation and the coexistence of tradition and change through time and space in Navajo social imaginary). When harsh conditions cause Pueblo and Spanish economies to collapse, the Navajo appear rich by comparison as they were never completely dependent on agriculture, and these differences are reflected in the Spanish historical accounts (Hill 1940; Reeve 1957, 1958, 1959, 1960).

TIME

Interpreting the Navajo oral tradition to help understand Navajo cultural emergence is not new. Matthews (1897) was one of the first anthropologists to estimate the time of Athapaskan entry into the American Southwest. Using a Bishop Ussher–like method,[2] Matthews estimated the lifetimes of prominent characters in the Navajo origin accounts and counted backward. He concluded that the Navajo were in the region by the fifteenth century or earlier.

Although we generally agree with Matthews' estimate, we take issue with his method. The origin accounts that Matthews was analyzing—those that express the traditional Navajo social imaginary—are based on a different conception of time, one Eliade (1959, 1965) calls the "time of origins."

Benjamin (1973:263) describes the modern sense of time as homogenous and empty. Anderson (1991) discusses the crucial importance of this linear sense of time to the modern (Western) social imaginary—the one within which Matthews was operating. However, the traditions of most cultures are based on the "time of origins," what Taylor (2007:57) describes as

> an "*illud tempus*," when the order of things was established, whether that of the creation of the present world, or the founding of our people with its Law. The agents in this time were on a larger scale than people today, perhaps gods, but at least heroes. In terms of secular time, this origin is in a remote past, it is "time out of mind" but it is not simply in the past, because it also something that we can re-approach, can get closer to again. This may be by ritual only, but this ritual may also have an effect of renewing and rededicating, hence coming closer to the origin. The Great Time is thus behind us, but it is also in a sense above us. It is what happened at the beginning, but it is also the great Exemplar, which we can be closer to or farther away from as we move through history.

Farella (1993:40), in talking about the Navajo Night Chant, says:

> In this ceremony, as in some others, men put on buckskin masks and appear as *Ye'ii*. Anglos always describe this as a reenactment of a mythical time, and the dancers as masked impersonators. But, here again, that isn't really

correct. It isn't so much a re-enactment as it is a re-creation, bringing the essence of that past moment, that prototypical time, into the present. Although that doesn't really capture it either, as what is represented here tends to be atemporal rather than arranged lineally into a past, a present, and a future.

The understanding that different cultures have different social and cosmic imaginaries can help us be sensitive to cultural differences and temper our interpretations. It can keep us from projecting our own ethnocentric prejudices onto others, and it can help us avoid interpreting other's accounts as just-so stories.

That said, it appears that a number of Navajo informants have tried to bridge the different concepts of time inherent in Navajo and non-Navajo social imaginaries in providing information to anthropologists (Matthews 1890:90; Van Valkenburg 1938:3; Witherspoon 1977:139; Wyman 1970:139; Zolbrod 1984: 409n3). Reichard (1950:243) says, "A large and unexplainable number is the reference to 102 as the age of man—probably the ideal of a long lifespan. Matthews was also told that 'seven times old age has killed'"—meaning that seven full generations of Navajo had existed up to the time that he had collected the legends.

By the implied reckoning, the narrative would be 714 years old, placing it, from the time of Matthews' recording, at AD 1176. Such a date is considerably older than that proposed by many archaeologists for Athapaskan entry into the Southwest; however, it is internally consistent with some of the Navajo accounts of Pueblo–proto-Navajo interactions at the old ancestral Puebloan centers (Brugge 1993:33), with the Jemez Pueblo oral history of their interaction with Athapaskans (Sando 1979:418), and with Seymour's (2005a) chronometric data on ancestral Chiricahua and Mescalero sites. Navajo agriculture from AD 1300 through the 1700s along the Upper San Juan River would account for maize in pollen samples reported by Eddy (1966:507–508; Brugge, this volume).

Another type of temporal interpretation of Navajo origin accounts is given by Young (1968:2), who views the Navajo account of the story of the movement of beings from the First to the present World on a horizontal rather than a vertical plane. He interprets the First World as the Arctic north, the Second World as the Northern Plains, culminating with the place of emergence into this World as the point at which the earliest ancestors of the Navajo entered the Southwest. Zolbrod (1984:359n39) calls Young's suggestion "fascinating" but warns that we should take care be not to "reduce the artistry of the story to facts of history as we like to reckon them in accounting for our own recorded past." He says "the narrative should be seen primarily as art and only secondarily as historic data." From the perspective of the modern, Western social imaginary, when we look at historic data, time is linear. Zolbrod's suggestion that the Navajo narrative should be approached aesthetically may help non-Navajos avoid confusing different kinds of time and assuming that their own social and cosmic imaginaries hold for all other peoples in all other times and places. It helps bridge traditional views and anthropologists' accounts. It helps us appreciate the subtleties expressed in traditional accounts such as that given by Bernard Second, a leading singer (*gutlą́ą́tl*) of the Mescalero Apaches (in Carmichael and Farrer, this volume), in which the informant is clearly seeking to communicate traditional stories in ways that will be understandable to his intended audience, bridging cultural differences in perception of time and space.

Not only does the traditional Navajo social imaginary reveal a different understanding of time—it also encompasses a different concept of space. Navajo understanding of sacred geography is different from the space-as-container concept familiar to Western modernity. The landscape itself figures prominently in Navajo accounts, and specific landscape features are cited as proof of the veracity of the stories. Kelley and Francis (1994:187) say that the "stories map the place and the landscape onto a dense structure of powerful cultural symbols, images, and beliefs that give meaning to that landscape and place." Wyman (1962:78) talks about the Navajo "passion for geography" and notes that "preoccupation with locality" is revealed in Navajo speech. In Navajo "movement is described in great detail." He claims the Navajo "lives conceptually and linguistically in a universe in motion." In a sense, Navajo geography is more dynamic than that of Western modernity, and non-Navajos must make extra effort to understand the Navajo emphasis on place and landscape. This has implications for the definition and understanding of sacred places and traditional use areas (Luckert 1977).

The Navajo's account of the creation of this world is centered on the emergence place in Dinétah and the sacred mountains that are at its limits. The emergence place is believed by most to be an actual, tangible place, the location of which is known to knowledgeable persons. By some accounts, it is Tó Aheedlí—where the rivers cross, where the water meet, and near where, according to Navajo tradition, the Hero Twins, Naayéé' Neizghání and Tó Bájísh Chíní, made their home. This location is often identified (e.g., Sylvia Many Goats in Kelley and Francis 1994:36) as the confluence of the San Juan and the Los Pinos Rivers, currently flooded by the U.S. Bureau of Reclamation's Navajo Reservoir. Others put the origin place at Hajíínáí, a lake or an island in a lake, in the San Juan Mountains near Pagosa Springs (e.g., Hastin Tlo'tsi Hee in O'Bryan 1956:12n44; see also Matthews 1897:219n43; Brugge 2005); or in the La Plata Mountains (e.g., Teddy Draper Sr. in Kelley and Francis 1994:76).

The Navajo origin stories all place the emergence of the Navajo divinities and the principal instance of the creation of the Navajo people in Dinétah. That these stories locate the center of the Navajo universe, Dinétah, not in the Navajo's current location but at a site to the east, in the vicinity of where we find the earliest Navajo archaeological sites, helps us locate where Navajo cultural identity emerged. The origin accounts are consistent with the archaeological record. We do not find evidence of emergent *Navajo* culture elsewhere. Prior to their arrival in Dinétah, the Southern Athapaskan–speakers were not Navajo. They were not Navajo for the 1,200 years that they were linguistically isolated from

FIGURE 7.4.
Rock art from
Delgadito Canyon
in Dinétah.
Photograph by
Douglas Dykeman.

their Tsuut'ina (Sarsi) and Dëne Suĺiné (Chipewyan) cousins in northern Canada. They were not Navajo at Avonlea, Besant, or Dismal River, or in the Wyoming, Utah, or Colorado Rockies; or any other place where anthropologists have theorized that these Athapaskan-speakers sojourned during their "migration" to the Southwest (translocation would be a better term—migrations do not take 1,100 years). But they did not become *Navajo* until they arrived in Dinétah, until they began to grow maize, build hogans in a ritually prescribed manner, and, importantly, until they embraced stories and accounts of the world that set them apart from other Apachean peoples. Navajo identity emerged in Dinétah. It is intimately tied to the place. Our theories should take the Navajo social imaginary into account. Those theories that argue that Navajo identity emerged elsewhere need to account for why they differ from the Navajo's own oral history of themselves, which they set down in rock art in the Dinétah region (Figure 7.4) and continue to celebrate in ritual.

We do not mean to imply that Navajo culture was set in the beginning and did not continue to change over time and space and in response to social, political, religious, economic, and environmental factors (see Carlson's comments, this volume, on Pueblo acculturation of the Navajo in the refugee period). However, many important elements we have come to recognize as characteristic of Navajo sites are present on the earliest known Navajo sites—Pueblo tradewares, evidence of corn agriculture, microblades and bipolar cores, arrow shaft straighteners, forked-stick hogans, sweat lodges, cardinal orientation of architecture, a general paucity of artifacts, scrupulous removal of ungulate bone from domestic sites with conspicuous exceptions, and so on. What is remarkable is that this constellation of cultural traits appears all at once, archaeologically, without the gradual change predicted by cultural evolutionists. We believe that is due, in large part, to the florescence of the Navajo social imaginary at the very beginning—at the time of Navajo emergence. When the Navajo became Navajo, they did so with vigor. One area in which we think Navajo culture did change profoundly over time under influence from the Pueblo and the Spanish is in response to disease.

DISEASE

What undoubtedly had a profound impact on the newly emergent Navajo culture, though difficult to discern archaeologically, was the devastating impact of European diseases. New World natives were, largely, immunologically defenseless against many diseases introduced by the arrival of Europeans. We do not know precisely when Old World diseases impacted the Navajo. The protohistoric period in native North America, the period between European arrival on the continent and the advent of sustained interaction, was characterized by the depopulation of some areas as a result of introduced epidemic diseases, and population coalescences in other areas from migrating dislocated populations. It seems likely that the effects of smallpox, chicken pox, measles, cholera, and other diseases were felt by native groups of the Upper San Juan region, perhaps even before their actual contact with the Spanish. Reff (1991) has documented smallpox epidemics in northwestern New Spain in 1518–1525 and 1530–1531. There was a measles epidemic in 1530–1534 and fever, possibly typhus, in 1545–1548, as well as plague, typhus, or other disease in 1576–1581. There were smallpox/measles epidemics again in 1590 and 1593–1594 in Durango, Mexico, and again in 1601–1602 and 1606–1607. Reff suggests that these epidemics might have extended as far north as Santa Fe. There were smallpox epidemics in 1612–1615 (including typhus), 1616–1617, 1625, 1637–1638, and 1636–1641 in Santa Fe, Hopi, and El Paso, and widespread smallpox in 1652. We can assume, depending on population contacts, that there were undocumented epidemics, which spread through the Upper San Juan region, possibly before the Spanish Entrada, though certainly after it. Calculations of mortality rates for native populations from European diseases are notoriously controversial, but many authorities agree that up to 90 percent of the native populations died from disease as a result of European contact (e.g., Dobyns 1984; Reff 1987; Thornton 1987).

Talking about the cultural geographic changes in the Rio Grande Pueblos, Barrett (2002a) notes:

> One way to measure the impact of the first phase of Spanish colonization (1598–1680) on the Rio Grande Pueblo peoples of New Mexico is to trace changes in the number and location pattern of their settlements (pueblos). During this period 62 percent of their pueblos were abandoned, and large parts of their territory were lost. The greatest loss occurred in the years from about 1636 to 1641, when Pueblo populations, already diminished as a re-

sult of various forms of Spanish exploitation, flight from the region, and, perhaps, earlier epidemics, suffered a major disease event that was a key factor in these abandonments, which particularly affected the Estancia, Socorro, and Albuquerque-Belen basins.

The evidence for change is less clear in the period before 1598, and Barrett (2002b) is more cautious about making claims for disease epidemics in the region for the earlier period.

Despite its impact—tearing the social fabric of the Navajo and other native societies, killing up to 90 percent of the population in a few generations—the effect of European diseases on early Navajo culture is difficult to see archaeologically either before or after 1598. We have not located and recorded enough early Navajo sites to be able to provide well-documented demographic analyses. However, one archaeological manifestation can be seen in the ceramic assemblages from three sites—LA 55979, LA 78178, and LA 79469—all near Tó Aheedlí, the place where the rivers cross, in the traditional Navajo homeland, Dinétah.

Dinetah Gray vessels found at the earliest well-dated Navajo site, LA 55979 (dated to the spring of 1541), show a very wide range and variety of surface treatments (Dykeman and Roebuck 2009a). David Brugge (personal communication 2009) suggests that the pockmarked surface treatment of these utility vessels became associated with the spread of smallpox and was therefore later abandoned as a ceramic surface finish. A Blessingway chanter, talking to Brugge about the Navajo story of the Destructive Storm, sheds light on Navajo thought concerning the shift away from the use of polychrome ceramics, and the shift from incised to smooth pottery as well:

> They [the predecessors of the Navajos] did not live peacefully, but were fighting among themselves and killed each other. They used clay to make the pots in which they boiled things. Pieces of these can be seen. Some were deep, some shallow, some were dippers. On this pottery some painted black, yellow, white, and red. There was part of their religion and tradition in painting pottery. Some of the pottery just had marks stamped on it, made with their fingers, which signified sores on the body. This caused all kinds of disease and epidemics. They wouldn't live right, so they were destroyed by fire, hail, and windstorms. It is not known who destroyed them but it is said that the Sun and Monster Slayer and Born for Water did it. (Brugge in Wyman 1970: 58–59)

At LA 78178 (Dykeman and Roebuck 2009b), the oldest Navajo site with a European artifact, tree-ring-dated between AD 1600 and 1602, the range of the surface treatments of Dinetah Gray pottery is already greatly restricted compared with that seen in the ceramic assemblage at LA 55979. We suggest that the impact of European diseases had already begun to be felt by the Navajo by AD 1602 and that they were searching for ways to cope with the epidemics, including changes in ceramic manufacture. Since, as noted by Brugge's Blessingway chanter, "part of their religion and tradition" was bound up in the decoration of their pottery, we see tangible evidence in the ceramic assemblage of this late Dinetah phase site of a ritual response to disease epidemics consistent with the reported oral history. Comparative data on surface treatments for Dinetah Gray ceramics from other Dinetah phase sites and additional evidence for disease epidemics among the Navajo will be necessary for us to evaluate the strength of this hypothesis.

This trend appears to continue into the Gobernador phase, when the Navajo started making polychrome pottery and, at least initially, appear to have substituted Gobernador polychrome for Puebloan polychrome wares (Langenfeld 1999, 2003). The earliest Navajo site with Gobernador polychrome, LA 79469, cross-dated to ca. AD 1625, also shows very limited surface treatments on the Dinetah Gray portion of its pottery assemblage (Dykeman and Roebuck 2009b).

Another likely effect of the impact of European diseases on Navajo culture, even less readily discernible archaeologically, is the emphasis on disease and healing ceremonies in Navajo religion (e.g., Franciscan Fathers 1910:346–421; Reichard 1963:80–122). Many of the principal ceremonies have curing as their primary focus.

In Navajo thought, it is generally the violation of Navajo norms that brings about disease (Reichard 1963:80–81; see also Wyman 1970 and Witherspoon 1974). The central premise of Navajo philosophy, *sq'a naghái bik'e hózhǫ́*—creating *hózhǫ́*, the ideal environment of beauty, happiness, balance, and order—is definable in distinction to disease and death. Witherspoon (1977:24–25) explains that for the Navajo, in order to maintain "positive health," one must have a proper relationship to everything in one's environment. The concept of health is much more than merely the proper functioning of one's physiological body. Negative things—ugly, disharmonious, or unhappy things/places/beings/environment—are called *hóchxǫ́*, which is considered by most commentators (e.g., Haile, Reichard, Wyman, and Witherspoon—but see Farella for a nuanced contrary view) to be the opposite of *hózhǫ́*. Disease comes from *hóchxǫ́*. It is the result of evil intentions and evil actions. It is not part of the normal, natural cycle of things. In that sense, Navajo curing rites are designed to restore health, along with beauty and harmony.

The term *nayéé* is usually translated as "monster." Many of the monsters described in the stories and ceremony *nayéé'ee* (Monsterway) would be thought of in most cultures as monsters, but the stories associated with *nayéé'ee* also include such "monsters" as old age, poverty, and disease.

Farella (1984:51) says the Navajos use *nayéé* to describe anything that gets in the way of a person living his or her life. These things are usually subjective and internal (such as obsessive thoughts or paranoia) rather than objective and external. But they include physical illness. Farella (1984:52) explains what the more than sixty curing rites are designed to accomplish:

> The initial step in any cure is to objectify that which is nebulous and intangible so as to be able more easily to externalize it or place it outside the patient. This is (at least on one level) what the ritual is all about. The stories describe nayéé' in incredibly vivid terms, the battle between them and the hero twins is re-created, and the bodies of these beings (and their other remains) can be seen all over the Reservation. The curing, then, first describes and objectifies. Then there is a battle and externalization which results in either the death of a particular nayéé' or in its management by the patient and the singer. Finally, there is a celebration of what is basically a new way of looking at the world.

Witherspoon (1977:24–25) says of that way of looking at the world:

> *Sq'a Naagháii* and *Bik'eh Hózhǫ́* are the central animating powers of the universe, and, as such, they produce a world described as *hózhǫ́*, the ideal environment of beauty, harmony, and happiness. All living beings, which includes the earth, the sacred mountains, and so on, have inner and outer forms, and to achieve well-being the inner forms must harmonize and unify with *Sq'ah Naagháii* and the outer forms must harmonize and unify with *Bik'eh hózhǫ́*.
>
> The desirable conditions of *sq'a naagháii bik'eh hózhǫ́* are disturbed and disrupted by improper, inadvertent, or inastute contact with things that are defined as dangerous (*báhádzid*) and by the malevolent deeds (witchcraft) of others. A variety of over sixty curing rites are designed to purify the patient made ill by contact with dangerous things or to neutralize and in some cases reverse the effects of witchcraft.

The concept *sq'a nagháí bik'e hózhǫ́* appears to have been shaped by the Navajo encounter with European diseases. It is a particularly powerful organizing principle around which to rebuild a culture decimated over a few generations by an up to 90 percent mortality rate from disease. It is an integral, core idea in all of the more than sixty curing ceremonies. Despite its centrality to Navajo thought and experience, so far we have been able to discern only very faint traces archaeologically. In addition to the changes in ceramic styles and treatments, these take the form of apparent ritual closing of hogans, including internal fire hearths containing ungulate bone for final firing where such bone has been scrupulously removed from elsewhere on the site, and traces of ritually important botanicals and objects in fire hearths but not elsewhere on the sites. More work on the transition from Dinetah phase to Gobernador phase Navajo sites will give us opportunities to find and test other hypotheses concerning material evidence of Navajo social imaginary in this critical time period.

Contrasting Accounts

The concept of the social imaginary applies to all cultures. It applies to our interpretations of both Navajo *and* non-Navajo thought, including our underlying assumptions regarding anthropological and historical theory. Recognizing the normative force that certain ideas have in shaping theory can help us understand practices in social science that may be culture bound. For example, many authors have noted contemporary Western society's bias toward written history over oral history (see Zolbrod 1984, 1995). Such a prejudice may be a subset of what Pearce (1953) calls *savagism*, a deep-seated prejudice of modern Western social imaginary against tribal peoples. Something of this may account, in part, for the fact that references to Spanish historical documents are far more frequent in the archaeological literature on the Navajo than are references to Navajo oral tradition. The tendency of many theorists to give greater credence to written history over oral history helps explain the vigor with which some archaeologists (e.g., Schaafsma 1996, 2002) have attempted to make their theories of Navajo origin coincide with specific interpretations of ambiguous Spanish historical documentation in support of the refugee hypothesis even in contradiction of Navajo and Pueblo oral accounts (see Brugge 1996:258).

The conflicts we see in the debate over written history versus oral history are repeated in discussions of empirical evidence versus historical evidence. Gunnerson's (1979) dismissal of all non-empirical evidence cited above is an example of a kind of prejudice in favor of naturalistic social science that ignores the beliefs and ideas of the people under study, apparently because they are "unscientific." However, unless all cultural changes occurred entirely in a fit of absence of mind, then we must have some recourse to human motivations to explain the social changes that are evoked as we attempt to understand transformations in Navajo culture during the protohistoric and historic periods.

Both prejudices may have a bearing on Seymour's (2005b) "low visibility archaeology," in which traces of mobile peoples are ignored in archaeological study, as mobile peoples are considered less civilized or less important than sedentary ones and the faint empirical evidence of their presence is ignored or overwhelmed by the architecture and ceramics and substantial thermal features of more sedentary peoples.

When we look at the context of our theories, we note there is a certain intellectual and emotional appeal to the refugee hypothesis of Navajo cultural emergence—it is clear and simple and ties the emergence of an entire cultural identity to a single historical event (recorded in writing and in a European tradition). Its assumption that the culture change that occurred when the two cultures met was largely one-way—from Pueblo to Navajo—reinforces our notions of progress. It accounts for several Puebloan elements in Navajo thought and practice. However, it ignores Athapaskan elements adopted by Puebloan cultures. As discussed above, the incorporation of cultural traits that occurred from the encounter of Puebloans and Athapaskans ran both ways. Athapaskans introduced new bow-and-arrow technology and new motifs in rock and kiva art that appear around AD 1400. There is good evidence that the Jemez traded obsidian with people living on the Southern Plains at about this time, and several researchers have speculated on the role played by Athapaskans in that trade (Baugh and Nelson 1987; Baugh et al. 1999; see also Gordon, Brunswig, Gilmore and Larmore, and Carlson, this volume). As an example of its enduring power, Kelley and Francis (1994:188) recur to the refugee hypothesis in discussing the syncretism in Navajo thought, which shares symbols and stories with neighboring Zunis, Hopis, other Puebloans, and Apaches: "The emergence of the Navajos as a distinct ethnic group [was] forged in the crucible of Spanish rule from pieces of many disparate communities, mainly Puebloans and Athapaskan. The story we construct suggests the possibility of a nativistic movement to forge the various stories and customs of these refugees from Spanish rule into a coherent belief system to help unite these resisters, fighters for the land, at a time when organization and unity were essential for survival." The refugee hypothesis has a romantic appeal, underlying current Western modernity's social imaginary relating to colonialism, indigenous resistance to colonialism, and pan-Indian cooperation, and also, perhaps, to the continuing application of the Black Legend (Juderías 1917) in Anglophone countries.

It is difficult to give up such appealing stories even in light of the mounting evidence that Navajo culture existed, flourished, and had already forged a coherent belief system at least 150 years before the 1680 Pueblo Revolt and the 1692 Reconquista. Our new stories regarding the Navajo will have to take the new evidence into account. However, the appeal of the old theory is strong enough that it will likely take some time to die out.

Just as the refugee hypothesis has been refuted, so too the acculturation hypothesis must be set aside in light of the new archaeological evidence. The acculturation theory reinforces modern notions of slow, gradual, progressive cultural evolution through fixed stages from primitive cultures up to ourselves. It has an underlying assumption that nomadic hunting-and-gathering societies will gradually evolve into sedentary agricultural ones upon exposure to them. Instead, in the archaeological record, we see evidence that Puebloan and Athapaskan cultures existed side by side, perhaps for hundreds of years, without the Athapaskans becoming acculturated. The Navajo cultural emergence demonstrates that cultural change need not be slow or gradual—it can be abrupt, as it was in this case. Furthermore, the Navajo adopted agriculture but managed to preserve both their northern hunting tradition and relative mobility. Like the refugee hypothesis, the acculturation hypothesis tends to ignore evidence that the incorporation of cultural traits that occurred from the encounter ran both ways. Pueblos adopted Athapaskan cultural elements, and Athapaskans adopted Puebloan elements.

The devastating effects of European diseases may account for rapid culture change between the mid-sixteenth century and the refugee period of the late seventeenth century. More work and more evidence from Dinetah and Gobernador phase sites will reveal the nature of these changes more clearly and help flesh out alternative theories to gradual acculturation.

Navajo cultural emergence did not occur because the Navajo adopted maize agriculture—other Apachean groups also adopted maize agriculture but did not become Navajo. It did not occur because the Navajo became more sedentary—the Western Apache were also relatively sedentary as compared with other Southern Athapaskan groups. It did not occur because the Navajo adapted some Pueblo ideas, rituals, or religious practice—the Navajo, Western Apache, Jicarilla, and Lipan all share origin stories based on "emergence" into this world from below and several other aspects of religious belief and practice, as discussed above. What were critical to the emergence of Navajo cultural identity were specific stories and symbols tying the Navajo people to a particular place, Dinétah, and the social and cultural practices of the people who shared those stories. These stories constitute a collective nationalist historiography. Foreign ideas and practices were incorporated into Navajo culture, but they were symbolically *Navajo-ized* (Vogt 1961; Brugge 1963) as part of the Navajo practice of changing to preserve tradition (Farella 1984; Langenfeld 2003; Dykeman 2004).

If we understand something about how protohistoric peoples comprehended the landscapes they inhabited, we can potentially see those landscapes in a new light. Understanding Navajo social imaginary has great utility for developing models that can be tested by archaeological information. Social imaginary is a useful concept for approaching the Navajo oral tradition and bridging Navajo concepts with Spanish historical accounts and with modern archaeological thought.

Archaeological information should be the basis for archaeological theory of Navajo cultural emergence. Absent evidence to the contrary, we need to avoid thinking of Navajo culture emerging outside Dinétah and the Navajo subsequently migrating to Dinétah from the north, as many archaeologists focused on migration have suggested. Athapaskan-speakers moved to the Southwest, but we take Navajo historiography and information from the Fruitland projects' archaeological sites as evidence for Navajo cultural genesis in Dinétah. To date, the earliest Navajo archaeological sites are found in Dinétah. Furthermore, we need to let go of the comforting, but incorrect, acculturation and refugee hypotheses. A new appreciation for the mobility and archaeological signatures of early Southern Athapaskan peoples and the complexity of their interaction with other Southwestern peoples commensurate with the archaeological evidence demands that we revise our theories.

A deeper knowledge and appreciation for the Navajo social imaginary gives us some insight into Navajo cultural patterns in the protohistoric period and how Navajo thought may have influenced the sites we find on the ground. This can change the way we gather archaeological data (what we look for and how we interpret it) and help us see evidence that may have been ignored in the past. It can temper our projection of our own ethnographic prejudices onto the practice of archaeology and the interpretation of data. Seeking the best interpretation of data from all sources helps us flesh out our understanding of Navajo cultural landscapes and place them in time and space. That, in turn, improves the quality of the archaeological analysis and interpretation that scholars can provide and gives us deeper insight into Navajo ethnogenesis.

Notes

1. Site LA 55979 was excavated by Cultural Resources Management Consultants in 1996–1997, but the company was disbanded before the final excavation report could be produced. The site was mentioned in progress reports by Dice (1997) and Hancock (1997). The analysis and write-up of the excavation was completed by Langenfeld, Dykeman, and Roebuck on behalf of Scaleable Editing Services and submitted to the Bureau of Land Management in 2009.
2. Bishop Ussher (1581–1656, primate of Ireland 1625–1656) famously calculated the date of the creation of the world as 23 October 4004 BC Julian by adding together the ages of people mentioned in the Bible. He is the source of the notion that the earth was created 6,000 years ago.

References

Anderson, Benedict
1991 *Imagined Communities: Reflections on the Origin and Spread of Nationalism*. London: Verso.

Austin, J. L.
1962 *How to Do Things with Words*. Oxford: Clarendon Press.

Baldwin, Stuart J.
1997 *Apacheans Bearing Gifts: Prehispanic Influence on the Pueblo Indians*. Arizona Archaeologist No. 29. Phoenix: Arizona Archaeological Society.

Barrett, Elinore M.
2002a The Geography of the Rio Grande Pueblos in the Seventeenth Century. *Ethnohistory* 49(1):123–169.
2002b *Conquest and Catastrophe: Changing Rio Grande Pueblo Settlement Patterns in the Sixteenth and Seventeenth Centuries*. Albuquerque: University of New Mexico Press.

Baugh, Timothy G., and F. W. Nelson Jr.
1987 New Mexico Obsidian Sources and Exchange on the Southern Plains. *Journal of Field Archaeology* 14(3):313–329.

Baugh, Timothy G., John Torres, and Ronald Towner
1999 Comparative Approaches to Dinetah and Plains Exchange from the Late Prehistoric through Historic Periods. Paper presented at the 64th Annual Meeting of the Society for American Archaeology, Chicago.

Benally, Clyde F., Andrew O. Wiget, John R. Alley, and Garry Blake
1982 *Dinéjí Nákéé' Nááhane': A Utah Navajo History*. San Juan School District, Monticello, Utah. From the collection of Floyd A. O'Neil. University of Utah Printing Service.

Benjamin, Walter
1973 *Illusions*. London: Fontana.

Blue Eyes
n.d. Male Shooting Chant: Its Story. Manuscript recorded by Fr. Berard Haile of oral account of Blue Eyes; free translation by Gladys A. Reichard. Leland Clifton Wyman Papers on Navajo Myths and Sandpaintings, Box 1, Folder 23. Center for Southwest Research, University of New Mexico, Albuquerque.

Brugge, David M.
1963 *Navajo Pottery and Ethnohistory*. Window Rock, Arizona: Navajo Museum.
1981 *Navajo Pottery and Ethnohistory*. Navajo Nation Papers in Anthropology No. 4. Window Rock, Arizona: Navajo Nation Cultural Resource Management Program.
1983 Navajo Prehistory and History to 1850. In *Southwest*, edited by Alfonso Ortiz, pp. 489–501. Handbook of North American Indians, Vol. 10, William C. Sturtevant, general editor. Washington, D.C.: Smithsonian Institution.
1986 *Tsegai: An Archaeological Ethnohistory of the Chaco Region*. Washington, D.C.: National Park Service.
1993 Eighteenth-Century Fugitives from New Mexico among the Navajos. In *Papers of the Third, Fourth, and Sixth Navajo Studies Conferences*, edited by Alexandra Roberts, Jenevieve Smith, and June-el Piper, pp. 279–283. Window Rock, Arizona: Navajo Nation Historic Preservation Department.
1996 Navajo Archaeology: A Promising Past. In *The Archaeology of Navajo Origins*, edited by Ronald H. Towner, pp. 255–271. Salt Lake City: University of Utah Press.
2005 Navajo Clan Origins. In *Inscriptions: Papers in Honor of Richard and Nathalie Woodbury*, edited by Regge N. Wiseman, Thomas C. O'Laughlin, and Cordelia C. Snow, pp. 15–31. Papers No. 30. Albuquerque: Archaeological Society of New Mexico.

Campbell, Lyle
1997 *American Indian Languages: The Historical Linguistics of Native America*. Oxford: Oxford University Press.

Cleveland, Elaine, Antoinette Kurley-Begay, and Marlene Arviso-Kakos
1999 Diné Perspectives on the Dinétah in Northwestern New Mexico. Paper presented at the 64th Annual Meeting of the Society for American Archaeology, Chicago.

Dice, Michael
1997 *Archaeological Investigations for Williams Field Services Trunk S Pipeline Reroute: 1996 Field Season Interim Report*. Technical Report No. 96-024. Farmington, New Mexico: Cultural Resources Management Consultants.

Dittert, Alfred E., Jr., James J. Hester, and Frank W. Eddy
1961 *An Archaeological Survey of the Navajo Reservoir District, Northwestern New Mexico*. Monographs of the School of American Research No. 23. Santa Fe: School of American Research and Museum of New Mexico.

Dobyns, Henry F.
1984 Native American Population Collapse and Recovery. In *Scholars and the Indian Experience*, edited by William R. Swagerty, pp. 17–35. Bloomington: Indiana University Press.

Doolittle, William E.
2000   *Cultivated Landscapes of Native North America*. Oxford: Oxford University Press.
Doolittle, William E., and Jonathan B. Mabry
2006   Environmental Mosaics, Agricultural Diversity and the Evolutionary Adoption of Maize in the American Southwest. In *Histories of Maize: Multidisciplinary Approaches to the Prehistory, Linguistics, Biogeography, Domestication, and Evolution of Maize*, edited by John E. Staller, Robert H. Tykot, and Bruce F. Benz, pp. 109–121. Amsterdam: Elsevier Academic Press.
Dykeman Douglas, D.
2000   Accuracy and Precision in Archaeological Dating: A Correlation of Tree-Ring, Thermoluminescence and Radiocarbon Techniques. Paper presented at the 65th Annual Meeting of the Society for American Archaeology, Philadelphia. Anthropological Investigations No. 7. Farmington, New Mexico: Dykeman Roebuck Archaeology. http://www.drarchaeology.com/publications/datingLA55979.pdf.
2003   *The Morris Site 1 Early Navajo Land Use Study: Gobernador Phase Community Development in Northwestern New Mexico*. Navajo Nation Papers in Anthropology No. 39. Window Rock, Arizona: Navajo Nation Archaeology Department.
2004   Shifting for Success in the Southwest: Early Navajo Culture Change, AD 1500–1800. Paper presented at the Fall Arizona Archaeological Council Meeting. Anthropological Investigations No. 6. Farmington, New Mexico: Dykeman Roebuck Archaeology. http://www.drarchaeology.com/publications/shiftingforsuccess.pdf.
Dykeman, Douglas D., and Paul Roebuck
2009a   Navajos in the AD 1500s: Archaeological Excavations at LA 55979, Dinétah, New Mexico. Draft submitted to the Bureau of Land Management, Farmington Field Office. Farmington, New Mexico: Scaleable Editing Services.
2009b   Early Navajo Culture Change and Continuity in the Seventeenth Century: Excavations at LA 78178 and LA 79469, Dinétah, Northwestern New Mexico. Draft submitted to the Bureau of Land Management, Farmington Field Office. Farmington, New Mexico: Scaleable Editing Services.
Eddy, Frank W.
1966   *Prehistory in the Navajo Reservoir District, Northwestern New Mexico*. Museum of New Mexico Papers in Anthropology No. 15. Santa Fe: Museum of New Mexico Press.
Eliade, Mircea
1959   *The Sacred and the Profane: The Nature of Religion*. Translated by Willard R. Trask. New York: Harcourt Brace.
1965   *The Myth of the Eternal Return*. Translated by Willard R. Trask. Princeton, N.J.: Princeton University Press.
Farella, John R.
1984   *The Main Stalk: A Synthesis of Navajo Philosophy*. Tucson: University of Arizona Press.
1993   *The Wind in a Jar*. Albuquerque: University of New Mexico Press.
Farmer, Malcolm F.
1942   Navajo Archaeology of the Upper Blanco and Largo Canyons, Northern New Mexico. *American Antiquity* 8(1):65–79.
Fishler, Stanley A.
1953   *In the Beginning: A Navaho Creation*. Anthropological Papers No. 13. Salt Lake City: Department of Anthropology, University of Utah.

Foster, Michael K.
1996 Language and the Culture History of North America. In *Languages*, edited by Ives Goddard, pp. 64–170. Handbook of North American Indians, Vol. 17, William C. Sturtevant, general editor. Washington, D.C.: Smithsonian Institution.

Franciscan Fathers
1910 *An Ethnologic Dictionary of the Navaho Language*. Saint Michaels, Arizona: St. Michaels Press.

Gill, Sam D.
1983 Navajo Views of Their Origin. In *Southwest*, edited by Alfonso Ortiz, pp. 502–505. Handbook of North American Indians, Vol. 10, William C. Sturtevant, general editor. Washington, D.C.: Smithsonian Institution.

Goddard, Pliny Earle
1933 *Navajo Texts—Hastin Sandoval*. Edited by Gladys A. Reichard. Anthropological Papers Vol. 34, Pt. 1. New York: American Museum of Natural History.

Goodwin, Grenville
1939 *Myths and Tales of the White Mountain Apache*. Memoirs Vol. 33. New York: American Folklore Society.

Gunnerson, Dolores A.
1956 The Southern Athabascans: Their Arrival in the Southwest. *El Palacio* 63(11–12): 346–365.

Gunnerson, James H.
1956 Plains-Promontory Relationships. *American Antiquity* 22(1):69–72.
1979 Southern Athapaskan Archaeology. In *Southwest*, edited by Alfonso Ortiz, pp. 162–169. Handbook of North American Indians, Vol. 9, William C. Sturtevant, general editor. Washington, D.C.: Smithsonian Institution.

Habermas, Jürgen
1989 *The Structural Transformation of the Public Sphere*. Translated by Thomas Burger. Cambridge, Massachusetts: MIT Press. Originally published as *Strukturwandel der Öffentlichkeit Luchterhand* (Neuwied, 1962).

Haile, Father Berard
1938 Navaho Chantways and Ceremonials. *American Anthropologist* 40(4):639–652.

Hall, Edward T., Jr.
1944 Recent Clues to Athapascan Prehistory in the Southwest. *American Anthropologist* 46(1):98–105.

Hancock, Patricia M.
1997 Dendrochronology Dates of the Dinetah. Paper presented at the Fruitland Conference, Farmington, New Mexico.

Halpern, Katherine Spencer, and Susan Brown McGreevy (editors)
1997 *Washington Matthews: Studies of Navajo Culture, 1880–1894*. Albuquerque: University of New Mexico Press.

Hester, James J.
1962 *Early Navajo Migrations and Acculturation in the Southwest*. Museum of New Mexico Papers in Anthropology No. 6. Santa Fe: Museum of New Mexico Press.

Hewett, Edgar L.
1906 Origin of the Name Navaho. *American Anthropologist,* in *Anthropologic Miscellanea* 8(1):193.

Hill, W. W.
1938 *The Agricultural and Hunting Methods of the Navajo Indians*. Yale University Publications in Anthropology No. 18. New Haven, Connecticut: Yale University Press.

1940   Some Navaho Culture Changes during Two Centuries (with a Translation of the Early Eighteenth Century Rabal Manuscript). In *Essays in Historical Anthropology of North America*. Smithsonian Miscellaneous Collections Vol. 100. Washington, D.C.: Smithsonian Institution.

Hodge, Frederick W.
1895   The Early Navajo and Apache. *American Anthropologist* 8(3):223–240.

Hodge, Frederick Webb, George P. Hammond, and Agapito Rey
1945   *Fray Alonso de Benavides' Revised Memorial of 1634*. Albuquerque: University of New Mexico Press.

Hogan, Patrick, Janette M. Elyea, and Peter Eschman
1991   *Overview and Research Design for the Fruitland Coal Gas Development Area*. Albuquerque: University of New Mexico Office of Contract Archeology.

Hoijer, Harry
1938   The Southern Athapaskan Languages. *American Anthropologist*, new series, 40(1):75–87.
1956   The Chronology of the Athapaskan Languages. *International Journal of American Linguistics* 22(4):219–232.
1971   The Position of the Apachean Languages in the Athapaskan Stock. In *Apachean Culture History and Ethnology*, edited by Keith H. Basso and Morris E. Opler, pp. 3–6. Anthropological Papers of the University of Arizona No. 21. Tucson: University of Arizona Press.

Hovezak, Timothy D., and Leslie M. Sesler
2002   *Archaeological Investigations in the Fruitland Project Area: Late Archaic, Basketmaker, Pueblo I, and Navajo Sites in Northwestern New Mexico*. Research Papers No. 4. Dolores, Colorado: La Plata Archaeological Consultants.

Huscher, Betty H., and Harold A. Huscher
1942   Athapascan Migration via the Intermountain Region. *American Antiquity* 8(1):80–88.
1943   The Hogan Builders of Colorado. *Southwestern Lore* 9(2):21–25.

Juderías, Julián
1917   *La leyenda negra: Estudios acerca del concepto de España en el extranjero*. Barcelona: Editorial Araluce.

Kelley, Klara, and Harris Francis
1994   *Navajo Sacred Places*. Bloomington: Indiana University Press.

Keur, Dorothy L.
1941   *Big Bead Mesa: An Archaeological Study of Navaho Acculturation, 1745–1812*. Memoirs No. 1. Menasha, Wisconsin: Society for American Archaeology.

Kidder, Alfred V.
1920   Ruins of the Historic Period in the Upper San Juan Valley, New Mexico. *American Anthropologist* 22(4):322–329.

Klah, Hasteen
1942   *Navajo Creation Myth: The Story of the Emergence*. Recorded by Mary C. Wheelwright. Navajo Religion Series No. 1. Santa Fe: Museum of Navajo Ceremonial Art.

Kluckhohn, Clyde
1949   *Mirror for Man*. New York: Whittlesey House.

Kluckhohn, Clyde, and Dorothea Leighton
1946   *The Navajo*. Cambridge, Massachusetts: Harvard University Press.
1962   *The Navajo*. Natural History Library. Garden City: Anchor Books, Doubleday.

Kooyman, Brian, Leonard V. Hills, Paul McNeil, and Shayne Tolman
2006   Late Pleistocene Horse Hunting at the Wally's Beach Site (DhPg-8), Canada. *American Antiquity* 71(1):101–121.

Krauss, Michael E.
1973   Na-Dene. In *Linguistics in North America*, edited by Thomas Sebeok, pp. 903–978. Current Trends in Linguistics Vol. 10. The Hague: Mouton.

Lange, Charles H.
1979   Relations of the Southwest with the Plains and Great Basin. In *Southwest*, edited by Alfonso Ortiz, pp. 201–205. Handbook of North American Indians, Vol. 9, William C. Sturtevant, general editor. Washington, D.C.: Smithsonian Institution.

Langenfeld, Kristin
1999   Pottery as a Measure of Change and Continuity in Early Navajo Households. Paper presented at the 64th Annual Meeting of the Society for American Archaeology, Chicago.
2003   Pottery of the Morris Site 1 Early Navajo Land Use Study. In *The Morris Site 1 Early Navajo Land Use Study: Gobernador Phase Community Development in Northwestern New Mexico*, edited by Douglas D. Dykeman, pp. 233–296. Fruitland Data Recoveries Series No. 4. Navajo Nation Papers in Anthropology No. 39. Window Rock, Arizona: Navajo Nation Archaeology Department.

Luckert, Karl W.
1977   *Rainbow Mountain and Rainbow Bridge Religion*. American Tribal Religions Vol. 1. Flagstaff: Museum of Northern Arizona.
1979   *Coyoteway: A Navajo Healing Ceremonial*. Tucson: University of Arizona Press; Flagstaff: Museum of Northern Arizona Press.

Matthews, Washington
1890   The Gentile System of the Navajo Indians from Their Creation and Migration Myth. *Journal of American Folklore* 3(9):89–110.
1894   Songs of Sequence of the Navajos. *Journal of American Folklore* 7(26):185–194.
1897   *Navaho Legends*. Boston: Houghton Mifflin. Reprinted. Salt Lake City: University of Utah Press, 1994.

McAllister, J. Gilbert
1949   Kiowa-Apache Tales. In *The Sky Is My Tipi*, edited by Mody C. Boatright, pp. 1–141. Publications No. 22. Dallas: Texas Folklore Society.

McNeley, James Kale
1973   The Navajo "Wind" Theory of Life and Behavior. Unpublished Ph.D. dissertation, University of Hawaii, Honolulu.
1981   *Holy Wind in Navajo Philosophy*. Tucson: University of Arizona Press.

O'Bryan, Aileen
1956   *The Dîné: Origin Myths of the Navajo Indians*. Bureau of American Ethnology Bulletin No. 163. Washington, D.C.: Smithsonian Institution.

Opler, Morris E.
1938   *Myths and Tales of the Jicarilla Apache Culture*. Memoirs No. 31. New York: American Folklore Society.
1940   *Myths and Tales of the Lipan Apache Indians*. Memoirs No. 36. New York: American Folklore Society.
1942   *Myths and Tales of the Chiricahua Apache Indians*. Memoirs No. 37. New York: American Folklore Society.
1983   The Apachean Culture Pattern and Its Origins. In *Southwest*, edited by Alfonso

Ortiz, pp. 368–392. Handbook of North American Indians, Vol. 10, William C. Sturtevant, general editor. Washington, D.C.: Smithsonian Institution.

Parsons, Elsie Clews
1939 *Pueblo Indian Religion*. Vol. 2. Chicago: University of Chicago Press.

Pearce, Roy Harvey
1953 *The Savages of America: A Study of the Indian and the Idea of Civilization*. Baltimore: Johns Hopkins Press.

Perry, Richard J.
1980 The Apachean Transition from the Subarctic to the Southwest. *Plains Anthropologist* 25 (90):279–296.
1991 *Western Apache Heritage: People of the Mountain Corridor*. Austin: University of Texas Press.

Reeve, Frank D.
1957 Seventeenth Century Navaho-Spanish Relations. *New Mexico Historical Review* 32(1):36–52.
1958 Navaho-Spanish Wars, 1680–1720. *New Mexico Historical Review* 33(3):204–231.
1959 Navaho-Spanish Peace, 1720s–1770s. *New Mexico Historical Review* 34(1):9–40.
1960 Navajo-Spanish Diplomacy, 1770–1790. *New Mexico Historical Review* 35(3): 200–235.

Reff, Daniel T.
1987 The Introduction of Smallpox in the Greater Southwest. *American Anthropologist* 89(3):704–708.
1991 *Disease, Depopulation, and Culture Change in Northwestern New Spain, 1518–1764*. Salt Lake City: University of Utah Press.

Reichard, Gladys A.
1928 *Social Life of the Navajo Indians*. Columbia University Contributions to Anthropology No. 7. New York: Columbia University Press.
1950 *Navajo Religion: A Study in Symbolism*. 2 vols. Bollingen Series No. 18. New York: Pantheon Books.
1977 [1939] *Navajo Medicine Man Sandpaintings*. New York: Dover.

Riley, Carroll L.
1954 Survey of Navajo Archaeology. *University of Colorado Studies in Anthropology* 4: 45–60.

Rockman, Marcy
2003 Knowledge and Learning in the Archaeology of Colonization. In *Colonization of Unfamiliar Landscapes: The Archaeology of Adaptation*, edited by Marcy Rockman and James Steele, pp. 3–24. New York: Routledge.

Roebuck, Paul
2007 *Navajo Ethnobotany—Diné Nanise and Ethnobotanical Analysis of Early Navajo Site LA 55979*. Anthropological Investigations No. 3. Farmington, New Mexico: Dykeman Roebuck Archaeology. http://www.drarchaeology.com/pub lications/earlynavajoethnobot.pdf.

Roessel, Robert A., Jr.
1983 *Dinétah: Navajo History*. Vol. 2. Rough Rock, Arizona: Rough Rock Demonstration School.

Sando, Joe S.
1979 Jemez Pueblo. In *Southwest*, edited by Alfonso Ortiz, pp. 418–429. Handbook of North American Indians, Vol. 9, William C. Sturtevant, general editor. Washington, D.C.: Smithsonian Institution.

Schaafsma, Curtis F.
1979 Archaeological Excavations and Lithic Analysis in the Abiquiu Reservoir District, New Mexico, Phase IV. Ms. on file, School of American Research, Santa Fe, New Mexico.
1981 Early Apacheans in the Southwest: A Review. In *The Protohistoric Period in the North American Southwest, AD 1450–1700*, edited by David R. Wilcox and W. Bruce Masse, pp. 291–320. Anthropological Research Papers No. 24. Tempe: Arizona State University.
1996 Ethnic Identity and Protohistoric Archaeological Sites in Northwestern New Mexico: Implications for Reconstructions of Navajo and Ute History. In *The Archaeology of Navajo Origins*, edited by Ronald H. Towner, pp. 19–46. Salt Lake City: University of Utah Press.
2002 *Apaches de Navajo: Seventeenth-Century Navajos in the Chama Valley of New Mexico*. Salt Lake City: University of Utah Press.

Sesler, Leslie M., and Tim D. Hovezak
2002 Synthesis: Cultural and Adaptational Diversity in the Fruitland Study Area. In *Archaeological Investigations in the Fruitland Project Area: Late Archaic, Basketmaker, Pueblo 1, and Navajo Sites in Northwestern New Mexico, Volume 1; Introductory Chapters and Synthesis*, edited by Tim Hovezak, Leslie Sesler, and Steve Fuller, pp. 109–240. Research Papers No. 4. Dolores, Colorado: La Plata Archaeological Consultants.

Seymour, Deni J.
2005a Archaeological Evidence of Early/Ancestral Chiricahua Apache in Southern Arizona. *Glyphs* (Arizona Archaeological and Historical Society) 55, no. 7 (January).
2005b The Implications of Mobility, Reoccupation, and Low Visibility Phenomena for Chronometric Dating. Unpublished manuscript.

Smith, James G. E.
1981 Chipewyan. In *Subarctic*, edited by June Helm, pp. 271–284. Handbook of North American Indians, Vol. 6, William C. Sturtevant, general editor. Washington, D.C.: Smithsonian Institution.

Spencer, Katherine
1947 *Reflection of Social Life in the Navajo Origin Myth*. University of New Mexico Publications in Anthropology No. 3. Albuquerque: University of New Mexico Press.

Stephen, A. M.
1930 Navajo Origin Legend. *Journal of American Folklore* 43(1):88–104.

Taylor, Allan Ross
2004 An Instructive Subject of Study: The When and How of the Arrival of the Ancestral Navajos in the Southwest. Unpublished Master's thesis, Department of Anthropology, University of Colorado, Boulder.

Taylor, Charles
2004 *Social Imaginary*. Durham, North Carolina: Duke University Press.
2007 *The Secular Age*. Cambridge, Massachusetts: Belknap Press of Harvard University Press.

Thornton, Russell
1987 *American Indian Holocaust and Survival: A Population History since 1492*. Norman: University of Oklahoma Press.

Torres, John A.
1999 Adapting Old Lithic Traditions to a New World Order. Paper presented at the 64th Annual Meeting of the Society for American Archaeology, Chicago.

2003   Early Navajo Lithic Technology of Dinetah. In *The Morris Site 1 Early Navajo Land Use Study: Gobernador Phase Community Development in Northwestern New Mexico*, edited by Douglas D. Dykeman, pp. 191–232. NNAD Fruitland Data Recoveries Series No. 4. Navajo Nation Papers in Anthropology No. 39. Window Rock, Arizona: Navajo Nation Archaeology Department.

Van Valkenburgh, Richard F.
1938   *A Short History of the Navajo People*. Window Rock, Arizona: Navajo Service, U.S. Department of the Interior.

Vogt, Evon Z.
1961   Navajo. In *Perspectives on American Indian Culture Change*, edited by Edward H. Spicer, pp. 278–336. Chicago: University of Chicago Press.

Warner, Michel
1990   *The Letters of the Republic*. Cambridge, Massachusetts: Harvard University Press.

Wilcox, David R.
1981   The Entry of the Athabaskans into the American Southwest: The Problem Today. In *The Protohistoric Period in the American Southwest, AD 1450–1700*, edited by David R. Wilcox and W. Bruce Masse. Anthropological Research Papers No. 24. Tempe: Arizona State University.

Witherspoon, Gary
1974   The Central Concepts of the Navajo World View. *Linguistics* 119:41–59.
1977   *Language and Art in the Navajo Universe*. Ann Arbor: University of Michigan Press.

Wyman, Leland C.
1962   *The Windways of the Navajo*. Colorado Springs, Colorado: Taylor Museum.
1965   *The Red Antway of the Navaho*. Santa Fe, New Mexico: Museum of Navaho Ceremonial Art.
1970   *Blessingway*. Tucson: University of Arizona Press.

Young, Robert W.
1968   *The Role of the Navajo in the Southwestern Drama*. Gallup, New Mexico: Gallup Independent.
1983   Apachean Languages. In *Southwest*, edited by Alfonso Ortiz, pp. 303–400. Handbook of North American Indians, Vol. 10, William C. Sturtevant, general editor. Washington, D.C.: Smithsonian Institution.

Zolbrod, Paul
1984   *Diné bahane': The Navajo Creation Story*. Albuquerque: University of New Mexico Press.
1995   *Reading the Voice: Native American Oral Poetry on the Written Page*. Salt Lake City: University of Utah Press.

CHAPTER 8

We Do Not Forget; We Remember

Mescalero Apache Origins and Migration as Reflected in Place Names

DAVID L. CARMICHAEL AND CLAIRE R. FARRER

The chapters in this book present archaeological and linguistic evidence for the relatively recent migration of Athapaskans into the Southwestern United States. Such a view is consistent with mainstream anthropological discourse (Gunnerson 1979, 1987; Opler 1983, 2001; Schweinfurth 2002), so the idea that Mescalero Apache migrated to what is now New Mexico in late prehistoric times should perhaps not be in doubt, at least not among archaeologists. However, in recent years, especially in the context of land and water claims, many Native Americans, including some Mescalero Apache, have found it useful to speak of their origins with statements such as "We have always been here" or "We have been here since time immemorial."

Such statements can be understood in different ways and could reflect various intended meanings. The statement, "We have always been here" might or might not mean "We originated in the place we still occupy today." Some Native American origin stories do have this intended meaning, especially those involving emergence rather than migration. For others, the intended meaning may not be so clear. It is possible that "here" could mean "on this continent" or "in this part of the country" or "at this particular place on the landscape which is currently subject of a land dispute." Webster's (2000:227–228) insightful analysis of place names on the west side of the Mescalero reservation indicates that names sometimes embody political statements. In reference to a narrative recorded by Hoijer in the 1930s, he makes a strong case that Mescalero names for places near Sierra Blanca functioned, at least in part, as a response to the efforts of Albert Fall (first as New Mexico senator and later as secretary of interior in the Harding administration) to remove lands from the Mescalero reservation so they could be used for his private ranch operations. Thus, the act of naming and remembering a place can be a political act, making a claim to the place.

It is also possible that there has been a gradual revision of the Apache migration tradition as a result of the passage of time and the passing of tribal elders. Luckert (1975) documents such a change among the Navajo by comparing narratives about early hunter traditions collected in 1929 by Father Bernard Haile with narratives collected in the 1970s. Luckert identifies a change from the earlier Navajo hunter tradition, with its references to ancestral knowledge and places north of the Dinétah region, to a fading of the hunter pantheon and the subsequent psychological mapping-on of Navajos to the Southwest. Most importantly, he outlines the gradual acceptance of an origin story based on emergence rather than migration, through a process he calls "gradual Puebloization" (1975: 7). It is conceivable that a similar process is under way among the Mescalero, albeit as a result of contact with Navajo or Western Apache instead of Pueblo peoples.

It could also be that different versions of the origin stories are maintained by different families and communities within the Mescalero Tribe. The Mescalero Tribe includes members who identify as Chiricahua and Lipan, as well as Mescalero Apache, and there are details of dialect, iconography, clothing, and oral tradition that still maintain the boundaries of these internal communities. As is the case with other types of narratives we have heard, creation stories are known in different versions while still being variations on a theme (Farrer 1991:17).

It is beyond the scope of this chapter to examine why an alternative view of Mescalero origins may be increasing in popularity at the present time. Instead, we present the story as it has been told to us—the story that reportedly contains the most anciently held knowledge of tribal origins. It is a story of migration from what is now the Canadian Subarctic, down the Great Plains along the front ranges of the Rocky Mountains, to the mountains and plains of New Mexico. It is a story that still seems to be the traditional narrative among the Mescalero. Luckert summarizes a personal communication from Opler to this effect: "As far as the emergence myth among the non-Navajo Apacheans is concerned, only the Jicarillas seem have a well-developed one. The Lipans have a fragment of it; the Chiricahuas and Mescaleros consider the idea of emergence as 'a funny notion'" (Luckert 1975:194n). The place names and stories reported herein indicate the general route and approximate time line for the migration, details that have implications for researchers studying Apache archaeology.

LANDSCAPE AS MEMORY: ORAL HISTORY METHODOLOGY

On the ocean, an old salt has a sense of direction and distance;
we have that too. We have been in this land for thousands of years,
and the understanding is in us. Of course, we use geographical
landmarks and place names to remember the way.

| BS 7/5/86 |

The information presented here comes largely from ethnographic interviews conducted by the authors with the late Bernard Second, a leading singer (*gutlą́ą́tl*) or holy man of the Mescalero Apache. We had the privilege of being adopted by his family and working with him for a total of 20 years (6 years and 14 years, respectively) up until his passing in 1988.

Why did we listen to him? We listened to Bernard Second because the Mescalero people listened to him and because other Mescalero singers listened to him and turned to him for historical accounts. Very few people within the tribe have access to the deep history of the group, and fewer yet were or are authorized to reveal it to outsiders. During the time we worked with Bernard, many Mescalero considered him to be the ranking holy man, and he was often expected to lead the other singers in the Holy Lodge during the Mescalero Apache girls' puberty ceremony (Farrer 1980, 1991). Even Wendell Chino, former president of the Mescalero Tribe, indicated that it was necessary to speak to Bernard about matters of history. One works with those who are able, willing, and authorized to provide the information, and in this case we were clearly dealing with the person recognized by the tribe as the appropriate person.

How can we "know" that what Bernard knew is correct? More appropriate to anthropological inquiry: What methodologies were used to ensure that the most accurate rendition of these oral accounts were obtained? We carefully asked and listened over a long period of time and, in the process, listened for consistencies and discrepancies. We also obtained corroboration from other people when possible to reinforce the accuracy of this knowledge and to seek variations in its telling. Although Bernard was the primary source for place names and associated stories, we made efforts to corroborate the stories by eliciting information from other individuals who provided information, including Sidney Baca, Meredith Begay, and Fred Peso. These people are not related to Bernard Second. (Attributions for specific information recorded in ethnographic notes are indicated in the text by the consultants' initials and the date of the discussion.) We also elicited oral history in the field at places where landscape features help recall the narrative details. This approach is consistent with the Mescalero way of remembering, as indicated by the epigraph to this section. We sought further verification by examining physical evidence in the field. We used all these recognized and rigorous methods in our data collection to ensure that elder knowledge was subject to verification and methods of collection were scrutinized.

Mescalero ritual dance, specifically the girls' puberty ceremony, has been described as a four-part fugue (Farrer 1978:6). One of the main elements of the fugue is the dancing of the *gą⁷he*, or Mountain Gods. The *gą⁷he* are perhaps the most recognizable symbol of Mescalero ceremonialism, at least to outsiders; their images serve as the tribal logo and are prominently displayed throughout the reservation, as at the Inn of the Mountain Gods Casino and Resort. Earlier versions are depicted at the nearby Three Rivers petroglyph site, where they have been made part of the landscape (Figure 8.1). The dancing of the *gą⁷he* is

FIGURE 8.1. Mountain Spirit (*gą⁷he*) rock art image at the Three Rivers petroglyph site, approximately five miles west of the Mescalero Apache reservation, Otero County, New Mexico. The panel marks a location that still serves as a place of spiritual power for one of the extant Mountain Spirit dance groups. Photograph by David Carmichael.

complemented by another part of the fugue, perhaps less familiar or visible to outsiders. The girls who are participating directly in the ceremony dance inside the Holy Lodge, under the supervision of singers and godmothers (*naaik⁷eesh*) — holy men and women. This element of the fugue is older than the performance of the Mountain Gods, as the Holy Lodge was part of ancestral Mescalero belief and ritual before the Mescalero's arrival in the Southwest.

Over four nights, the girls in the Holy Lodge dance to a long, intricate series of sacred songs; on the last night they dance all night. It is these sacred songs that contain and maintain the knowledge of the deep antiquity of tribal history. The singers are retelling the tribal history while the girls are reenacting it, becoming

White Painted Woman, the Mescalero cultural heroine from mythic time. The stories are remembered through the memorization and proper sequencing of ancient songs containing place names and their associated stories. In this context, Bernard served as a repository for the deep history of his people, recited in the ritual language reserved for religious ceremonies. By reciting the history in song (prayer), Bernard was a vehicle for its reenactment, during which participants actually experience the origin times and reaffirm the basic principles of proper Apache life.

As Basso (1996) demonstrates, a place is a metaphor for entire stories, and knowing a place name is part of understanding one's Apache identity. Knowing place names is also asserting a claim about a place (Webster 2000:229). And recalling place names is a way of constructing memories of the past, of remembering deep antiquity. The Mescalero Apache girls' puberty ceremony involves singing for life and running for the future (Farrer 1978, 1980), but it also involves remembering the past. In this sense, it is part of a process of memory-work (Kuchler 1993:86), in which some places are forgotten and some remembered: details of the landscape condition what is remembered and how it is shaped into an understanding of the past.

Memorable Places

Mescalero Apache have names for places far to the north, dating back to the distant past, before their arrival in the Southwest. The landmarks are still known even though the people have not occupied or used those regions for many generations. When discussing these places, Bernard often emphasized the northern roots, high degree of mobility, and the Plains affiliation of the Mescalero, in contrast to many other peoples in the Southwest. The Mescalero still use tipis, and the Holy Lodge constructed during the girls' puberty ceremony is a ceremonial tipi. They still know how to make snowshoes for use in deep snow, a skill they learned in the Northern Plains for which they have little need in the Southwest. The best Apache hunting bows are backed with horn and sinew; this technology is not common among Native Americans of the United States, but the Apache brought it with them from the Subarctic. Before confinement on the reservation, "when we were still a free people," the Mescalero used scaffold burials like other Plains groups (BS 8/27/83).

Mescaleros never made pottery, and they were the last of the Apache groups to migrate south. They were preceded in the Southwest by three earlier groups: hunting peoples, those who made pottery, and the small "ancient people" (ńda saane). The Mescalero knew they had reached the end of their wanderings when they found the alternating layers of red and yellow earth in the southern Sacramento Mountains, as had been foretold in their prophecies. The Mountain Gods were brought by Old Man Treas in the late nineteenth century; he had married a Western Apache woman and transmitted the knowledge of $gq^{\prime}he$ ceremonialism to the Mescalero.

The Mescalero were made in a Land of Ever Winter, near a lake you could not see across (*Tuduubitsʔqtlidaa*, Water cannot see over)—Great Slave Lake or Lake Athabasca, according to different variations of the story (Figure 8.2, site 2; Figure 8.3). "Ever Winter" is Farrer's translation of Bernard's term. It is intended to convey that the region is cold and that snow can occur at any time of year. The origin place is called House of Winter or House of Ice (*Kughaʔbikine*) in Apache (Farrer 1991:18). The northern location of this Apache ancestral land is demonstrated and remembered by references to people, places, and natural phenomena of the region. The traditional name for the aurora borealis is *'abaha'ch'i*, meaning "red above them." Although popular wisdom suggests that the name "apache" is derived from a Zuni word meaning "enemy," Bernard believed that it may instead recall their northern ancestry: *apa'ach'e*, in reference to the northern lights.

The ancestral Apache had close contact with the Dogrib and Slave peoples, and their languages are closely related. Once, while attending a Lakota ceremonial in South Dakota, Bernard spoke to a companion in Apache, commenting that he hoped the meat they were being served was not from reservation dogs. A Dogrib man overheard the remark and understood it, and shared a laugh with the Apaches at the expense of their Lakota hosts. The ritual Mescalero Apache names for Great Bear Lake (*Shush bitu*, Bear, its water) and Slave Lake (*Chede' tu*, Figure 8.2, site 2) are the same as those used by the Northern Athapaskans still living in those regions today (BS 6/15/85).

Great Bear Lake (Figure 8.2, site 1) is revered as the birthplace of the Twin Warrior Brothers, who are fathers to the Mescalero. The older brother, Destroyer of Enemies, cleared off the earth for the Mescalero, removing all the unpleasant and unclean things from the land. The younger twin, Born of Water, made available plants and animals as food for the Mescalero (Farrer 1991: 20–21; BS 2/4/84). It so happened that while the Mescalero were in these northern regions, troubles developed between them and other peoples, some of them relatives. There was a great catastrophe, and the Mescalero were being devastated; they were fighting near the shore of Lake Athabasca. The Twin Warrior Brothers interceded on their behalf and helped them defeat their enemies, driving them into the water. It is for this reason that the Mescalero have an aversion to large bodies of freshwater, for they are considered unclean (BS 7/5/86; SB 6/9/91) since the defeated warriors were eaten by lake fish. The story is also the foundation of the Apacheas aversion to freshwater fish. Following this battle, the Apache were surrounded by goodness and beauty; they became a people and started drifting south (Farrer 1991:21). The beginning of this southward migration was also the time of their separation from the Slave Indians, estimated at about 600 years ago (BS 6/22/85).

The ancestors moved southwest along the Athabasca River drainage (Figure 8.2, site 4), bringing them into contact with the Sarsi people. Over the years, the Apache became closely related to the Sarsi, especially in the area west of

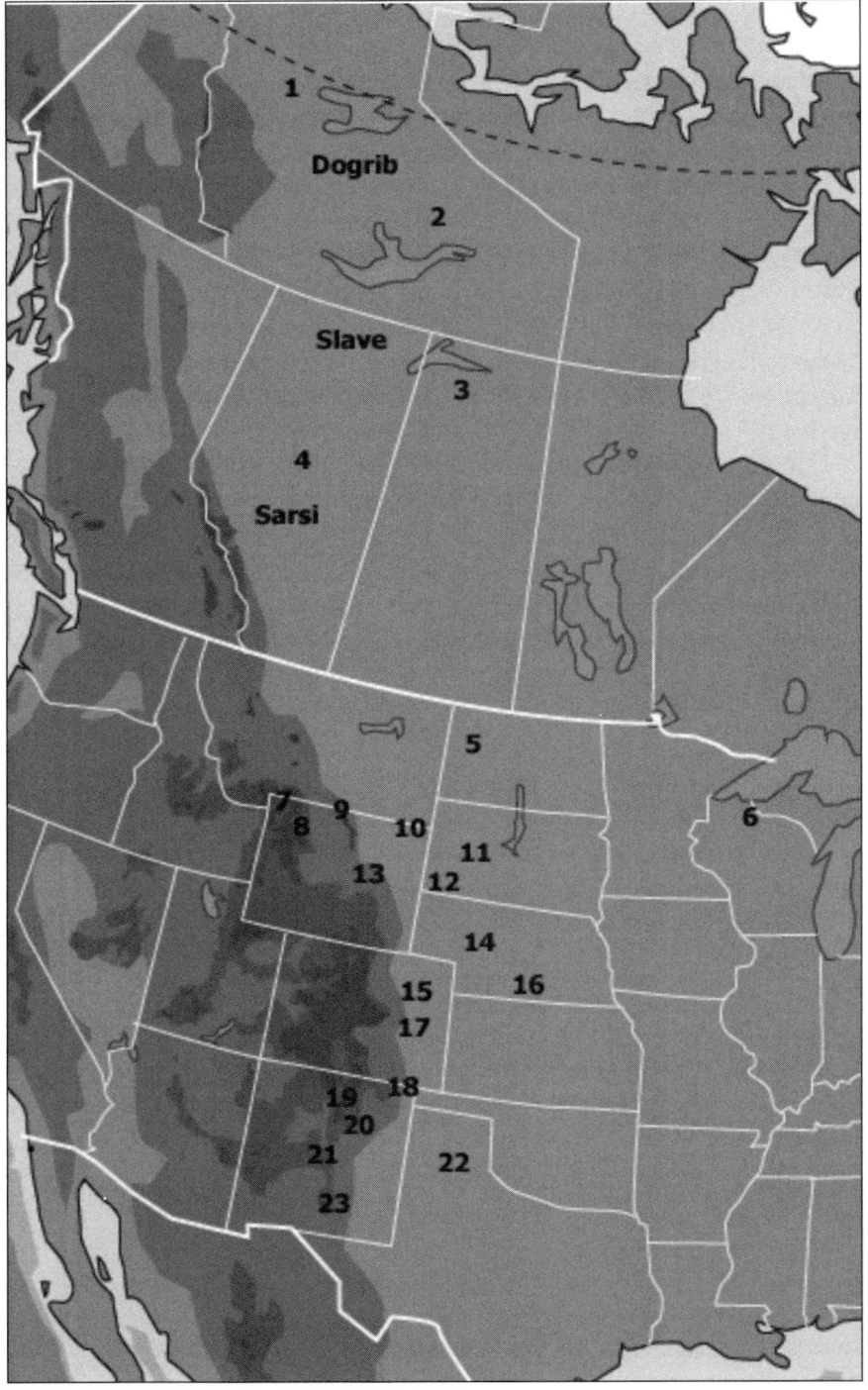

FIGURE 8.2. Map of the locations of traditional Apache place names mentioned by number in the text. The distribution of place names illustrates the route of Mescalero migration from the Arctic Circle to the Southern Plains via the eastern Rocky Mountain front ranges. (1) Great Bear Lake, (2) Great Slave Lake, (3) Lake Athabasca, (4) Athabasca River, (5) Missouri River, (6) Great Lakes, (7) Yellowstone and Obsidian Cliffs, (8) Green River headwaters, (9) Bighorn Medicine Wheel, (10) Devil's Tower and Little Missouri River, (11) Bear Butte, (12) Black Hills, (13) North Platte River, (14) Platte River, (15) South Platte River, (16) Republican River, (17) campsite near present-day Colorado Springs, (18) Raton, near Rabbit Ear Butte, (19) mesa north of Española, New Mexico, (20) Santa Fe, (21) Tijeras Canyon, near Albuquerque, (22) Palo Duro Canyon, (23) Mescalero Apache reservation. Image by David Carmichael.

FIGURE 8.3. Obsidian Cliff (*Beshtłizhee*) in Yellowstone National Park, an important location for the ancestral Mescalero and the site that is referenced by the traditional Apache name for Yellowstone country in general. Photograph by David Carmichael.

present-day Edmonton. One of Bernard's grandmothers was Sarsi, and even after the Apache moved farther south, they exchanged children with the Sarsi so that both groups would always remember the closeness of their relationship. The closeness is also indicated by language similarity. For instance, at a powwow in Alberta, Canada, Bernard was sitting in front of a group of young Sarsi men who were jokingly counting off the women dancing in women's traditional dress. There were five young men, so they counted from one to five in Sarsi. On the count of five, Bernard turned around to them and said, "*Duuda! Du shila'an; diylehedaa.*" (No! Not "my hand" [the meaning of *shila'an*—five fingers]; *dilyehe*—the way of saying "five" in Mescalero.) The six of them began sharing other common terms, including those for water, fire, and mother. They were all amazed that they could understand each other, and both Bernard and the Sarsi men had stories of their having separated from each other a long time ago. Our field notes contain many other such instances of corroboration.

As the people continued to move south and east along the Rocky Mountain front ranges, they traveled out on the plains, often at a distance of a five-day ride (about 300 miles) from the mountains. It was not unusual for them to travel to the Missouri River (Figure 8.2, site 5) to hunt buffalo and to trade with other tribes and the French. Sometimes they traveled across the northern Great Plains as far as the Great Lakes (Figure 8.2, site 6; *Tu skaane*). The wife of one of Bernard's great-great-great-grandfathers was French: she was taken from the St. Louis area in about 1756 and was purchased by the Mescalero at a Taos trade fair from the Pawnee with whom she was living. This fact is still sometimes used as a reason to tease members of the family: "Your wavy hair comes from your

French saddle blanket!" The other peoples with whom the Apache had contact at this time included the Mandan (*ze'edaje'e ndaa*, mouth tattooed people), Sioux (*yaa yuu ndaa*, big bead people), Arapaho (*ja hish kish ndaa*, ear cut people), and Cheyenne (*ja'aghatas ndaa*, ear split people). Aside from other Apache bands, and perhaps more recently the Navajo, most intermarriage has traditionally been with the Cheyenne (BS 10/14/82). It was during this early time in the Northern Plains that the ancestral Mescalero broke off from the ancestors of the Western Apache; the date of the split is estimated at 500 years ago. In contrast, the close relationship with the Sarsi was maintained longer and over considerable distances through regular visits. The eventual split with the Sarsi is estimated to have occurred only about 250 years ago (BS 6/22/85).

There are a number of traditional Mescalero names for places in Wyoming, in Yellowstone country, and in the plains to the east, presumably because of the amount of time they spent in the region and the importance of some of the events and places. The Yellowstone area (Figure 8.2, site 7) is referred to as *Ka' besh' ach'i* (Where one digs for stone [i.e., raw material for flintknapping]). Clearly, this is a reference to the high-quality obsidian source within Yellowstone National Park, well known to modern archaeologists as well as prehistoric Native Americans. However, there is another Mescalero name (*Besh tłizhee*, Rock black) for the specific site they once used at the outcrop at Obsidian Cliff (Figure 8.3). The emphasis on this site is likely due to the importance of obsidian to the ancestral Mescalero. Certainly obsidian was important to many Native Americans; it produces the sharpest cutting edge known to humans and is therefore a highly desirable raw material from which to fashion stone tools. But to the Mescalero it is something more; obsidian is imbued with sacred power. Some Mescalero singers include obsidian arrowheads in their ritual paraphernalia, sometimes tying them into the mescal bean necklaces worn on ceremonial occasions. When asked about this, one holy man recited a portion of his power song:

> I am coming, I am riding in, I am coming on a black horse,
> I am coming in and bringing the rain and thunder.
> I am powerful, and I am protected from my enemies.
> I am protected by blades of black stone.
> Blades of black stone are whirling around me on my horse,
> None of my enemies can reach me or harm me. (SB 6/10/91)

There are no significant sources of obsidian on the southern High Plains or in the vicinity of the Mescalero reservation, and there is little indication that obsidian artifacts have been especially important in the Mescalero tool kit since the group's arrival in the Sacramento Mountains. The gravels of the ancestral Rio Grande contain obsidian but only in the form of small pebbles unsuitable for manufacturing knives or even moderately sized arrowheads. The nearest source of sizable pieces of obsidian is in the Jemez Mountains, northwest of Santa Fe

(*Tu yuu*, Water bead; Figure 8.2, site 20, named for freshwater shells, not obsidian in the distant mountains). In the absence of readily available obsidian sources, most Apache lithic artifacts in southern New Mexico seem to have been made of chert and rhyolite, and then glass obtained from Euro-American sites. After it became available, metal rapidly replaced glass and chert as the preferred material for knives and arrowheads (BS 10/14/82). Yet obsidian remains important in spiritual contexts, and the traditional name for one of the most important obsidian sources is maintained in that context.

While living in Yellowstone country, the ancestral Mescalero separated from the Navajo people. This happened at a specific place in the headwaters of the Green River (which we were never able to visit together), placing the location in or adjacent to the Wind River Mountains (Figure 8.2, site 8). The parting of ways occurred an estimated 400 years ago, and the Mescalero moved east out onto the plains (BS 7/4/85). During this time, the Mescalero lived, traveled, and hunted in the drainages of the North Platte River (*K'a besh tu'*, Obsidian Arrow[head] water; Figure 8.2, site 13), the Platte River (*'A bah besh tede tu*, Upper flint water; Figure 8.2, site 14), the South Platte River (*Deł chil tu'*, Shell water; Figure 8.2, site 15), and the Republican River (Figure 8.2, site 16), habitually moving well out in the plains. Also during this time, while living in present-day Wyoming, the Mescalero first received the shoe game, or moccasin game, a guessing game that involves concealing stones or bullets in a moccasin. The first shoe game was held as a competition between the creatures of day and of night. The small animals (rodents) won the game by outsmarting the night creatures, who were cheating, thereby establishing daytime and nighttime as separate parts of each day (MB 3/3/92).

It was while the Mescalero were living in Wyoming and Montana, along the tributaries of the Missouri and Little Missouri Rivers, that they regained the horse. Bernard spoke on several occasions about "regaining" the horse (as opposed to receiving it), with the intentional implication that they had the horse in earlier times but it became lost to them. While reciting the origin story, he noted that God called on an animal, using a name that most Apaches wouldn't recognize today because it is an old name. God called forth the animal, *Netłíįye*, "Beast of burden," "the one who carries for me" (Farrer 1991:25). Bernard's grandparents understood this animal to be the horse; this was an old name for the horse, one that had been in use long before the White Man was in this land, when the Mescalero were still in the north, in the Land of Ever Winter (BS 6/15/85). Bernard didn't speak about how the horse was lost to his people, but the story seems to suggest that his ancestors knew the horse before it became extinct in North America at the end of the Pleistocene. Of course, it also suggests that some elements of oral tradition refer to events reaching very far back in time.

After the separation from the Navajo, the Mescalero developed attachments to several important holy sites on the plains, including the Bighorn Medicine Wheel (*Tse tłenditlii*, Rocks coming together; Figure 8.2, site 9), Bear Butte (site

11), Devil's Tower in the Little Missouri River drainage (site 10), and the Black Hills (*Tsi ta klish en'ah*, Blue Mountains ridge, site 12).

These places are sacred, at least in part, because they were used for vision quests by many Plains Indian groups, including the Mescalero. And they remain sacred to the Mescalero today. Once, when speaking about the Bighorn Medicine Wheel, Bernard expressed ongoing concern for the proper reverence for and protection of the site. Even though his people have not used it recently, he still spoke of it in a way that would define it as a traditional cultural property (TCP), in the parlance of modern cultural resources management. That is, the site is associated with traditional cultural practices and beliefs of the Mescalero community, and it is important to the maintenance of Mescalero cultural identity (as part of the tribe's creation story). As a practical matter, concerns about protecting and maintaining access to the site for traditional uses are given over to the tribes now living closer to it, in a preservation ethic that might be termed serial stewardship. It is expected and understood that tribes that still live in the vicinity of sacred sites formerly used by the Mescalero will take responsibility for their protection today. Similarly, the Mescalero consider themselves the current stewards of sacred sites in southeastern New Mexico and western Texas even though they were used in the past by other groups that are no longer extant or no longer live in the area or frequent the sites.

For a time, the Black Hills figured prominently in the Mescalero sacred landscape. In telling this part of the story, Bernard emphasized its legitimacy by speaking the words of the spirits, a literary device described by Webster (2000: 227). The story is remembered in song, a portion of which says, "In your country there are four plains, and there is a Blue Ridge Mountain...that is where you became a people." [That is, it is the place where the ancestral Mescalero were reconfigured after their separation from the Navajo.] Commenting on the story, Bernard noted that Apache were in the Black Hills long before the Crow and Cheyenne. The Crow, Pawnee, Mandan, and Hidatsa were all river people until they got the horse. They got the horse from the Apache, and that changed everything. "If those other groups had not obtained the horse from us, the Apaches would probably still be living in Alberta or Montana" (BS 7/4/88).

The Mescalero were the last of the Apache to come down [to leave the area of the Black Hills and migrate to the south]. "Horses were like a magnet to us; they kept us coming south." The first tribes encountered by the Mescalero in the southern region (i.e., the plains of New Mexico, Texas, and Oklahoma) were the Wichita, Tejas, Ponca, and Caddo (*'Kloga ndaa*, Grass lodge people). The Apache allied with the Cheyenne, Arapaho, Kiowa Apache, and Comanche to fight the Ponca. The Mescalero also fought the Pawnee in retaliation for their raiding to obtain virgin captives for sacrifice in the Morning Star ceremony. During these times, the Mescalero regularly used a concealed campsite located near present-day Colorado Springs on the west side of Pike's Peak (Figure 8.2, site 17), but they were being pressured by other Plains tribes and the westward expansion of the United States. Palo Duro Canyon (*Nił'e'aguteł*, Canyon in the plains; Figure

8.2, site 22), near present-day Amarillo, was the location of a major battle, likely in the early nineteenth century, in which four tribes—Apache (including Kiowa Apache), Arapaho, Cheyenne, and Comanche—fought the United States. Such alliances were shifting, however, and Palo Duro Canyon is more darkly remembered by the Apache as the site of a bloody battle with the Comanche, in which the Mescalero lost many people, resulting in their being displaced farther south.

The remaining place names shown in Figure 8.2 are within the area identified by Basehart (1974) as the Mescalero habitual use area by the mid-nineteenth century. The northern extent of seasonal movements at that time was in the area of Rabbit Ear Butte, near Raton, New Mexico (*Tse ha'a'*, Mountain rock standing up; site 18). Several other named locations in northern New Mexico document the Mescalero's familiarity with and regular use of the areas around Española (*Besh dilighai'a'*, Knife white sticking up; site 19), Santa Fe (*Tu yuu*, Water bead; site 20), and Tijeras Canyon (*Nakai'e naagishuł*, Mexican they dragged; site 21). The historic range of Mescalero seasonal movements extended well to the south of the location of the reservation established in 1873 (Figure 8.2, site 23), but place names in northern Mexico have been omitted here as they do not bear on the ancestral migration from the north and because many are identified by Basehart (1974).

ORAL HISTORY AS HISTORY

Most of you have grown up to believe and accept the preponderance of non-Indian history. [But] those of us who have come forth from these great Apache personalities—Cochise, Victorio, Naiche, and Geronimo—we can vouch for the oral history of our people. This oral history is more valid than some of the things that have been written about our people.
| Wendell Chino, president, Mescalero Apache Tribe, 1990 |

It has become fashionable for some students of culture to question the reliability of elder knowledge among indigenous peoples. Nevertheless, since the 1950s, there has been proof of the accuracy of elder knowledge, especially in the folklore literature, where there has long been a concern with oral tradition and accuracy. Albert Bates Lord's work (1960, 1995, 2000) was concerned with the question of whether Homer's *Iliad* and *Odyssey* could have actually been preserved for so long in oral format. Lord demonstrated that there were still singers in the Middle East who not only could recite the tales but also had various verbal resources on which to draw to elaborate or truncate the recitation or song depending on audience reaction.

Jan Vansina reported his work in West Africa in *Oral Tradition* (1961); he demonstrated how *griots*, singers of oral genealogies, maintained accounts that were isomorphic with written ones recorded by Portuguese priests in church records, despite the *griots* not being literate in Portuguese. Subsequent research reported in *Oral Traditions as History* (1985) reaffirmed and expanded on his earlier work.

Similar accounts of oral traditions involving verifiably ancient events are known among Native Americans as well. We have heard of a Kutenai flood story that is supported by geological evidence for regional flooding that resulted when the ice dam holding back Pleistocene glacial Lake Missoula broke and the outflow scoured the northern Plateau region. We have learned of Lakota people living in Whitewater, South Dakota, who maintain oral traditions about celestial alignments with local landform features. The alignments are slightly off today, but elders insisted they "used to be on"; after computer modeling was used to account for the effects of precession, it was discovered that the alignments were precise 2,000 years ago. Carmichael has obtained oral histories from a Lakota holy man that include knowledge of the Mount Mazama volcanic eruption about 7,600 years ago, as well as references to the hunting of the "long-nosed buffalo" (i.e., mammoths), the skulls of which are still used in ceremonial contexts.

The Mescalero Apache story of origins and migration related here is not the story of an old man with failing memory. Bernard passed away at the age of 46, so when he recited his oral histories he was vital and in the prime of life. Bernard was a polymath who loved to debate with linguists, historians, and theologians. For a time, he was part of a comparative religion tour in New England with the Right Reverend Sloan Coffin and Norman Vincent Peale. He attended college at the University of Colorado–Boulder and spoke three dialects of Apache, as well as Navajo, Spanish, English, German, and Japanese. He was always very clear about what his "grandfathers" said and what he learned elsewhere. We are aware of the phenomenon of feedback between researchers and indigenous consultants, but we never provided information from which Bernard could construct his vision of the past. He provided us with traditional place names, and the landmarks necessary to find the specific places, as a demonstration of the validity of his people's story as he learned it. One might be inclined to question a Mescalero emergence story as being a recent revision, but we are confident that the ancient migration story is indeed ancient, embedded as it is in the most ancient of the surviving Mescalero ceremonial practices. This is but one means of verification we used to authenticate the temporal depth of this knowledge.

Reconciling Heredity and Ethnicity

One summer afternoon during the Mescalero Apache girls' puberty ceremony, we were sitting in Bernard's tipi at the feast grounds, where he had received a group of visitors traveling with some people from Laguna Pueblo. Several of the visitors were from foreign countries, including a man from Japan. Bernard had been learning to speak Japanese on his own, and he relished the opportunity to practice the language and learn about Japanese culture. He spent a couple of hours in deep conversation with the Japanese man. After the visitors departed, Bernard spoke excitedly about his observations.

Clearly, there were some similarities in physical appearance between the Japanese man and at least some Apache people. But Bernard was more impressed by some specific similarities between their two cultures. The visitor traced his family roots to the samurai tradition, and even though the samurai influence in Japanese society declined in the late nineteenth century and officially ended after World War II, the family maintained knowledge of its ancestral traditions. Bernard and the Japanese visitor spoke at length about what it means (or meant) to be a warrior in the traditional sense. To Bernard's surprise, there were a number of detailed similarities between the samurai code of *Bushido* and the Mescalero Apache "Way of the Warrior." The similarities included not only the sorts of behaviors expected of warriors in each society (such as the importance of duty, honor, and self-sacrifice) but also the underlying spiritual insights on which the codes are based.

Bernard had long been aware of the standard anthropological view that the ancestors of Native Americans were ultimately derived from Asian populations who had migrated to the New World via the Bering land bridge. Nevertheless, while he respected our views about Native American origins as the product of serious professional study, he remained skeptical. After all, he knew that his own people had originated "here," on this continent, on the shores of a Lake You Can't See Over, in a Land of Ever Winter. Until meeting the Japanese visitor, he had had no firsthand exposure to any Asian culture that might lend credence to the notion of an ancient connection between his people and an Asian population. But after that meeting, the possibility of a connection to another continent became an observable reality. Moreover, it became a matter of personal intellectual interest for Bernard to reconcile the existence of such a connection with his knowledge of the origin of his people. He accomplished the reconciliation in a very simple yet elegant way—by drawing a distinction between biological heredity and cultural identity. That is, "We became a people near Lake Athabasca, but we have earlier biological connections to Asian populations." Viewed from this perspective, being from "here," whether that means North America or southern New Mexico, does not rule out the validity of earlier connections to peoples in other regions, precisely the sort of reality one might expect for a migratory group. Thus, in the same way that the Mescalero could have become a people in what is now northern Canada while still having a biological connection to Asia, it is possible to simultaneously be "from here" (southern New Mexico) while still having earlier connections to other parts of the continent. Such adaptability, and a willingness to accept what had been suspect data, seems to be an important trait that the Mescalero needed in their migrational history.

Wendell Chino, former president of the Mescalero Apache Tribe, delivered an eloquent eulogy at Bernard's funeral in 1988, in which he noted that with Bernard's passing, the tribe had lost a great deal of information about its traditions. He was thankful that Bernard had passed on some of his knowledge to us, and it is our hope that this outline of his version of the Mescalero migration story will benefit his people as well as scholars who are interested in researching the Mescalero Apache past.

REFERENCES

Basehart, Harry W.
1974 *Mescalero Apache Subsistence Patterns and Socio-Political Organization.* New York: Garland.

Basso, Keith
1996 *Wisdom Sits in Places: Landscape and Language among the Western Apache.* Albuquerque: University of New Mexico Press.

Farrer, Claire R.
1978 Mescalero Ritual Dance: A Four-Part Fugue. *Discovery 1978*:1–13. Santa Fe, New Mexico: School of American Research.
1980 Singing for Life: The Mescalero Apache Girls' Puberty Ceremony. In *Southwestern Indian Ritual Drama*, edited by Charlotte J. Frisbie, pp. 125–159. Advanced Seminar Series. Santa Fe, New Mexico: School of American Research.
1991 *Living Life's Circle: Mescalero Apache Cosmovision.* Albuquerque: University of New Mexico Press.

Gunnerson, James H.
1979 Southern Athapaskan Archeology. In *Southwest*, edited by Alfonso Ortiz, pp. 162–169. Handbook of North American Indians, Vol. 9, William C. Sturtevant, general editor. Washington, D.C.: Smithsonian Institution.
1987 *Archaeology of the High Plains.* Cultural Resource Series No. 9. Denver: U.S. Bureau of Land Management, Colorado State Office.

King, Thomas F.
2003 *Places That Count: Traditional Cultural Properties in Cultural Resources Management.* Walnut Creek, California: Altamira Press.

Kuchler, Susanne
1993 Landscape as Memory: The Mapping of Process and Its Representation in a Melanesian Society. In *Landscape: Politics and Perspectives*, edited by Barbara Bender, pp. 85–106. Providence, Rhode Island: Berg.

Lord, Albert Bates
1960 *The Singer of Tales.* Cambridge, Massachusetts: Harvard University Press.
1995 *The Singer Resumes the Tale.* Ithaca, New York: Cornell University Press.
2000 *The Singer of Tales.* 2nd ed. Edited by Stephen Mitchell and Gregory Nagy. Harvard Studies in Comparative Literature No. 24. Cambridge, Massachusetts: Harvard University Press.

Luckert, Karl W.
1975 *The Navajo Hunter Tradition.* Tucson: University of Arizona Press.

Opler, Morris E.
1983 The Apachean Culture Pattern and Its Origins. In *Southwest*, edited by Alfonso Ortiz, pp. 368–392. Handbook of North American Indians, Vol. 10, William C. Sturtevant, general editor. Washington, D.C.: Smithsonian Institution.
2001 Lipan Apache. In *Plains*, edited by Raymond J. DeMallie, pp. 941–952. Handbook of North American Indians, Vol. 13, William C. Sturtevant, general editor. Washington, D.C.: Smithsonian Institution.

Schweinfurth, Kay Parker
2002 *Prayer on Top of the Earth: The Spiritual Universe of the Plains Apaches.* Boulder: University Press of Colorado.

Vansina, Jan
1961 *Oral Tradition.* Chicago: Aldine.

1985   *Oral Tradition as History.* Madison: University of Wisconsin Press.
Webster, Anthony
2000   The Politics of Apache Place Names: Or Why "Dripping Springs" Does Not Equal "*Tonoogah.*" Proceedings of the Seventh Annual Symposium about Language and Society, Austin. *Texas Linguistic Forum* 43:223–232.

CHAPTER 9

Finding and Not Finding Athapaskans in the Archaeological Record Using Percentage Stratigraphy

DALE WALDE

Discussion of the timing and route of precontact Athapaskan movements from an inferred homeland in the northwestern Canadian boreal forest is a classic example of ongoing debate regarding identification of ethnicity and migration in the archaeological record and continues to be relevant to the issues of population movement treated in this book. As Brugge (this volume) notes, archaeological evidence serves a very strong role in determining the timing and route of the migration, although linguistic and genetic evidence certainly play a part (e.g., Webster, this volume; Malhi, this volume). Recognizing distinctly Athapaskan material culture in the archaeological record has been problematic (Seymour, Chapter 5, this volume), although Magne (this volume) makes some strong suggestions. Establishing the timing of the movement has also proven problematic, and estimates vary considerably (also see Hughes, Brunswig, and Carmichael and Farrer, this volume). Clearly, methodological and theoretical approaches must be thoroughly explored as we seek to refine our understanding of the Athapaskan archaeological record.

The question of archaeologically distinguishing in situ cultural developmental sequences from replacement through migration has intrigued archaeologists, to a greater or lesser extent, from the inception of the discipline (e.g., Anthony 1990; Binnema 2001; Clark 1994; Dumond 1998; Härke 1998; Rouse 1986). Following an extended hiatus, general interest in the question has been increasing, especially as indigenous and other inhabitants of former European colonies seek to explore their national and ethnic histories. In one former colony, on the Canadian Plains (Figure 9.1), the question of migration versus in situ development implicates the ethnogenesis of present-day Canadian Plains aboriginal peoples and has relevance to ongoing questions of traditional territories and legal land claims (Walde 2006a). In prehistoric contexts, projectile point styles have been and continue to be used as the primary source of evidence in discus-

Finding and Not Finding Athapaskans Using Percentage Stratigraphy · 199

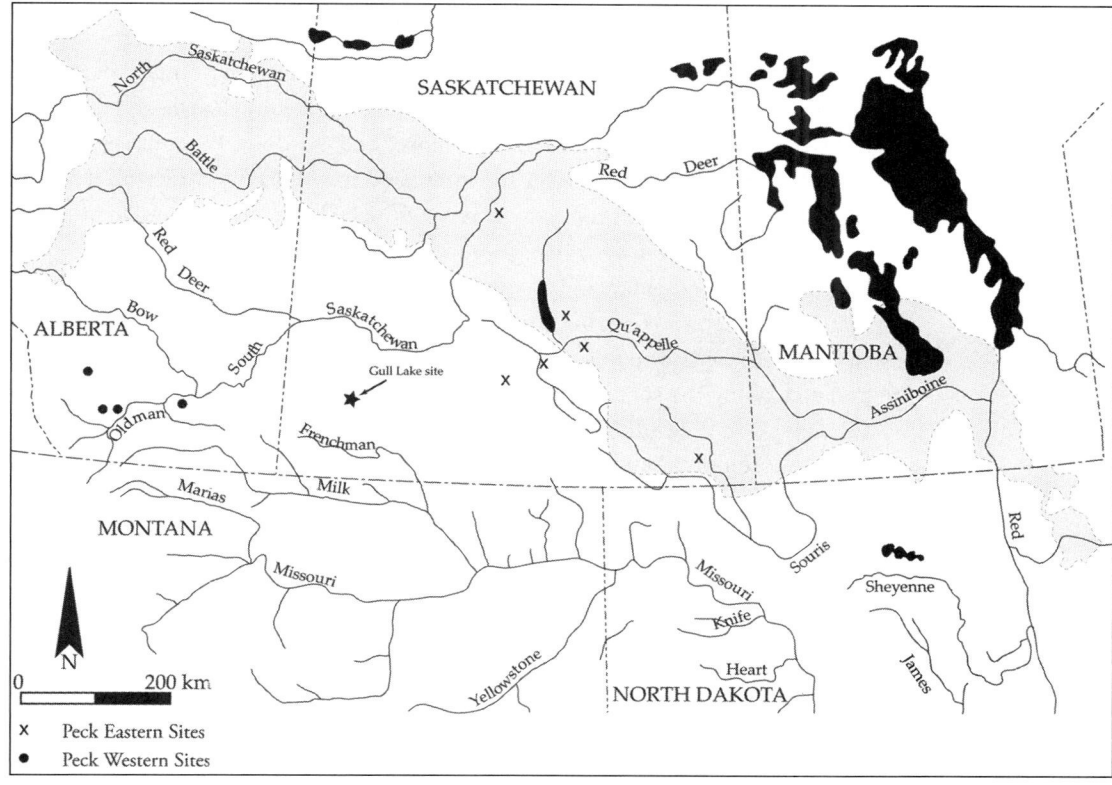

FIGURE 9.1. Canadian Plains overview map with location of Gull Lake site. Shaded area illustrates the Aspen Parkland area of the Canadian Plains. Image by Dale Walde.

sions of ethnicity and in interpretations of migration and replacement as agents of culture change on the Canadian Plains (e.g., Kehoe 1966; Peck 1996; Peck and Ives 2001; Walde 2006a, 2006c). The context of these discussions has changed considerably since their beginnings during the mid-twentieth century. They are now part of a wider social and legal debate, and it is even more important that archaeologists make the strengths and weaknesses of their interpretations clear to the larger circle of interested parties.

Kehoe (1966, 1973) made a significant early contribution to the exploration of Athapaskan history in proposing that the Avonlea horizon point style was produced by Athapaskans and that its appearance on the Canadian and northern U.S. Plains was both an indication of the timing of Athapaskan migration and a record of the route taken toward what is now the Southwestern United States. His work at the Gull Lake site in southwestern Saskatchewan (see Figure 9.1) was instrumental in establishing the idea that Athapaskans migrated through the Canadian Plains some two thousand years ago or so. That interpretation remains popular to the present day (see also discussions by Brunswig, Gilmore and Larmore, Gordon, and Magne, this volume), and it is important that it be reinvestigated as new approaches and understandings in archaeological method and theory come to the fore.

I have elsewhere suggested that the association of Avonlea projectile points with Athapaskan peoples is problematic, and I have proposed an alternative interpretation of the dynamics of adoption of that projectile point form (Walde 2006a, 2006b; see also Avonlea=Athapaskan discussions elsewhere in this volume, e.g., Brunswig, Gilmore and Larmore, and Gordon). I do not repeat that argument here but instead refer the interested reader to the works cited above. One aspect of Kehoe's argument, however, which I have not explored in previous work involves the post-Avonlea projectile point forms found on the Canadian Plains. This development of Late period projectile point typologies on the Canadian Plains seems to have been motivated by questions of both Avonlea and post-Avonlea ethnicity and ongoing human migration. For example, in establishing and discussing the sequence of Late period projectile point types (with varietal subclasses) in the Gull Lake site (EaOd-1) assemblage, Kehoe (1973:77–78) suggests that temporal change in form is associated with sequential migrations of ethnic groups into the area. As noted above, Avonlea projectile points are held to represent a migration of Athapaskan-speaking people onto the Canadian Plains. On this interpretation, the Athapaskans were supplanted by Algonquian-speaking peoples represented by Prairie side-notched type arrowheads. The Algonquians were, in their turn, replaced by (Siouan-speaking) Middle Missouri makers of Plains side-notched type points. The presence of these diagnostic point types in Gull Lake site components is used to support assertions with regard to ethnicity and mode of change. This interpretation follows Kehoe's earlier work (Kehoe 1966) in establishing and explaining a projectile point typology and sequence for the Late period Canadian Plains and serves as the basic model for many archaeologists, especially those working in Saskatchewan, for the identification of late precontact projectile point types in the area to this day, although attempts at modification have been made during the subsequent decades (e.g., Peck 1996; Peck and Ives 2001). Kehoe's (1966) use of the terms "Prairie side-notched" and "Plains side-notched" follows their introduction by MacNeish (1954:40) and subsequent use in Saskatchewan (Wettlaufer 1955; Wettlaufer and Mayer-Oakes 1960), although he is critical of their usage (Kehoe 1966:830) and redefines the types in his own work.

The basic notion that seems implicitly to underlie Kehoe's (1966, 1973) work concerns the nature of the archaeological record. Apparent discontinuities in Late period projectile point forms are read as evidence of migration and replacement of one group of people by another. Continuities in point form would then, presumably, be read as cultural and ethnic continuity. I should emphasize here that Kehoe (1966, 1973) does not explicitly address these issues in these terms, although they seem to be implicit in his discussion. The interpretation of his work presented here is, therefore, entirely my own construction and does not directly reflect an explicit argument made by Kehoe. My construct seems to follow logically and reasonably from Kehoe's stated opinions and does not, I believe, represent a "straw man" argument built selectively and reductively for later demolition. It must be clearly understood, however, that Kehoe did not structure his interpretations using the terms and framework introduced here. While Kehoe can hardly be held to account for an argument developed some four decades after his pioneering effort, it is nonetheless appropriate to reevaluate his approach and results in light of the changes and advances in archaeological analysis and explanation that have occurred over those same four decades. Following a long period of relative lack of interest among North American archaeologists, questions of how to distinguish archaeologically between migration or group replacement and in situ changes, such as local innovation and local adoption of externally developed ideas (diffusion), have started to regain higher research status and new approaches to older methods are being developed (e.g., Lipo et al. 1997). The work described below is part of this larger effort.

Given my own suggestions (Walde 2006a, 2006b) and those of others (e.g., Matson and Magne 2007) that Athapaskans are unlikely to be represented by Avonlea projectile points, and in view of the implications of new approaches to the classification of Late period projectile points (e.g., Peck 1996; Peck and Ives 2001), it is appropriate to reexamine the projectile point sequence proposed by Kehoe. It is also useful to explore further its implications for our present understanding of Athapaskan ethnicity and migration as reflected in the archaeological record. Using the Gull Lake site projectile point assemblage excavated by Kehoe (1973) during 1960 and 1963 as an example, I explore these questions as they have developed through the study of Late period point forms.

Canadian Plains Culture History Overview

Before launching into a discussion of arguments concerning cultural historical dynamics on the precontact Canadian Plains, however, I want to summarize briefly the culture history here. Detailed culture histories of the Canadian Plains for the periods discussed here (Middle and Late periods) are given by Forbis (1992), Reeves (1983), Syms (1977), Walde (2006a, 2006b) and Walde and others (1995).

Canadian Plains prehistory is conventionally divided into three periods: Early, Middle, and Late. There is little consensus in the naming of these periods with, for example, the Middle period identified variously as the Archaic, Plains Archaic, Middle Prehistoric, Middle Pre-contact, or Mesoindian period (Walde 2006c), but the tripartite division is generally recognized. This division is based first on perceived changes in weapons technology, specifically in projectile point form, with the large spear points of the Early period being replaced by medium-sized atlatl dart heads during the Middle period, only to be supplanted in turn by the appearance of arrowheads at the beginning of the Late period.

The Early period occurs immediately after deglaciation on the Canadian Plains at about 11,000 BC through about 6000 BC and can be characterized as an Upper Paleolithic lifeway with a focus on hunting now-extinct Late Pleistocene–Early Holocene fauna such as mammoth, giant bison, and, as recently noted by Kooyman and others (2006), horses.

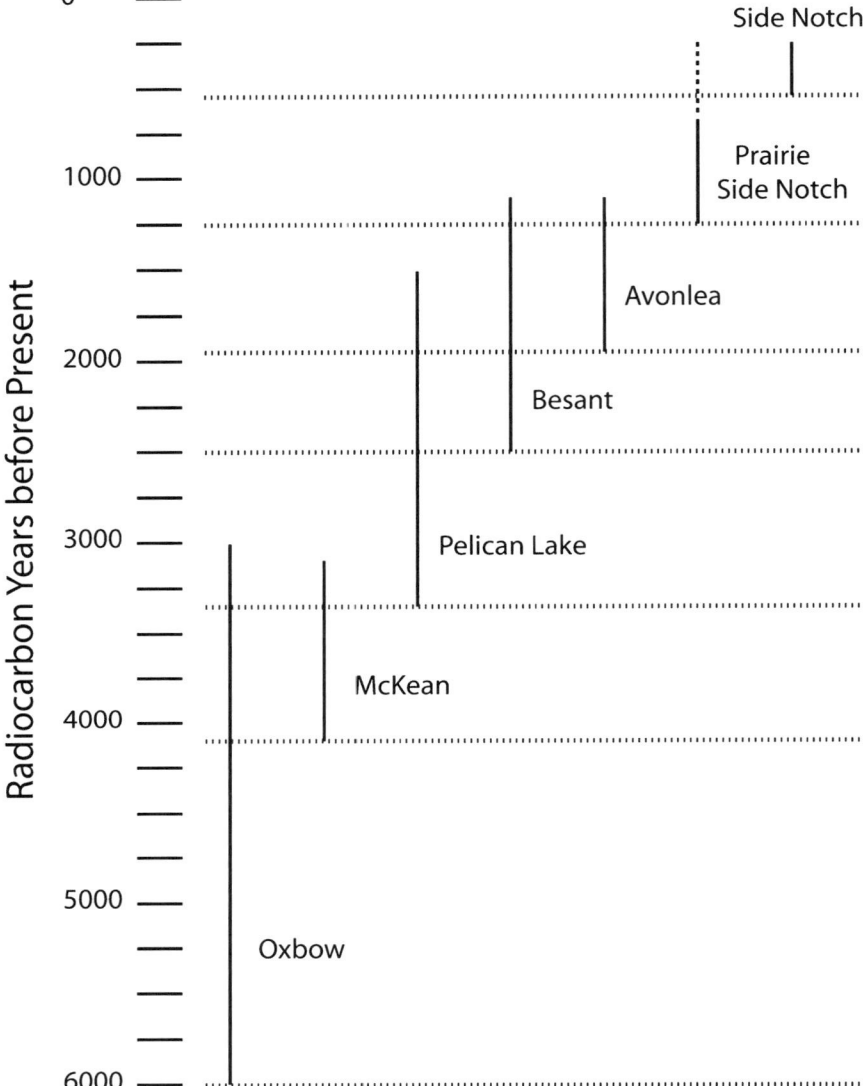

FIGURE 9.2. Sequence of cultural historical entities on the Canadian Plains. Solid vertical lines indicate the range of radiocarbon dates for each entity. Image by Dale Walde.

The Middle period begins at roughly 6000 BC and extends through about 550–250 BC (Walde 2006c:293). Relatively small band-level groups, possibly practicing a broader-spectrum hunting-and-gathering lifeway (Robertson 2004; Forbis 1992:53) but focusing on bison hunting (Brumley 1975:99; Forbis 1992: 53), characterize this period. Several named cultural historical entities based on sequential projectile point form (style) changes provide internal structure to this period, especially for the time following about 4000 BC (Figure 9.2). It is generally acknowledged that radiocarbon dates for these entities overlap (Figure 9.2), but this issue tends to be little discussed.

The end of the Middle period and the beginning of the Late period between about 550 and 250 BC is marked by widespread adoption of the bow and arrow and/or ceramics. This change was accompanied by the incorporation of large-scale communal bison hunting into the plains lifeway by tribally organized groups (Walde 2006c). Again, several sequential (although overlapping) cultural historical categories based initially on projectile point form provide internal structure to this period, with later categories identified through more regionally variable ceramic styles that add spatial complexity (see Figure 9.2).

Approaches to the Explanation of Culture Change on the Canadian Plains

Migration versus in situ development scenarios have formed the basis for many interpretations of Canadian Plains prehistory. Certainly for the period of the last 6,000 years, culture change has been largely discussed in these terms. The Oxbow phase (ca. 4100–1100 BC) has generally been regarded as an in situ cultural development arising from the earlier, rather ill-defined Mummy Cave complex (e.g., Reeves 1969; Forbis 1992; Walker 1992), although Mayer-Oakes (1959) suggested an Eastern Woodlands origin. The general agreement as to the mechanism for culture change disappears, however, with the advent of the McKean phase at about 2600 BC.

The McKean complex is characterized by three point types—McKean, Duncan, and Hanna—and is thought to have originated to the south of the Canadian Plains. There is little agreement, however, as to where the originating location might have been, how the points came to be on the Canadian Plains, and to which contemporary ethnolinguistic group the complex might be assigned (see, for example, Husted 1969:89, 91; Reeves 1969:32–33; Syms 1970:137; Brumley 1975:100, 102; Benedict 1981:87; Spurling and Ball 1981; Vickers 1986:71, 73). Similar disagreements surround the Pelican Lake phase, recognized by the presence of corner-notched points, which appears on the Canadian Plains by about 1550 BC (see, for example, Reeves 1969:33; Dyck 1983:107), as well as the Besant phase, appearing first on the Canadian Plains about 550 BC (Syms 1977:92; Dyck 1983:114; Reeves 1983:10, 191; Vickers 1986:86; Dyck and Morlan 1995:538; Toom and Jackson 2001:14.2).

A plethora of interpretations of ethnicity, origins, and migration (or not) based on Middle period point style is present, but no clear criteria for accepting or rejecting any or all of these arguments appear to be recognized. Authors seem often simply to ignore or gainsay alternative perspectives, expending little effort on developing methods and theory aimed at examining point style and resolving these issues.

As noted above, questions of ethnicity and migration also seem to underlie the development of Late period point typologies on the Canadian Plains. To recapitulate briefly, Kehoe (1973:77–78) suggests that temporal change in form is associated with sequential migrations of ethnic groups into the area. Avonlea

FIGURE 9.3. Projectile point types from the Gull Lake site: (a) Avonlea, (b) Prairie side-notched, and (c) Plains side-notched. Image by Dale Walde.

arrowheads (Figure 9.3a) are held to represent a migration onto the Canadian Plains at about AD 200 of Athapaskan-speaking people who were replaced at about AD 730 by Algonkian-speaking peoples who made Prairie side-notched type points (Figure 9.3b). The Algonkians were, in their turn, replaced at about AD 1300 by (Siouan-speaking) Middle Missouri migrants who made and used Plains side-notched type points (Figure 9.3c). The sequential appearance of these diagnostic point types in Gull Lake site components (see Figure 9.1) is used to support assertions with regard to ethnicity and mode of change.

Forbis (1962, 1977), working roughly contemporaneously with Kehoe, took a different approach to the construction and interpretation of Canadian Plains Late period point types, creating a series of nine post-Avonlea arrowhead types. In some contrast to Kehoe (1966, 1973), these types were not considered to be, strictly speaking, diagnostic of particular time periods or ethnic groups. Forbis produced percentage stratigraphy diagrams (see Lyman et al. 1998) of his types as they occurred in the various components of the Old Women's Buffalo Jump site (EcPl-1) and used those assemblages to establish a seriation chronology (Forbis 1977). His work suggested continuities in point style from about AD 600 through about AD 1753 in southern Alberta. Gradual change or evolution of point style over a broad area of the Canadian Plains is implicitly suggested (Forbis 1977:55). Although unenthusiastic about assigning ethnicity to the archaeological record, Forbis (1962:70) suggested that the Old Women's Buffalo Jump "was almost certainly a Blackfoot site, at least in the most recent period."

Peck (1996) and Peck and Ives (2001) also use point style to approach questions of ethnicity, migration, and change during the Late period. Peck (1996) examines variability in assemblages dating between about AD 700 and roughly AD 1750. Variation is regarded as so continuous in southern Alberta and perhaps southwestern Saskatchewan (the western portion of their study area) that separation of the points into types is not feasible. Peck and Ives (2001) conclude that the Prairie-Plains distinction suggested by Kehoe (1966, 1973) and the multiple types proposed by Forbis (1962, 1977) are untenable. Instead, western points are assigned to the Cayley series, which they attribute to ancestors of present-day Blackfoot groups (Old Women's phase).

For the eastern portion of his study area (southern and central Saskatchewan; see Figure 9.1), Peck (1996) finds that variation in assemblages dating between AD 700 and 1300 is very similar to that in the western assemblages (see Figure 9.1). He suggests that cultural continuity with the western assemblages is indicated and assigns the early eastern assemblages to the earlier stages of the Cayley series. Following AD 1300, Peck finds an abrupt change in point variation in the eastern assemblages. The geographic range of this change coincides spatially with the distribution of Mortlach phase (Walde 1994) and, as Peck (1996: 110) notes, supports empirically my impressionistic statement that points associated with Mortlach phase ceramics "were significantly different in lithic raw materials used and in size and shape from other Plains Side-Notch points associated with the Old Women's Phase in Alberta" (Walde 1994:87–88). While not including lithic raw material among their considered attributes (a feature I consider to be of great importance), Peck (1996) and Peck and Ives (2001) are able to statistically distinguish point assemblages associated with Mortlach phase ceramic assemblages from Cayley series point assemblages of the same age. Again suggesting that typological approaches, such as those proposed by Kehoe (1966, 1973) and Forbis (1962, 1977), are inappropriate, they assign this later spatially and temporally coherent range of variability to a stylistically distinct Mortlach group of points. The sudden appearance of Mortlach group assemblages at about AD 1300 is interpreted as an in-migration of another ethnic group represented by the Mortlach phase, which has been suggested to represent ancestral Assiniboine groups (Walde 1994; also see Peck 1996; Peck and Ives 2001).

The pattern of recognition of local development and replacement migration may be of more interest in the present context than the details of ethnic assignment. Peck (1996) and Peck and Ives (2001), following an approach that uses many of Forbis's (1962, 1977) point attributes and his original point assemblages, reach much the same conclusion with regard to continuity in point style between roughly AD 700 and 1700. That is, the assemblages vary continuously and there is little reason to suggest a rapid replacement by in-migrating groups (see Lipo et al. 1997:310 for a discussion of factors underlying continuity and discontinuity of styles in the archaeological record). Alternatively, in southern Saskatchewan, where Kehoe (1966, 1973) recognizes replacement of one ethnic group by another, Peck (1966) and Peck and Ives (2001) ultimately duplicate his conclusion that an in-migration and replacement of one ethnic group by another is evident in southern Saskatchewan because of the rapid replacement of projectile point types.

An area of disagreement occurs in the case of the Gull Lake site. Kehoe (1973) discusses a migration-and-replacement scenario using the entire Late period sequence from his Avonlea levels through Prairie side-notched to Plains side-notched levels. Peck (1996:28, 93) did not have an opportunity to look at this assemblage in detail but suggests that, for the Prairie-Plains levels, the sequence might better be associated with the continuous Cayley series.

My own recent suggestions that the Old Women's culture in Alberta extended back to Avonlea horizon times (Walde 2006b:102; Walde and Meyer 2003:142) projects the potential time frame for point style continuities somewhat deeper in time than does Peck's (1996; Peck and Ives 2001). If in situ development of Old Women's culture (Cayley series) in southern Alberta and southwestern Saskatchewan involved the Avonlea horizon, then we might expect to find continuities at Gull Lake rather than abrupt changes in style. A record of continuous in situ stylistic development from Avonlea horizon times in this area would also tend to support an argument that the makers of Avonlea points did not leave the area for the Southwestern United States but evolved culturally and stylistically in place through the following millennium and were, therefore, highly unlikely to have been Athapaskan-speakers.

Gull Lake Cultural Components

It is appropriate to pause here to describe briefly the Gull Lake site (Kehoe 1973) and the sequence of assemblages examined below. Gull Lake, a multicomponent bison kill site in southwestern Saskatchewan (see Figure 9.1), was excavated by Kehoe during the 1960 and 1963 field seasons. Situated on the northern edge of the Cypress Hills Upland, the site overlooks to the north a grass-covered glacial lake basin (Kehoe 1973:6). To the south, the upland landscape consists of grass-covered knob-and-kettle terrain. Bison were gathered on this upland area and driven into the kill area to be dispatched and processed. The site appears to have been in use from about AD 50 to the latest precontact times (ca. AD 1650).

The first component, located at the base of the excavation, contained no diagnostic artifacts such as projectile points or pottery and yielded a radiocarbon date of 1900 ± 65 BP (S-256; Kehoe 1973:39). (Note that all radiocarbon dates quoted here are uncalibrated one-sigma dates from samples processed in 1960 and 1964 at the University of Saskatchewan; Kehoe 1973:43.) That component is not considered further here. The second component (Assemblage 1; see Figure 9.4) occurs in Layers 32–30 and is associated with a radiocarbon date of 1740 ± 60 BP (S-255; Kehoe 1973:39). Avonlea points are characteristic of this component and the following two. The third component (Assemblage 2; Figure 9.4) occurs in Layers 29–27. The fourth component (Assemblage 3; Figure 9.4) occurs in Layer 26. Kehoe (1973:39) notes the occasional presence of Prairie side-notched points in Layer 26. A radiocarbon date of 1290 ± 60 BP (S-254) is associated with Layer 26 (Kehoe 1973:32).

The fifth component (Assemblage 4; Figure 9.4) is identified as a Prairie side-notched occupation by Kehoe (1973:39), although he notes the presence of Avonlea points (Kehoe 1973:43). This component occurs in Layers 24–21 and is associated with a radiocarbon date of 1220 ± 80 BP in Layer 24 (S-149; Kehoe 1973:39). The sixth component (Assemblage 5; Figure 9.4) is also identified as a Prairie side-notched occupation (Kehoe (1973:40). This component occurs in Layers 19–15, which Kehoe (1973:39) suggests date between AD 1000 and 1200.

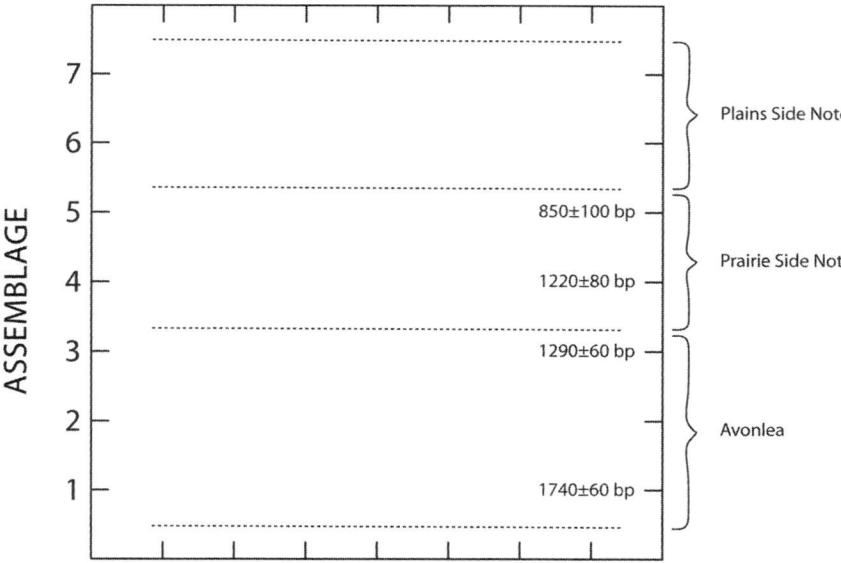

FIGURE 9.4. Distribution of Kehoe's (1973) projectile point types by assemblage. Image by Dale Walde.

The seventh component (Assemblage 6; Figure 9.4) occurs in Layers 8–6 (Kehoe 1973:39) and contains Plains side-notched points, and the eighth component (Levels 5–1; Assemblage 7; Figure 9.4) represents all Plains side-notched materials above the First Bone Bed in Layers 8–6 (Kehoe 1973:42).

CLASSIFICATION AND TYPOLOGY

Lipo and others (1997:301–302) suggest that much archaeological classification is concerned with recognition of ethnographic entities (cultures), resulting in a tendency to create "whole cultural" units, such as phases, based on similarities and differences in assemblages. On the Canadian Plains the general tendency has been to create phases based on similarities and differences in projectile points alone, despite efforts by Reeves (1983) to expand the range of data used. These "whole cultural" units tend to have loosely defined characteristics and, over time, become less well defined as newly discovered assemblages are added to existing cultural historical units without reassessment. Eventually, the empirical existence of these cultural historical entities becomes questionable (Lipo et al. 1997:303).

O'Brien and others (2003:137) note a lack of redundancy in characters used to classify Paleoindian points, and a similar lack of redundancy is apparent in the characters used to define point classes on the Canadian Plains. Characters are selected on a more or less ad hoc basis, and it is extremely difficult to assess continuity or lack thereof in point style in the absence of redundant characteristics (cf. Peck 1996). Types on the Canadian Plains and elsewhere (O'Brien et al. 2003:137) tend to be defined extensionally: "the definitions are derived by sorting through a collection of specimens, placing similar specimens together, and using average properties of the specimens…to create the type definition"

(O'Brien et al. 2003:137; see also O'Brien et al. 2001:1126, following Dunnell 1986). O'Brien and others (2003:137) also note that a "major problem arises when more specimens are introduced and type boundaries are reconfigured to include new variation." This approach on the Canadian Plains has led to the present situation in which point classes have become so poorly defined that many archaeologists practicing in the area have given up assigning new materials to established classes and have despaired of finding meaning in these materials, resorting to a generic "late side-notched" category (Brink et al. 1985; Brumley and Dau 1988).

O'Brien and others (2003:137), following Dunnell (1971) and O'Brien and Lyman (2000), attempt to overcome the problem of extensional class definition by using a paradigmatic classification scheme to create taxa. Investigators using a paradigmatic approach define a priori a set of apparently useful characters and their states: "Each specimen is then classified by noting the states of each character. Any state belonging to a single character can combine with any state belonging to any other character" (O'Brien et al. 2003:137). Classes are intentionally defined using a consistent character set, and any new materials that do not fit classes established in this manner must be assigned to new classes as defined by the paradigm. This is the approach used here.

As cultural historical entities become defined and settled in the literature, their very nature results in the creation of boundaries, "regardless of the structure of the archaeological record" (Lipo et al. 1997:303). This makes the development of new understandings of the past difficult, as new data are too often simply incorporated into predetermined classes and are not used to challenge, improve, and change them. Drawing on their understanding of an evolutionary archaeology approach, Lipo and others (1997) utilize modified frequency seriation to develop "a new means to describe interaction between populations in space and time" (Lipo et al. 1997:303). While not all readers will agree with all aspects of the evolutionary archaeology theory underlying their method, it nonetheless seems clear that their approach permits an empirically based assessment of continuity, change, and interaction in the archaeological record. And application of evolutionary archaeology theory provides a very strong warrant for interpreting patterns in the archaeological record and for understanding the modes of cultural transmission explored in this book.

Seriation may be used to provisionally confirm a suggestion of ongoing local development, and "the *failure* of a set of assemblages to seriate (rather than success) might be exploited to test hypotheses about the history of interaction in a region" (Lipo et al. 1997:310). Percentage stratigraphy may be used in a similar manner but is different from seriation in important ways, although many archaeologists tend to conflate the two procedures (Lyman et al. 1998). Like seriation, percentage stratigraphy diagrams plot frequencies of artifact classes in assemblages, but unlike seriation, in which temporal order is based on external criteria, the ordering of the assemblages is based on superposition (Lyman et al.

Finding and Not Finding Athapaskans Using Percentage Stratigraphy · 209

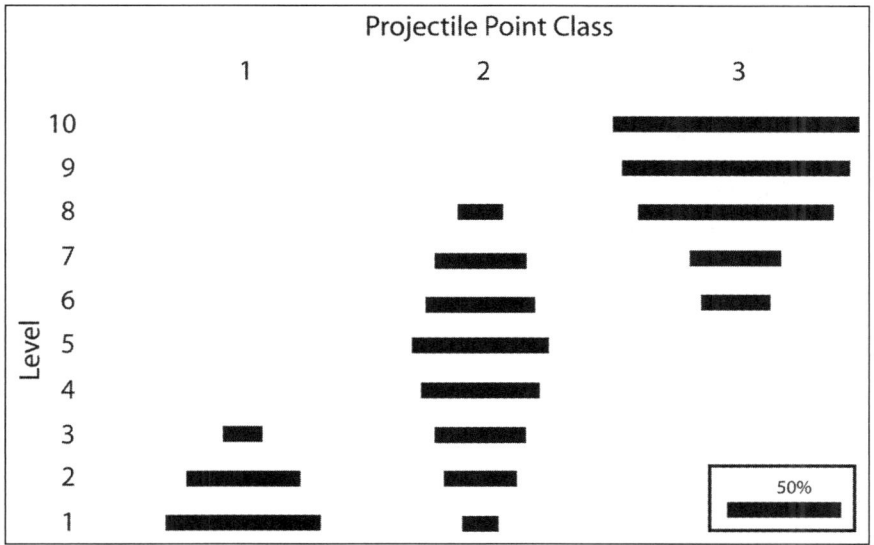

FIGURE 9.5. Idealized schematic model illustrating the overlapping unimodal class frequency distributions expected in cases of local style development and historical continuity. Image by Dale Walde.

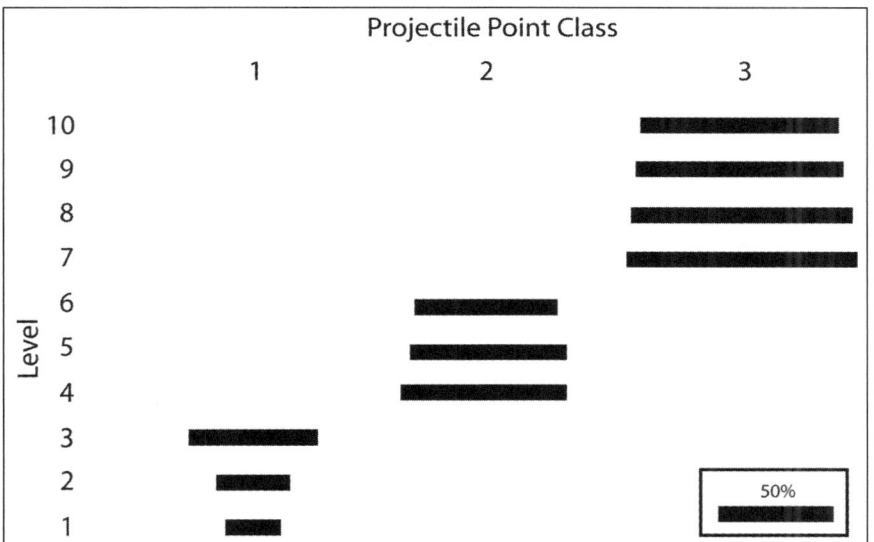

FIGURE 9.6. Idealized schematic model illustrating the non-overlapping style class frequency distributions expected in cases of interrupted local style development and population replacement (migration). Image by Dale Walde.

1998). The order of the assemblages cannot be changed. Historical relationships and continuity in cultural transmission of traits is indicated by overlapping, unimodal class frequency distributions (e.g., Figure 9.5). In this chapter, a failure of a percentage stratigraphy diagram of the Gull Lake projectile point assemblages to form overlapping, unimodal distributions of point classes might be taken to suggest an interruption in local development and, perhaps, a replacement of population—that is, such a failure would not contradict Kehoe's contention (e.g., Figure 9.6). Should such a diagram form overlapping, unimodal distributions, however, shared histories and continuity in cultural transmission would be indicated and a scenario of multiple migrations could not be supported.

This chapter represents an initial effort, using percentage stratigraphy, to develop an understanding of cultural development and cultural interaction at the Gull Lake site and to assess the likelihood that the sequence there might reasonably be interpreted as a migration or population replacement scenario. That is, an empirical test is conducted of Kehoe's assertion that at the Gull Lake site the Avonlea horizon style represents an intrusion of Athapaskan-speakers who were later replaced by two subsequent migrations of other linguistic groups after AD 700. Results from a study of a single multicomponent site clearly cannot entirely settle the question of the presence of Athapaskans on and subsequent migration from the Canadian Plains during the early Late period. Reexamination of the site assemblage that, in large part, formed the basis for this widely accepted scenario, however, may allow for a new assessment and for suggestions regarding directions for future research.

Selecting Variables

Before a typology can be constructed and classification can begin, however, decisions must be made as to which point characteristics should be used and how those characteristics should be measured. It is well recognized that the social context of construction of lithic projectile points on somewhat recalcitrant material has resulted in a very diverse data set, even within classes we generally consider to be relatively well defined. One of the biggest problems is the fact that the points were all made by individuals and that the individuals involved varied considerably from site to site (spatially), and certainly temporally as well. I have suggested elsewhere (Walde 1994, 2003, 2006a) that these individuals would have lived in loosely tribally organized societies. In those societies, it appears that a premium was placed on individual achievement and expression in craft production (Walde 2003:82) within a broadly defined reservoir of acceptable action and approaches to style (David et al. 1991:177). In such a scenario, the question of how one conducts a search for regularities and continuities, or discontinuities and abrupt changes, in artifact forms in an area characterized by a highly eclectic and context-specific mode of production is very much to the forefront.

Attempts to develop a classification for and an interpretation of Late period point styles often seem to founder on the problem of the extreme range of variation present in the point assemblages. Lucas (2001:103–104) discusses a similar issue with regard to European Neolithic beakers, which he feels are too variable to allow for successful typological analysis. He suggests that with too much variability "one cannot know where one type might begin and another end" and that "a great deal of archaeological material is going to be unclassifiable except in a broad sense using generic identities which must change according to context" (Lucas 2001:104). This complaint is very similar to the one noted above by Canadian Plains archaeologists with regard to the problem of classifying Late period projectile points.

This is, I think, an overly pessimistic view of the possibility of constructing classifications or, at the very least, of developing meaning from the extremely diverse assemblages created within relatively egalitarian societies. As Peck (1996) notes, variation in the metric attributes of Late period projectile points is, indeed, continuous. However, the possibilities for study of how combinations of these attributes might be created to support a chronologically meaningful classification have not been exhausted. It may well prove to be the case that not all classes will be temporally informative, but some might well be and they should be used.

Style and Function

Because the present study depends on percentage stratigraphy as an approach to the differentiation of in situ development versus migration as sources of temporal change in artifact assemblages, it is appropriate to explore briefly the roles of style and function in producing distribution curves. O'Brien and Lyman (2000: 285) note that successful seriation depends on the notions of transmission and heritable continuity in artifact form. I suggest that the same argument applies to the production of unimodal distributions by percentage stratigraphy. Following Dunnell (1978), O'Brien and Lyman (2000) suggest that stylistic forms can be expected to produce unimodal distributions that are unaffected by variations in the selective environment that could be expected to affect the distributional behavior of functional forms. These authors recognize that separation of stylistic from functional properties is not always possible, in that the two forms may not always be mutually exclusive and that seriations produced by use of such properties can result in "less than perfect unimodal frequency distributions" (O'Brien and Lyman 2000:335). Similar problems may well be expected for percentage stratigraphy diagrams. Bettinger and others (2003) also note that it would be unrealistic to expect to be able to completely separate stylistic from functional distributional patterns, but they suggest that meaningful interpretations can nonetheless be derived from temporal distribution curves. While it was recognized that style and function are not necessarily always separable, attempts were made to ensure that functional variation played as small a role as possible in the present study.

Peck (1996:31) recognized the style-function problem in conducting his study and indicates that he "had hoped to include only sites interpreted as bison kill sites in order to limit the functional context of the projectile points. Hence, any projectile point morphological variability across space or through time would theoretically be more readily attributable to 'stylistic' rather than 'functional' considerations." He was, however, forced to use points from campsites as well in order to obtain a reasonable sample of materials from across the Northern Plains. Peck (1996:31) suggests that he is not aware "of any study that demonstrates that projectile points from kill sites differ substantially from those related to occupation sites, or for that matter, to any other type of functionally

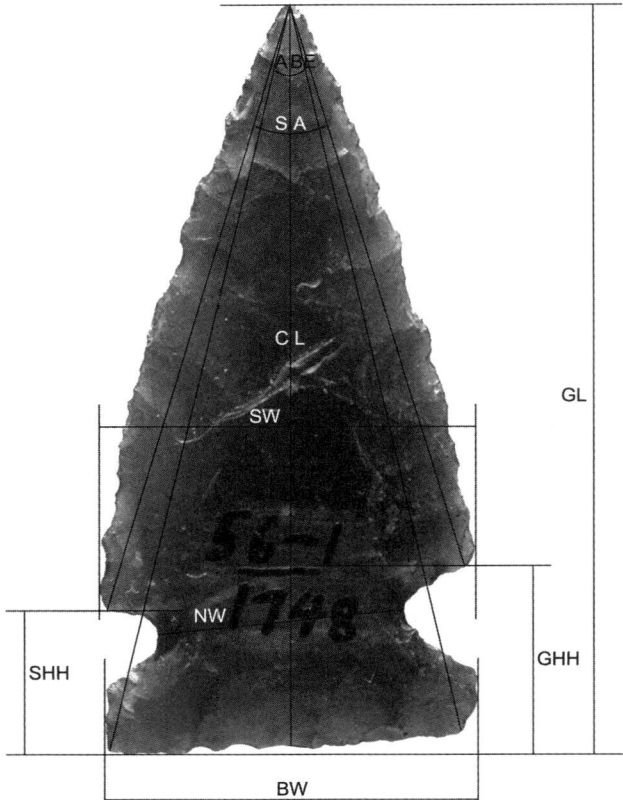

FIGURE 9.7. Measurements taken on digital images of projectile points (see text for definitions of measurement abbreviations). Image by Dale Walde.

specific site." This is may be true as far as it goes, although it should be mentioned that Peck (1996:23) notes the problems Brink and others (1985:105–136) encountered in attempting to classify late side-notched projectile points from their excavations in the camp area at Head-Smashed-In Buffalo Jump, a collection not used in Peck's (1996) analysis. I am also not aware of any study of Late period projectile point morphological variability that was placed in functional context, but it may be that such a study is needed to explore this question. However, the question is moot here as the present study is restricted to a multicomponent kill site (Gull Lake) and the question of functional context does not arise, at least not immediately.

For the present study, choosing the characters on which arrowhead classes might be defined was a relatively complex process. Using the work of Kehoe (1973), Forbis (1997), and Peck (1996) to define a wide constellation of potentially useful variables, I developed a procedure for scanning the points from the Gull Lake assemblage, measuring the resulting digital images, and recording the data.

The following characters were defined and measured digitally (Figure 9.7) on 410 points and point fragments, although not all characters were present on all examples: smallest haft height (SHH), greatest haft height (GHH); base width

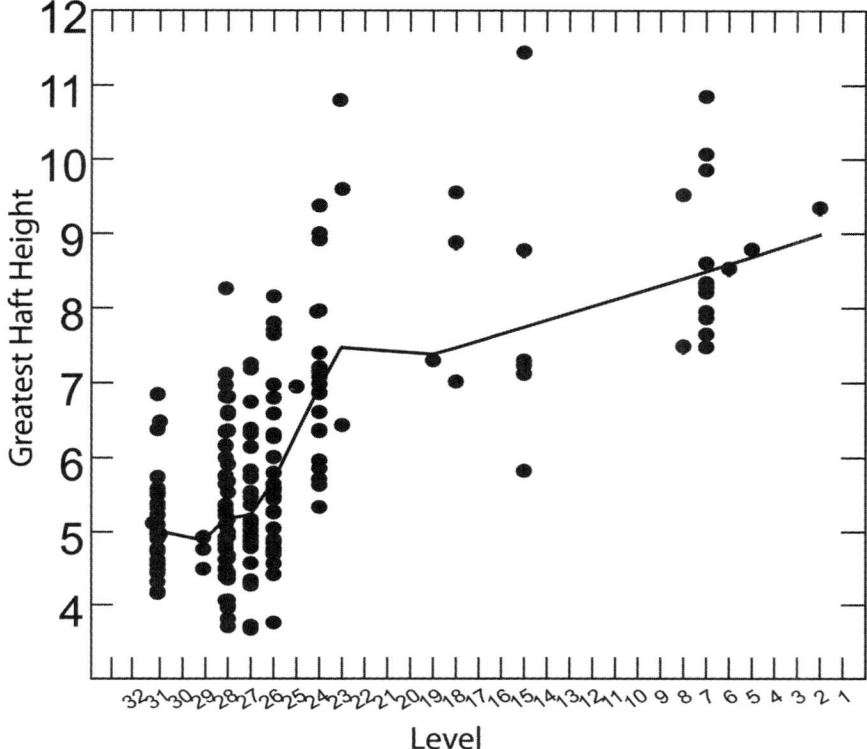

FIGURE 9.8. Distribution of greatest haft height by level. Image by Dale Walde.

(BW), shoulder width (SW), angle to base edges (ABE), angle to shoulders (AS), greatest length (GL), minimum neck width (NW), and length of central axis (CL). Neck thickness (NT) and maximum thickness (MT) were measured with digital calipers.

Because the method of choice for this study (percentage stratigraphy) requires large data sets, several characters were removed from further consideration. As is common in many Canadian Plains point assemblages, many of the specimens are broken and not all characters are present on all specimens. Insisting on use of all potential characteristics would have severely limited the sample size and compromised the validity of any results. Point bases are the most commonly available partial specimens in the collection, and characters not present in the basal (hafting) area were excluded from further analysis, leaving the hafting characters smallest haft height (SHH), greatest haft height (GHH), base width (BW), minimum neck width (NW), and neck thickness (NT). All hafting character data were imported into a statistical program—Systat 10 (SPSS 2000)—for data exploration.

Characters were plotted against level as a proxy measure of time. SHH, GHH (Figure 9.8), BW, and NT all increased in size from earlier to later levels while NW decreased (Figure 9.9). NW was selected as one character to be used in classification in part because it was present on the largest number of specimens,

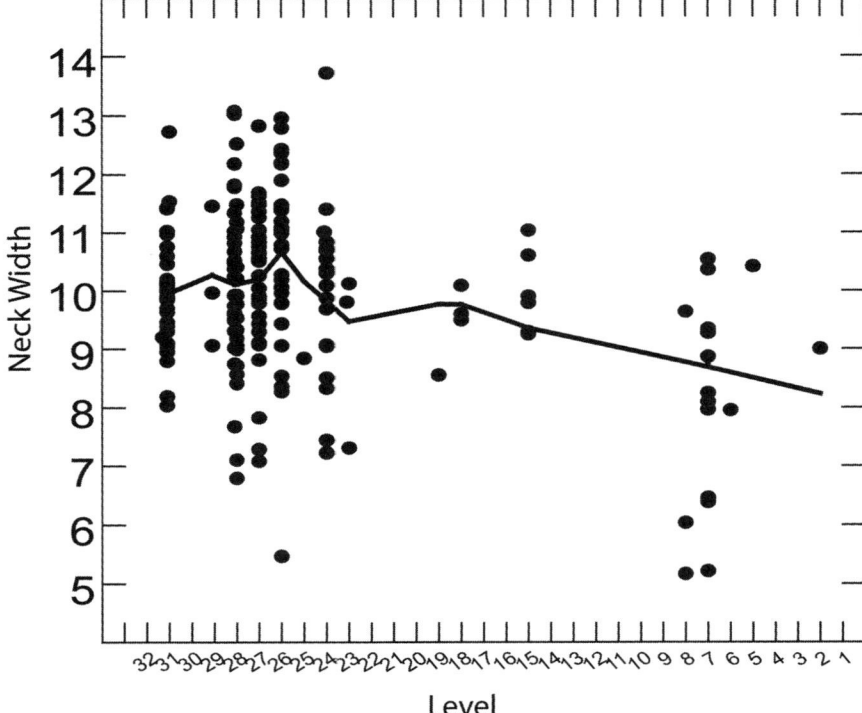

FIGURE 9.9. Distribution of neck width by level. Image by Dale Walde.

thereby maintaining the largest possible sample size, and also because it changes size in a direction opposite to GHH and the other characters under consideration. It was reasoned that including NW would emphasize time-related changes in projectile point shape. GHH was also selected as a character to be used in classification in part because it was the second-most frequently present character in the collection, thereby preserving sample size as much as possible, and also because it showed the greatest change in size of the characters that increased in value through time. GHH and NW are not correlated ($r^2 = 0.0$, $p = 0.998$), and the locally weighted sum of squares fitted lines (see Figures 9.8 and 9.9) show a certain amount of structure in the distributions of each variable, suggesting time-related "jumps" in size changes. The characters rejected did not demonstrate significant change through time and would have biased the test described below in favor of a "no population replacement" scenario. It is important to note here that use of characters that showed the greatest change through time was an effort to ensure that population replacement could be detected and that Kehoe's interpretation could be supported by the data selected.

Adding further point hafting characters to the classification greatly reduced both overall and within-class sample sizes by creating increasing numbers of point classes, greatly obscuring any possible patterns in the data while rendering any results suspect due to small sample size. The two character data sets (GHH and NW) to be included in the classification were then graphed in stem-

Finding and Not Finding Athapaskans Using Percentage Stratigraphy · 215

Greatest Haft Height Assemblage						Minimum Neck Width Assemblage					
GHH Stem (cm)	1 (n = 32)	2 (n = 80)	3 (n = 29)	4 and 5 (n = 33)	6 and 7 (n = 16)	NW Stem (cm)	1 (n = 32)	2 (n = 81)	3 (n = 29)	4 and 5 (n = 33)	6 and 7 (n = 17)
3		667	7		SMALL						
3		899									
4	111	00									
4	3	233333									
4	44445	44455	45								
4	6677	6667777	677								
4	9999	8888899999	88								
5	011	0001111	0			5	SMALL				1
5	2233	222333	22	3		5					2
5	5555	455	4455	INTERMEDIATE		5		4			
5	7	6677777	677	67		5					
5		89				5					
6		0111	0			6					0
6	3	3333	23	33		6					3
6	4	5	5	4		6					4
6		67		6		6		7			
6	8	889	899	889		6					
7		11		0011		7		01			
7		2		2223		7		2		223	
7				4	44	7				4	
7			67		6	7		6			
7			8	99	89	7		8			99
8			1			8	01				0
8		2			223	8			23	3	2
8					5	8		45	5		
8			7		67	8	7	77			
8				89		8	9	89	8		8
9				0		9	01	0000011	0	00	0
9				3	3	9	233	233		22	23
9				55	5	9	4	44555555	4	45	
9						9	667	6777	77	67	6
9					8	9	8899	899999	9	889	
10					0	10	00011	01	01	001	
10						10	2	2223	2	333	3
10						10	4	4444555		5	45
10				7		10	67	667	77	667	
10					8	10	9	8899	9	8	
11						11	0	0001	00	00	
11						11		233	23		
11				4	LARGE	11	445	4445	44	4	
						11		667		INTERMEDIATE	
						11		8	9		
						12		1	1		
						12			23		
						12		5	4		
						12	7		7		
						12		8	9		
						13		00			
						13					
						13					
						13			7	LARGE	

FIGURE 9.10. Stem-and-leaf display of GHH and NW data sets. Image by Dale Walde.

and-leaf diagrams (Figure 9.10) that were examined for natural break points in the assemblage distributions that could be used to establish character states. Not all break points in each assemblage coincided at all times, and the character states were ultimately decided with a judgmental mix of natural break points and distribution end points. The objective was to create sets of character states that would allow for maximum differentiation of point classes. In the end, a typology based on two characters (greatest haft height and neck width) with three states each was used (Table 9.1).

This approach allowed use of the largest number of points (190) while providing larger numbers of examples of each class. The paradigm created nine

TABLE 9.1. Gull Lake Projectile Point Class Paradigm.

		GREATEST HAFT HEIGHT		
		SMALL (3.600–5.299 mm)	INTERMEDIATE (5.300–7.399 mm)	LARGE (7.400–11.442 mm)
NOTCH WIDTH	Small (5.100–5.399 mm)			Type 7
	Intermediate (5.400–11.079 mm)	Type 2	Type 4	Type 6
	Large (11.080–13.799 mm)	Type 1	Type 3	Type 5

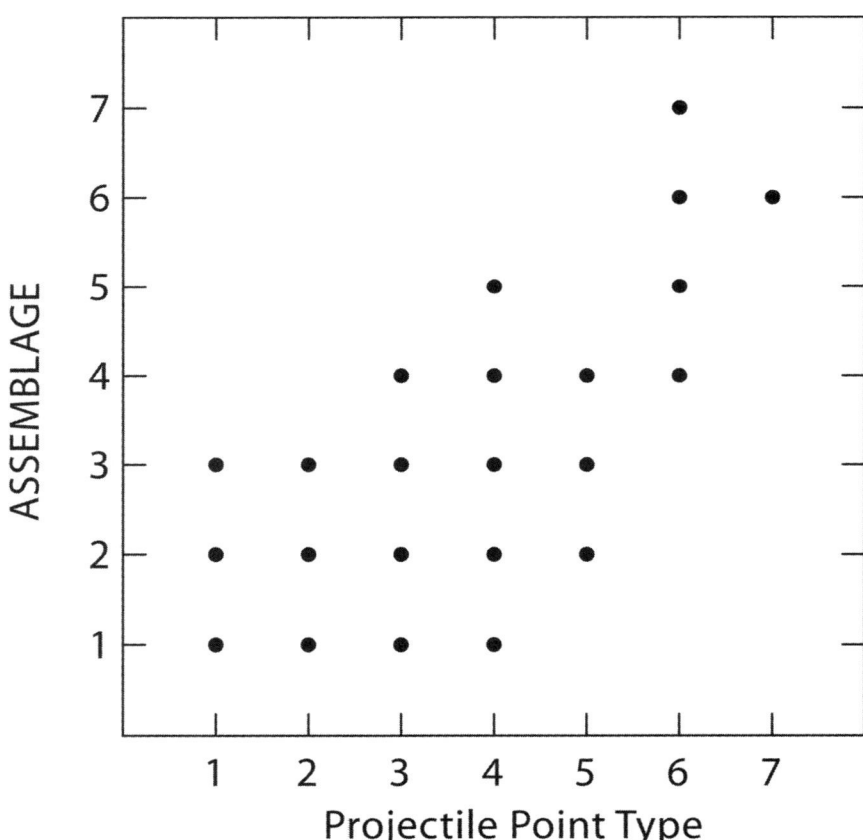

FIGURE 9.11. EaOd-1 projectile point class distribution by assemblage. Image by Dale Walde.

point classes, seven of which are present in the Gull Lake assemblage (Classes 1–7; see Table 9.1 and Figure 9.11). Percentage representation of the seven classes in each assemblage was calculated (Table 9.2) and a percentage stratigraphy diagram constructed by plotting percentage representation against archaeological level. Results are presented below.

TABLE 9.2. Gull Lake Site Percentage Stratigraphy.

ASSEMBLAGE	GULL LAKE POINT CLASSES							TOTAL	N
	1	2	3	4	5	6	7		
7	0.000	0.000	0.000	0.000	0.000	100.000	0.000	100.000	2
6	0.000	0.000	0.000	0.000	0.000	85.714	14.286	100.000	14
5	0.000	0.000	0.000	60.000	0.000	40.000	0.000	100.000	10
4	0.000	0.000	4.348	60.870	4.348	30.435	0.000	100.000	23
3	20.690	17.241	6.897	41.379	13.793	0.000	0.000	100.000	29
2	8.750	50.000	10.000	30.000	1.250	0.000	0.000	100.000	80
1	6.250	62.500	6.250	25.000	0.000	0.000	0.000	100.000	32
Total	7.895	34.211	6.842	33.684	3.158	13.158	1.053	100.000	
N	15	65	13	64	6	25	2		190

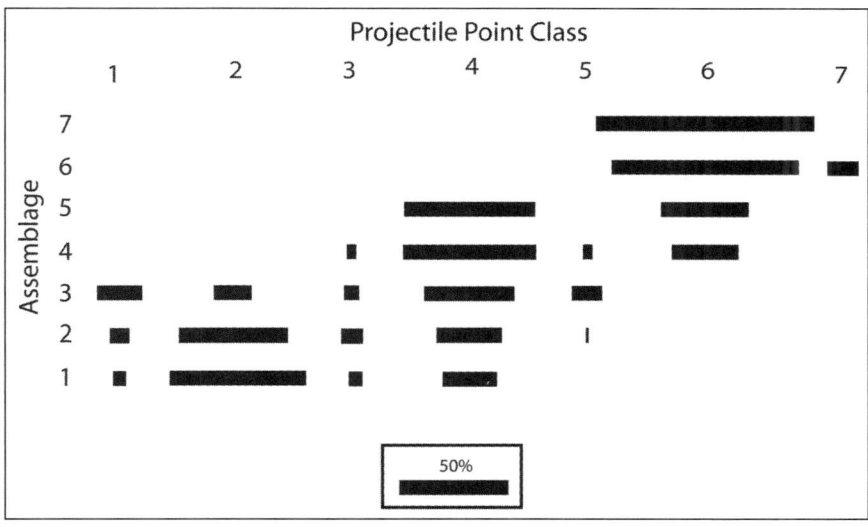

FIGURE 9.12. Percentage stratigraphy of projectile point classes by assemblage. Image by Dale Walde.

RESULTS

Distribution of the very small sample of 15 Class 1 arrowheads is restricted to Assemblages 1, 2, and 3; percentages increase from early to late in the sequence. Sixty-five Class 2 points are present in the lowermost three assemblages; percentage representation decreases from early to late in the sequence. Thirteen members of the sparsely represented Class 3 were noted in Assemblages 1, 2, 3, and 4. Percentages rise from Assemblage 1 to Assemblage 2 and then decrease to the final expression in the Assemblage 4. Sixty-four Class 4 points were recorded in Assemblages 1, 2, 3, 4, and 5. Representation increases from early to late in Assemblages 1 through 3 and then achieves its highest percentage in Assemblage 4 before decreasing in Assemblage 5. A very small sample of six Class

5 specimens appears in Assemblages 2, 3, and 4. Percentages increase from Assemblage 2 to Assemblage 3 and then decrease in Assemblage 4. Twenty-five Class 6 points appear in Assemblages 4, 5, 6, and 7. Representation increases from early to late in the sequence. Two members of the underrepresented Class 7 are present in Assemblage 6. This type is unique to the latest precontact times at the site.

Discussion and Conclusions

The concept of heritable continuity (e.g., O'Brien et al. 2001:1115) is useful for interpreting the results of the analysis described above. The largely unimodal percentage distribution patterns produced are the results of formal similarities among the arrowheads in the sample, formal similarities that are present because the specimens follow a common line of descent with modification through time. This is not to imply that arrowheads reproduce themselves (see also O'Brien et al. 2001:1117). Arrowhead makers do reproduce, certainly biologically, but, more to the point, their knowledge and ways of doing things do so because they are transmitted culturally. Cultural transmission of knowledge and approaches to work creates, among other things, tool traditions based on repeated personal inheritance of knowledge of preexisting forms. Given Peck's (1996) demonstration that continuity in projectile point characters is not demonstrated in his Cayley to Mortlach transition, it seems unlikely that the continuity demonstrated here is simply the result of constraints placed on form by function, material, and a general side-notch tradition. Similarity of sequent forms evident in the present study results from heritable continuity of characters, recorded in this case quite literally in stone but created by social learners who were simultaneously the transmitters and sources of variation of those characters (see also O'Brien et al. 2001:1134).

Most likely, the specific unimodal form of the distribution patterns produced is primarily a result of stylistic variation through time. Functional variation is acted on by environmental factors (broadly defined) and often shows directional temporal variation, whereas stylistic variation tends to be neutral and less subject to directional change (Dunnell 1978, 1982). While, as noted above, complete separation of stylistic and functional variation is seldom possible, it has been shown that the temporal distribution of style-based classes is unimodal within regional populations owing to the probabilistic nature of transmission (Lipo et al. 1997:305 following Dunnell 1982). Unimodal distributions of stylistic classes represent unique histories of transmission within regional populations (Lipo et al. 1997:305).

Some directional change in form related to function may be indicated by the overall pattern in Figure 9.9. The number of classes per assemblage increases from three in Assemblage 1 to five in Assemblages 2 and 3 and then consistently decreases from four in Assemblage 4 to two in Assemblages 5 and 6 and finally to one in Assemblage 7. Lyman and others (2008) note that variation in form increases when experimentation aimed at improving the performance of an artifact type is undertaken, then decreases as better-performing designs are adopted and less effective forms are discarded. Avonlea points represent the first widespread adoption of the bow and arrow on the Canadian Plains, although probably not its initial introduction (see, for example, Dyck and Morlan 1995), and the hafting characters selected for the present study would certainly be relevant to the function of the weapon system. It may be that some of the overall pattern of change in the number of classes per assemblage represents functional improvement of bow-and-arrow technology between about 2,000 and 400 years ago on the southwestern Saskatchewan Plains. Further research is necessary to explore this question.

Percentage stratigraphy of the Gull Lake data (see Table 9.2 and Figures 9.8 and 9.9), however, with the exception of the small sample of Class 1 points, shows generally consistent and overlapping unimodal patterns of appearance, increasing use, and decline. The abrupt breaks in the pattern that would be expected to result from the intrusion of and replacement with externally developed styles with different transmission histories are not present. The pattern found supports an interpretation of the evolution of a stylistic tradition within a regional population and does not support Kehoe's (1973) migration or replacement scenario on the southwestern Saskatchewan Plains. Given that the end of the Gull Lake sequence closely approaches the time of Euro-Canadian contact and that Athapaskan-speakers were not noted as long-time residents of the area, his assignment of Athapaskan ethnicity to the Avonlea horizon there is also not supported.

Results of the present study do not allow me to make any suggestions as to ethnic or cultural historical assignment of the Gull Lake sequence. While continuity based on ceramic wares between the Old Women's phase and the Avonlea horizon through the Upper Kill phase in southern Alberta has been suggested elsewhere (Walde and Meyer 2003), it is highly improbable that all phases throughout the Canadian Plains that include the Avonlea point horizon marker in their assemblages are precursors to Old Women's (i.e., are ancestors of present-day Blackfoot peoples) (Walde 2006b). Furthermore, while Peck (1996: 93) suggests that the upper levels of the Gull Lake sequence might be associated with the Cayley series (Old Women's phase), it must be noted that a chi-square test of the fit between his count of basal edge shapes in the Prairie side-notched (Early Cayley series) layers and his ideal Early Cayley assemblage configuration (Table 9.3) indicates significant differences ($p < .05$). Assignment of the Gull Lake sequence to an existing cultural historical entity or ethnic group is not appropriate at this time. There is, in fact, no a priori reason to suggest that the Gull Lake sequence must fit extensively into previously established sequences or entities. An opportunity for testing the range of those entities may very well be indicated by the results of this study.

Now that a classification and a local developmental sequence have been established at Gull Lake, it is important that future research explore, refine, and expand the classification using other assemblages to develop ideas with

TABLE 9.3. Comparison of Peck's (1996) Ideal Early Cayley Basal Edge Shape Frequencies (%) with Peck's (1996:93) Count of Basal Edge Shape Frequencies (%) in the Prairie Side-Notched Levels at the Gull Lake Site.

Point Group	Basal Edge Shape Percentages			
	Straight	Concave	Convex	Other
Early Cayley	49.5	28.9	17.8	3.8
Gull Lake Prairie Side-Notched	40.0	20.0	30.0	10.0

regard to synchronous spatio-temporal continuities and discontinuities across the Canadian Plains. It is highly unlikely that local sequences will be identical or that point class frequencies will be the same across that very broad study area (see also Lipo et al. 1997). Determined study of projectile point form has a significant potential when combined with other studies of material culture to help archaeologists develop stronger and much more detailed interpretations of what was surely a very dynamic human past on the Canadian Plains. Similarly, replicable percentage stratigraphy and seriation studies with predefined explicit criteria and expectations may prove helpful in studies of patterns of change and interaction within and among prehistoric hunter-gatherer societies elsewhere.

Kehoe's (1973) work at Gull Lake was the catalyst behind the notion that Athapaskans migrated through the Canadian Plains during Avonlea times. This reanalysis of his original excavated materials in the light of new approaches and understandings is an important step in examining and, ultimately, rejecting that notion. Use of the methodology described here might also very well help in the search for the Athapaskan migration route through Canada, but it seems most probable that local non-Athapaskans produced most if not all of the Avonlea horizon and that the search for the Athapaskan migration route might more profitably be conducted somewhere other than the Canadian Plains.

References

Anthony, David W.
1990 Migration in Archeology: The Baby and the Bathwater. *American Anthropologist* 92(4):895–914.

Benedict, James B.
1981 *The Fourth of July Valley*. Research Report No. 2. Ward, Colorado: Center for Mountain Archeology.

Bettinger, Robert L., Robert Boyd, and Peter J. Richerson
2003 Style, Function, and Cultural Evolutionary Process. In *Style, Function, Transmission: Evolutionary Archaeological Perspectives*, edited by Michael J. O'Brien and R. Lee Lyman, pp. 33–52. Salt Lake City: University of Utah Press.

Binnema, Theodore
2001 *Common and Contested Ground: A Human and Environmental History of the Northwestern Plains*. Norman: University of Oklahoma Press.

Brink, Jack W., Milt Wright, Bob Dawe, and Doug Glaum
1985   *Final Report of the 1983 Season at Head-Smashed-In Buffalo Jump, Alberta*. Archaeological Survey of Alberta Manuscript Series No. 1. Edmonton: Alberta Culture.

Brumley, John H.
1975   *The Cactus Flower Site in Southeastern Alberta: 1972–1974 Excavations*. Mercury Series, Archeological Survey of Canada, Paper No. 55. Ottawa, Ontario: National Museum of Man.

Brumley, John H., and Barry J. Dau
1988   *Historical Resource Investigations within the Forty Mile Coulee Reservoir*. Archaeological Survey of Alberta Manuscript Series No. 13. Edmonton: Alberta Culture.

Clark, Geoffrey A.
1994   Migration as an Explanatory Concept in Paleolithic Archaeology. *Journal of Archaeological Method and Theory* 1:305–343.

David, Nicholas, Kodzo Gavua, A. Scott MacEachern, and Judy Sterner
1991   Ethnicity and Material Culture in North Cameroon. *Canadian Journal of Archaeology* 15:171–177.

Dumond, Don E.
1998   The Archaeology of Migrations: Following the Fainter Footprints. *Arctic Anthropology* 35(2):59–76.

Dunnell, Robert C.
1971   *Systematics in Prehistory*. New York: Free Press.
1978   Style and Function: A Fundamental Dichotomy. *American Antiquity* 43(2):192–202.
1982   Science, Social Science and Common Sense: The Agonizing Dilemma of Modern Archaeology. *Journal of Anthropological Research* 38(1):1–25.
1986   Methodological Issues in Americanist Artifact Classification. *Advances in Archaeological Method and Theory* 9:9–207. New York: Academic Press.

Dyck, Ian G.
1983   The Prehistory of Southern Saskatchewan. In *Tracking Ancient Hunters: Prehistoric Archaeology in Saskatchewan*, edited by Henry Epp and Ian Dyck, pp. 63–139. Regina: Saskatchewan Archaeological Society.

Dyck, Ian, and Richard G. Morlan
1995   *The Sjovold Site: A River Crossing Campsite in the Northern Plains*. Mercury Series, Archaeological Survey of Canada, Paper No. 151. Hull, Ottawa: Canadian Museum of Civilization.

Forbis, Richard G.
1962   The Old Women's Buffalo Jump, Alberta. *National Museum of Canada Bulletin* 180, Part 1:56–123. Ottawa, Ontario: National Museum of Canada.
1977   *Cluny: An Ancient Fortified Village in Alberta*. Occasional Paper No. 4. Calgary, Alberta: Department of Archaeology, University of Calgary.
1992   The Mesoindian (Archaic) Period in the Northern Plains. *Revista de Arqueología Americana* 5:27–70.

Härke, Heinrich
1998   Archaeologists and Migration. *Current Anthropology* 39(1):19–45.

Husted, Wilfred M.
1969   *Bighorn Canyon Archaeology*. River Basin Survey Publications in Salvage Archaeology No. 12. Lincoln, Nebraska: Smithsonian Institution.

Kehoe, Thomas F.
1966   The Small Side-Notched Point System of the Northern Plains. *American Antiquity* 31(6): 827–841.

1973 *The Gull Lake Site: A Prehistoric Bison Drive Site in Southwestern Saskatchewan.* Publications in Anthropology and History No. 1. Milwaukee, Wisconsin: Milwaukee Public Museum.

Kooyman, Brian, Leonard V. Hills, Paul McNeil, and Shayne Tolman
2006 Late Pleistocene Horse Hunting at the Wally's Beach Site (DhPg-8), Canada. *American Antiquity* 71(1):101–121.

Lipo, Carl P., Mark E. Madsen, Robert C. Dunnell, and Tim Hunt
1997 Population Structure, Cultural Transmission, and Frequency Seriation. *Journal of Anthropological Archaeology* 16(4):301–334.

Lucas, Gavin
2001 *Critical Approaches to Fieldwork: Contemporary and Historical Archaeological Practice.* London: Routledge.

Lyman, R. Lee, Todd L. VanPool, and Michael J. O'Brien
2008 Variation in North American Dart Points and Arrow Points When One or Both Are Present. *Journal of Archaeological Science* 35(10):2805–2812.

Lyman, R. Lee, Steve Wolverton, and Michael J. O'Brien
1998 Seriation, Superposition, and Interdigitation: A History of Americanist Graphic Depictions of Culture Change. *American Antiquity* 63(2):239–261.

MacNeish, Richard S.
1954 The Stott Mound and Village, near Brandon, Manitoba. Annual Report of the National Museum of Canada for the Fiscal Year 1952–53. *National Museum of Canada Bulletin* 132:20–65.

Matson, R. G., and Martin P. R. Magne
2007 *Athapaskan Migrations: The Archaeology of Eagle Lake, British Columbia.* Tucson: University of Arizona Press. http://www.anth.ubc.ca/fileadmin/user_upload/anso/LOA_PDFs/Matson_2007/AppendixIc.pdf.

Mayer-Oakes, William J.
1959 Relationship between Plains Early Hunter and Eastern Archaic. *Journal of the Washington Academy of Sciences* 49(5):46–156.

O'Brien, Michael J., John Darwent, and R. Lee Lyman
2001 Cladistics Is Useful for Reconstructing Archaeological Phylogenies: Palaeoindian Points from the Southeastern United States. *Journal of Archaeological Science* 28(10):1115–1136.

O'Brien, Michael J., and R. Lee Lyman
2000 *Applying Evolutionary Archaeology: A Systematic Approach.* New York: Kluwer Academic/Plenum Press.

O'Brien, Michael J., R. Lee Lyman, John Darwent, and Daniel S. Glover
2003 Cladistics and Archaeology: Taxa, Characters, and Outgroups. In *Style, Function, Transmission: Evolutionary Archaeological Perspectives*, edited by Michael J. O'Brien and R. Lee Lyman, pp. 125–166. Salt Lake City: University of Utah Press.

Peck, Trevor R.
1996 Late Side-Notched Projectile Points on the Northwestern Plains. Unpublished Master's thesis, Department of Anthropology, University of Alberta, Edmonton.

Peck, Trevor R., and Jack W. Ives
2001 Late Side-Notched Projectile Points on the Northwestern Plains. *Plains Anthropologist* 46(176):163–193.

Reeves, Brian O. K.
1969 The Southern Alberta Paleo-Cultural-Paleo-Environmental Sequence. In *Post-*

Pleistocene Man and His Environment on the Northern Plains, edited by Richard G. Forbis, Leslie B. Davis, Ole A. Christensen, and Gloria Fedirichuk, pp. 6–46. Calgary, Alberta: Calgary Archaeological Association.

1983 *Culture Change in the Northern Plains: 1000 BC–AD 1000*. Archaeological Survey of Alberta Occasional Paper 20. Edmonton: Alberta Community Development.

Robertson, Elizabeth

2004 Communal Hunting as a Social Model for the Paleoindian to Early Archaic Transition on the Plains. In *Archaeology on the Edge: New Perspectives from the Northern Plains*, edited by Brian Kooyman and Jane Kelley, pp. 211–229. Calgary, Alberta: University of Calgary Press.

Rouse, Irving

1986 *Migrations in Prehistory: Inferring Population Movement from Cultural Remains*. New Haven, Connecticut: Yale University Press.

SPSS

2000 *SYSTAT 10*. Chicago: SPSS, Inc.

Spurling, Brian E., and Bruce F. Ball

1981 On Some Distributions of the Oxbow "Complex." *Canadian Journal of Archaeology* 5:89–101.

Syms, E. Leigh

1970 The McKean Complex in Manitoba. In *Ten Thousand Years: Archaeology in Manitoba*, edited by Walter M. Hlady, pp. 123–138. Winnipeg: Manitoba Archaeological Society.

Syms, E. Leigh

1977 *Cultural Ecology and Ecological Dynamics of the Ceramic Period in Southwestern Manitoba*. Memoir No. 12. *Plains Anthropologist* 22(76, Pt. 2).

Toom, Dennis L., and Michael A. Jackson

2001 Discussion and Conclusions. In *Besant-Sonota on the Little Missouri River: The Doaks Butte site (32BO222), Bowman County, North Dakota*, 2 vols., edited by Dennis L. Toom, 1:14.1–14.8. Anthropology Research Contribution No. 362. Grand Forks: University of North Dakota.

Vickers, J. Roderick

1986 *Alberta Plains Prehistory: A Review*. Archaeological Survey of Alberta Occasional Paper No. 27. Edmonton: Alberta Culture Historical Resources Division.

Walde, Dale

1994 The Mortlach Phase. Unpublished Ph.D. dissertation, Department of Archaeology, University of Calgary, Calgary, Alberta.

2003 *The Mortlach Phase*. Occasional Papers No. 2. Calgary: Archaeological Society of Alberta.

2006a Avonlea and Athabaskan Migrations: A Reconsideration. *Plains Anthropologist* 51(198):185–197.

2006b *A Descriptive Analysis of Little Bow Ceramic Assemblages*. Report to FMA Heritage Resources Consultants. On file at FMA Heritage Resources Consultants, Calgary, Alberta.

2006c Sedentism and Pre-contact Tribal Organization on the Northern Plains: Colonial Imposition or Indigenous Development? *World Archaeology* 38(2):291–310.

Walde, Dale, and David Meyer

2003 Precontact Pottery in Alberta: An Overview. In *Archaeology in Alberta: A View from the New Millennium*, edited by Jack W. Brink and John F. Dormaar, pp. 132–152. Medicine Hat: Archaeological Society of Alberta.

Walde, Dale, David Meyer, and Wendy Unfreed
1995   The Late Period on the Canadian and Adjacent Plains. *Revista de Arqueología Americana* 9:7–66.

Walker, Ernest G.
1992   *The Gowen Sites: Cultural Responses to Climatic Warming on the Northern Plains (7500–5000 BP)*. Mercury Series, Archaeological Survey of Canada, Paper No. 145. Hull, Ottawa: Canadian Museum of Civilization.

Wettlaufer, Boyd N.
1955   *The Mortlach Site in the Besant Valley of Central Saskatchewan*. Anthropological Series No. 1. Regina: Saskatchewan Museum of Natural History.

Wettlaufer, Boyd N., and William J. Mayer-Oakes
1960   *The Long Creek Site*. Anthropological Series No. 2. Regina: Saskatchewan Department of Natural Resources.

CHAPTER 10

Variation in the Production of Ceramics by Athapaskans in the Western United States

David V. Hill

Ceramics have been used as an indicator of the presence of Athapaskans in the Southwest. In this chapter I show that our current conceptual and methodological tools are inadequate for identifying one aspect of material culture that has been presented for recognizing Athapaskans in the archaeological record and propose more appropriate methods to address the issue. Two problems hinder our ability to identify early Athapaskan pottery in archaeological contexts.

- Previous classification schemes for describing pottery produced by Athapaskans and mobile people in general often do not attempt to understand the materials and processes that produce the attributes that are recorded.
- The effect of long-term social interaction between contemporary peoples has not been adequately taken into account.

By taking an explicit analytical approach that focuses on methods that identify the sources of variability in the ceramics recovered from Athapaskan and other protohistoric sites on the southern Great Plains, the Colorado Mountains, and the Greater Southwest, we can work toward reliably comparing ceramic assemblages (Figure 10.1). It is only through the creation of analytically comparable units that we can examine the technological variability that is presented to us in the archaeological record.

Pottery classification systems that have been developed over the last century in the U.S. Southwest have focused on the variability in ceramics made primarily by settled peoples. The ways in which mobile groups make and use pottery differ substantially from those of sedentary groups (Bright and Ugan 1999; Hill 2006; Hoopes and Barnett 1995; Jordan and Zvelebil 2009). Our lack of understanding of the sources of variation in the use of raw materials and of the forming technologies that contribute to our classification systems has confounded our ability to identify social groups in the archaeological record (Middleton

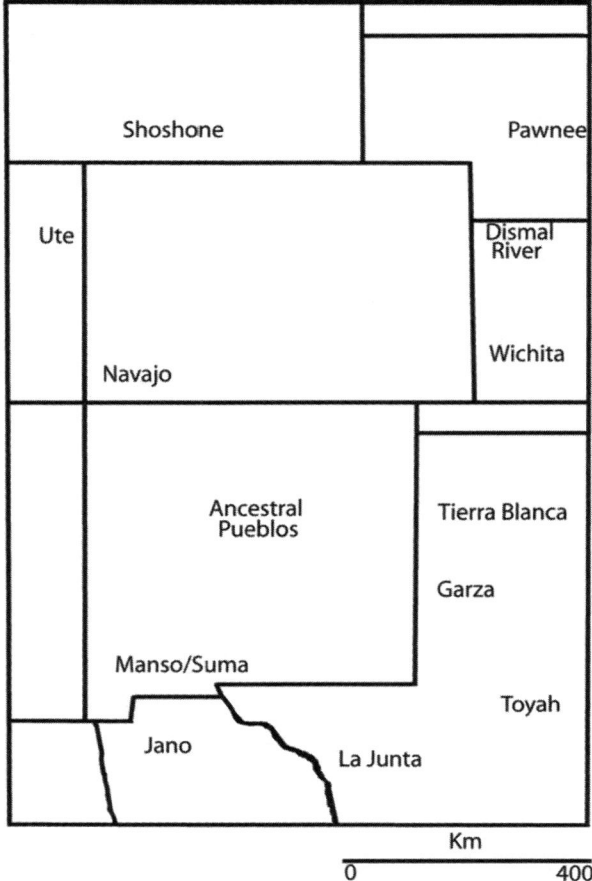

FIGURE 10.1. Selected cultural groups and archaeological complexes in the southern Great Plains during the late prehistoric and early historic periods. Image by David Hill.

et al. 2007; Seymour 2008). The following discussion focuses on the properties of different types of clay and the potential effects different technologies used to form ceramic vessels have on their appearance. Differences in ceramic technologies are also explored in light of ethnographic and archaeological data derived primarily from the U.S. Southwest and contemporary protohistoric archaeological cultures, some of which have been attributed to Athapaskans.

Qualities of Raw Materials: Effects on the Appearance of Pottery

The major function of pottery for hunting-and-gathering people is for the preparation of food. Foods such as dried meat and seeds need to be broken down to provide nutrients to the very young and very old, who lack the dentition to consume hard foods (Reid 1989). In this case, cooking is about providing heat to a vessel to raise the temperature of its liquid contents, and thus vessels with a large amount of surface area would be the most efficient for cooking (Skibo et al. 1989).

Vessels used in cooking tend to have similar overall forms. The raw materials used to produce ceramic vessels profoundly affect the appearance of the finished product. Cooking vessels are usually constructed of clays with coarser-grained natural or added inclusions that result in uneven surfaces, or in archaeological parlance, "crude" vessels (Arnold 1985). "Crude" also tends to equate with "little-studied."

One aspect that frequently goes unrecognized in the study of the ceramics of hunter-gatherers is the physical characteristics of raw materials used to produce vessels. Natural clays have a wide range of physical properties, including plasticity, shrinkage, and the ability to be polished (Rice 1987). Smectites, or three-layer clays, are characterized by the small size of their mineral structure, high plasticity, high rate of shrinkage, and low luster. Smectite clays are most common in fluvial and lacustrine environments. Two-layer clays, such as illite and kaolinite, have larger mineral structures, lower shrinkage rates, variable plasticity, and a natural luster, and can be used for pottery slips (Rice 1987). Because of these characteristics, illitic and kaolinitic clays can be used to produce the long rope-like coils that are used to make the pottery of the Pueblo region of the Greater Southwest. Illitic and kaolinitic clays can also be polished and used as slips. Smectites can be easily molded but, because of the fineness of their mineral structures, only into small structural elements. In such cases, vessels have to be constructed with short sections or overlapping patches of clay (Fewkes 1940; Vandiver 1987). As a result of differences in the physical properties of different clays, it is possible that different manufacturing techniques, such as the use of paddle-and-anvil and coil-and-scrape, could reflect behavioral responses to the physical characteristics of clays.

Some researchers suggest that ceramic vessels made by hunting-and-gathering peoples in the Great Basin lack a smooth finish as a result of the group's highly mobile lifestyle (Simms et al. 1997). Because of high group mobility, vessels were produced in an expedient manner and such steps as smoothing were omitted. Yet vessels made with smectite-rich clays cannot be as well smoothed or polished as ceramics made with illitic and kaolinitic clays. Thus it is also just as possible that the lack of a smooth surface in Great Basin vessels is the result of the use of clays with a smectitic composition. In this case, the clay itself would inhibit the formation of a smooth surface through polishing.

Mineral inclusions are another aspect of the appearance of ceramics that is controlled by raw materials. With the advent of resource surveys conducted in the context of technological studies of ceramics in the Southwest, the presence of a possible added temper is now a research issue rather than a given condition (Hill 2006, 2009; also see Shepard 1964). Petrographic studies that were supported by resource surveys of local clays and sediments have found that Ancestral Pueblo and Navajo ceramics that would previously have been described as tempered were made using clays that contain sediments as a natural constituent (Hill 1995, 1996; Wilson 1999).

Ceramics produced by mobile peoples are made with a variety of materials. Sedentary peoples tend to obtain their clays within 7 km of their settlements (Arnold 1985:109). For mobile peoples, the choice of ceramic resources is much more open. While moving across the landscape, mobile peoples become familiar with a wider number of clay resources and their physical properties. Consequently, the pottery made by mobile peoples is likely to reflect this flexibility in the choice of clay, resulting in increased variability in the composition of ceramics recovered from archaeological contexts (Seymour 2008). For example, the Shivwits, a mobile Paiute group resident in southwestern Utah, used two primary clay sources, one located just south of their reservation and the other near the Colorado River (Lowie 1924). Ceramics produced by the same group of Shivwits Paiute would appear to represent different pottery types: those made with clays from the uplands near Shivwits, Utah, have a less smooth appearance than those made with clays from the Colorado River. Without additional information regarding seasonal movement and the qualities of the two clay sources, the two types of pottery would likely be assigned to two different Paiute groups, to different time periods, or to other pottery-producing peoples.

Petrographic analysis and neutron activation analysis combined with field examinations of raw materials can aid in the identification of potential sources for archaeological ceramics. Petrographic analysis of ceramics collected from 5GF308, a multicomponent Ute site located near Rifle, in northwestern Colorado, and occupied during the late nineteenth century, identified both highly micaceous and nonmicaceous pastes in the ceramics. The two types of pottery were produced with similar construction techniques, including smoothing the vessel surfaces by scraping with a tree branch, resulting in deep parallel striations on the exterior of the sherds (Hill 1987). So even though ceramics produced by Ute potters may have differed in composition, they shared forming and shaping technologies. Such commonalities in ceramic technology could serve in the future to differentiate Athapaskan pottery from ceramics made by other contemporary peoples.

When choosing the attributes that are used to define specific ceramic types, archaeologists need to understand the sources of variability that distinguish their types. The presence of mica in the pastes of ceramics from the Colorado Front Range and western Nebraska and Kansas has been attributed to the Dismal River aspect and afforded the ceramic types Lovitt Plain and Lovitt Mica Tempered (Brunswig, this volume; Gunnerson 1960:247). Despite its low hardness and good cleavage, mica is a very durable mineral in sediments. Mica is elastic, and because of its flaky shape it can move around harder mineral grains during transport (Folk 1974:87). The continued attribution of sherds from Rocky Mountain National Park and the Colorado Front Range that contain mica as Dismal River–type Lovett Plain (Brunswig, this volume) ignores the fact that mica is found in the local sediments derived from the granites present throughout the Rocky Mountains of Colorado. Consequently, many sources of pedogenic and alluvial clays found in central or eastern Colorado contain at least a trace of mica. Because of the abundance of mica in the environment, virtually any pottery made in the Rocky Mountains or on their eastern flanks that contains mica could potentially be classified as a variety of Dismal River pottery. It is this sort of classificatory "lumping" that inhibits our ability to examine one source of variability in the archaeological record of this region. Future studies of ceramics from possible Athapaskan sites in Colorado should include comparison of the recovered ceramics with fired samples of local clays so as to identify ceramics that may have been made on the site as opposed to vessels brought from elsewhere.

Petrographic analysis of Apache and non-Apache pottery from the Cerro Rojo site (LA 37188) reported that while considerable variation was observed in the amount, size, and content of the inclusions, observed sherds that were classified as Apache were made with clays that could have been collected in the nearby environment (Hill 2002; Seymour 2008). The Apache ceramics could be distinguished from other undecorated pottery on the site that had been obtained from contemporary indigenous peoples in the region through trade or raiding (Seymour 2002).

Manufacturing Techniques and Their Effect on Clay

Not only do different types of clay exhibit different characteristics during smoothing, but specific manufacturing techniques may be needed to adjust to the requirements of the clay. Smectitic clays, for example, are sticky, and different methods of ceramic manufacture have been developed to address the sticky surface of vessels during construction. One of these, the paddle-and-anvil technique used to thin the walls of ceramic vessels, is common in the Great Plains and portions of the Greater Southwest (Gifford 1928). Potters often facilitated paddle-and-anvil technology by wrapping some material such as cordage around the wooden paddle or perhaps carving the surface with decorative patterns so that only small areas of the paddle were pressed against the surface at any one time (Fewkes 1940). In dry climates or with less sticky clays, a smooth paddle may have been used (Fontana et al. 1962). After hand smoothing, the results of paddling on the surface of a vessel would often be obliterated.

There has been little interest by archaeologists working on the Southern Plains in understanding how the ceramics they study were formed. Simple-stamping, so called because of the parallel impressions present on the exterior surfaces of vessels, likely indicates that the ceramics were made with the paddle-and-anvil technique. Simple-stamped impressions are observed from culturally distinct contemporary peoples, such as the Wichita of south-central Kansas (Figure 10.2) and the Dismal River culture (Figure 10.3), believed to represent an ancestral Athapaskan population (Gunnerson 1960; Wedel 1959). However, not all scholars accept that the Dismal River archaeological culture represents the presence of Apache (Opler 1983). A recent reexamination of Dismal River archaeology indicates that the extreme variation in site types, subsistence, mobility, and

FIGURE 10.2. Great Bend aspect, late prehistoric Wichita vessel from the Kendall-Shaw site. The vertical ridging on the vessel is caused by simple-stamping. Photograph used with permission of the Department of Anthropology at Wichita State University.

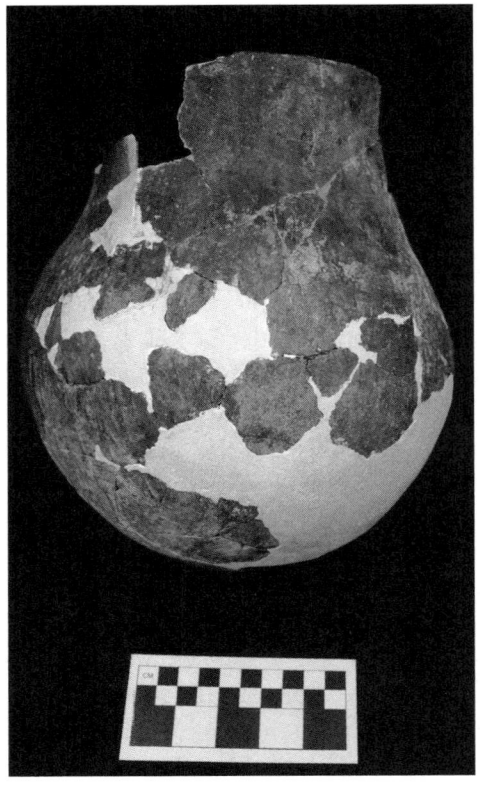

FIGURE 10.3. Ceramic vessel from 14SC01, the type site of the Dismal River ceramic type. The surface of this vessel bears the same kind of parallel impressions as those present on the vessel in Figure 10.2, indicating that the vessel was also smoothed by simple-stamping. Photograph used with permission of the Department of Anthropology at Wichita State University.

FIGURE 10.4. Ceramic vessel from 14SC01. The surface of this vessel has been smoothed, obliterating the visible presence of marks left by simple-stamping, yet it is still considered a Dismal River type. Photograph used with permission of Robert Hoard, Kansas State Historical Society.

FIGURE 10.5. Isolated Apache vessel from Otero Mesa on McGregor Range, Fort Bliss, Texas. Observe the smooth surface and thick parallel ridges that encompass the middle and lower portion of the vessel that represent coil joins. Photograph by Deni Seymour.

material culture, specifically ceramics, has made the term meaningless as a classificatory unit (Gulley 2000:62). However, hand-smoothing during manufacture can easily remove the shallow parallel impressions of simple-stamping on a vessel from the surface of the pot. With little effort a potter could create different surface treatments that archaeologists would classify as different types, such as Simple-Stamped and Plain (Figure 10.4).

Navajo and Apache potters in the Southwestern United States form vessels using a coil-and-scrape technology (Gifford 1940; Hill 1937) (Figure 10.5).

Recently, it has been suggested that some Apache ceramics from southern Arizona and southern New Mexico were also produced with the paddle-and-anvil technique (Seymour 2008). Whether the regional differences in the manufacturing technologies used by Athapaskan potters in various parts of the Southwest result from differences in types of clay or reflect social factors such as exogamy and cross-cultural learning cannot be assessed without characterization of ceramic clays and accurate identification of manufacturing techniques.

X-raying ceramic vessels and large sherds is an appropriate but underutilized technique to determine how pottery vessels were made (Ellingson et al. 1988; Middleton 2005). Recent breakthroughs in imaging technology, such as at the High Resolution X-ray CT Facility at the University of Texas–Austin, have contributed to advances in geology, paleontology, and conservation science (see http://www.ctlab.geo.utexas.edu/index.php). Application of these types of advanced imaging technologies will improve our knowledge of how pottery was made.

Social Relationships between Contemporary Peoples

Athapaskans acquired ceramic technology sometime after their migration from what is now western Canada and Alaska. The mechanisms of where and how ceramic technology was transferred to Athapaskan groups before or after their arrival in the Greater Southwest need to be explored. Studies of the transfer of ceramic technology require an understanding not only of the sources of variation in the materials and techniques used by Athapaskans to produce pottery but also of the materials and technology of the peoples with whom they would have interacted.

Athapaskan groups in the Southwest and elsewhere are known to have developed a complex web of social relationships with adjacent cultures (Goss 1968; Hester 1962). The establishment and maintenance of these social relationships include a wide range of behaviors, among them trade, intermarriage, kidnapping, and the adoption of members from neighboring tribes (Seymour 2008). The result of Navajo interaction with Ancestral Pueblo peoples resulted in the Navajo's adoption of painted ceramic and masonry architecture and incorporation of Pueblo deities into their spiritual practice (Hester 1962). The appearance of colonial Spanish–style masonry architecture among the Jicarilla Apache is another case of Athapaskans borrowing from nearby cultures (Gunnerson 1969).

The mutualistic relationship between Athapaskans, Ancestral Pueblos, and Plains Caddo during the protohistoric period is also highlighted by ceramic studies conducted in the Texas Panhandle (Baugh 1984) (Figures 10.6 and 10.7). Two roughly contemporary protohistoric archaeological cultures have been identified there: Tierra Blanca and Garza. Various scholars have attributed at least one of these entities to the appearance of Apaches in Texas, while the other represents an extension of protohistoric Caddoan-speaking peoples onto the Plains (Baugh 1984, 1986; Boyd 1997, 2001; Habicht-Mauche 1992; Hughes, this

FIGURE 10.6. Garza complex (Apache) vessel, West Texas. Photograph by Judith A. Habicht-Mauche, Department of Anthropology, University of California, Santa Cruz.

FIGURE 10.7. Rim sherds from cooking jars from a fourteenth-century Ancestral Pueblo site located in Albuquerque, New Mexico. Note the similarity in form with that of the vessel in Figure 10.5. Photograph by Hayward Franklin.

volume). The presence at Tierra Blanca and Garza of small amounts of obsidian and lead-glazed pottery that originated in the Galisteo Basin, the Salinas Pueblos, and the Rio Grande Valley provides evidence for trade with Ancestral Pueblo people. Undecorated pottery recovered from Tierra Blanca and Garza affiliated sites in the Texas Panhandle was believed to represent indigenous, locally made products (Habicht-Mauche 1987, 1988; Hughes, this volume). An instrumental neutron activation analysis (INAA) study of ceramics recovered from sites attributed to the Tierra Blanca and Garza cultures found that there was considerable compositional overlap between plainwares of unknown origin and the redwares and glazewares presumed to have an origin in the Ancestral Pueblo communities (Boyd et al. 2002:118). It is highly unlikely that the Ancestral Pueblo–style glazewares and redwares were produced in West Texas. The compositional overlap of Ancestral Pueblo– and Plains-derived plainwares may be due to the similarity in the geology of eastern New Mexican and the Texas Panhandle (Boyd et al. 2002:119). It is also possible that the sample of Plains-derived sherds that were analyzed in this study represented such a high degree of compositional variability that the statistical techniques failed to assign individual sherds to different composition groups. To better control the potential number of sources involved, future petrographic and INAA studies of Tierra Blanca Plain and other types of protohistoric utility wares from the Texas Panhandle should focus on examining collections of likely Plains-derived ceramics from a limited number of sites before comparing the results with Ancestral Pueblo materials. Limiting the potential number of sources of ceramics will allow for the establishment of valid composition groups. These composition groups can then be compared with future technological studies of plainwares from the Texas Panhandle.

Social interaction and group exogamy can provide sources of variation in access to clay and in ceramic technology. Ethnographic research reported that in north-central New Mexico, Jicarilla Apaches and Pueblo peoples used the same source of clay for making pottery (Harrington 1916:581). Recent research has found that Utes living in southwestern Colorado likewise used the same source of micaceous clay for pottery making (Eiselt 2004). Ethnographic data collected from the Southern Ute shows that they "learned" how to make pottery from Tiwa-speaking Taos Pueblo (Stewart 1942; Opler 1939). "Learned," in this case, indicates intermarriage and/or access to the source of micaceous clay that was used by several contemporary ethnic groups. Consequently, we should be careful about assigning undecorated pottery, in this case micaceous plainware, to a specific ethnic group (Seymour 2008).

Conversely, considerable variability can exist within the ceramic technology of a single linguistically related group. Apaches living near Plains groups apparently used the paddle-and-anvil technique for thinning the walls of vessels, while Apachean groups living closer to the Pueblos produced vessels that were thinned by the coil-and-scrape method (Baugh and Eddy 1987; Seymour 2008). The formal and technological similarity of Apachean pottery to that of adjacent social groups is likely the result of group exogamy (Habicht-Mauche 2000).

Owing to the presence of contemporary hunting-and-gathering peoples who also produced pottery, the identification of ceramics that were produced by Athapaskans in Colorado is perhaps even more difficult. Mobile pottery-making peoples, such as the Ute, the Shoshone, and the Wichita and other Plains groups, were also present in the western Great Plains during the time of the entrance of Athapaskans into the Southwest (Downing 1981:Figure 4b; Haspel 1984; Mueller and Firor 2009; Reed 1994). Given the variations in overall vessel shapes and surface treatments exhibited by complete vessels that display a continuous base-to-rim profile and have been identified as Apache elsewhere (Ellwood 2002; Ferg 2004), assigning an individual site to an Athapaskan origin based on only a few body sherds is no longer tenable.

Rather than reject the identification of Athapaskans or other ethnic groups as the subject of archaeological inquiry, we should develop analytical techniques that are grounded in theory to examine how ethnic groups can be recognized in the archaeological record. Recent developments in the application of practice theory and the recognition of shared patterns of cultural learning in the production of pottery can be fruitfully applied to the identification of Athapaskan pottery from archaeological contexts (Dobres and Robb 2000:4–9; Jones 1997:87–92; Stark 2006). Culturally interacting potters who share a common learning network produce vessels that are characterized by the use of a common set of ceramic raw materials and construct vessels with similar forms and decoration (Seymour 2008). The notion of potters as members of a larger interacting community allows archaeologists to identify distinctive prehistoric social groups across the landscape and through time, by understanding the adoption(s) and development of ceramic technology by Athapaskans.

Conclusions

Ceramics made by hunting-and-gathering people need to be studied in a different way than those produced by more settled people (Seymour 2008). Unless we look for more creative ways to characterize pottery, we will not be able to understand how it was used by protohistoric peoples in the Southern Plains or to attribute a specific body of characteristics to a distinct ethnic population. By taking an approach that focuses on understanding the sources of variability in possible Athapaskan ceramics and their associated artifact assemblages, we can advance our ability to identify ethnic groups in the archaeological record. These types of studies need not wait for the "next possible Athapaskan site" but can be applied to collections from previously excavated sites. Previously excavated artifact assemblages can be reanalyzed: ceramics from museum and avocational collections can be x-rayed, thin-sectioned, sampled for neutron activation, and directly dated through such techniques as optically stimulated luminescence.

By examining the sources of raw materials and how those materials are combined, we can learn how and where ceramics were produced and how the physical qualities of those raw materials affect and constrain the types of forming technologies and surface treatments that can be used to create successful vessels. Before we approach trying to understand variability in ceramic technology at an intraregional level, we need to understand how pottery was produced at one site or a small sample of sites. Well-developed research strategies that focus on how and why Athapaskans adopted and used pottery in the Southern Plains and Greater Southwest will make a substantive contribution to anthropological theory and archaeological knowledge.

References

Arnold, Dean E.
1985 *Ceramic Theory and Cultural Process.* New York: Cambridge University Press.

Baugh, Timothy G.
1984 Southern Plains Societies and Eastern Frontier Pueblo Exchange during the Protohistoric Period. *Papers of the Archaeological Society of New Mexico* 9: 154–167.

1986 Culture History and Protohistoric Societies in the Southern Plains. In *Current Trends in Southern Plains Archaeology*, edited by Timothy G. Baugh, pp. 167–187. Memoir No. 21. *Plains Anthropologist* 31(114, Pt. 2).

Baugh, Timothy, and F. W. Eddy
1987 Rethinking Apachean Ceramics: The 1985 Southern Athapaskan Ceramics Conference. *American Antiquity* 52(4):793–799.

Boyd, Douglas K.
1997 *Caprock Canyonlands Archaeology: A Synthesis of the Late Prehistory and History of Lake Alan Henry and the Texas Panhandle-Plains.* Reports of Investigations No. 110, Vol. 2, pp. 337–486. Austin, Texas: Prewitt and Associates.

2001 Querechos and Teyas: Protohistoric Hunters and Gatherers in the Texas Panhandle-Plains, AD 1540–1700. *Bulletin of the Texas Archeological Society* 72: 5–22.

Boyd, Doug K., Kathryn Reese-Taylor, Hector Neff, and Michael D. Glascock
2002 Protohistoric Ceramics from the Texas Southern Plains: Documenting Plains-Pueblo Interaction. In *Ceramic Production and Circulation in the Greater Southwest: Source Determination by INAA and Complementary Mineralogical Investigations*, edited by Donna M. Glowacki and Hector Neff, pp. 14–151. Cotsen Institute of Archaeology Monograph No. 44. Los Angeles: University of California.

Bright, Jason R., and Andrew Ugan
1999 Ceramics and Mobility: Assessing the Role of Foraging Behavior and Its Implications for Culture-History. *Utah Archaeology* 12:17–30.

Dobres, M. A., and J. E. Robb
2000 Agency in Archaeology: Paradigm or Platitude? In *Agency in Archaeology*, edited by M. A. Dobres and J. E. Robb, pp. 3–18. London: Routledge.

Downing, Barbara J.
1981 A Re-analysis of Old Archaeological Collections: The Renaud Collection. Unpublished Master's thesis, Department of Anthropology, University of Denver, Denver, Colorado.

Eiselt, Bernice Sunday
2004 Historic Micaceous Pottery Production and Raw Material Procurement in a Southwestern Horse Nomad Society: The Jicarilla Apache of Northern New Mexico. Paper presented at the 69th Annual Meeting of the Society for American Archaeology, Montreal.

Ellingson, William A., Pamela B. Vandiver, Thomas K. Robinson, and John J. Lobick
1988 Radiographic Imaging Technologies for Archaeological Ceramics. In *Materials Issues in Art and Archaeology*, edited by Edward V. Sayre, Pamela B. Vandiver, James Druzik, and Christopher Stevenson, pp. 25–32. Symposium Proceedings Vol. 123. Pittsburgh: Materials Research Society.

Ellwood, Priscilla B.
2002 *Native American Ceramics of Eastern Colorado.* Natural History Inventory of Colorado No. 21. Boulder: University of Colorado Museum.

Ferg, Alan
2004 *An Introduction to Chiricahua and Mescalero Apache Pottery.* Arizona Archaeologist No. 35. Phoenix: Arizona Archaeological Society.

Fewkes, Vladimir, J.
1940 Methods of Pottery Making. *American Antiquity* 6(2):172–173.

Folk, Robert L.
1974 *Petrology of Sedimentary Rocks.* Austin, Texas: Hemphill.

Fontana, Bernard L., William J. Robinson, Charles W. Cormack, and Ernest E. Leavitt Jr.
1962 *Papago Indian Pottery.* Seattle: University of Washington Press.

Gifford, Edward W.
1928 Pottery Making in the Southwest. *University of California Publications in American Archaeology and Ethnology* 23(8):353–373.
1940 *Culture Element Distributions, XVII: Apache-Pueblo.* Anthropological Records Vol. 4, No. 1. Berkeley: University of California Press.

Goss, James A.
1968 Culture-Historical Inference from Utazteckan Linguistic Evidence. In *Utazteckan Prehistory*, edited by Earl H. Swanson, pp. 1–42. Occasional Papers No. 22. Pocatello: Idaho State Museum.

Gulley, Cara C.
2000 A Reanalysis of Dismal River Archaeology and Ceramic Typology. Unpublished Master's thesis. Boulder: Department of Anthropology, University of Colorado.

Gunnerson, James H.
1960 *An Introduction to Plains Apache Archeology—The Dismal River Aspect.* Anthropological Papers No. 58, Bureau of American Ethnology Bulletin No. 173, pp. 131–260. Washington, D.C.: Smithsonian Institution.
1969 Apache Archaeology in Northeastern New Mexico. *American Antiquity* 34(1): 23–39.

Habicht-Mauche, Judith A.
1987 Southwestern-Style Culinary Ceramics on the Southern Plains: A Case Study of Technological Innovation and Cross-Cultural Interaction. *Plains Anthropologist* 32(116):175–191.
1988 An Analysis of Southwestern Style Ceramics from the Southern Plains in the Context of Plains-Pueblo Interaction. Unpublished Ph.D. dissertation, Department of Anthropology, Harvard University, Cambridge, Massachusetts.
1992 Coronado's Querechos and Teyas in the Archaeological Record of the Texas Panhandle. *Plains Anthropologist* 37(140):247–259.
2000 Pottery, Food, Hides, and Women: Labor, Production, and Exchange across the Protohistoric Plains-Pueblo Frontier. In *The Archaeology of Regional Interaction: Religion, Warfare, and Exchange across the American Southwest and Beyond*, edited by Michelle Hegmon, pp. 209–231. Boulder: University Press of Colorado.

Hancock, Patricia M.
1997 Dendrochronological Dates from the Dinétah. Paper presented at the 1997 Pecos Conference, Chaco Canyon National Park, New Mexico.

Harrington, John P.
1916 *The Ethnogeography of the Tewa Indians.* Twenty-ninth Annual Report of the Bureau of American Ethnology. Washington, D.C.: Smithsonian Institution.

Haspel, Howard
1984 The Study of Shoshonean Ceramics from Wyoming: The Bugas-Holding Ceramic Assemblage. *Wyoming Archaeologist* 27(3–4):25–40.

Hester, James J.
1962 *Early Navajo Migrations and Acculturation in the Southwest.* Museum of New Mexico Papers in Anthropology No. 6. Santa Fe: Museum of New Mexico Press.

Hill, David V.
1987 Petrographic Analysis of Selected Ceramics from 5GF308 (Squaw's Camp). Ms. on file, Bureau of Land Management, Glenwood Springs, Colorado.
1995 Appendix 2: Petrographic Analysis of Ceramics and Clay Samples from Eight Gobernador Phase Sites in Northwestern New Mexico. In *A Chapter in Early Navajo History: Late Gobernador Phase Pueblito Sites of the Dinetah*, assembled by Michael P. Marshall. Albuquerque: Office of Contract Archeology, University of New Mexico.
1996 Appendix I: Petrographic Analysis of Ceramics and Clay Samples from Las Campanas and Elsewhere in the Santa Fe Area. In *Las Campanas de Santa Fe Sunset Golf Course, and Estates IV, Estates V, and Estates VII Excavations: Small Sites in the Piñon-Juniper Piedmont North of the Santa Fe River, Santa Fe County, New Mexico*, by Stephen S. Post. Archaeology Notes No. 193. Santa Fe: Office of Archaeological Studies, Museum of New Mexico.
2002 Appendix C: Ceramic Compositional Studies. In *Conquest and Concealment: After the El Paso Phase on Fort Bliss: An Archaeological Study of the Manso, Suma, and Early Apache*, by Deni J. Seymour. Fort Bliss, Texas: Conservation Division, Directorate of the Environment, United States Army Air Defense Artillery Center.
2006 Theoretical and Methodological Approaches to the Study of the Ceramics of Protohistoric Hunter-Gatherers. Paper presented at the Mogollon Conference, Tucson, Arizona.
2009 Regional Mobility and the Sources of Ceramics Recovered in Southeastern New Mexico and West Texas. Paper presented at the 74th Annual Meeting of the Society for American Archaeology, Atlanta.

Hill, W. W.
1937 *Navajo Pottery Manufacture.* University of New Mexico Bulletin, Anthropological Series, Vol. 2, No. 3; Whole No. 317. Albuquerque: University of New Mexico.

Hoopes, John W., and William K. Barnett
1995 The Shape of Early Pottery Studies. In *The Emergence of Pottery: Technology and Innovation in Ancient Societies*, edited by William K. Barnett and John W. Hoopes, pp. 1–7. Washington, D.C.: Smithsonian Institution.

Jones, Sian
1997 *The Archaeology of Ethnicity.* London: Routledge.

Jordan, Peter, and Marek Zvelebil
2009 *Ex Oriente Lux*: The Prehistory of Hunter-Gatherer Ceramic Dispersals. In *Ceramics before Farming*, edited by Peter Jordan and Marek Zvelebil, pp. 33–90. Walnut Creek, California: Left Coast Press.

Lowie, Robert H.
1924 *Notes on Shoshonean Ethnography.* Anthropological Papers Vol. 20, Pt. 3. New York: American Museum of Natural History.

Middleton, Andrew
2005 Ceramics. In *Radiography of Cultural Material*, 2nd ed., edited by Janet Lang and Andrew Middleton, pp. 76–95. Oxford: Elsevier Butterworth-Heinemann.

Middleton, Jessica L., Patrick M. Lubinski, and Michael D. Metcalf
2007 Ceramics from the Firehole Basin Site and Firehole Phase in the Wyoming Basin. *Plains Anthropologist* 52(201):29–41.

Mueller, Jenn, and James Firor
2009 Excavations at the Long Knife Site (5MF5827). In *The Rockies Express Pipeline Archaeological Data Recovery Project, Moffat County, Colorado*, Vol. 5, edited by Alan D. Reed. Montrose, Colorado: Alpine Archaeological Consultants.

Opler, Marvin K.
1939 Southern Ute Pottery Types. *Masterkey* 13:161–163. Los Angeles: Southwest Museum.

Opler, Morris E.
1983 The Apachean Culture Pattern and Its Origins. In *Southwest*, edited by Alfonso Ortiz, pp. 368–392. Handbook of North American Indians, Vol. 10, William C. Sturtevant, general editor. Washington, D.C.: Smithsonian Institution.

Reed, Alan D.
1994 Numic Occupation of Western Colorado and Eastern Utah during the Prehistoric and Protohistoric Periods. In *Across the West: Human Population Movement and the Expansion of the Numa*, edited by David B. Madsen and David Rhode, pp. 188–199. Salt Lake City: University of Utah Press.

Reid, Kenneth C.
1989 A Materials Science Perspective on Hunter-Gatherer Pottery. In *Pottery Technology: Ideas and Approaches*, edited by Gordon Bronitsky, pp. 167–180. Boulder, Colorado: Westview Press.

Rice, Prudence M.
1987 *Pottery Analysis: A Sourcebook*. Chicago: University of Chicago Press.

Rogers, Malcolm J.
1936 *Yuman Pottery Making*. Papers No. 2. San Diego, California: San Diego Museum of Man.

Seymour, Deni J.
2002 *Conquest and Concealment: After the El Paso Phase on Fort Bliss; An Archaeological Study of the Manso, Suma, and Early Apache*. With contributions by Mark E. Harlan and David V. Hill. Lone Mountain Report 525/528. Conservation Division, Directorate of the Environment, United States Army Air Defense, Artillery Center, Fort Bliss, Texas. Qualified researchers may obtain this document by contacting martha.yduarte@us.army.mil.
2003 *Protohistoric and Early Historic Temporal Resolution*. Lone Mountain Report 560-003. Conservation Division, Directorate of the Environment, Fort Bliss. Qualified researchers may obtain this document by contacting martha.yduarte@us.army.mil.
2008 Apache Plain and Other Plainwares on Apache Sites in the Southern Southwest. In *Serendipity: Papers in Honor of Frances Joan Mathien*, edited by R. N. Wiseman, T. C. O'Laughlin, C. T. Snow, and C. Travis, pp. 163–186. Papers No. 34. Albuquerque: Archaeological Society of New Mexico.
2009 Manso Tipis and Other Non Sequiturs Relating to the Protohistoric Southwest. In *Proceedings of the 2007 Jornada Mogollon Conference*. El Paso, Texas.

Shepard, Anna O.
1964 Temper Identification: "Technological Sherd-Splitting" or an Unanswered Challenge. *American Antiquity* 29(4): 518–520.

Simms, Steven R., Jason R. Bright, and Andrew Ugan
1997 Plain-Ware Ceramics and Residential Mobility: A Case Study from the Great Basin. *Journal of Archaeological Science* 24:779–792.

Skibo, James M., Michael B. Schiffer, and Kenneth C. Reid
1989 Organic Tempered Pottery: An Experimental Study. *American Antiquity* 54(1): 122–146.

Stark, Miriam T.
2006 Glazeware Technology, Social Lives of Pots, and Communities of Practice in the Late Prehistoric Southwest. In *The Social Life of Pots: Glaze Wares and Cultural Dynamics in the Southwest, AD 1250–1680*, edited by Judith Habicht-Mauche, Suzanne L. Eckert, and Deborah L. Huntley, pp. 17–33. Tucson: University of Arizona Press.

Stewart, Omer C.
1942 *Culture Element Distributions, XVII: Ute-Southern Paiute.* Anthropological Records Vol. 6, No. 4. Berkeley: University of California Press.

Vandiver, Pamela B.
1987 Sequential Slab Construction: A Conservative Southwest Asiatic Ceramics Tradition, ca. 7000–3000 BC *Paleorient* 13(2):9–35.

Wedel, Waldo R.
1959 *An Introduction to Kansas Archeology.* Bureau of American Ethnology Bulletin No. 174. Washington, D.C.: Smithsonian Institution.

Wilson, C. Dean
1999 Ceramic Trends at Luna Project Sites. In *Archaeology of the Mogollon Highlands: Settlement Systems and Adaptations, Vol. 4: Ceramics, Miscellaneous Artifacts, Bioarchaeology, Bone Tools, and Faunal Analysis*, edited by Yvonne R. Oakes and Dorothy A. Zamora, pp. 139–172. Archaeology Notes No. 232. Santa Fe: Office of Archaeological Studies, Museum of New Mexico.

CHAPTER 11

DNA Evidence of a Prehistoric Athapaskan Migration from the Subarctic to the Southwest of North America

RIPAN S. MALHI

The geographic distribution of the Athapaskan language family in North America is hypothesized to have resulted from long-distance population movements (Goddard 1996). Specifically, Hoijer (1956) hypothesized that the proto-Athapaskan homeland was in the Subarctic and that the distribution of Athapaskan languages along the Pacific coast and in the Southwest was the result of recent migrations. The Southern Athapaskans are widely dispersed throughout the central region of the Southwest and speak languages that are closely related to Chipewyan, an Athapaskan language found in the Subarctic (Hoijer 1956). However, genetic studies of Southern Athapaskans are mainly based on the analysis of only two groups, the Navajo and Western Apache. Future sampling and studies of Jicarilla, Lipan, Mescalero, and Chiricahua Apaches are needed to provide a complete understanding of the genetic diversity and structure of Southern Athapaskans.

Multiple genetic systems have been used to test the hypothesis of migration of Athapaskans from the Subarctic to the Southwest, or the classic Southern Athapaskan migration hypothesis (Smith et al. 2000; Malhi et al. 2003; Hunley and Long 2005; Malhi et al. 2008). In this chapter, I provide an overview of the genetic systems used and inferences of the genetic data evaluating the Southern Athapaskan migration hypothesis. The genetic data support two main inferences about the Southern Athapaskan migration: (1) the migration from the Subarctic to the American Southwest was likely accomplished by a small group of individuals; (2) Athapaskans absorbed non-Athapaskan individuals after the migration to the Southwest (Dykeman and Roebuck, this volume) and potentially absorbed individuals along the migration route to the Southwest. The analysis of mitochondrial DNA (mtDNA), DNA from the non-recombining Y-chromosome (NRY), and Albumin polymorphisms support these conclusions.

MITOCHONDRIAL GENOME

The mitochondrial genome consists of mtDNA, which exhibits unique characteristics compared with nuclear DNA because it is located in every mitochondrion in the cytoplasm of a cell. The location of mtDNA in the cytoplasm of a cell creates a system of maternal inheritance: mtDNA is passed from mother to offspring, but only a daughter will be able to pass her mtDNA to the next generation. Because of its unique maternal inheritance, mtDNA provides information that can be used to infer female population history. Also, because paternal mtDNA is not transmitted to offspring, there is no recombination and only mutation can cause changes in mtDNA from ancestors to descendants through generations. Significantly, mtDNA is found in high copy number (hundreds to thousands of copies) in a cell, compared with two copies of nuclear DNA. This accounts for the high percentage of success in extracting mtDNA from ancient samples relative to nuclear DNA (Kaestle and Horsburgh 2002).

Native Americans belong to one of five broad groups (A, B, C, D, and X) of mitochondrial genomes called haplogroups (Schurr et al. 1990; Torroni et al. 1993; Brown et al. 1998). These haplogroups consist of multiple individual mitochondrial genomes or lineages that all share mutations unique to each haplogroup. Ten of these lineages (A2, B2, C1b, C1c, C1d1, C1d*, C4c, D1, D2, D4h3a) are widely distributed throughout the Americas and are posited to be the founding mitochondrial genomes that arrived with the original migrants who peopled the Americas over 15,000 years before present (ybp; Tamm et al. 2007; Perego et al. 2010). A nonrandom pattern of these haplogroups exists in Native American populations and suggests both regional and temporal continuity (Lorenz and Smith 1996; O'Rourke et al. 2000; Smith et al. 1999). In other words, geographically proximate Native American groups exhibit similar patterns of haplogroup frequencies (except as demonstrated in the Southeastern United States; Bolnick and Smith 2003), and distantly located groups exhibit different haplogroup frequencies. This phenomenon likely results from a significant amount of admixture among neighboring groups occupying the same region of North America throughout prehistory (Malhi et al. 2002). Evidence for the pattern of temporal continuity comes from genetic data of ancient populations. The data from these prehistoric populations were used to investigate the mtDNA patterns that existed before the time of European contact. The mtDNA patterns from prehistoric populations (2,000 years in age or younger) in a geographic region are similar to the mtDNA patterns of contemporary groups from that same region in many, but not all, cases (O'Rourke et al. 2000).

Athapaskans residing in the Subarctic all exhibit a near fixation of haplogroup A whereas the Athapaskan-speaking groups of the Southwest (Navajo and Western Apache) exhibit approximately 50 percent frequency of haplogroup A and ~50 percent combined frequencies of haplogroups B, C, D, and X (Lorenz and Smith 1996; Smith et al. 2000; Malhi et al. 2003). It is hypothesized that the haplogroup A from the Navajo and Western Apache is descended from Athapaskans in the Subarctic and the combined haplogroups B, C, D, and X in the Navajo and Western Apache are a result of intermarriage or admixture with non-Athapaskan groups in the Southwest (Lorenz and Smith 1996; Smith et al. 2000; Malhi et al. 2003). Within haplogroup A, sub-haplogroup A2a is exhibited in moderate frequency among Subarctic Athapaskan groups (e.g., 25 percent A2a in the Dogrib); however, A2a is exhibited at 100 percent frequency in the Western Apache and presumably high frequency in all Southern Athapaskans (Malhi et al. 2003; Tamm et al. 2007). The large difference in the frequency of A2a between Athapaskans of the Subarctic and the Southwest is likely a result of a founder effect (Malhi et al. 2003). This suggests that it was a small group of Athapaskan migrants who traveled from the Subarctic to the Southwest.

Non-recombining Y-Chromosome (NRY)

A portion of the Y-chromosome does not recombine and is referred to as the non-recombining Y-chromosome (NRY). It is this part of the chromosome that can change only through mutation and results in variation that can be used to trace ancestor/descendant relationships. Only males have Y-chromosomes, and therefore NRYs are transmitted through generations from father to son. As a result of this unique inheritance system, the NRY can be used to trace male population history. Like mtDNA, the NRY system is organized into haplogroups that are defined by a change of a single nucleotide position or a point mutation. The majority of Native Americans belong to haplogroups Q, C, and R (Zegura et al. 2004). Variation within a haplogroup is defined by mutations called short tandem repeats (STR) or microsatellites. Unlike a point mutation, STR loci are defined by repeats of nucleotide motifs (e.g., ATAGATAGATAG = 3 repeats of the ATAG motif). Variation of an STR is the result of a different number of repeats (and lengths) for each allele.

Haplogroup Q is widely distributed and often in high frequency throughout North and South America (Zegura et al. 2004; Malhi et al. 2008). Haplogroup C is in highest frequency in northern regions of North America such as the Arctic and Subarctic (Zegura et al. 2004; Malhi et al. 2008). Unlike haplogroups Q and C, haplogroup R is hypothesized to be the result of recent (postcolumbian) admixture with Europeans (Zegura et al. 2004). This hypothesis is supported by the presence of numerous exact matches between European and Native American NRYs defined as lineages of haplogroup R (Bolnick et al. 2006). Haplogroup R is exhibited in approximately 73 percent of Native North American populations; frequencies range from 4 to 88 percent (Malhi et al. 2008). This is a very different pattern from that of mtDNA, in which only approximately 1 percent of all Native North Americans exhibit an mtDNA of European ancestry (Smith et al. 1999). From this pattern, Malhi and colleagues (2008) infer that European colonization strongly influenced the genetic structure of Native North American men relative to Native North American women. Because European colonization had such a strong influence on the structure and diversity of North American NRYs, ancient DNA of pre-European contact human remains is likely to be the most robust manner to assess Native American NRY diversity and inference of pre–European contact male population history.

Even with the strong influence of European colonization on Native North American NRY diversity and structure, a clear pattern of the Southern Athapaskan migration is inferred from the NRY data (Malhi et al. 2008). While NRY haplogroup C is exhibited in moderate frequencies in Subarctic Athapaskan populations, the only Southwest populations that exhibit haplogroup C are the Southern Athapaskans (Malhi et al. 2008). In addition, like mtDNA A haplotypes, the NRY C haplotypes exhibit a pattern consistent with a founder effect in the Southern Athapaskans. Therefore, inference from both mtDNA and NRY suggest that a small number of Athapaskan individuals migrated from the Subarctic to the Southwest. A small group of migrants with a mobile, dynamic, and light-footed lifestyle may explain why traditional methods of identifying Athapaskans in the archaeological record have been largely unsuccessful (Seymour 2010; Seymour, Chapters 5 and 17, this volume; Dykeman and Roebuck, this volume).

Albumin Polymorphisms

A large body of data exists from classic genetic studies of human genetic variation (Cavalli-Sforza et al. 1994). The majority of this data is in the form of protein polymorphisms, such as Albumin. Although Albumin polymorphism studies are low resolution and provide limited information for autosomal DNA variation, they have still been informative about the population history of Southern Athapaskans. Specifically, the Albumin*Naskapi and Albumin*Mexico variants are informative about gene flow between Southern Athapaskans and non-Athapaskan groups in the Southwest (Smith et al. 2000; Brugge, this volume). The Albumin*Naskapi variant is exhibited in populations in the Subarctic and Northwest Coast and also in Southern Athapaskan populations. The presence of Albumin*Naskapi in Southern Athapaskans provides a third line of genetic evidence supporting the classic Southern Athapaskan migration hypothesis. Non-Athapaskan populations in the Southwest do not exhibit the Albumin*Naskapi variant. Populations in Mexico and the Southwest, including Southern Athapaskan populations, exhibit the Albumin*Mexico variant (Smith et al. 2000). It is hypothesized that Southern Athapaskans gained the Albumin*Mexico variant through recent admixture with non-Athapaskan Southwest groups (Smith et al. 2000). This pattern is similar to variation in mtDNA, in which Southern Athapaskans exhibit mtDNAs (haplogroups B, C, D, and X) that were likely absorbed through gene flow with non-Athapaskan Southwest populations; however, nearly all non-Athapaskan Southwest populations do not exhibit mtDNA haplogroup A2a, a variant in high frequency in Southern Athapaskan popula-

TABLE 11.1. Genetic Variants of Athapaskans.

GENETIC SYSTEM	NATIVE AMERICAN	SOUTHERN ATHAPASKAN
mtDNA	A2, A2a, B2, C1b, C1c, C1d, C1d*, C4c, D1, D2, D4h3	A2a
NRY	Q, C, R	C
Albumin	Albumin*Mexico, Albumin*Naskapi	Albumin*Naskapi

tions. The patterns observed in Albumin and mtDNA suggest one-way gene flow of non-Athapaskan Southwest individuals being incorporated into Southern Athapaskan culture. It is also possible that Southern Athapaskans may have absorbed non-Athapaskan individuals along the migration route to the Southwest, although this is unlikely because the Albumin*Mexico variant is found only in populations of Mesoamerica and the Southwest (Table 11.1).

FUTURE GENETIC STUDIES

Biotechnology is advancing rapidly, and future genetic studies may be more informative about the timing and route of the Southern Athapaskan migration. High-resolution, genome-wide data are currently being generated for contemporary Native North American populations (Rasmussen et al. 2010). Similar genome-wide data for Southern Athapaskans can potentially be used to assess whether genetic variants from Southern Athapaskans, presumed to be the result of gene flow with non-Athapaskans, originate from populations in the Southwest or from populations from other regions, along the migration route, of North America. With additional sampling from the Jicarilla, Lipan, Mescalero, and Chiricahua Apaches, hypotheses of multiple Southern Athapaskan migrations from different source populations in the Subarctic can also be addressed with high-resolution, genome-wide data. However, the timing at which the hypothesized migration(s) occurred in the past is unlikely to be resolved by the analysis of contemporary, genome-wide data because the confidence intervals around the point estimate of the date generated by the genetic data will likely span thousands of years.

A strategy of using ancient DNA analysis may have more success in assessing the migration route and timing of Southern Athapaskans' arrival in the Southwest. Specifically, if ancient DNA can be analyzed from biological sources at archaeological sites along the hypothesized migration route, the presence of Athapaskan-specific genetic markers, such as mtDNA haplogroup A2a, would provide strong support that Athapaskans occupied the site. Similarly, the first appearance of mtDNA haplogroup A2a in human remains spanning a wide range (e.g., 2,000–300 ybp) in the Southwest would help construct the time frame for when Southern Athapaskans first arrived in the Southwest.

Conclusion

Genetic studies of Athapaskans have been informative about the nature of the Southern Athapaskan migration. These studies suggest that it is likely that only a small group of Athapaskans migrated to the Southwest. In addition, these migrants absorbed non-Athapaskans once they arrived in the Southwest and possibly along the migration route. Advances in biotechnology are already providing high-resolution data sets on Native North American individuals and will likely provide additional information and details on the Southern Athapaskan migration. However, a full understanding of how and why the Southern Athapaskan migration occurred will come only from a holistic view that combines information from multiple disciplines, such as those discussed in this book.

References

Bolnick, D. A., D. L. Bolnick, and D. G. Smith
2006   Asymmetric Male and Female Genetic Histories among Native Americans from Eastern North America. *Molecular Biology and Evolution* 11:2161–2174.

Bolnick, D. A., and D. G. Smith
2003   Unexpected Patterns of Mitochondrial DNA Variation among Native Americans from the Southeastern United States. *American Journal of Physical Anthropology* 122:226–254.

Brown, M. D., S. H. Hosseini, A. Torroni, H. J. Bandelt, J. C. Allen, T. G. Schurr, R. Scozzari, F. Cruciani, and D. C. Wallace
1998   MtDNA Haplogroup X: An Ancient Link between Europe/Western Asia and North America? *American Journal of Human Genetics* 63:1852–1861.

Cavalli-Sforza, L. L., P. Menozzi, and A. Piazza
1994   *The History and Geography of Human Genes*. Princeton, New Jersey: Princeton University Press.

Goddard, Ives
1996   The Classification of the Native Languages of North America. In *Languages*, edited by Ives Goddard, pp. 240–323. Handbook of North American Indians, Vol. 17, William C. Sturtevant, general editor. Washington, D.C.: Smithsonian Institution.

Hoijer, Harry
1956   The Chronology of the Athapaskan Languages. *International Journal of American Linguistics* 22(4):219–232.

Hunley, K., and J. C. Long
2005   Gene Flow across Linguistic Boundaries in Native North American Populations. *Proceedings of the National Academy of Sciences* 102:1312–1317.

Kaestle, F. A., and K. A. Horsburgh
2002   Ancient DNA in Anthropology: Methods, Applications, and Ethics. *American Journal of Physical Anthropology Supplement* 35:92–130.

Lorenz, J. G., and D. G. Smith
1996   Distribution of Four Founding mtDNA Haplogroups among Native North Americans. *American Journal of Physical Anthropology* 101:307–329.

Malhi, R. S., J. A. Eshleman, J. A. Greenberg, D. A. Weiss, B. A. Schultz Shook, F. A. Kaestle, J. G. Lorenz, B. M. Kemp, J. R. Johnson, and D. G. Smith
2002   The Structure of Diversity within New World Mitochondrial DNA Haplogroups:

Implications for the Prehistory of North America. *American Journal of Human Genetics* 70:905–919.

Malhi, Ripan Singh, Angelica Gonzales-Oliver, Kari Britt Schroeder, Brian M. Kemp, Jonathan A. Greenberg, Solomon Z. Dobrowski, David Glenn Smith, Andres Resendez, Tatiana Karafet, Michael Hammer, Stephen Zegura, and Tatiana Brovko
2008   Distribution of Y Chromosomes among Native North Americans: A Study of Athapaskan Population History. *American Journal of Physical Anthropology* 137(4):412–424.

Malhi, R. S., H. M. Mortensen, J. A. Eshleman, J. G. Lorenz, F. A. Kaestle, J. R. Johnson, C. Gorodesky, and D. G. Smith
2003   Native American mtDNA Prehistory in the American Southwest. *American Journal of Physical Anthropology* 120:108–124.

O'Rourke, D. H., M. G. Hayes, and S. W. Carlyle
2000   Spatial and Temporal Stability of mtDNA Haplogroup Frequencies in Native North America. *Human Biology* 72:15–34.

Perego, U. A., N. Angerhofer, M. Pala, A. Olivieri, H. Lancioni, B. H. Kashani, V. Carossa, J. E. Ekins, A. Gomez-Cabralla, G. Huber, B. Zimmermann, D. Corach, N. Babudri, F. Panara, N. M. Myres, W. Parson, O. Semino, A. Salas, S. R. Woodward, A. Achilli, and A. Torroni
2010   The Initial Peopling of the Americas: A Growing Number of Founding Mitochondrial Genomes from Beringia. *Genome Research*. Ahead of print. http://www.genome.org/cgi/doi/10.1101/gr.109231.110.

Rasmussen, M., Y. Li, S. Lindgreen, J. S. Pedersen, A. Albrechtsen, I. Moltke, M. Metspalu, E. Metspalu, T. Kivisild, R. Gupta, M. Bertalan, K. Nielsen, M. T. Gilbert, Y. Wang, M. Raghavan, P. F. Campos, H. M. Kamp, A. S. Wilson, A. Gledhill, S. Tridico, M. Bunce, E. D. Lorenzen, J. Binladen, X. Guo, J. Zhao, X. Zhang, H. Zhang, Z. Li, M. Chen, L. Orlando, K. Kristiansen, M. Bak, N. Tommerup, C. Bendixen, T. L. Pierre, B. Gronnow, M. Meldgaard, C. Andreasen, S. A. Fedorova, L. P. Osipova, T. F. Higham, C. B. Ramsey, T. V. Hansen, F. C. Nielsen, M. H. Crawford, S. Brunak, T. Sicheritz-Ponten, R. Villems, R. Nielsen, A. Krogh, J. Wang, and E. Willerslev
2010   Ancient Human Genome Sequence of an Extinct Palaeo-Eskimo. *Nature* 463:757–762.

Schurr, T. G., S. W. Ballinger, Y. Y. Gan, J. A. Hodge, D. A. Merriwether, D. N. Lawrence, W. C. Knowler, K. M. Weiss, and D. C. Wallace
1990   Amerindian Mitochondrial DNAs Have Rare Asian Mutations at High Frequencies, Suggesting They Derived from Four Primary Maternal Lineages. *American Journal of Human Genetics* 46:613–623.

Seymour, Deni J.
2010   Contextual Incongruities, Statistical Outliers, and Anomalies: Targeting Inconspicuous Occupational Events. *American Antiquity* 75(1):158–176.

Smith, D. G., J. G. Lorenz, B. K. Rolfs, R. L. Bettinger, B. Green, J. Eshleman, B. Schultz, and R. S. Malhi
2000   Implications of the Distribution of Albumin Naskapi and Albumin Mexico for New World Prehistory. *American Journal of Physical Anthropology* 111:557–572.

Smith, D. G., R. S. Malhi, J. Eshleman, J. G. Lorenz, and F. A. Kaestle
1999   Distribution of mtDNA Haplogroup X among Native North Americans. *American Journal of Physical Anthropology* 110:271–284.

Tamm, E., T. Kivisild, M. Reidla, M. Metspalu, D. G. Smith, C. J. Mulligan, C. M. Bravi, O. Rickards, C. Martinez-Labarga, E. K. Khusnutdinova, S. A. Fedorova, M. V. Golubenko,

V. A. Stepanov, M. A. Gubina, S. I. Zhadanov, L. P. Ossipova, L. Damba, M. I. Voevoda, J. E. Dipierri, R. Villems, and R. S. Malhi
2007 Beringian Standstill and Spread of Native American Founders. *PLoS ONE* 2:e829.

Torroni, A., R. I. Sukernik, T. G. Schurr, Y. B. Starikorskaya, M. F. Cabell, M. H. Crawford, A. G. Comuzzie, and D. C. Wallace
1993 MtDNA Variation of Aboriginal Siberians Reveals Distinct Genetic Affinities with Native Americans. *American Journal of Human Genetics* 53:591–608.

Zegura, S. L., T. M. Karafet, L. A. Zhivotovsky, and M. F. Hammer
2004 High-Resolution SNPs and Microsatellite Haplotypes Point to a Single, Recent Entry of Native American Y Chromosomes into the Americas. *Molecular Biology and Evolution* 21:164–175.

CHAPTER 12

Linguistic Evidence Regarding the Apachean Migration

KEREN RICE

The close relationship among languages of the Dene (Athapaskan) family,[1] Eyak, and, at somewhat more remove, Tlingit has long been recognized (see, for instance, Campbell 1997; Foster 1996; Krauss 1973, 1986 for discussion; see also Kari and Potter 2010 on the hypothesis that Dene languages are related to the Yeniseian languages of Siberia). This family is generally considered to be a spread family (e.g., Golla 2000:62), with the languages found in three discontinuous zones in North America. Given both the clear relationship among the languages and the widespread geographic distribution, the family has long been an object of fascination for those interested in many different areas—archaeology, linguistics, genetics, anthropology, and ethnohistory, among others.

The goal of this chapter is a narrow one, namely, to examine what linguistics can tell us about two important questions regarding one branch of the family, the Apachean languages of the American Southwest. First, what can linguistics tell us about whether the Apachean group has a common origin, with a single migration from the north and later splitting, or whether there was more than one wave of migration, perhaps along different routes from the start? And second, what can linguistics tell us about the time of separation of what became the Apachean group from its northern homeland? We will see that, in response to the first question, linguistic evidence points both to northern origins for the Apacheans (as argued in a classic article by Sapir 1936) and to a common origin, with language differentiation occurring later. In response to the second question, we will examine the evidence for what can be said about time.

Before we begin, a note on names is in order. The word "Athapaskan" (with its various spellings, as indicated in note 1) has been used for this family for many years. Recently, the term "Dene" (person) has become common as the name for the family, and I use these two terms interchangeably. With respect to language names, these are undergoing shifts as well, from names proposed by postcontact European settlers to names proposed by the speakers. I use the more recent names; on first mention, the traditional name is given in parentheses.

THE DENE LANGUAGE FAMILY: SOME BACKGROUND

The Dene language family is geographically the most widespread of the language families in North America (see, e.g., Mithun 1999), spanning an area from the far north of Canada and the United States to the Pacific coast to the American Southwest, with the three groups being geographically discontinuous. Major questions that have occupied those interested in this family concern where the Athapaskan homeland was and the routes and numbers of migrations.

In discussion of the Athapaskan language family, three major groups are identified: Northern Athapaskan, Apachean or Southern Athapaskan, and Pacific Coast Athapaskan. These are geographically rather than linguistically defined units. There is no real agreement about the internal structure of the northern group, and Krauss (2005:118) emphasizes that "Athabaskan 'languages'... are really parts of a dynamic complex of more or less constant interaction and influences," making it difficult to define these languages in a standard way.

The Athapaskan homeland is usually considered to be eastern interior Alaska, the upper drainage of the Yukon River, and northern British Columbia, or some part of this area (Krauss and Golla 1981:68), although Kari (2010:210) notes that there is no real support for this region as the homeland beyond its being near the area of great divergence of the branches. Again, see Kari (2010) for an interesting discussion.

Proto-Athapaskan is generally posited as being a linguistic unit of some sort until 2,000 to 2,500 years ago, splitting from Eyak around 1500 BC, or 3,400 ± 500 years ago; the split with Tlingit is proposed to have taken place around 4,500 years ago (see Golla 2007:71; Krauss 1973:950–953; Krauss 1980:11–13; Kari 2010:200; see Campbell 1997:110 for a summary). Fortescue (1998) suggests that the Na-Dene speech community probably entered North America around 6,000 years ago. See Kari (2010) for a longer-term proposal, the suggestion that from around 12,000 years ago until around 3,000 years ago there was a continuous proto-Athapaskan occupation from northwest Alaska to parts of western Canada, with a long-term range expansion in the Subarctic (Kari 2010: 209). This hypothesis is very interesting, but I do not pursue it here as it is connected more with Northern Athapaskan than it is with Apachean, whose date Kari does not dispute. The Pacific Coast Athapaskan groups branched first, perhaps 1,500 years ago (see Golla 2007:71; Krauss 1980:12; Krauss and Golla 1981: 68); see below for discussion of the timing of Apachean branching.

As noted earlier, the close linguistic relationship between the languages of the Athapaskan family has long been evident. In this section, I review a few of the many types of linguistic evidence that show this close relationship despite the passage of time.

I begin with cognates, or morphemes/words that are related to morphemes/ words in a related language by virtue of having descended from the same morpheme/word in the proto-language (mother language). In working with

TABLE 12.1. Cognates in Several Dene Languages.

	Ahtna	Tsuut'ina	Dëne Sųłiné	Hupa	Navajo	Jicarilla Apache	Chiricahua Apache	Lipan Apache
louse	ya'	yà'	yá	yà	yaa'	yaa'	yaa	yaa
eye	-naegge'	-nàgh	-naghá	-naa'	-náá'	-ndáá	-ndáa	-ndáa
rope	tł'uuł	tł'úł	tł'ulɛ	tł'ohł	tł'óół	tł'ół	tł'óół	tł'óół
water	tuu	tú	tu	too	tó	kó	tó	kó
horn	-de'	-da'	-dɛ́	-de'	-dee'	-dee'	-dee'	-dii'

Note: Data are from Hoijer (1956), with the exception of Ahtna, which is from Kari (1990).

cognates, I follow a widely accepted method in linguistics for determining relationships between languages, the comparative method. This method involves the comparison of vocabulary and structural features of languages in order to reconstruct the proto-language. Through the comparison of cognates, family-internal relationships can also be discerned. See Campbell (2004) for clear discussion. Here I aim simply to present some cognates to provide a small indication of how similar the languages of this family are.

The most valuable cognates for the comparative method are words such as body parts, close kinship terms, and basic geographical terms, words that are likely to be preserved from the proto-language rather than borrowed, and I thus draw vocabulary from these areas. In Table 12.1 I compare cognates from a number of languages. The currently used language name is given first, followed by alternative names, if any, and the location of the language in parentheses. The languages used are Ahtna (Northern [Alaska]), Tsuut'ina (Sarcee or Sarsi; Northern [Canada]), Dëne Sųłiné (Chipewyan; Northern [Canada]), Hupa (Pacific Coast [California]), Navajo (sometimes called Diné; Apachean [Arizona, New Mexico]), Jicarilla Apache (Apachean [New Mexico]), Chiricahua Apache (Apachean [New Mexico]), and Lipan Apache (Apachean [New Mexico]). I use a common orthographic system for Athapaskan languages. The raised comma represents a glottal stop, *gh* is a voiced velar fricative, *ł* is a voiceless lateral fricative, ´ indicates high tone, and ` indicates low tone. A hook under the vowel indicates nasalization.

I have chosen words in which the regular sound changes that have occurred are minor and do not obscure the overall similarity of the words. The number of clear cognates across the family is very high—Kari (2010:201) notes that there appear to be somewhere between 1,300 and 1,500 cognate roots and morphemes in the comparative Athapaskan lexicon (Leer 1996)—and the cognates provide strong evidence for the linguistic relationship between the languages despite their being geographically far-flung.

In addition to cognate vocabulary, Dene languages are similar in many other ways. The verb word in an Athapaskan language is typically quite complex,

TABLE 12.2. General Template Showing the Overall Order of Prefixes in the Verb of Dene Languages.

one or more adverbial prefixes
iterative (lacking in some languages)
pluralizing (distributive)
object pronoun
deictic subject
zero, one, or two adverbial prefixes (qualifier)
prefix marking mode, tense, aspect (conjugation marker)
subject pronoun
classifier (voice/valence)
stem

Note: Drawn from Hoijer (1971a:125); more recent names for positions are given in parentheses.

consisting of an obligatory verb stem preceded by a potentially large number of prefixes. The similarities are striking enough that Hoijer (1971a) pointed out that the order of prefixes is much the same in all languages of the family (Table 12.2).

While many North American languages have verb words with complex morphology, the verb in Dene languages differs from that of nearby languages. The following statements are vastly oversimplified but provide an indication that the prefixing status of the Dene languages is unusual. For instance, the verb word in Eskimo-Aleut languages is suffixing, and the verb word in Algonquian languages has a complex stem that combines with prefixes and suffixes. Salish languages are largely suffixing, with some prefixes. Uto-Aztecan languages have both prefixes and suffixes, and Siouan languages are predominantly prefixing, although suffixes occur as well. Thus, the strong prefixing nature of Athapaskan languages, coupled with the ordering of the prefixes within the verb word, is characteristic of Dene languages and not of the languages of neighboring families.

Athapaskan languages are also known for a kind of verb called a "classificatory verb." This is cross-linguistically a rather uncommon type of system that exists across the Athapaskan family. In these verbs, properties of the subject of an intransitive verb and the object of a transitive verb are indicated by the form of the verb stem itself. For instance, verb stems for expressing location, independent movement, and handling of an object differ according to the nature of the object—whether it is stick-like, flat and flexible, and so on. A subset of the classificatory verb stems of location is given in Table 12.3. For example, to say in Navajo that a roundish object (e.g., ball, drum, egg, chunk of meat) is in a particular place, one would use the verb *si'ą́*, with the stem -*'ą́*, while for slender

TABLE 12.3. Dene Classificatory Verb Stems Meaning "Object Is Located" (a Subset).

	Ahtna	Tsuut'ina	Dëne Sųłiné	Hupa	Navajo	Chiricahua Apache	Jicarilla Apache
Roundish object	-'aan	-'ón	-'ą	-'a:n	-'ą́	-'ą́	-'ą́
Slender stiff object	-taan	-tón	-tą	-ta:n	-tą́	-tą́	-ką́
Living being	-taen	-tíh	-tį	-te:n	-tį́	-tį́	-kį́į́
Open rigid container and contents	-kaan	-kón	-ką	-xa:n	-ką́	-ką́	-ką́
Source	Kari 1990	Cook 1984	Carter 1976	Golla 1996	Hoijer 1945	Hoijer 1945	Phone et al. 2007; Willem de Reuse, pers. comm. 2011

Note: Spellings are from the sources listed.

TABLE 12.4. Dene Irregular Verb Stems.

'DO TO O'	Imperfective	Perfective	Inceptive	Future	Customary
Ahtna	laex	laak	le'	liił	ł+'iis
Navajo	lééh	laa	le'	lííł	ł+'įįh

Note: From Kari 2010.

stiff objects (e.g., horn, arrow, ear of corn, spoon, thorn), one would choose *sitą́*, with the stem *-tą́* (from Young and Morgan 1987). Underlining is used in Jicarilla Apache spelling to represent nasalization, parallel to the hook that is used in other languages. While there are regular sound changes that take place, the similarity between these verb stems in the different languages should be evident.

Another feature that is found across the Dene family is a complex system of stems. Kari (2010:9) provides the comparison of Ahtna and Navajo shown in Table 12.4, which illustrates verb stem forms that differ by aspect. Imperfective is similar to present and perfective to past; inceptive indicates the beginning of an event, and customary is used for something that happens on a periodic basis (e.g., every year). While Athapaskan languages typically show variation in stem form depending on aspect, the particular variation seen here is unusual, and the customary form is completely different from the other forms. The similarity between the languages despite the irregular nature of the stem forms is striking: leveling might have been expected.

While many more similarities between the languages of the family could be mentioned, I note just one more, discussed in Kari (2009): the similarity in the form of place names across the language family. Kari identifies six different

TABLE 12.5. Dene Place Names Compared.

	AHTNA	NAVAJO	HUPA
Noun+Postposition	t'aghes tah "among cottonwoods"	diné tah "among people"	mis q'id "on bank"
Noun+Noun	ketseni t'ox "hawk nest"	gini bit'oh "hawk nest"	taa kye' "water tail"
(Noun+)Verb+suffix	naghilen den "water flows down place"	tsé íí'ahí "rock that extends place"	nowilin ding "current flows to place"

Note: From Kari 2009:7–8.

structures associated with place names, giving names from Ahtna, Hupa, and Navajo to represent the three different geographic branches of the family. A few examples are provided in Table 12.5. The first row shows place names formed of a noun followed by a postposition (similar to a preposition, but following rather than preceding the noun). The second row shows place names formed from two nouns, and the third row shows place names that may contain a subject noun and obligatorily include a verb word followed by a suffix that makes it into a noun. These patterns, and others, are found across the family; Kari (2009), citing personal communication from Johanna Nichols, suggests that this type of stability of form of place names is very unusual on a worldwide basis.

From the perspective of the linguist, then, the languages of this family have much in common, from cognate vocabulary to very similar verb structures to the formation of words. This conservatism is a point of interest to linguists; see Kari (2010) for recent discussion.

CHARACTERISTICS OF APACHEAN LANGUAGES

Having examined some characteristics of the languages of the Athapaskan family as a whole, we now turn to characteristics of the Apachean group to see what types of features distinguish it from the other languages of the family. Apachean is sometimes thought to consist of three major groups: Plains (Kiowa) Apache, Western Apachean (containing Chiricahua Apache, Mescalero Apache, Navajo, and Western Apache), and Eastern Apachean (containing Jicarilla Apache and Lipan Apache); see Young (1983) and references therein for details. San Carlos Apache is a variety of Western Apache, and in general, Western Apache data in this chapter represent this variety.

There is general agreement in the Athapaskan linguistics literature that the Apachean branch represents a fairly recent expansion into the Southwest and a common origin; see Hoijer (1938: 86) for a fairly early statement and references. Work by Hoijer (1956) on glottochronology (see the section "Linguistic Evidence for Time Depth," below) suggests that the proto-Apacheans split from the Northern Athapaskan group around AD 1000, reaching the Southwest around AD 1400, with a later split into what are now recognized as distinct languages. Foster (1996) gives the earliest divergence times as 1,300–1,500 years ago, in general agreement with times given by Campbell (1997), Krauss and Golla (1981:68), Kari (2010), Ives (1990, 2003, 2010), and others.

Ives (1990, 2003, 2010), and Ives et al. (2002) suggest that 1,200 to 1,500 years ago the Apachean ancestors spread from the Peace River country of northeastern British Columbia and east across the southern Subarctic; Ives (2010) notes that there may have been Apachean ancestors in the western Canadian Parkland ecotone and the northern edge of the Plains region as well. Golla (2008, cited in Ives 2010 and based on discussions with de Reuse (Willem de Reuse, personal communication 2011) has recently reinforced the conclusion that the linguistic evidence points to a single relatively undifferentiated proto-Apachean group with later diversification into independent groups. More specifically, Golla suggests early separation from this group of what came to be known as Plains Apache, as well as early separation of what became Navajo, with the speakers of the intermediate dialects (precursors of Jicarilla, Mescalero, Chiricahua, and Lipan Apache) lingering longer on the Plains. This assumes a Plains path, something disputed in many of the chapters in this book. De Reuse (personal communication 2011) adds that there is a U-shaped linguistic continuum of what were originally dialects, going from the least Plains-culture influenced and most Puebloan-culture influenced (Navajo) to the most Plains-culture influenced and least Puebloan-culture influenced (Plains Apache), with the continuum being Navajo–Western Apache–Chiricahua Apache–Mescalero Apache–Jicarilla Apache–Lipan-Plains Apache.[2] Linguists are not, with current knowledge, able to provide definitive linguistic evidence for the pathway of southern movement and whether there was a single pathway or more than one, as advanced in many of the chapters in this book, but can provide evidence for the likelihood that there was a common origin with differentiation along the way.

In terms of specific northern relations, surprisingly little has been written. Krauss and Golla (1981:68) suggest that the closest ties of Apachean languages are with Tsuut'ina, but, they note, it is not likely that this is evidence for the Apacheans having moved southward through the High Plains and they do not present specific linguistic support for their claim.

What kinds of linguistic evidence might be brought to support the claim that the Apachean languages form a distinct subgroup, and a unified subgroup, represented by a single migration that later diversified? As we saw, the comparative method, with evidence drawn from the lexicon and language structure, is adduced to point to a language being part of a family. This method can also be used to argue that a subset of the languages of a family forms a distinct group, as suggested by the existence of cognates within that group but not elsewhere, and structural properties.

It is worthwhile to begin this discussion with mention of work by Sapir (1936). Sapir aims not so much to establish the similarities between the Apachean languages as to provide linguistic evidence for their northern origins, taking the similarities of the group as a given. Sapir's objective is to see how linguistic evidence might be useful for reconstructing aspects of a culture, that is, using linguistic evidence to understand prehistory. In this seminal article, Sapir argues for the northern origin of the Navajo and, by extension, of the other Apachean groups.

Sapir begins his article by pointing to the difficulties of using linguistic evidence to make inferences about culture, noting that it is often "tricky as to what of a factual nature can be gathered from it, for words may change their meanings radically and, furthermore, it is often difficult to tell whether community of nomenclature rests on early linguistic relationship or on linguistic borrowing attending cultural diffusion" (Sapir 1936:224). He also states that linguistic evidence can be difficult to handle, with a "closeness of knowledge that is often out of proportion to what little can be obtained from it for tangible cultural inference" (Sapir 1936:224).

Sapir argues that there is tangible evidence from Navajo, and other Apachean languages, for the "secondary origin of apparently fundamental elements of Navajo culture...that...seems to point to an early association of the culture of these people with a more northern environment than their present one" (Sapir 1936:224). Sapir draws evidence from four words; I review one of these here, the Navajo word for gourd.

The gourd is very important in Navajo culture. The word for 'gourd, gourd ladle, dipper, ladle, horn' in Navajo is 'àdè:' (current spelling [Young and Morgan 1987]: 'adee'). This word is itself composed of two pieces: 'a-, a prefix meaning 'somebody's, something's', followed by the noun stem -dee' (current spelling). The cognate form in Chiricahua Apache and Mescalero Apache also means 'horn, cup, dish, dipper' although not 'gourd'. Sapir proposes that the Navajo 'gourd ladle' derives from 'ladle', which itself derives from '(animal's) horn'. In other Athapaskan languages, the cognates of the Apachean word mean '(animal's) horn' (e.g., Chipewyan -dé, Sarsi [Tsuut'ina] -dà') but not 'ladle'. (These spellings are from Sapir 1936.)

Sapir concludes that the gourd was absent in an early phase of the culture of the Navajo-Apache tribes, while horn spoons were present at this phase, and the word that originally meant 'horn' was used. As the Navajo encountered gourds, they extended this word to mean 'gourd ladle' and then 'gourd'. Sapir proposes a particular path of semantic development: the original meaning, 'animal horn', was found in the northern languages; this was extended to mean 'something made out of a horn' (specifically, a ladle made out of a horn) and then generalized to 'ladle'. This opened the door to the meaning of 'gourd ladle' and, from there, to 'gourd', or something that a ladle is made out of. This kind of change is an example of a linguistic phenomenon known as metonymy (a word or phrase is substituted for one with which it is closely associated). This type of evidence, Sapir argues, supports the theory that the Apachean groups migrated to the Southwest: the extensions in the use of the word are of a common type. Sapir concludes that all the Southern Athapaskan languages—Navajo, Western Apache, Mescalero Apache, Chiricahua Apache, Lipan Apache, and Kiowa (Plains) Apache—"obviously form a close-knit dialectic unity which contrasts with the more dialectic ramifications of Pacific and northern Athapaskan" (Sapir 1936:234). Sapir thus argues from semantic development that the gourd is not an original element of Apachean culture and that horn spoons were present at an early stage of this culture, given that the Apachean languages all share this meaning.

Sapir (1936) is largely concerned with showing that linguistic evidence can suggest the northern origin of the Apachean groups. Arguments from lexical items can also be used as evidence for a common origin in the north rather than more than one origin, with the differences that mark the various Apachean languages taking place later, once the migrating group split. The reasoning is as follows: if there are meaning shifts shared by the Apachean languages that are not present in the other languages, as with the meaning 'ladle', this argues for a stage at which that shift occurred when the groups were still together. Thus, shared vocabulary argues for a period at which the languages that share that vocabulary were one, distinct from their predecessors.

The case discussed above involved a shift in meaning of a word with cognates across the family, with a similar shift in meaning in the Apachean group but not elsewhere. Ives and Rice (2006) give additional examples of this sort of extension of meaning of core Dene roots. One of these is the northern word 'thorn', extended to 'cactus' in the Apachean languages for which it is recorded. Other terms for items encountered along the way that derive from common Athapaskan vocabulary include bison/cattle, lodge pole, lizard, and mountain lion; see Ives and Rice (2006).

In other cases, as new items were encountered in the journey southward, or once the Apacheans reached their destinations, new words were created from the existing Athapaskan lexical stock. This is a particularly common way of forming new words in Dene languages. As noted earlier, Athapaskan languages are known for their resistance to borrowing, another frequent way of extending the vocabulary of a language. Sapir (1921:209) remarked on this: "The Athabaskan languages of America are spoken by peoples that have astonishingly varied cultural contacts, yet nowhere do we find that an Athabaskan dialect has borrowed at all freely from a neighboring language." Clear borrowing exists, but it is more recent, from Spanish and English.

As Ives and Rice (2006) show, there are a number of words for things that do not exist in the north that share in form across all Apachean languages for which they are recorded. One word they offer is based on work by Sapir (1936): the word for 'corn, maize'. The Navajo word is *na:dą́:'*, and forms in other Apachean languages are shown in Table 12.6. In a true tour de force, Sapir (1936:228–231) argues that the word *na:dą́:'* is a possessive form, composed *of na:* 'enemy' and *dá:n* 'food, possessed form', literally meaning 'food of the enemy'.

TABLE 12.6. Apachean Words for 'Corn'.

Navajo	nà:dą́:'	
Chiricahua Apache	nà:dą́:'	Sapir 1936: perhaps borrowed from Navajo
Jicarilla Apache	naadą́'	Phone et al. 2007
San Carlos Apache (and Western Apache generally)	nadą́'	de Reuse 2006

Note: Spellings are from the sources given.

TABLE 12.7. The Words for 'Corn' in Northern and Pacific Coast Dene Languages.

Dëne Sųłiné	jie tth'oghé	'berry + yellow'	(Ives and Rice 2006)
Ahtna	xoos ghu'	'horse + teeth' ('horse' from English)	(Kari 1990)
Hupa	ka:n	(from English)	(Golla 1996)

Note: Spellings are from the sources given.

When we look at the northern and Pacific Coast languages, we find that there is not a single word for 'corn'; the word varies from one language to another in the languages for which a word is recorded, as shown in Table 12.7.

The existence of a common word in the Apachean languages when no such word is found in the other languages suggests a common origin in Apachean, at a time when the people whose ancestors became the Apacheans were together. It is worth noting here that Sapir (1936:229) speculates that the Chiricahua Apache term for 'corn' might have been borrowed from Navajo, perhaps because the Chiricahua (and the Mescalero) did not grow corn until very late (Deni Seymour, personal communication 2011). Thus, it is possible that this particular lexical item illustrates both common origin and diffusion.

It is worth noting as well that there are also new words where the various Apachean languages differ. A few of these are given in Table 12.8 for Navajo, Jicarilla Apache, San Carlos Apache, and, for some of them, Mescalero Apache.

The cognate and noncognate Apachean vocabulary discussed above is different in nature: the cognate vocabulary represents innovative items likely to have been encountered early in migration, while the noncognate vocabulary generally names innovative items introduced after contact. For instance, some of the words in Table 12.8 were adapted from Spanish.

While the use of cognates is the most common type of evidence for a common origin, other, more complex types of linguistic evidence can be adduced in support of this claim. One of these comes from the use of the well-known third-person pronouns *y*- and *b*- in the Apachean languages. In the Apachean languages for which there is adequate documentation, we find that a direct object

TABLE 12.8. Noncognate Apachean Words.

	NAVAJO	JICARILLA APACHE	SAN CARLOS APACHE	MESCALERO APACHE
'cowboy'	'akałii 'the one characterized by leather', 'akał bistłee'ii 'the one characterized by leather stockings'	magéelo (from Spanish 'vaquero')	idilohí 'roper'	mageedu (from Spanish 'vaquero')
'candle'	'ak'ah diltłi'í 'grease, fat, oil, tallow that burns', 'ak'ahko̞ níyizígíí 'grease, fat, oil, tallow + fire that is rod-like in shape'	tłamiko̞ ' 'grease' + 'its flame'	jeehko̞' 'gum, pitch' + 'fire'	
'donkey'	dzaanééz 'long ears'	ja'áá (?? 'ear' + ?)	túłgaiyé 'white chest'	ja'ę́ntų́é (ja'ę́ 'donkey' [jaa 'ear'] + ntu 'worthless, no good')
'key'	bee 'ą̨ą́ ńdítį́hí 'the one with which it is repeatedly opened'	yáabi (from Spanish 'llave')	bee ha'igę̨ę̨sé, bagę̨ę̨sé 'twisting open is done with it'	

Note: Navajo forms are from Young and Morgan (1987), Jicarilla Apache forms are from Phone et al. (2007), San Carlos Apache forms are from de Reuse (2006), and Mescalero Apache forms are from Breuninger et al. (1982).

TABLE 12.9. Distribution of the Object Pronoun y- in Navajo.

a.	'ashkii	'at'ééd	**y**íníł'į́
	boy	girl	3 sees *y*
	'The boy sees the girl.' (Young and Morgan 1987:65)		
b.	*'ashkii	'at'ééd	níł'į́
	boy	girl	3 sees

TABLE 12.10. Distribution of the Object Pronoun y- in Jicarilla Apache.

chiníí	moosha	**y**inoołchééł
dog	cat	3 is chasing *y*
'The dog is chasing the cat.' (Axelrod 2007:15)		

pronoun is required in the verb word. The sentence in Table 12.9a is acceptable when this pronoun is present, but not without it (as indicated by the asterisk before the sentence in Table 12.9b). I gloss (translate) this pronoun '*y*'—it is a third-person direct object in these examples. The abbreviation "3" stands for third-person, and in these examples it indicates that the subject of the sentence

TABLE 12.11. Distribution of the Object Pronoun *y-* in Tsuut'ina.

a. dìní   tsììlìh
   man   3 hires
   'He'll hire the man.' (Cook 1984:203)
b. tsìyìlìh
   3 hires *y*
   'He'll hire him.' (Cook 1984:203)

TABLE 12.12. Incorporated Noun in Tsuut'ina.

tsì-dìnìsí-t'ó   'I turned my head.' (Cook 1984:136)
tsì   'head'

TABLE 12.13. Incorporated Noun in Dëne Sųłiné.

bεghą nį́ **yat**ini:'ą   'I passed the words to him.' (Li 1946:417)
yatei   'word'

is third-person. For Navajo, see Table 12.9. For Jicarilla Apache, which is similar, see Table 12.10.

Outside Apachean, if a nominal object is present, there is not generally a pronominal object as well. This is illustrated in Table 12.11 with an example from Tsuut'ina. In Table 12.11a, the sentence has a nominal direct object, and no pronoun is present in the verb word. In the absence of the nominal object, the pronominal prefix is obligatory (Table 12.11b).

The languages differ as follows. The object pronoun is obligatory in the Apachean languages whether a nominal object is present or not, while in northern languages the pronoun is required only when the object is pronominal; conditions vary across languages as to whether it can occur, and, if so, when it might occur, if the object is nominal. While there are roots for the co-occurrence of the noun and the pronoun in the northern languages, it seems likely that this was a development in the Apachean group.

Another difference between Apachean and the northern languages comes from noun incorporation, or the inclusion of a noun inside the verb word. The northern languages allow for somewhat productive noun incorporation, as in the examples in Table 12.12 and Table 12.13. Here we see a noun that can appear independently occurring within the verb word.

Noun incorporation does not exist in the same sense in the Apachean languages: remnants of it can be found, but it is not productive, meaning that new words are not formed with noun incorporation. Axelrod (2007:60–62) points

TABLE 12.14. Numbers in Tsuut'ina and Some Apachean Languages.

	20	30
Tsuut'ina	'àká-dii	tó-dii
Navajo	nà:-dì:n	tá-dì:n
Jicarilla Apache	náa-din	káa-din
San Carlos Apache	na-din	tá-din

Note: The Tsuut'ina and Navajo forms are from Leer (2005); the Jicarilla Apache forms are from Phone et al. (2007), and the San Carlos Apache forms are from de Reuse (2006).

out that in Jicarilla Apache there are examples of noun incorporation but it is fairly nonproductive.

The linguistic evidence cited in this section suggests that the Apachean languages form a close-knit group with a common origin in the north, dividing into different groups along the journey south. Given the variation in these particular properties in the north and the similarity in Apachean, the most likely scenario is the development of these various characteristics before the Apachean languages split from each other.

What about the relationships of the Apachean group with northern languages? As noted earlier, Krauss and Golla (1981) speculate that the closest northern language to Apachean is Tsuut'ina, although, as we saw, they do not offer any linguistic evidence. Leer (2005) includes some ways in which Tsuut'ina and the Apachean languages (he uses the term "Southern Athabaskan") are similar.

First, Leer (2005:291) notes that Apachean languages and Tsuut'ina share the presence of a suffix that is found in stative verbs to denote negative qualities or with stative verbs containing a semantic component roughly translatable as "-ish." Second, Leer (2005:293) identifies a "system of counting decades," with its second part coming from the form meaning 'person', that is common to both Tsuut'ina and Apachean languages, as shown in Table 12.14. Finally, Leer (2005: 301–302) points to a similar form of the word for 'trousers, pants'. In most of the northern languages, a reflex of the form *səs-ł (nonpossessed), *-səs-łe' (possessed) occurs. For Tsuut'ina and Apachean, Leer posits the following forms instead, labeling them "regional Proto-Athabaskan": nonpossessed *həs-łe:, possessed *-(ə)s-łe'.

De Reuse (2005:210) points to a possible similarity between Plains Apache and Tsuut'ina: proto-Athapaskan reduced vowels have a mid tone in these two languages. However, the tone is low rather than mid in the remainder of the Apachean languages, making it difficult to know just how to evaluate this evidence.

While the evidence given here is not in itself sufficient to establish a definite link between Tsuut'ina and the Apachean languages, the similarities are interesting and definitely worth pursuing.

Linguistic Evidence for Time Depth

Having established that there is evidence of various sorts that the Apachean languages form a very close-knit group, and that, in all likelihood, the people who became today's Apacheans left the north in a single group, let us now turn to another question, the use of linguistic evidence for establishing time depth. As discussed earlier, in the Athapaskan literature, the following dates are commonly proposed for the formation of the proto-groups:

Proto-Athapaskan: 2,400 ± 500 years
Proto-Apachean: 1,200 years

What kind of linguistic evidence are these numbers based on?

The most common technique in linguistics for establishing time depth involves glottochronology. Glottochronology, also sometimes called lexicostatistics (there are some differences between them, but they are similar enough for our purposes to be lumped together), rests on the assumption that languages change at a uniform constant rate that can be quantified through a study of the part of the lexicon that expresses core universal, noncultural meanings. Vocabulary is drawn from a list commonly called the Swadesh word list. This list was created based on the assumption that there is a set of vocabulary that might be universal. It includes pronouns, some adjectives (e.g., 'big', 'long', 'small'), some verbs, and words such as 'woman', 'man', 'fish', 'dog', 'louse', 'tree', and body part terms. The words include those that are important in the comparative method, introduced in the section on characteristics of Apachean languages above.

In addition to a set of vocabulary, a way of determining length of separation is important; glottochronology starts with the assumption that stages separated by 1,000 years exhibit around 86 retentions out of 100 words, or 86 percent retention over this time period, with a 14 percent replacement.[3] The time depth of a split is computed with a formula (see Campbell 2004:201–210 for an introduction).

Krauss (1973:950–953) provides an overview of the literature on the use of glottochronology in the Athapaskan (and Na-Dene) families, giving a list of publications between 1951 and 1962 on this topic. The most important work was done by Hoijer (1956), who, using glottochronology, argues that the proto-Apachean split from the Northern Athapaskan languages occurred around AD 1000. He further proposes lengths of times of divergence for the Apachean languages, as shown in Table 12.15 along with updates computed by Sally Rice (personal communication 2011).

Hoijer also compares these with the times for a split from the northern languages established through glottochronology; I illustrate with Tsuut'ina (Sarcee) and Dëne Sųłiné (Chipewyan) (Table 12.16). Again, reported time depths are given based on Hoijer (1956), with Rice's (personal communication 2011) updates. The third number in Table 12.16 indicates the approximate year AD of separation (from Rice, personal communication 2011).

TABLE 12.15. Time Divergences for Apachean Languages Proposed by Harry Hoijer in 1956 and Sally Rice in 2011.

	NAVAJO	CHIRICAHUA APACHE	SAN CARLOS APACHE	JICARILLA APACHE
Chiricahua Apache	149 / 203			
San Carlos Apache	279 / 333	227 / 281		
Jicarilla Apache	279 / 333	200 / 254	335 / 389	
Lipan Apache	335 / 389	227 / 281	419 / 473	227 / 281

Note: The first number in each entry is from Hoijer (1956:226); the second is from Sally Rice (personal communication 2011).

TABLE 12.16. Time Divergences for Apachean, Dëne Sųłiné, and Tsuut'ina Proposed by Harry Hoijer in 1956 and Sally Rice in 2011 and Approximate Year of Separation.

	NAVAJO	CHIRICAHUA APACHE	SAN CARLOS APACHE	JICARILLA APACHE	LIPAN APACHE
Dëne Sųłiné	628 / 682 / 1329	660 / 714 / 1297	790 / 844 / 1167	724 / 778 / 1233	724 / 778 / 1233
Tsuut'ina	928 / 982 / 1029	928 / 982 / 1029	1036 / 1090 / 921	928 / 982 / 1029	1000 / 1054 / 957

Note: The first number in each entry is from Hoijer (1956:230); the second number and the year are from Sally Rice (personal communication 2011).

In a 1971 publication, Hoijer views the material slightly differently, from the perspective of shared percentages of vocabulary among the Apachean languages (Hoijer 1971b:5). These percentages are shown in Table 12.17.

Krauss (1973:952) cites a 1963 personal communication from Hoijer in which Hoijer said he was discouraged with glottochronology and repudiated the earlier dates he had proposed. Krauss (1973:952) remarks, "Part of this disenchantment is unjustified, in that the Alaskan materials were collected by investigators who were not trained in linguistics or in Athapaskan, with the result that there was far less uniformity in style of elicitation and, especially, far less communication between informant and investigator as to what was wanted." Krauss further notes that, in his own experiments with dating, he consistently arrived at a maximum divergence within Athapaskan of 2,400 ± 500 years.

Despite Krauss's remarks, many linguists reject glottochronology (see, for instance, Campbell 2004:204–210 for explicit discussion), while others continue to work with it and have tried to refine it. Whatever stance one takes on the value of glottochronology, it is extremely important to keep in mind that it does not have the accuracy of the radiocarbon or tree-ring dating methods that archaeologists often use. The problems that have been noted with glottochronology include whether there is a core universal set of vocabulary and whether the assumptions around constant and uniform rates of change are valid. A number of factors have been identified that might influence rates of change. These include

TABLE 12.17. Percentages of Shared Cognates in Apachean Languages.

	SAN CARLOS	CHIRICAHUA APACHE	MESCALERO APACHE	JICARILLA APACHE	LIPAN APACHE	KIOWA APACHE
Navajo	94	95	95	94	92	75
San Carlos Apache		96	94	93	90	74
Chiricahua Apache			97	95	93	75
Mescalero Apache				96	95	74
Jicarilla Apache					94	76
Lipan Apache						75

Note: From Hoijer 1971b:5.

the type of society (hunter-gatherer or agricultural), social relationships, geography, and latitude. Bowern (2010) provides a recent review of proposed correlates of language change in hunter-gatherer and other "small" languages, and I summarize some of her discussion here in order to show the complexity of this area. See also Nichols (2008) for discussion of some of the geographic factors that might play a role in rates of language spread.

Some have proposed that the rates of linguistic change that are used to determine time depths are applicable only to sedentary agricultural societies (e.g., Dixon 1997; Nettle 1999), and not to hunter-gatherer and other small societies. In the case of nonagricultural societies, a number of factors that might influence the rate of language change have been discussed. Nonagricultural communities are smaller than agricultural groups, being more tightly constrained by available food resources. One might expect that population size could affect language change and the rate of change. On the one hand, change in languages spoken by small populations might be slower than in larger groups because of the dense social network structures (see Milroy and Milroy 1985 on types of social networks); alternatively, change might be faster because it takes less time to diffuse through a smaller population. As Bowern points out, there is no agreement as to whether the rate of change in smaller populations is faster or slower than in larger groups.

Bowern further notes that predictions about change in terms of social structure are contradictory, that there is no clear evidence about how geography affects the speed of spread, and that there is little discussion about what the effect of cultural attitudes might be. Overall, Bowern (2010:673) argues that the notion of hunter-gatherer is not a unified one since there is no single factor that distinguishes agriculturalists from nonagricultural groups. She concludes that it is necessary to look at rates of change with respect to an array of factors, including population size, social structure, geography, and climate.

What factors might be involved in the conservatism of Athapaskan languages? Kari (2010) examines this question in some detail, proposing what he dubs the "Athabascan Geolinguistic Conservatism Hypothesis." Kari suggests that certain linguistic features of Dene languages contribute to their conservatism. For example, northern Dene societies are egalitarian and lack intense contact and convergence with people speaking other, unrelated languages. While Kari suggests that this was the case in the north, many of the chapters in this book note that Apacheans had contact with other groups. As mentioned earlier, Sapir (1921:209) notes that Dene languages tend not to borrow lexicon or grammar, nor do they influence other languages. Ives (2010:313), focusing on Apachean groups, remarks, "Even where Apachean speakers are in a distinct minority, Dene languages persist, with genuine resistance to the borrowing of terms. Despite this language conservatism, however, Apachean speakers (like Pacific Coast Athapaskans) have clearly been willing to adopt extensive suites of material and ceremonial culture from neighboring societies." Ives (2010:315) continues, "Intriguingly, in that trilogy of language, culture and genes, the Apachean evidence would suggest that Dene language may very well be the most resistant to change."

Conclusion

What conclusions can be drawn about Apachean migrations on the basis of linguistic evidence? First, the family is conservative in terms of language change. Second, the Apachean branch has several characteristics that distinguish it from Northern Athapaskan languages, suggesting a common origin for Apachean and later differentiation into the groups we recognize now. And third, there has been very little lexical borrowing in Athapaskan languages; the meaning of the existing lexical stock has been extended and new words created by regular and persistent Athapaskan word formation processes. A study of loanwords in a language provides strong evidence of contact between languages. Given the dearth of loanwords from people encountered along the way, there is no clear direct evidence from the lexicon and word formation in the languages about the people with whom the Apacheans came into contact, and thus of the southward route. (See Ives et al. 2010 for interesting discussion of linguistic evidence for contact with the Blackfoot.) In the rest of this conclusion, I elaborate on what types of linguistic data might be sought that would provide evidence for contact and, thus, for encounters with other peoples.

What else might further linguistic evidence reveal? First, continued work on the lexicon, with a focus on items that the Apacheans might have encountered through their journeys, might reveal whether there is an occasional loan from a non-Athapaskan language. More work on cognates, again with an in-depth look into the lexicon across the family, could also be helpful for understanding core meanings and meaning change; see Rice (2009) on eating and drinking verbs in Athapaskan languages for an example. Such a study of lexical items might reveal words in a particular language that do not appear to be found in other Athapaskan languages, and could potentially provide evidence of contact with other peoples on the journey south. See the Pan-Athapaskan Comparative Lexicon Project at the University of Alberta, a project that is focusing on material culture, biota, and social structure, for this type of research (http://www.linguistics.ualberta.ca/Research/Projects/PanAthapaskanComparativeLexico.aspx).

While words are a traditional focus of study for understanding potential contact effects, other avenues might prove to be fruitful as well. Expanding the domain of study in order to obtain an overall finer-grained understanding of the similarities and differences between the languages, combined with an understanding of pockets in which to look for contact effects beyond the lexicon, could be revealing. Thus while Athapaskan languages have been resistant to borrowing in obvious ways—the borrowing of words—there may well be other effects of contact that could reveal something about migration paths. Study beyond the lexicon and word formation, as in Webster's (this volume) examination of the use of certain discourse-level particles, might help identify contact languages along the journey. Contact effects can be identified beyond borrowed words and word structures through the study of patterns of expression and stylistic choices. This level of study of Apachean languages and the languages of the groups the Apacheans interacted with could well be revealing. See Mithun (2010) for interesting discussion of such evidence for contact in languages of the Americas.

Finally, a deeper understanding of dialects and of interactions between speakers of different languages over time is of interest. I have worked under the assumption that common vocabulary and structures in the Apachean languages but not with the northern languages reflect shared innovations, implying common origins of the Apachean languages, while different vocabulary in the different Apachean languages indicates items created after the Apachean groups split, and as discussed in this chapter, this hypothesis is broadly accepted in the linguistics literature. There is, however, an alternative—diffusion, with the similarities arising not because of common origin but because of borrowing across the Apachean languages. The linguistic evidence on its own cannot absolutely confirm common origin as opposed to diffusion, and evidence from other areas may be important here. (See, for instance, work by Babel et al. [2012] on descent and diffusion in Western and Central Numic.) However, the shared lexicon in Apachean languages reflects innovations that people would have encountered soon after leaving the north, as opposed to later, postcontact items, and this pattern suggests common origins, as do the structural similarities shared by the Apachean languages and not the northern languages (e.g., distribution of *y-/b-* pronouns). Thus, while diffusion is a possibility, the linguistic evidence in this case suggests a common origin of the Apachean languages, with movement and splitting as well as continuing interaction of peoples later on. This lack of a match between the linguistic evidence and the archaeological evidence reported in this book shows how much more we have to learn.

Linguistic work has an important contribution to make to the understanding of origins and migrations and, perhaps, how and when they took place. Linguistic evidence forms just one piece of the important puzzle of Apachean migration. Coupled with work in archaeology, ethnohistory, anthropology, and genetics, it may someday help us understand the full story of the Athapaskans' migration to the south.

Acknowledgments

I would like to thank Deni Seymour for inviting me to contribute to this volume, and for very helpful feedback on the paper. Thank you also to Willem de Reuse, Jack Ives, and Sally Rice for discussion of the issues and for their comments.

Notes

1. See http://www.uaf.edu/anlc/resources/athabascan/ for discussion of the history of the spelling of the name of this language family. The name "Dene" is often used now rather than the traditional Athapaskan/Athabaskan/Athabascan/Athapascan, replacing a Cree-origin word with a word from the language family.
2. Deni Seymour (personal communication, 2011) points out that Chiricahua and Mescalero should not be as Pueblo-culture influenced but influenced by the groups that surrounded them, namely, non-Puebloan groups.
3. This represents a simplification. There are two wordlists, a 100-word list and a 200-word list. The assumption is that there will be 86 percent retention of the 100-word list and 81 percent retention of the 200-word list each 1,000 years. Campbell (2004: 202) notes that the 200-word list is not sufficiently culture-free and thus the 100-word list is more commonly used.

References

Axelrod, Melissa
2007 Grammatical Sketch of Jicarilla Apache. In *Dictionary of Jicarilla Apache/Abáachi Mizaa Iłkee' Siijai*, edited by Wilhelmina Phone, Maureen Olson, and Matilda Martinez, pp. 9–67. Albuquerque: University of New Mexico Press.

Babel, Molly, Andrew Garrett, Michael Hauser, and Maziar Toosarvandani
2012 Descent and Diffusion in Language Diversification: A Study of Western Numic Dialectology. *International Journal of American Linguistics*.

Bowern, Claire
2010 Correlates of Language Change in Hunter-Gatherer and Other "Small" Languages. *Language and Linguistics Compass* 4(8):665–669.

Breuninger, Evelyn, Elbys Hugar, Ellen Ann Lathan, and Scott Rushforth
1982 *Mescalero Apache Dictionary*. Mescalero, New Mexico: Mescalero Apache Tribe.

Campbell, Lyle
1997 *American Indian Languages: The Historical Linguistics of Native America*. Oxford: Oxford University Press.
2004 *Historical Linguistics: An Introduction*. 2nd ed. Edinburgh: Edinburgh University Press.

Carter, Robin M.
1976 Chipewyan Classificatory Verbs. *International Journal of American Linguistics* 42(1):24–30.

Cook, Eung-Do
1984 *A Sarcee Grammar*. Vancouver: University of British Columbia Press.

de Reuse, Willem J.
2005 The Tonology of the Western Apache Noun Stem. In *Athabaskan Prosody*, edited by Sharon Hargus and Keren Rice, pp. 209–228. Amsterdam: John Benjamins.
2006 *A Practical Grammar of the San Carlos Apache Language*. With Phillip Goode. Munich: Lincom Studies in Native American Linguistics.

Dixon, R. M. W.
1997 *The Rise and Fall of Languages*. Cambridge: Cambridge University Press.

Fortescue, Michael
1998 *Language Relations across Bering Strait: Reappraising the Archaeological and Linguistic Evidence*. London: Cassell.

Foster, Michael K.
1996 Language and the Culture History of North America. In *Languages*, edited by Ives Goddard, pp. 64–110. Handbook of North American Indians, Vol. 17, William C. Sturtevant, general editor. Washington, D.C.: Smithsonian Institution.

Golla, Victor
1996 *Hupa Language Dictionary/Na:tinixwe Mixine:whe'*. 2nd ed. Hoopa, California: Hoopa Valley Tribal Council.
2000 Language Families of North America. In *America Past, America Present: Genes and Languages in the Americas and Beyond*, edited by Colin Renfrew, pp. 5–72. Papers in the Prehistory of Languages. Cambridge, U.K.: McDonald Institute for Archaeological Research.
2007 Linguistic Prehistory. In *California Prehistory: Colonization, Culture, and Complexity*, edited by Terry L. Jones and Kathryn A. Klar, pp. 71–82. Lanham, Maryland: AltaMira Press.
2008 Discussant comments for the symposium "Ways of Becoming: Dynamic Processes in the Creation of Athapaskan Identities and Landscapes." 73rd Annual Meeting of the Society for American Archaeology, Vancouver, British Columbia.

Hoijer, Harry
1938 The Southern Athapaskan Languages. *American Anthropologist*, new series, 40(1):75–87.
1945 Classificatory Verb Stems in the Apachean Languages. *International Journal of American Linguistics* 11(1):13–23.
1956 The Chronology of the Athapaskan Languages. *International Journal of American Linguistics* 22(4):219–232.
1971a Athapaskan Morphology. In *Studies in American Indian Linguistics*, edited by Jesse Sawyer. *University of California Studies in Linguistics* 75:113–148.
1971b The Position of the Apachean Languages in the Athapaskan Stock. In *Apachean Culture History and Ethnology*, edited by Keith H. Basso and Morris E. Opler, pp. 3–6. Anthropological Papers of the University of Arizona No. 21. Tucson: University of Arizona Press.

Ives, John W.
1990 *A Theory of Athapaskan Prehistory*. Boulder, Colorado: Westview Press; Calgary, Alberta: University of Calgary Press.
2003 Alberta, Athapaskans and Apachean Origins. In *Archaeology in Alberta: A View from the New Millennium*, edited by J. W. Brink and J. F. Dormaar, pp. 256–281. Medicine Hat: Archaeological Society of Alberta.
2010 Dene-Yeniseian, Migration, and Prehistory. In *The Dene-Yeniseian Connection*, edited by James Kari and Ben A. Potter, pp. 324–334. Anthropological Papers of

the University of Alaska, Vol. 5, new series, Nos. 1–2. Fairbanks: Department of Anthropology, University of Alaska.

Ives, John W., and Sally Rice
2006 Correspondences in Archaeological, Linguistic and Genetic Evidence for Apachean History. Poster presented at the Languages and Genes Conference, University of California–Santa Barbara.

Ives, John W., Sally Rice, and Stephanie Heming
2002 On the Dispersal of Athapaskan Peoples in Western North America. Paper presented at ARCLING II, Second Conference on the Archaeology and Linguistics of Australia, National Museum of Australia and the Australian Institute of Aboriginal and Torres Strait Islander Studies, Canberra.

Ives, John W., Sally Rice, and Edward J. Vajda
2010 Dene-Yeniseian and Processes of Deep Change in Kin Terminologies. In *The Dene-Yeniseian Connection*, edited by James Kari and Ben A. Potter, pp. 223–256. Anthropological Papers of the University of Alaska, Vol. 5, new series, Nos. 1–2. Fairbanks: Department of Anthropology, University of Alaska.

Kari, James
1990 *Ahtna Athabaskan Dictionary*. Fairbanks: Alaska Native Language Center, University of Alaska, and Ahtna, Inc.
2009 Some Issues in Dene-Yeniseian Prehistory. Paper presented at the Athabascan Languages Conference, University of California–Berkeley.
2010 The Concept of Geolinguistic Conservatism in Na-Dene Prehistory. In *The Dene-Yeniseian Connection*, edited by James Kari and Ben A. Potter, pp. 194–222. Anthropological Papers of the University of Alaska, Vol. 5, new series, Nos. 1–2. Fairbanks: Department of Anthropology, University of Alaska.

Kari, James, and Ben A. Potter (editors)
2010 *The Dene-Yeniseian Connection*. Anthropological Papers of the University of Alaska, Vol. 5, new series, Nos. 1–2. Fairbanks: Department of Anthropology, University of Alaska.

Krauss, Michael E.
1973 Na-Dene. In *Linguistics in North America*, edited by Thomas Sebeok, pp. 903–978. Current Trends in Linguistics, Vol. 10. The Hague: Mouton.
1980 *Alaska Native Languages: Past, Present, and Future*. Research Papers No. 4. Fairbanks: Alaska Native Language Center.
1986 Edward Sapir and Athabaskan Linguistics. In *New Perspectives in Language, Culture, and Personality: Proceedings of the Edward Sapir Centenary Conference (Ottawa, 1–3 October 1984)*, edited by William Cowan, Michael K. Foster, and Konrad Koerner, pp. 147–190. Studies in the History of the Language Sciences No. 41. Amsterdam: John Benjamins.
2005 Athabaskan Tone. In *Athabaskan Prosody*, edited by Sharon Hargus and Keren Rice, pp. 51–136. Amsterdam: John Benjamins.

Krauss, Michael E., and Victor K. Golla
1981 Northern Athapaskan Languages. In *Subarctic*, edited by June Helm, pp. 67–85. Handbook of North American Indians, Vol. 6, William C. Sturtevant, general editor. Washington, D.C.: Smithsonian Institution.

Leer, Jeff
1996 *Comparative Athabaskan Lexicon*. Alaska Native Language Archive. Fairbanks: Alaska Native Language Center. http://www.uaf.edu/anla/collections/ca/cal/.

2005   How Stress Shapes the Stem-Suffix Complex in Athabaskan. In *Athabaskan Prosody*, edited by Sharon Hargus and Keren Rice, pp. 277–318. Amsterdam: John Benjamins.

Li Fang-Kuei

1946   Chipewyan. In *Linguistic Structures of Native America*, edited by Harry Hoijer, pp. 398–423. Publications in Anthropology No. 6. New York: Viking Fund.

Milroy, James, and Lesley Milroy

1985   Linguistic Change, Social Network and Speaker Innovation. *Journal of Linguistics* 21(2): 339–384.

Mithun, Marianne

1999   *The Languages of Native North America*. Cambridge: Cambridge University Press.

2010   Contact and North American Languages. In *The Handbook of Language Contact*, edited by Raymond Hickey, pp. 673–694. Malden, Massachusetts: Wiley-Blackwell.

Nettle, Daniel

1999   *Linguistic Diversity*. New York: Oxford University Press.

Nichols, Johanna

2008   Language Spread Rates and Prehistorical American Migration Rates. *Current Anthropology* 49(6):1109–1117.

Phone, Wilhelmina, Maureen Olson, and Matilda Martinez

2007   *Dictionary of Jicarilla Apache: Abáachi Mizaa Iłkee' Siijai*. Albuquerque: University of New Mexico Press.

Rice, Sally

2009   Athapaskan Eating and Drinking Verbs and Constructions. In *The Linguistics of Eating and Drinking*, edited by John Newman, pp. 109–152. Amsterdam: John Benjamins.

Sapir, Edward

1921   *Language: An Introduction to the Study of Speech*. New York: Harcourt, Brace & World.

1936   Linguistic Evidence Suggestive of the Northern Origin of the Navaho. *American Anthropologist* 38(2):224–235.

Young, Robert W.

1983   Apachean Languages. In *Southwest*, edited by Alfonso Ortiz, pp. 393–400. Handbook of North American Indians, Vol. 10, William C. Sturtevant, general editor. Washington, D.C.: Smithsonian Institution.

Young, Robert W., and William Morgan Sr.

1987   *The Navajo Language: A Grammar and Colloquial Dictionary*. Rev. ed. Albuquerque: University of New Mexico Press.

CHAPTER 13

Apache Names in Spanish and Early Mexican Documents

What They Can Tell Us about the Early Contact Apache Dialect Situation

WILLEM J. DE REUSE

By the end of the eighteenth century, Spanish missionaries and military commanders had written an impressive collection of documents regarding the indigenous people inhabiting northern New Spain. These documents are a gold mine for the study of the Apache, particularly if one recalls that Spanish-speakers have had a long history of contact (both friendly and hostile) with Apachean-speaking groups, starting in the late sixteenth century. The history of Spanish-Apache relations is thus about 250 years longer than the history of Anglo-Apache contacts.[1] Spanish-language archival research with a focused interest in Apache history, ethnohistory, and biography started relatively recently and has resulted in the work of Griffen (1983, 1988, 1998), John (1984, 1988, 1989, 1991), and Sweeney (1991, 1998).

What I propose to do in this chapter is to find out whether such archives can tell us something about Apachean languages, in their earliest recorded forms, in view of the fact that these documents contain words, mostly personal names of Apaches and names of Apache groups, presumably written in an Apachean language. While such names cannot reveal when and how Apacheans arrived in the Southwest, they can provide us with precious information about the early contact dialect situation. Indeed, in thinking about Apachean groups, we tend today to recognize seven ethnolinguistic groups: Navajo, Western Apache, Chiricahua, Mescalero, Jicarilla, Lipan, and Plains Apache (or Kiowa-Apache). However, a number of other groups, in particular Gileño and Mimbreño, are named in the earlier literature. It has been assumed that such names refer to groups that can be neatly subsumed under the modern ethnolinguistic groups. In this chapter, I provide evidence that this assumption is ill-founded. I argue that some of the early group names do not match any of the other names and might correspond to ethnolinguistic groups of importance in the early contact situation but currently extinct.[2]

I have not had the opportunity to consult the original archives myself, but I trust the secondary works mentioned above to accurately reproduce words in an Apachean language. The archives and reports were not interested in linguistic pursuits, but insofar as they were valuable administrative, military, legal, or religious documents, they had to mention the proper names of Apaches involved, especially leaders, as well as, when relevant, group names. Occurrences of Apache words that are not personal or group names are exceedingly rare.[3] The first wordlists were compiled (mostly by Anglo-Americans) about a hundred years later than the first reliable mentions of Apache personal or group names in Spanish documents.

The Linguistic Significance of Apache Personal Names

The study of Apachean personal names in Spanish and early Mexican documents is interesting for several reasons. The first to point this out was William Griffen, in a 1998 preface to his seminal work *Apaches at War and Peace: The Janos Presidio, 1750–1858*, originally published in 1988. Griffen's (1998:ix) suggestion is intriguing enough to be quoted in full:

> While we may never know much about the Apaches' views of outsiders in the earlier periods, any hints from written sources certainly should be investigated. For example, documentary evidence indicates that some Apaches in the early nineteenth century lived in or close to Opata Indian communities in eastern Sonora. Not only did they learn the Opata language, but many also appear in the written sources under their Opata names (Apache "real" or sacred names, of course, would never be learned by outsiders). Nicknames often reveal some personal characteristic or bit of personal history, such as the names Mangas Coloradas ("red sleeves") and Cuchillo Negro ("black knife"). The apparently Opata-derived names probably do the same—Chirimi perhaps refers to "sparks" or "fire," for example. Other names may be Tarahumare or perhaps even Yaqui-Mayo, or may come from Indian groups contacted earlier such as the Jano, Jocome, Chiso, or Suma. Examples of these non-Apache and non-Spanish nicknames are Compá, Esquinalini, Esquiriba, Naperú, Nagué, Nasá, Pegá, Raji, Sanapa, Tadocha, Estadiya, Teboca, and Quidé. Any pattern that emerges in future investigation will be of help in interpreting Apache history.

I agree with Griffen's assessment, and the rest of this chapter attempts to refine and modify it from a more linguistic perspective. It should be noted that most recorded names of Apache people are not actually of Apachean or other indigenous origin: they are of Spanish origin.[4] The reason why Apaches provided outsiders with Spanish (or Opata) names is indeed due to the Athapaskan taboo against uttering one's own name, which I have mentioned previously (de Reuse 1996, 2002). It is also true that there are in the sources a number of indigenous names that are most likely not Apachean. Chirimi is a good example, and Yayame (Griffen 1998:130) is another.[5]

However, I disagree with Griffen's suggestion that the proportion of Opata or other non-Apache indigenous names is substantial. In particular, I think that most of the names he gives in the quotation above will turn out to have good Apachean etymologies. It certainly looks like the Athapaskan taboo was operative; otherwise there would not have been so many Spanish names in the documents. At the same time, however, quite a few Apaches volunteered genuine names. Maybe they thought the documents were important enough to deserve their real names because there was enough confidence in the document writer's ability to be discreet about it. After all, writing an Apache name down in a document destined for non-Apache readers is quite different from uttering it in front of another Apache. But this is speculation. In any event, my impression is that Opata or other non-Apache indigenous names are not numerous, and that many non-Apache-looking names will turn out to have Apache etymologies on closer examination.

I compiled a list of all the Apache-looking personal names in three of Griffen's works (1983, 1988, and 1998). It is certainly not a complete list for the area or period, since a few more names or spelling variants can be found in other secondary works, such as John (1991) and Sweeney (1991). The names from Griffen cover the period 1762–1857 and are from documents dealing with northern Chihuahua and the northeastern edge of Sonora. Including spelling or other variants of the same name, I came up with 144 names.

Plausible etymologies and linguistic analyses for each name are needed in order to prove that they are indeed Apache. Here are two examples of rather successful cases.

The earliest Apache name on my list is Natanijú,[6] recorded first in 1762, belonging to a leader who was from either the Gileño or the Mimbreño group. Variants are Natanejú, Natanijuí, and Natenajuyé. This name can be analyzed as follows. The *Nata* part is *naat'á* [7] 'chief, leader' (Opler 1983b:411), and the *nijú* part is the verb *niihoo* 'to be happy, content', according to Hoijer's *Chiricahua Stem List* (n.d.:68). The final *í* in the second spelling variant and the final *yé* in the last spelling variant are the relativizing enclitics *-í* and *-yé*. The word would thus be *naat'ániihoo*, with the variants *naat'ániihoo'í* or *naat'ániihooyé*, 'happy or content leader'.

A second example is Canslude, the only woman's name in the list.[8] It can be explained as Chiricahua *ganłóódí* 'the one with sore(s) on (her) arm', from *gan* 'arm' (Hoijer n.d.:44), *łóód* 'sore, scab' (Hoijer n.d.:109), and *-í*, the relativizing enclitic.

I discuss below a list of 30 names (a subset of the complete list of 144 names) that contain the same interesting part—*Jasque-*, *Jasquie-*, or its variants—and draw linguistic and dialectological conclusions.

Evidence from Apache Names Containing the Element *Jasque-*, *Jasquie-*

Lieutenant Colonel Don Antonio Cordero's influential description of the Apache, written in 1796, contains the following:

> The Apache is proud of nothing, except of being brave, this attitude reaching such a degree, that he despises the man of whom no bold deed is known, and on account of this he adds to his name that of "Jasquie", which means gallant, placing it before the one by which he is known, as Jasquietajusitlan, Jasquiedecja, etc. This idea and custom is prevalent among the Gileños and the Mimbreños who, actually, are the boldest. (Matson and Schroeder 1957:341)

The names that seem to contain this element *Jasque-*, *Jasquie-* in Griffen's works are listed in Table 13.1. All the names mentioned here are for male leaders (either war leaders or more permanent leaders). Apparently, only those individuals deserved a name starting in *Jasque-*, *Jasquie-*. Regarding the town names, I would expect Bacoachi and Bavispe (Sonora, Mexico) to be mostly a residence for the Chiricahua group, and Janos (Chihuahua, Mexico) for the Gileño and Mimbreño groups and to a lesser extent the Chiricahua group.

We are now ready for some philological commentary on the element *Jasque-*, *Jasquie-*. This element is well documented in Western Apache, Chiricahua, and Mescalero, the three recorded Apachean languages that are the potential descendants of eighteenth-century Chiricahua, Mimbreño, and Gileño varieties.[9] The element is a third-person verb form, Chiricahua *hashké* 'she/he is fierce, pugnacious' (Hoijer [n.d.]:52), Mescalero *haashké* 'she/he is mean' (Breuninger et al. 1982:152),[10] and Western Apache *hashkéé* 'she/he is mad, angry, mean'. Goodwin (1942:522) says that the Western Apache form implies fierceness, bravery, and fighting ability combined.[11]

There is quite a bit of spelling variation in the sources. If the *h-* is not heard, the element can be spelled *Asque-* or *Asquie-* (nos. 1–6 in Table 13.1); the initial syllable can also be written as *es-*, resulting in *Esque-*, *Esqui-*, or *Esquie-* (nos. 8–13 in Table 13.1). Escriba (no. 7) is a shortened version, perhaps from the influence of Spanish *escribir* or the Spanish surname Escrivá. Griffen (1998:ix), as shown by the quotation above, did not recognize the variant with initial *es-* and therefore assumed it was not Apache. We can be fairly sure that *es-* is a reduction of *ha(a)sh-*, since Western Apache names with *hashkéé* are invariably spelled in English with *es-*. Examples of Western Apache chiefs' names are Eskelta *hashkéé (i)łta* 'angry, he scatters it about' (Goodwin 1942:525, 581), Eskenasbas *hashkéé násbas* 'angry circular' (Goodwin 1942:579), and Eskimenzine *hashkéé bá nzín* 'angry, men stand in line for him' (Goodwin 1942:580). Finally, in more garbled spellings, the syllable *ha(a)sh-* can be dropped entirely, as in numbers 26–29 in Table 13.1, or just the *s* of the syllable can remain, as in number 30.

The variation in the spelling of the second syllable is more revealing from a phonetic point of view. There is variation between *-que-* (nos. 1–4, 8–9, 14–17)

TABLE 13.1. Apache Names Containing the Element *Jasque-* or *Jasquie-*.

NAME	DATE (IF MENTIONED IN ORIGINAL DOCUMENT)	GROUP [OR TOWN]
1. Asquedega = Jasquedegá		
2. Asquegocá	ca. 1787	Gileño
3. Asqueguigoca = Asquegocá		
4. Asquelite	1766	Gileño
5. Asquiedenchul		[Bavispe]
6. Asquiegocá = Asquegocá		
7. Escriba = Esquiriba		
8. Esquedegad = Jasquedegá		
9. Esquenelid	1794–1796	Chiricahua
10. Esquielnoctén = Squielnoctero		
11. Esquinalini[a]	1844	Chiricahua/Gileño
12. Esquiné[b]	1842	Mescalero?
13. Esquiriba[c]	1846–1850	[Bacoachi]
14. Jasquedegá[d]	1795–1849+	Gileño/Mimbreño
15. Jasquekanecjal[e]		Gileño/Mimbreño
16. Jasquenelté[f]	1790–1828+	Chiricahua
17. Jasquenilté = Jasquenelté		
18. Jasquiatil	1842	Gileño/Mimbreño
19. Jasquie-ja = Jasquieljal		
20. Jasquiedegá = Jasquedegá		
21. Jasquiegocá = Asquegocá		
22. Jasquieljal	1791–1797	Chiricahua
23. Jasquielté = Jasquenelté		
24. Jasquienachi	1787–1791	[Janos]
25. Jasquienolté[g] = Jasquenelté		
26. Quiejal = Jasquieljal		
27. Quielnelté = Jasquenelté		
28. Quienelté = Jasquenelté		
29. Quietjal = Jasquieljal		
30. Squielnoctero	1789	Mimbreño

Note: Names are from Griffen (1983, 1988, 1998). An equals sign means the same person as; a plus sign follows the year of death of the person bearing the name. When there is some uncertainty about the group name, I give two group names; when the group name is not mentioned or cannot be inferred, I give the town name in square brackets.
a. In Sweeney (1991), Esquinaline or Esconolea, a Chiricahua.
b. Escani in Sweeney (1991)?
c. Chiricahua, according to Sweeney (1991).
d. Jasquiédegá in Merino (John 1991:166) and apparently Jasquiedecja in Cordero (Matson and Schroeder 1957).
e. Another name for Natanijé, discussed in the text.
f. Jasquié Nelté in Merino (John 1991:166); Asquienalte and Asquenitery in Sweeney (1991).
g. In Merino (John 1991:166), there is mention of a Jasquié Nolten from the town of Guajoquillo, Nueva Vizcaya, who is not the same person as Jasquenelté.

and -*quie*- (5–6, 10, and 19–30). Thus for the same name, one has the alternation Jasquedegá (no. 14) and Jasquiedegá (no. 20). The alternant -*quie*- points to a strongly palatalized velar aspiration of the /k/ [k^{xy}] before front vowels, which is typical of Chiricahua and Mescalero Apache but does not exist in Western Apache (Hoijer 1942). This is evidence that the language involved here is closer to Chiricahua or Mescalero than to Western Apache.

What about the part following *ha(a)shké*? According to Goodwin (1942: 522), the second element is also a verb, typically a verb of movement. In the light of this Western Apache evidence, it is possible to interpret at least a few of these second elements. Thus Jasquedegá (no. 14) can be analyzed as Chiricahua *hashké deghá* 'angry, he is going to go' (Hoijer 1938:87),[12] and Esquiriba (no. 13) can be analyzed as Chiricahua *hashké dibá* 'angry, he is going on the warpath' (Hoijer [n.d.]:10). We cannot be completely sure of the interpretation because a translation of these names is never provided. That might be additional evidence that they were true names rather than nicknames.

Can we draw conclusions about what variety or varieties of Apache the names are in? The easy solution would be to say that they are Chiricahua, since Opler (1941, 1983b) started using the cover term "Chiricahua" for Chiricahua proper, Gileño, and Mimbreño because they are now so close culturally. Hoijer's (n.d.) linguistic work of the 1930s certainly has conveyed the impression that there is only one language here, with minute dialectal variation, which he also calls "Chiricahua" for convenience.

However, the data about names with *ha(a)shké* throw a monkey wrench into this easy solution. In Opler's most detailed ethnographic account of the Chiricahua (1941), there are many discussions of names, but not a word about names starting with the word "fierce" or "angry." In Griswold's comprehensive compilation (1958–1962) of names of Fort Sill Apaches from Oklahoma, which included descendants of Mimbreño and Chiricahua groups, there are only three names starting with something reminiscent of *ha(a)shké*: Esk-kel-lain (also spelled Ish-kaa-lin or Ish-kall-lee), "said to have no meaning" (p. 22), Ish-kay-znn (also spelled Eskin-zion) (p. 96), and Ish-key-eh-ahts-onzeh (p. 62). All three are identified as Warm Springs, an American-period term, which possibly refers to descendants of the Mimbreño.[13]

On the other hand, in Goodwin's equally detailed ethnographic account of the Western Apache (1942:522–523, 577–581), there is extensive discussion of names beginning with the word *hashkéé*, and it is stated that of 117 men's names recorded, 45 started with *hashkéé*. Since Cordero (Matson and Schroeder 1957) stated that the *Jasquie*-initial names were most common among the Gileño and Mimbreño, presumably Chiricahua-speakers, and since Western Apache are definitely not Chiricahua-speakers, the discrepancy merits an explanation.

There are five hypotheses that can be used to explain this discrepancy:
1. Goodwin obtained genuine men's names. The Chiricahua men managed to hide their genuine names from Opler, giving him nicknames instead, and

Opler was never told any *ha(a)shké* names. However, in view of the fact that both Goodwin and Opler were adept at obtaining personal information from their consultants (Goodwin 1942; Opler 1941), I find this hypothesis unlikely.

2. The Chiricahua/Gileño/Mimbreño drastically changed their naming patterns from the early nineteenth century to the early twentieth century. I find this hypothesis unlikely.
3. The names in Griffen's works are actually Western Apache, and the Western Apache at that time lived farther east, in territory later occupied by Chiricahua/Gileño/Mimbreño, and they moved west later. Thus the names are merely mentioning what geographical area (river or mountain) a particular group happened to live near and they do not tell us anything about dialect. This is a possibility, since there is historical evidence that other Apacheans, such as the Navajo, moved west into Hopi or Southern Paiute territory, and that Western Apache moved west into Yavapai territory (in the north) and into Sobaipuri territory in the San Pedro River Valley (in the south). However, there is linguistic evidence that the names are not Western Apache, since they have some Chiricahua phonetic characteristics. One is the strongly palatalized velar aspiration of the /k/ before front vowels, mentioned above.
4. The names in Griffen's works are actually Western Apache. These Western Apache were in constant contact with Chiricahua-speakers in northern New Spain, and under the influence of Chiricahua, or dialect mixture with Chiricahua, they started pronouncing their names with Chiricahua phonetic features while maintaining Western Apache naming patterns. It is true that there was contact between Chiricahua and Western Apache, and it is impossible to conclude that this would not result in phonetic influence. In the nineteenth century, there were attempts to concentrate all Apaches of Arizona (i.e., Chiricahua and Western Apache) on one reservation; descendants of Chiricahuas now living on the Western Apache reservations in Arizona speak Western Apache only, but a Chiricahua accent is detectable. However, since there was a degree of enmity and distrust between Chiricahua and Western Apache in pre-reservation times, it is not clear that dialect mixtures would have arisen then. Perhaps more convincingly, the names in Griffen often contain morphemic elements recorded only in modern Chiricahua, and not in Western Apache. For example, the verb *niihoo* 'to be happy, content', occurring in Nataniju, discussed above, exists only in recorded Chiricahua and has not been documented in Western Apache.[14]
5. These names belong to dialectal variants of Apache that are neither Chiricahua, as reported by Opler and Hoijer, nor Western Apache, as reported by Goodwin and myself. Possibly, this dialect is intermediate between Western Apache and recorded Chiricahua, which would explain why it has both Chiricahua phonetic features, such as the velar aspiration of /k/ before front

vowels mentioned already, and naming patterns that are more like Western Apache than Chiricahua proper. This is the hypothesis I suggest here.

Since the Gileño were located geographically (roughly) north of the Chiricahua and southeast of the Western Apache, one might tentatively label this intermediate dialect "Gileño." We need to keep in mind, however, that the term "Gileño" is a problematic one, since the Gila River Basin covers a large area of the Southwest and it is clear from the literature that any native groups (Apache, or O'odham- or Yuman-speakers) living near the Gila River at some point in history might have been called Gileño (Schroeder 1974a:257; Opler 1983a:388–389). What I assume is that in Griffen's sources and in Cordero's report, the term "Gileño" referred to a specific Apache group residing on the Gila River at a point in history. Furthermore, it is interesting that the term "Gileño" had become obsolete by the early American period (Opler 1983a:389), whereas there are still modern Apache who self-identify as Mimbreño or Chiricahua. Possibly, the term "Gileño" had become too vague to be of any use.

Also, it is likely that the naming pattern described in this section is Mimbreño as well, as Cordero says, and that it included some Chiricahua subgroups, since the list of names beginning in *Jasque-, Jasquie-* appears to contain Mimbreños and Chiricahuas. Possibly, the intermediate dialect would cover Gileño groups, as well as some (but certainly not all) eighteenth-century Mimbreño and Chiricahua groups. Indeed, since some modern Apache identify themselves as Mimbreño (or Warm Springs) or as Chiricahua but do not speak the intermediate dialect, one must assume that these modern Mimbreño and Chiricahua are not the descendants, in the linguistic sense, of the groups called Mimbreño and Chiricahua by Cordero and other early Spanish chroniclers.

EVIDENCE FROM CORDERO'S LIST OF APACHE GROUPS OR TRIBES

I now focus on Cordero's report, particularly his list of Apache groups or tribes.[15] Cordero's list appears to be carefully written and phonetically consistent, particularly in comparison with the earlier list of tribes made by Hugo O'Conor, written in 1771–1776 (Brugge 1961:60–62; Opler 1983a:388), which appears to be quite confused. Cordero's account became authoritative, and later military reports borrowed freely from it (John 1989, 1991). It also appears that Cordero knew Apache (Matson and Schroeder 1957:336), and it is likely that he got his information from one particular dialect. Assuming that, one might ask, What Apache dialect is the list written in? Cordero's list appears in Table 13.2.

Basehart (1959:31–33), who made the first detailed study of this list, also finds it quite useful, and suggests that the names were elicited from Chiricahua-speakers. I come to a different conclusion. I discuss the names of the list in the order in which they appear.

Vinni ettinen-ne 'Tontos' is interpretable as Chiricahua or Mescalero *bínii édiné n^{n}dé* (Goodwin 1942:6; Breuninger et al. 1982:88) or Western Apache *bíni'*

TABLE 13.2. Cordero's 1796 List of Apache Tribe Names.

"Names They Have for Themselves"	"Spaniards' Names"
Vinni ettinen-ne	Tontos
Segatajen-ne	Chiricaguis
Tjuiccujen-ne	Gileños
Iccujen-ne	Mimbreños
Yntajen-ne	Faraones
Sejen-ne	Mescaleros
Cuelcajen-ne	Llaneros
Lipajen-ne	Lipanes
Yutajen-ne	Navajos

Note: From Matson and Schroeder 1957:336.

édiné nnēē 'people with no mind'.[16] This is a term used by modern Chiricahua and Mescalero to refer to Western Apache. There is a propensity among Apaches (as among many other groups) to use the most descriptive or derogatory names for groups other than themselves. Western Apache do not call themselves by such a derogatory term, and thus we have good evidence that the list is not written in Western Apache itself.

Segatajen-ne 'Chiricaguis' is interpretable as Mescalero *tséghát'ahé nⁿdé* 'rock pocket people' (Breuninger et al. 1982:86; Opler 1983b:418), nowadays used for a Chiricahua division. This is a descriptive name, so possibly it was not used by the Chiricahua themselves. Indeed, it is not recorded by Opler or Hoijer as used by the Chiricahua themselves. It is thus unlikely that our mystery dialect is Chiricahua.

Tjuiccujen-ne 'Gileños' and Iccujen-ne 'Mimbreños' do not look very descriptive and probably contain a locative adverbial element *-kó-* or *-ko-* 'here, there' (Hoijer n.d.: 54); they never recur in the literature after Cordero's report. The *Tju-* in the first word is obviously *tó* [txú] 'water', possibly referring to the Gila River, and is the only element separating the two names. The first name is possibly translatable as 'river people from here' and the second one as 'people from here'. My guess is that either of those might have been self-denominations for the Apache-speaker providing the list.

Yntajen-ne 'Faraones' is interpretable as Mescalero or Chiricahua **iⁿdaahé nⁿdé* or Western Apache **ndaahé nnēē* 'enemy people'.[17] This is evidence that the person providing the list was not a Faraon.

I cannot analyze Sejen-ne 'Mescaleros'; it is not a contemporary Mescalero, Chiricahua, or Western Apache name.

Cuelcajen-ne 'Llaneros' is interpretable as Mescalero *guułgahé nⁿdé* 'plains people', the name for a modern Mescalero division (Breuninger et al. 1982:87).

Lipajen-ne 'Lipanes' is interpretable as Mescalero or Chiricahua *łibáhé n^{n}dé or Western Apache *łibáhé nnēē. However, this is not a contemporary Mescalero, Chiricahua, or Western Apache name, nor is it the Lipan self-designation (Opler 2001:951–952).

Yutajen-ne 'Navajos' is interpretable as Western Apache yúdahé nnēē 'people above or up'. This is what the Western Apache (but not the Chiricahua or Mescalero) call the Navajo, and is evidence of linguistic similarity of our mystery dialect to Western Apache, as well as geographical proximity to the Western Apache, since for the Western Apache, as well as for the person providing the list, they lived in the same direction (i.e., farther north).

Since there are several names in this list that are interpretable as Mescalero Apache, one might ask if the list could be Mescalero. There is phonetic evidence that it is not. The last element, n-ne, in each Apache group name means 'people'. I assume this spelling is an attempt at rendering the pronunciation nné, a word starting with a syllabic n followed by another n. The pronunciation nnēē of this word is typical for most Western Apache dialects. The recorded Chiricahua and Mescalero varieties have n^{n}dé for this word with a prenasalized ^{n}d instead of a simple n. The d part of the prenasalized ^{n}d is stronger in Mescalero; the n part is stronger in Chiricahua (Hoijer 1938:3). Certainly, if the list was Mescalero (and maybe even if it was Chiricahua), Cordero would have written nde, rather than the somewhat unusual n-ne.

Then again, the phonetic evidence of Tju- 'water' in Tjuiccujen-ne points to the pronunciation with velar aspiration [txu], which is typical of recorded Chiricahua or Mescalero, and not of Western Apache, since the Western Apache pronunciation is [t^{h}u:] (Hoijer 1942).

My hypothesis here is the same as the hypothesis under (5) in the previous section: Cordero's list is not written in modern Chiricahua, Western Apache, or Mescalero. Instead, it is a dialectal variety intermediate between modern Chiricahua and Western Apache, because it has name-giving and phonetic characteristics of both. Cordero's group or tribe name list is likely to represent a Gileño dialect or a Mimbreño dialect that is not the linguistic ancestor of present-day Chiricahua or Mimbreño. It is also likely that the list is in a Gileño or Mimbreño dialect because the Mimbreño and Gileño were the groups that Cordero was most familiar with, both in peace settlements and when fighting them.

Conclusion

I have argued, on the basis of evidence from Apache personal names and from Cordero's list of Apache tribe or group names, that at least some of the Gileño and Mimbreño with whom eighteenth-century and early nineteenth-century Spanish-speakers were in contact were neither Western Apache– nor Chiricahua-speakers, but spoke a variety linguistically intermediate between the recorded Western Apache and Chiricahua languages. This is the most likely explanation for why many Gileño (and some Mimbreño and Chiricahua) names have linguistic characteristics of both modern Chiricahua and Western Apache but have a uniquely Western Apache naming pattern.

One might ask what happened to these groups. Since they were the ones most in touch with Spaniards and early Mexicans, through complex patterns of raiding and trading and friendship, one would expect that some of them merged with New Spain's settlements, either voluntarily or through slavery, and that some were exterminated. It is possible that what was called the Southern Chiricahua band in reservation times (*nédnaa'í* 'enemy people'; Opler 1983b:401) would have contained some of the remnants of these groups. In any event, it is not at all unlikely that some Apache ethnolinguistic groups disappeared from history without leaving a clear linguistic trace in the remaining modern languages. Such a likelihood is only one of the reasons why a philological inspection of Apache names in early Spanish and Mexican documents is a rewarding pursuit.

Acknowledgments

This chapter is a revised and updated version of an article published as "Apache Personal Names in Spanish and Early Mexican Documents: Their Linguistic and Dialectological Significance," *Memorias del VII Encuentro de Lingüística en el Noroeste*, Vol. 2, pp. 235–251 (Hermosillo: Universidad de Sonora, 2004). I am indebted to the editors of the *Memorias* for their gracious permission to republish the article in this book. In addition, I thank the audiences at the VII Encuentro and the Linguistics Colloquium at the University of Oklahoma, November 21, 2002, for their comments. This chapter also owes a great deal to suggestions from Philip Greenfeld, Michael Krauss, and Deni Seymour. It was inspired by Muriel Saville-Troike's work on Apachean philology and benefited from comments from Michael Darrow. Thanks to all of you.

Notes

1. Nevertheless, there exist more book-length treatments of the history of Anglo-Apache contacts than of the history of Spanish-Apache contacts. Notable cases of the latter are the pioneering general works of Thomas (1932, 1941), Spicer (1962), and Moorhead (1968). For Apachean groups, there is Forbes's *Apache, Navaho and Spaniard* (1960), which covers the period ca. AD 1535–1698 and has always been somewhat controversial because of its strong anti-Spanish bias. Schroeder's reports (1974a, 1974b), written for the Indian Land Claims Commission, include useful surveys.
2. From an archaeological point of view, it might be the case that these extinct groups left an archaeological mark in the Southwest that does not neatly correspond to any of the present-day Apachean ethnolinguistic groups.
3. The earliest Apache word in Spanish sources that is not a personal name appears to be *nitisi* 'immortal, desert milkweed', a plant name in Nentvig's *Rudo Ensayo* of 1764 (Nentvig 1980:50). A possible interpretation of this word might be *i'níí tsįh* 'lightning stick', which, in modern Western Apache, is the name for honeysuckle (*Lonicera* sp.) (Randall and Cassa 2002:56).

4. These are nicknames such as Coleto Amarillo, El Fuerte, El Zurdo, Feroz, and Mano Mocha; or first names such as Andrés, Cristóbal, Francisquillo, and Matías; or names derived from Spanish (or Basque) surnames such as Narbona and Irigoyen.
5. I have not been able to find good etymologies for these presumably Opata names in Opata lexical compilations. Thanks to David Shaul for sending me some Opata materials.
6. The spellings of Apache names in the Spanish documents follow the conventions of the Spanish spelling system. For example, the letter <j> represents the sound [x] or [h] of the International Phonetic Alphabet.
7. The spellings of the Apache names follow the system set out for Western Apache in de Reuse 2006. In this system, diacritics to be noted are the following: an acute accent indicates a high tone; a macron indicates a mid tone; an ogonek (hook under a vowel) indicates the nasalization of a vowel; the slash through the letter <l> indicates that it is a voiceless fricative similar to Welsh ll; an apostrophe between two vowels or at the end of a word indicates a glottal stop; and an apostrophe following a consonant indicates that that consonant is glottalized.
8. Indeed, Apache names for women are severely underrepresented in the documents. This could be because women were not often leaders or because Spanish-speakers tended not to take female leaders into account in their documents.
9. I assume that each of these Apache groups or tribes, as defined by Cordero (Matson and Schroeder 1957; see discussion below), might have had its own distinctive language variety of Apache.
10. The spellings of Mescalero names from Breuninger and others (1982) have been modified to accord with Hoijer's (1938) transcriptions of Mescalero Apache.
11. Interestingly enough, this same word also exists in Hopi—*haskye* 'aggressive, vicious, hostile' (Hopi Dictionary Project 1998:63)—apparently borrowed from the Navajo cognate *hashké* 'he is angry, he is mean, warrior'.
12. It is interesting that the form from Merino given in Note d to Table 13.1—Jasquiédegá—is written as one word but with two stress marks, which is counter to Spanish spelling conventions of one stress mark per word. The Apache syllables with stress marks are definitely the two Apache syllables that would have a measure of stress. But in this word the two syllables so marked are also the only ones with a high tone, so it is possible that some Spanish writers wrote stress marks because they perceived a high tone as stress.
13. Michael Darrow, tribal historian of the Fort Sill Chiricahua–Warm Springs Apache Nation (personal communication 2004) agrees that contemporary Chiricahua names do not contain *hashké*, and suggests that the three names from Griswold are more likely to contain a Chiricahua word for 'boy' than Chiricahua *hashké*.
14. Intriguingly, this person is also known with a Western Apache–looking *Jasqué*- name: Jasquekanecjal. This by itself is not evidence of the person's group affiliation, because it is possible to argue that Natanijú was the name the Chiricahuas gave him and Jasquekanecjal was the name the Western Apaches gave him.
15. I do not take a position on whether the Apache names on this list refer to "tribes" or some other sort of subdivision such as a "group." Cordero alternates between "groups" and "tribes," so I assume that a distinction is not relevant here.
16. I assume that the gloss 'No face people' given in Breuninger and others (1982:88) is a misinterpretation.
17. Starred forms are my constructions.

References

Basehart, Harry W.
1959 *Chiricahua Apache Subsistence and Socio-Political Organization, Section I*. A report of the Mescalero-Chiricahua Land Claims Project, Contract No. 290-154. Albuquerque: University of New Mexico.

Breuninger, Evelyn, Elbys Hugar, Ellen Ann Lathan, and Scott Rushforth
1982 *Mescalero Apache Dictionary*. Mescalero, New Mexico: Mescalero Apache Tribe.

Brugge, David M.
1961 Notes on the Apaches in the Late 18th Century. *Katunob* 2(1):59–63. Magnolia, Arkansas.

de Reuse, Willem J.
1996 The Functions of Spanish Loanwords in 19th Century Sources on the Western Apache Language. In *Memorias del III Encuentro de Lingüistica en el Noroeste*, Vol. 1, pp. 151–179. Hermosillo: Universidad de Sonora.
2002 Palabras Comanches en las lenguas de los Apaches Llaneros. In *Memorias del VI Encuentro de Lingüistica en el Noroeste*, Vol. 2, pp. 229–238. Hermosillo: Universidad de Sonora.
2006 *A Practical Grammar of the San Carlos Apache Language*. With Phillip Goode. Munich: Lincom Studies in Native American Linguistics.

Forbes, Jack D.
1960 *Apache, Navaho, and Spaniard*. Norman: University of Oklahoma Press.

Goodwin, Grenville
1942 *The Social Organization of the Western Apache*. Chicago: University of Chicago Press. Reprinted. Tucson: University of Arizona Press, 1969.

Griffen, William B.
1983 The Compas: A Chiricahua Apache Family in the Late 18th and Early 19th Centuries. *American Indian Quarterly* 7(2):21–49.
1988 *Utmost Good Faith: Patterns of Apache-Mexican Hostilities in Northern Chihuahua Border Warfare, 1821–1848*. Albuquerque: University of New Mexico Press.
1998 *Apaches at War and Peace: The Janos Presidio, 1750–1858*. Norman: University of Oklahoma Press. First published by University of New Mexico Press, 1988.

Griswold, Gillett
1858– The Fort Sill Apaches: Their Vital Statistics, Tribal Origins, Antecedents. Ms. on
1962 file, U.S. Field Artillery and Fort Sill Museum, Fort Sill, Oklahoma.

Hoijer, Harry
N.d. Chiricahua Apache Stems. Ms., copy in Alaska Native Language Center Archives, University of Alaska, Fairbanks.
1938 *Chiricahua and Mescalero Apache Texts, with Ethnological Notes by Morris Opler*. Chicago: University of Chicago Press.
1942 Phonetic and Phonemic Change in the Athapaskan Languages. *Language* 18(3): 218–220.

Hopi Dictionary Project
1998 *Hopi Dictionary = Hopìikwa Lavàytutuveni: A Hopi-English Dictionary of the Third Mesa Dialect*. Tucson: University of Arizona Press.

John, Elizabeth A. H.
1984 A Cautionary Exercise in Apache Historiography. *Journal of Arizona History* 25(3):301–315.
1988 Bernardo de Galvez on the Apache Frontier. A Cautionary Note for Gringo Historians. *Journal of Arizona History* 29(4):427–430.

1991 Views from a Desk in Chihuahua: Manuel Merino's Report on Apaches and Neighboring Nations, ca. 1804. *Southwestern Historical Quarterly* 95(2):138–204.

John, Elizabeth A. H. (editor)

1989 *Views from the Apache Frontier: Report on the Northern Provinces of New Spain.* By José Cortés. Translated by John Wheat. Norman: University of Oklahoma Press.

Matson, Daniel S., and Albert H. Schroeder

1957 Cordero's Description of the Apache—1796. *New Mexico Historical Review* 32(4): 335–356.

Moorhead, Max L.

1968 *The Apache Frontier: Jacobo Ugarte and Spanish-Indian Relations in New Spain, 1769–1791.* Norman: University of Oklahoma Press.

Nentvig, Juan, S.J.

1980 *Rudo Ensayo: A Description of Sonora and Arizona in 1764.* Translated, clarified, and annotated by Alberto Francisco Pradeau and Robert R. Rasmussen. Tucson: University of Arizona Press.

Opler, Morris E.

1941 *An Apache Life-Way: The Economic, Social, and Religious Institutions of the Chiricahua Indians.* Chicago: University of Chicago Press. Reprinted. Lincoln: University of Nebraska Press, 1996.

Opler, Morris, E.

1983a The Apachean Culture Pattern and Its Origins. In *Southwest*, edited by Alfonso Ortiz, pp. 368–392. Handbook of North American Indians, Vol. 10, William C. Sturtevant, general editor. Washington, D.C.: Smithsonian Institution.

1983b Chiricahua Apache. In *Southwest*, edited by Alfonso Ortiz, pp. 401–418. Handbook of North American Indians, Vol. 10, William C. Sturtevant, general editor. Washington, D.C.: Smithsonian Institution.

1983c Mescalero Apache. In *Southwest*, edited by Alfonso Ortiz, pp. 419–439. Handbook of North American Indians, Vol. 10, William C. Sturtevant, general editor. Washington, D.C.: Smithsonian Institution.

2001 Lipan Apache. In *Plains,* edited by Raymond J. DeMallie, pp. 941–952. Handbook of North American Indians, Vol. 13, William C. Sturtevant, general editor. Washington, D.C.: Smithsonian Institution.

Randall, Vincent, and Jeanette Cassa

2002 *Nigosdzan Bił Dagodotł'izhí: Western Apache Trees and Shrubs.* San Carlos, Arizona: San Carlos Apache Tribe, White Mountain Apache Tribe, Yavapai-Apache Nation, and Tonto Apache Tribe.

Schroeder, Albert H.

1974a A Study of the Apache Indians, Part IV: The Mogollon, Copper Mine, Mimbres, Warm Spring, and Chiricahua Apaches. In *Apache Indians*, edited by David Horr, pp. 1–189 (renumbered 1–219). American Indian Ethnohistory: Indians of the Southwest. New York: Garland.

1974b A Study of the Apache Indians, Part V-A: "Tonto" and Western Apaches. In *Apache Indians*, edited by David Horr, pp. 1–50 (renumbered pp. 327–451). American Indian Ethnohistory: Indians of the Southwest. New York: Garland.

Spicer, Edward H.

1962 *Cycles of Conquest: The Impact of Spain, Mexico, and the United States on the Indians of the Southwest, 1533–1960.* Tucson: University of Arizona Press.

Sweeney, Edwin R.
1991   *Cochise, Chiricahua Apache Chief.* Norman: University of Oklahoma Press.
1998   *Mangas Coloradas, Chief of the Chiricahua Apaches.* Norman: University of Oklahoma Press.

Thomas, Alfred Barnaby
1932   *Forgotten Frontiers: A Study of the Spanish Indian Policy of Don Juan Bautista de Anza, Governor of New Mexico, 1777–1787.* Norman: University of Oklahoma Press.
1941   *Teodoro de Croix and the Northern Frontier of New Spain, 1776–1783.* Norman: University of Oklahoma Press.

CHAPTER 14

Southern Athapaskan Quotative Evidentials

A Discursive Areal Typology

ANTHONY K. WEBSTER

This chapter concerns an areal discursive typology of the Southwest, that is, a typology of discourse features irrespective of language family. I take as the center of this comparative project the Southern Athapaskan languages. I compare the use of an independent verb of speaking with dependent enclitic markings for quotative evidentials. I then compare the resulting division with selected Northern and Pacific Athapaskan languages and finally with other Southwestern languages (see Rice, this volume, on the general outlines of the Athapaskan language family). I then make (1) an internal division of Southern Athapaskan languages based on a discursive typology, (2) a genetic comparison of that division with related Northern and Pacific Athapaskan languages, and (3) an areal comparison with unrelated Southwestern languages. In doing so, I argue that a discursive typology (based on form and function) cross-cuts earlier divisions based on lexical and phonological distinctions within Southern Athapaskan languages. I conclude by suggesting that such a division may be explained by two possible hypotheses (both in need of further testing): a more prolonged presence for Southern Athapaskan speakers in the Southwest and/or a more intensive interactional relation between what I term the Eastern discursive Apachean subgroup and non-Apachean peoples. This chapter also suggests that there was only one migration into the Southwest (see also Webster 2008). Finally, in respect to methodology, I argue that ethnopoetics may be of crucial value in historical linguistics, especially a historical linguistics that focuses on discursive typologies.

Both Kroskrity (1998) and Beier et al. (2002) argue for approaching areal linguistics from a discursive perspective (both investigate evidentials). By a discursive approach to areal linguistics, I mean that it is not enough to simply note the presence or absence of certain grammatical features; rather, we need to understand their discursive use as well. For example, as noted by Kroskrity (1998), Rio Grande Tewa, Arizona Tewa, and Hopi all have an "evidential particle" that marks information as outside firsthand experience. Rio Grande Tewa and Arizona Tewa are related languages, whereas Hopi is a Uto-Aztecan language and

TABLE 14.1. Division Based on /t/ → /k/ Split.

WESTERN APACHEAN /T/		EASTERN APACHEAN /K/	
Language	'water'	Language	'water'
Navajo	tó	Jicarilla Apache	kó
Chiricahua Apache	tó		
		Lipan Apache	kó
Mescalero Apache	tú		
		Plains Apache	kóó
Western Apache	tóó		

not related to the Kiowa-Tanoan Tewa languages. However, both Arizona Tewa and Hopi use the evidential particle (*ba* and *yaw*, respectively) far more commonly in genres of traditional narratives than do Rio Grande Tewa. Kroskrity (1998) argues that it is the influence of Hopi rhetorical patterns on Arizona Tewa that has led to a "discursive convergence." Thus while all three languages have a putative evidential particle, an examination of the discursive use of that particle reveals historical connections and interactions.

TWO TRADITIONAL WAYS OF DIVIDING SOUTHERN ATHAPASKAN LANGUAGES

I begin by briefly discussing two ways that Southern Athapaskan languages have been divided into Eastern and Western language groupings. The first way concerns phonology. As Hoijer (1942) noted, there is a general division based on a /t/→/k/ shift in Southern Athapaskan languages. Navajo, Chiricahua Apache, Mescalero Apache, and Western Apache all have a stem initial /t/. On the other hand, Jicarilla Apache, Lipan Apache, and Plains Apache all have a stem initial /k/. Table 14.1 gives the East/West division and a prototypical emblem of that shift (the word for water).

Haas (1968) noted that in Chipewyan (Northern Athapaskan) there is also an internal East/West /t/→/k/ shift. According to Haas (1968), the Yellowknife Chipewyan dialect had shifted from the base Athapaskan /t/ to /k/. More recently, Cook (1989) has suggested that the shift is not peculiar to any particular dialect of Chipewyan, but rather can be found in various Chipewyan dialects, though it seems localized in Fond du Lac, Saskatchewan, and Snowdrift, Northwest Territories. Indeed, Saville-Troike (1974) has suggested that there was an internal /t/→/k/ dialect difference that followed the Lukachukai and Chuska Mountains and separated an internal East/West division. If so, then Navajo

TABLE 14.2. Divergence Times (in Years) Based on Cognates.

	NAVAJO	CHIRICAHUA	SAN CARLOS	JICARILLA
Chiricahua	149			
San Carlos	279	227		
Jicarilla	279	200	335	
Lipan	335	227	419	227

Note: From Hoijer 1956a:226.

resembled Chipewyan in having an internal distribution of /t/ →/k/ (see, however, Brugge, this volume).

Another way that Southern Athapaskan languages have been divided has been based on lexico-statistics, or glottochronology; (see also Rice, this volume). Hoijer (1956a, 1971) presented lexico-statistic data that were used to augment his (1938a) earlier division of Southern Athapaskan languages based on phonological features (see Table 14.1). And while lexico-statistics has faced enormous (and I believe devastating) scrutiny by several linguists, including Hoijer (1956b) himself, it is interesting to note that Hoijer's lexico-statistic evidence suggested a more complicated view of Southern Athapaskan languages. In Table 14.2, I reproduce Hoijer's (1956a) results for time of divergence based on a comparison of 100 core words for Navajo, Chiricahua, San Carlos, Jicarilla, and Lipan Apache.

As Hoijer (1956a) notes, the above numbers suggest that the Southern Athapaskan languages diverged only relatively recently, a little more than four hundred years ago. However, this method, as Hoijer notes, completely obscures the phonological differences revealed in the /t/ →/k/ split. Chiricahua Apache, a /t/ language, shares more cognates with Jicarilla Apache, a /k/ language, than it does with San Carlos Apache, a fellow /t/ language, which is roughly the same amount it shares with Lipan Apache, another /k/ language. Chiricahua Apache is nearest to Navajo, also a /t/ language. Below I present one plausible division based on the lexico-statistic results (this is a decidedly Chiricahua Apache–centric view):

Navajo   Lipan   San Carlos
Chiricahua
Jicarilla

Such a division flies in the face of the historical information we have. As Hoijer (1956a:226) notes, "These discrepancies may well result from the fact that all five languages have been in more or less close contact for the last two or three hundred years. The same factor may account for the generally low times of divergence." In other words, Apachean peoples have continued to talk to one another.

TABLE 14.3. Quotative Evidentials Used in Southern Athapaskan Languages.

Language	Evidential Used in Traditional Narrative
Navajo	jiní (ji + ní) 'one says, they say' (Sapir and Hoijer 1942)
Chiricahua Apache	-ná'a 'they say, so they say' (Hoijer 1938)
Jicarilla Apache	-ná 'so they say, how it is told' (Tuttle and Sandoval 2002: 111; Sandoval 1984:163)
Lipan Apache	-ná 'they say' (Hoijer 1975)
Mescalero Apache	-ná'a 'so they say' (Hoijer 1938)
Western Apache	ch'in̲i̲i̲ 'it is said' (ch'i + -n̲i̲i̲) lęk'eh 'it is said' (de Reuse 2003) léni 'it's said to have happened' (Nevins and Nevins 2004:286)

A Discursive Typological View

Hoijer's point, that we must take into account the interactional histories of languages, seems warranted here. It is also crucial to view these interactional histories not so much as "languages" but rather as clusters of speakers who have interacted. A discursive typological approach does just this. In what follows I present the results of a survey of six of the seven generally recognized Southern Athapaskan languages. Plains Apache has been excluded due to a lack of relevant data. For purposes here, I have used the following data sets:

1. Chiricahua Apache: Hoijer 1938b
2. Mescalero Apache: Hoijer 1938b
3. Jicarilla Apache: Goddard 1911
4. Western Apache:
   White Mountain Apache: Goddard 1920
   San Carlos Apache: Goddard 1919
5. Lipan Apache: Hoijer 1975
6. Navajo: Sapir and Hoijer 1942; Goddard 1933

In inspecting these texts, I have attempted to discern the ways that certain evidentials are used. Specifically, I have been concerned with how traditional narratives are marked by the repeated use of evidential devices. In work by Toelken and Scott (1981), Webster (1999a, 1999b, 2004, 2006), and de Reuse (2003), the use of evidentials has been described for Navajo, Chiricahua, Mescalero, Lipan, and Western Apache. Indeed, for all six languages under consideration here (Chiricahua, Mescalero, Navajo, Lipan, Western Apache, and Jicarilla), traditional narratives that are understood to be outside the narrator's firsthand experience are marked by the recurrent use of an evidential marker. In Table 14.3 I provide the relevant information.

The evidentials in the table all occur in various traditional narrative genres. For example, most of these forms occur in Coyote narratives (a traditional genre of trickster narratives). In Navajo the evidential *jiní* seems to act as a verse-marking device (depending on the speaker, it can also act as a framing device or a line-marking device). Likewise, -ná'a seems to work as a line-marking device in Chiricahua Apache but functions more as a verse-marking device in Mescalero Apache (Webster 1999a, 1999b). There seem to be a variety of Western Apache forms, but here we restrict ourselves to *ch'inii* 'it is said' because it is the most common form found in the Goddard texts.

Below I provide an example of each, culled from one of the above-mentioned sources. For purposes here, an underline indicates nasality on the vowel, an acute accent indicates high tone, ['] is a glottal stop, and [ł] is a voiceless lateral fricative. The relevant forms are in boldface.

Navajo example:
'ałk'idą́ą́' ma'ii jooldlosh, **jiní**
long ago coyote trotting along it is said (Sapir and Hoijer 1942:20)

Chiricahua Apache example:
yiiłndi**ná'a**
He (Coyote) said to him, they say. (Hoijer 1938b:16:22:2)

Jicarilla Apache example:
Dá'ko didé ńkeenádiidą́í'íí , ań koshí igał**ná**
He had on a big warm coat, they say. (Tuttle and Sandoval 2002:111)

Lipan Apache example:
tsínaaslá dá'á'ii gokídaa'yaa**ná**.
Pairs of Stones Lie About right there [was] their country, it is said. (Hoijer 1975:8, 25)

Mescalero Apache example:
'ákoo 'inoodzá**ná'a**
And then he went away, they say. (Hoijer 1938b:157)

Western Apache example:
akogo Geda dezla **tc'i ni n**
Then they planted them they say (Goddard 1919:151)

In Southern Athapaskan narrative traditions, we see two general forms of the quotative evidential. In one group we have independent verb forms that have the fourth-person subject pronominal prefix, used for persons who are "socially distant" (i.e., relatives by marriage and the dead). Navajo is an example of this. Here we see the verb of speaking *-ní* prefixed with the fourth-person subject pronoun *ji-*, which lends a glossing of "one says." This fourth-person pronominal can be found in all Southern Athapaskan languages. In Navajo and Western

TABLE 14.4. East/West Split Based on Discursive Typology.

EASTERN APACHEAN (NARRATIVE ENCLITIC)	WESTERN APACHEAN (VERB OF SPEAKING)
Chiricahua Apache	Navajo
Jicarilla Apache	Western Apache
Lipan Apache	
Mescalero Apache	

Apache, the quotative evidentials give a sense that one is citing the words of the ancestors. In the other grouping of languages, we find an enclitic that is attached to the final verb in a clause or sentence within a traditional narrative. This form, -ná'a or -ná, is not segmentable into readily apparent morphemes like the Western Apache or Navajo forms.

We should also note that while there are two basic forms, jiní and -ná'a/-ná, the quotative evidential appears to function in a similar manner across languages and its relative placement clause finally is also consistent. In reviewing the literature regarding the function of these quotative evidentials, we find that they are commonly cited as organizing devices within certain genres of traditional narratives (see Basso and Tessay 1994; Nevins and Nevins 2004; de Reuse 2003; Toelken and Scott 1981; Webster 1999a, 1999b, 2004). It would appear that while Southern Athapaskan languages use quotative evidentials as ethnopoetic organizing devices within narratives (that is, the evidentials aid in organizing narratives into a series of poetic lines), they differ between independent verbs of speaking and dependent "narrative" enclitics. The function, then, is roughly the same, but the form varies (more work needs to be done to validate this impression). Organizing Southern Athapaskan languages along a discursive typological axis based on relatively dependent and morphologically opaque forms (enclitics) versus independent and morphologically analyzable forms (pronoun plus verb of speaking) of quotative evidentials reveals the grouping shown in Table 14.4.

Notice that such an organization cross-cuts both the lexical and phonological divisions. It should be stated explicitly here that a fourth person plus a verb of speaking (jiní) exists in Chiricahua, Jicarilla, Lipan, and Mescalero Apache, but it is not used in the same rhetorical or ethnopoetic manner as it is in Navajo and Western Apache. On the other hand, as far as I have been able to discern, a concomitant narrative enclitic (-ná'a/-ná), as found in the Eastern typological branch, has not been recorded in either Navajo or Western Apache. The narrative enclitic appears to be restricted to Jicarilla, Chiricahua, Mescalero, and Lipan. Throughout the rest of this chapter I use this division of Apachean languages.

It should be noted that simply looking at the presence or absence of the narrative enclitic in traditional narratives gives us a division that has some support from Southern Athapaskan kinship. Opler (1936) divided Southern Athapaskan kinship into two general patterns based on the kinship terms of the seven languages. These he called "Chiricahua" and "Jicarilla":

Chiricahua	**Jicarilla**
Chiricahua	Jicarilla
Mescalero	Lipan
	Plains Apache
	Western Apache
	Navajo

There is an even more basic way to divide Southern Athapaskan groups based on kinship. We may simply note the presence or absence of clans (specifically matrilineal clans). Such a division reveals the following groupings:

Clan:	Navajo, Western Apache
No Clan:	Chiricahua Apache, Jicarilla Apache, Lipan Apache, and Mescalero Apache

This division is exactly the same as the division based on the presence of a narrative enclitic in traditional narratives. Note that the Hopi also have matrilineal clans and use an independent quotative in their narratives (see below).

Northern and Pacific Athapaskan Marking

Having introduced a discursive typology to distinguish an Eastern and Western Apachean grouping, I now turn to a comparison with Athapaskan languages found in Canada and Alaska and on the American Pacific Coast. In doing so, I wish to investigate any potential discursive influences from genetically related languages. Let me first make clear that what follows is a tentative first approximation. The comparison is not complete, and the current results are suggestive rather than definitive. Here again, more work needs to be done.

I looked at six Northern Athapaskan languages and three Pacific Coast Athapaskan languages. I present the results of the survey of the use of quotative evidential devices in traditional narratives in Table 14.5.

We see three patterns here, I believe. First, many Northern Athapaskan languages are not reported to have a quotative evidential that functions in the same way as Southern Athapaskan devices. In Chilcotin there is a framing device—*Yedanx'egúh, sedanx* 'Long ago, before my time'—which locates the following narrative within a set of genre expectations (Dinwoodie 2002:72). This form works very much like the Navajo formula *Ałk'idídą́ą́ ' adajiní ńt'éé'* 'Long ago they say', which can be found at the opening of various traditional narratives. Of the six Northern Athapaskan languages I looked at, only Tsetsault appears to have a narrative enclitic. This form seems to function like a narrative enclitic

TABLE 14.5. Quotative Evidentials in Selected Athapaskan Languages.

NORTHERN ATHABASKAN LANGUAGES	QUOTATIVE EVIDENTIAL
Chipewyan (Goddard 1917a)	None
Beaver (Goddard 1917b)	None
Koyukon (Attla 1989)	Kk'edon Ts'ednee 'the distant past, it is said'
Tsetsault (Boas and Goddard 1924)	-d'ɛ´ᵃ 'it is said'
Ten'a (Jetté 1908)	tsedĕnī 'we say' tsedeni 'one says'
Chilcotin (Dinwoodie 2002)	None
Pacific Coast Athabaskan Languages	
Wailaki (California) (Seaburg 1977)	ya'nin 'they say' reduced ya-ch'i-n-in
Tolowa (Northern California) (Collins 1998)	-lah 'it is said'
Galice (Oregon) (Jacobs 1968)	-hʷaⁿ· 'so people say'

in the Tsetsault narrative collected by Boas, that is, it occurs at least twenty-nine times in the short narrative presented and like its Southern Athapaskan counterpart it does not occur within quoted speech within the narrative but rather frames the narrative as quoted speech of the ancestors. Nevertheless, it seems to be directly related to either the Tsetsault verb form 'to speak' -dɛ or 'to talk' -dɛ (my impression is that these forms may be identical; they also—according to Goddard (Boas and Goddard 1924)—appear to be cognate with the Navajo form -ti' 'to talk'). In Ten'a (Koyukon) we see the use of a fully formed verb of speaking tsedĕnī [ts'ednee] 'we say' that Jetté (1908:304) translates as 'says the old tradition.' Attla (1989) gives these forms as a verb of speaking in the framing device kk'edon ts'ednee 'the distant past, it is said' or 'in legendary times, it is said' (Jetté and Jones 2000:437). Again, ts'ednee is a verb of speaking. These forms are, then, similar to the Navajo and Western Apache examples. However, judging from a review of Jetté's Ten'a texts, it appears to occur only at the beginning of traditional narratives. (As a comparative note, one Navajo consultant has suggested a preference for that usage with *jiní*.)

The Pacific Coast examples present a division very similar to what we see in the Southwest. While Seaburg (1977:330) describes for Wailaki the form *ya'nin* as a "narrative enclitic," he also reconstructs it as a reduced fully inflected verb of speaking *ya-ch'i-n-in* 'they say'. The reduction in form is similar, I should add, to what one finds in Navajo concerning *jiní* where that form can be reduced to a monosyllabic form (either *jiin* or *jn*). It might be better to call *ya'nin* a narrative quotative evidential and not an enclitic and restrict enclitic to the examples we find in the Eastern Apachean languages and the forms we find in Galice, -hʷaⁿ 'so people say', and Tolowa, -*lah* 'it is said'. Jacobs (1968:183) described the function of the Galice enclitic as follows: "Mr. Simmons tagged it unpredictably to

TABLE 14.6. Southwestern Quotative Evidentials (Non-Apachean).

Language	Quotative Evidential
Arizona Tewa	ba 'so they say' (Kroskity 1998)
Hopi	yaw 'it is said' (Shaul 2002)
Southern Paiute	ukwa (quotative demonstrative), -pixai (narrative past) (Bunte 2002)
Zuni	inoote 'long ago' (Tedlock 1972)
Tohono O'odham	na'ana 'once upon a time, long ago' (Saxton and Saxton 1973)
Tonkawa	-lakno'o 'so they say' (Hymes 1987)

one word or another word, more often a phrase-final, in every third or fourth utterance in both myth and non-myth dictations." Without giving it the thorough investigation it deserves, I can at minimum suggest that it functions very much like the narrative enclitic in Mescalero Apache (where it seems to mark larger discourse units than a line, as we find in Chiricahua Apache). Like other quotative evidentials in Athapaskan, it does not appear inside quoted speech. It is of some interest to see a North/South split concerning the verb of speaking versus a narrative enclitic in the Pacific Coast (north having the narrative enclitic and south the verb of speaking). Again, these are tentative results.

A final note, before we turn to the Southwest again, concerns the comment Jacobs made that the narrative enclitic occurs in both myths and nonmyths. More work needs to be done to understand Athapaskan ethnopoetics and the uses of these quotative evidentials. Far from being a minor element in linguistic anthropology, I believe ethnopoetics will prove to be of fundamental value in historical linguistics, especially a historical linguistics that focuses on discursive typologies.

An Areal Discursive Typological View of the Southwest

I want now to turn to the final pieces of data to be presented in this chapter. Here I survey a number of Southwestern languages outside the Athapaskan languages we have so far discussed. Again, the focus is on quotative evidentials (narrative devices) that occur in traditional stories. In Table 14.6 I present the results of a survey for quotative evidentials in the following languages: Arizona Tewa (Kiowa-Tanoan) (Kroskrity 1998), Hopi (Uto-Aztecan) (Shaul 2002), Tohono O'odham (Uto-Aztecan) (Saxton and Saxton 1973), Southern Paiute (Uto-Aztecan) (Bunte 2002), Tonkawa (language isolate) (Hymes 1987), and Zuni (language isolate) (Tedlock 1972). I chose these languages for several reasons: (1) all of them have been analyzed ethnopoetically so we can more easily understand the discursive uses of the quotative evidentials, (2) all have had extended contact and interaction with Southern Athapaskan–speaking people, (3) and all have had narratives published in the Native language original.

Zuni, in the example published by Tedlock (1972), does not appear to have a quotative evidential used in Coyote narratives. Instead, as Tedlock describes, the rhetorical and poetic structuring of Zuni narratives seems to rely on pause structures. Tedlock notes the use of a framing initial word *inoote* 'long ago', but this does not seem to have an evidential quality to it. The Tohono O'odham form *na'ana* seems to act as a framing device at the beginning of narratives (similar to the Chilcotin and Navajo examples above). Like the Zuni form, they do not have a quotative feel to them, and unlike the forms found in Southern Apachean languages or the other Southwestern forms that I now turn to, they do not recur. Arizona Tewa, Hopi, and Tonkawa all use quotative evidentials pervasively in traditional narratives. As Kroskrity (1998) has documented for Arizona Tewa, the function of the evidential particle *ba* seems to be a convergence with Hopi rhetorical uses of their evidential particle *yaw*. There are, however, some differences. For example, in Hopi traditional narratives *yaw* can occur sentence or clause initially and repeatedly within a sentence, whereas in Arizona Tewa there are no attested examples of *ba* occurring clause or sentence initially. Instead, it can appear multiple times within a sentence (Kroskrity 1998). The related Southern Paiute gives us two forms, *ukwa* or *-pixai*. Neither acts exactly like the Arizona Tewa or Hopi quotative evidential, though *ukwa* comes closer. Also, neither consistently occurs clause or sentence finally, but—in distinction to Arizona Tewa and Hopi—they can occur clause finally. It is important to note here that the Southern Paiute, who live at Kaibab-Paiute Reservation and in the San Juan communities within the Navajo Nation, have a long history with the Navajo.

Tonkawa has a narrative enclitic *-lakno'o* 'so they say'. This form attaches to the final verb of a clause. Tonkawa, like Apachean languages and Hopi, is generally an SOV (Subject Object Verb) language. Arizona Tewa is a verb-final language, but the word order is relatively fluid. In many respects, *-lakno'o* seems to function very much like Chiricahua Apache *-ná'a*.

Table 14.7 compares Arizona Tewa, Hopi, Tonkawa, Eastern Apachean, and Western Apachean, and certain patterns and connections can be noted. First, I think we can make a strong argument that the use of quotative evidentials in traditional narratives is a discursive areal feature in the American Southwest. Languages from three language families and a language isolate all use some form of a quotative evidential in traditional narratives. They differ, however, in clause placement, in recurrence within a sentence or clause, in their morphological form, and in their independence. These differences are most likely due to language-specific factors and, as Kroskrity (1998) notes, certain rhetorical convergences we see between Hopi and Arizona Tewa. It is worth noting that the Eastern Apachean division and Tonkawa look very similar. We know that the Tonkawa historically interacted with Mescalero and Lipan Apaches (Webster 1999b) and resided to the east of the Apachean-speaking peoples in Texas. The Western Apachean group looks similar to the Southern Paiute, the Arizona Tewa, and the Hopi (though, as Kroskrity [1998] notes, the Arizona Tewa

TABLE 14.7. Comparison of Selected Languages and Quotative Evidentials.

	ARIZONA TEWA	HOPI	SOUTHERN PAIUTE	TONKAWA	EASTERN APACHEAN	WESTERN APACHEAN
Dependent enclitic or independent form	Independent	Independent	Independent	Enclitic	Enclitic	Independent
Verb of speaking	No	No	No	No	No	Yes
Single or multiple occurrence per clause	Multiple	Multiple	Single	Single	Single	Single
Clause final	No	No	Yes/No	Yes	Yes	Yes

probably looks similar to Hopi because of convergence). They differ in the use of a verb of speaking versus a quotative particle. Based on the above comparison, we might, tentatively, offer the following grouping:

Hopi   Tonkawa
Southern Paiute Chiricahua Apache
Arizona Tewa   Jicarilla Apache
Navajo   Mescalero Apache
Western Apache Lipan Apache

In a previous article (Webster 1999b), I noted that in the attested versions of Coyote narratives in Lipan Apache (one in Hoijer n.d. and fragments in Goddard n.d.) the narrative enclitic does not occur. It does, however, occur in the long narrative told by Augustina Zuazua (Hoijer 1975) when Zuazua is recounting the early movements of the Lipan Apache as told to her by an elderly Lipan Apache. For a variety of reasons (see Webster 2007), I believe Zuazua had greater command of Lipan Apache than did Lisandro Mendez, the narrator of the Coyote story in Hoijer n.d. I now believe that the exclusion of the narrative enclitic in Mendez's Coyote story either was due to socio-linguistic factors related to the indexing of Lipan-ness or was an indicator of the rapid decline in use of the Lipan Apache language.

When we compare Northern Athapaskan quotative evidentials with Southern Athapaskan evidentials, we see that the quotatives are relatively uncommon in the Northern corpus I examined. However, when they do occur, they are either an enclitic or an independent verb of speaking, but in both cases they are traceable to a verb of speaking. The Tsetsault form is clearly related to the verb forms of 'to talk' and 'to speak'. This matches the Navajo and Western Apache uses of a verb of speaking. Tsetsault differs from Navajo and Western Apache in the independence of the form, but over time, one can see how the verb of speaking might become reduced and attached to the clause final verb. Note that in both Navajo and Wailaki an independent verb of speaking is often reduced in form. From the comparison described above, we can suggest that the narrative enclitic as a single semi-bound morpheme does not appear to occur in Northern Athapaskan languages. The narrative enclitic does appear in both the Pacific Coast and the Southwest. The Tsetsault form seems to mirror the rhetorical use in the Southern Athapaskan languages of the quotative evidential. The Ten'a (Koyukon) forms seem to function rhetorically in a way similar to at least one Navajo consultant's view of how *jiní* should be used.

The Pacific Coast Athapaskan data seem to mirror the Southwest Athapaskan data. There are two general patterns: an independent verb of speaking and a dependent enclitic. And, at least according to Seaburg (1977), the Wailaki form was a narrative enclitic.

Inferences from a Comparison of Athapaskan Forms

First, I think it plausible that the narrative enclitics began as independent verbs of speaking and were reduced and attached to the clause final verb over time. Thus Navajo, Wailaki, and Ten'a (Koyukon) show the older form to varying degrees. Where there is no use of quotative evidentials in the Northern Athapaskan languages, I suspect that the form has been lost completely. Such a reduction is obviously not obligatory, as the Tsetsault example suggests. Likewise, reduction to a narrative enclitic is also not obligatory, as the Navajo and Wailaki examples attest. The process can be diagrammed as follows (where parentheses indicate optional processes):

Verb of speaking (→ narrative enclitic (→ zero))

That Navajo and Western Apache show the older form suggests that the migration south occurred before a complete reduction in the north. Likewise, the fact that the phonetic shapes of the narrative enclitics in the north, the Pacific, and the Southwest do not align could suggest that the migration occurred before the reduction to narrative enclitics. The logic behind this claim would be that, in essence, each group had to create its own phonological path to the narrative enclitic. More work needs to be done on this.

Inferences from a Comparison with the Southwest

In the Southwest, we see three general patterns from an areal discursive typological view. The first pattern is the zero occurrences of quotative evidentials. We find this in Zuni and to a large degree in Tohono O'odham, where we find a framing device used at the beginning of traditional narratives. More common is the second pattern, in which we find the use of independent quotative particles. Hopi, Southern Paiute, Arizona Tewa, and Western Apachean all exhibit this pattern. Finally, a third pattern is found in Tonkawa and Eastern Apachean, in which a narrative enclitic is used.

Conclusion

To conclude, I wish to construct a possible accounting for the division found in Southwest Athapaskan uses of quotative evidentials. Judging by a comparison with Northern Athapaskan and Pacific Coast Athapaskan, it is entirely possible that the proto-Apachean-speakers had *both* the dependent and independent forms when they migrated into the Southwest. As the data concerning Chipewyan and Navajo /t/→/k/ suggest, two divergent forms can be held at the same time in Athapaskan languages (both Chipewyan and Navajo have internal phonological variation between /t/ and /k/). Thus proto-Apacheans on the migration southward may have begun reducing the verb of speaking to a narrative enclitic. It is also likely that they had the Western Apachean system when they entered the Southwest. What is not likely is that they had only the Eastern Apachean system, which then became elaborated. Reduction is more likely than addition. This leads to two questions: (1) Why did Navajo and Western Apache not reduce to a narrative enclitic or lose the form completely? and (2) Why did Eastern Apachean languages stop at the narrative enclitic, that is, why did they not completely lose the form (though Lipan seems to be doing some of that)?

I think the answer to this question may be found in the interactions of proto-Apachean peoples with speakers of other languages. We know from historical and ethnohistorical records that the Lipan Apache and Mescalero Apache interacted frequently and extensively with the Tonkawa. We know that the Mescalero and Lipan Apache also interacted with the Jicarilla and the Chiricahua. Because of the level interaction with the Tonkawa, who used a narrative enclitic in traditional narratives which bears a surface phonological resemblance to the Eastern Apachean narrative enclitic (*-lakno'o* and *-ná'a, -ná*), there may have been a stabilizing influence produced by an extended cross-linguacultural interaction. Likewise, the Southern Paiute and Hopi have had extended interactions with the Navajo, and the Navajo have had extended interactions with the Western Apache. The influence of the two Uto-Aztecan groups—and especially the Hopi—may have provided a stabilizing influence for retaining an independent quotative evidential. Thus the influence of the discursive areal feature of the use of a quotative evidential has led to a stabilizing of a quotative evidential in the two Southern Athapaskan divisions. However, inter-linguacultural interaction between Eastern Apachean and Tonkawa and between Western Apachean and Hopi, Arizona Tewa, and Southern Paiute has led to what form the quotative evidential has been stabilized as, either dependent or independent.

As Kroskrity (1998) notes, Arizona Tewa–speakers take pride in their language as an identity marker. This may suggest why there has been a discursive convergence without a concomitant borrowing of a Hopi form. Arizona Tewa has borrowed a discursive device, but it uses an Arizona Tewa form. As Hoijer (1939) and Young (1989) have pointed out for Southern Athapaskan languages, they appear relatively resistant to borrowings of outside lexical items (see also de Reuse, this volume). Instead, lexical elaboration and innovation using existing lexical stock is the norm. Thus we would not expect either the Western or Eastern Apachean groups to borrow discursive evidentials from Uto-Aztecan or Tonkawa. Instead, as I have argued, the convergence of discursive function influenced the shape or form of the evidential. Such discursive convergence may have occurred as people sat and told stories to each other, listening to the poetics of each language. We need to avoid thinking that ethnopoetic structurings arose in isolation; rather, we should seek to glimpse dialogue in the calibration of ethnopoetic structurings.

This chapter has been an initial attempt at outlining a discursive areal typological accounting of the use of quotative evidentials in the American Southwest and beyond. I have attempted to use the evidential as way to understand the migration history of the Southern Athapaskans and to suggest a possible accounting for the division in form of the quotative evidential. This is clearly a preliminary report: more work needs to be done on Northern Athapaskan languages as well as on a wider comparison of languages of the Southwest. However, I hope this chapter suggests two methodological points: (1) ethnopoetics, far from being a marginal pursuit, can be of great value to historical reconstructions of past migrations, and (2) a discursive areal typological perspective can lead to new and interesting ways to understand the interactions of peoples who spoke distinct languages but still engaged in linguacultural exchanges.

REFERENCES

Attla, Catherine
1989   *Bakk'aatugh Ts'uhuniy: Stories We Live By*. Fairbanks: Alaska Native Language Center.

Basso, Keith, and Nashley Tessay Sr.
1994   Joseph Hoffman's "The Birth of He Triumphs over Evils": A Western Apache Origin Story. In *Coming to Light*, edited by Brian Swann, pp. 636–656. New York: Vintage Books.

Beier, Chris, Lev Michael, and Joel Sherzer
2002   Discourse Forms and Processes in Indigenous Lowland South America: An Areal-Typological Perspective. *Annual Review of Anthropology* 31:121–145.

Boas, Franz, and Pliny Goddard
1924   Ts'ets'aut: An Athapascan Language from Portland Canal, British Columbia. *International Journal of American Linguistics* 3(1):1–35.

Bunte, Pamela
2002   Verbal Artistry in Southern Paiute Narratives: Reduplication as a Stylistic Process. *Journal of Linguistic Anthropology* 12(1):3–33.

Collins, James
1998   *Understanding Tolowa Histories*. New York: Routledge.

Cook, Eung-Do
1989   Is Phonology Going Haywire in Dying Languages? Phonological Variations in Chipewyan and Sarcee. *Language in Society* 18(2):235–255.

de Reuse, Willem J.
2003 Evidentiality in Western Apache (Athabaskan). In *Studies in Evidentiality*, edited by Alexandra Aikhenvald and Robert M. W. Dixon, pp. 79–100. Amsterdam: John Benjamins.

Dinwoodie, David
2002 *Reserve Memories: The Power of the Past in a Chilcotin Community.* Lincoln: University of Nebraska Press.

Goddard, Pliny Earle
1911 *Jicarilla Apache Texts.* Anthropological Papers Vol. 8. New York: American Museum of Natural History.
1917a *Chipewyan Texts.* Anthropological Papers Vol. 10, Pt. 1. New York: American Museum of Natural History.
1917b *Beaver Texts.* Anthropological Papers Vol. 10, Pt. 5. New York: American Museum of Natural History.
1919 *San Carlos Apache Texts.* Anthropological Papers Vol. 24, Pt. 3. New York: American Museum of Natural History.
1920 *White Mountain Apache Texts.* Anthropological Papers Vol. 24, Pt. 4. New York: American Museum of Natural History.
1933 *Navajo Texts—Hastin Sandoval.* Anthropological Papers Vol. 34, Pt. 1. New York: American Museum of Natural History.
n.d. Lipan Apache Texts. Circa 1909. Unpublished papers stored at Archives of Traditional Music, Indiana University, Bloomington.

Haas, Mary R.
1968 Notes on a Chipewyan Dialect. *International Journal of American Linguistics* 34(3):165–175.

Hoijer, Harry
1938a The Southern Athapaskan Languages. *American Anthropologist*, new series, 40(1):75–87.
1938b *Chiricahua and Mescalero Apache Texts, with Ethnological Notes by Morris Opler.* Chicago: University of Chicago Press.
1939 Chiricahua Loan Words from Spanish. *Language* 15(2):110–115.
1942 Phonetic and Phonemic Change in the Athapaskan Languages. *Language* 18(3): 218–220.
1956a The Chronology of the Athapaskan Languages. *International Journal of American Linguistics* 22(4):219–232.
1956b Lexicostatistics: A Critique. *Language* 32(1):49–60.
1971 Athapaskan Morphology. In *Studies in American Indian Linguistics*, edited by Jesse Sawyer. *University of California Studies in Linguistics* 75:113–148.
1975 The History and Customs of the Lipan, as told by Augustina Zuazua. *Linguistics* 161:5–37.
n.d. Lipan Apache Texts. Circa 1938. Unpublished notebook housed at the American Philosophical Society, Philadelphia.

Hymes, Dell H.
1987 Tonkawa Poetics: John Rush Buffalo's "Coyote and Eagle's Daughter." In *Native American Discourse: Poetics and Rhetoric*, edited by Joel Sherzer and Anthony Woodbury, pp. 17–61. Cambridge: Cambridge University Press.

Jacobs, Melville
1968 An Historical Event Text from a Galice Athabaskan in Southwestern Oregon. *International Journal of American Linguistics* 34(3):183–191.

Jetté, Jules, and Eliza Jones
2000   *Koyukon Athabaskan Dictionary.* Fairbanks: Alaska Native Language Center, University of Alaska.

Jetté, Rev. J.
1908   On Ten'a Folk-Lore. *Journal of the Royal Anthropological Institute of Great Britain and Ireland* 38(July–December):298–367.

Kroskrity, Paul
1998   Discursive Convergence with a Tewa Evidential. In *The Life of Language,* edited by Jane Hill, P. J. Mistry, and Lyle Campbell, pp. 25–34. Berlin: Mouton de Gruyter.

Nevins, M. Eleanor, and Thomas Nevins
2004   He Became an Eagle. In *Voices from the Four Directions,* edited by Brian Swann, pp. 283–302. Lincoln: University of Nebraska Press.

Opler, Morris E.
1936   The Kinship System of the Southern Athabaskan-Speaking Tribes. *American Anthropologist* 38(4):620–633.

Sandoval, Merton
1984   The Syntactic Function of the Yi-/Bi- Alternation in Jicarilla Apache. In *Coyote Papers,* Vol. 5, edited by Stuart Davis, pp. 153–190. Tucson: University of Arizona Press.

Sapir, Edward, and Harry Hoijer
1942   *Navaho Texts.* Iowa City, Iowa: Linguistic Society of America.

Saville-Troike, Muriel
1974   Diversity in Southwestern Athabaskan: A Historical Perspective. *Navajo Language Review* 1(2):67–84.

Saxton, Dean, and Lucille Saxton
1973   *O'othham Hoho'ok A'agitha: Legends and Lore of the Papago and Pima Indians.* Tucson: University of Arizona Press.

Seaburg, William
1977   A Wailaki (Athapaskan) Text with Comparative Notes. *International Journal of American Linguistics* 43(4):327–332.

Shaul, David Leedom
2002   *Hopi Traditional Literature.* Albuquerque: University of New Mexico Press.

Tedlock, Dennis
1972   *Finding the Center.* New York: Dial Press.

Toelken, Barre, and Tacheeni Scott
1981   Poetic Retranslation and the "Pretty Languages" of Yellowman. In *Traditional Literatures of the American Indians,* edited by Karl Kroeber, pp. 65–116. Lincoln: University of Nebraska Press.

Tuttle, Siri, and Merton Sandoval
2002   Jicarilla Apache. *Journal of the International Phonetic Association* 32(1):105–112.

Webster, Anthony K.
1999a   Sam Kenoi's Coyote Stories: Poetics and Rhetoric in Some Chiricahua Apache Narratives. *American Indian Culture and Research Journal* 23(1):137–163.
1999b   Lisandro Mendez's "Coyote and Deer": On Narrative Structures, Reciprocity, and Interactions. *American Indian Quarterly* 23(1):1–24.
2004   Coyote Poems: Navajo Poetry, Intertextuality, and Language Choice. *American Indian Culture and Research Journal* 28(4):69–91.
2006   On Speaking to Him (Coyote): The Discourse Functions of the yi-/bi- Alternation

in Some Chiricahua Apache Narratives. *Southwest Journal of Linguistics* 25(2): 143–160.

2007 Lipan Apache Place Names of Augustina Zuazua: Some Structural and Discursive Features. *Names: A Journal of Onomastics* 55(2):103–122.

2008 A Note on Plains Apache Warpath Vocabulary. *International Journal of American Linguistics* 74(2):257–261.

Young, Robert W.

1989 Lexical Elaboration in Navajo. In *General and Amerindian Ethnolinguistics*, edited by Mary Ritchie Key and Henry Hoenigswald, pp. 303–320. Berlin: Mouton de Gruyter.

CHAPTER 15

The Ancestral Chipewyan Became the Navajo and Apache

New Support for a Northwest Plains–Mountain Route to the American Southwest

BRYAN C. GORDON

And then on the fourth day [Bik'éguindan-n] made Man; [Bik'égu'dé] made Apache. (Now, I get into a time when my people's history when our people were made.) We were made in a Land of Ever Winter, a House of Ice and Winter, which we call in Apache, Kugha'bikine, House of Winter or House of Ice—Home, not House, on the shores of a big lake called Tuduubits'alidaa, Water That You Cannot See Over.... We looked around. But that there was always something to the south, that drew us. And we started drifting in that way. And, as we left our birthplace as a people, our Spirit Brother Warriors told us: "Go forth as a people. You will see many things and do many things. And there will be heartaches; there will be lonesomeness. There will be brutality; and there will also be happiness for you. For there is a land that you will enter, that you do not know. You will see the blood of your people spilled. You will cry, but it will not break your heart. And henceforth you will be a people. And in this world you will call yourselves Ndé, The People."

| Elder Bernard Second of Mescalero (Farrer 1991) |

Linguistic, genetic, ethnographic, and archaeological evidence corroborate an Apache legend of a northern origin. Although linguistic relationships between Navajo, Apache, and Chipewyan have been recognized for more than 150 years (Turner 1852), proof of such relationships from other anthropological disciplines have emerged more slowly and with more difficulty. The route taken by a small group of Chipewyan as it migrated south from the Canadian Barrenlands to the Southwestern United States has been one of the most elusive factors.

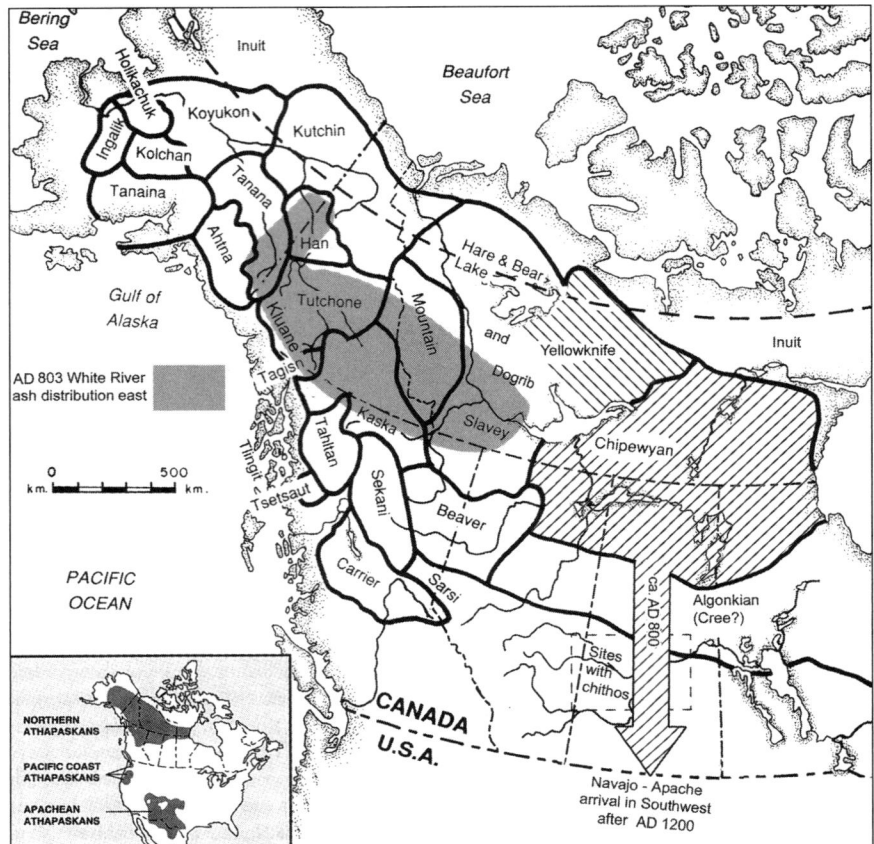

FIGURE 15.1. Proposed origin of the Navajo-Apache from Chipewyan ca. AD 800. Image by Bryan Gordon and Canadian Museum of Civilization.

Small sites, scattered along plains, valleys, and mountains, have been difficult to recognize and interpret as Dene, while varying approaches and interpretations have clouded the data. Legend has added some insight. Carmichael and Farrer (this volume) trace Apache origin to Great Bear, Great Slave, and Athabasca Lakes, the land of the Dogrib, Slave, and Chipeywan, who have similar terms for these lakes. Carmichael and Farrer also use material culture (snowshoes), natural phenomena (the aurora borealis), and topographic links. While I think the Northern Dene exodus was farther east along a Northwest Plains route, their legend-based dating at 600 years ago is quite compatible with my radiocarbon dates of 800–1200 years. This chapter outlines some of the evidence for the transformation of Chipewyan into the Southwestern manifestations of proto-Navajo and proto-Apachean and identifies the regional archaeological findings and complexes most likely to provide support for this early arrival. My suggestion is that the Chipewyan changed into Navajo and Apache en route, probably when they assumed a different subsistence pattern on the Green River, and arrived as two groups at the Four Corners (Figures 15.1 and 15.2).

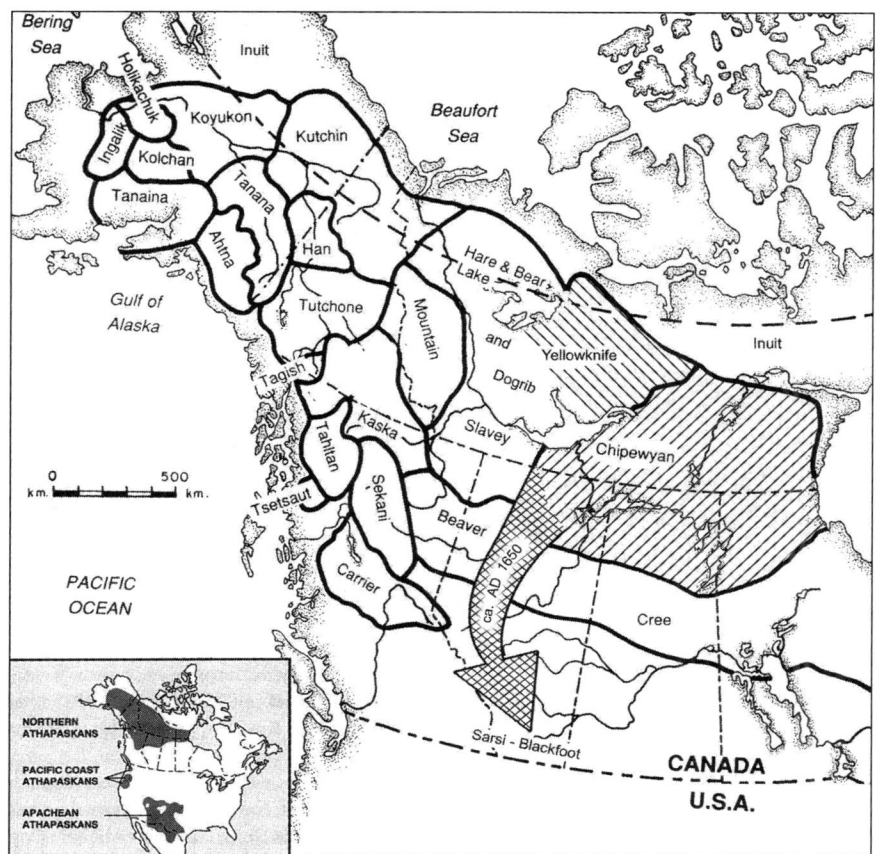

FIGURE 15.2. Proposed Dene movement to become Sarsi ca. AD 1650. Image by Bryan Gordon and Canadian Museum of Civilization.

RELATIONSHIPS BETWEEN NORTHERN AND SOUTHERN DENE

Linguistics

In 1790 Peter Fidler recorded not only the name Lake Athabasca but also its descriptive term "Lake of the Hills," translated from the Cree name *Tootoosakaheegan*, which means Breast Lake, referring to the northwest shore, where the hills seem high and rounded at a distance. At first this seems close to the Apache name, *Tuduubits'alidaa*, but the Chipewyan name for breast is also *toutou*; west is *yada*, and northwest, or "direction from which the wind blows," is *bétθiyé*, for a combination of *toutou bétθyada*. This translation is much closer to Apache than Cree. *Tootoosakaheegan* could have been derived by the Cree from old Chipewyan in a time 1,000 years before the Cree were at Lake Athabasca. That would have been when some ancestral Chipewyan migrated south to evolve into Navajo-Apache. Although I could not find similar Apache spellings for *Bik'éguindan-n* (Creator) or *kugha'bikine* (snow-packed hut) in Chipewyan or Denesuline dictionaries, it is certain that variations of Ndé, the People, are what the Chipewyan, Navajo, and Apache call themselves.

Edward Sapir (1931, 1936) linguistically tied the Chipewyan to the Navajo and Apache 70 years ago. His research was instrumental for my attempt to track the route of these ancestral Apacheans south across the Plains and Rockies from Canada.[1] Table 15.1 shows the work of eight linguists, noting 217 words in two or more languages. In this table we see that Apache, Chipewyan, and Navajo, and Apache and Chipewyan, have the same number of correspondences (18); that Chipewyan and Navajo have the highest number of correspondences (41); and that the greatest disparity is between Chipewyan and Apache—three pieces of evidence I interpret as due to at least two ancestral Chipewyan groups arriving separately in the Southwest. Hoijer (1942:) found a range of phonetic variation in 't' and 'k' from high in San Carlos or Western Apache to a "palatal spirantal glide" in Chiricahua and Mescalero Apache [tx] and [kx], but in Northern Dene this [x] fricative release occurs only in Chipewyan, suggesting a closer Chipewyan-Chiricahua-Mescalero link. On a more general issue, the Chipewyan and Navajo words for bow (*k'a* and *k'ā*) are alike, supporting the idea that the name for bow was transported from north to south.

Hoijer (1956) and Hymes (1957:Figure 2) used glottochronology to estimate dialect divergence dates, and their estimates are averaged in the righthand column of Table 15.2. Chipewyan traveling in the Southwest have slightly more trouble speaking with Navajo than with Apache (Hank Epp, personal communication 2010). This supports my concept of a small Chipewyan group moving down the Northwest Plains from Saskatchewan, crossing the Rockies portal in eastern Wyoming to the Green River, dividing into proto-Apache and proto-Navajo according to different hunting transitions from bison to pronghorn, and arriving in the Southwest at about AD 1000–1200. Some of the proto-Apache likely went east through Pueblo country to Texas to form the ancestral Jicarilla and Lipan Apache; others later formed the Plains Apache, who followed the bison migrations north across the Southern and Central Plains, possibly becoming hunters of the Dismal River aspect. This opposes any accepted interpretation of the Southwest Dene originating via the Dismal River people, as proposed by the Gunnersons (1971), but better fits the timing because the aspect is proto-historic. Using Apachean settlement and differentiation in their historically known homeland, Forbes (1960) even suggests the Western Apache were as far west as western Arizona by AD 1400. Before this happened, the late-coming proto-Navajo from the Intermountain route became the Navajo.

Genetics

Old, documented, small-scale, distant out-migrations like the one I propose for the Chipewyan are uncommon and difficult to find. One example is that of a small Inuit party of nine females and seven males from Iglulik, Baffinland, who made a five-year journey to Qaanaaq in Greenland in 1861 (Gilberg 1984). It heavily influenced Qaanaaq's mtDNA gene pool, increasing the A2a haplotype frequency and demonstrating the after-effects of a mobile group that was even smaller than any proposed Chipewyan group moving to the Southwest.

TABLE 15.1. Comparative Wordlist of Apache, Chipewyan, and Navajo.

Language	Apache	———	Chipewyan	———	Navajo
Source	Bourke (Condie 1980)	Haas 1968; Scollon 1979 in italics	Morice 1907; general N. Dene in italics	Hohn 1973; Li 1946 in italics	Franciscan Fathers 1910; Young & Morgan 1987 in italics
above				dà *dà*	kídœ *'aką́ą́*
arrow	k'â		'ka *'kra*	ká *ká*	kā' *k'aa'*
aurora borealis	gŭznadílkl'a				nahoogaii
autumn				xàiťází	'aak'eed
away from			yuta *yuto*	t'càzí	sits'áji *'ats'ąą*
awl				tθàł	tsăgaí *tsah*
ax	chí-hi-k'é			tθèł	nĭł *tséníł*
baby	ishkin			tsìyè	shiyázh *'awéé'*
back (my)				nən-ɛ *nànɛ́*	shináe'de *'anághah*
bag				tcɛð	dă'nagłzí *'azis*
ball				dzòlɛ́	joł *jooł*
bark				t'u'zɛ́	azhí *'azhííh*
bead	yô			t'su'z	yō *yoo'*
bear	shoz			sàs *sàs*	shâsh *shash*
beaver	chá	tsá		ts'a	chā *chaa'*
bedding				tèy-ɛ́	yātqéł *yaateeł*
belly (ribs)	shi		-bit *bœt*	bàyà *tcàyá*	bitsá *'átsą*
below			yuya (*yuyo*)	yèyà	yádœ *biyaadi*
belt				bèðéyą	sĭs *sis*
berry				dj'íyè	dzĭdzé *dzidzé*
beyond				'ází	'alááh
big	inchá		tso *tco*	tcòy	tsoh
birch				kəl' *k'aì*ᶜ	k'ishchíí'
bird				jí·zɛh	tsídi *tsídii*
bison				edsheeré *èdjèrè*	'ayání
black				zàn	łizhín *łizhin*
blanket	chît			tìl	beêdlé *beeldléí*
blow				yúł	yích'ííh
blue	duklíj			tłís	dotł'ísh *dootł'izh*
boat				t'sì	yŏłtsinaa'eeł
bone			d'sœn	t'θàn	d'zin *ts'in*
bow	eltin		œłthin	tín	ałtqín *'ałtíí*
break (v)	ni-í-zôntz			j-djɛ́z	bighádlaad

TABLE 15.1. (cont'd.) Comparative Wordlist of Apache, Chipewyan, and Navajo.

Language	Apache		Chipewyan		Navajo
breast			t'θừ		shitqél 'abe'
cane			táθ-έ		gish
card			xál·jł		naaltsoos
charcoal			t'és		t'ēsh t'eesh
clothes			yú		'éé'
cloud	yâ-kôz	'kos 'kwos	kwòθ k'wòθ		kŏs k'os
coat			'ì		ăbáni (shirt) 'éétsoh
cold	zuzkôs	nez'kaz	k'áð		hakáz hak'az
cook (v)	ishpéj		bέz		yibéézh
corpse	nizéltin		té		dsǏstaí
cough			kwòθ		dokhós dikos
count			tá		má'i
coyote	bâ		nunnit, shallé alie		mâ'i dił'qíłi mạ'ii
cup			t'θái		beqa'ízhâhi
darkness	jíne		xíł t'łèyè		nîhojí chahaheeł
daughter			lị-έ		sitsí' hach'é'é
day or dawn	ek'áyi	dziné	yīkai yœkhaih	kàiᶜ	nt'œ, qa'í'â
dog	jlîn	shee		łį	łichái łééchąą'í
door			tịdá		cliǽětqin dáádílkał
dream			tị		shibíł na'iidzeeł
dress			'ì		bīl tł'aakał
drum	é-kot-tatza		tᵃ₂γəli		tsá 'ásaa'
duck	tayína-eth		tsheth tcəð		nāl'éł i naal'eełí
eagle			detone dèt'ánεtòy		atsá 'atsá
ear	shi-chá		dzày-á		ăjá' 'ajaa'
east	chígo-na-áy-akâz		yal'·né		ha'a'aah
egg	igúej		gyὲzὲ		biyézhi 'ayẹẹzhii
elbow			t'súz		ōzhlá' 'ach'oozhlaa'
enemy			ná (Cree)		'ana'í
eyes	shindá	-na -na	nàyá		aná 'anáá
fall (season)			xàit'a'zị		aakhád
far off		Nizá neza	ðà		nízad nízaad
father	shitá		tá		'azhé'é
feather	k'â-t'â		l'εts'əé		bit'á 'at'a'

TABLE 15.1. (cont'd.) Comparative Wordlist of Apache, Chipewyan, and Navajo.

Language	Apache	— Chipewyan —	Chipewyan	Navajo
female			t'sɛ̀	tsa'ii
finger	shúlajuz		tθàł-ɛ̀	hála 'ála'
fire	k'ûn		kún	khû ko'
fish	jlûi	ło ło	łŭwɛ̀	łō' łóó'
five			sàsŭláyɛ̀	ăshdlá'
flesh		-tsî'	təən	bitsí 'atsi̧'
food	í-t'ân		dąnɛ́	ch'iyáán
foot	shik'é	ke khé	kɛ́	khĕ 'akee'
fox			gyìð-ɛ	mâ'iłtsoi
four		dín	dìγì	dī díí'
freeze	i-nânésti		tən	yistaín yishtin
frog			t'sàl	châł ch'ał
girl			t̆ɛ̀rɛ̀	'at'ééd
goose	nâlelthi		cha xà	nat'ági
grass	?	tło	t'łòy	tlo
grease			t'łɛ̀s	bił
grey			bà	tabá'
ground			t'sɛ́τ	tēsh
grouse, ptarmigan	t'dee or etchay		k'àzbà	dih
hair	tzi-zil		yà	tsīgha
half	dáiji-nígo		tànìzi̧	'ałníí'
hand	shik'ôn		('n)là	yīlá'
handle			káθ	bitsiin
hat	châ		t'sà	ch'ah
he, himself			ɛ̀di̧nì	t'áá bíhí
head	sitzín		tθí	sĭtsīts'ín
heart	ichí		dzìyɛ́	ajĕidíshjŏl
heavy			dáð	nisdaaz
heel			kξ̧ttál	ăkhétqāl
hide, skin	k'águe		ðəð	abáni
hold			tŭn	
horn	itlé		dɛ́	dē
horse	jlîn		sheetsho łitšŏg	lĭ
house	k'ĭn		yɛ̀	khĭn or hogan
husband			sɛ̀₂ɛ̀nɛθɛ́	hastqín
ice	tîn	kai khe	tən	tqi̧n

TABLE 15.1. (cont'd.) Comparative Wordlist of Apache, Chipewyan, and Navajo.

Language	Apache	——— Chipewyan ———		Navajo
intestines			t'sìyέ	ăch'í
kidney	chégoschúje		t'səzέ	ătśashkáshi
knee	pi-k'ût		gwóτ	ăwhód
knife	pêsh	bec bés	bès	besh
lake	tû-si-k'ân		tǐτέ	river
land			nən-έ	kéyah
language			təì	sād
laugh	cho-kl'ô		dlóy	anáshdlō
leaf		il -œl	t'ą	-'tan
leg	si-chat		dzà	ăjád
lie down		Saka sœka	t'sí	
liver	izzít		ðə,	ăzíd
louse		yā yā	yá	yaa'
lynx			Tseeshé tc'ìzέ	nash duił baí
maggot			náy-ì	chŏsh
man		díne diné	yu'də'nèù	díné
many		Łani łane	łą	łani
meat	itzí		bər,εgyànέ	'atsi'
Milky Way	yâ-ta-kô-kay			yikáísdáhí
moccasin			kέ	khĕ
month	dágiltân		ðá	ji
moon	kl'égo-na-ay			oljé
mosquito	chínzi-olté		djǐτlì	tsīdānǽzi
mother	shima		à à	'amá
mountain		dził dzœł	céθ	dził
mouse			donné	na'ăstsósi
mouth	sizzé	-ze	ðè	-zé
mud/adobe	gûshklij		t'łés	hashtl'ísh
muskrat		dzen	tshenn dzən	tqábâ'
name			('n)zí	'azhi'
neck	shi-kôz		kwòð	khăs
needle	bi-nak'addi		tθàtìłì tθàtìkì	tsă ts'ósi
nest	bikk'ín	-'do -'to	t'òy	bit'ó'
night	kl'égo		təð-έ tàð-έ	tlégo
north	nílkôz-indé		Toí	náhookos
North Star (Polaris)	iltzônt-ze-tu-nâdi-tá			náhokhŏs bokhó

TABLE 15.1. (cont'd.) Comparative Wordlist of Apache, Chipewyan, and Navajo.

Language	Apache	Chipewyan	Navajo
nose	inchí	(ń)tsì	ăchí
ochre	tsékhô		tséko'
old	ostín	yąn-ὲ	sá'
one	tazlá	ì-łá	łá'i
otter		bìy ὲ	tsōstqíni
outerwear	i·-inchâ	'ì (Li: coat)	
pan	pêzá		'asaa'
pemmican		gγàné	'atsi'
people		hòřìnɛ	dine'é
pine	indilchi	gyàn-ὲ	destsín
porcupine	tsee	t'sì	dă'sáni
quill		t'còy	baghá
rabbit	k'â	ga gyà	gă
rain	nágoltîn	tcà	niłtsá'
red	lichí	k'wóz	łichí
river	tû-slân-hunli	dès	tooh ńlínígíí
roast (v)		bέłt'sέθ	sĭt'égo
rock, flint		tθέ	tsétl'eł
root		xai, yày-έ	'akétł'óól
rope	tłoł t'łoł	t'łúlὲ	tl'ōl
rot (v)		djὲr	diłdzííd
salt	inshi	ðài	áshî
sand	kl'ésh	θài	sai
scrape hair		djὲ	akhάł yíshē
scraper		('n)γwòł (n)ywòł	bee 'aldzéhí
sheep		debe tepe	debé
shoes	k'énkl'îzé		ké
shoot (bow)	ka'beche diltûo	tàs	dishł'ó
shore		thaba thapa	tabaah
sinew		t'θέ	ats'íd
sing		-djən	hatqáł
sit down	zestágo	nìdái -dài'	nishdaah
skin		ðəð	'akági
skunk		Nooltsee nùltsį̀	wŏlízhi
sky	yâ ? ya ya	yà	yă
small	alchisé		yázhí

TABLE 15.1. (cont'd.) Comparative Wordlist of Apache, Chipewyan, and Navajo.

Language	Apache	Chipewyan		Navajo
smoke	jlît	łit łét	łər	łĭd
snake			nádu'ðεh	nat'áni
snare			bìł	bewúdlĕhe
snow	tzôs t'ô		yàθ	yás (zăs)
snowshoe			'ài 'ài	yasíkhe
son	shi-jarje	yé' yé'	siγ/yεse	yé'
south	sitûc-zindédi		nàsì	shádi'aah
spear			θùθ tθúł	tsii'détáán
spoon	pê-tônne		łùs	adé (bésh'idē)
springtime	t'án-go		łùk'έ	dā
spruce			t'sù	chǒ'ká
stick		tsin tcèn	tcìn	tsĭn
stone	tzé	tsĕ tsĕ́	tθέ	tsĕ
stranger	indá		xástàn εxáztànὲ	'eyóní
string			t'łùł	tł'óółts'ósí
sugar	kl'ík'ânné			'áshiih łikan
sun	chígo-na-ay	ca sa	sà	shă
swamp	bi-tû-sik'ăn		'εl-	
swan			Gagoos gyàgwòs	yáhazhjōl
sweet		łakan	kàn	lakhán
table	bik'átánni			bikáá'adání
tail	itzé'	tse tcé	tcέ	bitsé
talk	yâ-iti			yáshti'
tear	datŭnalí			'iidlaad
tent	k'olk'âykungûa		Nìbálὲ nìbálὲ	níbaal
there			'èyèr	'aadi
three		tha tha	tàyè, tà	tgā'
throat	shi-táye		kàs-έ k'às-έ	ădáyĭ'
tongue	sizzat		Tθù tθù, setsú	ătsó
trail, road	ittin	thin	tənε tən-ὲ	'atiin
trap			ʔεłdzùzì	beeljízhi
twilight			hòbà hòbà	nahootsooi
two	nagíu		nákὲ	nākhí
water			Tà	taō
weasel			łechkalé tὲlk'àłì	dlú'i
west	chígo-na-áy-ona-táya		Yadá	'e'e'aah

TABLE 15.1. (cont'd.) Comparative Wordlist of Apache, Chipewyan, and Navajo.

LANGUAGE	APACHE	CHIPEWYAN	NAVAJO
white	lek'ay	Gài	łagaí
wife	ad	t'séyàné	asdzáni
wing		bit'á t'sə	ăsts'ín
winter	huestango	xàyɛ xàyɛ̀	qaĭ
wolf	bâ-chu	Nunneesa nùnìyɛ̀	m'a'itso
woman	ts'ékuyi	t'sɛ́kùyì	asdzáni
year	kl'égôntza		náqai
yellow	litzoe	Tθòy	łitso

Note: Condie (1980) says Bourke's *jl, thl, th*, etc., is modern *ł*, while glottalized consonants were subscript 2, and *n* or supra *n* nasalized vowels.

TABLE 15.2. Northern and Southern Dene Language Divergence.

DENE (ATHAPASKAN GROUP)	HOIJER 1956 (YEARS)	HYMES 1957 (YEARS)	YEARS (MEAN)	MEAN YEAR AD
Navajo and Chipewyan	628	864	746	1210
Chiricahua and Chipewyan	660	907	784	1172
San Carlos and Chipewyan	790	1089	940	1016
Jicarilla and Chipewyan	724	996	860	1096
Lipan and Chipewyan	724	996	860	1096

Note: Mean year AD uses Hymes 1957/Hoijer 1956 baseline.

Navajo and ancestral Apache share a characteristic Dene genetic marker with Chipewyan, the loss of an RsaI site at locus 16329, and their sequences are very different from Amerind sequences (Torroni et al. 1992). Their having only a haploid A group precludes their being related to either British Columbia mountain peoples or Utah Fremont peoples, who have B and C (Brugge 2003; cf. Jones 2004:21).

In a widespread study, Malhi and others (2008) found that the Subarctic Dene were ancestral to the Southwest Dene on the basis of the Y chromosome. They also found significant admixture between Navajo and Pueblo groups (see Malhi, this volume).[2] Unfortunately, they also accept traditional Southwest archaeological dogma that the Dene arrived after AD 1500 (also see Seymour 2009). Nonetheless, their data are valuable if applied to Dene arrival in the Southwest 500 years earlier. Their mtDNA and Y chromosome frequencies point to a migration of mainly males moving south and marrying Pueblo females. Both dental patterns and preliminary mtDNA data show immigration during the Pueblo III period, but Malhi et al. (2008) do not have dental and mtDNA data from specific northern source populations to identify the immigrants.

Within the Southwest, data for timing southern movement to the Middle San Juan from Mesa Verde is vague (Durand et al. 2010) but agrees with Duff and Wilshusen's (2000) model for migration into northwestern New Mexico at AD 950–1300. It would be interesting to see if this supports the arrival of ancestral Chipewyan from Canada.

Supernatural Beliefs

Similar supernatural beliefs between the Chipewyan and the Apacheans include a concept of supernatural heightened personal power existing with Chipewyan as *inkoze*, or as secret knowledge (Smith 1973; Sharp 1988) with Apache and Navajo (Perry 1991). Dene had a heightened fear of the dead and destroyed the possessions of the deceased. Removal of the dead through the north wall of a dwelling was pan-Dene (David Brugge and Bonnie Clark, personal communication 2006), and their names are not spoken. Chipewyan bushmen resemble Navajo and Chiricahua Apache whistling night ghosts, described by Brugge (1978: 309–328). All believed in an underworld origin and stockroom for animals—caribou for Northern Dene and deer, pronghorn, and bighorn sheep for Navajo (Luckert 1975). Both have a similar legend of a giant bridging their land (Franciscan Fathers 1910:120–121). *Yakke-elt'ini* was killed and petrified, providing a bridge for the Northern Dene and their caribou from the Yellowknife and Chipewyan all the way to New Mexico. His head is *Yei-two*, a hill northeast of Mount San Mateo, while New Mexico's numerous lava flows represent his blood as petrified wood (*yei-tśo*). The Windway and other ceremonial narratives teach that there was a time when Navajo families were highly mobile.

Social Organization

The Dene all share matrilocal residency and matrilineal kin reckoning. Henry Sharp (personal communication 2009) suggests that any trickle of hunters and even fewer women across the Plains may have strengthened matrilineality, which is strong among the Navajo-Apache. Driver (1972:1147) said the Apache acquired matrilocal residence on their way south via contact with Plains Hidatsa, Mandan, Arikara, Pawnee, and Wichita women farmers, but my data suggest that Dene acquisition of matrilineality was much earlier and stemmed from their origin in northwest Canada and Alaska.

Northern and Southern Dene tend to have weak leadership in "chiefs" and have a consensus-based society. All had close same-sex siblings and tended to avoid those of the opposite sex who were unrelated. Women assisted in communal hunts.

Gaming

Chipewyan, Apache, and Navajo all play a gambling game (Opler 1938:231), which the Chipewyan call the "bone game." Two opposing teams of about four players are separated by a raised blanket (a moose hide in the Subarctic). A bone is passed under the blanket or hide while members of the opposing team try to guess which person (Chipewyan) or what moccasin (Apache or Navajo) has the bone or token. Sticks are often used as counters.

DEFINING PRE-CHIPEWYAN (TALTHEILEI) AND CHIPEWYAN TOOLS AND FEATURES IN THE BARRENLANDS

From 8,000-year-old Paleo-Indian Northern Plano times, most Canadian Barrenland hunters lanced caribou at water crossings.[3] This practice continued through the occupation of Early and Middle Taltheilei phases, which represent the ancestral Chipewyan. Temporally and typologically continuous caribou hunting features include drivelanes and lookout areas for game at tundra water crossings, plus blinds farther south in the forest where herds dispersed for winter.

The Early Taltheilei people entered the Barrenlands during a warming trend after 650 BC and became communal caribou hunters. Magne (this volume) shows that they reached the central Barrenlands at about AD 1000, but I believe they were there almost two millennia earlier, merging into Middle and Late Taltheilei. Late Taltheilei merged in turn into Historic Chipewyan and continued likewise, preying on specific caribou herds at precise water crossings along their migration routes (Gordon 1979, 1996). In winter they split into smaller groups to hunt the caribou, which dispersed into small, widespread groups according to the availability of tree lichens in the boreal forest. Stratified Barrenland sites reveal characteristic hunting, food-preparation, and hide-processing tools in successive Taltheilei to Chipewyan levels. Smaller and widespread sites within the boreal forest confirm the long-term migratory pattern of the Dene.

Chipewyan tools include lance points, side-notched arrowheads, beveled knives, chithos, scrapers, and an overabundance of flake tools (Figure 15.3). Most lance heads are asymmetric, crudely retouched quartzite. They became cruder with time, possibly because notched arrowheads surpassed them in importance in hunting. Knives are mostly ovoid, but some are semi-lunar or lanceolate with square bases or round tips. Tundra knives are mainly quartzite; forest ones are quartzite, quartz, and chert material. Many forest knives are unifacial (Gordon 1996:65). Scrapers are mostly crude flakes.

At about AD 800 Saskatchewan's Northern Plains grassland advanced during the Medieval Warm period into the aspen parkland.[4] The Plains Indians had abandoned the parkland, and the ancestral Chipewyan moved in, skirting west of what later became Algonkian Selkirk sites (Meyer and Hamilton 1994:118, 123). They found arrowheads and perhaps even discarded bows and learned

FIGURE 15.3. Chipewyan tools: (a) Dene Klo-Kut or Kavik arrowhead; (b) four Late Taltheilei arrowheads; (c) scraper; (d) three chithos. Image by Bryan Gordon and Canadian Museum of Civilization.

how to use them. Earlier scouting parties may have also observed the use of the bow. In any case, they brought the bow north to the crossings, allowing hunting on the open tundra. Here hunter visibility was minimized by the use of shallow blinds and a horizontally held bow, as documented in the 1790s by Thompson (1916:166). The arrow is held on the string by two fingers below and the thumb above, with the string drawn to the chest only. This limits accuracy, pull, and range by two-thirds, but these limitations are partly overcome by the kinetic energy released from this powerful sinew-backed bow.

Late Taltheilei bowmen added bison to their game in the aspen parkland and Northwest Plains. The horizontal bow allowed wolf skin–disguised hunters to stalk the bison, a low-profile technique seen in Plains Indian paintings. Later and farther south it would have been a definite asset against hostile Plains Indians, who used a more visible standing stance. Prairie and Plains side-notched arrowheads occur throughout the caribou range. Four found on the upper Thelon River dating to AD 800–1200 (Gordon 1996:Table 3.4.1) resemble hundreds found in central Saskatchewan and farther south. There Kehoe (1974) defined Prairie side-notched arrowheads as being asymmetric, mediocre bifaces with notches wider than deep and base narrower than blade—traits common to AD 700 Late Taltheilei (Gordon 1996:Figure 4.4). The earlier Klo-Kut or Kavik arrowhead in the Yukon (Figure 15.3) is very different and remained west of the Rockies.

Chithos are used to soften or abrade hides, their shape varying with local stone. The Chipewyan and their ancestors used roundish sandstone tablets, gradually wearing their edges and sometimes their faces. The Yukon, Alaskan, and British Columbian Dene simply broke river cobbles to get plano-convex cortex spalls for the same purpose. Both types have trimmed edges that show wear or right-angled striae from being dragged almost perpendicularly over a hide to break or flex fibers (Lowie 1963:67). Chithos may occur with metapodial bone beamers, but only in late periods, as podzol soil acids dissolve bone. Leather, wood, and antler materials also perished, but preservation is possible. A 1,400-year-old Yukon Ice Patch moccasin had no seam from the toes toward the ankle on the upper section, quite unlike historic Dene moccasins and more like those of the Cree. In fact, the historic Dene adopted the Cree moccasin style. Moccasins as route tracers are fraught with problems because specific traits, such as upper seams and heel tabs, occur in completely unrelated tribes across North America. Hence any comparison between the Yukon Ice Patch moccasin and those in the Promontory Caves and deemed Dene (Ives 2005) need more than corresponding radiocarbon dates.

Chipewyan Departure from Their Ancestral Range

The Chipewyan and their ancestors aligned their seasonal movements with those of the caribou. In winter both lived in small groups in the forest. In summer both massed at tundra water crossings, the hunters walking great distances to join these hunts. As any minor change in herd movement led to starvation, hunters followed the herds to survive. Hunters at the southern Barrenland edge were not as fortunate because herds were thin and distances great, making nearby bison attractive game.

The number of wives in this polygamous society reflected male social importance (Henry Sharp, personal communication 2008), and most Chipewyan women accompanied the more numerous, successful, and aggressive hunters to the tundra. Women were critical food and hide processors, a shortage of whom was detrimental to group survival. Fewer caribou wintered at the southern Barrenland edge in the Medieval Warm period, so disenfranchised bachelor bowmen turned entirely to bison. Genetic similarity between Southwest and Barrenland Dene Y chromosomes suggests that the Northern Dene emigrants were mainly male. Being good hunters adept at stealth and not averse to violence, they readily entered the Plains with their fewer women.

Derry (1975), Workman (1979), Magne (this volume, Figures 16.2 and 16.3), and Ives (1990:42–46; 2003:267) link a Dene exodus from northwestern Canada to the AD 803 White River ash deposition from Mount Churchill in southeastern Alaska (Figure 15.1). Moodie and Catchpole (1992) say the blast height exceeded 25 km, resulting in a heavy, 12-hour acid precipitation that created an uninhabitable desert. Workman (1974:260, 1979:350–352) favors a winter ashfall, which is supported by Hanson (1965) and West and Donaldson (2000, 2002).

Workman estimates that some 500 people were seriously affected by this eruption and ashfall, based on a population density of one person per 100–250 km^2. Although the ash thickness is 1 m near its vent, it lessens to a discontinuous 5 mm 1,300 km away (Robinson 2001:158). Steve Robinson (personal communication 2006; Robinson and Moore 2000) says the ash fouled rivers, sterilized soil (see also King and Brewster 1978), and killed trees. Ives (1990:42) adds that pre- and post-ash vegetation differences based on pollen are insubstantial and that if only 50 to 100 people were affected, they could easily have been absorbed by neighboring groups. He sees the ashfall as having a ripple effect on surrounding groups, possibly triggering the Dene migration south. I doubt that absorption of these few people by neighbors had any effect on out-migration.

Using atmospheric patterns and topography to understand ash effects on aquatic ecosystems, Bunbury (2004) collected lake sediment cores along a transect at increasing distances from Mount Churchill. For mid-range, she says land and water biota survived, their full recovery taking a few years. Land animals were less affected than fish, which take longer to recover. This same result is seen in long-term effects on fish due to ash from Mount St. Helens, Washington, another exploding strato-volcano (Crisafulli and Hawkins 1998; McDowall 1996; Pringle and Scott 2001). Forest thinning caused by widespread firing of ground litter may have led to a change in game species, bringing new ones that were easier to hunt with the bow and arrow than with the older atlatl and dart. Pre-ash game had more food value (44 percent beaver, 25 percent whitefish) than post-ash game (29 percent beaver, 9 percent whitefish), possibly due to cultural preference, game shortages, and taphonomic effects on fauna. Be that as it may, lower food values were insufficient to cause a Yukon exodus.

Broad similarities in settlement and subsistence patterns suggest an in situ stratigraphic and cultural development across the White River ashfall (Thomas 2003:103). At the Tatlmain Lake site near Pelly Crossing in central Yukon, Thomas (2003:99–101) says game selection patterns differed above and below the White River ash, yet distant trade continued throughout, especially in Edziza and Hoodoo Mountain tool-making obsidian. If people in traditionally occupied areas such as Tatlmain Lake, 150 km downwind from the volcano, had normal winter stores of meat and fish and lived in the usual skin or semi-subterranean shelters, then we can conclude that not only did most survive, but few likely out-migrated.

Kuhn and others (2010) find partial genetic replacement of woodland caribou at the time of the White River ashfall by possibly more southern caribou. They also say that "caribou were probably able to recolonize the large region in the southern Yukon as a result of their ability to expand in numbers and migrate into newly available habitats as cooler temperatures...prevailed" (Kuhn et al. 2010:1321). Until we know much more about pre-ash diet other than caribou remains found at high elevations in the Ice Patches, we really cannot say what effect the ash had on human exodus. Even Thomas (2003:99–101) does not hazard a guess that woodland caribou replacement was evident in his site. Kuhn and others (2010) quote Robinson (2001) as linking the ash to widespread archaeological upheaval in the southern Yukon. Yet peat specialist Steve Robinson (personal communication 2006) used ash only as a chronomarker, not assuming that burnt wood in his Mackenzie Valley peat cores hundreds of kilometers east reflects anything other than widespread local burning of dry, dead trees, and not positing that it was caused by Alaskan-Yukon volcanism. Further, Robinson (2001) took no stand on southern Yukon archaeological upheaval.

The Dene Did Not Take a Foothills Route to the Southwest

Because of the presence of similar side-notched arrowheads in northwestern and southwestern Alberta, Ives (2003) suggests that the Dene took a Rockies Foothills route. But Brian Reeves (personal communication 2006), an expert on southwestern Alberta, says such arrowheads differ much more than they appear to do in Ives's photograph and that no data exist for a Foothills route and "none likely will ever be found." Seymour (this volume, Chapter 17) quotes Cole (1988) as saying that the ancestral Chiricahua moved south along the Foothills route "between the treeless heights and the treeless plains," which in her words would "explain the early dates in the Mogollon, Datil, Peloncillo, and Dragoon mountains and in the Four Corners" (Seymour 2004a, 2008a). Lewis (1942), Wedel (1961), Buckles (1968), Wright (1978), and Wilcox (1981:224) reject any Foothills route because it was more densely occupied prehistorically and passage would not be unopposed.

The Dene Did Not Take a Full Plains Route to the Southwest

Sapir (1936) supported a Plains route based on cultural links between the Sarsi and Kiowa Apache. The Sarsi are Northwest Plains Dene who were adopted by early historic Alberta Blackfoot and contacted the Black Hills Kiowa (Figure 15.2). Sapir's Plains route is unsupported by early Apachean dates because the only possible Dene manifestation, that of the Tierra Blanca complex (see below), is too late in the Texas Panhandle for arrival. Tierra Blanca forebears likely came from New Mexico via the Intermountain route. Any alternate Plains route via the Oklahoma Panhandle was also blocked at AD 1200–1500 by Antelope Creek bison-hunting farmers and at AD 1000–1400 by Nebraska Plains Village farmers. Dittert and others (1961) also favored a Plains route, with Dene groups moving through eastern Colorado and dividing into Navajo and Apache in the Southwest, the Apaches keeping their Plains orientation and the Navajos adopting Southwest culture. Some Plains and Foothills route enthusiasts suggest that the Sarsi became Mountain Navajo, but the Navajo reached the Southwest centuries before the Sarsi joined the Blackfoot.

Archaeologists favoring a Full Plains route relied heavily on Avonlea side-notched arrowhead distribution, which they thought began in the Barrenlands and terminated far down the Plains. In Alberta, Saskatchewan, and Montana,

Kehoe (1973) defined Avonlea culture on tiny late prehistoric thin-eared, concave-based arrowheads used to kill bison. Except for their deep, narrow sidenotches, they slightly resemble the thin harpoon endblades of the much earlier and unrelated Barrenland Arctic Small Tool tradition. Extrapolating from mixed surface collections of Arctic Small Tool and Dene components making up the now disproved Canadian Tundra tradition (Noble 1971), Wilcox (1981:219) said Avonlea represents Dene moving south over an unrealistic AD 0–1600 duration (Morlan 1988:Figures 2–4), based on a transition to Plains side-notched arrowheads. Avonlea in Alberta and Saskatchewan (AD 150–250, Vickers 1994), Montana, the Dakotas, Wyoming, and Colorado is Algonkian (Meyer et al. 1988:41); Reeves (personal communication 2009) added an Algonkian link to the Benson's Butte-Beehive Avonlea complex. Ives (2003:263) says Avonlea is not Dene, based on its absence in the lower Athabasca Valley and Peace River, which are traditional Dene areas. Walde (2006:192–193; this volume) concluded that Avonlea consisted of a variety of ethnic groups, but not Dene. In sum, a Full Plains route on the basis of Avonlea arrowheads and occupation by horticulturists is not an option either culturally or archaeologically.

The Dene Did Not Reach the Southwest from British Columbia

As noted under the section on genetics, the loss of an RsaI site at locus 16329 among ancestral Apacheans and Chipewyan precludes Magne's (this volume) Apachean origin around Eagle Lake, British Columbia. His Figures 16.3 and 16.4 show first an exodus from the Yukon's White River ash fallout to Eagle Lake of the Chilcotin region, and then along the spine of the Rockies (Idaho and Montana border) to Wyoming. I doubt his suggestion that the ash might have caused a Dene exodus to Eagle Lake. Genetics does not support his claim, and neither does topography or subsistence. The Rockies are very high and difficult to cross here, and it would be especially difficult to follow their spine. Why would they wish to cross this barrier devoid of much fish and game? He mentions root crops and small ungulates "in relative abundance from north to south," yet I think this possible scenario does not apply above the Rockies foothills.

There are no stratified artifacts at Eagle Lake on which to confirm a route to Wyoming. Why are microblades in Eagle Lake absent in any proven Dene sites in Idaho, Montana, and Wyoming? Why do Kavik points, a Dene diagnostic west of the Rockies and present in the Hedley Rockshelter region west of the Okanagan Valley (Copp 2008) and at Eagle Lake (Matson 2007:8), not occur in these states? Instead, they appear south among the Oregon Coast or Pacific Dene. British Columbia Coastal tribes zealously protected their salmon rivers from any downriver attempts to capture this resource by the interior Dene. As this would include Eagle Lake and the Hedley area, the Dene could approach only the less protected Oregon and California coasts. For the Southwest, Magne proposes a route to Wyoming via possible (?) microblades in Copp's (2008) Hedley Rockshelter, but there are no proven Dene microblades here or farther along on any route to the United States. Rather, Copp has possible Salishan, Penutian, and Dene microblades.

Of interest here is Magne's (this volume) allusion to Gilmore's (2006) Dene "seasonal transhumance" near the Rockies entrance to my Northwest Plains–Intermountain route, well beyond any British Columbia route. I thank Magne (this volume) for acknowledging that "the archaeological picture of Athapaskan migrations is very sketchy for the intermediate Great Basin and southern Plateau zones." Finally, Southwest and British Columbia archaeologists always link the Southwest Dene, invariably the Navajo, to the mountains, yet ignore most Apache, some of whom, such as the Barrenland Chipewyan, occupied open country.

My Proposed Plains-Intermountain Route for the Dene

I summarize existing evidence for identifying and dating a route for ancestral Chipewyan movement south and appeal for help from avocational and professional archaeologists from Canada, the Southwest, and the Mountain States to examine collections for diagnostic Dene artifacts and features that may have been misidentified as Ute, Paiute, or Shoshone. I begin with a discussion of the conservative nature of herd followers as they changed from caribou to bison to pronghorn on their route south. Then I discuss the erroneous dating of the Numic expansion, which precluded any consideration of their southern movement. Finally, I attempt to show that using pottery as evidence of the Dene's arrival is wrong. But first a cautionary note is needed.

The main problem in finding ancestral Chipewyan sites along my proposed Northwestern Plains–Intermountain route to the Southwest is that all Dene, including Plains Apache (Wedel 1986:147–148), adapted well to different environments, resulting in generalized tool kits (see Seymour, this volume, Chapter 17). They and the Navajo were "forced to contend with many different...environments...and in their willingness to accept innovation, [also] borrow[ed] only that which was useful and rework[ed it]...without any loss of cultural integrity" (Griffin-Pierce 1992:23). Unlike the Chipewyan, who still hunt caribou, the Apache stopped bison hunting after nineteenth-century herd extermination, becoming shepherds, "a reinforcement of the interest in hunting and the tendency for moving about" (Spicer 1961:530). It is reasonable to suggest that the proto-Apacheans hunted first caribou as ancestral Chipewyan, then bison, then pronghorn, mule deer, and desert bighorn sheep, before returning to bison centuries later in the Central Plains. We know of the Mountain Apache hunting mule deer, and below I discuss the Navajo corralling pronghorn and the Plains Apache hunting the bison. The proto-Apacheans changed prey on the Plains-Intermountain route, but not their migratory life, as caribou, bison, and pronghorn herds linked their transitory camps from Canada to the Southwest.

Caribou Hunting

Using aerial photos, I pinpointed potential Barrenland hunting camps in the early 1970s by studying the migratory habits of the caribou, a behavior pattern learned much earlier by human hunters. Before climate warming and the inroads of civilization, herd migration was generally stable and predictable. Ninety percent of camps were identified in photos of river narrows and lakes with islands and sand spits. Deeply stratified sites at these water crossings confirm long and predictable hunter and herd use. In the forested plateau and foothills west of the Rockies, where some researchers believe the Dene originated, such sites are absent because the topography and migratory herds are missing. These researchers base their ideas on Navajo belief and current residence in hilly areas. But the Navajo's closest linguistic and genetic relatives are the Dogrib, Yellowknife, and Chipewyan in the flat caribou ranges east of the Rockies. A thousand years ago, Chipewyan hunters wintered at the aspen parkland interface between the southernmost caribou range and the northernmost bison range. They learned the bison's migratory habits and adopted the bow, crucial to open-terrain bison hunting. Those farther north continued lancing caribou but also adopted Plains side-notched arrowheads (as seen in Barrenland arrowheads in Figure 15.3b). From south to north, such arrowheads show the Dene camped at Chartier on the Upper Churchill River (Millar 1983) and Black Lake (Minni 1976) in northern Saskatchewan, deep in the forest at IgNj-1, at treeline in KeNi-4, and on tundra at KjNb-7. Hunters wintering at the interface took these tools, along with their Barrenland hide-smoothing chithos, south across Saskatchewan by following bison migrations into the United States.

Switching from Caribou to Bison at the Northern Aspen Parkland Interface

Dene at the interface adopted the "spoke-and-axle" seasonal movements of the Northwest Plains bison. By spoke-and-axle, I mean a herd migrating along a spoke in spring to the central axle, or calving ground, joining other herds entering on other spokes. Hunters did the same. The Northwest Plains enclosed this half-wheel, a huge succession of semi-circular arcs of grasses that ripened in different seasons. An arc of long and fescue grasses within the outer arc of the aspen parkland interface ripened in spring and autumn. Extending from southeastern Manitoba over central Saskatchewan to western Alberta, it provided pre- and post-calving herds with food and ensured a return migration. The next arc of mixed grass, from northwest North Dakota and adjacent southeastern Saskatchewan, extended northwest to Alberta, then turned southwest to Montana. It surrounded the north end of a central core, axle, or calving ground of short-grass prairie straddling the 49th parallel and continuing to Mexico. Twice yearly, Northwest Plains bison from the interface crossed these arcs according to the grass-ripening sequence. Interface Dene could return to winter with the bison in the aspen parkland (Malainey and Sherriff 1996:345–346) or its

The Ancestral Chipewyan Became the Navajo and Apache · 323

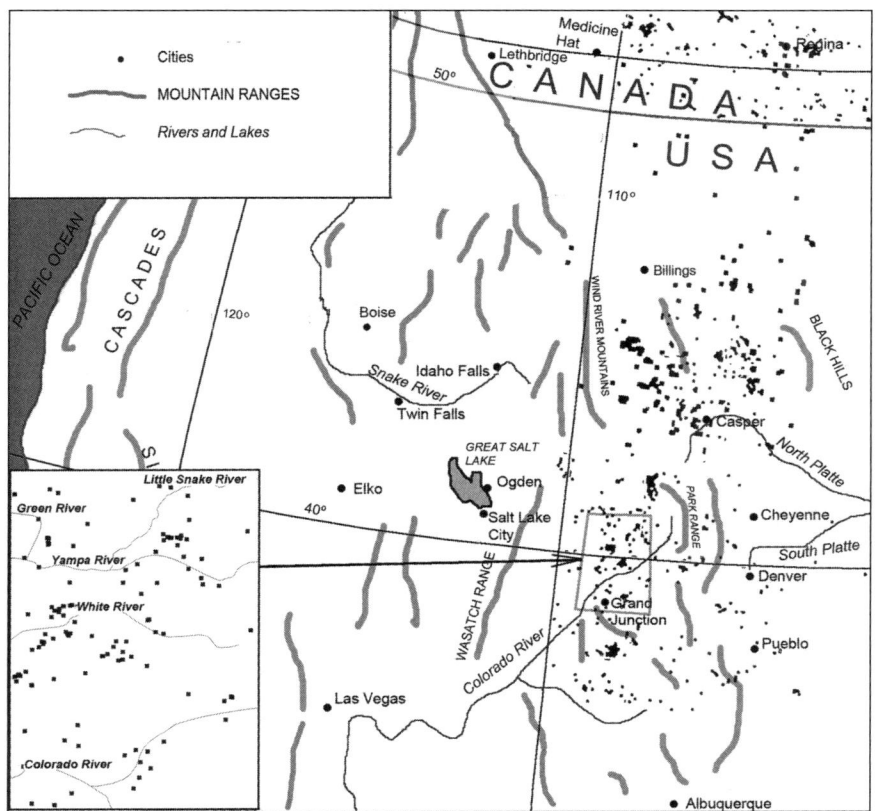

FIGURE 15.4. Archaeological sites suggesting on the basis of side-notched points the proposed route the ancestral Subarctic Chipewyan followed in AD 800–1200 to become Navajo-Apache. Image by Bryan Gordon and Canadian Museum of Civilization.

boreal forest edge (Meyer and Epp 1990:328–330). They could also track a herd west on a spoke to the Alberta and Montana foothills (Morgan 1979:144–146) or one southwest to Wyoming. Figure 15.4 shows their camps as small dots, some of which are in dense clusters, with larger dots representing modern cities for scale. Their camps are more widespread than north-south caribou hunter sites and may yet retain evidence of seasonal occupation related to herd movement.

Strengthening my model of pre-Chipewyan crossing the half-wheel are Northwest Plains arrowheads and edge-ground disk-like chithos in bison kill sites: Sjovold on the South Saskatchewan River at AD 850–1250 (Wettlaufer 1955:31, Plate 3, no. 18; Dyck and Morlan 1995:202–203, 215–216, Figure 8.6) and EfNg-1 Lake Midden in the Qu'Appelle Valley dating to AD 1000–1500 (Canadian Museum of Civilization collection XB-363, 432, 547, 548). Chithos also appear as split edge-ground cobbles in Montana (Darroch 1974), Wyoming, Colorado, and Utah but retain their tanning, flexing, or hide-smoothing function. Some flat, bevel-edged cobbles in Wyoming and Montana (Lewis 1944:336–338) may even be Chipewyan chithos. The latter are thin, 5–12-cm-long, edge- and face-ground disks, usually of rough sandstone, but would vary with available stone; I hope these will be recognized in Montana, Wyoming, Colorado, Utah, and New Mexico collections.

Switching from Bison to Pronghorn Antelope

As bison were fewer at their range limit, the Chipewyan may have formed the proto-Apache and proto-Navajo as they switched at different times to pronghorn at the west end of the wide Plains extension through the Wyoming Rockies. Here pronghorn migrate north-south through the tight Trapper's Point corridor (Sawyer 2005) on the Green River and have done so for 6,000 years. A good part of the route is shared by mule deer. Pronghorn bone here (48SU1006) and at Oyster Ridge (48UT35) shows a late April–early May occupation (Fenner and Walker 2008) before the herd moved north to calve. In fall, the herd forced its way through Trapper's Point, then occupied by Northern Dene bison hunters. Just upriver, Carmichael and Farrer (this volume) believe they separated into the Apache and Navajo. Hunters may have stayed to hunt both animals in spring or autumn before moving permanently as two groups south to the Colorado River. Here in the Blue Mountains they may have corralled mule deer in the same way as the historic Navajo. They may have followed pronghorn and mule deer along the Green and Colorado Rivers to the Uncompahgre Plateau. Reed (1994) did not find chithos here, but he suggests one-handed manos or cobbles as possible alternatives. Around the Four Corners, historic Navajo pronghorn drivelanes and corrals resemble those used for caribou. They are at La Plata, Chaco Canyon (Hill 1938:96), and Thoreau in New Mexico, and Lukachukai, Keams, Jeddito, and White Cone Canyons in Arizona.

ARE SOME NUMIC TOOLS REALLY DENE?

Between AD 1400 and 1776, pottery-making Fremont hunter-farmers in Utah's Great Basin were replaced by Numic-speaking Ute, Paiute, and Shoshone from the west (Loosle and Knoll 2003). Surviving at low desert or mountain subsistence levels, they left thousands of small hunting sites with simple artifacts not unlike those of the Dene. These include side-notched arrowheads, simple scrapers and knives, and abundant retouched flake tools. Early Wyoming and Great Basin surveys were done by archaeologists whose professors maintained that most post-Fremont artifacts were Numic. Most of these likely are, but the uncritical dogma left no room for Dene sites. Tiny scatters of worked flakes, beveled bifaces, side-notched arrowheads, hearths, and tipi rings so typical of Dene may have been misidentified as Numic. I too can be accused of culturally aligning simple tools in my review below, as there are no Dene tools that are identical along their route south; they varied their tool styles according to usage. A sandstone chitho used to soften caribou skin may have been replaced by a bone metapodial beamer to deflesh and soften a bison hide, with chithos regaining importance when smaller game, such as pronghorn or mule deer, were hunted along the Intermountain route. The same is true for side- and corner-notched points, which assume many styles across the Plains and through the Rockies. Butchering knives may also change stylistically simply due to different applications and ways to work available stone. If younger people surveying the route or restudying collections can keep these ideas in mind when examining old or new collections, I will have accomplished my goal.

My survey of possible Dene sites on the Intermountain route begins near the entrance of the wide Plains corridor through the Rockies and goes west across the Wyoming Basin, then south on the Green River. Hundreds of tiny Basin sites suggest drought-diminished bison (Gilmore 2004), but thousands of potential sites are unrecorded because much of the eastern entrance is private land (Figure 15.4). A promising site is T-W Diamond, southwest of Cheyenne and 35 km into Colorado (Flayharty and Morris 1974:161). Called Shoshone, its side-notched and triangular points, ridge-top location, bison-hunting subsistence, and dates of AD 1020 ± 230 and 1170 ± 220 favor Dene. Also south of Cheyenne in Arapaho Pass, Indian Peaks, and the Fourth of July Valley of Colorado's Front Range (Figure 15.4), Benedict (1981, 1985, 1996, 2000a, 2000b, 2005) found alpine drivelanes, hunting blinds, and cairns resembling those of the Chipewyan. As a geologist, he did not assign ethnicity, but his late radiocarbon dates and point types suggest contemporaneity with the Dene. The drivelanes he found were used to direct mountain sheep, elk, and possibly bison (personal communication 2010), which also follow drivelanes (e.g., Alberta's Head-Smashed-In Buffalo Jump). Dene presence is also based on diagnostic first molars in 3 of 13 burials at the Trinidad Reservoir, as well as micaceous pottery (Winter 1988). This fits well with my theory of ancestral Apache reaching southeastern Colorado and Texas from the Four Corners, but it is too late for a Plains route south.

To the northwest, in the south-central part of the Plains extension, the Bairoil site has 180 1.8–5.6-m tipi rings, and its arrowheads (Jess and Berrigan 1982: Figures 10b, d, 11a, d) are very like Dene (Gordon 1996:Figure 4.4, upper row). Arrowheads at Flaming Gorge on the lower Green River are also Dene-like (Day and Dibble 1963:1–86, Figure 5a, d, e; cf. Gordon 1996:Figure 4.4: KeNi-4:40, KkNb-19:7, and JkNf-1:47 and 48). The Twin Buttes site near Flaming Gorge has tipi rings (Sharrock 1966:173, Figure 47f–h), again with Dene-like points (Gordon 1996:Figure 4.4). Nearby, Smith and Creasman's (1988:B30, 31, 94, 106) features and fire-cracked rock in Taliaferro's late prehistoric component VI are part of a Paiute wickiup, but its artifacts and features resemble Dene. Its 1,170-year-old date matches my concept of Dene transit and is much too old for Paiute. Wickiups, dwellings domed with long curved sticks and covered with grass, brush, bark, rushes, mats, or reeds, were used transiently where these materials were easily available. Tipis, conical dwellings made from a circle of long poles converging at the top and covered with animal skins, require dozens of prepared hides, rawhide ropes, wooden stakes, and precut poles. They were important enough to Plains and Barrenland Dene that they were transported unassembled by families and their dogs (and later the horse on the Plains) for hundreds of miles as they followed the bison or caribou. The Dene varied wickiup and tipi usage according to conditions. Both Paiute and Dene used wickiups and simple tool kits and can best be separated with the use of radiocarbon dates, but special care must be taken not to use "old wood." The Dene should date about 1,000 to 800 years ago on the Intermountain part of my route, while the Paiute, Ute, and Shoshone should approach the protohistoric period.

Downriver, some of Breternitz's (1970) Dinosaur National Monument tools labeled Numic may be Dene: a chipped disk and scraper resembling chithos from 42UN119 Dam (p. 78; Figures 4c and 13c); arrowheads in MacLeod 42UN121 and Ford 42UN120 (pp. 52–53; Figure 12 and p. 79; Figure 3a, b, c); those dug by Anderson and Higel (p. 98; Figure 6; Gordon 1996:Figure 4.4); Jennings and Wade's Lowell Spring 5MF224 (p. 83; Figure 9-IIIa–e; Gordon 1996:Figure 4.4, top row); Anderson and Higel's Deerlodge Midden 5MF202 (p. 101); Leach's Swelter Shelter 42UN40 (p. 127; Figure 4); and Swedlund and Lageson's Serviceberry Shelter (p. 83; Figure 11 "blades" and Figure 4.8). Anderson and Higel (see Breternitz 1970:101) compared the Deerlodge Midden and Serviceberry Shelter arrowheads with those of the Northwest Plains. Dene traces may also appear in the Castle Park site (see Huscher and Huscher 1942; Burgh and Scoggin 1948:79). The Dene may also have followed the Yampa River, a Green tributary, where Burgh and Scoggin (1948:79) and later surveyors found many sites, some possibly Dene. Jason Labelle (personal communication 2009) also found many sites. A topographically easier route south on the White River to the San Juan Valley and the Four Corners justifies a second look at tools. I favor the Green River route because of its distant pronghorn migrations and its link to a Plains bison extension into Wyoming. Since leaving the Yukon and British Columbia 2,600 years ago, the ancestral Chipewyan had adopted a migratory lifestyle and would not readily have abandoned it.

Farther downriver, most Colorado stone rings are above deep canyons or on mesas and bluffs (Raynaud 1942:35, 38). Their inhabitants left large numbers of stone chips and artifacts while looking for game and strangers. All these ancestral traits are present for the Southwest Apacheans (Seymour 2002, 2008a) and Chipewyan. Raynaud (1942:47) even compared his ring distribution with those of the prehistoric ancestral Navajo and Apache. His thin long slab uprights in blinds closely resemble Chipewyan blinds.

The Green and Colorado Rivers meet on the Colorado Plateau. East on the Uncompahgre Plateau of western Colorado, Alan Reed (personal communication 2007) is unopposed to ancestral Dene but, like others, has difficulty recognizing its stone tools because his resemble Ute. He says "old wood" affects Numic dating, acknowledging that his many calibrated radiocarbon dates (Reed and Gebauer 2004:104, Figure 2) suggest Numic presence at AD 1300–1450 but actual arrival is possibly post-1500. "Old wood," taken from the ground instead of freshly cut, provides dates for tools and structures with 300-, 500-, and even 1,000-year errors. There is no Numic evidence in the Four Corners before AD 1300, and little more even after the Pueblo exodus (Lipe 1995:161). Furthermore, linguistic data and genetic haplogroup distribution (Kaestle and Smith 2001:1–2) show that Numic-speakers were recent visitors. Numic and Dene traits are chronologically distinct, so continuing discontent with Numic dating may open a Dene door long closed. Dene transit at AD 1100–1200 is possible with corrected Numic dates. In central Colorado, three radiocarbon dates in Fremont County's Castle Gardens Access Road site span a suggested Dene passage in AD 1170–1290 (Walker and Todd 1984:14). Some later side-notched, concave-based arrowheads (Walker and Todd 1984:Figure 14) resemble Dene (Gordon 1996:Figure 4.4; JkNf-1:47). Dene assemblages can be separated from Ute assemblages, even on surface sites, by the presence of chithos, early radiocarbon dates, and a seasonal sequence of sites across the land that result from following migratory herds. My route needs proof, but there are many collections to reexamine. Across the Continental Divide, the link between the Plains, Wyoming Basin, Green River, and Southwest is unmatched as a possible Dene route to the Southwest (Figure 15.4, right center, site gap southwest of Black Hills). Its size, accessibility, low elevation, and orientation formed a natural conduit for flora and fauna, particularly bison and pronghorn.

DENE ARRIVAL IN THE SOUTHWEST MUST NOT BE BASED ON POTTERY

According to many researchers, the Dene entered north-central and northeastern Colorado at AD 1300–1400 (Brunswig 1995:174–177; 2005:87–88, 92–93, 122–123, 207–210; Cassells 1997:234–240; Clark 1999:309–313; Gilmore 2004, 2006; Kindig 2000:106–107). I think they were there a century earlier, entering the Southwest at AD 1000–1200, hunting from simple brush shelters. But some archaeologists mark their arrival on the basis of hogans and corn remains, plus crude pottery at the time of the Spanish entrada—the earliest date being 1541.

Reed and Hensler (1999) think the Dene derived their pottery from Promontory-Fremont or Dismal River. Aikens (1967:198–199, 203–205) and Haskell (1987) say Promontory represents Dene Lipan bison hunters with Woodland pottery reaching Utah from the Plains via Colorado in the interval AD 885–1700, with precise dates of AD 885 ± 120 and 1110 ± 75. These dates match those for my proposed migration of the Chipewyan, but I believe they went directly south from Wyoming to Colorado without pottery. I also think the Lipan dating range of almost a millennium is far too imprecise. Warburton and Begay (2005:552–553) say the earliest Navajo in the Four Corners did not have pottery. The Windway and other ceremonial narratives teach that there was a time when Navajo families were not making pottery. Neither Coronado on his trip to central Kansas in AD 1541 nor Mescalero Apache oral tradition mentions pottery (Wedel 1986:136; see Carmichael and Farrer, this volume). Hancock (1997) says the Navajo imported pottery before AD 1541, as seen at LA 55979. Many believe Apachean pottery came from Puebloan neighbors. Genetic evidence of Dene men marrying Pueblo women supports this (Mahli et al. 2008:414). But most Southwest archaeologists maintain the Dene arrived with pottery. It is interesting that in 1870–1880 Bourke said the Apache were not potters because their term for pot (*izá*) actually meant basket and "proves linguistically what is known to be true historically—that the Apaches have never been potters; always basket-makers" (Condie 1980:vii, 68).

Dittert and others (1961) and Hester (1962) define the earliest Navajo on the basis of Dinétah pottery dating to AD 1500. But using Dinétah or thin gray Apache plainware as evidence excludes all pre–AD 1400 sites. In my plotting of possible Plains side-notched sites in northern Colorado (Figure 15.4), I found only 32 sites with pottery, none of it Dene. Of these, most had Uncompahgre and grayware, then a few micaceous, plainware, black-on-white, Dismal River, and corrugated, with one each of Dinétah, Uintah Gray, Numic, and Intermountain ware. Dismal River and Numic pottery are too late. Uintah Gray is Utah Fremont and too early. Fremont, Woodland, and Dinétah and Gobernador pottery differ, while micaceous and plainware are ubiquitous. So we must relinquish pottery as an arrival marker (also see Seymour 2008a:158, 2008b).

The Gunnersons (J. Gunnerson 1960:246, 1969:36; J. and D. Gunnerson 1971:9) believe that paddle-and-anvil-made Ocate Micaceous pottery accompanied the first Apache to the Southwest. But this technique may have diffused from their Puebloan neighbors. Ferg (2004) says most post-arrival vessels exhibit a "classical Apache shape," with wide mouths, high shoulders, and pointed bottoms, but Seymour (2002:322–324) suggests that most of the traits associated with later Apache pottery may represent late additions or be unique to specific bands. In this volume (Chapter 5), Seymour suggests that at least a third of the vessels pictured by Ferg are actually non-Apachean. After all is said and done, I feel that it is unlikely that the first Apacheans had pottery, a position shared by a number of other scholars (Warburton and Begay 2005:552–553; Hancock 1997; Wedel 1986:136; Carmichael and Farrer, this volume). Carmichael and Farrer are to be complimented for their insightful position on pottery.

DENE MOVEMENT IN THE SOUTHWEST

From the Four Corners, some Dene spread south and east to form the Plains Apache. Like all Dene, the Plains Apache adapted well to different environments, resulting in generalized tool kits (Wedel 1986:147–148). This, then, is the main problem in finding Dene sites, whether along my proposed migration route or in the Dene motherland. Unlike Chipewyan caribou hunting, which is still carried out today, bison hunting by the Apache completely disappeared with nineteenth-century herd extermination, as did their specialized hunting tools.

My conclusions on Dene arrival at AD 1300–1400 with distinct cultural traits agree with those of Seymour (2002:322–324). Consistent with her findings, game overlooks, concealed sites, sinew-backed bows, and chitho hide abraders, plus appropriate seasonality and radiocarbon dates, are supported by 10 dates for the 1200–1300 period (Seymour 2008a:8, 12, Table 3); dates in my Table 15.3 are from Seymour (2008a). She (2004:133) says Apache were mountain-oriented from the beginning in the Southwest (though she says they also seasonally occupied the valleys and foothills), but I think this orientation was learned

TABLE 15.3. North and South Dene ^{14}C Dates.

Normalized/Calibrated AD Age (Lab No.)	Method	Site by Decreasing Distance from Canada to American Southwest
940 ± 70 (S-1021)	^{14}C (1σ)	KkLn-4, Migod site, lower Dubawnt River, Nunavut (wood charcoal)
930 ± 230 (S-1158a)	^{14}C (1σ)	KkLn-4, Migod site, lower Dubawnt River, Nunavut (wood charcoal)
900 ± 100 (S-1009)	^{14}C (1σ)	KkLn-4, Migod site, lower Dubawnt River, Nunavut (wood charcoal)
1105 ± 115 (S-717) Prairie & Plains side-notched points	^{14}C (1σ)	KjNb-7, Duc site, upper Thelon River, NWT (wood charcoal)
800 ± 85 (S-716) Prairie side-notched points	^{14}C (1σ)	KjNb-7, Duc site, upper Thelon River, NWT (wood charcoal)
990 ± 130 (I-4973)	^{14}C (1σ)	KeNo-2, E Arm, Great Slave Lake, NWT (hearth bone collagen)
860 ± 160 (GaK-1258)	^{14}C (1σ)	KeNo-2, E Arm, Great Slave Lake, NWT (hearth bone collagen)
995 ± 95 (S-587)	^{14}C (1σ)	KfNm-3, Hennessey, Artillery Lake, NWT (hearth bone collagen)
910 ± 70 (S-1441) Prairie side-notched points	^{14}C (1σ)	KeNi-4, Whitefish Lake, Southwest Barrenlands, NWT (wood charcoal)
910 ± 80 (S-1530) Prairie side-notched points	^{14}C (1σ)	KeNi-4, Whitefish Lake, Southwest Barrenlands, NWT (wood charcoal)
990 ± 60 (S-1529) Prairie side-notched points	^{14}C (1σ)	KeNi-4, Whitefish Lake, Southwest Barrenlands, NWT (wood charcoal)
1350 ± 80 (S-1528) (MT)	^{14}C (1σ)	KeNi-5, Whitefish Lake, Southwest Barrenlands, NWT (wood charcoal)
1390 ± 50 (S-1143) (MT)	^{14}C (1σ)	JjNe-6, Jarvis Lake, Southwest Barrenlands, NWT (wood charcoal)
1320 ± 90 (S-1156) (MT)	^{14}C (1σ)	JjNk-2, Rennie Lake, Southwest Barrenlands, NWT (wood charcoal)
1340 ± 50 (S-1140) (MT)	^{14}C (1σ)	JkNf-1, Jarvis Lake, Southwest Barrenlands, NWT (wood charcoal)
1010 ± 50 (S-1142)	^{14}C (1σ)	http://www.canadianarchaeology.ca/localc14/detail.php?id=5914, JiNc-3 Firedrake Lake, Southwest Barrenlands, NWT (wood charcoal)
920 ± 65 (S-1141)	^{14}C (1σ)	JiNf-7, Firedrake Lake, Southwest Barrenlands, NWT (wood charcoal)
1235 ± 60 (S-1136)	^{14}C (1σ)	JjNd-1, Firedrake Lake, Southwest Barrenlands, NWT (wood charcoal)
690 ± 170 (GaK-3798)	^{14}C (1σ)	IgOo-1, Big Bay, Lake Athabasca, Northern Alberta
1325 Prairie side-notched point	^{14}C	IgNj-1, Black L, N Saskatchewan; based on Manitoba date (Minni 1976:54)

TABLE 15.3. (cont'd.) North and South Dene ^{14}C Dates.

Normalized/Calibrated AD Age (Lab No.)	Method	Site by Decreasing Distance from Canada to American Southwest
1180 ± 80 (GaK-2341)	^{14}C (1σ)	IeLk-4, Shethanei Narrows, Seal River, Northern Manitoba
1175 ± 90 (I-6000)	^{14}C (1σ)	IhLa-1, Caribou Hill site, Manitoba
960 ± 110 (I-3032)	^{14}C (1σ)	IiLk-1, Duck Lake Narrows site, Northern Manitoba
660 ± 110 (I-3033)	^{14}C (1σ)	IiLk-1, Duck Lake Narrows site, Northern Manitoba
675 ± 75 (S-2240)	^{14}C (1σ)	GlOc-20, Martin Chartier 3 site, Northern Saskatchewan
1270–1320 (Cal. BP 680–630) & Cal. 1350–1390 (Cal. BP 600–560) (Beta-203376)	^{14}C (2σ)	AZ CC:7:11[BLM], Whitlock Mts, Arizona, grass in Early Dene storage platform (annual without "old wood" dating problems), also LA 16265 below (Seymour 2008a)
1415–1490 (Cal. BP 535–460) (Beta-188760)	^{14}C (2σ)	LA 117112/FB 16265, Rough Canyon, NM, E Dene storage platform, grass (no old wood problems; Seymour 2002, 2003, 2008a)
1450–1670 & 1780–1795 (Beta-126400)	^{14}C (2σ)	LA 117165/FB 16318, Juniper Canyon, Otero Mesa, NM; from Early Dene ocotillo and leaves storage platform (see Seymour 2002, 2003, 2008a)
1520–1580 (Cal. BP 430–380) & Cal. 1630–1690 (Cal.BP 320–260), Cal. 1730–1810 (Cal. BP 220–140) (Beta-203378)	^{14}C (2σ)	AZ CC:12:58[ASM], Peloncillo Mts, yucca from storage platform in rockshelter with Early Dene charcoal gq'he pictographs (yucca does not have "old wood" dating problems; Seymour 2008a and Chapter 5, this volume)
1430–1520 (Cal. BP 520–430) & Cal. 1580–1630 (Cal.BP 380–320) (Beta-166882)	^{14}C (2σ)	Dragoon 1, Dragoon Mts, Arizona, burned sugary plant material from small Early Dene roasting pit (no "old wood" dating problems; Seymour 2002, 2003, 2008a)
1354 ± 40 (1324–1404) (Oxford X1874)	TL	Dragoon 1, Dragoon Mts, Arizona, rock in tiny Early Dene roasting pit (Seymour 2002, 2003, 2008a)
1420 ± 80 BP ; 1340–1500 (Oxford X1517)	OSL	LA 37188/FB 9609, Hueco Mts, NM, Llano Plainware sherd, probably Apache (Seymour 2002, 2003, 2008a)
Cal. 1270–1400 (Cal. BP 680–550) (Beta-169609)	^{14}C (2σ)	LA 84424, F1, Mogollon Mts, NM, Early Dene roasting pit charcoal (see Seymour 2008a)
Cal. 1400–1450 (Cal. BP 550–500) (Beta-172175)	^{14}C (2σ)	LA 84424, F2, Mogollon Mts, NM, Early Dene roasting pit charcoal (see Seymour 2008a)
1240–1440 (Beta-64068)	^{14}C (1σ)	LA 70189, Mogollon Mts, NM (Early Dene; Oakes and Zamora 1999; see Seymour 2008a)
1220–1430 (Beta-69815)	^{14}C (1σ)	LA 70189, Mogollon Mts, NM (Early Dene; Oakes and Zamora 1999; see Seymour 2008a)
1400–1470 (Beta-64067)	^{14}C (1σ)	LA 70188, Mogollon Mts, NM (Early Dene; Oakes and Zamora 1999; see Seymour 2008a)

Note: Canadian dates are normalized using an accepted oak standard of −25 parts per mil based on isotopic fractionation correction of ^{12}C/^{13}C ratios, with difference from −25 = 16 years. NWT is Northwest Territories, Canada, north of the Prairie provinces. My dates are Late Taltheilei (Early Dene) except MT (Middle phase; see http://www.canadianarchaeology.ca/localc14/c14search.htm). Pre-Coronado Apachean dates are calibrated and obtained from Seymour (2008a), who examined contexts of dates and associated material culture to ascertain reliability of dates.

in the Green and San Juan valleys. They wintered in low-lying small camps on south-facing slopes, in canyon mouths and wash confluences, as indicated by several dozen artifacts. A good example is the early southern Arizona Dragoon Mountain site with paired structures, roasting pits, caches, a gaming circle, and only 18 centrally placed artifacts (Seymour 2002).

Seymour (2002) says Apachean archaeology is challenging because many sites are palimpsests with artifacts from other cultures intermixed, with few artifacts, and these must be separated culturally. The itinerant life of the proto-Apacheans left few remains, but was distinct from that of their sedentary Puebloan and non-Puebloan farming neighbors. Compounding the problem is the perishable nature of their baskets and wood and fiber items, and the fact that their camps were 50 miles or more apart and sometimes seldom revisited, making for incomplete assemblages. Seymour (this volume, Chapter 5) reveals the need to observe dozens of sites to obtain a balanced picture of Apachean life. Like the Sarsi Dene of the southwestern Alberta Blackfoot Confederacy, all Apachean and Dene descendants were inveterate borrowers whose stone tools submerge in the tool kits of those whose lands they shared (Seymour, this volume, Chapter 5; Gilmore and Larmore, this volume).

FOUR CORNERS ABANDONMENT BY PUEBLOANS AND DENE SURVIVAL

Low-frequency environmental degradation began about AD 1150, the Great Drought lasting from AD 1276 to 1299 (Douglass 1929), when Chaco Canyon, Mesa Verde, Hovenweep, and Wupatki were suddenly emptied (Plog 1982: 26–27). People left northern Black Mesa at AD 980–1010, reoccupied it for 125 years, and permanently abandoned it about AD 1130 (Plog and Hantman 1990). There and at Vermillion Cliffs, Larsen and others (1996:221) say tree-ring evidence indicates highly variable soil moisture at AD 1000–1050, 1100–1150, and 1200–1270, with the periods 1120–1200 and 1270–1300 having drought severe enough that even with increased labor input, food storage, and trade, abandonment was inevitable. By AD 1225, lowland farming was greatly reduced, but intense widespread occupation of the Kayenta area continued through Pueblo II to about AD 1225 (Lindsay et al. 1968:364–365). By AD 1250, permanent occupants had left Kayenta, possibly for Navajo Mountain, which had more suitable conditions. Widespread abandonment occurred in the terminal Pueblo II period before heavy peopling in Pueblo III.

Late Pueblo III people in the northern Rainbow Plateau left in the AD 1270s, with full abandonment by AD 1300. By AD 1300, all the northern and most of the central plateau were abandoned in favor of the Rio Grande to the east and a southern transitional zone, both with greater summer rainfall. Lipe (1995:140, 143) says that drought caused the estimated 10,000 Puebloans living in the Four Corners up to about AD 1250 to disappear by 1300. He adds that if one "considers artifact counts rather than site numbers," these low-density scatters represent a fraction of the northern San Juan archaeological record.

Puebloan ability to overcome resource and technical change was overwhelmed by severe conditions from AD 1150 to 1350 (Basgall 1999). Post–AD 1050 impact on all inhabitants was significant, especially on the heavily populated Rainbow Plateau (Dean et al. 1985; Dean 1988; Plog et al. 1988; Larsen and Michaelsen 1990; Van West and Lipe 1992). A current disregard for a direct link between drought and cultural change stems from a reaction to overly deterministic approaches in archaeology on the effect of the Altithermal on cultural change. Jones et al. (1999:137) say that "many ecologically oriented archaeologists...equate environmental causality with determinism, [rejecting] environment as a potential cause of cultural change." Dean (1988) cautions against relating moisture phase transitions to environmental change.

Davis (1965:353–355) asked, "Why should the well-adapted inhabitants... endure 800 years of cyclical droughts and suddenly collapse in the midst of one of them?" And Carla Van West (1994) showed that the Mesa Verde cliff dwellers could have raised enough corn despite the drought. Jones and others (1999: 156) say that "severe environmental downturns should not be ignored as potential causes of demographic stress." Still, hunter-gatherers "could transcend low-intensity/low-frequency environmental flux" (Jones et al. 1999:164; Basgall 1987). I believe the newly arrived proto-Apacheans, some of whom adopted agriculture in the Southwest, survived by reverting to their earlier hunter-gatherer lifeway. They hunted the highly drought-tolerant Plains bison and mountain pronghorn and could find perennial water sources even in the desert. If hunter-gatherers relied on piñon nuts, which mature every three to seven years, the Colorado Plateau, including the San Juan, was poor for hunter-gatherers (Matson 1991:221–243). I believe Apacheans had a broader food base than this, one that they learned during their lengthy intermountain sojourn.

As for warfare as a cause for abandonment of these areas by Puebloans, Gumerman (1984:107) found "little archaeological evidence for internecine warfare," but later researchers saw evidence for warfare between Pueblo and Apache. Adler (1996:15–16) says village aggregation was a response to tensions between Pueblo farmers and Apachean nomads, based on the latter's raiding lifestyle.

Intergroup violence started in the AD 1240s, intensifying over the next 30 years, with raiding becoming an adaptive strategy during local shortages (Haas and Creamer 1999). Jones et al. (1999:162) say warfare at Kayenta occurred "when [moisture] spatial variability was consistently low (Plog et al. 1988)," that is, when there would have been competition for limited resources.

The mid-nineteenth-century find of abandoned cliff dwellings near the Four Corners prompted early-twentieth-century speculation about the timing and cause of their desertion, but over a decade ago, LeBlanc (1999) said:

> We start seeing ever-increasing evidence for warfare beginning AD 1200, and...by the 1300s the entire Southwest was engulfed in conflict...mas-

sacres...sites massively burned...scalping.... Smaller settlements abandoned.... Caves (or cliff overhangs) used to house large communities.... Mesa Verde and Kayenta...Tonto Basin, Sierra Ancha, and Upper Gila.... Unburied bodies, decapitated heads, and isolated limbs.... By around AD 1300 almost the entire Southwest was broken up into these...site clusters [which then] began disappearing...until only three were left (Hopi, Zuni, and Acoma).... The most recent population estimates for the Southwest [show]... the population declined to one-quarter or less by AD 1400. Warfare and its consequences are partly to blame, but...the climate began to deteriorate at a rapid pace, and by the 1300s...much of the Southwest was unusable by farmers.... Fierce competition ensued and warfare broke out.... As if this was not enough...the sinew-backed recurved bow was introduced.... [It] did not cause the increase in warfare, but it may have made it more deadly.

Based on their history, the fearsome Apache raiders and their deadly sinew-backed recurved bow were blamed until the mid-twentieth century. Jett (1964: 281) had favored Apache intrusion based on "legend, glottochronology and indirect archaeological evidence in the Largo-Gallina area," stating that Puebloan defensive architecture could have been overcome with guerrilla-type raids. Even Haas and Creamer (1993:50) do not rule out raiding, but the Apache were thought to be too few to uproot the numerous Pueblo villagers. Keith Kintigh (personal communication 2008) thinks that only a nontrivial number of Dene could have caused 20,000 well-established and successful villagers to move 300 kilometers. Nonetheless, a broken side-notched arrowhead of unknown origin found in a man's pelvis in the Kayenta region of northeastern Arizona might be Dene (Haas and Creamer 1993).

Data now show that proto-Apache traded and intermarried with Puebloans (Malhi et al. 2008; Malhi, this volume) so the conflict between them may not have been as intense as some relate. An elaborate Puebloan line-of-sight warning system between neighboring settlements may not have been adequate to protect against intervillage feuds. Upham (1984:248–249) raises another possibility: "abandonment does not require...a catastrophe precipitated by drought, disease, Athapaskan intrusion, arroyo cutting, or erosion. Instead, the cycle of adaptive shifts from hunting and gathering to agriculture to hunting and gathering again provides a much more parsimonious explanation for abandonments [of] areas [that] were inhabited by hunter-gatherers." Yet Upham's adaptive shift cannot explain the construction of widespread defensive structures or the presence of mutilated corpses.

LeBlanc (1999) and Jones and others (1999) favor internal Puebloan warfare over scarce resources, but this does not explain why *everyone* left. Plog and Hantman (1990) cite political and social reasons for the abandonment of Black Mesa rather than deteriorating climate. Others suggest village disputes, political collapse, religious failures, witchcraft, disease, or interrupted trade, but these were likely local. Cordell (1995) says the villages felt "pushed" by combined social and environmental factors and "pulled" elsewhere by anticipated settled weather, irrigable land, safer communities, and spiritual enlightenment. Another debatable consideration raised by amateur archaeologist Don Dove and reported by Fred Plog (1982:26–27) is wood fuel depletion.

Renfrew (2000) suggests that a late Pueblo III abandonment caused by an AD 1250–1300 drought allowed early Dene entry, but I think the Dene were already there surviving in the dry environment. Neily (1983) concludes that communities became more independent in the late AD 1100s and 1200s. I can see why Navajo farmers reverted to hunting-gathering and remained near the Four Corners, but I cannot visualize Puebloans embracing a more mobile lifestyle.

IF THE DISMAL RIVER ASPECT REPRESENTS A REVERSE DENE MIGRATION, IS PROMONTORY POINT RELATED TO THE ORIGINAL MIGRATION SOUTH?

Schaafsma (1996), the major late-arrival enthusiast, suggests a post–AD 1700 arrival west of the Continental Divide, after the Pueblo Revolt and Reconquest; in this view, pre-1700 material is from the Ute or other already resident groups. But most researchers believe the Navajo entered before the early 1500s, while Schaafsma's interpretation is problematic if "old wood" samples were used to date material.

The Dismal River aspect is the often accepted midpoint of Dene movement south, but I believe it is too late and too far east to be considered. Moreover, it has corn and pottery, traits I think were missing in ancient Dene inventories. I suggest its lateness more accurately reflects a reverse migration of Plains Apache from the Southwest some centuries after their arrival as Apacheans. Promontory Point is more complex because its occupation dates to Dene entry, but it is in Utah in the Great Basin and quite far west of my route. Nonetheless, it remains a possibility.

Dismal River

Dismal River sites in Nebraska (one south-central, three north-central) and three in southeastern Wyoming are often cited as evidence for a Dene migration route south to become the Navajo and Apache. Quite distant from the mountains, these sites are used to support Rockies, Foothills, and Plains routes on the basis of some artifacts and their joint occupation of the High Plains, the Sandhills, and the Colorado Piedmont, with sites implied for western Kansas and eastern Colorado. But even in its earliest description, Gunnerson (1960) says the migration was of 1700s Plains Apache, not northern Dene, as does Wedel (1953: 508), with only a 50-year time span and no Plains antecedents. Their houses with five central posts represent a compromise between the Plains earth lodge and the Navajo hogan with its three main and two entrance posts. Despite all this evidence for a late migration from the Southwest, Gunnerson (1979:163) and Gunnerson and Gunnerson (1971:15) favor a route between Canada and the Southwest through northwestern Nebraska, the Angostura Reservoir, and the Badlands south of the Black Hills. Gilmore (2006:29) thinks the western branch of Dismal River culture denotes an eastern Apachean move from Colorado to the Central Plains ca. AD 1500, but adds that migration was often two-way along Colorado's Front Range (Gilmore and Larmore 2005). If so, the many pictographs and overlook sites along the Green River suggest that Dismal River people may have moved north along its banks from eastern Utah to the Great Plains. As this is tenuous support, I favor the Southern Plains route north from the Southwest. Finally, Judith Habicht-Mauche (personal communication 2006) rejects Dismal River entirely as Dene, saying it "reflects Plains Village groups who moved west to the High Plains, gave up farming, and may have become Apacheized."

Promontory Point

Steward (1937) suggests that Promontory artifacts were made by northern bison hunters or ancestral Dene; they are believed to date to about AD 1200–1300, according to Ives (2005). Without specifying, Gunnerson (1960:244) links Promontory Point to Dismal River on the basis of "sufficiently numerous...similarities between the two complexes." Ives (2005) suggests a link between Promontory and the Yukon's Ice Patch moccasin and an Albertan pictograph, adding that Promontory is midway between the northern and southern Dene, but does not suggest a route south. I await his forthcoming book.

CERRO ROJO COMPLEX AS THE FIRST SOUTHWEST APACHEAN-RELATED COMPLEX?

Seymour defines the Cerro Rojo complex using about 100 sites in southeastern Arizona, New Mexico, parts of southwest Texas, and northern Chihuahua and Sonora (Chapter 5, this volume, 2002, 2004b). Many of its tools and traits resemble what I consider to be those of the earliest Apacheans to arrive via my Northwest Plains–Intermountain route. She even has some radiocarbon dates from the period in which I (and she) think they arrived—the AD 1200s. Indeed, the earliest part of her Cerro Rojo complex may represent the earliest arrivals, but this remains unproven until more pre–AD 1200 sites are found to the north near the Four Corners, where I end my Intermountain route. Stratified sites with Apachean levels dated before AD 1200 must be found here before we can prove anything, yet as Seymour (personal communication 2010) points out, stratified Apachean sites in the southern Southwest are not known, as the Apacheans' use of the landscape tended to be transient. Another major problem is determining whether the first arrivals had pottery, as Seymour, Brunswig, and Gilmore and Larmore (this volume) point out. Gilmore and Larmore allude to pottery associated with the Dismal River aspect, which I reiterate is far too late and should be dropped from discussion.

The Cerro Rojo type site is a mixed Apache and non-Apache Canutillo complex hilltop ranchería in southern New Mexico that dates intermittently from the AD 1400s to the late 1700s on the basis of luminescence dates on pottery and burned-hearth caliche and radiocarbon dates. The site was reused over time, resulting in evidence for 212 structures. The latest occupation shows a defensive response to southern and western Comanche advance. Early Dene–dated material at this and/or other Cerro Rojo complex sites includes storage platforms, pictographs, roasting pits, pottery, burned hearth stones, and hearth charcoal. Stone tools at some sites include small thin side-notched points, bifacial knives, drills, side and end scrapers, and slab metates.

My reading of Seymour's (2003:24, 57) Elephant Mountain site data suggests that there is a pre–AD 1300 Cerro Rojo occupation that postdates the use of its pueblo by the Jornada Mogollon and dates Apache use of this site. Some of Seymour's early pre-Coronado Dene sites with Cerro Rojo material located elsewhere are dated in Table 15.3. Of the 70-plus dates she collected, I include the 12 that are pre-Coronado (Seymour 2008a). By AD 1400, early Dene were well distributed, their artifacts quite unlike those of historic Southwest Dene as new adaptations, technologies, identities, and social practices were adopted. Seymour has made a point of locating sites in widely dispersed areas in an effort to address the issues of route, timing, and geographic variability. Many of her (2008a:Figure 38) pre-Coronado sites in the Mogollon Highlands and south to the international border are so dispersed geographically that they suggest widespread quick Apachean expansion following initial entry.

A Later Apachean-Related Complex: Tierra Blanca and Apachean Arrival

Tierra Blanca has few well-reported or dated sites even in the type site area in the Texas Panhandle (Boyd 1997b:368; Hughes, this volume). Its artifacts are vaguely defined and include the ubiquitous Washita, Harrell, and Fresno-like points, plus Plains diamond-shaped beveled knives, snub-nosed scrapers, and drills. Tierra Blanca pottery is confined to part of the Red River in the Texas Panhandle (Habicht-Mauche 1987, 1988) and defined as micaceous plainware, its origin controversial.[5] As "Apache pottery" may be mixed with late Southern Plains plainware, it cannot be used to define these Tierra Blanca sites (Boyd 1997a:211). Hughes (this volume) states that "until such time as at least one site that represents the Tierra Blanca complex is fully reported, the minutiae of elements within the complex cannot be assessed." He reiterates Boyd as saying the Tierra Blanca transition to the Dene is a "working hypothesis." Some Tierra Blanca sites have tipi rings on canyon rims and thatched-roof adobe huts on sheltered terraces with separate hunting and planting areas used later by Jicarilla, Sierra Blanca, Carlana, Penxaye, Paloma Apache, and Cuartelejo bison hunters from 1696 to 1719 (Thomas 1935). Important Plains artifacts and raw materials in Pueblo sites are found largely along the eastern border (Spielmann 1983:262).

Habicht-Mauche (1992:251) infers an AD 1450–1650 range for Tierra Blanca, while one of Spielmann's (1982:287) dates is consistent with Jelinek's AD 1380 ± 60 date from the Middle Pecos. Most radiocarbon dates and Southwestern glazed ceramics show Tierra Blanca to be protohistoric. Seymour (2002; Chapter 5, this volume) thinks her tri-notched points from El Paso–Fort Bliss are likely Apachean. Tierra Blanca may represent semi-sedentary, semi-nomadic, pre–Plains Apache (Hughes 1978, 1989; Katz and Katz 1976:55) bison hunters who may have grown corn (Hogan 2006:4:14–22).

The proximity of Tierra Blanca sites to Alibates quarries implied to Spielmann (1983:265–268) that the Apache controlled trade north of Amarillo after AD 1450. Apache bison hunters in southern Colorado traveled to the headwaters of the Cimarron River in New Mexico and the Colorado River in Colorado to collect or trade for Alibates chert (Kingsbury and Gabel 1983:325). This northern trade is inferred to have led to Apache bison products at Pecos Pueblo and Pueblo trade sherds in Tierra Blanca, with east-west trade soon following (Hughes 1991; Schroeder 1994:300). The strength of Plains and Puebloan trade starting in the mid-1400s suggests an earlier date than that proposed by Gunnerson (1974). By AD 1400, Mogollon-Hohokam southern trade declined (Hughes 1991; Maestas 2003:46–47) and Tierra Blancans were displaced deeper into the South Texas Plains by the equestrian Plains Comanche.

One thing seems certain: the Tierra Blancans were not the earliest Dene entering the Southwest or Plains. Rather, I believe some of the ancient Dene arriving on an Intermountain route went east and assumed a Plains lifeway characteristic of the Tierra Blancans and gradually evolved into protohistoric Plains Apache.

A Contemporaneous but Non-Apachean-Related Complex: Toyah Complex and Apachean Arrival

Toyah complex sites follow the Austin phase and occur in north-central, central, and southern Texas (Johnson 1994; Prewitt 1981, 1985; Ricklis 1992) and possibly northeastern Chihuahua (Mallouf 1987). The complex's earliest sites occupied an advanced savanna and grassland, a moist period also seeing inroads by early Apacheans to the northwest. Toyah sites, such as 41LK201 and 41MC222, along the Frio River, had abundant bison bone, the latter site dating to AD 1260–1290 (Hester 1980; Highley 1986). Deer were important prey (Black and McGraw 1985), while the South Texas Hinojosa site (41JW8), dating to AD 1300–1500, had a subsistence base of fish, softshell turtle, waterfowl, mussels, deer, bison, and pronghorn (Black 1986). Some Toyah tools, such as thin alternately beveled bifacial knives, abundant end scrapers, flake drills or perforators, bone awls, and bison bone tools, bear general resemblance to Dene tools, but definitive traits are missing. Toyah arrowheads, cordage, corn (Prewitt 1981:84), basketry, and bone-tempered ceramics (Black 1986, 1989; Creel 1991; Hester 1980, 1995; Jelks 1962; Johnson 1994; Kelley 1986; Prewitt 1981) are also non-Dene. Rather, I suggest that Toyah represents protohistoric bison trade. Toyah hunters seem to have come from the Plains and date to AD 1300–1700 in central Texas, and were too far southeast of both the Dene and later Plains Apache.

Conclusion

I have summarized published and unpublished data on the suggested post–AD 500 Dene movement from British Columbia, Alberta, and Saskatchewan to the American Southwest. These areas have dedicated Dene archaeologists whose work I have tried to interpret correctly. In view of this work, my Northwest Plains–Intermountain route seems the most probable path for the migration of the ancestral Chipewyan to the south. I believe they changed into proto-Navajo and proto-Apache en route, probably in separate transitions from bison to pronghorn subsistence near the Green River, and arrived as two groups near the Four Corners at AD 1000–1200. Linguistics, glottochronology, and Saskatchewan and Barrenland archaeological site material, along with my radiocarbon dates, support this suggestion.

Linguistics and folk tradition support a minimum Apachean divergence of a millennium from Chipewyan. The divergence seems to have occurred well within the AD 800–1200 period of Plains side-notched points described for ancestral Chipewyan of the Late Taltheilei archaeological tradition. Arrowheads resembling Plains side-notched "swept the Anasazi world during Pueblo II times...its sudden popularity [suggesting Apachean arrival] about 900 to 1000" (Brugge 1988:283). New archaeological data in the form of late prehistoric Prairie and Plains side-notched arrowheads and some chithos or their variants are traced from Saskatchewan's Beverly caribou range south much of the way to the Four Corners. As the Dene traveled, they switched from hunting Barrenland caribou to Plains bison, then to Rocky Mountain pronghorn in the Green River Valley of Wyoming, then to deer and forest and desert fauna in the American Southwest. After the proto-Navajo and proto-Apache arrived separately in the Southwest, the latter moved east to hunt the bison, becoming the Plains Apache. After a long drought, when the bison returned to the Southern Plains, the Apache followed their northern migration to become the Dismal River aspect.

A major problem in the study of when the Chipewyan became the Navajo and the various Apache groups is that we have been thrown off the scent because earlier archaeologists misinterpreted some of their data. The 1,700-year radiocarbon range of Avonlea and its link to Canada's Arctic Small Tool tradition are both absurd and unfounded. Promontory Point data should continue to be considered until it proves unrelated. Abundant but sparse Montana, Wyoming, and Colorado collections ascribed to Numic-speakers should be reexamined now that many "old wood" dendrochronological dates are centuries too early. We must forget the idea of the Dene arriving in the Southwest with agriculture, hogans, and pottery. In the Southwest, Seymour (2002, 2004b, this volume,

Chapter 5) uses type and location of structures, specific side-notched arrowheads, overabundant worked flakes, bifacial and beveled knives, and other traits to define the proto-Apache in ways that look similar to assemblages of the ancestral Chipewyan. We must identify chithos as distinct from ubiquitous choppers and similar stone tools and attempt to trace a line of seasonal hunting camps across the landscape, assuming, of course, that coverage is regularly distributed. Caribou, bison, and pronghorn all migrate, and herd followers do not easily relinquish their lifeway.

AIDS TO MOUNTAIN AND SOUTHWEST ARCHAEOLOGISTS IN TRACING THE APACHEANS SOUTH

Regarding an AD 800 Chipewyan move from Canada to the American Southwest to become Apache and Navajo at AD 1000–1200, we must examine collections from eastern Montana, through western and central Wyoming, and along the Green and San Juan Rivers to the Four Corners. Modern state boundaries must not hinder this search. We must question why, how, and when they went, who and what game they encountered, as well as what environments and climates influenced their passage. We must avoid emotive evaluations (e.g., Great Basin archaeologists opposing the idea of a recent Numic spread, despite good evidence to the contrary; David Brugge, personal communication 2006). Southwest and Mountain State archaeologists must reexamine existing sites and collections for the following:

1. Concealed campsites, because the Dene were in others' territory or overlooking game movements
2. Confined scatters of overrepresented worked flakes with few if any "finished" tools
3. Sites linked to raiding or hunting with side- or corner-notched arrowheads
4. Sandstone disc or cobble spall "chithos" under other names
5. Simple brush shelters (wickiups) where rock circles were unneeded because sand was placed over flaps or poles embedded in the ground
6. Exposed C-shaped, three-rock-lined hearths opening east because of the dominant west wind
7. Roasting pits or skin-lined depressions with fire-cracked rock used for marrow extraction by boiling
8. Few tools directly east of exposed hearths due to windblown smoke and cinders because the wind in open areas is mainly western (this will change in valleys with prevailing winds)
9. Bones from dogs the size of water spaniels

ACKNOWLEDGMENTS

I thank Frank Bayerl for gathering and editing references over the winter of 2006–2007 and for continuous editing prior to publication. I thank Pavel Dvorak for drawing and adding to the maps where needed, and Spencer Sutton for stitching together the Utah,

Wyoming, Colorado, Montana, and Saskatchewan site locations so Pavel could incorporate them into the main migration map. Spencer used site databases sent by Arie Leeflang (Utah Division of State History); Ross Hillman, Mary Hopkins, and Chris Young (Wyoming State Historic Preservation Office); Mary Sullivan (Colorado Office of Archaeology and Historic Preservation); Damon Murdo (Montana State Historic Preservation Office); and Nathan Friesen (Heritage Resources Branch, Saskatchewan Tourism, Parks, Culture, and Sport). I thank all these individuals for their trust and quick response to often demanding inquiries. I thank Deni Seymour for inviting me to write this chapter and sharing her early Apachean data from southern Arizona, New Mexico, and Texas. She also made valuable editorial comments. Doug Boyd of Lubbock convinced me that there is little early Apache evidence north of the Texas and Oklahoma Panhandles to support a Southern Plains route, an area occupied by Plains agriculturists. The list of archaeologists who sent articles for review is too long for me to acknowledge them individually, but I thank Ray Le Blanc and David Brugge for special assistance. I also thank those who sent personal communications whose names are noted in the text. I especially thank my wife, Marjory, for undertaking a revision that was too daunting for past participants and myself. She too tired after her major condensation, so I persisted and am responsible for any errors and omissions.

Notes

1. In this chapter I use "Apachean" to include both Apache and Navajo. For linguistic comparison, I use their separate terms.
2. By adopting a now-outdated view of Southwestern Dene prehistory, Malhi perceives this mixing as a post-1680 phenomenon, when it really occurred centuries earlier (Seymour 2009), likely in Pueblo II–III times, in my view.
3. The Chipewyan continued to prefer lancing at water crossings even after rifles were introduced, but the arrow permitted medium-distance hunting away from the crossings without the necessity of trips to a fort to obtain shot and powder.
4. Bélanger and Pinno (2008:65) and Nicolas Bélanger (personal communication 2009) found a northerly-advanced boreal forest southern border during the Medieval Warm period, with anticipated simultaneous advance of the aspen parkland and prairie.
5. Mica occurs naturally in some Southwest clays and cannot be used indiscriminately to identify sherds as Apachean, especially in the southern Southwest (Seymour 2002, 2008b).

References

Adler, M. A.
1996 *The Prehistoric Pueblo World, AD 1150–1350*. Tucson: University of Arizona Press.
Aikens, C. Melvin
1967 Plains Relationships of the Fremont Culture: A Hypothesis. *American Antiquity* 32(2):198–209.
Basgall, Mark E.
1987 Resource Intensification among Hunter-Gatherers: Acorn Economies in Prehistoric California. *Research in Economic Anthropology* 9:21–52.
1999 Comments. *Current Anthropology* 40(2):157.
Bélanger, Nicolas, and Bradley D. Pinno
2008 Carbon Sequestration, Vegetation Dynamics and Soil Development in the Boreal Transition Ecoregion of Saskatchewan during the Holocene. *Catena* 74(1):65–72.

Benedict, James B.
1981 *The Fourth of July Valley.* Research Report No. 2. Ward, Colorado: Center for Mountain Archeology.
1985 *Arapaho Pass.* Research Report No. 3. Ward, Colorado: Center for Mountain Archeology.
1996 *The Game Drives of Rocky Mountain National Park.* Research Report No. 7. Ward, Colorado: Center for Mountain Archeology.
2000a Excavations at the Fourth of July Mine Site. In *This Land of Shining Mountains: Archeological Studies in Colorado's Indian Peaks Wilderness Area,* edited by E. S. Cassells, pp. 159–188. Research Report No. 8. Ward, Colorado: Center for Mountain Archeology.
2000b Game Drives of the Devil's Thumb Pass Area. In *This Land of Shining Mountains: Archeological Studies in Colorado's Indian Peaks Wilderness Area,* edited by E. S. Cassells, pp. 8–94. Research Report No. 8. Ward, Colorado: Center for Mountain Archeology.
2005 Tundra Game Drives: An Arctic-Alpine Comparison. *Arctic, Antarctic, and Alpine Research* 37:425–434.

Black, Stephen. L.
1986 *The Clemente and Herminia Hinojosa Site, 41JW8: A Toyah Horizon Campsite in Southern Texas.* Special Report No. 18. San Antonio: Center for Archaeological Research, University of Texas.
1989 South Texas Plains. In *From the Gulf to the Rio Grande: Human Adaptation in Central, South, and Lower Pecos Texas,* by T. R. Hester, S. L. Black, D. G. Steele, B. W. Olive, A. A. Fox, K. Reinhard, and L. C. Bement, pp. 39–62. Research Series No. 33. Fayetteville: Arkansas Archeological Survey.

Black, S. L., and A. J. McGraw.
1985 *The Panther Springs Creek Site: Cultural Change and Continuity within the Upper Salado Creek Watershed, South-Central Texas.* Archaeological Survey Report No. 100. San Antonio: Center for Archaeological Research, University of Texas.

Boyd, Douglas K.
1997a *Caprock Canyonlands Archaeology: A Synthesis of the Late Prehistory and History of Lake Alan Henry and the Texas Panhandle-Plains,* Vol. 1. Reports of Investigations No. 110. Austin, Texas: Prewitt and Associates.
1997b *Caprock Canyonlands Archaeology: A Synthesis of the Late Prehistory and History of Lake Alan Henry and the Texas Panhandle-Plains,* Vol. 2. Reports of Investigations No. 110. Austin, Texas: Prewitt and Associates.

Breternitz, David A. (editor)
1970 *Archaeological Excavations in Dinosaur National Monument, Colorado-Utah, 1964–1965.* Boulder: University of Colorado Press.

Breuninger, Evelyn, Elbys Hugar, Ellen Ann Lathan, and Scott Rushforth
1982 *Mescalero Apache Dictionary.* Mescalero, New Mexico: Mescalero Apache Tribe.

Bright, Jason R., and Andrew Ugan
1999 Ceramics and Mobility: Assessing the Role of Foraging Behavior and Its Implications for Culture-History. *Utah Archaeology* 12:17–30.

Brinckerhoff, Sidney B.
1967 The Last Years of Spanish Arizona, 1786–1821. *Arizona and the West* 9(1):5–20.

Brink, Jack W., Milt Wright, Bob Dawe, and Doug Glaum
1985 *Final Report of the 1983 Season at Head-Smashed-In Buffalo Jump, Alberta.* Ar-

chaeological Survey of Alberta Manuscript Series No. 1. Edmonton: Alberta Culture.

Britten, Thomas A.
2009 *The Lipan Apaches: People of Wind and Lightning.* Albuquerque: University of New Mexico Press.

Broecker, Wallace S.
2001 Was the Medieval Warm Period Global? *Science* 291(5508):1497–1499.

Brown, Gary M.
1991 *Archaeological Data Recovery at San Juan Coal Company's La Plata Mine, San Juan County, New Mexico.* Technical Report No. 355. Albuquerque: Mariah Associates.
1996 The Protohistoric Transition in the Northern San Juan Region. In *The Archaeology of Navajo Origins*, edited by Ronald H. Towner, pp. 47–69. Salt Lake City: University of Utah Press.
1998 The Transition from Prehistory to History in the Mimbres Region. Paper presented at the conference "The Transition from Prehistory to History in the Southwest," Albuquerque.

Brown, Gary M., and Pat M. Hancock
1992 The Dinetah Phase in the La Plata Valley. In *Cultural Diversity and Adaptation: The Archaic, Anasazi, and Navajo Occupation of the Upper San Juan Basin*, edited by Lori S. Reed and Paul F. Reed, pp. 69–90. Cultural Resources Series No. 9. Santa Fe: New Mexico Bureau of Land Management.

Brugge, David M.
1978 A Comparative Study of Navajo Mortuary Practices. *American Indian Quarterly* 4(4):309–328.
1988 Comments on Athapaskans and Sumas. In *The Protohistoric Period in the North American Southwest, AD 1450–1700*, edited by David R. Wilcox and W. Bruce Masse, pp. 282–290. Anthropological Research Paper No. 24. Tempe: Arizona State University.
2003 DNA and Ancient Demography. In *Climbing the Rocks: Papers in Honor of Helen and Jay Crotty*, edited by Regge N. Wiseman, Thomas C. O'Laughlin, and Cordelia T. Snow, pp. 49–56. Papers No. 29. Albuquerque: Archaeological Society of New Mexico.

Brunswig, Robert H., Jr.
1995 Apachean Ceramics East of Colorado's Continental Divide: Current Data and New Directions. In *Archaeological Pottery of Colorado: Ceramic Clues to the Prehistoric and Protohistoric Lives of the State's Native Peoples*, edited by Robert H. Brunswig, B. Bradley, and S. M. Chandler, pp. 172–207. Occasional Papers No. 2. Denver: Colorado Council of Professional Archaeologists.
2005 *Prehistoric, Protohistoric, and Early Historic Native American Archeology of Rocky Mountain National Park: Final Report of Systemwide Archeological Inventory Program Investigations by the University of Northern Colorado (1998–2002).* Greeley: Department of Anthropology, University of Northern Colorado.

Brunswig, Robert H., Jr., Bruce Bradley, and Susan M. Chandler
1995 *Archaeological Pottery of Colorado: Ceramic Clues to the Prehistoric and Protohistoric Lives of the State's Native Peoples.* Occasional Papers No. 2. Denver: Colorado Council of Professional Archaeologists.

Buckles, William G.
1968 Archaeology in Colorado: Historic Tribes. *Southwestern Lore* 34(3):53–67.

Bunbury, Joan
2004 The White River Ash, Microorganisms and Yukon Lakes. *Kluane Lake Research Station Newsletter,* Fall, p. 6.

Burgh, Robert F., and Charles R. Scoggin
1948 *The Archaeology of Castle Park, Dinosaur National Monument.* University of Colorado Studies, Anthropology Series No. 2. Boulder: University of Colorado.

Cassells, E. Steve
1997 *The Archaeology of Colorado.* Boulder, Colorado: Johnson Books.

Clark, Bonnie
1999 The Protohistoric Period. In *Colorado Prehistory: A Context for the Platte River Basin,* edited by Kevin P. Gilmore, Marcia Tate, Mark L. Chenault, Bonnie Clark, Terri McBride, and Margaret Wood, pp. 309–335. Denver: Colorado Council of Professional Archaeologists, Colorado Historical Society.

Cole, Donald C.
1988 *The Chiricahua Apache: From War to Reservation, 1846–1876.* Albuquerque: University of New Mexico Press.

Condie, Carol J.
1980 *Vocabulary of the Apache or Indé+ Language of Arizona & New Mexico, Collected by John Gregory Bourke in the 1870s and 1880s.* Occasional Publications in Anthropology No. 7 (Linguistic Series). Greeley: Museum of Anthropology, University of Northern Colorado.

Copp, Stanley Arthur
2006 Similkameen Archaeology (1993–2004). Unpublished Ph.D. dissertation, Department of Archaeology, Simon Fraser University, Burnaby, British Columbia.
2008 Okanagan–Similkameen Projectile Points: Origins, Associations, and the Athapaskan Question. In *Projectile Point Sequences in Northwestern North America,* edited by Roy L. Carlson and Martin P. R. Magne, pp. 251–272. Burnaby, British Columbia: Archaeology Press.

Cordell, Linda S.
1995 Tracing Migration Pathways from the Receiving End. *Journal of Anthropological Archaeology* 14(2):203–211.

Creel, D.
1991 Bison Hides in Late Prehistoric Exchange in the Southern Plains. *American Antiquity* 56(1):40–49.

Crisafulli, Charles M., and Charles P. Hawkins
1998 Ecosystem Recovery Following a Catastrophic Disturbance: Lessons Learned from Mount St. Helens. In *Status and Trends of the Nation's Biological Resources,* edited by M. F. Mac, P. A. Opler, C. E. Pucket Haecker, and P. D. Doran. Reston, Virginia: U.S. Department of the Interior. http://biology.usgs.gov/s%Bt/SNT/noframe/np105.htm (retrieved April 14, 2006).

Darroch, John I.
1974 Edge-Ground Cobbles: A Discussion. *Archaeology in Montana* 15(2):52–73.

Davis, Emma Lou
1965 Small Pressures and Cultural Drift as Explanations for Abandonment of the San Juan Area. *American Antiquity* 30(3):353–355.

Day, Kent C., and David S. Dibble
1963 *Archaeological Survey of the Flaming Gorge Reservoir Area, Wyoming–Utah.* Anthropological Paper No. 65. Salt Lake City: University of Utah Department of Anthropology.

Dean, Jeffrey S.
1988   A Model of Anasazi Behavioral Adaptation. In *The Anasazi in a Changing Environment*, edited by George G. Gumerman, pp. 25–44. New York: Cambridge University Press.

Dean, Jeffrey S., Robert C. Euler, George J. Gumerman, Fred Plog, Richard H. Hevly, and Thor N. V. Karlstrom
1985   Human Behavior, Demography, and Paleoenvironment on the Colorado Plateaus. *American Antiquity* 50(3):537–554.

Derry, D. E.
1975   Later Athapaskan Prehistory: A Migration Hypothesis. *Western Canadian Journal of Anthropology* 5:134–147.

Dittert, Alfred E., Jr.
1958   *Preliminary Archaeological Investigations in the Navajo Project Area of Northwestern New Mexico*. Navajo Project Studies No. 1. Santa Fe: Museum of New Mexico and School of American Research.

Dittert, Alfred E., Jr., James J. Hester, and Frank W. Eddy
1961   *An Archaeological Survey of the Navajo Reservoir District, Northwestern New Mexico*. Monographs of the School of American Research No. 23. Santa Fe: School of American Research and Museum of New Mexico.

Douglass, Andrew Ellicott
1929   The Secret of the Southwest Solved by Talkative Tree Rings. *National Geographic* 56(6):736–770.

Driver, Harold E.
1972   Reply to Opler on Apachean Subsistence, Residence, and Girls' Puberty Rites. *American Anthropologist* 74(5):1147–1151.

Duff, Andrew I., and Richard H. Wilshusen
2000   Prehistoric Population Dynamics in the Northern San Juan Region, AD 950–1300. *Kiva* 66(1):167–190.

Durand, Kathy Roler, Meradeth Snow, David Glenn Smith, and Stephen R. Durand
2010   Discrete Dental Trait Evidence of Migration Patterns in the Northern Southwest. In *Human Variation in the Americas: The Integration of Archaeology and Biological Anthropology*, edited by Benjamin M. Auerbach, pp. 113–134. Occasional Paper No. 38. Carbondale: Center for Archaeological Investigations, Southern Illinois University.

Dyck, Ian, and Richard G. Morlan
1995   *The Sjovold Site: A River Crossing Campsite in the Northern Plains*. Mercury Series, Archaeological Survey of Canada, Paper No. 151. Gatineau, Quebec: Canadian Museum of Civilization.

Farrer, Claire R.
1991   *Living Life's Circle: Mescalero Apache Cosmovision*. Albuquerque: University of New Mexico Press.

Fenner, J. N., and D. N. Walker
2008   Mortality Date Estimation Using Fetal Pronghorn Remains. *International Journal of Osteoarchaeology* 18(1):45–60.

Ferg, Alan
2004   *An Introduction to Chiricahua and Mescalero Apache Pottery*. Arizona Archaeologist No. 35. Phoenix: Arizona Archaeological Society.

Flayharty, R. A., and Elizabeth A. Morris
1974   T-W Diamond, a Stone Ring Site in Northern Colorado. *Plains Anthropologist* 19(65):161–172.

Forbes, Jack D.
1960 *Apache, Navaho, and Spaniard*. Norman: University of Oklahoma Press.

Franciscan Fathers
1910 *An Ethnologic Dictionary of the Navaho Language*. Saint Michaels, Arizona: St. Michaels Press.

Gilberg, R.
1984 Polar Eskimos. In *Arctic*, edited by David Damas, pp. 577–594. Handbook of North American Indians, Vol. 5, William C. Sturtevant, general editor. Washington, D.C.: Smithsonian Institution.

Gilmore, Kevin P.
2004 Way Down upon the South Platte River: Southern Avonlea Manifestations in Colorado and a Population-Based Scenario for Athapaskan Migration. In *Ancient and Historic Lifeways in North America's Rocky Mountains: Proceedings of the 2003 Rocky Mountain Anthropological Conference, Estes Park, Colorado*, edited by Robert H. Brunswig and William B. Butler, pp. 146–167. Greeley: Department of Anthropology, University of Northern Colorado.
2006 And Miles to Go Before I Sleep: A Model for Prehistoric Athapaskan Migration Along the Western High Plains Margin. Paper presented at 71st Annual Meeting of the Society for American Archaeology, San Juan, Puerto Rico.

Gilmore, Kevin P., and Sean Larmore
2005 *Archaeology of the Eureka Ridge Site (5TL3296), Teller County, Colorado*. Submitted by RMC Consultants to the USDA Forest Service, Pike National Forest, Pueblo. On file at the Office of Archaeology and Historic Preservation, Denver, and USDA Forest Service, Pueblo, Colorado. Lakewood, Colorado: RMC Consultants.

Gordon, Bryan C.
1979 *Of Men and Herds in Canadian Plains Prehistory*. Archaeological Survey of Canada, Mercury Series No. 84. Ottawa, Ontario: National Museum of Man.
1996 *People of Sunlight, People of Starlight: Barrenland Archaeology in the Northwest Territories of Canada*. Archaeological Survey of Canada, Mercury Series No. 154. Gatineau, Quebec: Canadian Museum of Civilization.

Griffin-Pierce, Trudy
1992 *Earth Is My Mother, Sky Is My Father: Space, Time, and Astronomy in Navajo Sandpainting*. Albuquerque: University of New Mexico Press.

Gumerman, George J.
1984 *A View from Black Mesa*. Tucson: University of Arizona Press.

Gunnerson, James H.
1956 Plains-Promontory Relationships. *American Antiquity* 22(1):69–72.
1960 *An Introduction to Plains Apache Archeology—The Dismal River Aspect*. Anthropological Papers No. 58, Bureau of American Ethnology Bulletin No. 173, pp. 131–260. Washington, D.C.: Smithsonian Institution.
1969 Apache Archaeology in Northeastern New Mexico. *American Antiquity* 34(1): 23–39.
1974 *The Jicarilla Apaches: A Study in Survival*. DeKalb: Northern Illinois University Press.
1979 Southern Athapaskan Archaeology. In *Southwest*, edited by Alfonso Ortiz, pp. 162–169. Handbook of North American Indians, Vol. 9, William C. Sturtevant, general editor. Washington, D.C.: Smithsonian Institution.

Gunnerson, James H., and Dolores A. Gunnerson
1971 Apachean Culture: A Study in Unity and Diversity. In *Apachean Culture History*

and Ethnology, edited by Keith H. Basso and Morris E. Opler, pp. 7–28. Tucson: University of Arizona Press.

Haas, Jonathan, and Winifred Creamer
1993 *Stress and Warfare among the Kayenta Anasazi of the Thirteenth Century AD.* Fieldiana Anthropology (new series) No. 21, Publication No. 1450. Chicago: Field Museum of Natural History.
1999 Comments. *Current Anthropology* 40(2):160.

Haas, Mary R.
1968 Notes on a Chipewyan Dialect. *International Journal of American Linguistics* 34(3):165–175.

Habicht-Mauche, Judith A.
1987 Southwestern-Style Culinary Ceramics on the Southern Plains: A Case Study of Technological Innovation and Cross-Cultural Interaction. *Plains Anthropologist* 32(116):175–191.
1988 An Analysis of Southwestern Style Ceramics from the Southern Plains in the Context of Plains-Pueblo Interaction. Unpublished Ph.D. dissertation, Department of Anthropology, Harvard University, Cambridge.
1992 Coronado's Querechos and Teyas in the Archaeological Record of the Texas Panhandle. *Plains Anthropologist* 37(140):247–259.

Hancock, Patricia M.
1997 Dendrochronological Dates from the Dinétah. Paper presented at the 1997 Pecos Conference, Chaco Canyon National Park, New Mexico.

Hanson, L. W.
1965 Size Distribution of the White River Ash, Yukon Territory. Unpublished Master's thesis, Department of Geology, University of Alberta, Edmonton.

Haskell, J. Loring
1987 *Southern Athapaskan Migration, AD 200–1750.* Tsaile, Arizona: Navajo Community College Press.

Hester, James J.
1962 *Early Navajo Migrations and Acculturation in the Southwest.* Museum of New Mexico Papers in Anthropology No. 6. Santa Fe: Museum of New Mexico Press.
1980 *Digging into South Texas Prehistory: A Guide for Amateur Archeologists.* San Antonio, Texas: Corona Publishing.
1995 The Prehistory of South Texas. *Bulletin of the Texas Archeological Society* 66:427–459.

Highley, C. L.
1986 *Archaeological Investigations at 41LK201: Choke Canyon Reservoir, Southern Texas.* Choke Canyon Series Vol. 11. San Antonio: Center for Archaeological Research, University of Texas.

Hill, W. W.
1938 *The Agricultural and Hunting Methods of the Navajo Indians.* Yale University Publications in Anthropology No. 18. New Haven: Yale University Press.

Hogan, Patrick F.
2006 *Development of Southeastern New Mexico Regional Research Design and Cultural Resource Management Strategy.* With contributions by Richard Chapman, Don Clifton, Glenna Dean, Peggy Gerow, Stephen Hall, Cynthia Herhahn, John Speth, and Regge Wiseman. Prepared for Stephen Fosberg, New Mexico State Office, USDI Bureau of Land Management Santa Fe, Contract NAC000002, UNM Report No. 185-849.

Hohn, O. E.
1973   Mammal and Bird Names in Indian Languages of the Lake Athabasca area. *Arctic* 26:163–171.

Hoijer, Harry
1942   Phonetic and Phonemic Change in the Athapaskan Languages. *Language* 18(3): 218–220.
1956   The Chronology of the Athapaskan Languages. *International Journal of American Linguistics* 22(4):219–232.

Hughes, Jack T.
1978   Archaeology of Palo Duro Canyon. In *The Story of Palo Duro Canyon*, edited by D. Guy, pp. 35–58. Canyon, Texas: Panhandle-Plains Historical Society.
1989   Terminal Archaic Bison Kills in the Texas Panhandle. In *The Light of Past Experience: Essays in Honor of Jack T. Hughes*, edited by Beryl C. Roper, pp. 183–204. Publication No. 5. Amarillo, Texas: Panhandle Archaeological Society.
1991   Prehistoric Cultural Development on the Texas High Plains. *Bulletin of the Texas Archeological Society* 60:1–55.

Huscher, Betty H., and Harold A. Huscher
1942   Athapascan Migration via the Intermountain Region. *American Antiquity* 8(1): 80–88.

Hymes, Dell H.
1957   A Note on Athapaskan Glottochronology. *International Journal of American Linguistics* 22(4):291–297.

Ives, John W.
1990   *A Theory of Athapascan Prehistory*. Boulder, Colorado: Westview Press; Calgary, Alberta: University of Calgary Press.
2003   Alberta, Athapaskans and Apachean Origins. In *Archaeology in Alberta: A View from the New Millennium*, edited by J. W. Brink and J. F. Dormaar, pp. 256–281. Medicine Hat: Archaeological Society of Alberta.
2005   Was Julian Steward Right about the Promontory Culture? Abstract. Paper presented at the 63rd Annual Plains Anthropological Conference, Edmonton, Alberta. Available at http://canadianarchaeology.com/caa/node/2922.

Jelks, E. B.
1962   *The Kyle Site: A Stratified Central Texas Aspect Site in Hill Country, Texas*. Archeology Series No. 5. Austin: Department of Anthropology, University of Texas.

Jess, Edward J., and Dianne M. C. Berrigan
1982   The Bairoil Tipi Ring Site (48SW2369), Sweetwater County, Southwestern Wyoming. *Wyoming Contributions to Anthropology* 3:39–60. Laramie: University of Wyoming.

Jett, Stephen C.
1964   Pueblo Indian Migrations: An Evaluation of the Possible Physical and Cultural Determinants. *American Antiquity* 29(3):281–300.

Jett, Stephen C., and Virginia E. Spencer
1981   *Navajo Architecture: Forms, History, Distributions*. Tucson: University of Arizona Press.

Johnson, I.
1994   *The Life and Times of Toyah Culture Folk as Seen from the Buckhollow Encampment: Site 41KM16, Kimble County, Texas*. Office of the State Archeologist, Report No. 38. Austin: Texas Historical Commission and Texas Department of Transportation.

Jones, Peter N.

2004 *American Indian mtDNA and Y Chromosome Genetic Data: A Comprehensive Report of Their Use in Migration and Other Anthropological Studies.* http://www.iiirm.org/publications/Articles%20Reports%20Papers/Genetics%20and%20Biotechnology/Jones%20DNA.pdf.

Jones, Terry L., Gary M. Brown, L. Mark Raab, Janet L. McVickar, W. Geoffrey Spaulding, Douglas J. Kennett, Andrew York, Phillip L. Walker, Mark E. Basgall, Robert L. Bettinger, Katalin T. Biró, Jonathan Haas, Winifred Creamer, José Luis Lanata, Ian Lilley, and Thomas A. Wake

1999 Environmental Imperatives Reconsidered: Demographic Crises in Western North America during the Medieval Climatic Anomaly [and Comments and Reply]. *Current Anthropology* 40(2):137–170.

Kaestle F. A., and D. G. Smith

2001 Ancient Mitochondrial DNA Evidence for Prehistoric Population Movement: The Numic Expansion. *American Journal of Physical Anthropology* 115(1):1–12.

Katz, Susana R., and Paul Katz

1976 *Archeological Investigations in Lower Tule Canyon, Briscoe County, Texas.* Office of the State Archeologist, Survey Report No. 16. Austin: Texas Archeological Commission.

Kehoe, Thomas F.

1973 *The Gull Lake Site: A Prehistoric Bison Drive Site in Southwestern Saskatchewan.* Publications in Anthropology and History No. 1. Milwaukee: Milwaukee Public Museum.

1974 The Large Corner-Notched Point System of the Northern Plains and Adjacent Woodlands. In *Aspects of Upper Great Lakes Anthropology: Papers in Honor of Lloyd A. Wilford*, edited by E. Johnson, pp. 103–114. St. Paul: Minnesota Historical Society.

Kelley, J. C.

1986 *Jumano and Patarabueye: Relations at La Junta de los Rios.* Anthropological Paper No. 77. Ann Arbor: Museum of Anthropology, University of Michigan.

Kindig, Jean Matthews

2000 Two Ceramic Sites in the Devil's Thumb Valley. In *This Land of Shining Mountains: Archeological Studies in Colorado's Indian Peaks Wilderness Area*, edited by E. Steve Cassells, pp. 95–123. Research Report No. 8. Ward, Colorado: Center for Mountain Archeology.

King, R. H., and G. R. Brewster

1978 The Impact of Environmental Stress on Subalpine Pedogenesis, Banff National Park, Alberta. *Arctic and Alpine Research* 10(2):295–312.

Kingsbury, Lawrence A., and Lorna H. Gabel

1983 Eastern Apache Campsites in Southeastern Colorado: An Hypothesis. In *From Microcosm to Macrocosm: Advances in Tipi Ring Investigation and Interpretation*, edited by Leslie B. David, pp. 319–326. Memoir No. 19. *Plains Anthropologist* 28 (2, Pt. 2).

Kuhn, Tyler, Keri A. McFarlane, Pamela Groves, Arne Ø. Mooers, and Beth Shapiro

2010 Modern and Ancient DNA Reveal Recent Partial Replacement of Caribou in the Southwest Yukon. *Molecular Ecology* 19:1312–1323.

Larsen, D. O., and J. Michaelsen

1990 Impacts of Climatic Variability and Population Growth on Virgin Branch Anasazi Cultural Developments. *American Antiquity* 55(2):227–249.

Larsen, D. O., H. Neff, D. A. Graybill, J. Michaelsen, and E. Ambos
1996 Risk, Climatic Variability, and the Study of Southwestern Prehistory: An Evolutionary Perspective. *American Antiquity* 61(2):217–241.

LeBlanc, Steven A.
1999 Southwestern Warfare: Reality and Consequences. *Archaeology Southwest Newsletter* 13(2):1–11. Tucson: Center for Desert Archaeology.

Lewis, O.
1942 *The Effects of White Contact upon Blackfoot Culture, with Special Reference to the Role of the Fur Trade*. Monograph No. 6. Washington, D.C.: American Ethnological Society.
1944 Edged (Tanning) Stones from South Central Montana and North Central Wyoming: Their Possible Use and Distribution. *American Antiquity* 9(3):336–338.

Li, Fang-Kuei
1946 Card files. University of Calgary Library, Calgary, Alberta. http://www.ucalgary/archives/Cookcardlista.htm.

Lindsay, A. J., J. R. Ambler, M. A. Stein, and P. H. Hobler
1968 *Survey and Excavations North and East of Navajo Mountain, Utah, 1959–1962*. Bulletin No. 45, Glen Canyon Series No. 8. Flagstaff: Museum of Northern Arizona.

Lipe, William D.
1995 The Depopulation of the Northern San Juan: Conditions in the Turbulent 1200s. *Journal of Anthropological Science* 14(2):143–169.

Loosle, Byron, and Michelle Knoll
2003 Fremont Numic Transitions. Paper presented at the Rocky Mountain Anthropological Conference, Estes Park, Colorado.

Lowie, Robert H.
1963 *Indians of the Plains*. American Museum Science Books. Garden City, New York: Natural History Press.

Luckert, Karl W.
1975 *The Navajo Hunter Tradition*. Tucson: University of Arizona Press.

Maestas, Enrique Gilbert-Michael
2003 Culture and History of Native American Peoples of South Texas. Ph.D. dissertation, University of Texas, Austin.

Malainey, Mary E., and Barbara L. Sherriff
1996 Adjusting Our Perceptions: Historical and Archaeological Evidence of Winter on the Plains of Western Canada. *Plains Anthropologist* 41(158):333–357.

Malhi, Ripan Singh, Angelica Gonzalez-Oliver, Kari Britt Schroeder, Brian M. Kemp, Jonathan A. Greenberg, Solomon Z. Dobrowski, David Glenn Smith, Andres Resendez, Tatiana Karafet, Michael Hammer, Stephen Zegura, and Tatiana Brovko
2008 Distribution of Y Chromosomes among Native North Americans: A Study of Athapaskan Population History. *American Journal of Physical Anthropology* 137(4):412–424.

Mallouf, R. J.
1987 *Las Haciendas: A Cairn-Burial Assemblage from Northeastern Chihuahua, Mexico*. Office of the State Archaeologist, Report No. 13. Austin: Texas Historical Commission.

Matson, R. G.
1991 *The Origins of Southwestern Agriculture*. Tucson: University of Arizona Press.
2007 Appendix 1: Artifacts and Fauna. In *Athapaskan Migrations: The Archaeology of*

Eagle Lake, British Columbia. http://www.anth.ubc.ca/fileadmin/user_upload/anso/LOA_PDFs/Matson_2007/AppendixIc.pdf.

Matson, R. G., and Martin P. R. Magne
2007 *Athapaskan Migrations: The Archaeology of Eagle Lake, British Columbia*. Tucson: University of Arizona Press.

McDowall, Robert M.
1996 Volcanism and Freshwater Fish Biogeography in the Northeastern North Island of New Zealand. *Journal of Biogeography* 23(2):139–148.

Meyer, David, and Henry T. Epp
1990 North-South Interaction in the Late Prehistory of Central Saskatchewan. *Plains Anthropologist* 35(132):321–342.

Meyer, David, and Scott Hamilton
1994 Neighbors to the North: Peoples of the Boreal Forest. In *Plains Indians, AD 500–1500: The Archaeological Past of Historic Groups*, edited by K. H. Schlesier, pp. 96–127. Norman: University of Oklahoma Press.

Meyer, David, Olga Klimko, and James Finnigan
1988 Northernmost Avonlea in Saskatchewan. In *Avonlea Yesterday and Today: Archaeology and Prehistory*, edited by Leslie B. Davis, pp. 33–42. Saskatoon: Saskatchewan Archaeological Society.

Millar, James F. V.
1983 The Chartier Sites: Two Stratified Campsites on Kisis Channel near Buffalo Narrows, Saskatchewan. Northern Heritage Ltd., Consulting Archaeologists, Ms. 2599. Gatineau, Quebec: Canadian Museum of Civilization.

Minni, Sheila Joan
1976 *The Prehistoric Occupations of Black Lake, Northern Saskatchewan*. Archaeological Survey of Canada, Mercury Series No. 53. Ottawa, Ontario: National Museum of Man.

Moodie, D. W., and A. J. W. Catchpole
1992 Northern Athapaskan Oral Traditions and the White River Volcano. *Ethnohistory* 39(2):148–171.

Morgan, Grace R.
1979 *An Ecological Study of the Northern Plains as Seen through the Garratt Site*. Occasional Paper No. 1. Regina, Saskatchewan: Department of Anthropology, University of Regina.

Morice, A. G.
1907 The Unity of Speech among the Northern and Southern Déné. *American Anthropologist* 9(4):720–737.

Morlan, Richard
1988 Avonlea and Radiocarbon Dating. In *Avonlea Yesterday and Today: Archaeology and Prehistory*, edited by Leslie B. Davis, pp. 291–309. Saskatoon: Saskatchewan Archaeological Society.

Neily, Robert B.
1983 The Prehistoric Community on the Colorado Plateau: An Approach to the Study of Change and Survival in the Northern San Juan Area of the American Southwest. Unpublished Ph.D. dissertation, Department of Anthropology, Southern Illinois University, Carbondale.

Noble, W. C.
1971 Archaeological Surveys and Sequences in Central District of Mackenzie, N.W.T. *Arctic Anthropology* 8(1):102–135.

Oakes, Yvonne R., and Dorothy A. Zamora
1999   *Archaeology of the Mogollon Highlands: Settlement Systems and Adaptations.* Archaeology Notes No. 232. Santa Fe: Office of Archaeological Studies, Museum of New Mexico.

Opler, Morris E.
1938   *Myths and Tales of the Jicarilla Apache Culture.* Memoirs No. 31. New York: American Folklore Society.
1941   *An Apache Lifeway: The Economic, Social, and Religious Institutions of the Chiricahua Indians.* Chicago: University of Chicago Press.
1983   The Apachean Culture Pattern and Its Origins. In *Southwest*, edited by Alfonso Ortiz, pp. 368–392. Handbook of North American Indians, Vol. 10, William C. Sturtevant, general editor. Washington, D.C.: Smithsonian Institution.

Perry, Richard J.
1991   *Western Apache Heritage: People of the Mountain Corridor.* Austin: University of Texas Press.

Plog, Fred
1982   The Original. In http://www.traumwerk.stanford.edu:3455/contemporary issues/admin/download.html?attachid=155424 (no longer available online).

Plog, F., G. J. Gumerman, R. C. Euler, J. S. Dean, R. H. Hevley, and T. N. V. Karlstrom
1988   Anasazi Adaptive Strategies: The Model, Predictions, and Results. In *The Anasazi in a Changing Environment*, edited by George J. Gumerman, pp. 230–276. New York: Cambridge University Press.

Plog, S., and J. L. Hantman
1990   Chronology Construction and the Study of Prehistoric Culture Change. *Journal of Field Archaeology* 17(4):439–456.

Prewitt, E. R.
1981   Cultural Chronology in Central Texas. *Bulletin of the Texas Archaeological Society* 52:65–89.
1985   From Circleville to Toyah: Comments on Central Texas chronology. *Bulletin of the Texas Archaeological Society* 54:201–238.

Pringle, Patrick, and Kevin Scott
2001   *Postglacial Influence of Volcanism on the Landscape and Environmental History of the Puget Lowland, Washington: A Review of Geologic Literature and Recent Discoveries, with Emphasis on the Landscape Disturbances Associated with Lahars, Lahar Runouts, and Associated Flooding.* Proceedings of Puget Sound Research 2001, Fifth Puget Sound Research Conference. http://www.psat.wa.gov/Publications/01_proceedings/sessions/oral/4d_pring.pdf (retrieved April 14, 2006).

Randall, Vincent, and Jeanette Cassa
2002   *Nigosdzan Bił Dagodotł'izhí: Western Apache Trees and Shrubs.* San Carlos, Arizona: San Carlos Apache Tribe, White Mountain Apache Tribe, Yavapai-Apache Nation, and Tonto Apache Tribe.

Raynaud, E. B.
1942   *Indian Stone Enclosures of Colorado and New Mexico.* Archaeological Series, Second Paper. Denver: Department of Anthropology, University of Denver.

Reed, Alan D.
1994   The Numic Occupation of Western Colorado and Eastern Utah during the Prehistoric and Protohistoric Periods. In *Across the West: Human Population Movement and the Expansion of the Numa*, edited by David B. Madsen and David Rhode, pp. 188–199. Salt Lake City: University of Utah Press.

Reed, Alan D., and Rachel Gebauer
2004 *A Research Design and Context for Prehistoric Cultural Resources in the Uncompahgre Plateau Archaeological Project's Study Area, Western Colorado.* http://www.blm.gov/pgdata/etc/medialib/blm/co/field_offices/uncompahgre_field/documents.Par.94071.File.dat/Uncompahgre%20Archeological%20Project%20Study%20Area.pdf. Montrose, Colorado: Alpine Archaeological Consultants.

Reed, Paul F., and Kathy N. Hensler
1999 *Anasazi Community Development in Cove-Redrock Valley: Final Report on the Cove–Red Valley Archaeological Project along the N33 Road in Apache County, Arizona.* Navajo Nation Papers in Anthropology No. 33. Window Rock, Arizona: Navajo Nation Archaeology Department.

Renfrew, Colin
2000 At the Edge of Knowability: Towards a Prehistory of Languages. *Cambridge Archaeology Journal* 10(1):7–34.

Ricklis, Robert A.
1992 The Spread of a Late Prehistoric Bison Hunting Complex: Evidence from the South-Central Coastal Prairie of Texas. *Plains Anthropologist* 37(140):261–273.

Robinson, S. D.
2001 Extending the Late Holocene White River Ash Distribution, Northwestern Canada. *Arctic* 54(2):157–161.

Robinson, S. D., and T. R. Moore
2000 The Influence of Permafrost and Fire upon Carbon Accumulation in High Boreal Peatlands, Northwest Territories, Canada. *Arctic, Antarctic, and Alpine Research* 32(2):155–166.

Sapir, Edward
1931 The Concept of Phonetic Law as Tested in Primitive Languages by Leonard Bloomfield. In *Methods in Social Science: A Case Book*, edited by S. A. Rice, pp. 297–306. Chicago: University of Chicago Press.
1936 Linguistic Evidence Suggestive of the Northern Origin of the Navaho. *American Anthropologist* 38(2):224–235.

Sawyer, Hall
2005 Pronghorn Migration in Western Wyoming. *Wildlife Society Bulletin* 33(4):1266–1273.

Schaafsma, Curtis F.
1996 Ethnic Identity and Protohistoric Archaeological Sites in Northwestern New Mexico: Implications for Reconstructions of Navajo and Ute History. In *The Archaeology of Navajo Origins*, edited by Ronald H. Towner, pp. 19–46. Salt Lake City: University of Utah Press.

Schroeder, Albert H.
1994 Development in the Southwest and Relations with the Plains. In *Plains Indians, AD 500–1500: The Archaeological Past of Historic Groups*, edited by K. Schlesier, pp. 290–307. Norman: University of Oklahoma Press.

Scollon, R.
1979 236 Years of Variability in Chipewyan Consonants. *International Journal of American Linguistics* 45(4):332–342.

Seymour, Deni J.
2002 *Conquest and Concealment: After the El Paso Phase on Fort Bliss; An Archaeological Study of the Manso, Suma, and Early Apache.* With contributions by Mark E. Har-

lan and David V. Hill. Lone Mountain Report 525-528. Conservation Division, Directorate of the Environment, United States Army Air Defense, Artillery Center, Fort Bliss, Texas. Qualified researchers may obtain this document by contacting martha.yduarte@us.army.mil.

2003 *Protohistoric and Early Historic Temporal Resolution.* Lone Mountain Report 560-003. Conservation Division, Directorate of the Environment, United States Army Air Defense, Artillery Center, Fort Bliss, Texas. Qualified researchers may obtain this document by contacting martha.yduarte@us.army.mil.

2004a Before the Spanish Chronicles: Early Apache in the Southern Southwest. In *Ancient and Historic Lifeways in North America's Rocky Mountains: Proceedings of the 2003 Rocky Mountain Anthropological Conference, Estes Park, Colorado*, edited by Robert H. Brunswig and William B. Butler, pp. 120–142. Greeley: Department of Anthropology, University of Northern Colorado.

2004b A Ranchería in the Gran Apachería: Evidence of Intercultural Interaction at the Cerro Rojo Site. *Plains Anthropologist* 49(190):153–192.

2008a Despoblado or Athapaskan Heartland: A Methodological Perspective on Ancestral Apache Landscape Use in the Safford Area. In *Crossroads of the Southwest: Culture, Ethnicity, and Migration in Arizona's Safford Basin*, edited by David E. Purcell, pp. 121–162. New York: Cambridge Scholars Press.

2008b Apache Plain and Other Plainwares on Apache Sites in the Southern Southwest. In *Serendipity: Papers in Honor of Frances Joan Mathien*, edited by R. N. Wiseman, T. C. O'Laughlin, C. T. Snow, and C. Travis, pp. 163–186. Papers No. 34. Albuquerque: Archaeological Society of New Mexico.

2009 Comments on Genetic Data Relating to Athapaskan Migrations: Implications of the Malhi et al. Study for the Apache and Navajo. *American Journal of Physical Anthropology* 139(3):281–283.

Sharp, Henry S.
1988 *The Transformation of Bigfoot: Maleness, Power, and Belief among the Chipewyan.* Washington, D.C.: Smithsonian Institution.

Sharrock, Floyd W.
1966 *Prehistoric Occupation Patterns in Southwest Wyoming and Cultural Relationships with the Great Basin and Plains Culture Area.* Anthropological Papers No. 77. Salt Lake City: University of Utah.

Smith, C. S., and S. D. Creasman
1988 *The Taliaferro Site: 5000 years of Prehistory in Southwest Wyoming.* Cultural Resource Series No. 8. Cheyenne, Wyoming: Bureau of Land Management.

Smith, D. M.
1973 *Inkonze: Magico-Religious Beliefs of Contact-Traditional Chipewyan Trading at Fort Resolution, Northwest Territories, Canada.* Mercury Series, Ethnology Division Paper No. 6. Ottawa, Ontario: National Museum of Man.

Spicer, Edward H.
1961 Types of Contact and Processes of Change. In *Perspectives in American Indian Culture Change*, edited by E. H. Spicer, pp. 517–544. Chicago: University of Chicago Press.

Spielmann, Katherine
1982 Inter-societal Food Acquisition among Egalitarian Societies: An Ecological Study of Plains/Pueblo Interaction in the American Southwest, Volume 1. Unpublished Ph.D. dissertation, Department of Anthropology, University of Michigan, Ann Arbor.

1983 Late Prehistoric Exchange between the Southwest and Southern Plains. *Plains Anthropologist* 28(102):257–272.

Steward, Julian H.
1937 *Ancient Caves of the Great Salt Lake Region*. Bureau of American Ethnology Bulletin No. 116. Washington, D.C.: Smithsonian Institution.

Thomas, Alfred Barnaby
1935 *After Coronado: Spanish Exploration Northeast of New Mexico, 1696–1727*. Norman: University of Oklahoma Press.

Thomas, C. D.
2003 *Ta'Tla Mun: An Archaeological Examination of Technology, Subsistence Economy and Trade at Tatlmain Lake, Central Yukon*. Occasional Papers in Archaeology No. 13. Yukon: Tourism and Culture.

Thompson, David
1916 *David Thompson's Narrative of His Exploration in Western America, 1784–1812*. Edited by J. B. Tyrrell. Publications Vol. 12. Toronto: Champlain Society.

Torroni, A., T. G. Schurr, C. C. Yang, E. J. Szathmary, R. C. Williams, M. S. Schanfield, G. A. Troup, W. C. Knowler, D. N. Lawrence, and K. M. Weiss
1992 Native American Mitochondrial DNA Analysis Indicates that the Amerind and the Nadene Populations Were Founded by Two Independent Migrations. *Genetics* 130:153–162.

Turner, William W.
1852 The Apaches. *Literary World* 20(272):281–282.

Upham, Steadman
1984 Adaptive Diversity and Southwestern Abandonment. *Journal of Anthropological Research* 40(2):235–256.

Van West, Carla R.
1994 *Modelling Prehistoric Climatic Variability and Agricultural Production in Southwestern Colorado: A G.I.S. Approach*. Report of Investigations No. 67. Pullman: Department of Anthropology, Washington State University.

Van West, Carla R., and William D. Lipe
1992 Modelling Prehistoric Climate and Agriculture in Southwestern Colorado. In *The Sand Canyon Archaeological Project: A Progress Report*, edited by W. D. Lipe, pp. 105–119. Occasional Paper No. 3. Cortez, Colorado: Crow Canyon Archaeological Center.

Vickers, J. Roderick
1994 Cultures of the Northwestern Plains: From the Boreal Forest Edge to Milk River. In *Plains Indians, AD 500–1500: The Archaeological Past of Historic Groups*, edited by Karl H. Schlesier, pp. 3–33. Norman: University of Oklahoma Press.

Walde, Dale
2006 Sedentism and Pre-contact Tribal Organization on the Northern Plains: Colonial Imposition or Indigenous Development? *World Archaeology* 38(2):291–310.

Walker, Danny L., and Lawrence C. Todd (editors)
1984 *Archaeological Salvage at 48FRI398: The Castle Gardens Access Road Site, Fremont County, Wyoming*. Occasional Papers on Wyoming Archaeology No. 2. Laramie.

Warburton, Miranda, and Richard M. Begay
2005 An Exploration of Navajo-Anasazi Relationships. *Ethnohistory* 52(3):533–561.

Wedel, Waldo R.
1940 Culture Sequences in the Central Great Plains. In *Essays in Historical Anthropol-*

ogy of North America, edited by Julian Steward, pp. 291–352. Smithsonian Miscellaneous Collections Vol. 100. Washington, D.C.: Smithsonian Institution.
1953 Some Aspects of Human Ecology in the Central Plains. *American Anthropologist* 55(4):499–514.
1961 *Prehistoric Men on the Great Plains*. Norman: University of Oklahoma Press.
1986 *Central Plains Prehistory*. Lincoln: University of Nebraska Press.

West, K. D., and J. D. Donaldson
2000 Evidence for Winter Eruption of the White River Ash (Eastern Lobe), Yukon Territory, Canada. Paper presented at GeoCanada 2000: The Millennium Geoscience Summit, Calgary, Alberta.
2002 Resedimentation of the Late Holocene White River Tephra, Yukon Territory and Alaska. In *Yukon Exploration and Geology 2002*, edited by D. S. Emond, L. H. Weston, and L. L. Lewis, pp. 239–247. Ottawa, Ontario: Exploration and Geological Services Division, Yukon Region, Indian and Northern Affairs, Canada.

Wettlaufer, Boyd N.
1955 *The Mortlach Site in the Besant Valley of Central Saskatchewan*. Anthropological Series No. 1. Regina: Saskatchewan Museum of Natural History.

Wilcox, David R.
1981 The Entry of the Athabaskans into the American Southwest: The Problem Today. In *The Protohistoric Period in the American Southwest, A.D. 1450–1700*, edited by David R. Wilcox and W. Bruce Masse. Anthropological Research Papers No. 24. Tempe: Arizona State University.

Winter, Joseph
1988 *Stone Circles, Ancient Forts and Other Antiquities of the Dry Cimarron Valley: A Study of the Cimarron Seco Indians*. Santa Fe, New Mexico: Historic Preservation Program.

Workman, W.
1974 The Cultural Significance of a Volcanic Ash Which Fell in the Upper Yukon about 1400 Years Ago. In *International Conference on the Prehistory and Palaeoecology of Western North American Arctic and Subarctic*, edited by S. Raymond and P. Schledermann, pp. 239–261. Calgary, Alberta: Archaeological Association, University of Calgary.
1979 The Significance of Volcanism in the Prehistory of Subarctic Northwest North America. In *Volcanic Activity and Human Ecology*, edited by P. D. Sheets and D. K. Grayson, pp. 339–371. New York: Academic Press.

Wright, Gary A.
1978 The Shoshonean Migration Problem. *Plains Anthropologist* 23(80):113–137.

Young, Robert W., and William Morgan
1980 *The Navajo Language: A Grammar and Colloquial Dictionary*. Albuquerque: University of New Mexico Press.

CHAPTER 16

Modeling Athapaskan Migrations

MARTIN P. R. MAGNE

Through their work in British Columbia (Figure 16.1), Matson and Magne (2007) have recently proposed a model for the timing of the Athapaskan migrations and a method for investigating the archaeological evidence for those movements. What they have not explored very completely are theoretical models and implications of how and why the migrations occurred as process. Using the results of that work in British Columbia and recent work by Seymour (e.g., 2008, 2009) in Arizona and New Mexico, in this chapter I borrow from and modify elements of recent thinking about colonization, applying theoretical principles about migratory processes to the particulars of the Athapaskan case. Given the geographic scale under discussion (1,000–2,000 km), concepts relating to selection of place through time (Seymour 2009) are also specifically relevant to interpreting archaeological signatures of particular groups and their lifeways. This merging of method and theory yields a clearer understanding of how we need to construct models and methods for future investigations into the routes of the migrations and signs of their occurrence.

The Athapaskan migrations were a remarkable series of events and processes (Figure 16.2). From Subarctic origins, Athapaskans appear to have populated both the southern northwest coast (northern California) and the U.S. Southwest within about 1,000 to 700 years. On the archaeological time scale, this is very quick, but on a human life scale, it represents about 30 generations. Thus, over this time period, people modified their entire way of life, from northern hunter-gatherers to semi-sedentary coastal fishers and semi-arid horticulturalists, with each of those more extreme sedentary groups being neighbored by relatives still maintaining highly mobile adaptations. Athapaskans moved through some areas that were populated, some areas that were not (at least not densely), and other areas that were likely recently abandoned.

So how did several groups of people make this happen? How can a viable population move into an area, establish relationships with existing groups, scout further routes, acquire knowledge and skills, and plan and execute the next step in relatively short periods of time? What was pushing them or pulling them? Did those motivations remain constant, or did they shift over time or in response

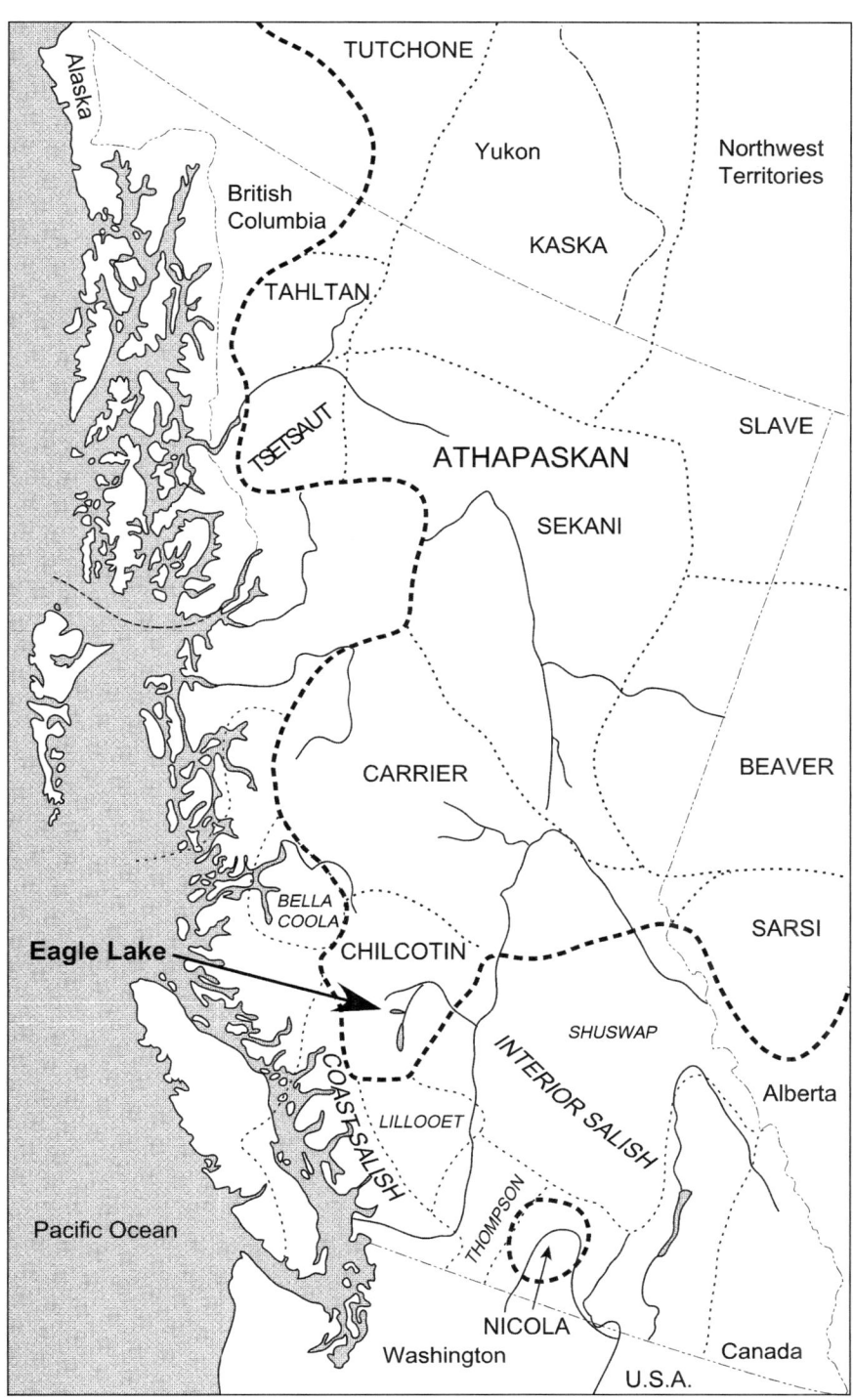

FIGURE 16.1. Location of Eagle Lake and Athapaskan groups in British Columbia, western Alberta, and southern Yukon and Alaska. Base map by Susan Matson.

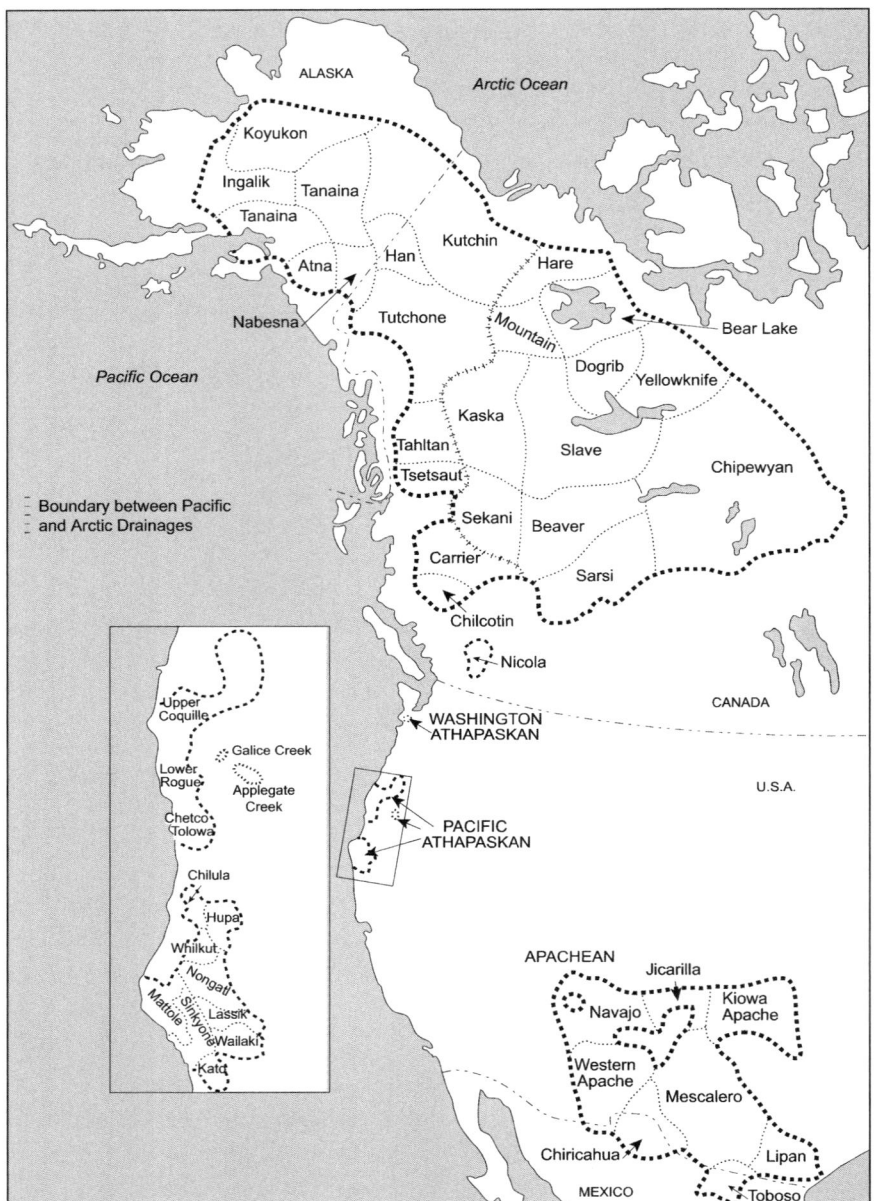

FIGURE 16.2. Distribution of Athapaskan-speakers in North America. From Matson and Magne (2007). Image by Susan Matson.

to new conditions? Did their strategies change over time? Did they always succeed? Surely their advances were not unknown, so what motivations did existing groups have to either welcome or deter them?

Migration Theory: Rockman

Marcy Rockman's (2003) work, "Knowledge and Learning in the Archaeology of Colonization," is a stimulating overview of contemporary migration thinking that I believe can be used to further develop methodologies to examine the

Athapaskan case. Rockman (2003:8) proposes that "at present, the issue of knowledge in archaeological approaches to colonization occurs in two primary aspects. The first lies in the motivations that are considered for colonization and the second in the actual physical orientations of movement presented in colonization models." This chapter looks at these processes as they may apply to the Athapaskan migration.

Motivation

With respect to motivation, Rockman adheres to Anthony's (1990) concept of "push" and "pull" models, which I have referred to before (Magne 2001), paraphrasing Anthony to the effect that "migrants never go where they haven't been before," a concept I return to later.

In the scenario that Matson and Magne developed from the work of other researchers and from the results of their own work (Figure 16.3), the initial primary motivation, or "push" factor, for the Athapaskan migration was escape from the effects of the White River ash falls, of which there were two principal occurrences: the first at about AD 300, the second at about AD 800 (Clague et al. 1995). However, once the initial migrations had occurred, what would have continued to push people, or pull them, well beyond the ash falls? Vacant territory by itself could be attractive as a "pull" factor in those situations, or if the migrants faced hostile groups. Indeed, several southern Athapaskan groups' settlement patterns are notable for their occupations of semi-marginal areas or areas recently abandoned by others (Figure 16.4), as noted by Moratto (1984) for northern California groups. This implies sufficient environmental awareness and technological means to allow groups to seek areas that were becoming unsuitable for others. Climatic episodes, such as the Medieval Warm period, likely had significant influence on those kinds of choices, and Matson and Magne (2007) have outlined how occupation of certain areas of the U.S. Southwest by Athapaskans was made possible by such areas' abandonment by agriculturalists during these arid times. Still, one must ask how far ahead knowledge of distant environments would be known or perceived by a "staging" group. Plateau Athapaskans, in the Similkameen area of southern British Columbia, would probably have known of coastal salmon peoples on the Washington-Oregon coasts, but would they have known of Puebloan horticulture?

The continuing push and pull factors are simply not clear. Motivation may be the most difficult factor to explore archaeologically. At some geographic point, the initial push, if it was motivated by the devastating environmental effects of the ash falls in the Yukon, becomes adaptationally irrelevant. The ash falls may in fact have little to with the entire movement. But whatever the motivation, the question remains as to whether it remained constant or whether the reasons for moving changed over the course of the migration. Was it simply expansion for its own sake or to reach more favorable environmental areas, or perhaps to fulfill a prophecy or shared destiny?

FIGURE 16.3. Matson and Magne's (2007) Athapaskan migration scenario, 500 BC–AD 1800: (1) Hypothesized initial distribution, ca. 500 BC. (2) Initial SE/NW push effect of first, smaller White River ash eruption, ca. AD 300. (3) Greater S+SE push effect of later eruption, ca. AD 800. (4) Continuing movement south on Interior Plateau and to coastal United States, ca. AD 1000–1200. (5) Placement of Apachean, Pacific Athapaskans, and Canadian groups just before any ethnohistoric contact; continued Interior Plateau movement, ca. AD 1400. (6) Full ethnohistoric distribution, ca. AD 1600–1800; Fur Trade era Cree/Sarsi push on eastern slopes and western plains Kiowa Apache movement. Image by Susan Matson.

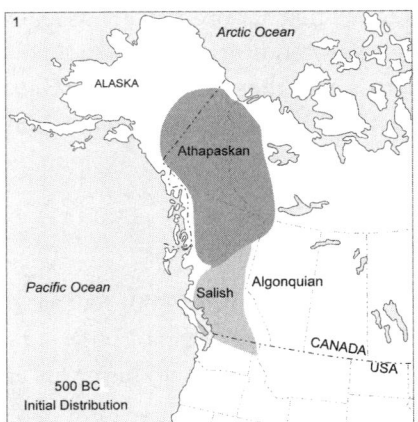
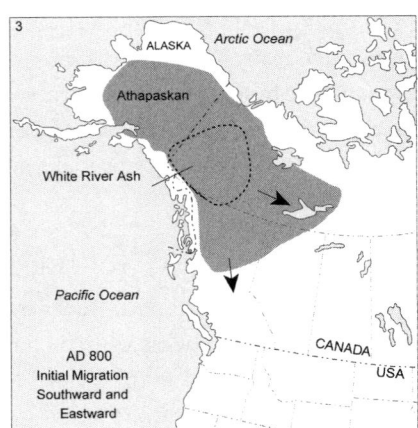
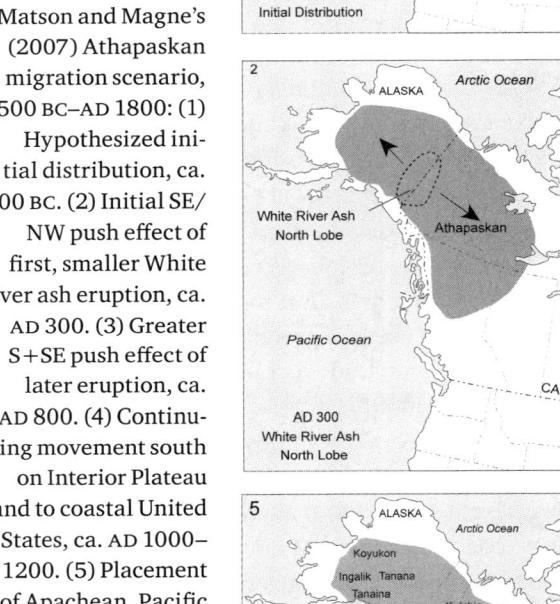
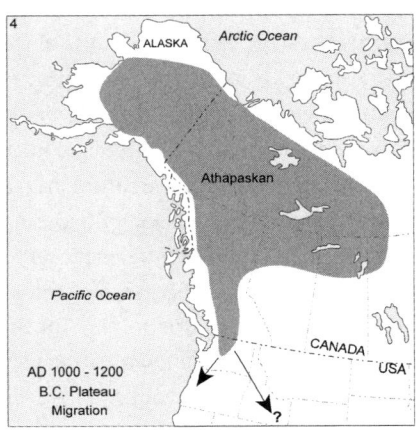
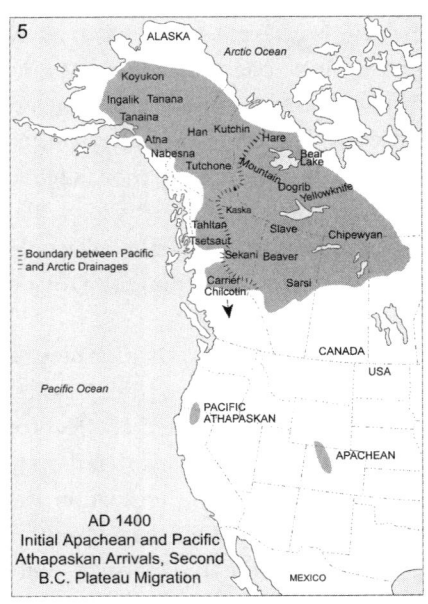
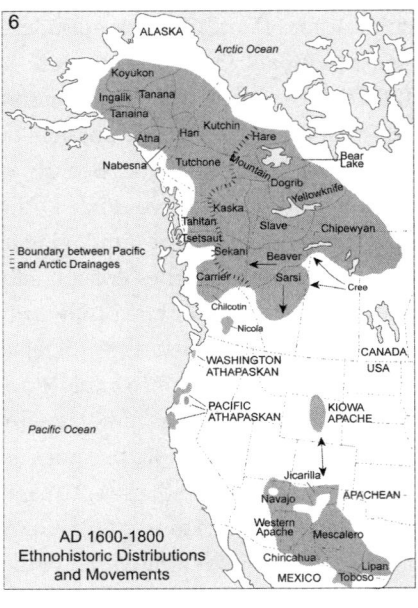

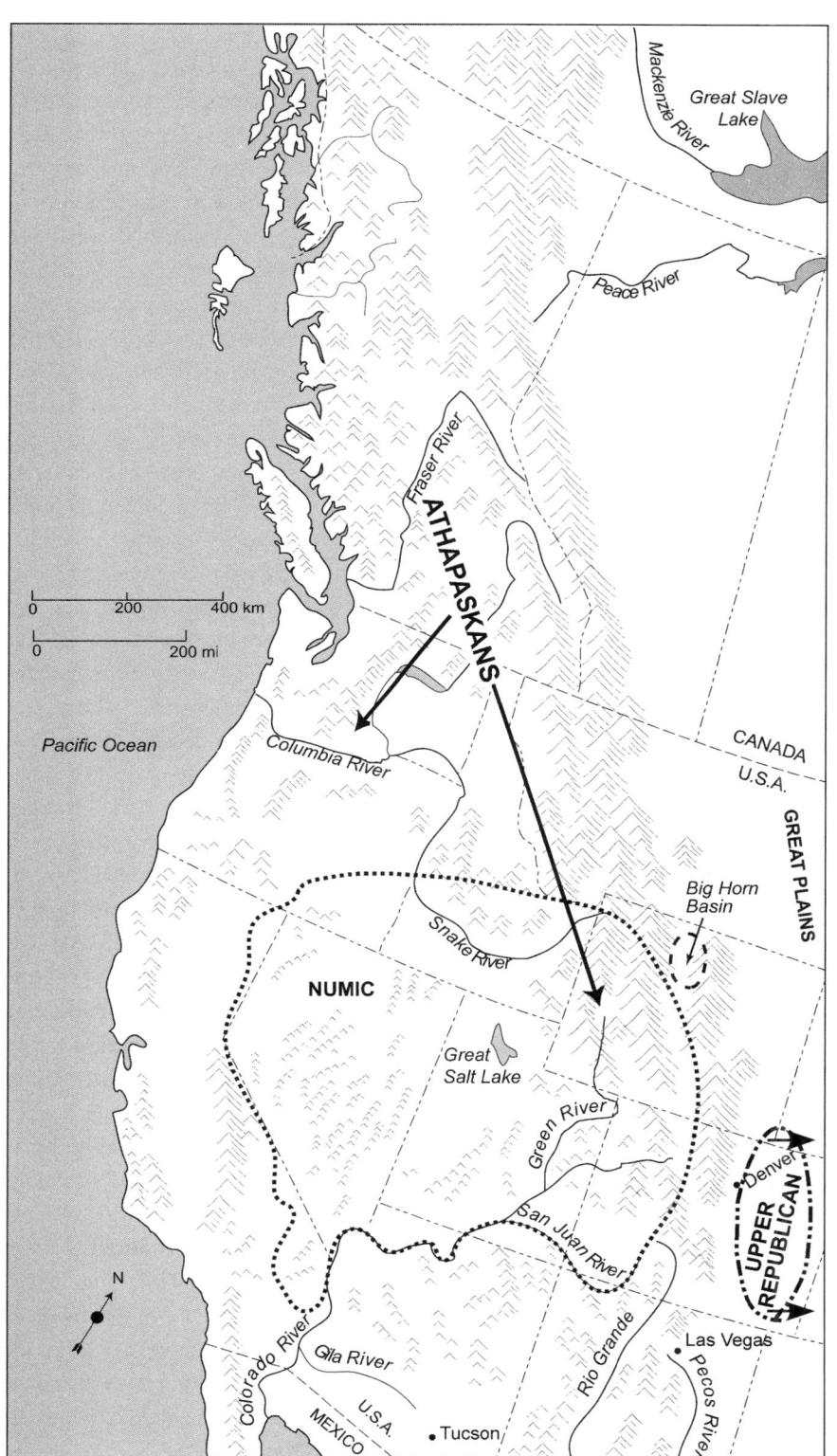

FIGURE 16.4. Hypothesized movement of Athapaskans into abandoned areas of the Southwest and to the U.S. Pacific Coast following detrimental environmental effects on horticultural Numic Shoshone/Ute peoples and eastern movement of Upper Republican cultures. Staged from southern British Columbia, ca. AD 1100–1400. From Matson and Magne (2007). Image by Susan Matson.

Migratory Patterns

The principal movement models in use today are envisioned as "point and arrow" (or "streaming") and "advancing front," which I refer to simply as a "wave" model (Figure 16.5). Point-and-arrow movements leave the areas in between uncolonized, and the movements can go both ways. Scouting is important here, since people had to obtain advance information in some way. Furthermore, in contrast, say, to a Clovis advancing-front scenario (e.g., Hamilton and Buchanan 2007; Waters and Stafford 2007), there are huge geographic gaps in the Athapaskans' distribution. According to Rockman (2003), in the advancing-front model, "sites in a newly colonized area are not likely to differ strongly from each other in terms of the learning level that they represent." Learning thus has "a low level effect on the archaeological record" and is "effectively invisible"; the archaeological signatures are highly similar at both ends. Therefore, being very distinct from Northern Athapaskans in their final manifestations, the Apacheans, as well as the Pacific Athapaskans, do not fit the advancing-front model in their migrations, which are in this argument more likely to have been point-and-arrow. A point-and-arrow scenario involves a record in which learning has a greater effect, so sites at either end are very different. Thus identifiable "signatures" between the southern cultures and the Canadian ones are currently very scarce, owing to this form of migration. Even if one accepts Dismal River (e.g., Gunnerson 1960) on the Central Plains as an Athapaskan "signature," a large gap in recognized Athapaskan attributions exists on the Northwestern Plains. Dismal River similarities overall are far more southern than northern, even though Wilmeth (1978:105–107) finds spurred end scrapers at Anahim Lake that are similar to those in Dismal River assemblages.

The greatest ethnic-material culture similarities among Athapaskan assemblages are within the greater southern and northern culture areas, with a large gap in any identification between British Columbia and Colorado. But as Rockman (2003) points out, the evidence for point-and-arrow migrations in the intervening areas is not fully explored, so archaeological gaps can be expected.

Following this argument further, one may expect geographical gaps in the Athapaskan migrations' archaeological signature but also perhaps fairly long-range two-way evidence as well, since a point-and-arrow pattern implies information feedback to at least immediate ancestors, but probably over multiple generations. Perhaps the distances spanned by two or three generations would be the limits for archaeologically recognizable acquisition of new lithic sources or faunal or floral resources. Trade items or materials obtained directly, some hundreds of kilometers from their sources, should be expected if kin remained in contact over extended periods of time. These kinds of studies have yet to be undertaken in Athapaskan archaeology, but worldwide hunter-gatherer studies indicate that individuals can acquire very detailed environmental knowledge over huge distances, in fact over tens of thousands of square miles. Relevant here to the possibility of this kind of kin-trade evidence is the recent work by Whitaker

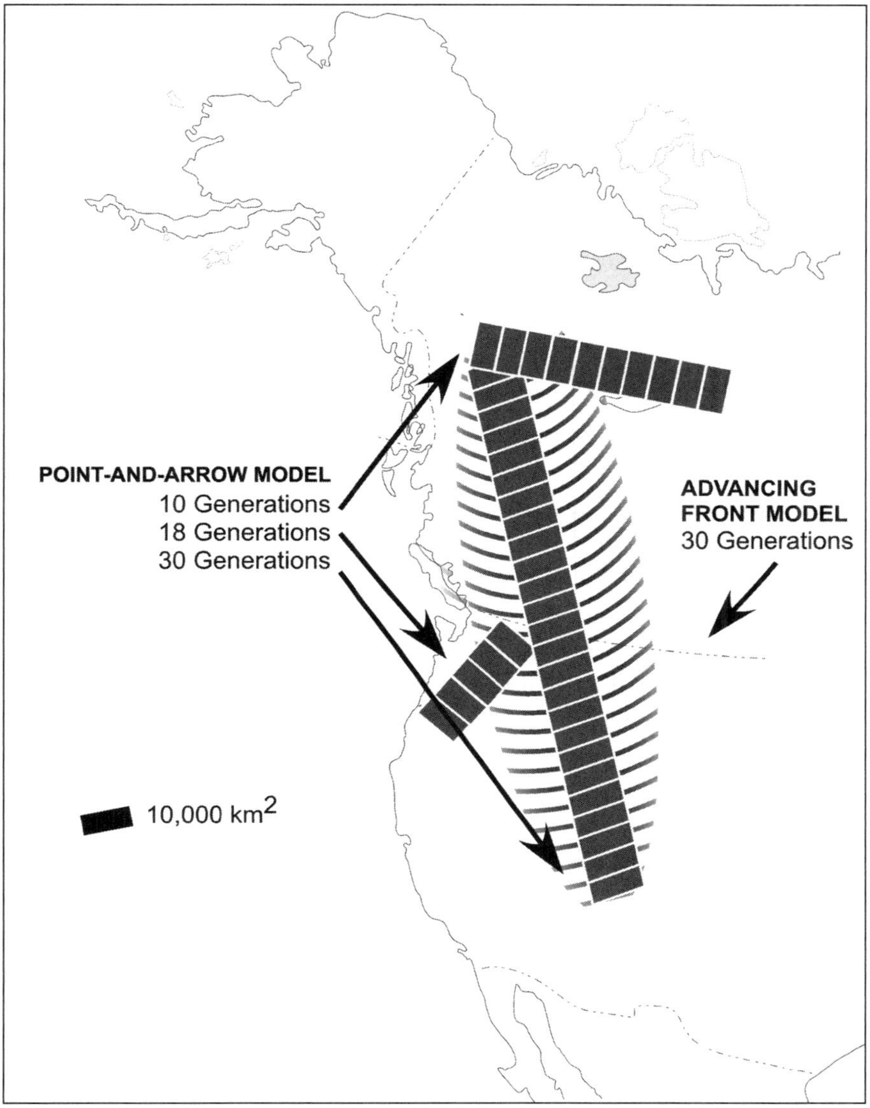

FIGURE 16.5. Point-and-arrow model and advancing-front model as alternative generational scenarios for Athapaskan migration, each across 30 generations over 1,000 years. Image by Martin Magne.

et al. (2008) concerning obsidian trade by northern California coastal Athapaskans. Rather than trade with immediately neighboring Algic socio-linguistic groups, the coastal groups preferred obsidian from more distant sources that was acquired through their linguistic relatives; at the same time, they were able to obtain other interior montane resources and, presumably, other information as well.

GENERATIONAL ADAPTATION

Rockman (2003) suggests, "Most likely... it takes a least a generation to develop familiarity with resources, their fluctuations, their potentials, and their carrying capacity on a scale that influences human activity." Thus the Athapaskan scale of 30 generations over 700 years (23.3 years/generation) can be examined for "patterns of familiarity." I equate this with Binford's (1980) "mapping on" signatures, in which, for example, initial learning of species distribution could be contrasted with later occupants' or migrants' fuller knowledge, predictability being reflected in more frequent and perhaps less efficient usage. Stevenson (1986) applied this concept to the well-stratified Peace Point site in northern Alberta, where he was able to demonstrate, over about 2,000 years, an increasing familiarity with faunal resources through time. The same kinds of learning would, theoretically, apply to lithic sources.

In Figure 16.5, applying the point-and-arrow and wave scenarios to the migration south, to the central Subarctic, and to the Pacific, I have mapped 25-year distances over 700 years, from a Yukon origin, to illustrate the extent of the landscapes over which people could have taught their descendants how to adapt to new areas on a generational scale. I ask whether what we see in that map is unreasonable or simply remarkable. In addition to learning environmental adaptation, successive generations need to adapt socially to the changing composition of their communities—both to new neighbors and to incoming relatives. A wealth of social factors must have been involved, including considerations of how to maintain contacts with ancestors and how to best approach other populations and make initial contacts. Social factors can be enhancing as well as limiting. In this vein, Ives's (1990) Dravidian kinship model for northern Athapaskans has crucial implications for the occupation of new areas, as does his model for group growth versus group alliance (Figure 16.6), when seen as alternative means of migratory adaptation: in one, groups grow larger and expand into new areas, and in the other, groups merge with existing ones. By all evidence, Athapaskans have a tremendously adaptive kinship system (Ives 1990). Bilateral cross-cousin marriage and its varieties generally would have been favorable to alliance building and knowledge gain. How better to start to learn an area and move confidently than to have extended family members with knowledge of areas one has yet to visit, as well as family left behind? Ives's model, as I describe below, partly provides a way to link generational modeling to archaeological assemblage structures resulting essentially from learning behavior. Seymour (Chapter 5, this volume) discusses how understanding the patterned behavior is key to discovering what may be faint occupational evidence in regions where even reoccupation may have left very few material remains.

Modeling Methods:
Assemblage Structure and Periodicity

What Matson and Magne (2007) did at Eagle Lake is a form of what Rockman (2003:13) calls "retrogressive analysis," in which "research and interpretation move from well-known landscapes of the recent past back through a sequence of progressively earlier antecedent phases." In adjoining regions, they successfully described Athapaskan versus Salishan lithic styles, and corresponding structures in lithic, faunal, and residential assemblages (Figure 16.7).

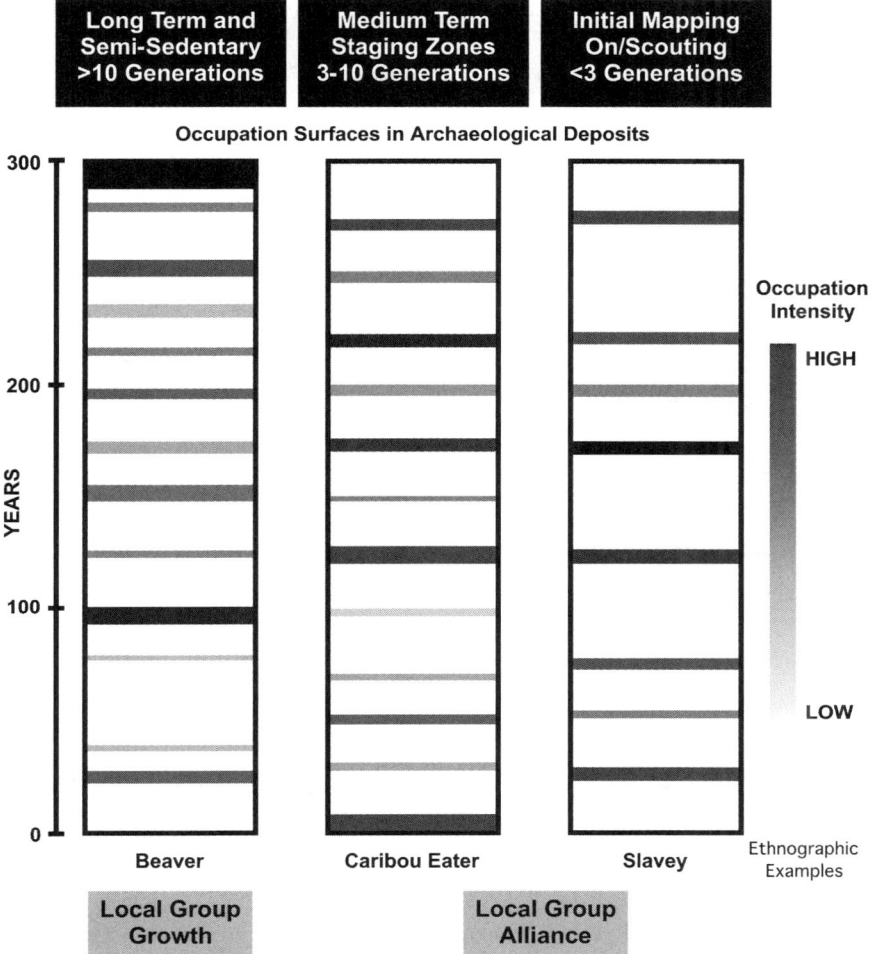

FIGURE 16.6. Generational model concepts integrated with Ives's (1990) group alliance and group growth models of site formation. Different degrees of local permanence, site occupation duration, and group growth likely occurred during the Athapaskan migration, leading to varying densities and periodicities of archaeological assemblage formation and accumulation. Modified from Ives (1990:324). Image by Martin Magne.

In our view, the application of detection methods across broad regions is the logical approach to take so that assemblage structures are understood between previous and new inhabitants of areas, as well as particular artifact attributes, whether those are lithic, ceramic, or habitation types. Demonstrating key environmental similarities across two regions, in detailed botanical community, geomorphology, and site locational preferences was an integral component of the Eagle Lake–Mouth of Chilcotin regional investigations. At the local and regional scales we can further develop ways to identify something different about new occupants versus long-established ones. Seymour (2002, 2003, Chapter 5 in this volume) demonstrates quite convincingly, for example, that assemblage structure is crucial to identifying Apachean occupations even when traded ceramics are part of the mix. The most useful measures that Seymour applies are principally lithic types (coarse versus fine stone), stylistic attributes of flaked-stone tools, and residential remains. Matson and Magne (2007) applied a similar methodology using particular technological types at Eagle Lake.

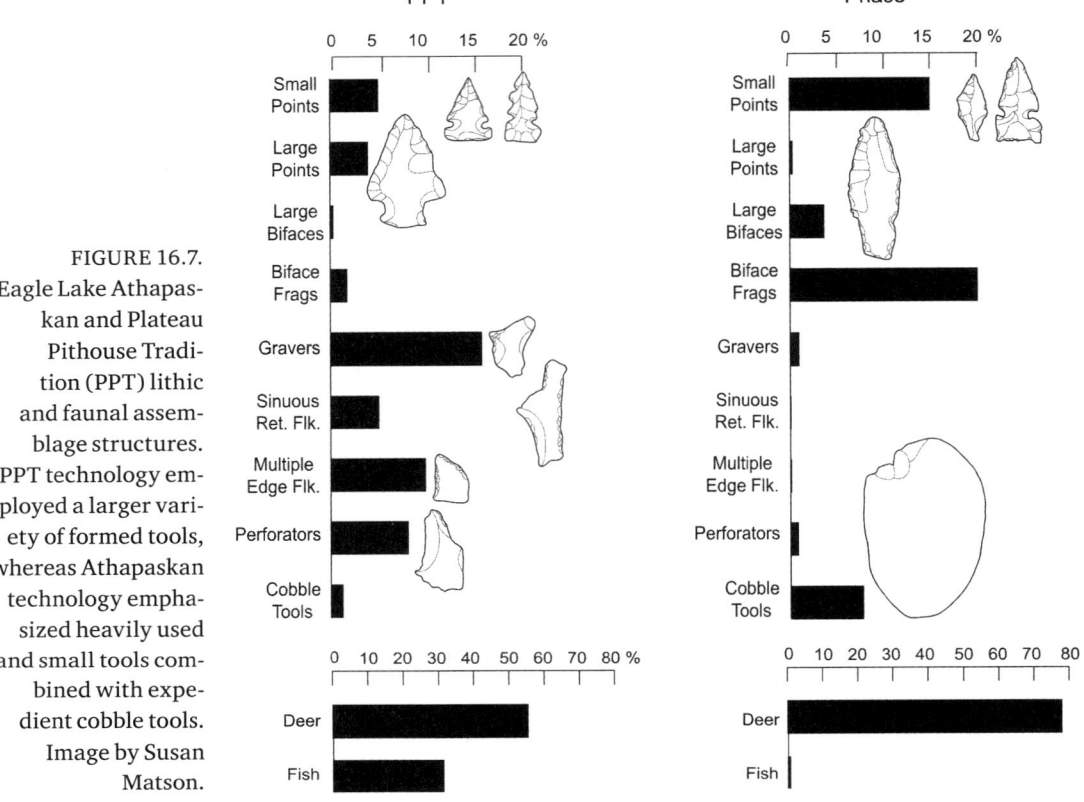

FIGURE 16.7. Eagle Lake Athapaskan and Plateau Pithouse Tradition (PPT) lithic and faunal assemblage structures. PPT technology employed a larger variety of formed tools, whereas Athapaskan technology emphasized heavily used and small tools combined with expedient cobble tools. Image by Susan Matson.

Extending Binford's (1983) concept of "long term range occupancy," or generational residence locations, Ives (1990) developed a preliminary model of how Northern Athapaskan assemblage structures may vary in predictable ways under conditions of local group growth versus those of local group alliance. In Ives's terms, we can understand a migration as requiring a long-term process involving a train of alliances over a long range yet also requiring a series of stages from which communities would operate. Given sufficient resolution, these staging and "mapping on" locations should show assemblage structures with patterns distinct from those of groups that have fully mapped on to the regional environment. In Figure 16.6 I have modified Ives's model to accommodate generational sequences of initial arrival and scouting, medium-term staging, and long-term occupations. Demonstrating patterns of differing assemblage structures is precisely what Matson and Magne (2007) were able to accomplish at Eagle Lake, showing recognizable distinctions in the lithic assemblages of the Athapaskan sites versus those of the earlier Plateau Pithouse Tradition peoples. What Matson and Magne lacked to fill Ives's model was good stratified sites, but this deficiency was alleviated in large measure by controlled regional sampling. Moreover, stratified sites are not a realistic expectation for a recently arrived highly mobile people (Seymour 2003, 2010). A similar application of their methodology in another adjoining region would be highly informative. Interestingly, Copp's (2008) ascription of Athapaskan archaeological presence in the Canadian Okanagan region known as the Similkameen, precisely in the area occupied by the ethnohistorically isolated Nicola Athapaskans, where he has employed some of Matson and Magne's more northern diagnostics (projectile point styles and possibly microblades), would be just about the ideal one- to two-generational distance from Eagle Lake that could be expected for an area of sustained "jumping off" occupations. Specifically, a distance such as this of about 300 km would be well within the environmental and social frame of reference for a highly mobile group, and perhaps over a considerable period of time.

Ethnographic Knowledge

The knowledge I have of Athapaskan mythology leads me to believe that regional migratory oral traditions are significant among Athapaskans (e.g., Carmichael and Farrer, this volume). Long-range origin legends are rare but nonetheless present. In fact, travel-related traditions among Athapaskans are fascinating to review with migration in mind. Appropriately, an example that Rockman uses to illustrate environmental learning is from Basso's (1996) work with Western Apache. His studies of Western Apachean relationships among culture, language, and landscape are revealing of the degree to which environmental knowledge was essential to the Athapaskan migration. Basso (1996) describes how Apache children are invited to travel with learned people, to acquire knowledge that can be recalled quickly. He observes that "images evoked by place names cause them to travel in their minds," and that travel is both forward into space and backward in the footsteps of their ancestors (Basso 1996: 89). This practice is so evocative that a single place name can take the place of an entire historical tale. The Western Apache call this "speaking with names."

Another relevant case is Ridington's (1982) research among the Dunne-Za, or Beaver, of northeastern British Columbia. Ridington (1982) argues that technical knowledge has greater value than material items in hunter-gatherer technology. In agreement with Basso's observations of Western Apache communicating with the environment, Ridington notes that Dunne-Za were taught to "think like game animals in order to predict their behaviour. They were trained to interpret the environment from an animal's perspective"; furthermore, the "quality of their interpersonal relations was reflected in the quality of their relations with animals." In what could be considered closely related to success in migration, Ridington observes: "Traditional Beaver world view centred around their image of the trail.... Success depended upon being able to make decisions about how best to move in relation to the complex network of trails emerging from the past and merging into the future. Hunters believed that in the dream state they could resolve a larger pattern of interrelated trails than would be possible in ordinary waking consciousness.... Hunters slept with their heads toward the place where the sun would rise, in expectation of being able to travel in dreams ahead of their physical trail on earth." Central to Beaver people is a tradition of shamans known as Dreamers, who travel to lands beyond the sky and return in roles as "messengers from the trails that lay ahead.... Dreamers could see ahead on the trails of an entire community" (Ridington 1982:476). Dunne-Za behavior is mirrored in the Southwest. Stockel (2007; also see Seymour 2008: 143) observes that the Apache way of life recognized the "medicine man's suggestion as to when they finally arrived at the end of their travels." A comparative study of these ways of life with the Shoshone, Crow, or Cheyenne "intervening" societies could be revealing: is environmental learning, evident as band-level belief systems for success in travel among Southern and Northern Athapaskans, an equally important social element in those Great Basin and western Plains societies?

INTEGRATIVE MODELING:
BIOGEOGRAPHY AND REGIONAL DEMOGRAPHICS

How do models of colonization, such as initial migration or migration into areas with resident populations, shed light on the Athapaskan migrations? The entire Athapaskan movement was likely through "occupied areas," though some of those areas were probably not very densely occupied. One would not expect a dense Athapaskan presence through most of the journey, although local densities likely built up in periodic stagings. The barriers also likely fluctuated in their degrees of filtration along the way. Nevertheless, the sheer rapidity of the Athapaskan migration implies that for the most part, social and environmental barriers were quite low.

In a fascinating study of ecological productivity and its variability through time across areas occupied by various ethnolinguistic groups of northern California, Gmoser (1993) finds, first of all, "a well conformed fit of ethnographic linguistic boundaries with...productivity distribution"; he also notes that the "highest productivity peaks also fit predictions in regard to the location of isolate languages," namely, the non-Athapaskan Wiyot, Yurok, and Karok. The Athapaskan groups, in contrast, "have peak areas that are smaller" and "appear to have surrounded the isolate territories" (1993:256). In other words, the Athapaskans there occupied the less-productive areas surrounding the better ones. In a method that would be worth combining with Gmoser's, Gilmore (2006; Gilmore and Larmore, this volume) has been working in the Colorado High Country (see also Brunswig, this volume), attempting to identify an Athapaskan presence, principally through affiliations with western Dismal River aspect assemblages of the Plains. One of the most interesting components of his study is a compilation of radiocarbon dates that, when used as proxy population curves in various environmental zones, may represent Athapaskan "seasonal transhumance."

As Rockman and Anthony suggest, continual acquisition of relevant information is critical to successful migration, and some form of advance scouting must have been well engrained in these cultures. I suggest that scouting by Athapaskans at the generational level could have been very long range down the Rocky Mountains and their east and west slopes. The reason for this is an essential suite of similarities in alpine and montane environments, including common seasonal and altitudinal factors that offer less risk for a highly "residential mobile" population than plains or coastal environments, particularly during a move into already occupied areas. Kelly (2003) reinforces this point by quoting Nelson's (1986) observation that a Kutchin trapper could more easily find his way in unfamiliar mountainous terrain than in forests. In the same work, Kelly (2003:49) offers the view that "linear mountain chains (or their foothills), major rivers, and coastlines might provide the easiest terrain to navigate and relate to other known places." In the Athapaskan case, large-scale environmental adaptations along the Rocky Mountains must have been the norm, fitting well with Beaton's (1991) concept of "megapatch" adaptations for long-range colonizations. I suggest that Athapaskan adaptations at general scales of settlement patterns could be fruitfully investigated within a series of distinct biogeographic zones, as pictured in Figure 16.8.

I believe that the distribution of individual species down the Rockies is not in itself a critical factor; rather, the similarity in food types, altitudinal variability, and seasonality, combined with a highly mobile lifestyle, produced the most effective, adaptable way to move long distances (see also Seymour 2008). Root crops, large to medium-sized ungulates, and small game are all found in relative abundance north to south, through similar altitudinal clines and in extremely variable seasons whether one is in Colorado or British Columbia.

Seymour's (2002, 2004a, 2004b, 2008, 2009, Chapter 5 of this volume) work in Arizona and New Mexico advances Athapaskan migration research considerably in the Southwest by directing problems in group identification and ethnohistoric sources toward the mobile Apache (such as the Mescalero and Chiricahua) rather than the agricultural Navajo. Through substantial regional survey and comparisons of sparse lithic assemblages, very occasional ceramics, faint architectural features, and landscape attributes, she finds recognizable Apache signatures. These sites push the commonly accepted radiocarbon dates of about AD 1450 for Athapaskans in the Southwest to the mid-AD 1300s (Seymour 2008:140–141). That these sites are found in mountainous areas (Mogollon Mountains, Peloncillo Mountains, and environs) results from the deliberate application of a mobile settlement pattern model, and this approach also reveals the erroneous logic in a reliance on ethnohistoric accounts, particularly well-known Spanish ones such as those of the Coronado expedition of 1540, which suggest that large areas were uninhabited, even by Apache. The conclusion may be drawn that lack of historic record is far from irrefutable evidence that the mountains were unoccupied: the Spaniards' observations came mainly

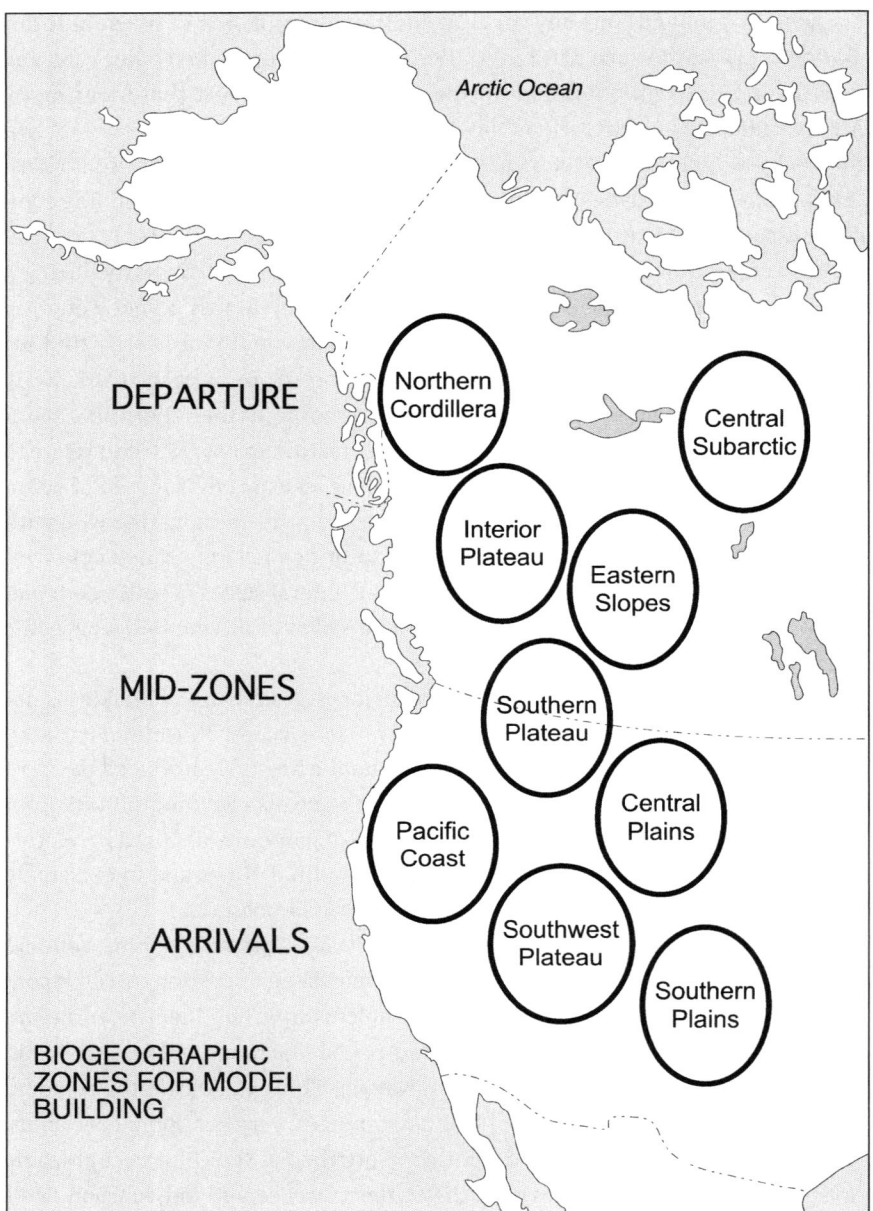

FIGURE 16.8. Biogeographic zones within which Athapaskan migrational events could be explored on generational scales. Image by Martin Magne.

from lowland areas, and the Athapaskans had highly developed abilities to hide and observe from a distance (Seymour 2008).

Theoretically, this recent Apache research also advances thinking about what early arrivals look like, particularly when these arrivals are likely represented by only a light and inconspicuous addition to the landscape. The nature of mountain Apache archaeology seriously questions Anthony's (1990) assertions that migrations are readily identifiable and that they have distinct effects on the archaeological record (Seymour 2004b, 2008). It makes sense that the first arrivals would be few and that we may not be able to see when this process of change started in a particular area, only once it was well under way (Seymour 2008). Another theoretical implication of Seymour's work is that modeling is a matter of scale, in this instance both continental and local. The local Apache adaptation and regional movement patterns appear to be those of surging and blanketing, rather than highly directional, though that may (or may not) have been the case at the continental scale.

Conclusion: Migrational Biogeography

First, models of the Athapaskan migrations have to reference all groups, including those of the central Subarctic. Second, as the preceding discussion indicates, a purely blind migration is highly unlikely. Therefore, a mountain migration is probable because if the Athapaskan migrants had a high degree of relevant, existing environmental knowledge, the intervening areas would have offered them few challenges requiring efforts to obtain new information. Moreover, that balance of effort could have been expended on social relations favoring rapid movement—knowing the environments and their predictability over long distances would greatly facilitate alliance formation, trade, and expansion of kin relations.

Moving for the most part through similar mountain environments, leapfrogging areas that were unsuitable for subsistence reasons, social reasons, or both, would seem a good solution. Thus, if an unfriendly neighbor was encountered, rapid displacement was less of an issue than moving to a new environment. Moving rapidly was probably even less of a challenge with the Athapaskans' cultural traditions of travel. One needs to ask seriously if the Athapaskans could have stayed for long in Shoshone territory, for example. As for demonstrating technological traditions, I believe that Carr's (1995) concepts of hierarchical style apply here, particularly his development of theory as to the "geographic distribution of the alternative states" of artifact attributes (Carr 1995:172). This is another dimension of examining the migrations at different geographic scales. In a similar vein, also applicable are the considerations of "technological embeddedness" that Clark (2001) developed in relation to Puebloan migrations, with reference to Carr's model of style, using a worldwide sample of ethnoarchaeological evidence. Clark (2001:18) found "substantial support [for] the strategy of using attributes with low physical and contextual visibility to identify groups with different enculturative backgrounds and settlement histories," or what one might call ethnolinguistic groups. The visibility of lithic technological patterns versus projectile point styles, in contrast to housing or burial styles, is variable in different settlement systems. We shouldn't expect Chilcotin side-notched points to look like Apache ones, but on the other hand, higher-elevation Chilcotin camp assemblages may look an awful lot like those of sixteenth-century mountain Apache. These contrasts are difficult to predict, but general modeling nonetheless helps establish comparative methods by which to examine Southwestern

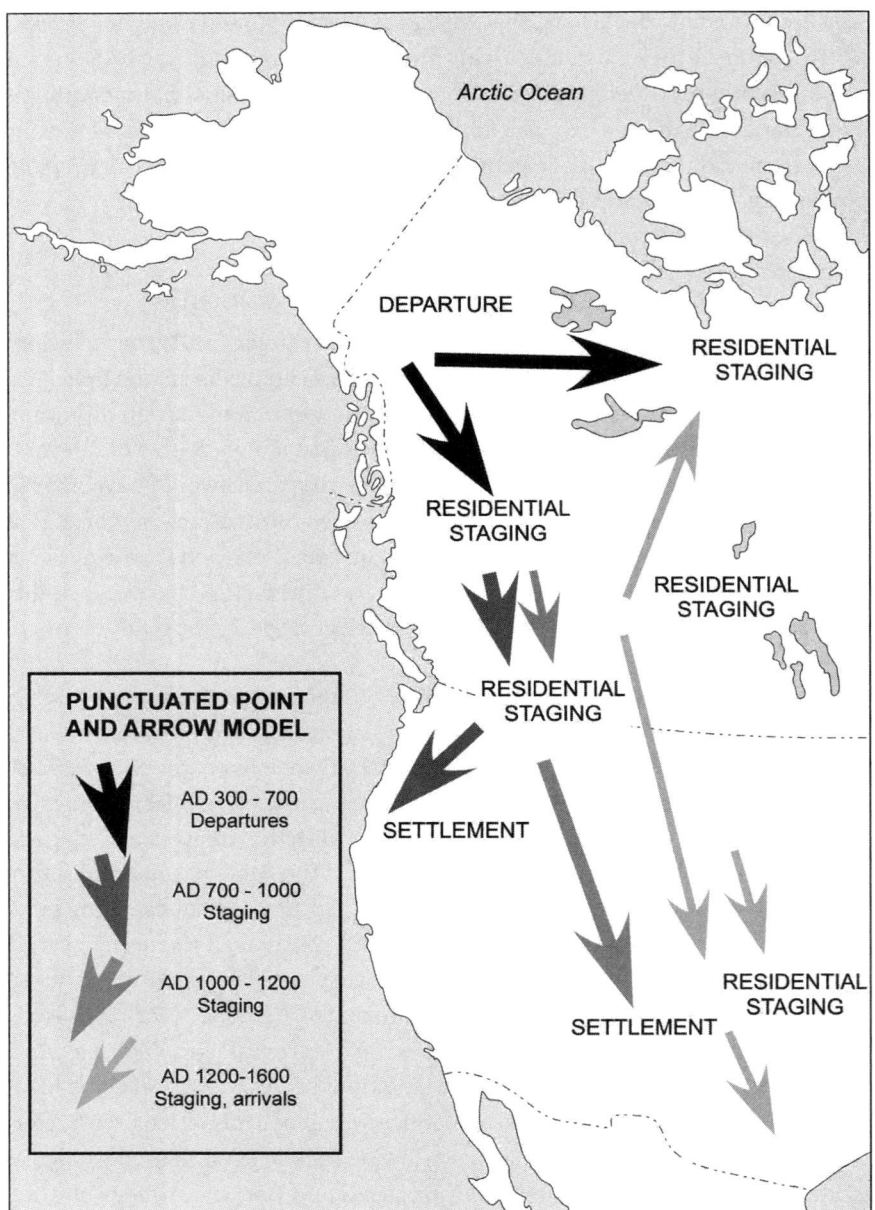

FIGURE 16.9. Punctuated point-and-arrow model for Athapaskan migration showing principal areas of residential staging over the course of approximately 1,000 years. Image by Martin Magne.

Navajo, Apache, and Pueblo assemblages. We really don't know how change at the level of assemblage or artifact attribute occurred in Athapaskan adaptations through time and across the midcontinental space of the migration. Low-level adaptations likely occurred, but again, the basic mountain settlement pattern adaptation remained fairly constant. The Apache sites that Seymour (2008) describes in Arizona and New Mexico are in many ways not that different from the smallest surface lithic and cultural feature scatters of the Interior Plateau, but they are in contrast to the predominant settlement patterns of the late prehistoric Southwest.

To find those patterns archaeologically, I believe a "punctuated point-and-arrow" model is appropriate, as shown in Figure 16.9, one that recognizes different phases of the migrations in the north, the central areas, and the south. At a sequential series of zones, the propensity for certain artifact styles to be retained, or to change, can be contrasted with the technological organization of the assemblages in those regions. That type of archaeological evidence is gathering on the Canadian Plateau and in the Southwest, and Gilmore's (2006; Gilmore and Larmore, this volume), Wilshusen's (2010), and Brunswig's (this volume) work may be filling in the picture on the west-central Plains, but the archaeological picture of Athapaskan migrations is very sketchy for the intermediate Great Basin and southern Plateau zones.

Integrating large-scale migration modeling with artifact style and assemblage theory is a promising research avenue, and intensive regional studies at about 200–300-km target zones should be a fruitful approach. We can expect the course and timing of the Athapaskan migrations to be shown through a series of periodic, zonal patterns of residential and logistical assemblage structures.

NOTE

This chapter was presented in preliminary form at the session "Agriculture to Athapaskans, Sampling to Salmon: Papers in Honour of R. G. Matson," Society for American Archaeology, Vancouver, British Columbia, March 2008.

REFERENCES

Anthony, David W.
1990 Migration in Archeology: The Baby and the Bathwater. *American Anthropologist* 92(4):895–914.

Basso, Keith
1996 *Wisdom Sits in Places: Landscape and Language among the Western Apache.* Albuquerque: University of New Mexico Press.

Beaton, John M.
1991 Colonizing Continents: Some Problems from Australia and the Americas. In *The First Americans: Search and Research*, edited by Tom D. Dillehay and David J. Meltzer, pp. 209–230. Boca Raton, Florida: CRC Press.

Binford, Lewis
1980 Willow Smoke and Dog's Tails: Hunter-Gatherer Settlement Systems and Archaeological Site Formation. *American Antiquity* 45(1):4–20.
1983 Long Term Land-Use Patterning: Some Implications for Archaeology. In *Working at Archaeology*, edited by Lewis R. Binford, pp. 379–386. New York: Academic Press.

Carr, Christopher
1995 A Unified Middle-Range Theory of Artifact Design. In *Style, Society, and Person: Archaeological and Ethnological Perspectives*, edited by C. Carr and J. E. Neitzel, pp. 171–258. New York: Plenum Press.

Clague, John, S. G. Evans, V. N. Rampton, and G. J. Woodsworth
1995   Improved Age Estimates for the White River and Bridge River Tephras, Western Canada. *Canadian Journal of Earth Sciences* 32:1172–1179.

Clark, Jeffery J.
2001   *Tracking Prehistoric Migrations: Pueblo Settlers among the Tonto Basin Hohokam.* Tucson: University of Arizona Press.

Copp, Stanley A.
2008   Okanagan-Similkameen Projectile Points: Origins, Associations, and the Athapaskan Question. In *Projectile Point Sequences in Northwestern North America*, edited by Roy L. Carlson and Martin P. R. Magne, pp. 251–272. Burnaby, British Columbia: Archaeology Press.

Gilmore, Kevin
2006   And Miles to Go Before I Sleep: A Model for Prehistoric Athapaskan Migration along the Western High Plains Margin. Paper presented at the 71st Annual Meeting of the Society for American Archaeology, San Juan, Puerto Rico.

Gmoser, Glenn J.
1993   Co-evolution of Adaptation and Linguistic Boundaries in Northwest California. In *There Grows a Green Tree: Papers in Honor of David A. Fredrickson*, edited by Greg White, Pat Mikkelsen, William R. Hildebrandt, and Mark E. Basgall, pp. 243–264. Center for Archaeological Research at Davis, Publication No. 11. Davis: Department of Anthropology, University of California.

Gunnerson, James H.
1960   *An Introduction to Plains Apache Archeology—The Dismal River Aspect.* Anthropological Papers No. 58, Bureau of American Ethnology Bulletin No. 173, pp. 131–260. Washington, D.C.: Smithsonian Institution.

Hamilton, Marcus J., and Briggs Buchanan
2007   Spatial Gradients in Clovis-Age Radiocarbon Dates across North America Suggest Rapid Colonization from the North. *Proceedings of the National Academy of Sciences* 104(40):15626–15630.

Ives, John W.
1990   *A Theory of Athapascan Prehistory.* Boulder, Colorado: Westview Press; Calgary, Alberta: University of Calgary Press.

Kelly, Robert
2003   Colonization of New Land by Hunter-Gatherers: Expectations and Implications Based on Ethnographic Data. In *Colonization of Unfamiliar Landscapes: The Archaeology of Adaptation*, edited by Marcy Rockman and James Steele, pp. 44–58. New York: Routledge.

Magne, Martin P. R.
2001   Plateau and Plains Athapaskan Movements in Late Prehistoric and Early Historic Periods. Paper presented at the 66th Annual Meeting of the Society for American Archaeology, New Orleans.

Matson, R. G., and Martin P. R. Magne
2007   *Athapaskan Migrations: The Archaeology of Eagle Lake, British Columbia.* Tucson: University of Arizona Press.

Moratto, Michael
1984   *California Archaeology.* New York: Academic Press.

Nelson, Richard
1986   *Hunters of the Northern Forest.* Chicago: University of Chicago Press.

Ridington, Robin
1982 Technology, World View, and Adaptive Strategy in a Northern Hunting Society. *Canadian Review of Sociology and Anthropology* 19(4):469–481.

Rockman, Marcy
2003 Knowledge and Learning in the Archaeology of Colonization. In *Colonization of Unfamiliar Landscapes: The Archaeology of Adaptation*, edited by Marcy Rockman and James Steele, pp. 3–24. New York: Routledge.

Seymour, Deni
2002 *Conquest and Concealment: After the El Paso Phase on Fort Bliss; An Archaeological Study of the Manso, Suma, and Early Apache*. With contributions by Mark E. Harlan and David V. Hill. Lone Mountain Report 525/528. Conservation Division, Directorate of the Environment, United States Army Air Defense, Artillery Center, Fort Bliss, Texas. Qualified researchers may obtain this document by contacting martha.yduarte@us.army.mil.
2003 *Protohistoric and Early Historic Temporal Resolution*. Lone Mountain Report 560-003. Conservation Division, Directorate of the Environment, Fort Bliss. Qualified researchers may obtain this document by contacting martha.yduarte@us.army.mil.
2004a A Ranchería in the Gran Apachería: Evidence of Intercultural Interaction at the Cerro Rojo Site. *Plains Anthropologist* 49(190):153–192.
2004b Before the Spanish Chronicles: Early Apache in the Southern Southwest. In *Ancient and Historic Lifeways in North America's Rocky Mountains: Proceedings of the 2003 Rocky Mountain Anthropological Conference, Estes Park, Colorado*, edited by Robert H. Brunswig and William B. Butler, pp. 120–142. Greeley: Department of Anthropology, University of Northern Colorado.
2008 Despoblado or Athapaskan Heartland: A Methodological Perspective on Ancestral Apache Landscape Use in the Safford Area. In *Crossroads of the Southwest: Culture, Ethnicity, and Migration in Arizona's Safford Basin*, edited by David E. Purcell, pp. 121–162. New York: Cambridge Scholars Press.
2009 Distinctive Places, Suitable Spaces: Conceptualizing Mobile Group Occupational Duration and Landscape Use. *International Journal of Historical Archaeology* 13(3):255–281.
2010 Cycles of Renewal, Transportable Assets: Aspects of Ancient Apache Housing. *Plains Anthropologist* 55(214):133–152.

Stevenson, Marc G.
1986 *Window on the Past: Archaeological Assessment of the Peace Point Site, Wood Buffalo National Park, Alberta*. Studies in Archaeology, Architecture and History. Ottawa, Ontario: Parks Canada.

Stockel, Henrietta
2007 Rocks, Waters, Earth: Chiricahua Apache Spiritual Geography. *Journal of the West* 46:18–27.

Waters, Michael, and Thomas W. Stafford
2007 Redefining the Age of Clovis: Implications for the Peopling of the Americas. *Science* 315:1122–1126.

Whitaker, Adrian R., Elmer W. Hearkens, Amy M. Spurting, Edward L. Smith, and Michelle A. Gras
2008 Linguistic Boundaries as Barriers to Exchange. *Journal of Archaeological Science* 35(4):1104–1113.

Wilmeth, Roscoe
1978   *Anahim Lake Archaeology and the Early Chilcotin Indians*. Mercury Series, Archaeological Survey of Canada, Paper No. 82. Ottawa, Ontario: National Museum of Man.

Wilshusen, Richard H.
2010   The Diné at the Edge of History: Navajo Ethnogenesis in the Northern Southwest, 1500–1750. In *Across a Great Divide: Continuity and Change in Native North American Societies, 1400–1850*, edited by Laura L. Scheiber and Mark D. Mitchell, pp. 192–211. Tucson: University of Arizona Press.

CHAPTER 17

"Big Trips" and Historic Apache Movement and Interaction

Models for Early Athapaskan Migrations

DENI J. SEYMOUR

The way many mobile groups migrate, and specifically the way ancestral Apacheans accomplished this process of moving from one area to another in the historic period, provides a sense of how longer-range migrations might have occurred. The way mobile groups migrate is related to their use of the land and so, because they are distinct from more geographically stable peoples (e.g., Dumond 1998), requires different migration theory than that applied to sedentary or semi-mobile systems (e.g., Seymour 2008). By understanding late Apache forms of moving into new territory and practices of Apache landscape encompassment, we can formulate more effective models for understanding certain forms of long-distance movement, or "big trips," as occurred between the Subarctic and the American Southwest. This extra-long-distance move probably consisted of a series of more restricted "big trips" that resulted in the transfer of discrete groups of people from one "distinct center of occupation" to another farther along their route. Concepts such as these, which are derived from historic Chiricahua Apache oral accounts, are discussed later in this chapter.

This perspective on the movement of ancestral Apacheans is aided by an understanding of their mode of intercultural interaction, specifically with respect to forms of social recruitment and the adoption (incorporation, borrowing) of neighbors' technologies and ways of life. Such factors have implications for how to look for evidence of this migration. These perspectives also have the potential to account for material cultural and land-use changes along the way, thereby explaining why we do not see a mirror image of Subarctic Athapaskans in the earliest Southwestern Athapaskan assemblages. These changes also explain why there is so much diversity in how early Athapaskans are manifest archaeologically (for examples, see chapters in this volume) as they moved south and once they got there. Theirs was not a site-unit intrusion, as often occurs among many more stationary groups, in which a cultural package is transplanted intact into a new area. Rather, Athapaskan migrations involved the acquisition and discard of attributes along the way.

Migration Theory for Mobile Groups

Migration, by definition, represents the movement to new, previously unoccupied territory. It is widely accepted that "a methodology for examining prehistoric migration must be dependent upon an understanding of the general structure of migration as a patterned behavior" (Anthony 1990:895). Many of the relevant behavioral patterns, however, differ in substantial ways between fundamentally mobile and primarily stationary groups. Degrees and types of mobility matter. This is because mobility activates a different set of relationships with the land and with neighbors than are experienced by staunchly or territorially stationary peoples. Mobile groups are not necessarily burdened with fixed boundaries, dependent on stored resources, tethered to arable land and growing seasons, or limited by the requirements of their architectural template (Seymour 2008). Moreover, how new, previously unoccupied territory is defined differs between mobile and more stationary groups. Mobile people may use, raid into, and occupy an area on a limited basis before that location becomes part of their distinct center of occupation. Because migration among mobile groups involves a different set of processes than migration for relatively stationary groups, distinct material and spatial evidence is expected.

Migration versus Seasonal Movement

It is useful to point out that there is a confusion of terms pervasive in the regional literature regarding movement between places within a previously defined and regularly used territory and the process of long-distance migration. For example, Basehart (1960:107) comments: "The large-scale migration was a gradual process, rather than a unitary movement. Family units would break camp over the course of several weeks, and meet with other members of the group at a designated rendezvous." What Basehart means is that as people moved from one known residential locale to another known residential locale within an existing territory, they moved at their own pace (Figure 17.1). This is not migration in the sense used here but instead is seasonal movement. Movements he refers to as "long distance" or "large-scale" (Basehart 1960:108–110) are actually movements *within* territories, whereas I reserve these terms for actual migrations. Citing Basehart, Henderson (1990:228) also uses inaccurate language to suggest movements between residential sites: "Matrilocal bands moved from resource sites when an item was exhausted and new material was needed. Males who had successfully identified a new location of resource supplies led the migration." Henderson, like Basehart, is referring to the seasonal round, sometimes called a seasonal *migration*. This terminology, however, leads to confusion in cases in which big trips or migrations represent gradual or punctuated encompassment of new territory rather than movements within known, regularly used, and ensconced territorial boundaries (Figure 17.2).

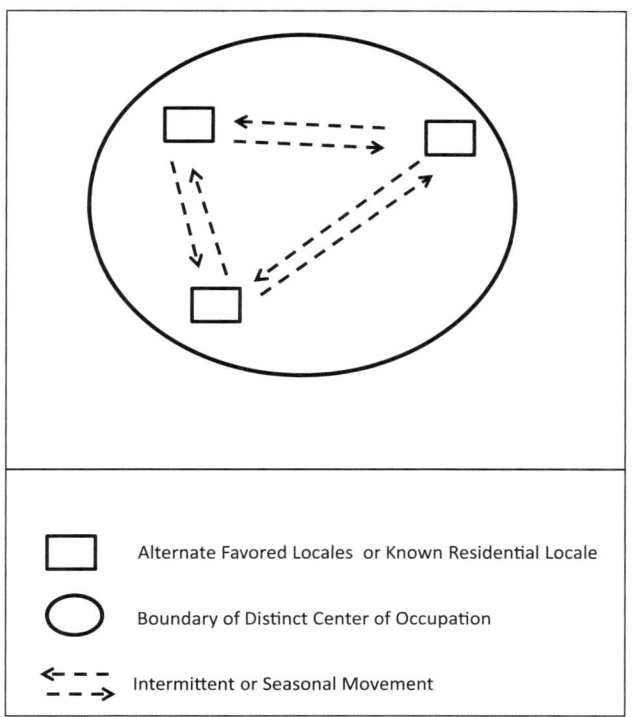

FIGURE 17.1. Movements within a known range occur on a seasonal basis and for political, social, and economic reasons. People moved from one known residential locale to another known residential locale within an existing territory. Image by Deni Seymour.

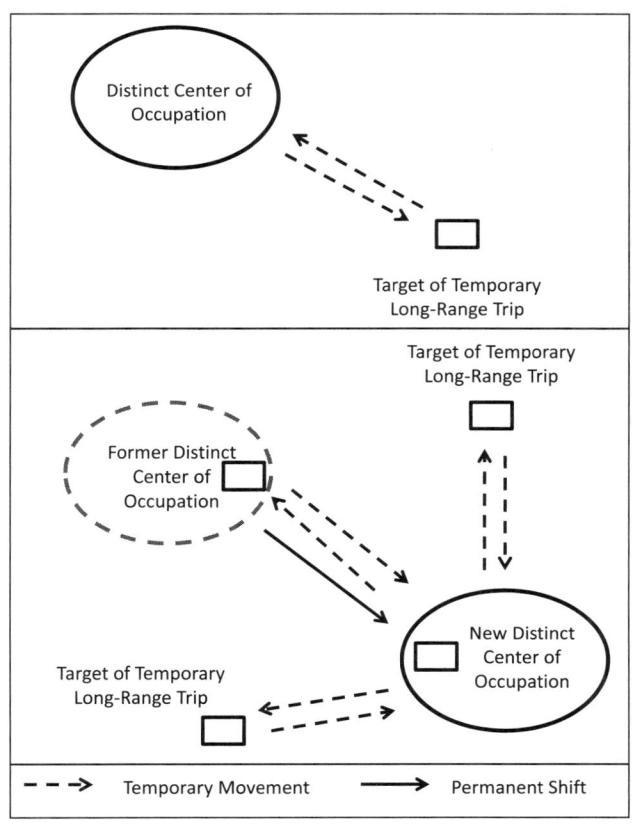

FIGURE 17.2. Big trips, or migrations, represent the end result of gradual or punctuated encompassment of new territory rather than movements within known and regularly used territorial boundaries. Image by Deni Seymour.

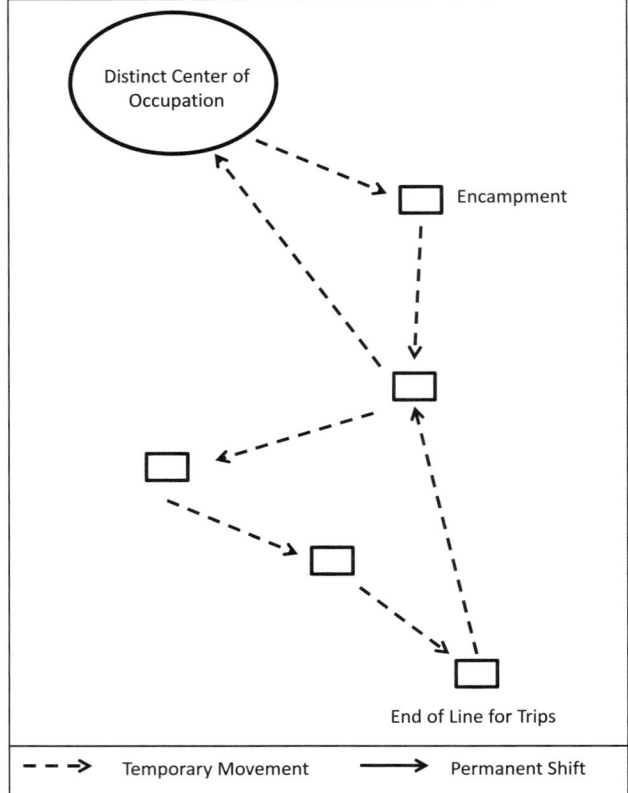

FIGURE 17.3. Migration was probably initiated as temporary long-distance movement into new territories for seasonal or task-specific purposes. Image by Deni Seymour.

To "Move at Their Own Pace"

Basehart (1960:107) notes that particular leaders' favoring of certain geographic regions influenced the timing and direction of within-territory movement. In a similar sense, male leaders would also likely determine the timing and direction of actual long-distance migrations to new territories. Still, such decisions would have been made on a consensus basis, and the process of Athapaskan migrations also likely involved this proclivity to "move at their own pace." Consequently, movement resulting in migration (big trips) probably occurred over an extended period of time by small groups that were going about their daily affairs. Migration probably began as temporary long-distance movement into new territories for seasonal or task-specific purposes, movement that ultimately and regularly returned the group to known habitation places within distinct centers of occupation (Figure 17.3).

Mobility versus Migration

A clearer understanding of the processes involved in long-distance migration arises when the distinction is made between mobility and acts of migration. Researchers who study stationary farming groups sometimes suggest that people who move every 4 or 16 years or perhaps every century or two are mobile (Bernbeck 2008:47; Kelly 1983, 1992; Varien 1999:3, 195). Scholars do this to counteract the long-held notion that people stay in one place for centuries once they establish a village. As they note, even these persistent places may experience a punctuated and intermittent series of occupations. This type of movement for groups that are residentially stable for many years at a time, however, distinctly contrasts with the routine movements of more mobile people throughout the year.

Moreover, mobility in the sense discussed here is different from migration. High mobility occurs within a specific territory or range where members move from place to place on an annual round, to and from familiar resources and places (see Figure 17.1). Established residential sites (or persistent places) for both large and small groups form a sense of place and belonging. Members are drawn back to familiar places, anchoring most of their routine activities to these areas. Despite this, one locale of group coalescence may substitute for another, depending on a variety of factors, as reflected in the ethnographic, ethnohistoric, and historic records:

a. Time of year
"They go there temporarily to gather fruit, seeds, walnuts, hunt there. Don't stay there all the time" (Sam Kenoi interview in Henderson 1957:584). "With the advent of spring, groups began to move gradually from the winter bases, in part in order to gather mescal" (Basehart 1959b:101–102).

b. Actions of neighbors
So that they could not go there; "in case the first one [residential site] proved to be unsafe or couldn't be reached" (Betzinez and Nye 1959:68).

c. Restrictions on travel routes
"We circled wide from Fort Cummings, and set out north" (Ball 1970:174). "When they discovered by the dust that they were being cut off from the south, they turned toward their old home" (Ball 1970:52).

d. Presence of or discovery by enemies
"The Nantan Lupan had stationed guards at the waterholes and dangerous crossings" (Ball 1970:179, 184); they were "fired upon by the Mexicans lying in ambush" (Betzinez and Nye 1959:53); "the Blue Coats lay in ambush waiting for us" (Ball 1970:76).

e. Resource availability
"Favored hunting and gathering sites might be unproductive in a given year" (Basehart 1959b:99); so they could access mescal in areas guarded by the enemy (Griffen 1988:38, 39). "All places known to be frequented by Apaches [camps, water holes, and mescal harvesting areas] were to be scoured" (Griffen 1988:46, 58). "We moved camp to a new location…where there was plenty of water and abundant supplies of wild fruit" (Betzinez and Nye 1959:89). "No ammunition for these [guns] was obtainable in Mexico, so it was necessary to make a raid into the United States to get some cartridges" (Betzinez and Nye 1959:88).

Non-exclusive Territories, Territorial Attachment, and Gradual Encompassment

Significantly, territories were not exclusive, and they overlapped with those of other Apache groups and of their non-Apachean neighbors (Basehart 1959b:87, 105–106; 1960:85, 86; Opler 1971:316). In this sense, the term "territory" is used loosely. Anthropologists are most comfortable envisioning indigenous groups as occupying circumscribed space and producing distinct forms of material culture that can be classified and then referred to by type names. This concept of culture area that dominates modern archaeological understanding is, however, fundamentally misleading when applied to mobile populations such as the ancestral Apache. Their movements were more fluid, shifting between alternate favored locales depending on a number of evaluated circumstances. Their territories of use were defined to a large degree by the activities of their neighbors, whether these neighbors were other Apaches, other Native American groups (such as the Sobaipuri-O'odham), or European-derived populations. Understanding these factors is fundamental to conceptualizing the way mobile groups move across space and adjust to internal and external social and political pressures and group factionalization.

Foremost, as Basehart (1960:132) notes for the Mescalero:

> Leaders definitely were not associated with named territorial divisions, nor did they represent particular geographic regions. At the same time, leaders and their followers did have favorite areas for seasonal concentration, even though no claim to the specific locality was involved. As one very old man said of named geographical districts, the people "didn't think they had any more claim on the portion of land they live on than any other part of the country. It's just because they want to live over at a certain place; that's all there was to it." Essentially, territorial linkages consisted of generalized, long-term preferences for certain geographical areas, other things being equal. But "other things," especially subsistence problems, were seldom equal.

While Basehart (1960:132–133) suggests some differences between the Mescalero and Chiricahua regarding band organization, on the points quoted above they seem quite similar. While these highly mobile people felt a strong attachment to their range (Opler 1983b:411), the Chiricahua and Mescalero did not have the same type of attachment to or perception of territory as other Athapaskan groups that were relatively more stationary (such as the Western Apache, Jicarilla, and Navajo; also see Opler 1971:313–315). These distinctions are important because the act of settling-in presupposes a kind of relationship with the land that involves recognition of and respect for or knowledge of territorial boundaries, and changes in behavior as these boundaries are violated (Seymour 2008).

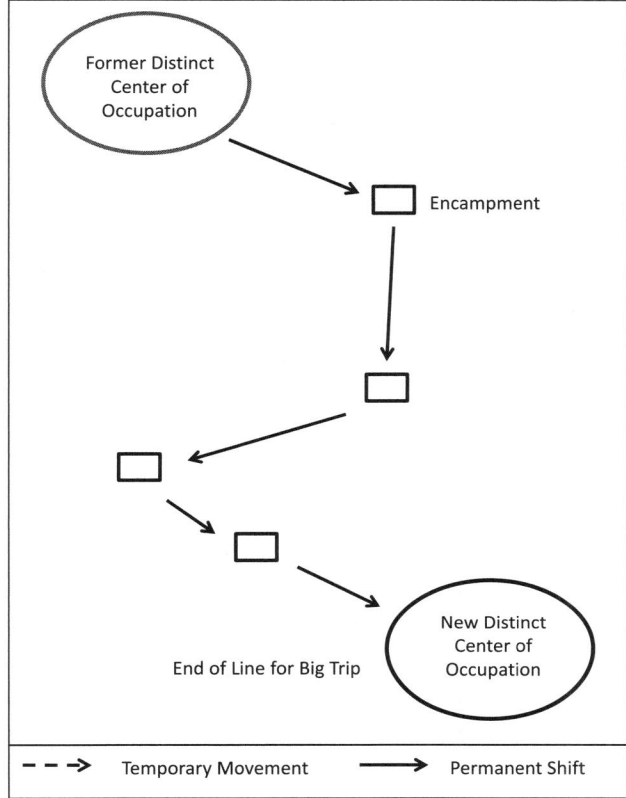

FIGURE 17.4. Gradual or punctuated encompassment of new territory occurs with a shift in the distinct center of occupation, following routes established through short-term, long-range trips into unknown territory. Image by Deni Seymour.

Among these southernmost Apache (Chiricahua and Mescalero), an overlap into another's territory occurred in a variety of ways, including mutual use zones at the fringes of core use areas or favored areas (Christian Naichee interview in Henderson 1957:796). Multiband use of particular territories was common, and people might not know they were in another tribe's territory until they met someone from the other tribe (Christian Naichee interview in Henderson 1957:58). "Groups with different band membership utilized the same geographical areas, sometimes at different seasons, but also at the same time" (Basehart 1959b:105). Yet as Basehart (1959b:88; also see Opler 1941:462) notes, "Although band territories overlapped at the extreme margins, there were distinct centers of occupation for each band which were not confused by informants."[1] As discussed below, however, these "distinct centers of occupation" shifted over time, and such shifts are what mark the migration into new areas (Figure 17.4), rather than just the use of or temporary expansion into a new area.

Overlap between Chiricahua and Western Apache band areas also occurred and was relevant to the shifting of band use areas and to longer-term migration patterns. While "there were frequent exchanges of visits between the two groups, and intermarriage was common," with groups even raiding together (Basehart 1959b:89), land-claims work documented friction between the Chiricahua and others (Western Apache and Navajo) who were perceived as having infringed on Chiricahua territory (Basehart 1959b:89–90; Eugene Chihuahua interview in Henderson 1957:57, 71, 101–102). Similarly, as Goodwin (1969 [1942]:9) noted, Western Apache groups "had recognized territorial limits, and any intrusion into the land of another group was only temporary," although these boundaries were more defined than they were for the Chiricahua and Mescalero. Extension and protraction occurred during periods of resource shortages or when key resource areas were removed from consideration by the actions of neighbors. Once familiar, these new zones of use accessed through extension or short-term expansion became potential springboards for subsequent longer-term movement and a shifting of the centers of occupation.

Another way this overlap between bands and tribes occurred is through the use of travel corridors through another's territory. Well-documented travel routes passed through the Boot Heel of New Mexico and along the San Pedro River in Arizona (Basehart 1960:Map 5; Brinckerhoff 1967:6; Goodwin 1969; Schroeder 1974a:45, 1974b:37), where more northern groups (Mimbreño, Warm Springs, and Western Apache) moved through the southern portion of Chiricahua territory (Basehart 1959a, 1959b; Goodwin 1969). In fact, loci of Western Apache pottery identified along the San Pedro River provide evidence of their historically documented presence (Seymour 2011c). This travel occurred both during raids, which in the late 1700s went as far south as Durango (Thomas 1941:6) Guadalajara, and Mexico City (Simmons 1991:57), and during relocation for winter, when groups in the late 1800s (such as the Warms Springs Apache) moved south as far as Sinaloa (Ball 1970; Basehart 1959a:64). Many sources suggest that the Apache thrust into Sonora and Chihuahua (actually the southern portions of these states) occurred shortly after the Pueblo Revolt of 1680 (e.g., Hastings 1961:336; Schroeder 1952:141); these raids were not such a substantial and consistent problem until the mid-1700s, especially after the Pima Revolt of 1751 (Dobyns 1976:23; Stern and Jackson 1988:471; Winter 1973:72; also see Seymour 2011a). At the terminus of these travel corridors, additional (short-term, task-specific, or seasonal) residential sites were established in or adjacent to the territories of still other non-Apache groups. After the raid or after the winter, these Apacheans then retracted to their northern homelands, zones perceived by them to be the source of their heritage, intimately known, and relatively safe from intruders (see Figure 17.3). By withdrawing to their homelands, they maintained a connection to their past and a link with their route southward.

On the other hand, knowledge of the character of these southern latitudes provided an inventory of alternative residential places or potential centers of occupation for future habitation if a group decided to stay rather than return north at the end of a season or event (see Figure 17.4). This easily accounts for the presence in Mexico's Sierra Madre of the Nednhi (Netdahe, Nednai) band of Chiricahua, which became established there as the result of an extended and

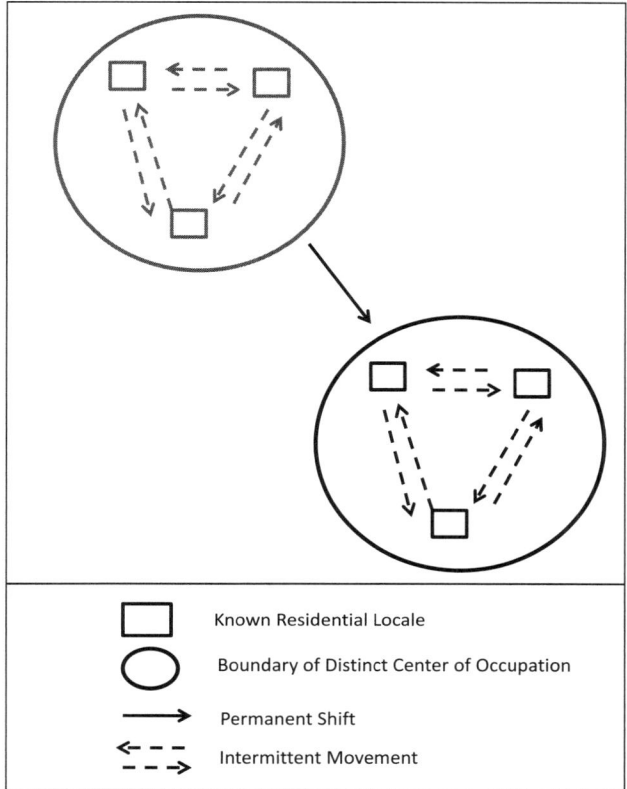

FIGURE 17.5. Alternate favored locales are used serially or as needed within the new distinct center of occupation. Image by Deni Seymour.

slow-paced familiarity with and then shift in residential emphasis south into Mexico (also see Basehart 1959a:33). This fundamental change in geographic focus (e.g., migration through mobility practices) is indicated by the group's routine withdrawal to this new safety zone south of the international border late in Chiricahua Apache history rather than to the north above the Gila River, as was the practice previously (see Figures 17.2 and 17.4). In late Chiricahua Apache history, this southern zone became the location from which they raided to the north or visited American-based reservations.

Migration through Mobility

The additional step in the migration process described above may be what distinguishes the Apachean form of migration from that practiced by more stationary groups. As Apacheans expanded into new territories, they did so initially for a limited purpose or time and then retracted into their recognized territorial zone, or distinct center of occupation. Over time, the distant target zone might be encompassed into their territory as groups shifted geographically to favor the new region, leaving the old one behind or revising their emphasis so that the original homeland became the secondary use zone (Figure 17.5). The intervening zone between old and new distinct centers of occupation would not necessarily continue to be occupied, especially after the shift was complete.

Knowledge of these new areas was not necessarily provided by scouts, as Anthony (1990:902–903) suggests. Rather, knowledge of a supply font, such as a raiding target, might be obtained from a non-Apache source, justifying a foray into the new terrain. Moreover, a social group as a whole was often involved in the move, following viable routes that produced suitable resources, whether raided, gathered, or hunted (see Figures 17.3 and 17.4).

It is true, however, that men would raid while women and children remained in safe base encampments (e.g., Basehart 1959b:102; Betzinez and Nye 1959: 49, 113; Maud Geronimo interview in Henderson 1957:625; Mary Botella interview in Henderson 1957:850; Sam Kenoi interview in Henderson 1957:561), so in many circumstances these raiding events would provide the first knowledge of new areas. Movement between seasonally appropriate places, however, was not a single mass movement of subgroups or bands as a whole, but rather involved "travel by small groups of allied families, often attached to a popular leader" (Basehart 1959b:102). Chiricahua (and Mescalero) occupational patterns consisted of the occasional coalescence of small groups of allied families into larger groupings in preparation for raids, ceremonies, or communal subsistence pursuits, and then a subsequent division into smaller groupings (e.g., Basehart 1959b:103), sometimes in different combinations of families than when the groups first arrived.

The frictional effects of distance Anthony (1990) describes are most applicable to more stationary groups laden with the burdens and benefits of highly focused food and technology niches. This friction is reduced when a group moves as a way of life, following routes that on a daily basis must provide for necessities: "We harvested food as we went" (Ball 1970:19); they went to Mexico in the fall, "living off the land as they went, killing game, harvesting fruit, and giving thanks to Ussen for the good things He had given" (Ball 1970:45). Southward movement would occur as an everyday process rather than a decisive event as groups followed game herds and the seasonal and geographic availability of plant resources (Basehart 1960, 1971, 1974; Opler 1974). Their movement was established by adherence to a lifestyle that favored resource knowledge over landscape knowledge (e.g., Kelly 2003; Seymour 2008). Moreover, for "big trips," the groups would follow a set route, year after year, following landmarks such as mountains and springs (Sam Chino interview in Henderson 1957:765–766) and using zones that were familiar. Use of high-elevation environments that shared attributes between regions would have mitigated the effects of differences that might otherwise be pronounced as groups moved south into new geographic areas (see Kelly 2003; Nelson 1986; also see Magne, this volume). As Kelly (2003:49) suggests, linear mountain chains or their foothills and other major topographic features may provide the easiest terrain to navigate and relate to other known places (and were also least favored by other groups). This preference may explain a Chiricahua Apache traditional story that relates their migration south along the forested flanks of the Rocky Mountains, "between the treeless heights and the treeless plains" (Cole 1981, 1988)—a pattern that seems to have continued as they moved south into Mexico along the Sierra Madre. This is consistent with data from Colorado as well (see Brunswig, this volume; Gilmore and Larmore, this volume). Gradually, through repeated temporary visits to an area or through expansion, new areas would be encompassed. Groups would use an area briefly and intermittently, and then, when "pressed kind of hard [by enemies], they would know where to go to [for refuge], because [they had] been there before" (Wheeler Tsnoltos interview in Henderson 1957:498). Pressure from neighboring groups is a fundamental factor affecting this process. Eventual saturation of an area would come only after primary and preferred residential sites ("distinct centers of occupation") were shifted south and tilted toward a new safety zone.

This conceptualization is similar to that envisioned by Perry (1991:9) of a population expanding into "a variety of niches at the margins of its range, with the result that in the process of adaptation to the situations they encounter, local contingents alter to produce variants of the former parent population." As Basehart (1959b:99–100) notes:

> One of the most significant conditioning factors [facilitating the Chiricahua pattern of environmental exploitation] was the availability of a wide range of territory, without which the pattern was likely to break down. The hunting, gathering, raiding mode of life placed a premium on mobility—individual and group flexibility was essential if available resources were to be exploited effectively.... Given sufficient territory and mobility... it was possible to locate a more productive area, and move rapidly to take advantage of its resources.

As part of a mobile strategy, movement was an ongoing process, and a place would not be occupied if there were not suitable adaptive mechanisms by which to exploit it.

Neighbors: Recruitment and Borrowing

The frictional effects of neighboring groups were instrumental in the historic period, suggesting that the nature of intergroup interaction was another primary factor in the direction and pace of movement. Some of the groups—both those left behind and those that moved southward—interacted amiably and routinely intermixed with neighboring groups. At other times interaction involved recruitment in aggressive ways, bring members of different groups together. Chiricahua informants sometimes mention that they originated from the south (e.g., Sam Kenoi in Henderson 1957:583). In such cases, links to Yaqui or Tarahumara are indicated (also see Cole 1988:7); these people were adopted into the tribe, becoming Apache but recalling their roots in these other geographic areas (also see discussion in Magne, this volume, and Carmichael and Farrer, this volume). In such cases, the Apacheans "knew the people whose land they crossed" (Ball 1970:45), and contact with these people might occur many years before any permanent shift in the distinct centers of occupation. Goodwin (1969:611) mentions O'odham clans among the Western Apache, and Bourke (1890:114) notes the absorption of certain Sobaipuri among the Aravaipa Apache (also see Forbes 1966:341; Schroeder 1952:153). These examples document the widespread occurrence of this process of indigenous acculturation and the frequency with which "others" were incorporated into Apache culture by various means of recruitment. Genetic studies (Malhi et al. 2008; Malhi, this volume), as well as oral historic and ethnographic data (see Seymour 2009b; also see Brugge, this volume), also document this process, in which Southwestern populations were incorporated into Apachean groups as individuals and as family groups or lineages (Malhi, this volume). Flexible social boundaries would help bridge geographic boundaries, allowing Apachean groups to incorporate and adapt to local knowledge (Seymour 2008). Southwestern Athapaskan groups are known for their proclivity to borrow from neighbors, incorporating new technologies into their cultural inventory (Kluckhohn and Leighton 1962). At the same time, these southern groups followed their northern cousins (e.g., Borden 1952) in mimicking a low level of investment in traditional technology, a practice that is consistent with borrowing and with raiding and the resulting routine and wholesale replacement of inventory: "The troops followed them into the sierra and unexpectedly found an abandoned ranchería whose inhabitants had all fled to the mountain peaks.... In the ranchería they had left behind all their possessions, tanned hides, and the remains of some horses they had just killed" (Naylor and Polzer 1986:640).

Neighbors: Friction

Of course, in many other instances, intergroup relations were not amicable. The pressure exerted by Americans in the nineteenth century is probably an appropriate analogy for similar influences along the southward route. Centered at the western edge of Apachean advancement, the American presence in southern Arizona was eventually able to shift the Chiricahua Apache migration track back to the east (still west of the Rio Grande) and south (as the Sobaipuri-O'odham had before them), out of heavily occupied areas and down the spine of the Sierra Madre. Detours forced by such powerful adversaries would involve a complex series of events, including (a) an initial period of becoming familiar, (b) a record of alternately amicable and hostile contact, (c) pressure at the common boundaries and mutual-use zones, (d) extension of some activities by each group into the territories dominated and claimed by the other, which in the case of raiding would usually be viewed as a contestation of boundaries, (e) a shifting of boundaries, and then (f) a readjustment or a slow-motion pinball-like repulsion of one group by the other (e.g., Sobaipuri-O'odham movement out of portions of the San Pedro; Western Apache shift of residential sites south of the Gila River; Chiricahua Apache movement to the east and south). These moves are discussed further below.

Defining Parameters

Before we proceed to a discussion of boundaries and movements, it is useful to clarify a few parameters relating to this discussion. Although still widely and implicitly practiced among archaeologists, the direct historical approach can be detrimental in research on the ancestral Apache. A resurgence of the direct historical approach comes with the popularity of community-focused studies that incorporate ethnographic data and oral interviews with little critical analysis that might expose discontinuities between past and present or variations between subgroups and factions. This proclivity is reinforced by some researchers' failure to actively consider archaeology-specific method and theory when attempting to address these particularly difficult issues. Nevertheless, lifeways changed so dramatically and frequently throughout the historic period that even historic documentary data must be seriated and checked with archaeological data if we wish to evaluate its applicability through time. Assessing which lifeways and organizational features remain intact is a necessary part of the process of using textual, oral, and ethnographic data.

Similarly, and often to the detriment of understanding, scholarly and popular perceptions of the Apache in the American Southwest derive largely from the Western Apache and Navajo. There are a number of reasons for this, including continued confusion in classing the Chiricahua with the Western Apache. As Marion Opler (1935:702) appropriately noted some years ago: "The latter term should be reserved strictly for the Apache groups now stationed upon the San Carlos and White Mountain reservations in Arizona (White Mountain or Coyotero Apache, Tonto Apache, San Carlos Apache, and Cibecue Apache)." The eastern Apache (Jicarilla, Lipan, and Plains Apache) versus western Apache (Navajo, Western Apache, Chiricahua, and Mescalero) distinction for the Southern Athapaskans is based on initial linguistic divisions suggested by Hoijer (1938) and continues to confuse discussions owing to its unfortunate use in relation to other aspects of life.[2]

Many other factors have led to the inaccurate use of Western Apache analogies for Chiricahua lifeways and hence, inappropriately, expectations for a convergence of material and spatial evidence between these groups. The most important is that the Western Apache (White Mountain or Coyotero Apache, Tonto Apache, San Carlos Apache, and Cibecue) have been studied the most intensively, both ethnographically and archaeologically. Because they were *relatively more sedentary* and because of their interaction with ancestral Puebloans (e.g., Opler 1983a:380), they accumulated a more diverse and divergent material culture set than their more mobile neighbors to the south and east. Consequently, their habitation sites are often easier to detect archaeologically than those of their more mobile neighbors.

As Marion Opler (1935:702) noted, the Western Apache are very different from the southernmost Apache, with Chiricahua and Mescalero being most similar. Most of what is known about the Apache, however, comes from studies of the Western Apache. We must therefore apply these conceptualizations when appropriate and refer to other sources when they are available. Fortunately, archaeology allows us to distinguish between many of the applicable and inapplicable attributes. When these documentary sources are combined with archaeological data, a somewhat different picture emerges regarding Apache land use, one that has relevance to migration among people who practice a mobile way of life. Specifically, we can profitably examine seventeenth- through nineteenth-century Chiricahua and Western Apache movements and boundaries in southeastern Arizona and conceptions of space and landscape to illustrate points made above regarding migration and movements. These can in turn be used to devise and evaluate models for migration of mobile populations in the terminal prehistoric and early historic periods.

Land Claims and Attachment to Place

The distribution of Southwestern Apachean groups was established during the land-claims work of the 1940s and 1950s under the Indian Claims Commission Act (although most culture distribution maps vary considerably). A pattern of land use was mapped out on paper for purposes of compensating defendant tribes for their losses owing to the colonial enterprise. As Basehart (1959b:83) notes, "It is important to emphasize that a map based on information secured from present-day Chiricahua underestimates the territory actually utilized by the historic peoples of the region.... But this certainly does not depict the full exploitation range of the /tcihene/, which was unknown to the modern, highly acculturated informants of this group." Significantly, the legal theory employed during this land-claims process required the establishment of exclusive use areas, in direct contrast to the realities of Apachean land-use practices.

Despite this and other cautionary statements, the patterns established during the land-claims work have been treated as if they embody considerable time depth and are representative of long-held "traditional homelands." For example, the Western Apache claim Mount Graham in the Pinaleño Mountains as their sacred mountain (Brandt 1996; Spoerl 2001, 2002a, 2002b; Welch 1997; Ferguson and Colwell-Chanthaphonh 2006), and given that the "tribe" level of organization (as a political unit among the Chiricahua and other Apaches) had a definite and exclusive territory (Basehart 1959a:5; Opler 1933:4), the claim by the Western Apache to this mountain would exclude this zone from Chiricahua territory. Yet my research and that of others (Forbes 1966:337; Wilson 1991) indicate that this mountain range initially fell within a territory used by both the Chiricahua tribe and the non-Apache Jocome, consistent with earlier tribal movements that are discussed below. There are also important Chiricahua places named in this mountain range and other mountains situated in this western portion of Chiricahua territory (Basehart 1959b:71–72, 77), providing evidence of early Chiricahua use of this zone. These temporally relevant data establish a basis for understanding changes in and the gradual eastward and southward movement of Chiricahua territorial boundaries through time and of their replacement, through a southern movement, by the Western Apache.

As was alluded to, one reason researchers operate with this conceptualization of enduring and distinct tribal boundaries is because the land-claims work fixed these otherwise elusive groups in space in a complex legal setting of tribal claims versus Justice Department claims. These culture area or tribal territorial boundaries, while somewhat useful for the land-claims efforts, are detrimental when one is attempting to characterize mobile Apachean groups. The way these boundaries changed through time can be informative, however, about the shifting nature of Apachean use zones and migration.

Another reason we are led to believe in the inviolability of these homeland boundaries is because of the way we have come to understand Western Apache attachment to the land. Basso (1996) has eloquently indicated that Western Apache historical events and identity are linked to places on the landscape. "What matters most to [the Western] Apaches is *where* events occurred, not when, and what they serve to reveal about the development and character of Apache social life" (Basso 1996:31; emphasis in original). Western Apache place names convey cultural meaning of place and derive from the historical experience of those places. In this way, many places are distinctly relevant to the local group.

Yet a commensurate and expected implication of this is that as Apache peoples are separated from certain sectors of the land, they tend to forget these links, once important places become less important and are replaced by new ones (also see Underhill 1956:19). This is apparent in the Chiricahua land-claims documents, in which fundamental changes in lifestyle and landscape-use patterns during a person's lifetime resulted in a more restricted geographic knowledge and in an absence of knowledge. Especially illuminating cases are contained in the land-claims materials in which geographic and landscape knowledge became more restricted among the Chiricahua owing to the danger of being shot if they ventured too far from Warm Springs (Tom Duffy interview in Henderson 1957:121) or to the cessation of raiding and warfare that had previously brought people much farther afield than in the early twentieth century (Sam Chino interview in Henderson 1957:198).

Although stories believed to be many generations old were told of more geographically dispersed places to the west and south and of more encompassing land-use practices, these were usually outside the individual's personal knowledge. Some of these places had names, but by then they usually were without an on-the-ground referent (Christian Naichee interview in Henderson 1957:136). These reflect contracting and shifting land-use patterns through the generations as altered subsistence pursuits and relations with neighbors changed the geographic focus of family and local groups and of bands as a whole. Those portions of the landscape that were no longer part of the lived landscape (e.g., Thomas 2001:173) fell away from memory. Under such circumstances, ancestral stories may take on entirely new meanings as they are adjusted to the new realities of life.

People who remain within specific geographic boundaries establish vital symbolic links to a particular locale (see Cribb 1991:21; Seymour 2008, 2010a), but this conceptualization need not assume a stationary attachment to and prolonged presence in a territory. In a synchronic sense, emphasis on place names—and their links to history and identity—does not capture or adequately account for changes brought by social, political, and environmental factors, especially those brought by colonialism. Places are named and may be thick with history and relevance through time, providing guidance as people move from place to place and navigate through life. But places that have names are often those that are not favored, returned to, or even within a group's normal zones of use (e.g., Jastrzembski 1995:189). Named places, such as those used as residential sites, may be abandoned to the ages because of proximity of enemies, depletion of resources, factionalism, death of residents, or occupation by another band or tribe (Opler 1983b:411).

Especially pertinent in this regard is the fact that many Chiricahua land-claims documents cite no specific memory of the Dragoon Mountains (or other ranges to the west; Eugene Chihuahua in Henderson 1957:245), which, as discussed below, was a favorite and documented range, occupied by the famous Chiricahua Apache leader Cochise and where numerous encampments have been identified. Thus current understandings of traditional homelands and ranges and the flexibility with which they were used is marred by a rigidly fixed modern notion of territorial stability, tribal unity, and sacredness of specific places in bounded and static territories anchored immemorially in time.

Notably, it is not tribal identity that is fixed by places on the landscape but rather local group identity. This critically important distinction between tribe and local group is made apparent by land-claims documents and ethnographies that clarify that it is the local group that occupies certain areas and gives and derives meaning from selected places. Local groups are those that congregate around a place. Families and often friends and acquaintances cluster or go together (Mary Botella in Henderson 1957:856; Sam Chino in Henderson 1957: 703; Seymour and Henderson 2010), moving between a select number of favored places. While there was considerable fluidity of local groups (Opler 1941:7; Henderson 1958:87), the basis for unity in these family alliances that compose the local group was their "mutual orientation to a favored spot and economic raiding cooperation" (Henderson 1958:6; Seymour and Henderson 2010). In these desirable locations, camps may be clustered or not, depending on the terrain, resource density, time of year, purpose for the gathering, and need for defense (Seymour and Henderson 2010).

These places took on special meanings for specific local groups and were given names by them. As discussed below, when these local groups moved away, the memory and significance of these places became lost, while new places were elevated in importance. Thus noteworthy attributes of the landscape allow participants to distinguish with "rich descriptive imagery" places of importance that are given "handsomely drafted names—bold, visual, evocative" (see Basso 1996:23; Seymour 2008:133). Yet the durability of these memories is dependent on continued connection to those places or to the transfer of similar concepts to new named places. This has important implications for conceptualizing migration.[3]

An essential distinction between the Western Apache and the southernmost bands (Mescalero and Chiricahua) is that the latter identified themselves by what leader they followed rather than by or in addition to the places they lived. This association is an expected attribute of highly mobile people. As Basehart (1960:117) notes for the Mescalero:

> Although people living in the vicinity of any of the place-names...could be referred to as the "People of Such-and-Such Place," usually they were not so called. Even if the named place was a favorite camping spot, others would be more likely to designate the group by reference to the leader. Indeed, leaders so overshadowed places in the Mescalero scheme of things that only persistent inquiry revealed the possibility of place-name usage. Named places are fixed and permanent; perhaps the leader's name is a more appropriate symbol for the flexible social organization of the Mescalero.

This statement about the Mescalero seems pertinent to the Chiricahua as well, as distinct from the relatively more sedentary Western Apache. Basehart's (1959b:87–88) Chiricahua work supports this, as does Opler's (1983b:411; also see Opler 1941:25), notwithstanding the emphasis chosen by the following statement: "the local group was always named after some prominent natural landmark of its range, though it could also be referred to by the name of its leader or 'chief.'...It is loyalty to this local group leader and trust in his wisdom which holds" the local group together (Opler 1941:464), and throughout the literature there are references to the people who follow a specific leader. Local groups (and landmarks) were geographically named (Basehart 1959a:8), but references to local groups were often to qualities of a people or their range, such as "sunset people," "prairie people," or "red paint people," or to a leader (Basehart 1959b:85–87), probably owing to the use of wide territorial ranges that often overlapped with those of other Chiricahua bands and the groups' movement into new areas via big trips or migration. When asked about the names given to local groups, one informant noted that the "name is not important" and that they "just call themselves that because they go there" (Sam Kenoi interview in Henderson 1957:586).

These distinctions are critical for recognizing that while places were named and thus accumulated layers of history and meaning that contributed to the identity of the people, such places did not anchor these people in the sense of fixing them eternally to a place. Being mobile, band members, followers of So-and-So Leader, readily followed leaders to new encampments or to new territories through big trips, if they chose to do so, or initiated movements independent of the leaders' participation or approval (Basehart 1960:122). Members were not attached to places the way people are who modify their terrain and build on their landscape, such as stationary farmers or farming Apache groups. Thus people moved in small groups, and occasionally circumstances warranted a big trip or cumulative short moves resulted a long-distance move.

Use of and Forgetting of the Dragoons and Pinaleño Mountains

The history of use and memory regarding the westernmost sectors of Apache territory during the historic period illustrates these points and sets the foundation for understanding historic movements. Review of documentary data indicates that several geographic adjustments had relevance to the final land-claims boundaries established in the 1950s. The eastern shift of Chiricahua bands, along with a southern movement of a Western Apache band, accounts for the south-dipping boundaries of the Western Apache shown by Goodwin (1969 [1942]:4, Map 1). His final maps illustrate Western Apache territory plunging far down along the San Pedro, while earlier documentary data suggest that this was Chiricahua or Gileño Apache territory (as well as Sobaipuri-O'odham, along the rivers). Opler (1941:1) appropriately qualifies the illustrated territorial boundaries from the land-claims efforts, noting that they are difficult to define accurately and that those conveyed pertain specifically to this late period.[4]

Despite numerous historic references to use of the westernmost mountains (Dragoons, Pinaleños, Santa Ritas, Huachucas), a lapse in memory and specific knowledge is apparent among many Chiricahua land-claims interviewees in the 1950s. This deficiency probably relates to historical events that led to the use of more eastern and southern portions of their range. Specifically, the Dragoon Mountains are not mentioned in the land-claims materials collected by Henderson (1957), so they are also absent from Basehart's work, other than minor place names that are mentioned. The Pinaleños or Mount Graham was mentioned by one informant (Wheeler Tsnoltos interview in Henderson 1957:496–498; Basehart 1959b:72) as a place of refuge, which is consistent with earlier historical accounts of ancestral Chiricahua being chased to this area by Spaniards. By the later historic period, the Pinaleño Mountains fell within the boundary of Western Apache territory after a period of co-use with the Chiricahua. For example, in 1866 Captain Dunkelberger encountered a Western Apache ranchería in the Pinaleño Mountains (Sweeney 1992:35). In 1871 Western Apache groups occupied Aravaipa Canyon during efforts toward establishing peace related to Camp Grant, some groups having originated from north of the Gila (Goodwin 1929–1939c). In 1873 Coyotero Apaches were present in the Dragoon Mountains following a raid in the Patagonia area (Sweeney 1991:386). These seem to suggest a southward movement of the Western Apache during the nineteenth century;

this inference is consistent with the opinions of others (Forbes 1966:337; Wilson 1991) and with archaeological evidence.

These territorial adjustments seem to have been reflected in the final land-claims boundaries established in the 1950s. The focus of interviews on more eastern-centered Chiricahua bands and their territories, movements, and memories accounts for why the western edge of Chiricahua territory is truncated and why Goodwin outlined such southern-reaching boundaries for the Western Apache. His final maps illustrate Western Apache territory dipping far down along the San Pedro, while earlier documentary data suggest that this was Chiricahua territory and, more specifically, an area used by both the Apache and the Jano and Jocome.

It is clear that the specific Chiricahua interviewed in the 1950s were not likely to have used the Dragoons and other westernmost ranges. One reason is that many of these interviewees descended from different local groups, so their ancestors frequented different preferred areas. For example, land-claim records indicate rather clearly that each group that followed a leader used preferred areas, occupying a couple of large sites (winter versus summer) and many small ones. (There were also likely super-sized sites where multiple bands came together.) The band territories overlapped to some degree, but by and large they focused on different areas and used different sets of preferred residential locations. The descendants of those who had used the westernmost mountains were not interviewed.

Another reason for this is that the ancestors in question had changed territories in the 1870s and 1880s owing to increasingly effective American military pressure. Dwindling numbers of free Apache also resulted in changes in alliances between Apache leaders and reconfigurations of local groups. For example, Cochise's son, Naichae, often camped with Geronimo, and both were pursued south of the international border, which was in Nednhi territory. Notably, Cochise's descendants had realigned themselves with Geronimo and used a different territory. This illustrates that memory is connected to active use of places by specific local groups and quickly falls away when those places are no longer used. It is therefore not surprising that encampments in the Dragoons are not mentioned and that the lower (northern) San Pedro and its bordering mountains were claimed by and included in the Western Apache territorial boundaries. It is significant, however, that these ranges have specific names known to the Chiricahua (e.g., Basehart 1959b:72).

THE SOBAIPURI-O'ODHAM FACTOR

Surrounding indigenous groups, specifically the Sobaipuri-O'odham, are another important element in this history of events relating to Apache band distributions. In the mid-1700s, Apache raids intensified on Sonoran ranches, missions, and mining camps, and represented a substantial change in this regard in central Sonora. Historians have suggested that this increase in Apache depredations was related to the abandonment of the San Pedro by the Sobaipuri, citing the Rudo Ensayo, which stated that the river was abandoned by the Sobaipuri by 1762 (Pradeau and Rasmussen 1980:73–74). This widely cited event was said to have opened a new corridor of raiding to the south (Dobyns 1976:23; Stern and Jackson 1988:471).

The problem with this conventionally held wisdom is that seldom-used documents from the 1780s indicate that the Sobaipuri remained in residence or returned to occupy the upper San Pedro, outlasting the 1775–1780 occupancy of the presidio of Santa Cruz de Terrenate (Seymour 2010b, 2011a; also see Rocha y Figueroa 1780a, 1780b, 1784). What does seem to have occurred is that the lower (northern) San Pedro had been abandoned by the Sobaipuri and consequently the Western Apache moved south into territory previously dominated by that northern Sobaipuri political entity, while a small contingent from the southern Sobaipuri faction remained within or returned to claim its traditional homeland. Wilson's (1991, 1992) historical work suggests this northern area south of the Gila River is first mentioned as under Western Apache control in 1814, and this would be consistent with the retraction of Sobaipuri south and west.

It may be at this time that the Chiricahua Apache also began moving east and south, out of the Pinaleños and adjacent mountains. The Dragoons and mountains south of Benson remained within Chiricahua Apache territory, but they were shared by Western Apache as the latter intensified raiding in the southern portions of Arizona and into Mexico. Raiding by Western Apache through this corridor continued, even after Cochise's Chokonen Chiricahua band made peace with the Americans in 1872 and after the Camp Grant Affair at Aravaipa Creek, involving the killing of more than a hundred Western Apache in 1871. Soon thereafter, some Chiricahua were occupying the Sierra Madre rather than simply raiding into northern Mexico. By the 1800s, Nednhi Chiricahua were spending time in the Sierra Madre, and by the late 1800s, this was known as Juh's hideout and became a common refuge for Geronimo after breakouts from the reservation.

If this reading of documentary history is correct, the southward movement began as raiding expeditions, which were soon followed by long-distance winter visits (big trips); then key ranges in Mexico were occupied, substituting for the now-obsolete northern safety zones north of and along the Gila River. As Basehart (1959b:100) notes, raiding required assessments of its productivity as well as "flexibility in dealing with defensive and punitive measures on the part of the enemy. Retreat strongholds were necessary features of a group's territory...[because]...raiding was an integral part of the Chiricahua way of life."

THE JANO AND JOCOME FACTOR

Early maps show Jano and Jocome in what later was solely Chiricahua territory. Sauer (1934:75), Forbes (1957, 1959, 1960), and Basehart (1959a:14–17) have suggested that Jano and Jocome were Athapaskan-speaking groups, but other researchers disagree (Naylor 1970, 1981; Seymour 2002, 2009a, 2011b). Numerous equally relevant examples from the documentary record can be cited that contradict the evidence used by Sauer, Forbes, and Basehart in their argument for an Athapaskan affiliation of these groups. For example, these same groups were able to converse, raid, and co-reside with Uto-Aztecan-speakers (Sobaipuri) as well as with the Athapaskan-speaking Apache (Seymour 2002). The documentary record suggests that the Jano and Jocome were ultimately absorbed by surrounding groups, including the Tigua and Piro of El Paso, the Sobaipuri of southern Arizona, and the various Apacheans who occupied the region as a whole. Thus the ability to communicate with others does not seem to have been a determining attribute of linguistic origin or a sign of ethnicity in this multilingual world (Seymour 2002).

Archaeological distributions of distinctive material culture complexes suggest that the Jano and Jocome were non-Athapaskan groups and represent one of the two distinct cultural complexes documented throughout the area occupied by historically referenced Athapaskan and non-Athapaskan mobile groups (Seymour 2002, 2004, 2009a, 2011b). The archaeological record supports the documentary record, which notes that these non-Apache groups sometimes co-resided with the Apache: some sites have been found with both Athapaskan and these non-Athapaskan materials on them. The clustering and spatial distribution of materials on larger sites, including but not limited to the Cerro Rojo site (FB 9609, LA 37188), suggest contemporaneous co-occupation of groups representing the Cerro Rojo and Canutillo complexes (Athapaskan and non-Athapaskan assemblages, respectively; Seymour 2002, 2004, 2009a). This is consistent with the documentary record, which mentions cohabitation and discusses such encampments as places of refuge for missionized Indians during uprisings from riverside mission settlements (Forbes 1960; Gerald 1974; Hendricks and Timmons 1998; Naylor and Polzer 1986:641, 644, 645, 647–648; Seymour 2002). As noted below, these larger sites where people coalesced were used for short periods and for specific purposes and then the groups dispersed.

Historic maps show the distribution of Jano, Jocome, Manso, and Suma in areas that were later occupied singly by various Chiricahua and Mescalero bands. Co-use of the area is indicated during the period of the first historic observations, but gradually these non-Athapaskan mobile groups (Jano and Jocome) faded and the Chiricahua and Mescalero Apache became the dominant users in these areas. The Jano and Jocome may be the mobile groups mentioned in traditional Chiricahua accounts in such statements as "The people encountered and fought another hunting people and drove them south before the Chokonen" (Cole 1981:12). Because Apache traditional stories often frame history in terms of cultural practices or are embedded in the timelessness of a distant era for didactic purposes, the timing of such events is lost, except as may be recoverable through archaeology.

Whether or not these specific groups are being referenced, the account just cited conveys a process that likely occurred more than once during the movement south. Unless empty niches were characteristic of the route(s) south, the migrants would have met resistance in some instances, while in others the ancestral Apache would have displaced existing populations. Some of the latter would have moved aside, still others were likely incorporated into ancestral Apache society, while others incorporated Apache into their own culture. In some circumstances the interaction changed the ancestral populations so substantially that they vary from the original proto-Athapaskan Subarctic pattern, much as has been inferred for the Kiowa-Apache. John (1989:77–79, 136–137n79) provides a description of a non-Athapaskan mortuary practice among an Apachean group at Janos Presidio that according to Griffen and Dobyns is suggestive of the incorporation of others (Janos, Jocomes, or Sumas) and adoption of their cultural practices. All these processes were likely at work. The final displacement of the Apache in the American period probably characterizes earlier processes as well, in which ancestral Athapaskans met with more persistently powerful groups and moved along their southern migration track.

Changing Historical Distributions and Implications for Long-Distance Migration

Using the documentary record in a matrix of archaeological data, I envision a scenario very similar to the one laid out a half century ago by Forbes (1966:337):

> At the beginning of the European contact period, in the 1600's, the territory of the Western Apaches lay somewhat to the north... and probably did not extend to the south of the Gila River. The region to the south of the Gila was occupied in the 1600's by the Sobaipuris, a Piman [O'odham] group (in the San Pedro River Valley) and by the Jocomes... to the east of the Sobaipuris. After the early 1700's the Jocomes were absorbed by the Western or Chiricahua Apaches and in 1762–63 the Sobaipuris retreated to the Santa Cruz Valley and their territory was occupied by the San Carlos division of the Western Apache and by Chiricahuas.[5]

These movements—inferred from the fragmentary but informative documentary record—are modeled in Figure 17.6 a–d. Key events are (a) the movement of the Sobaipuri out of the lower San Pedro, (b) the southward movement below the Gila River of the Western Apache, (c) the absorption of the non-Apache mobile groups into the Chiricahua, and (d) the eastern and southern movement of Chiricahua Apache. These adjustments demonstrate a southerly movement, an expansion and contraction, a west-to-east shift, and finally a southern extension into Mexico for a subset of group members as the end result of a big trip. (The figures do not show the Spanish, Mexican, or American occupational boundaries.)

Adding to this complex interplay were
 a. the *establecimientos de paz* (peace establishments) at various presidios,

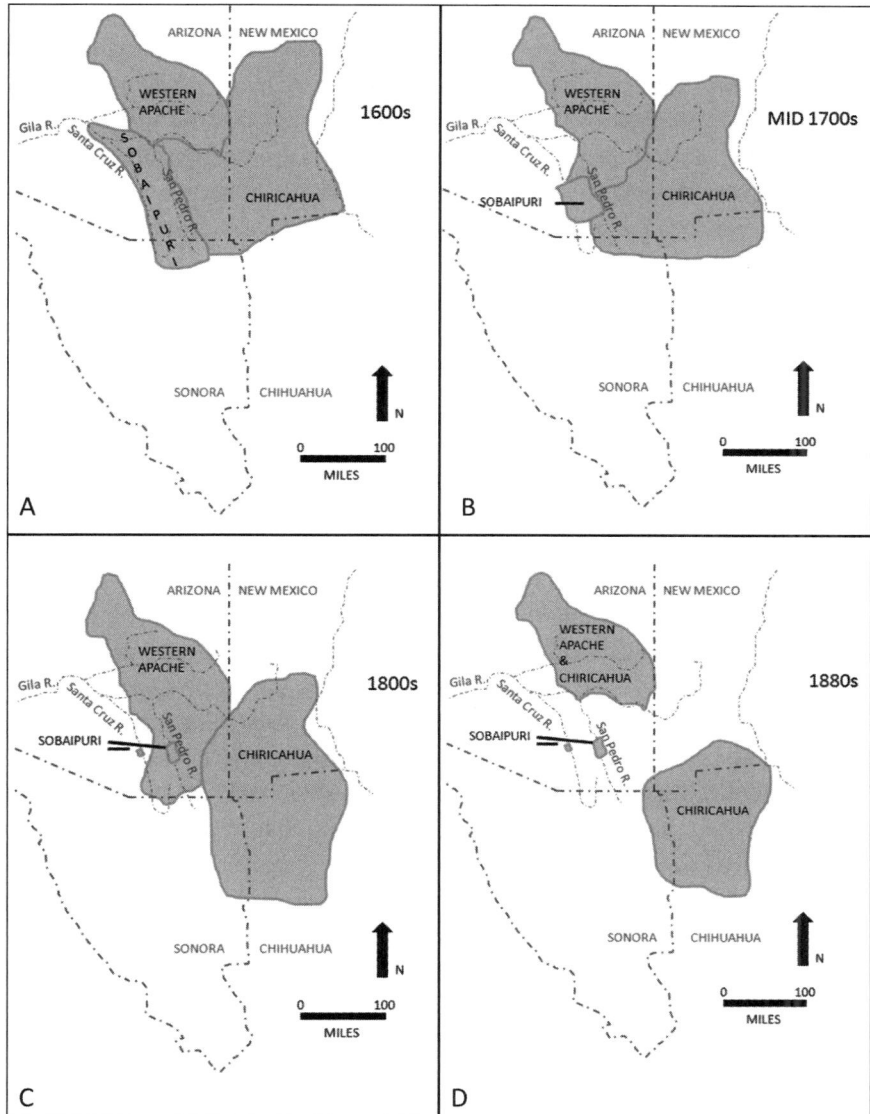

FIGURE 17.6. (a) Model of historic Chiricahua movements, 1600s; (b) Model of historic Chiricahua movements, mid-1700s; (c) Model of historic Chiricahua movements, 1800s; (d) Model of historic Chiricahua movements, 1880s. Image by Deni Seymour.

which drew Chiricahua and other Apachean populations south and ultimately invigorated their ranks (Griffen 1988:64, 267–268; 1991),

b. an increase and greater density of raiding targets in Sonora and Chihuahua as the century closed,

c. pressure from the four allied tribes (Comanche, Ute, Jicarilla, and Navajo), which, as Spanish allies, drove the Chiricahua southward in the late 1700s and early 1800s (Feather 1959; Reeve 1960), and

d. movement of settlements of other groups, such as the Navajo, into the Apachean heartland along the Gila River and its tributaries (Correll 1979).

These movements over many centuries may be an appropriate model for Athapaskan movements southward in general. A useful analogue is provided as the Chiricahua gradually shifted into new areas, with use areas adjusting to pressures from neighbors and then spilling out into an open (or less contested) niche farther south. This historical series of events provides an illustration of how migration or big trips under such circumstances are not likely to follow a straight line, but rather ebb and flow, contract and expand, speed up and slow down in response to the pressures (push and pull) of neighboring groups. The especially big trip from the Subarctic to the Southwest likely consisted of a series of more distance-restricted big trips on the scale of that which occurred between the Gila homeland and the Sierra Madre when the latter eventually became a new center of occupation for the Chiricahua.

Marked instability and substantial shifts in areas exploited are characteristic of highly mobile people because of their expansionist nature (Cribb 1991: 22) and the almost inevitable encroachment on the territories and resources of surrounding groups. Apaches impinging on and then ultimately taking over the territories of other Apachean and non-Apachean groups may have occurred in a surge-like fashion, with previous users retreating as new ones advanced. The leapfrog model (Anthony 1990:902; Seymour 2008:148) might characterize the longer-distance movements as groups found themselves occupying already familiar terrain many hundreds of miles from the next nearest kindred.

Three centuries of documentation, though sketchy, provides a sense of band movement within a generalized region, with shifting emphasis dependent on a number of social, political, and environmental factors. With movements as complex as a three-dimensional mechanical puzzle, groups pivoted around an established homeland, moving seasonally from those camping together in a "great bunch" or home base (Robert Geronimo and Sam Kenoi interviews in Henderson 1957:664, 589), or what Basehart (1960:60–61, 110) refers to as a "nuclear center," to occupy local-group encampments, while avoiding prolonged intrusion into the partially overlapping realms of adjacent bands and tribes. They moved between favored places, taking big trips to venture into distant regions to raid or establish seasonal camps. In the face of enemy threat, as if fixed to a core mechanism, the Chiricahua initially (within recorded history) withdrew to the mountainous and forest-covered zones above the Gila River, while later safety zones shifted south to the Sierra Madre in modern-day Mexico in response to effective American military pressure, restriction of Apaches to reservations, and increasing American populations north of the border. Residential sites and safety zones changed in response to enemy tactics and distributions, altering the configuration of use and necessitating that native groups adjust to and rotate around one another. Ultimately, the shift was oriented southward, halted only by prevailing political factors and population dynamics in Mexico. Thus, over 300 years, the occupational core or "distinct center of occupation" of the remaining free Apacheans had shifted between 250 and 300 miles south of that first indicated by the Spanish documentary record in the American Southwest, an average of a mile a year.[6] A "great bunch" had taken a big trip or ended up there through gradual movement after establishing familiarity through previous big trips.

CLOSING STATEMENT

These historic distributions provide a model of how the earliest Athapaskans might have migrated, taking on the attributes of surrounding groups as they intermarried and adopted new technologies while settling into a new area. The flexible social boundaries so typical of mobile groups would increase familiarity with conditions in distant territories. Intermarriage and other forms of recruitment would have facilitated moves into previously unoccupied zones.

These historic period examples also show the way various Apachean groups moved around a relatively small region in the southern portion of the American Southwest—within the southernmost extension of their occupational range. This is consistent with Basehart's (1959b:87, 88) suggestion that bands were "rather fluid divisions" and were "not unalterably fixed," and with Perry's (1991:4–5) view of individual alliances and ad hoc affiliations, in which groups "diverged, merged, and separated along different fault lines and converged to form new aggregates." Considerable co-use of areas is indicated by a variety of Athapaskan and non-Athapaskan (Jano, Jocome) groups, with the absorption of some smaller groups (Jano, Jocome) and the hardening of distinctions between others. The end result was a movement choreographed on the basis of the actions of neighbors, who drew or repelled Apachean groups as raiding or trading opportunities arose, as the balance of power changed, or as once-powerful groups adjusted their boundaries. Seen in this way, it is not so difficult to comprehend the elusiveness of these early Athapaskans and the distance between colonized residential sites (some areas skipped over entirely), to visualize the diversity of their material and spatial footprints as they moved south, and to understand how such different material culture signatures might develop at the southernmost end of their migration track.

NOTES

1. These "centers of occupation" may be the equivalent of the Jicarilla Apache conception that "the heart of the world lies here," or in line with their headquarters (Opler 1971:313).
2. *A History of the Southwest: The Land and Its People* is one such modern volume that refers to the Nedhni as Western Apache (Sheridan 1998:41).
3. This apparently was not the case for the Jicarilla and others who remember the "the heart of the world" quite vividly (Opler 1971:313).
4. To begin, it is useful to establish the fact of Chiricahua use of specific mountain ranges in this western area. As Opler (1941:2) noted, the Dragoon Mountains were one of three of the most famous strongholds of Cochise's band (others were in the Chiricahua and Dos Cabezas Mountains). Perhaps the best-documented account of Cochise's use of this range relates to the time when Thomas Jeffords and General

Oliver Otis Howard came in 1872 to negotiate peace. This several-week-long series of events took place along the western side of the Dragoon Mountains, and at least one of these residential sites has been identified, as confirmed by historic photographs (Seymour and Robertson 2008). The American and Mexican militaries left many accounts about encountering Apache or evidence of their recent presence in the Dragoons (Sweeney 1991:239, 265, 280–282, 310–315, 345, 1992:43, 46, 47, 50, 51, 52, 53).

In Spanish times the Dragoons were referred to by many different names, including the Sierra de la Penascola (Thomas 1959:iv), Sierra de Peñascosa (Thomas 1932: 214), Sierra Peñacosa (Schroeder 1974b:25/357), Sierra de Santa Cruz (Polzer and Burrus 1971:313), and perhaps even Sierra de Quiburi (e.g., Caraveo Martínez and Caraveo 2007:83; *quiburi* is an O'odham word that means "many houses" and refers to a Sobaipuri-O'odham settlement on the nearby San Pedro River). Unfortunately, records of encounters between Spanish and Apache in this range are rare and ambiguous. For example, when in September 1695 Captain Juan Fernández de la Fuente and his army crossed these mountains, they did not encounter anyone until they reached the western slopes of the Chiricahuas, where they found Jocomes, Sumas, Janos, and Apaches (Polzer 1971:313–315). Of course, this is not evidence that such groups did not inhabit the Dragoons, only that they were not present or seen at that time. In fact, the crossing and search of this range implies an expectation that Apache and their allies might be found there. One reason to think that these mountains were used by the Apache and their allies during this era is that when a combined force of these groups attacked the Sobaipuri-O'odham settlement of Santa Cruz de Gaybanipitea in 1698, the league distances given in accounts indicate that it was probably to both the Dragoon and the Tombstone Mountains that the aggressors retreated (e.g., Bolton 1948:1:178–181; Karns 1954:97–98). Later, in 1786, Captain Chiquito of the Chiricahua Apache was understood to be from the Dragoons (Sierra Peñascosa; Navarro García 1964:456). I have also documented early Athapaskan sites in this range from the terminal prehistoric period, indicating occupation and use before to European arrival.

The Chiricahua Apache were said to have also inhabited the Chiricahua Mountains, which in the 1600s included the modern-day Chiricahua, Dos Cabezas, and Pinaleño Mountains; to their north were the Santa Teresa Mountains, the eastern part of which was the Sierra de la Florida (Thomas 1959:iii). In 1872 a Chokonen (Chiricahua) ranchería was identified near the Pinaleño Mountains (Sweeney 1992:55). In 1795 Zúñiga searched the Pinaleño Mountains for a well-known Chiricahua chief (Esquigoca) and, while failing to find him, captured several Apache (Thomas 1959: 28). Both Chiricahua and "Gila" Apache were found flanking the Gila River. In the 1600s Apache were tracked fleeing north to and above the Gila River (Naylor and Polzer 1986:651). Their origin in the south suggests that these in all likelihood were ancestral Chiricahua Apache. Apache and other groups were found encamped together in the woods along the Gila River and in the Pinaleño Mountains. These allied tribes were those that tended to live to the south and east of the Gila, suggesting that this was a co-use zone of the ancestral Chiricahua and allied mobile groups. Land-claims interviews reinforce this notion.

5. To avoid confusion, I have omitted Forbes's (1966) reference to the Jocome as Athapaskan, as it is now thought that the Jocome were non-Apachean mobile groups (see Seymour 2009a). Also, it is documented that the first European encounters in the area (the southern Southwest north of the international border) occurred by

1539/1540, if not by 1536. Moreover, I have discussed elsewhere that the Sobaipuri did not abandon the San Pedro in 1762 (Seymour 2011a).

6. It is not known how the introduction of the horse would have altered this rate, though it is possible that the pace increased through time.

References

Anthony, David W.
1990 Migration in Archeology: The Baby and the Bathwater. *American Anthropologist* 92(4):895–914.

Ball, Eve
1970 *In the Days of Victorio: Recollections of a Warm Springs Apache.* Tucson: University of Arizona Press.

Basehart, Harry W.
1959a *Chiricahua Apache Subsistence and Socio-Political Organization, Section II.* A report of the Mescalero-Chiricahua Land Claims Project, Contract No. 290-154. Albuquerque: University of New Mexico.
1959b *Chiricahua Apache Subsistence and Socio-Political Organization, Section I.* A report of the Mescalero-Chiricahua Land Claims Project, Contract No. 290-154. Albuquerque: University of New Mexico.
1960 *Mescalero Apache Subsistence Patterns and Socio-Political Organization: Sections I and II: A Report of the Mescalero-Chiricahua Land Claims Project.* Albuquerque: University of New Mexico.
1971 Mescalero Apache Band Organization and Leadership. In *Apachean Culture History and Ethnology*, edited by Keith H. Basso and Morris E. Opler, pp. 35–51. Anthropological Papers of the University of Arizona No. 21. Tucson: University of Arizona Press.
1974 *Mescalero Apache Subsistence Patterns and Socio-Political Organization.* New York: Garland.

Basso, Keith H.
1996 *Wisdom Sits in Places: Landscape and Language among the Western Apache.* Albuquerque: University of New Mexico Press.

Bernbeck, Reinhard
2008 An Archaeology of Multisited Communities. In *The Archaeology of Mobility: Old and New World Nomadism*, edited by Hans Barnard and Willeke Wendrich, pp. 45–77. Los Angeles: Cotsen Institute of Archaeology, University of California.

Betzinez, Jason, and Wilbur Sturtevant Nye
1959 *I Fought with Geronimo.* Lincoln: University of Nebraska Press.

Bolton, Herbert E.
1948 *Kino's Historical Memoir of Pimería Alta.* 2 vols. Berkeley: University of California Press.

Borden, Charles
1952 Results of Archaeological Investigations in Central British Columbia. *Anthropology in British Columbia* 3:31–43.

Bourke, John G.
1890 Notes upon the Gentile Organization of the Apaches of Arizona. *Journal of American Folklore* 3(9):111–126.

Brandt, Elizabeth A.
1996 The Fight for Dził Nchaa Si'an, Mt. Graham: Apaches and Astrophysical Development in Arizona. *Cultural Survival Quarterly* 19(4):50–57.

Brinckerhoff, Sidney B.
1967   The Last Years of Spanish Arizona, 1786–1821. *Arizona and the West* 9(1):5–20.
Caraveo Martínez, Alfredo, and Carlos Caraveo
2007   Transcription of a document in El Archivo de Hidalgo del Parral. Transcripts and Other Documents, Special Collections Department, University of Texas, El Paso.
Cole, Donald C.
1981   An Ethnohistory of the Chiricahua Apache Indian Reservation, 1872–1876. Unpublished Ph.D. dissertation, University of New Mexico, Albuquerque.
1988   *The Chiricahua Apache: From War to Reservation, 1846–1876*. Albuquerque: University of New Mexico Press.
Correll, J. Lee
1979   *Through White Men's Eyes: A Contribution to Navajo History; A Chronological Record of the Navaho People from Earliest Times to the Treaty of June 1, 1868, Volume 1*. Window Rock, Arizona: Navajo Heritage Center.
Cribb, Roger L.
1991   *Nomads in Archaeology*. Cambridge: Cambridge University Press.
Dobyns, Henry F.
1976   *Spanish Colonial Tucson: A Demographic History*. Tucson: University of Arizona Press.
Dumond, Don E.
1998   The Archaeology of Migrations: Following the Fainter Footprints. *Arctic Anthropology* 35(2):59–76.
Feather, Adlai
1959   Colonel Don Fernando de la Concha Diary, 1788. *New Mexico Historical Review* 34(4):285–304.
Ferguson T. J., and Chip Colwell-Chanthaphonh
2006   *History Is in the Land: Multivocal Tribal Traditions in Arizona's San Pedro Valley*. Tucson: University of Arizona Press.
Forbes, Jack D.
1957   The Janos, Jocomes, Mansos and Sumas Indians. *New Mexico Historical Review* 32(4):319–334.
1959   Unknown Athapaskans: The Identification of the Jano, Jocome, Jumano, Manso, Suma, and Other Indian Tribes of the Southwest. *Ethnohistory* (6)2:97–159.
1960   *Apache, Navaho, and Spaniard*. Norman: University of Oklahoma Press.
1966   The Early Western Apache, 1300–1700. *Journal of the West* 5(3):336–354.
Gerald, Rex E.
1974   *Aboriginal Use and Occupation by Tiqua, Manso, and Suma Indians*. New York: Garland.
Goodwin, Grenville
1929–1939a   Dwellings of the White Mountain Apache. Manuscript 17, Goodwin Papers, 1929–1939. Arizona State Museum Archives, University of Arizona, Tucson.
1929–1939b   Miscellaneous Notes. Manuscript 17, Goodwin Papers, 1929–1939. Arizona State Museum Archives, University of Arizona, Tucson.
1929–1939c   Interview with bi ja gush kai ye. Manuscript 17, Box 3, Folder 34, Goodwin Papers, 1929–1939. Arizona State Museum Archives, University of Arizona, Tucson.
1969   [1942] *The Social Organization of the Western Apache*. Tucson: University of Arizona Press.

Goodwin, Grenville, and Keith H. Basso
1971   *Western Apache Raiding and Warfare*. Tucson: University of Arizona Press.
Griffen, William B.
1988   *Utmost Good Faith: Patterns of Apache-Mexican Hostilities in Northern Chihuahua Border Warfare, 1821–1848*. Albuquerque: University of New Mexico Press.
1991   The Chiricahua Apache Population Resident at the Janos Presidio, 1792 to 1858. *Journal of the Southwest* 33(2):151–199.
1998   *Apaches at War and Peace: The Janos Presidio, 1750–1858*. Norman: University of Oklahoma Press. Originally published by University of New Mexico Press, 1988.
Hastings, James Rodney
1961   People of Reason and Others: The Colonization of Sonora to 1767. *Arizona and the West* 3(4):321–340.
Henderson, Martha L.
1990   Settlement Patterns on the Mescalero Apache Reservation since 1883. *Geographical Review* 80(3):226–238.
Henderson, Richard N.
1957   Field notes of Mescalero-Chiricahua Land Claims interviews with various Chiricahua tribal members. Papers in possession of Deni Seymour.
1958   An Historical and Ethnographic Study of Problems in Chiricahua Apache Territory, Social Groupings, and Ecology. Draft Master's thesis, Department of Anthropology, University of New Mexico, Albuquerque.
Hendricks, Rick, and W. H. Timmons
1998   *San Elizario: Spanish Presidio to Texas County Seat*. El Paso: Texas Western Press.
Hoijer, Harry
1938   The Southern Athapaskan Languages. *American Anthropologist* 40(1):75–87.
Jastrzembski, Joseph C.
1995   Treacherous Towns in Mexico: Chiricahua Apache Personal Narratives of "Horrors." *Western Folklore* 54(2):169–196.
John, Elizabeth A. H. (editor)
1989   *Views from the Apache Frontier: Report on the Northern Provinces of New Spain*, by José Cortés. Translated by John Wheat. Norman: University of Oklahoma Press.
Karns, Harry J.
1954   *Luz de Tierra Incognita*. Tucson: Arizona Silhouettes.
Kelly, Robert L.
1983   Hunter-Gatherer Mobility Strategies. *Journal of Anthropological Research* 39(3):277–306.
1992   Mobility/Sedentism: Concepts, Archaeological Measures, and Effects. *Annual Review of Anthropology* 21:43–66.
2003   Colonization of New Land by Hunter-Gatherers: Expectations and Implications Based on Ethnographic Data. In *Colonization of Unfamiliar Landscapes: The Archaeology of Adaptation*, edited by Marcy Rockman and James Steele, pp. 44–58. New York: Routledge.
Kluckhohn, Clyde, and Dorothea Leighton
1962   *The Navajo*. Natural History Library. Garden City, New York: Anchor Books, Doubleday.
Malhi, Ripan Singh, Angelica Gonzales-Oliver, Kari Britt Schroeder, Brian M. Kemp, Jonathan A. Greenberg, Solomon Z. Dobrowski, David Glenn Smith, Andres Resendez, Tatiana Karafet, Michael Hammer, Stephen Zegura, and Tatiana Brovko
2008   Distribution of Y Chromosomes among Native North Americans: A Study of

Athapaskan Population History. *American Journal of Physical Anthropology* 137(4):412–424.

Navarro García, Luis

1964 *Don José de Gálvez y la Comandancia General de las Provincias Internas del Norte de Nueva España*. Escuela de Estudios Hispanoamericanos No. 148. Seville: Consejo Superior de Investigaciones Científicas.

Naylor, Thomas H.

1970 The Extinct Suma of Northern Chihuahua: Their Origin, Cultural Identity, and Disappearance. Class paper on file at the Arizona State Museum, Tucson.

1981 Athapaskans They Weren't: The Suma Rebels Executed at Casas Grandes in 1685. In *The Protohistoric Period in the North American Southwest, AD 1450–1700*, pp. 275–281. Anthropological Research Papers No. 24. Tempe: Arizona State University.

Naylor, Thomas H., and Charles W. Polzer, S.J.

1986 *The Presidio and Militia on the Northern Frontier of New Spain, 1570–1700*. Tucson: University of Arizona Press.

Nelson, Richard K.

1986 *Hunters of the Northern Forest*. Chicago: University of Chicago Press.

Opler, Marion E.

1935 A Note on the Cultural Affiliations of Northern Mexican Nomads. *American Anthropologist* 37(4, Pt. 1):702–706.

Opler, Morris E.

1933 An Analysis of Mescalero and Chiricahua Apache Social Organization in the Light of Their Systems of Relationship. Unpublished Ph.D. dissertation, University of Chicago, Chicago.

1941 *An Apache Life-Way: The Economic, Social, and Religious Institutions of the Chiricahua Indians*. Chicago: University of Chicago Press. Reprinted. Lincoln: University of Nebraska Press, 1996.

1971 Jicarilla Apache Territory, Economy, and Society in 1850. *Southwestern Journal of Anthropology* 27(4):309–329.

1974 *Lipan and Mescalero Apache in Texas*. Apache Indians X. New York: Garland.

1983a The Apachean Culture Pattern and Its Origins. In *Southwest*, edited by Alfonso Ortiz, pp. 368–392. Handbook of North American Indians, Vol. 10, William C. Sturtevant, general editor. Washington, D.C.: Smithsonian Institution.

1983b Chiricahua Apache. In *Southwest*, edited by Alfonso Ortiz, pp. 401–418. Handbook of North American Indians, Vol. 10, William C. Sturtevant, general editor. Washington, D.C.: Smithsonian Institution.

Perry, Richard J.

1991 *Western Apache Heritage: People of the Mountain Corridor*. Austin: University of Texas Press.

Polzer, Charles W., and Ernest J. Burrus

1971 *Kino's Biography of Francisco Javier Saeta, S.J.* Sources and Studies for the History of the Americas Vol. 9. Rome: Jesuit Historical Institute.

Pradeau, Alberto Francisco, and Robert R. Rasmussen

1980 *Rudo Ensayo: A Description of Sonora and Arizona in 1764*, by Juan Nentvig, S.J. Tucson: University of Arizona Press.

Reeve, Frank D.

1960 Navajo-Spanish Diplomacy, 1770–1790. *New Mexico Historical Review* 35(3): 200–235.

Rocha y Figueroa, Gerónimo de la
1780a Mapa de la frontera de Sonora para el establecimiento de la linea de presidios. Microfilm, Reel 55 of 105. Woodbridge, Connecticut, 2003. Manuscript No. Add. 17661 A, British Library, London.
1780b Diario de los reconocimientos hechos en la frontera de la provincia de Sonora en consecuencia de la superior orden del 19 de abril del presente año del señor comandante general de las Provincias Internas de Nueva España...por el teniente de infantería e ingeniero extraordinario de los reales ejércitos Don Gerónimo de la Rocha y Figueroa. (Diary of the facts made in the frontier of the Sonoran province under the orders of the general commander of the Provincias Internas of New Spain...by the engineer of the royal armies Gerónimo de la Rocha y Figueroa. Dated April 19th of 1780.) Houghton Library, Harvard University.
1784 Mapa del terreno que ha de vatir la expedición que deve executarse contra los Apaches Gileños, March 18, 1784. AGI location: Gobierno, Audiencia de Guadalajara, 103-5-4. Huntington Library filing location: Karpinski Collection, Box 15, #552.

Sauer, Carl
1934 *The Distribution of Aboriginal Tribes and Languages in Northwestern Mexico.* Berkeley: University of California Press.

Schroeder, Albert H.
1952 Documentary Evidence Pertaining to the Early Historic Period of Southern Arizona. *New Mexico Historical Review* 27(2):137–167.
1974a A Study of the Apache Indians, Part IV: The Mogollon, Copper Mine, Mimbres, Warm Spring, and Chiricahua Apaches. In *Apache Indians*, edited by David Horr, pp. 1–189 (renumbered 1–219). American Indian Ethnohistory: Indians of the Southwest. New York: Garland.
1974b A Study of the Apache Indians, Part V-A: "Tonto" and Western Apaches. In *Apache Indians*, edited by David Horr, pp. 1–50 (renumbered 327–451). American Indian Ethnohistory: Indians of the Southwest. New York: Garland.

Seymour, Deni J.
2002 *Conquest and Concealment: After the El Paso Phase on Fort Bliss; An Archaeological Study of the Manso, Suma, and Early Apache.* With contributions by Mark E. Harlan and David V. Hill. Lone Mountain Report 525/528. Conservation Division, Directorate of the Environment, United States Army Air Defense, Artillery Center, Fort Bliss, Texas. Qualified researchers may obtain this document by contacting martha.yduarte@us.army.mil.
2004 A Ranchería in the Gran Apachería: Evidence of Intercultural Interaction at the Cerro Rojo Site. *Plains Anthropologist* 49(190):153–192.
2008 Despoblado or Athapaskan Heartland: A Methodological Perspective on Ancestral Apache Landscape Use in the Safford Area. In *Crossroads of the Southwest: Culture, Ethnicity, and Migration in Arizona's Safford Basin*, edited by David E. Purcell, pp. 121–162. New York: Cambridge Scholars Press.
2009a The Canutillo Complex: Evidence of Protohistoric Mobile Occupants in the Southern Southwest. *Kiva* 74(4):421–446.
2009b Comments on Genetic Data Relating to Athapaskan Migrations: Implications of the Malhi et al. Study for the Apache and Navajo. *American Journal of Physical Anthropology* 139(3):281–283.
2010a Cycles of Renewal, Transportable Assets: Aspects of Ancestral Apache Housing. *Plains Anthropologist* 55(214):133–152.

2010b　The Waning Days of Quiburi: Sobaipuri-O'odham Occupation on the San Pedro River in 1780. Under review, *New Mexico Historical Review.*

2011a　1762 on the San Pedro: Reevaluating Sobaipuri-O'odham Abandonment and New Apache Raiding Corridors. *Journal of Arizona History* 52(2):169–188.

2011b　*Where the Earth and Sky Are Sewn Together: Sobaipuri-O'odham Contexts of Contact and Colonialism.* Salt Lake City: University of Utah Press.

2011c　*Data Recovery on Sobaipuri and Spanish Colonial Sites along the Middle and Lower San Pedro River on Bureau of Land Management Lands.* Report submitted to Bureau of Land Management, Tucson, Arizona.

Seymour, Deni J., and George Robertson
2008　A Pledge of Peace: Evidence of the Cochise-Howard Treaty Campsite. *Historical Archaeology* 42(4):154–179.

Sheridan, Thomas E.
1998　*A History of the Southwest: The Land and Its People.* Tucson: Southwest Parks and Monuments.

Simmons, Marc
1991　*Coronado's Land: Essays on Daily Life in Colonial New Mexico.* Albuquerque: University of New Mexico Press.

Spoerl, Patricia M.
2001　Mt. Graham (*Dził Nchaa Si'an*): A Western Apache Traditional Cultural Property, or Determination of Eligibility for the National Register of Historic Places, Mt. Graham (*Dził Nchaa Si'an*). Safford Ranger District, Coronado National Forest, Arizona. Final report (2001-05-079), on file at Coronado National Forest Supervisor's Office, Tucson.

2002a　Supplement to the Determination of Eligibility for Mt. Graham Traditional Cultural Property—Boundary Considerations. Report 2002-05-63, on file at Coronado National Forest Supervisor's Office, Tucson.

2002b　Determination of Eligibility Criteria for the NRHP and Mt. Graham as a Traditional Cultural Property. Report 2002-05-67, on file at Coronado National Forest Supervisor's Office, Tucson.

Stern, Peter, and Robert Jackson
1988　Vagabundaje and Settlement Patterns in Colonial Northern Sonora. *The Americas* 44(4):461–481.

Sweeney, Edwin R.
1991　*Cochise: Chiricahua Apache Chief.* Norman: University of Oklahoma Press.
1992　*Merejildo Grijalva: Apache Captive, Army Scout.* Southwestern Studies Series No. 96. El Paso: Texas Western Press.

Thomas, Alfred Barnaby
1932　*Forgotten Frontiers: A Study of the Spanish Indian Policy of Don Juan Bautista de Anza, Governor of New Mexico, 1777–1787.* Norman: University of Oklahoma Press.

1941　*Teodoro de Croix and the Northern Frontier of New Spain, 1776–1783.* Norman: University of Oklahoma Press.

1959　*The Chiricahua Apache, 1695–1876.* University of New Mexico, Mescalero-Chiricahua Land Claims Project, Contract Research #290-154. New York: Garland.

Thomas, Julian
2001　Archaeologies of Place and Landscape. In *Archaeological Theory Today*, edited by Ian Hodder, pp. 165–186. Cambridge: Polity Press.

Underhill, Ruth M.
1956   *The Navajos*. Norman: University of Oklahoma Press.

Varien, Mark D.
1999   *Sedentism and Mobility in a Social Landscape: Mesa Verde and Beyond*. Tucson: University of Arizona Press.

Welch, John R.
1997   White Eyes' Lies and the Battle for Dził Nchaa Si'an. *American Indian Quarterly* 21(1):75–109.

Wilson, John P.
1991   *Apache Use of the Pinaleno Mountain Range*. Report No. 55. Tucson, Arizona: Coronado National Forest.

1992   *Apache Use of the Pinaleno Mountain Range II*. Report No. 57. Tucson, Arizona: Coronado National Forest.

Winter, Joseph
1973   Cultural Modifications of the Gila Pima, AD 1697–AD 1846. *Ethnohistory* 20(1): 67–77.

CHAPTER 18

Issues in Athapaskan Prehistory

Roy L. Carlson

A particularly neat instance of the ofttimes conclusive nature of linguistic evidence for the determination of the direction of movement of population is that of the distribution of the Athabascan languages... it would seem that the historical centre of gravity was in the north rather than in either of the other two regions and that the occupation of these latter was due to a southern movement of Athabascan-speaking tribes.

| Edward Sapir (1916: 456–457) |

As in most studies in which the historical relationships between archaeological and ethnohistoric cultures are explored, the linguistic relationships are given precedence in structuring the research questions. The chapters in this book are no exception. The close relationship of the three groups of Athapaskan languages—Northern, Southern (Apachean), and Pacific—to each other and the movement of peoples speaking languages of the latter two groups from north to south are non-issues. Beyond that, almost everything about Athapaskans is or can be an issue: identification of ethnicity in the archaeological record, timing and cause of population movements including starting points and migration routes, size of the migrating population, time and degree of acculturation or incorporation of foreign elements into the cultural tradition, and the validity of both native oral histories and written Spanish records. The authors of the chapters in this book are sometimes in agreement on these issues and sometimes not. That these issues have not been resolved in spite of the vast accumulation of archaeological knowledge over the past half-century is closely related to the fact that archaeology is not an exact science but a science of probabilities in which conclusions are revised or restated as new data come to light and new analytical techniques are applied to old data. Competing cultural-historical models composed of multiple hypotheses are the rule rather than the exception, and each hypothesis can involve multiple issues. Chapter 15, by Gordon, exemplifies this aspect of archaeological discourse more than the other chapters by being much broader in coverage and attempting to reference all the competing hypotheses relating to Navajo and Apache culture history. Complicating the problem of working out models of this culture history are two technological revolutions that were responsible for changing the archaeological record in terms of ethnic identifiers, settlement patterns, and home territories: the development and spread of the bow and arrow in late prehistory and the introduction and spread of the horse in the early historic period changed the archaeological signatures of these cultures. It is no wonder there are problems in tracing the thread of history through these revolutions as well as through the periodic environmental changes.

Use of the comparative method is implicit throughout this book, but there is little explication of the theoretical principles that underlie this method as it is applied to material objects and their distributions in time and space. The most important of these principles is the principle of similarity: the greater the degree of similarity among objects found in the archaeological record, the greater the probability of a close historic relationship among these objects. This principle can be applied to either single artifact types or clusters of associated artifacts, depending or whether the researcher is interested in the history of a particular artifact type or in the culture or society identifiable by the cluster. It is also necessary to apply the principle of propinquity: the closer the artifact assemblages of similar content are in time and space, the greater the probability of the ethnic congruity of the people who occupied the sites and left the remains. Assemblages that contain the same or similar types of artifacts are considered to belong to the same culture or cultural tradition, providing that they are found in a continuous distribution in time and space and other aspects of the assemblages are not markedly different. A third principle, one articulated by Walde (Chapter 9), is that gradual change in sequent archaeological assemblages in a site or locality is indicative of cultural and ethnic continuity rather than replacement by migrating peoples. These principles and others are relatively easy to apply to the earliest periods of migrations in aboriginal North America when populations were small and somewhat isolated (Carlson 1996). However, in later periods, as populations grew and diverged and different degrees of acculturation took place, the problem of ethnic identification in the archaeological record is more difficult, and this difficulty is apparent in the attempts to find the archaeological evidence of the Athapaskan migration from the Subarctic to the Southwest.

ETHNIC IDENTIFIERS

Seymour (Chapter 17) points out that one reason Athapaskan migration out of Canada remains an unresolved problem is because archaeologists have not known what the migrants' material culture looked like at the time. There is consensus that the ancestors of the speakers of the NaDene language phylum spread into eastern Beringia from Asia during the Late Pleistocene or Early Holocene and subsequently diverged into speakers of Haida, Tlingit, Eyak, and

Athapaskan (although the inclusion of Haida is still debated), and that in late prehistory some of the Athapaskan-speakers spread to the Southwest and diverged into the Apachean and Navajo groups we know today. The research questions then become, What archaeologically identifiable material culture did the migrants bring with them? What persisted and what changed as adaptations to new environments and ethnic and linguistic divergence took place? Numerous ethnic identifiers, ranging from forked-stick hogans and the sinew-backed bow, to contrasting lithic products including various styles of arrowheads, microblades, spurred scrapers, the chitho, and bipointed bifaces with central lugs, to types of moccasins, arrow shaft smoothers, and different kinds of plain and decorated ceramics, have been proposed, as well as clusters of associated artifact types and particular settlement patterns. Unfortunately, none of these artifact types except perhaps microblades has been researched to its fullest extent, as, for example, in the study of snowshoes, in which Davidson (1937) concluded that snowshoes were introduced into North America by the ancestors of the Athapaskans. Snowshoes rarely survive in the archaeological record, however, and research has centered on nonperishable ceramics and lithics, of which microblades are the most fully studied.

Microblade Technology

Microblades are small stone flakes more than twice as long as they are wide, prepared from specialized cores and used as inserts in the sides or ends of wooden or bone points or hafts to form cutting or piercing tools. This technology is very different from the making of bifaces, tools with much the same function. Microblades are the dominant lithic technology in northeast Asia and adjacent Alaska during the Late Pleistocene and Early Holocene (Kuzmin et al. 2007). It was proposed some time ago that microblade technology was brought to northern North America by the ancestors of the NaDene speakers (Borden 1969; Dumond 1969; Carlson 1983), but it is only recently that the temporal and spatial distribution of this technology in western North America and Asia has been brought up-to-date, and this distribution correlates reasonably well with the speakers of Athapaskan and other NaDene languages in the north (Magne and Fedje 2007). Its earliest known occurrence in North America is at the Swan Point site in Alaska at 14,000 cal BP (Holmes 2007). The time-transgressive spread of this technology in western North America has been modeled by Magne and Fedje (2007); it was still used in the late prehistoric period by some Northern Athapaskans in British Columbia, but in the Chipewyan region east of the Rocky Mountains it is found only in Arctic Small Tool tradition sites and not in the later Athapaskan-related Taltheilei sites except in mixed assemblages (Bryan Gordon, personal communication 2011). The demise of microblade technology in some parts of Northern Athapaskan territory may have been part of the replacement of the atlatl and associated bone spear heads armed with inset microblade segments by the bow and arrow.

Interestingly, in the Southwest microblades are reported on the Hopi Mesas, Unshagi (Jemez), and Pecos, where they are attributed to an Athapaskan presence (Dykeman and Roebuck, Chapter 7), and in the El Paso area (Seymour 2003). As an ethnic identifier, microblades may work in some cases, but it must be recognized that this technology is diffusible and that other ethnic groups, such as the Inuit and some non-Athapaskan Northwest Coast groups, also used them. Cores specifically prepared for the detachment of microblades are the most diagnostic part of microblade technology, although some sizes and shapes of raw materials such as quartz crystals and some obsidian nodules lend themselves to microblade production by bipolar percussion without further core preparation. Only bipolar cores are described in the early Navajo Fruitland sites (Torres 2003), and at issue is whether the small blades present there are true microblades since there is no evidence of prepared cores. The question is whether microblades are defined by their form and intended use or by the technology that produced them. If these blades are related to the northern microblade industries, it is probable that they were introduced by Athapaskan migrants from the north, where microblade industries persisted into late prehistory (Magne and Fedje 2007) and the bipolar cores are an adaptation to the size and shape of local raw material.

Projectile Points

The advent of the bow and arrow revolutionized hunting practices throughout the West. Arrow points are present on the Northern Plains at the Sjovold site by 1800 BC and had replaced dart points there completely by 700 BC (Dyck and Morlan 1995). Most arrow points are small and side-notched, and several authors herein consider these points to be ubiquitous, nondiagnostic of ethnicity, and best understood as late-period horizon markers. The issue is whether any of the small side-notched arrow points that occur throughout the western Subarctic, Plateau, Plains, Southwest, and Great Basin after about 2000 BP can be used as ethnic identifiers. These points are consistently found in sites attributed to both Northern and Southern Athapaskans. They are also found in sites attributed to non-Athapaskans. A type of point of this class long thought to identify Athapaskans is the Avonlea point, dating upward from AD 200 and also thought to mark the introduction of the bow and arrow. Walde's (Chapter 9) analysis, using 11 attributes of the points and percentage stratigraphy from the Gull Lake site in southern Saskatchewan on which Tom Kehoe had based his sequence of point types with Avonlea at the bottom, casts considerable doubt on this attribution. Walde's analysis shows gradual change in point attributes through the sequence indicative of cultural and ethnic continuity rather than replacement of one ethnic group by another, which invalidates Kehoe's ethnic attributions unless all components are Athapaskan. Walde's work (Chapter 9) also casts doubt on the utility of the Avonlea, Prairie side-notched, and Plains side-notched point typology other than as a descriptive mechanism. The early Navajo

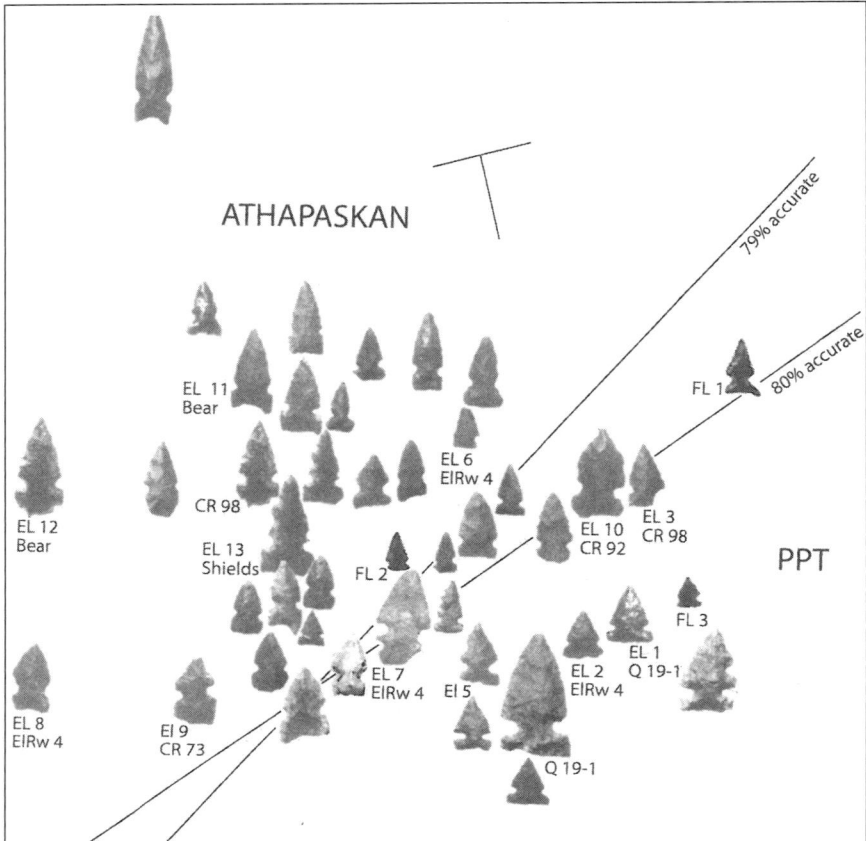

FIGURE 18.1. Multidimensional scaling of Athapaskan and Plateau Pithouse Tradition (Salish) small side-notched points. From "Projectile Points of Central and Northern British Columbia," in *Projectile Point Sequences in Northwestern North America* (2008), reprinted courtesy of authors M. P. R. Magne and R. G. Matson and Archaeology Press.

arrow points illustrated by Torres (2003:Figure 117) look very much like the Athapaskan points from the northern interior of British Columbia (Figure 18.1), as well as like other Plains, Prairie, Plateau, Southwest, and Desert side-notched arrow points. Is there any way to discover consistent similarities and differences indicative of ethnic affiliation between assemblages of these points?

Matson and Magne (2007), Magne (Chapter 16), Magne and Matson (2008, 2010) looked at this problem and, using a number of attributes, successfully differentiated small side-notched points from Northern Athapaskan contexts from points from adjacent Salish contexts using multiple discriminate analysis and multidimensional scaling (see Figure 18.1). The Athapaskan points have elongate blades narrow in proportion to their length, have wider and shallower notches, are generally thick, and sometimes have basal concavities or spurs on the base (Matson and Magne 2007:112). The basal spurred type is found in the high mountains of eastern Colorado in AD 1300–1650 along with Dismal River pottery and is used to infer Athapaskan movement along the Front Range (Gilmore and Larmore, Chapter 3).

Kavik and Klokut small contracting-stem arrow points are also used as ethnic identifiers of Athapaskans in the western Subarctic (Matson and Magne

2007:37, 140, Figure 644; Magne, Chapter 16) but have not been identified in the Plains, Rocky Mountains, or Great Basin, potential routes of Athapaskans moving south. Small side-notched points of the general form that were also used by Northern Athapaskans are found throughout these regions. Small contracting-stem points are found in the Great Basin (Thomas 1985:Figures 55–57) but are much less common than other forms. Until detailed comparisons of assemblages of small side-notched points from the Subarctic, Plains, Plateau, Great Basin, and Southwest are made with the use of selected attributes and complex quantitative techniques, the question of whether such points can be used as ethnic identifiers or only as horizon markers will remain an issue.

Ceramics

Hill (Chapter 10) tackles the problem of determining ethnic identity using pottery types. Pottery is generally taken to be the best ethnic identifier. However, Hill points out that different ethnic groups can and do use the same source of clay, and different techniques such as coil and scrape and paddle and anvil can be responses to the physical properties of different clays rather than indicators of cultural-historical relationships. As part of mobile or semi-mobile groups, potters would come in contact with different settled ceramic-producing cultures and different clay sources and might not produce an ethnically distinct type or might produce more than one type. Ute, Jicarilla, and some Puebloan peoples used the same source of micaceous clay (Hill, Chapter 10). Neither the Northern nor the Pacific Athapaskans made pottery, so it is assumed that the Southern Athapaskans acquired pottery-making techniques from their neighbors either during or after their movement south. The issues are largely when, where, and from whom. Hill points out that migrating groups may derive ceramic technology from many different sedentary groups with which they come in contact. It was only with petrographic and INNA analysis that origins of plainware pots such as those considered to be of local manufacture in Tierra Blanca and Garza sites in Texas were found to be imports from the Pueblos of the Rio Grande (Hill, Chapter 10).

Plainware or utility ware has been thought to have been adopted by the Navajo from late Puebloan Gallina types, from Jemez utility ware (Reiter 1938; Carlson 1965), or from Plains wares. How it compares with types in the Canadian prairies has not to my knowledge been explored. The earliest pottery attributed to Southern Athapaskans in this book is 640 BP (AD 1280–1400) (Brunswig, Chapter 2; Gilmore and Larmore, Chapter 3) in the context of an early western Dismal River occupation in the mountains of eastern Colorado. Is this earliest pottery proto-Athapaskan, just proto-Apache, or seasonal transhumance, or is Dismal River even an Athapaskan occupation?

Lovitt Plain, Lovitt Simple Stamped, and Ocate Micaceous are Dismal River types, with the latter type from southern Dismal River sites resembling Jicarilla and northern Pueblo types. The earliest Navajo pottery is Dinetah gray pock-marked, present at LA 55979 by AD 1541 in the Fruitland locality accompanied by maize but no Puebloan ground-stone industry (Dykeman and Roebuck, Chapter 7). Gilmore and Larmore (Chapter 3) consider Apachean pottery in San Luis to be possibly proto-Dinetah Gray. The La Plata Mine components are considered by the excavators to be Navajo, whereas Curt Schaafsma (2002) considers them more probably Ute on the basis of the pottery, which differs from that in the Chama Valley (which he considers Navajo). Perhaps both became Navajo. Brunswig (Chapter 2) notes the identification of Uncompahgre Brownware as Ute. It seems that only through consideration of other associated aspects of culture can ethnic attribution of plainware be possible.

Painted ware seems to have been made only by the Navajo and not the other Athapaskan-speakers, and while it fits with their more sedentary lifestyle, there are issues concerning its origin and relationships. Gobernador Polychrome is the primary painted type. It was long considered to have become a Navajo product through incorporation of Puebloan refugees from the Rio Grande following the Pueblo Revolts of 1680 and 1692. However, recent research indicates that Gobernador Polychrome is present earlier and was being made to the west of Dinétah in the Fruitland locality by AD 1625, well before the refugee period (Langenfeld 2003; Dykeman and Roebuck, Chapter 7). Reed and Reed (1996) relate Gobernador Polychrome to Hopi wares because of the yellow surface color, and they emphasize the presence of pan-Puebloan design elements. The surface color, however, is the result of the firing process and the clays used, so a slip was not necessary to provide the desired background color for the surface designs, although a partial red slip was sometimes used (Carlson 1965:52). Previous descriptions of Gobernador Polychrome emphasized the banded designs (Carlson 1965:Figures 13, 14) and their close similarities with banded designs on Jemez Black-on-white and the general similarity with Rio Grande types. Since Hopi yellow ware is very rare in early Navajo Fruitland sites (Langenfeld 2003) and in the early Navajo Reservoir District sites (Dittert 1958), Jemez Black-on-white is by far the most common intrusive type, and since Rio Grande types are much more common in these early sites with Gobernador Polychrome than are Western Pueblo types, it seems likely that Jemez Black-on-white and Tewa Polychrome were the primary sources of inspiration for this type, although there is no reason to think that Hopi wares could not have also been involved. The sources were probably Puebloan women who married into the Navajo, although Towner (2003:207) wonders if the Genizaros from Abiquiu could have been responsible. There is still confusion in differentiating Frances Polychrome, Gobernador Polychrome, and Navajo Polychrome and in determining where Frances Polychrome belongs in the sequence (Langenfeld 2003).

Other Ethnic Identifiers

While other individual artifact types such as the Promontory Point moccasins (Brugge, Chapter 6) and the double-bitted bifaces found in both Dismal River and Cerro Rojo (Gilmore and Larmore, Chapter 3; Seymour, Chapter 5) have been proposed as ethnic identifiers, more promising identifiers would be systematic quantitative comparisons of assemblages of associated artifacts. The early western Dismal River compared with the later eastern Dismal River (Gilmore and Larmore, Chapter 3; Brunswig, Chapter 2) compared with the Dinetah phase assemblage from the Fruitland sites (Dykeman 2003) compared with Cerro Rojo would be a good place to start. Kearns (1996:136–137) considers the small side-notched points from northwest New Mexico to be horizon styles and not culturally diagnostic, but he considers these points accompanied by multidirectional microcores, elongated flake knives, small hafted scrapers, gravers, rectangular arrow shaft straighteners, bifacial knives, and comals to be potentially diagnostic of early Navajo. Brunswig (Chapter 2) compares Dismal River assemblages in Colorado's Front Range and foothills with Dismal River assemblages on the eastern border of the High Plains, which are two centuries later. Gordon (Chapter 15) describes several site components he believes could be Athapaskan.

Ives (2011) has revived Julian Steward's (1937) earlier hypothesis that the Promontory Point component in Utah was left by migrating Athapaskans. The types of moccasins and the abundance of chithos are suggestive, and current research may well provide conclusive evidence.

Several authors employ assemblage structure based on coarse and fine stone use, stylistic attributes of flaked stone tools, and residential remains. Seymour (Chapter 5) promotes construction of models of what Apache prehistoric or protohistoric sites and assemblages should look like by selective mining of the ethnohistoric record and constructing matrices and spatial grids of material and spatial correlates. Her method resulted in the identification of the Cerro Rojo complex, dated between AD 1300 and 1850, with various dwelling types, Desert side-notched points, finely retouched bifacial knives, chithos, shaft smoothers, and rare ceramics identified as Apache.

ROUTES, TIMES, AND SIZE OF MIGRATIONS

There is general consensus that the ancestral Athapaskan-speakers arrived in northern North America after the earlier migration of Paleoindians and before the arrival of speakers of Eskimo-Aleut. In the New World, the problem of tracing Athapaskans becomes one of not only migration but divergence. Divergence is a product of migration, geographic separation, adaptation to new environments, and borrowing from neighbors. The Athapaskans were clearly originally adapted to the Subarctic environments of the north. When peoples are adapted to an ecological niche and aware of unfriendly neighbors, why do they move?

The various authors are fairly consistent in their use of the effect of environmental changes as causative in migration. Seymour (Chapter 5) and Magne (Chapter 16) discuss theory and the "push" and "pull" factors in human movement. Any major reduction in the kind and abundance of food staples is potentially a "push" factor in hunter-gatherer migrations. The White River ash fall around AD 800–1000 in the Yukon is cited as such a factor by Magne (Chapter

16). Recent research gives strong support to the idea of changes triggered by volcanic eruptions. DNA analyses by Kuhn et al. (2010) indicate that the caribou herds predating the volcanic ash fall of 1000 BP in the Yukon disappeared and were replaced at some later date by genetically different caribou, possibly from the south. The effect on other wildlife has not been determined, but to hunter-gatherers such as the Northern Athapaskans, the disappearance of caribou alone would have been detrimental to their food supply and causative of a push toward better-endowed regions.

Pull factors are the absence of human enemies and the presence of resources favored by the subsistence system. The abandonment of the Four Corners by the agricultural Puebloans as a result of a long severe drought is cited as a pull factor that brought both Athapaskan hunter-gatherers into that region from the north and east in the late twelfth or early thirteenth century and Numic (Ute, Shoshone) people from the Great Basin. Vacated territory is a strong pull factor as long as the subsistence base is there. Climate changes are cited to take early Dismal River peoples out of the mountains and onto the Plains (Gilmore and Larmore, Chapter 3).

There are issues regarding points of origin of ancestral Southern Athapaskans. Some data indicate (Gordon, Chapter 15) that the Southern Athapaskans are an offshoot of the caribou-hunting Chipewyan of the Subarctic northern tundra and boreal forest margins to the west of Hudson Bay, which is at odds with Matson and Magne (2007:34; Magne, Chapter 2). The latter interpret lexicostatistical data to mean that the Southern Athapaskans split from a still linguistically undifferentiated Carrier-Chipewyan group in the interior Plateau region of southern British Columbia, and thence traveled over the Rocky Mountains in Montana to the Big Horn Basin in the period ca. AD 1000–1200, with the Pacific Athapaskans moving south from the same region at the same time or slightly earlier. The Green River, an oasis in the midst of desolation, is favored as the logical route south through the mountains by several researchers; others propose the eastern fringe of the Rocky Mountains. Rice (Chapter 12), using linguistic comparisons, suggests a single southward migration of a very small ancestral group speaking Tsuut'ina (Sarcee or Sarsi) and/or Dëne Sųłiné (Chipewyan), and gives figures indicating divergence of the Southern Athapaskan–speakers from these ancestors between AD 921 and 1329, and subsequent divergence into the Navajo and Apache ethnic groups at various times between AD 1538 and 1808. This later period is of interest because it is mostly within the period when horses were acquired, which would have speeded up geographic separation and cultural divergence.

Brugge (Chapter 8) offers the most extreme position on Navajo origins, and that is that they originated from the Archaic peoples long resident in the Southwest from a much earlier time. This position echoes that of many Navajo themselves that they originated in Dinétah, the ancestral homeland around the San Juan River in northern Arizona and New Mexico, bounded by the four sacred mountains, and that their ancestors were always there. If the Navajo are identified solely by their biology (see Malhi, Chapter 11) rather than by their language, this model could well be correct. However, documentary evidence indicates that their DNA signature has been formed through considerable intermixture with their neighbors. Spencer (1947:60) analyzed the various versions of the Navajo origin myth that document the incorporation of groups met during the period of wanderings and the formation of new clans; seven of the 41 clans, one from the east and six from the west, formed the original nucleus. This group was later joined by outsiders, some of whom are identified as Apache, Zuni, Paiute, Ute, Spanish-Mexican, and other Puebloans. The mitochrondrial DNA (Malhi, Chapter 11) of the Navajo of today agrees with this traditional account of new clans being formed by alien progenitors, always women. The language spoken by the original clans is unknown, but the origin myths read as if the raconteurs either assumed or knew that the original clans spoke Navajo. One interesting feature of the Athapaskan languages (Rice, Chapter 12) is their profound resistance to the incorporation of linguistic traits from other languages, which would account for a continued dominance of Athapaskan in spite of considerable incorporation of peoples speaking languages belonging to other families.

Analysis of the Navajo and Western Apache genome data leads Mahli (Chapter 11) to infer that it was a small group of Athapaskans who migrated from the Subarctic, and that non-Athapaskans were incorporated after the migration and potentially along the route.

The Mescalero account of their traditional history (Carmichael and Farrer, Chapter 8) indicates that the ancestors were neighbors of the Dogrib and Slave and resided on Great Bear Lake and Slave Lake, which bear the same names in these northern languages as in Mescalero. The neighbors of these two Northern Athapaskan groups are the Chipewyan, whose territory abuts both these lakes, also known by them by these same names (Gordon, Chapter 15).

Acculturation and Divergence

Once the archaeological evidence clearly establishes the Athapaskan presence in the Southwest, the research emphasis changes from origins and migration routes to acculturation and divergence into the known ethnic divisions. The belief in spirit power and its importance for healing is endemic among all Northern Athapaskans, and in this central religious belief the Southern Athapaskans differ from the Pueblos, whose religion centers on fertility and the quest for rain. Linguistic, ethnological, and archaeological evidence all indicate that there have likely been varying degrees of acculturation by the different Southern Athapaskan groups to Puebloan culture and other farming cultures of the Southwest. There is also linguistic evidence (Webster, Chapter 14) of acculturation between some Apache and non-Athapaskan-speakers to the east. If Dismal River represents undifferentiated Athapaskans on the Plains, then it is clear that both Navajo and Apache ancestors made ceramics and grew maize before their expansion into the Southwest. Once lifeways changed as a result of the introduction of the horse, some Apache groups may well have lost these traits. Both ethnology and linguistics (Chapters 6 and 12) indicate greater adoption of Puebloan traits by the Navajo and Western Apache than by the other Apache groups. For example, the myth of ancestral emergence from the underworld that is central to Navajo and Western Apache cosmology goes back in time among the Puebloans to at least early Mimbres at AD 700 (Carlson 2005). Chiricahua and Mescalero consider emergence a "funny notion" (Opler summarized by Luckert 1975:194n, cited in Carmichael and Farrer, Chapter 8).

The refugee acculturation model that Navajo culture was intensely modified by incorporation of Puebloan refugees after the Pueblo Revolt was based on Kidder's (1920) suggestion that the pueblitos of the Gobernador region were built by Puebloan refugees, particularly from Jemez; the idea was later expanded by subsequent researchers. Early chinks in this model came with the tree-ring dating of the pueblitos as too late to initially accommodate Puebloan refugees and dating to the time of the later Ute and Comanche raids (Carlson 1965). Towner (2003) and Dykeman and Roebuck (Chapter 7) reject the model of the acculturation of the Navajo by refugees from the unsuccessful Pueblo Revolt of 1696. Dykeman and Roebuck reject it because of the discovery of plainware and Gobernador Polychrome, including a kiln (and other Navajo traits) in trash associated with a hogan dated ca. AD 1625, along with archaeological evidence that now shows that the Navajo grew corn and made painted pottery well before the Pueblo Revolt (1680) and Reconquest (1692). They also contend that incorporation rather than acculturation better describes the process. Towner (2003:194) rejects the refugee acculturation model on the basis of demography and tree-ring dating of sites. However, cross-dating of ceramics from the Navajo Reservoir sites (Hester 1962), which are undated by tree rings, indicate a time period when refugees from the Pueblo Revolt probably were harbored. While research clearly shows interaction and incorporation of Puebloan traits well before the Pueblo Revolt, it does not invalidate incorporation of additional Puebloan traits as a result of the influx of refugees during and after the revolt; it only extends the period of acculturation/incorporation backward about 150 years. Jemez Black-on-white is by far the most common intrusive decorated pottery type in both the early Navajo Fruitland sites (Langenfeld 2003) and the Navajo Reservoir District (Dittert 1958:20). The painted ware ceramic assemblages of the latter consist mostly of Jemez Black-on-white, Rio Grande glazes, and Gobernador Polychrome, which is an earlier ceramic assemblage than found in post-1700 sites (Carlson 1965). What Dykeman and Roebuck (Chapter 7) have documented is a long period of cultural exchange between the Pueblos and Navajo that does not invalidate a model of more intense cultural borrowing during the refugee period. The incorporation of emergence cosmology and other Puebloan beliefs and practices into the Athapaskan system of shamanic curing to create the distinctly Navajo ideology had to have taken place at some time. There are pictographs (P. Schaafsma 1963) in the Navajo Reservoir sites that indicate incorporation of Puebloan beliefs, and Curt Schaafsma (2002), in a review of Spanish documents of the refugee period, finds 21 Jemez who went to the Navajo and whose return cannot be accounted for. Were they agents of acculturation, joining relatives as part of a long-standing acculturative process? There are considerably more data that bear on this issue, including population estimates and tree-ring dates on pueblitos (see Towner and Johnson 1996; Towner 2003).

Oral Histories

While archaeologists are adept at formulating cultural-historical models based on current knowledge, they are not the only scholars capable of so doing. Literate Indians who have interacted over their lifetimes with archaeologists, linguists, anthropologists, and the published accounts of their history and prehistory are also fully capable of creating logical scenarios incorporating all their knowledge. The fascinating account complete with times of ethnic divergence gleaned from the relatively young Mescalero wise man, Bernard Second, by Carmichael and Farrer (Chapter 8) reads like such an account. The Mescalero Apache have the same names for Great Bear Lake and Slave Lake as do the Northern Athapaskans still living in the Subarctic, and Bernard Second's story supports migration "down the Great Plains along the front ranges of the Rocky Mountains," as Carmichael and Farrer note. How did Bernard Second arrive at the dates of Mescalero separation from the Slave 600 years ago, from the Western Apache 500 years ago, from the Navajo in Yellowstone country at the headwaters of the Green River 400 years ago, from the Sarsi 250 years ago, and the later encounter with the French on the Plains? Was Bernard Second aware of the correspondence in place names of Great Bear Lake and Slave Lake, or was this fact discovered by Carmichael and Farrar? The issue is how traditional is this traditional history. Gordon's epigraph (Chapter 15) suggests that many parts of it have been around for a long time.

The other contributor who relies heavily on oral tradition is Brugge (Chapter 6). As Dykeman and Roebuck (Chapter 7) point out, archaeologists should pay close attention to Navajo traditional history, and I would argue that this attention should perhaps be more for elucidation of the process by which the Navajo came into being than for other specifics. Traditional histories indicate that multiple archaeological complexes are potentially ancestral Navajo. As noted earlier, Spencer (1947) determined that the central theme in the Navajo origin myths is the incorporation of diverse peoples and the technologies such as pottery and basketry they brought with them. The question then becomes, "When is a Navajo?" Issues such as whether the brownware in the La Plata Mine sites north of the San Juan River is Ute or Navajo become impossible to answer. The problem is not in identifying one ancestral Navajo culture, but many.

Conclusion

This book contains both consensus and disagreement among scholars engaged in Athapaskan research. Issues in prehistory are normally not easily resolved; they increase in number and tend to become more complex as the archaeological database enlarges. Numerous authors make casual comparisons of similarities between different components or assemblages, implying some kind of cultural-historical relationship—chithos, dog husband myth, side-notched points, and so on—but do not plot or research the entire distribution of these traits, so their results are interesting but unconvincing. The new culture history requires new techniques of analysis to handle complex enlarged databases, and the chapters in this book point out questions that need to be answered. Ad hoc comparisons may point the way but are unsatisfactory to fully resolve issues. The Human Relations Area Files, a consortium that evolved to facilitate comparisons of ethnographic cultures, is now attempting to do the same thing for archaeology and is currently incorporating cultural sequences from the Southwest (Christiane Cunnar, personal communication 2010). The amount of data now available on North American archaeology needs such a database to facilitate comparisons of artifact attributes, types, assemblages, components, dates, contexts, and cultures so that researchers may make inferences and draw conclusions about relationships. Standardization of attributes is a prime necessity in constructing such a database in order to ensure that tangerines are not confused with navel oranges or crabapples with Red Delicious. With such a database, advanced quantitative techniques can be used to arrive at the probable resolution of issues such as those involved in the determination of Athapaskan migrations and relationships. A time should come when new data decrease the complexities and ambiguities in the interpretation of the archaeological record and increase the probability of conclusive results.

This book marks a milestone in the continuous movement toward synthesis of what has long been called "the Athapaskan question." There is obviously more than one question. Formulation of the problems associated with determination of ethnicity in the archaeological record is a major contribution of this volume. The strengthening of the model of the Chipewyan as ancestral Apache-Navajo (Chapter 15) is a big step forward, as is the evidence from the High Country of Colorado (Chapters 2, 3) that documents the presence of a complex both related to and earlier than the Dismal River complex, long thought to be ancestral Athapaskan. The persuasive arguments (Chapter 5) that the Cerro Rojo complex represents undifferentiated Apacheans in the southern Southwest at a very early date adds a new dimension to both the timing and extent of early Athapaskan penetration of this region, and is supported to some extent by linguistic evidence (Chapter 12). The summary of the recent archaeological work (Chapter 7) indicating that the Navajo were adopting Puebloan traits long before the Pueblo Revolt of 1680 certainly helps clarify Navajo-Pueblo acculturation models. The "Athapaskan question" is actually a continuing saga brought up-to-date with both exciting new data and new ideas presented by the contributors to this book.

REFERENCES

Borden, Charles
1969   Early Population Movements from Asia into Western North America. *Syesis* 2 (1–2):1–13. Victoria, B.C.

Carlson, Roy L.
1965   *Eighteenth Century Navajo Fortresses of the Gobernador District*. Series in Anthropology No. 10. Boulder: University of Colorado.
1983   The Far West. In *Early Man in the New World*, edited by Richard Shutler Jr., pp. 73–96. Beverly Hills, California: Sage.
2005   Mimbres and Zuni: Certainties and Probabilities. *Review of Archaeology* 26(2): 1–9.
1996   Introduction to Early Human Occupation in British Columbia. In *Early Human Occupation in British Columbia*, edited by Roy L. Carlson and Luke Dalla Bona, pp. 3-10. Vancouver, University of British Columbia Press.

Davidson, Daniel S.
1937   *Snowshoes*. Memoirs Vol. 6. Philadelphia: American Philosophical Society.

Dittert, Alfred E., Jr.
1958   *Preliminary Archaeological investigations in the Navajo Project Area of Northwestern New Mexico*. Navajo Project Studies No. 1. Santa Fe: Museum of New Mexico and School of American Research.

Dumond, Don E.
1969   Toward a Prehistory of the Na-Dene, with a General Comment on Population Movements among Nomadic Hunters. *American Anthropologist* 71(5):857–863.

Dyck, Ian, and Richard G. Morlan
1995   *The Sjovold Site: A River Crossing Campsite in the Northern Plains*. Mercury Series, Archaeological Survey of Canada, Paper No. 151. Hull, Ottawa: Canadian Museum of Civilization.

Dykeman Douglas, D.
2003   *The Morris Site 1 Early Navajo Land Use Study: Gobernador Phase Community Development in Northwestern New Mexico*. Navajo Nation Papers in Anthropology No. 39. Window Rock, Arizona: Navajo Nation Archaeology Department.

Hester, James J.
1962   *Early Navajo Migrations and Acculturation in the Southwest*. Museum of New Mexico Papers in Anthropology No. 6. Santa Fe: Museum of New Mexico Press.

Holmes, Charles E.
2007   The East Beringian Tradition and the Transitional Period: New Data from Swan Point. Paper presented at the annual meeting of the Alaska Anthropological Association, Fairbanks.

Ives, John W.
2011   Resolving the Promontory Culture Enigma. Paper presented at the 76th Annual Meeting of the Society for American Archaeology, Sacramento.

Kearns, Timothy M.
1996   Protohistoric and Historic Navajo Lithic Technology. In *The Archaeology of Navajo Origins*, edited by R. H. Towner, pp. 109–145. Salt Lake City: University of Utah Press.

Kehoe, Thomas F.
1973   *The Gull Lake Site: A Prehistoric Bison Drive Site in Southwestern Saskatchewan*. Publications in Anthropology and History No. 1. Milwaukee: Milwaukee Public Museum.

Kidder, Alfred V.
1920 Ruins of the Historic Period in the Upper San Juan Valley, New Mexico. *American Anthropologist* 22(4):322–329.

Kuhn, Tyler, Keri A. McFarlane, Pamela Groves, Arne Ø. Mooers, and Beth Shapiro
2010 Modern and Ancient DNA Reveal Recent Partial Replacement of Caribou in the Southwest Yukon. *Molecular Ecology* 19:1312–1323.

Kuzman, Y. V., S. G. Keates, and Chen Shen (editors)
2007 *Origin and Spread of Microblade Technology in Northern Asia and North America*. Burnaby, British Columbia: Archaeology Press, Simon Fraser University.

Langenfeld, Kristin
2003 Pottery of the Morris Site 1 Early Navajo Land Use Study. In *The Morris Site 1 Early Navajo Land Use Study: Gobernador Phase Community Development in Northwestern New Mexico*, edited by Douglas D. Dykeman, pp. 233–296. Fruitland Data Recoveries Series No. 4, Navajo Nation Papers in Anthropology No. 39. Window Rock, Arizona: Navajo Nation Archaeology Department.

Magne, Martin P. R., and Daryl Fedje
2007 The Spread of Microblade Technology in Northwestern North America. In *Origin and Spread of Microblade Technology in Northern Asia and North America*, edited by Y. V. Kuzmin, S. G. Keates, and Chen Shen, pp. 171–188. Burnaby, British Columbia: Archaeology Press, Simon Fraser University.

Magne, Martin P. R., and R. G. Matson
2008 Projectile Points of Central and Northern British Columbia. In *Projectile Point Sequences in Northwestern North America*, edited by R. L. Carlson, pp. 273–292. Burnaby, British Columbia: Archaeology Press, Simon Fraser University.
2010 Moving On: Expanding Perspectives on Athapaskan Migration. *Canadian Journal of Archaeology* 34(2):212–239.

Matson, R. G., and Martin P. R. Magne
2007 *Athapaskan Migrations: The Archaeology of Eagle Lake, British Columbia*. Tucson: University of Arizona Press.

Reed, L. S., and P. F. Reed
1996 Reexamining Gobernador Polychrome: Toward a New Understanding of the Early Navajo Chronological Sequence in Northwestern New Mexico. In *The Archaeology of Navajo Origins*, edited by R. H. Towner, pp. 83–108. Salt Lake City: University of Utah Press.

Reiter, Paul
1938 *The Jemez Pueblo of Unshagi, New Mexico*. University of New Mexico Bulletin No. 326. Albuquerque: University of New Mexico Press.

Sapir, Edward
1916 *Time Perspective in Aboriginal American Culture: A Study in Method*. Memoir No. 90, Anthropological Series No. 13. Ottawa, Ontario: Canada Department of Mines, Geological Survey.

Schaafsma, Curtis F.
2002 *Apaches de Navajo: Seventeenth-Century Navajos in the Chama Valley of New Mexico*. Salt Lake City: University of Utah Press.

Schaafsma, Polly
1963 *Rock Art in the Navajo Reservoir District*. Papers in Anthropology No. 7. Santa Fe: Museum of New Mexico.

Seymour, Deni J.
2003 *Protohistoric and Early Historic Temporal Resolution*. Lone Mountain Report 560-

003. Conservation Division, Directorate of the Environment, United States Army Air Defense, Artillery Center, Fort Bliss, Texas. Qualified researchers may obtain this document by contacting martha.yduarte@us.army.mil.

Spencer, Katherine
1947 *Reflection of Social Life in the Navajo Origin Myth*. University of New Mexico Publications in Anthropology No. 3. Albuquerque: University of New Mexico Press.

Steward, Julian
1937 *Ancient Caves of the Great Salt Lake Region*. Bulletin No. 116. Washington, D.C.: Bureau of American Ethnology.

Thomas, D. H.
1985 *The Archaeology of Hidden Cave, Nevada*. Anthropological Papers Vol. 61. New York: American Museum of Natural History.

Torres, John A.
2003 Early Navajo Lithic Technology of Dinetah. In *The Morris Site 1 Early Navajo Land Use Study: Gobernador Phase Community Development in Northwestern New Mexico*, edited by Douglas D. Dykeman, pp. 191–232. Fruitland Data Recoveries Series No. 4, Navajo Nation Papers in Anthropology No. 39. Window Rock, Arizona: Navajo Nation Archaeology Department.

Towner, Ronald H.
2003 *Defending the Dinétah: Pueblitos in the Ancestral Navajo Homeland*. Salt Lake City: University of Utah Press.

Towner, Ronald H., and Bryan P. Johnson
1996 *The San Rafael Canyon Survey: Reconstructing Eighteenth Century Navajo Population Dynamics in the Dinetah*. Report No. WCRM(F)087, Project No. 93042. Farmington, New Mexico: Western Cultural Resource Management.

Contributors

David M. Brugge
Retired, National Park Service,
Santa Fe
Independent Researcher
Albuquerque, New Mexico

Robert H. Brunswig
Professor
Department of Anthropology
University of Northern Colorado
Greeley, Colorado

Roy L. Carlson
Professor Emeritus
Department of Archaeology
Simon Fraser University
Burnaby, British Columbia

David L. Carmichael
Associate Professor
Department of Sociology and
Anthropology
University of Texas at El Paso
El Paso, Texas

Willem J. de Reuse
Adjunct Research Professor
Department of Linguistics and
Technical Communication
University of North Texas
Denton, Texas

Douglas D. Dykeman
Archaeologist
Dykeman Roebuck Archaeology
Farmington, New Mexico

Claire R. Farrer
Professor Emerita
California State University
Chico, California

Kevin P. Gilmore
Senior Archaeologist/Principal
Investigator
ERO Resources Corporation
Adjunct Instructor
Department of Anthropology
University of Denver
Denver, Colorado

Bryan C. Gordon
Curator Emeritus
Canadian Museum of Civilization
Gatineau, Quebec

David V. Hill
Adjunct Faculty
Department of Sociology,
Anthropology, and Behavioral
Science
Metropolitan State University of
Denver
Denver, Colorado

David T. Hughes
Associate Professor of Anthropology
Wichita State University
Wichita, Kansas

Sean Larmore
Cultural Resource Manager
ERO Resources Corporation
Durango, Colorado

Martin P. R. Magne
Director
Western and Northern Service Centre
Parks Canada
Calgary, Alberta

Ripan S. Malhi
Associate Professor
Department of Anthropology
University of Illinois at Urbana-Champaign
Urbana, Illinois

Keren Rice
Professor
Department of Linguistics
University of Toronto
Toronto, Ontario

Paul Roebuck
Archaeologist
Dykeman Roebuck Archaeology
Farmington, New Mexico

Deni J. Seymour
Research Associate
University of Arizona
Tucson, Arizona
Adjunct Researcher
University of Colorado Museum of Natural History
Boulder, Colorado

Dale Walde
Associate Professor
Department of Archaeology
University of Calgary
Calgary, Alberta

Anthony K. Webster
Associate Professor
Department of Anthropology
Southern Illinois University
Carbondale, Illinois

Index

abandonment: of eastern Colorado by Upper Republican and Apishapa peoples, 55; of Four Corners region by Puebloans, 331–34, 418

Aberle, David F., 130

acculturation: and acculturation hypothesis for Navajo culture emergence, 152, 171–72; of Southern Athapaskan groups to Puebloan and other Southwestern cultures, 419–21. *See also* borrowing

advancing-front model, of migration, 156, 362, *363*

agriculture. *See* maize

Ahtna (Alaska), 135, 251, 253, 254

Aikens, C. Melvin, 138, 327

Akimel O'odham (Riverine Pima and Sobaípuri), 140

albumin polymorphisms, 244–45

Aleut, 252

Algonquian-speaking peoples, 200, 204, 252

Anderson, Benedict, 157, 162

Antelope Creek phase, 79, 80, 85, 87

Anthony, David W., 38, 63, 64, 369, 370, 378, 386

anthropology: bridges and barriers between subdisciplines of, 4–5; and comparative method, 411; and middle-range theory, 66, 93, 95, 107, 115, 117n4; and theory on cultural identity formation, 9. *See also* ethnography

Apache(s): and ceramics, 42–44, 229, 231–32, 234, 327–28; and comparative wordlist, *307–13*; and cultural continuity with Cerro Rojo complex, 99–107, 108, 336; derivation of name, 187; and emergence of Navajo, 151–52; and group names in Spanish and early Mexican historic documents, 278–80, 282n15; mobility and historic movement and interaction of, 377–401; and raiding in Four Corners region, 333; and Tierra Blanca complex, 85, 86, 87, 119n17, 232–34, 337. *See also* Apachean peoples; Aravaipa Apache; Chiricahua Apache; Jicarilla Apache; Kiowa-Apache; Lipan Apache; Mescalero Apache; Plains Apache; San Carlos Apache; Western Apache; White Mountain Apache

Apachean peoples: and archaeology of Rocky Mountain National Park and Colorado Front Range, 20–32; languages of and personal names in early historic documents, 271–81; linguistic evidence for migration of, 249–67; and proto-Apache sites in Colorado high country, 46–55; and retention of lifeway attributes by descendant populations, 107–8; use of term, 340n1. *See also* Apache(s); Gileño complex; Mimbreño complex

Apache de Quinía, 128, 142n3

Apaches at War and Peace: The Janos Presidio, 1750–1858 (Griffen 1988), 272–73

Apishapa (Colorado), 53, 55, 57–58

Arapaho, 22, 190, 192

Aravaipa Apache, 388

archaeology and archaeological record: and Apachean peoples in eastern High Plains and mountains of Colorado, 20–32; and connections to historically referenced groups, 93–95; and ethnic identifiers, 411–12; and highly mobile groups, 95–98; and incorporation of data from Subarctic and Southwest into interpretation of Athapaskan

migration, 2–3; and multidisciplinary approach, 5; percentage stratigraphy and evidence of Athapaskans in, 198–220; of Tierra Blanca complex, 78–85. *See also* ceramics; dates and dating methods; lithic assemblages; "low visibility archaeology"
Archaic sites, in San Juan Basin, 140
Arctic Small Tool tradition, 320, 412
areal linguistics, discursive approach to, 286–99
Arizona Tewa, 286–87, 294–97, 298
Arroyo del Arenal site (Colorado), *47*, 48, *49*, 50, *51*, 52, 64, 67
"Athabascan Geolinguistic Conservatism Hypothesis," 265
Athabasca River and Lake Athabasca, 187, *188*, 305
Athapaskans, migration of from Subarctic to Southwest: and Cerro Rojo complex, 90–117; DNA evidence of, 241–46; and emergence of Navajo, 124–41; historic Apache movement and interaction as model for, 377–401; incorporation of cultural traits from encounters with Puebloans, 154, 171, 232–35; and Jemez, 155; and Mescalero Apache place names, 182–95; and migration models from perspective of eastern Colorado, 37–67; overview of issues in research on, 1–15, 410–22; percentage stratigraphy and evidence of in archaeological record, 198–220; and taboo against speaking personal names, 273; and Tierra Blanca complex, 59, 85–87, 232–34, 319; and variation in production of ceramics, 225–35. *See also* Apachean peoples; Chipewyans; languages and linguistics; migration; Northern Athapaskans; routes
Attla, Catherine, 293
aurora borealis, 187
Avonlea culture, 21, 39, 199–200, 203–4, 206, 219, 220, 320
Axelrod, Melissa, 260–61

Baca, Sidney, 184
background scatter, 117–18n7
Bairoil site, 325

Ball, Eve, 381, 386, 387
Barrett, Elinore M., 166–67
base camps, 78
Basehart, Harry W., 111, 193, 278, 378, 380, 381, 382, 383, 386, 387, 390, 393, 396, 400, 401
Basso, Keith H., 186, 367, 391
Baugh, Timothy G., *41*
Bear Butte, *189*, 191
Beaton, John M., 369
Beaver people, 126, 127, 136, 367–68
Begay, Meredith, 184
Begay, Richard M., 6, 327
Beier, Chris, 286
Bélanger, Nicolas, 340n4
Bella Coola, 130
Benavides, Fray Alonso de, 155
Benedict, James B., 27, 325
Benjamin, Walter, 162
Besant phase, 203
Bettinger, Robert L., 211
Betzinez, Jason, 381
bifacial knives, and Cerro Rojo complex, *110*, 113
Bighorn Medicine Wheel, *189*, 191, 192
Binford, Lewis, 364, 366
biogeography, and migration, *370*, 371–73
bison, hunting of: and Canadian Plains, 202, 203, 316; and plains-intermountain route for Athapaskan migration, 322–23, 338; and Tierra Blanca complex, 85, 86
Blackburn site (Texas), *80*, 83
Blackfeet, 127
Blackfoot, 204, 319
Black Hills, *189*, 192
Blakeslee, Donald J., 86
Blessingway (Navajo), 167, 168
Blue Bull site (Arizona), *133*
Boas, Franz, 293
Borman-Pikes Peak vessel, 29, *47*, 61
borrowing: Athapaskan languages and resistance to, 257, 265, 266; and recruitment form neighboring groups, 387–88. *See also* acculturation; ceramics
boundaries, land-claims process and tribal, 390–94
Bourke, John G., 388

bow-and-arrow technology: and Chipewyan peoples, 316; and culture history of Canadian Plains, 203; and Mescalero Apache, 186. *See also* projectile points
Bowern, Claire, 264
Boyd, Douglas K., 78, 85, 86, 87
Breternitz, David A., 326
Breuninger, Evelyn, 282n10, 282n16
Brink, Jack W., 212
Broken Jaw site (Texas), *80*
Brugge, David M., 3, 7, 9, 13, 15n2, 42, 61, 66, 152, 155, 158, 161, 167, 168, 198, 314, 338, 418, 421
Brunswig, Robert H., 13, 30, *41*, 335, 373, 416
Buckles, William G., 319
buffalo-horned images, in rock art, 101, *102, 103*
Bunbury, Joan, 318
Burgh, Robert E., 326

Caddo culture, 192, 232
Campbell, Lyle, 251, 255, 267n3
Canadian Plains: approaches to culture change on, 203–6; and Gull Lake cultural components, 206–20; overview of culture history of, 201–3. *See also* Chipewyans
Canadian Tundra tradition, 320
Cañon de los Embudos site, 99, 108
Canutillo complex, 397
Canyon City Club site (Texas), *80*, 83
caribou, hunting of, 315, 317, 318, 322, 338, 418
Carlson, Roy L., 14, 15n1, 116
Carmichael, David L., 3, 5, 6, 7–8, 9, 100, 194, 304, 324, 328, 421
Carr, Christopher, 371
Carrier people, 130
Castle Gardens Access Road site, 327
Castle Park site, 326
Catchpole, A. J. W., 317
Cedar Point Village site (Colorado), 41–42
Center for Mountain Archeology, 27
"centers of occupation," 377, 401n1
ceramics: adoption of by Apaches, 42–44; Apache sites and borrowing of technologies, 106–7; and Apachean sites in Colorado Front Range, 23–24, 25–26, 26–27, 29; and Athapaskan arrival in Southwest, 327–28; and Cerro Rojo complex, 114; and culture history of Canadian Plains, 203; differences of opinion on use of to identify Athapaskans, 8–9; and Dismal River sites, 40–41, 42, 44–45, 48, 50–51, *52*, 228, 229, *230*, 231, 415; and ethnic identity, 415–16; and Navajo sites, 167–68, 231–32, 327, 415–16; and Promontory Point culture, 137; social relationships and transfer of technology, 232–35; and Tierra Blanca complex, 85; variation in production of by Athapaskans, 225–35
Cerro Alto complex, 98–99
Cerro Rojo complex, 90–117, 229, 335–36, 397, 417
Chaco Canyon, 331
chain migration, 38, 63
Changing Woman (Navajo), 138–39, 140, 142n8
Cheyenne, 190, 192
Chilcolin language, 292
Chino, Wendell, 184, 195
Chipewyans: and evidence for migration route to Southwest, 303–39; and linguistics, 126, 241, 251, 287, 298; and Navajo cultural identity, 165
Chiricahua Apache: absorption of non-Apache mobile groups into, 398; and band organization, 382, 384, 385, 386; distinction between Western Apache and, 393; historic distribution of, 400; and imagery in rock art, 100, 101; and linguistics, 251, 258, 287, 288, *289*, 290, 298; and personal or group names, 274, 276, 277–78, 279–80, 282n13; territories of, 390–91, 392, 394, 395, 396, 401–402n4, 402n4; use of term, 118n13. *See also* Apache(s); Apachean peoples
chithos (tool type), 317, 323, 324, 327, 338, 339
Churchill, Mount. *See* White River ash deposition
Cita Mouth site (Texas), *80*, 85
clans: and kinship systems of Southern Athapaskan groups, 292; and Navajo social structure, 130-31, 139, 140,

419; and Western Apache, 125, 130, 388
Clark, Jeffrey J., 371
classificatory verbs, in Athapaskan languages, 252–53
clays, and production of ceramics, 227, 229–32
climate: and motivations for migration, 359, 418; and proto-Apache sites in eastern Colorado, 53–55, 65. *See also* drought; environmental changes; Medieval Climate Anomaly
Cochise (Chiricahua Apache leader), 392, 395, 396, 401n4
Cochise-Howard Treaty site, 99
cognates, and Athapaskan languages, 250–51, 256, 257, 258–60
coil-and-scrape technology, and ceramics, 231–32
Cole, Donald C., 5, 65, 319, 386
Colorado River, 326
Comanche, 21, 31, 192, 193, 337
comparative method, 251, 411
Condie, Carol J., 328
conflict, and intergroup relations of Apachean groups, 388. *See also* warfare
conservatism, of Athapaskan languages, 264–65
continuity: and concept of heritable continuity, 215; convoluted forms of in descendant populations, 99–102; gradual change as indicative of in archaeological assemblages, 411; and iterative approach to cultural identity, 105–7
Cook, Eung-Do, 287
cooking, and use of pottery, 226–27
Copp, Stanley Arthur, 320–21, 367
Cordell, Linda S., 118n12, 334
Cordero, Don Antonio, 274, 276, 278–80, 282n9, 282n15
Corecho. See Querecho
cores, and microblade technology, 413
correlate grids, 94, 95, *96*, 116
cosmology, of Navajo and Western Apache, 420. *See also* religious beliefs; supernatural beliefs
coyote narratives, 289–90, 296

Coyotero Apaches, 394
Creamer, Winifred, 333
Creasman, S. D., 325
creation story, and Navajo oral history, 138–40
Cree people, 305, 317
Crow tribe, 192
cultural context, and archaeological manifestations of Athapaskans on Great Plains, 39–40
cultural identity: and anthropological theory on identity formation, 9; attachment to place and tribal, 392; in historic period, 94; iterative approach to continuity of, 105–7
cultural interrelationships, between Navajo and other Athapaskan peoples, 129–38. *See also* social relationships
culture history, of Canadian Plains, 201–6. *See also* acculturation
Curtis, Edward, *104*

Dark-Circle-of-Branches ritual (Navajo), 132, 135, 142n4
Darrow, Michael, 282n13
dates and dating methods: and Apachean languages, 254–55; of ceramics from Apachean sites in Colorado Front Range, 24, 30; and Cerro Rojo complex, 110; and controversy on chronometric dating, 11–12; from Dismal River sites, 29, 50, 52, *53*; innovations in and reinterpretation of Athapaskan migration, 3; and Numic sites, 326; and "old wood" problem for radiocarbon, 27, 325–26, 338; and proto-Apache sites in Colorado, 46; of sites by decreasing distance from Canada to Southwest, *329–30*; and Tierra Blanca complex, 80
Davidson, Daniel S., 412
Davis, Emma Lou, 332
dead, and supernatural beliefs of Chipewyans and Apacheans, 314
Dean, Jeffrey S., 332
Deerlodge Midden site, 326
Dene. *See* Athapaskans; Chipewyans
de Reuse, Willem J., 7, 118n13, 255, 261, 289

Derry, D. E., 317
descriptive grids, 93–94
Devil's Thumb Trail site (Colorado), 27, 47, 50
Devil's Tower, 189, 192
Dice, Michael, 173n1
Dick, Herbert W., 44
Dinétah, and emergence of Navajo, 62, 150–73, 418–19
Dinetah Gray, 167–68, 415–16
Dinosaur National Monument, 326
direct historical approach, 90, 389
discursive areal typology, for Southern Athapaskan languages, 286–99
disease, impact of European on Navajo culture, 166–70, 172
Dismal River aspect: and ceramics, 40–41, 42, 44–45, 48, 50–51, 52, 228, 229, 230, 231, 415; division of into eastern and western types, 41–42, 59, 61, 65; and evidence for Athapaskan migration route, 334–35; proto-Apache ethic affiliation of, 21, 30, 39–40, 46–55; quantitative comparisons of assemblages of associated artifacts from, 417; and sources of obsidian, 31
distinct centers of occupation, 380, 383, 385, 387
Dittert, Albert E., Jr., 319, 328
DNA, and genetic evidence of Athapaskan migration, 241–46
dog, words for in Apachean languages, 127, 129
Dogrib people, 187
Donaldson, J. D., 317
Dove, Don, 334
Dragoon Mountains, 394–95, 401n4, 402n4
Dragoon Mountain site (Arizona), 331
Driver, Harold E., 314
drought, in Four Corners region from 1276 to 1299, 331. *See also* climate
Duff, Andrew I., 314
Dunnell, Robert C., 208, 211
Dyen, Isidore, 130
Dykeman, Douglas D., 3, 6, 7, 8, 173n1, 420, 421

Eagle Lake (British Columbia), 320, 357, 364–67
earthlodge architecture, and Dismal River sites, 41
Eastern Apachean languages, 254
Eddy, Frank W., 41, 163
Eiselt, Bernice Sunday, 42, 43, 44
Elephant Mountain site, 336
Eliade, Mircea, 162
Ellwood, Priscilla, 29
environmental changes, as cause of migration, 417. *See also* biogeography; climate; landscape; paleoenvironmental context
Eskimo, 131, 252. *See also* Inuit
Eskimo-Aleut language, 252
ethnicity: and development of Late period point typologies on Canadian Plains, 203–4; identifiers of in archaeological record, 411–17; and modeling of Athapaskan migration, 367–68; oral history and reconciliation of heredity with, 194–95
ethnography: and isolation of archaeological culture groups, 98–99; and multidisciplinary approach, 5
ethnopoetics, 294, 299
Eureka Ridge site (Colorado), 28–29, 31, 42, 47, 48, 49, 50, 51, 52, 59, 63, 64, 67
evidential markers, in oral narratives, 289–92
evolutionary theory, in archaeology, 208
extractive method, 97
Eyak, 249, 250

Fall, Albert, 182
family histories, of Navajo, 158
Farella, John R., 158, 162–63, 168–69
Farrer, Claire R., 3, 5, 6, 7–8, 9, 100, 304, 324, 328, 421
Fatheree site (Texas), 80, 85
Fedje, Daryl, 412
Ferg, Alan, 91, 328
Fidler, Peter, 305
Fifth Green site (Texas), 80, 81, 83, 84
Flaming Gorge site, 325
Flattop Game Drive site, 26–27
Fly, C. S., 99

food preparation, and function of pottery for hunter-gatherers, 226
Forbes, Jack D., 281n1, 306, 396, 398, 402n5
Forbis, Richard G., 201, 204, 205, 212
Forest Canyon Pass site (Colorado), 25–26
forked-pole hogans, as characteristic of Navajo, 135–36
Fortescue, Michael, 250
Fort Sill Apaches (Oklahoma), 276
Foster, Michael K., 254–55
Four Corners region: abandonment of by Puebloans, 331–34, 418; and drought from 1276 to 1299, 331; establishment of ancestral Puebloans in, 56–57
Frances Polychrome, 416
Francis, Harris, 164, 171
Franktown Cave site (Colorado), *47, 49,* 50, *51,* 52
Fremont culture, 125, 138, 141n1
Front Range mountains (Colorado), 20–32

Galice language, 293–94
gambling games, 315
Garza complex, 232–34
generational adaptation, and migration, 363–64
genetics: and DNA evidence of Athapaskan migration, 241–46; and incorporation of Southwestern populations in Apachean groups, 388; and multidisciplinary approach, 5; and Navajo, 125–26, 313, 419; oral history and reconciliation of ethnicity with, 194–95; small-scale, out-migrations and Chipewyan, 306, 313–14
Genizaros, 416
Geromino (Apache leader), 395, 396
Geronimo, Robert, 91
Gila River, 278, 402n4
Gileño complex, 119n18, 271, 273, 274, 276, 277, 278, 280, 281, 394
Gilmore, Kevin P., 13, 30, 31, 321, 335, 368, 373, 416
Gitksan, 130
Glasscock site (Colorado), *49*
glottochronology, 262–65, 288, 306

Gmoser, Glenn J., 368
Gobernador phase, 168, 416
Goddard, Pliny Earle, 293
Golla, Victor K., 255, 261
Goodwin, Grenville, 274, 276, 384, 388, 394
Gordon, Bryan C., 5, 13, 410–11, 421
gourd, in Navajo culture, 256–57
Great Bear Lake, 187, *188*
Great Lakes, *188,* 189
Great Slave Lake, 187, *188*
Green River, 326, 418
Griffen, William B., 271, 272–73, 274, 277, 381, 398
Griffin-Pierce, Trudy, 321
Griswold, Gillett, 276, 282n13
group names, of Apache tribes in Spanish and early Mexican documents, 278–80, 282n15
Gulley, Cara C., 40, 45
Gull Lake site (Saskatchewan), 199, 200, 201, 205, 206–20, 413
Gunnerson, James H. and Dolores A., 38, 39, 40, 43, 108, 155, 170, 306, 328, 334–35

Haas, Jonathan, 333
Haas, Mary R., 287
Habermas, Jürgen, 157
Habicht-Mauche, Judith A., 43, 45, 59, 78, 335, 337
Hancock, Patricia M., 173n1
Hanson, L. W., 317
Hantman, J. L., 333
haplogroups, 242–43
Haskell, J. Loring, 327
headdresses: depictions of in Apachean rock art, 101, *104*; and Navajo religious beliefs, 131–32
Head-Smashed-In Buffalo Jump, 212
healing ceremonies, and Navajo religion, 168–69
Henderson, Richard N., 378, 392, 394
Hensler, Kathy N., 327
heritable continuity, concept of, 218
Hester, James J., 328
Hidatsa people, 192
High Plains, and Colorado Front Range, 20–32

Hill, David V., 8, 107, 415
Hinojosa site, 337
historic documents: and connection of archaeological records to historically referenced groups, 93–95; Dragoons and Pinaleño Mountains and territories of Apache groups, 394; personal names in Spanish and early Mexican documents and Apache dialects, 271–81; references to Navajo in Spanish-language, 124, 155; and references to Plains Apaches in eastern High Plains and mountains of Colorado, 20; and selective use of source content, 117n3. *See also* Spanish
Hogup Cave, 138
Hoijer, Harry, 241, 252, 254, 262, 273, 282n10, 287, 288, 298, 306, 389
Holden, William C., 78, 81
Hopi, 130, *131*, 282n11, 286–87, 292, 294–97, 298, 416. *See also* Puebloan peoples
Hormiguero site, 100, 111
horse: change of lifeways after introduction of, 420; construction of word for and lexicons of Athapaskan groups, 61, 127–29; "regaining" of by Mescalero Apache, 191, 192
housing types: and Cerro Rojo complex, 112; in historic photographs, 99; and retention of Apachean lifeway attributes by descendant groups, 108. *See also* forked-pole hogans; hut rings; tipis and tipi rings; wickiups
Howard, Oliver Otis, 402n4
Hughes, David T., 13
Hughes, Jack T., 78, 80, 81, 83, 85, 86–87, 336
Human Relations Area Files, 422
hunting: Athapaskan technology of, 154; and Plains-intermountain route for Athapaskan migration, 321–24, 338; and seasonal camps in Colorado Front Range, 26, 30; and Tierra Blanca complex, 78. *See also* bison; caribou; pronghorn
Hupa, 140, 251, 254
hut rings, and Cerro Rojo complex, 111
Hymes, Dell H., 306

ideas: Athapaskan migration and transmission of, 60–61; and return migration, 64
identity. *See* cultural identity; ethnicity
illitic clays, 227
Indian Claims Commission Act, 390
Indian Peak's Wilderness (Colorado), 27
information, long-distance migration and transmission of, 63
Ingalik, 132
integrative modeling, of migrations, 368–71
interregional comparisons, and connections between archaeological complexes and historically referenced groups, 108–10
Inuit, 306. *See also* Eskimo
iterative approach, to continuity in cultural identity, 105–7
Ives, John W., 204, 205, 255, 257, 265, 318, 319, 320, 335, 364, 366, 417

Jacobs, Melville, 293, 294
Janetski, Joel C., 142n5
Jano, 118–19n16, 395, 396–98, 401
Jeffords, Thomas, 401n4
Jemez, 141n1, 155, 163, 171. *See also* Puebloan peoples
Jemez Black-on-White, 416
Jennings, Jesse D., 137
Jett, Stephen C., 136, 333
Jetté, Jules, 293
Jicarilla Apache: borrowing of technologies from nearby cultures, 232; and ceramics, 234; and Cerro Rojo complex, 111; and Dismal River culture, 43, 62; and "heart of the world," 401n1, 401n3; and linguistics, 127–28, 251, 258, *259*, 261, 287, 288, *289*, 290, 298; Navajo and religious beliefs of, 125; and oral history of Navajo, 161
Jocome, 118–19n16, 390, 395, 396–98, 401, 402n5
John, Elizabeth A. H., 124, 273, 398
Jones, Terry L., 332, 333
Jornada Mogollon, 336

Kalokowski, H. Paul, Jr., 87n1
kaolinitic clays, 227

Kari, James, 250, 251, 253–54, 255, 264–65
Kavik people, 414
Kearns, Timothy M., 417
Kehoe, Thomas F., 199–201, 203, 205, 206, 210, 212, 219, 220, 316, 320, 413
Kelley, Klara, 164, 171
Kelly, Robert L., 369, 386
Kendall-Shaw site, *230*
Kidder, Alfred V., 420
Kinaaldá (Navajo girls' puberty ceremony), 140
Kindig, Jean Matthews, 30
kinship, adaptiveness of Athapaskan systems, 364. See also clans; matrilineality
Kintigh, Keith, 333
Kiowa, and linguistics, 127, 141n1
Kiowa-Apache: alliance of Mescalero Apache with, 192; divergence date between Western Apache and, 65; and linguistics, 127, 128; and use of term "Plains Apache," 142n3
Klo-kut phase (Yukon), 137, 414
Kooyman, Brian, 201
Krauss, Michael E., 250, 255, 261, 262, 263
Kroskrity, Paul, 286, 287, 295, 298
Kuhn, Tyler, 318, 319, 418
Kurok people, 368
Kutenai people, 194

Labelle, Jason, 326
Lakota tribe, 187, 194
land claims, and Apache groups, 390–94, 395
"Land of Ever Winter," 2, 15n1, 187
landscape, and social imaginary of Navajo, 164. See also place; place names; territories
Langenfeld, Kristin, 173n1
languages and linguistics: and discursive areal typology for Southern Athapaskan languages, 286–99; and evidence for Apachean migration, 249–67; and evidence for Northwest Plains-mountain route of Athapaskan migration to Southwest, 303–39; geographic distribution of Athapaskan languages as evidence for long-distance population movement, 241;

and multidisciplinary approach, 5; and Navajo, 126–29, 251, 253, 254, 255, 256, *259*, 287–88, *289*, 290, 297, 298, *307–13*; personal names in early historic documents and Apachean, 271–81; and understanding of social imaginary, 161
Larmore, Sean, 13, 30, 31, 335, 416
Lawn Lake site (Colorado), 22–25, *47*, 52
leap-frogging, as model of migration, 38, 63, 64, 65, 371, 400
Le Blanc, Raymond, 137
LeBlanc, Steven A., 332–33
Leer, Jeff, 261
Leone, Mark P., 93, 94
lexico-statistics, 262, 288
lifeways: introduction of horse and changes in, 420; retention of attributes of by Apachean descendant populations, 107–8. See also food preparation; housing types; hunting
linguistics. See language and linguistics
Lipan Apache: and Dismal River culture, 62; and imagery in rock art, 101; and linguistics, 127–28, 251, 287, 288, *289*, 290, 296, 298; and oral history of Navajo, 161. See also Apache(s); Apachean peoples
Lipe, William D., 331
Lipo, Carl P., 207, 208
lithic assemblages: and Apachean sites in Colorado Front Range, 25, 28–29; and Cerro Rojo complex, 113–14; and Chipewyan tools, 315–17; and Gull Lake site in Saskatchewan, 206–20; and microblade technology, 412–13; and Numic-speaking peoples, 324–27; and proto-Apache sites in Colorado high country, 47–48; structure of, 365–67. See also bifacial knives; chithos; obsidian; projectile points; tool kits
Little Ice Age (LIA), 53–55, *56*
Llano Estacado Grayware, 85
loanwords, and Athapaskan languages, 265
Lockwood, Frank C., 2
Loendorf, Lawrence, 102
Lord, Albert Bates, 193
Lovitt Mica Tempered, 228

Lovitt Plain, 228, 415
Lovitt Simple Stamped, 50, 415
Lowell Spring site, 326
"low visibility archaeology," and highly mobile groups, 95–98, 170
Lucas, Gavin, 210
Luckert, Karl W., 183
Lyman, R. Lee, 208, 211, 218–19

Maestas, Enrique Gilbert-Michael, 85
Magne, Martin P. R., 4, 5, 63, 198, 315, 317, 320, 321, 356, 359, 364, 365, 366, 412, 414, 417, 418
maize: and Apachean languages, 257–58; and Athapaskan subsistence in eastern Colorado, 61; and emergence of Navajo, 153–54, 155
Malhi, Ripan Singh, 243, 313, 340n2, 419
Mandan tribe, 190, 192
Manso, 397
manufacturing techniques, for ceramics, 229–32
material culture: and Cerro Rojo complex, 98–99; controversy on definition of early Athapaskan, 8; difficulty of distinguishing Apachean from Ute, 21; Dismal River sites and diagnostic forms of, 40–46; and Tierra Blanca complex, 87. *See also* ceramics; housing types; lithic assemblages; moccasins; snowshoes
matrilineality, and social organization of Chipewyan and Apachean peoples, 314
Matson, R. G., 356, 359, 364, 365, 366, 414, 418
Matthews, Washington, 163
Mayer-Oakes, William J., 203
McKenzie Canyon site (Colorado), *47*
McKean complex, 203
Medieval Climate Anomaly (MCA), 53–55, *56*, 65, 359
"megapatch" adaptations, for long-range colonizations, 369
member recruitment behavior, by Apachean groups, 106–7. *See also* recruitment
Mescalero Apache: and Apachean languages, 258, *259*, 287, 290, 298; band organization and use of territories by, 382, 384; and Cerro Alto complex, 98; and Dismal River culture, 62; distinction between Western Apache and, 393; and mountain spirit imagery, 100; and personal or group names, 274, 276, 279–80, 282n10; reflection of origins and migration in place names of, 182–95, 419, 421. *See also* Apache(s); Apachean peoples
Mexico, and Apache personal names in early historic documents, 271–81
mica, in pastes of ceramics, 228–29, 340n5
microblade technology, and ethic identity, 412–13
middle-range theory, 66, 93, 95, 107, 115, 117n4
migration: and biogeography, *370*, 371–73; and generational adaptation, 363–64; and interpretations of Canadian Plains prehistory, 203; linguistic evidence for Apachean, 249–67; modeling of, 38, 362–71; motivations for, 359; and place names of Mescalero Apache, 182–95; push-and-pull factors and structure of, 63–64, 359, 417–18; references to in oral history of Navajo, 156; theory of, 358–59. *See also* Athapaskans; routes
Mimbreño complex, 271, 273, 274, 276, 277, 278, 279, 280
mineral inclusions, in raw materials for ceramics, 227
Missouri River, *188*, 189
Mithun, Marianne, 266
mitochondrial genome, and genetic evidence for Athapaskan migration, 242–43
mobility: and historic Apache movement and interaction as model for Athapaskan migration, 377–401; and "low visibility" archaeology of highly mobile groups, 95–98, 170; and variety of materials used to produce ceramics, 228, 235
moccasins, 137, 138, 317
modeling, of Athapaskan migration, 356–73
modified frequency seriation, and point typologies, 208

Moodie, D. W., 317
Moorhead, Max L., 281n1
Moratto, Michael, 359
morphemes/words, and Athapaskan languages, 250–51
mortality rates, from European diseases, 166
Mortlach phase, 205
motivations, for migration, 359
mountain spirit imagery, 100, 101, *102, 104*, 184–85
mule deer, 324
Mummy Cave complex, 203
Mummy Pass site (Colorado), 27

NaDene language phylum, 411–12
Naichae (son of Cochise), 395
narrative enclitic, in oral traditions, 291–92, 295, 296, 297
Navajo: adoption of Puebloan traits by, 420–21; and ceramics, 167–68, 231–32, 327, 415–16; coalescence of in Dinétah region, 62, 418–19; cultural interrelationships with other Athapaskan peoples, 129–38; differences of from other Athapaskan peoples, 124–25; Dinétah in social imaginary of, 150–73; genetics and Southwestern ancestry of, 125–26, 313, 419; and haplogroups, 243; historic distribution of, 399; impact of European diseases on culture of, 166–70, 172; and linguistics, 126–29, 251, 253, 254, 255, 256, *259*, 287–88, *289*, 290, 297, 298, *307–13*; and oral history, 138–41, 155, 156, 157–66, 170–73, 421; and religious beliefs, 131–35, 167, 168, 314, 327; separation of Mescalero from, 191; social structure and clan system of, 130–31, 139, 140, 419; and Western Apache, 280
Naylor, Thomas H., 388
Neily, Robert B., 334
Nelson, Richard, 369
Nentvig, Juan, S. J., 281n3
neutron activation analysis, of ceramics, 228
Nichols, Johanna, 254
Night Chant (Navajo), 162–63

non-recombining Y-chromosome (NRY), 243–44
Northern Athapaskans: and clan system, 130; and language family, 250, 287, 292–94, 296–97; and religious beliefs, 132, 135. *See also* Chipewyan
North Platte River, *189*, 191
noun incorporation, in Apachean languages, 260–61
nuclear centers, and Cerro Rojo complex, 111
Numic-speaking peoples: expansion of into eastern Utah and western Colorado, 56, *57*, 61, *62*, 65; expansion of into Puebloan periphery, 151; and lithic assemblages, 324–27
Nye, William Sturtevant, 381

object pronouns, in Apachean languages, 258–60
O'Brien, Michael J., 207, 208, 211
obsidian: and ritual paraphenalia of Mescalero Apache, 190–91; and trade at Apachean sites in Colorado Front Range, 29, 31
Obsidian Cliff (Yellowstone National Park), *188, 189*, 190
Ocate Micaceous, 44–45, 50, 328, 415
O'Conor, Hugh, 278
occupational core, of Apachean groups, 400–401
Old Man Mountain site (Colorado), 26
Old Women's Buffalo Jump site, 204, 206, 219
Olinger, B., 44
O'odham, 388, 395–96, 402n4. *See also* Akimel O'odham; Tohono O'odham
"open niche," concept of, 53
Opler, Marion E., 389
Opler, Morris E., 1–2, 6–7, 13, 65, 111, 118n13, 183, 276–77, 292, 393, 394, 401n4
oral history: Apachean languages and evidential markers in, 289–92; and ethnographic evidence for Athapaskan migration, 367–68, 421; importance of and controversy on as source of information, 3; and Jemez, 155; and multidisciplinary approach, 5; origins

and migration as reflected in Mescalero Apache place names and, 182–95, 419, 421; of Navajo, 138–41, 155, 156, 157–66, 170–73, 421; within-tribe variations in, 6
Oxbow phase (Canadian Plains), 203
Oyster Ridge site, 324

Pacific Coast Athapaskan language family, 250
paddle-and-anvil technology, and ceramics, 229
Paiute, 325, 326. *See also* Shivwits; Southern Paiute
paleoenvironmental context, of proto-Apache sites in eastern Colorado, 53–55
Palisades site (Hughes Rockshelter), *80*
Palluche Canyon Cache (New Mexico), *133*
Palmer Drought Severity Index (PDSI), 54, *55*
Palo Duro Canyon, *189*, 192–93
Pan-Athapaskan Comparative Lexicon Project, 266
Panhandle-Plains Historical Museum (Texas), 78, 83
Papago. *See* Tohono O'odham
paradigmatic classification scheme, for lithic assemblages, 208
Pawnee tribe, 192
Peace Point site, 364
Pearce, Roy Harvey, 170
Peck, Trevor R., 204, 205, 206, 211–12, 218, 219
Pecos complex, 119n18
Pelican Lake phase, 203
percentage stratigraphy, and evidence for Athapaskan migration, 198–220
Perry, Richard J., 10, 12, 63, 129, 387, 401
personal names, of Apaches in Spanish and early Mexican documents, 271–81
Peso, Fred, 184
petrographic analysis, of ceramics, 228, 229
Petsch Springs site (Colorado), *47, 48, 53*
Picuris Pueblo, 44
Pima Revolt of 1751, 384

Pinaleño Mountains, 394–95, 402n4
Pinnacle site (Colorado), 29, 42, *47*
Pinno, Bradley D., 340n4
Piro, 397
place: land claims of Apachean groups and attachment to, 390–94; political aspects of naming and remembering of, 182. *See also* landscapes; place names
place names, origins and migration of Mescalero Apache reflected in, 182–95, 419, 421
Plains Apache, 20, 254, 255, 261, 287, 289. *See also* Apache(s); Apachean peoples; Kiowa-Apache
Plains side-notched points, 200, 204, 316, 338
Plateau Pithouse Tradition, 366
Platte River, *189*, 191
Plog, Fred, 334
Plog, S., 333
point-and-arrow model, of migration, 362, *363*, 364, *372*, 373
politics, and naming or remembering of places, 182
polychrome wares, and Navajo ceramics, 167, 168, 416
Polzer, Charles W., 388
Ponca tribe, 192
population context, of proto-Apache sites in eastern Colorado, 52–53, *54, 56*
Potter, Parker B., 93, 94
Prairie side-notched points, 200, 204, 316
"pre-differentiation Athapaskans," use of phrase, 9–11
prefixes, and Athapaskan languages, 252
projectile points: and Avonlea horizon point style, 199–200; and Cerro Rojo complex, *109*, 113; as ethnic identifiers in archaeological record, 413–15; and Late period typologies on Canadian Plains, 203–4; and proto-Apache sites in Colorado high country, 47–48, *49*. *See also* lithic assemblages; Plains side-notched points; Prairie side-notched points
Promontory Point culture (Utah), 136–38, 335, 417

pronghorn, 324, 338
propinquity, principle of, 411
proto-Apache sites, in Colorado high country, 46–55
proto-Athapaskan culture, in southern Alaska, 12
proto-Athapaskan language, 250
Puebloan peoples: abandonment of Four Corners by, 331–34, 418; acculturation of Southern Athapaskan groups to culture of, 419; diffusion of ceramic technology from, 42, 44, 45, 327; establishment of ancestral in Four Corners region, 56–57; and genetics of Navajo, 125, 313; incorporation of cultural traits from encounter of Athapaskans and, 154, 171, 232–35; and Navajo clan system, 139. *See also* Hopi; Jemez; Taos Pueblo; Zuni
Pueblo Revolt of 1680, 44, 65, 139, 384, 420
punctuated point-and-arrow model, of migration, *372*, 373
push-and-pull factors, in migration, 63–64, 359, 417–18

Querecho, 45, 86, 87, 124
quotative evidentials, in oral narratives, 290–91, 294

Rabbit Ear Butte, *189*, 193
radiation model, of migration, 63
raiding: and characteristics of Apachean groups, 106; and ethnohistoric evidence of Apaches in Rocky Mountain National Park area, 22; and territories of Apache groups, 384, 386, 395, 396, 399. *See also* warfare
raw materials, and appearance of pottery, 226–29
Raynaud, E. B., 326
"readback," problem of in scholarly writing, 3–4
recruitment, and borrowing from neighboring groups, 387–88. *See also* member recruitment behavior
Reed, Alan D., 324, 326
Reed, Lori Stephens, 43, 66, 416
Reed, Paul F., 327, 416

Reeves, Brian O. K., 201, 207, 319, 320
refugee hypothesis, for Navajo cultural emergence, 152, 170–71, 420
Reichard, Gladys A., 163
religious beliefs: and differences between Southern Athapaskans and Pueblos, 419; of Navajo, 131–35, 168–69, 314, 327. *See also* cosmology; mountain spirit imagery; shamans; vision quests
Renfrew, Colin, 334
replacement migration, 205
Republican River, 191
retrogressive analysis, and modeling methods, 364
return migration, 38, 64, 65, 334–35
Rice, Keren, 4, 418
Rice, Sally, 257, 265
Ridington, Robin, 367–68
Rio Grande Tewa, 286–87
ritual dance, and Mescalero Apache, 184–86
Robinson, S. D., 318, 319
rock art: and Navajo religious beliefs, *134, 151, 165*; and ritual dance of Mescalero Apache, 184, *185*; symbolism in Apachean, 100–102, *103, 104*
Rockman, Marcy, 358–59, 362, 363, 364, 367, 369, 420
Rocky Mountain National Park (Colorado), 20–32
Roebuck, Paul, 3, 6, 7, 8, 173n1, 421
routes, of Athapaskan migration: differences in perspectives on, 13–14, 417–19; linguistic evidence for Northwest Plains-mountain route to Southwest, 303–39; plausibility of multiple, 66; proposed versions of, 37–38, *39*

St. Helens, Mount, 318
Salish groups and languages, 252, 414
Sammis site (Colorado), *49*
San Carlos Apache, 254, 258, 288, *289*. *See also* Apache(s); Apachean peoples
Sangre de Cristo culture, 21–22
San Juan Basin, and Navajo sites, 140
San Lorenzo de la Santa Cruz (mission), 108
Sapir, Edward, 255–57, 258, 265, 306, 319
Sarsi (Tsuut'ina) people: affiliation of

with Blackfeet, 127; and linguistics, 126, 165, 251, 255, 260, 261, 319; relation of Apache to, 187, 189, 190
Sauer, Carl, 396
savagism, and prejudice in Western social imaginary, 170
Saville-Troike, Muriel, 142n2, 287
Schaafsma, Curtis F., 334, 416, 421
Schiffer, Michael B., 117n4
Schroeder, Albert H., 2, 281n1
Scoggin, Charles R., 326
Scott, Tacheeni, 289
scouting, and migration, 362, 369
Seaburg, William, 293
seasonal movement, compared to migration, 378, *379*
Second, Bernard, 164, 184, 186, 189, 191, 194–95, 421
Servicebetty Shelter site, 326
Seymour, Deni J., 4, 5, 8, 13–14, 15n2, 21, 86, 156, 163, 170, 267n2, 319, 328, 331, 335, 336, 337, 338–39, 356, 365, 369, 370, 372, 417
shamans, and Northern Athapaskan religious beliefs, 135, 368, 420–21
Sharp, Henry, 314
Shivwits (Paiute), 228
shoe game (Mescalero Apache), 191
short tandem repeats (STR), 243
Shoshone, 326
similarity, principle of, 411
simple-stamped ceramics, 229
Siouan-speaking peoples, 200, 204, 252
Sioux, 190
Slave people, 187
smectitic clays, 227, 229
Smith, C. S., 325
snowshoes, 186, 412
Sobaípuri, 388, 395–96, 397, 398, 402n4. *See also* Akimel O'odham
social imaginary, and oral traditions of Navajo, 157–66, 170–73
social organization: and Navajo clan system, 130–31; and similarities between Chipewyan and Apachean peoples, 314; and social factors in migration, 364; and territories of Apache groups, 382–85
social relationships, and transfer of ceramic technology, 232–35. *See also* cultural interrelationships
Society for American Archaeology, 4
Sopris phase, 57
Southern Athapaskan Ceramic Conference (1985), 42
Southern Athapaskan language family, 250, 286–99
Southern Athapaskan migration hypothesis, 241, 244
Southern Paiute, 294–97, 298
Southern Plains Macroeconomy, 59, 60
Southern Ute, 234
South Platte River, *189*, 191
Southwest: acculturation of Southern Athapaskan groups to preexisting cultures of, 419–21; areal discursive typological view of languages of, 294–97. *See also* Athapaskans; Four Corners region; migration; Puebloans; routes
space, Navajo concept of, 164
Spanish: and epidemic diseases in Southwest, 166–70; and references to Dragoon Mountains, 402n4. *See also* historic documents
Specimen Mountain site (Colorado), 27
Spencer, Katherine, 159, 419, 421
Spencer, Virginia E., 136
Spicer, Edward H., 281n1, 321
Spielmann, Katherine, 60, 78, 81, 83, 337
Stevenson, Marc G., 364
Steward, Julian H., 335, 417
Stockel, Henrietta, 368
style-function problem, in lithic analysis, 211–16
Suma, 397
Sun Shield site (New Mexico), *134*
supernatural beliefs, similarity between Chipewyan and Apachean, 314
Swadesh word list, 262
Swan Point site (Alaska), 412
Sweeney, Edwin R., 271, 273
Syms, E. Leigh, 201
Systemwide Archeological Inventory Program (SAIP), 22

Tagish, 135
Tahltan, 130

Taltheilei sites, 315, 412
Tanoans, 125, 141n1
Taos Pueblo, 44, 234
Tarahumara, 387
Tatlmain Lake site (Yukon), 318
Taylor, Charles, 157, 162
Tedlock, Dennis, 295
Teguayo (place), 141n1
Tejas tribe, 192
Ten'a (Koyukon) language, 293, 297
territories, Apache groups and non-exclusive use of, 382–85
Tewa, 286–87, 294–97. *See also* Arizona Tewa
Tewa Polychrome, 416
Teya, 45, 86
Thomas, Alfred Barnaby, 281n1, 318–19
Thompson, David, 316
Three Rivers petroglyph, 184, *185*
Tierra Blanca complex (Texas), 59, 78–87, 119n17, 232–34, 319, 336–37
Tierra Blanca Plain, 85
Tigua, 397
time: and Apachean and Athapaskan language families, 262–65; frames of for proposed routes of Athapaskan migration, 38, 417–19; and Navajo oral history, 162–66. *See also* dates and dating methods
tipis and tipi rings: and Cerro Rojo complex, 112; and Dismal River sites, 42; and Mescalero Apache, 186; and similarities between Numic and Athapaskan sites, 325; and Tierra Blanca complex, 85
Tlingit, 130, 249, 250
Toelken, Barre, 289
Tohono O'odham (Papago), 140, 294–97
Tolowa language, 293
Tonkawa language, 294–97, 298
tool kits: and Cerro Rojo complex, 118n11; obsidian artifacts in Mescalero, 190
Torres, John A., 414
Towner, Ronald H., 416, 420
Toyah complex, 337–38
trade: and characteristics of Apachean groups, 106; and exchange of ideas and goods between Puebloans and Apacheans, 151, 171; in obsidian at Apachean sites in Colorado Front Range, 29, 31; and Tierra Blanca sites, 337
traditional cultural property (TCP), and Bighorn Medicine Wheel, 192
transformation, of Cerro Rojo into Cerro Alto complex, 98–99
translocation, and Athapaskan migration, 165
Trapper's Point site, 324
Trinidad Reservoir site, 325
Tsetsaut language, 292–93, 296
Tsuut'ina. *See* Sarsi people
Tule Mouth site (Texas), *80*, 85
Turner, William W., 124
Tutchone, 135
T-W Diamond site, 325
Twin Buttes site, 325
Twin Warrior Brothers (Mescalero Apache), 187

Uncompahgre Brownware, 24, 30, 416
Unglaub, LeRoy, 118n14
University of North Colorado (UNC), 23
Upham, Steadman, 333
Upper Kill phase (Alberta), 219
Upper Republican people, 53, 55, 57
Ussher, Bishop, 173n2
Utes: and cultural component at Lawn Lake site, 23, 24; and dating of sites, 326; difficulty of distinguishing material culture of from Apachean or Athapaskan, 21, 327; pottery of as distinct from Apachean, 24, 416; raw materials used in pottery production by, 228, 234; relations with Apache ancestral bands in Colorado Front Range, 30–31; and trade in obsidian, 29, 31. *See also* Southern Ute
Ute Trail, 25
Uto-Aztecan languages, 252, 286–87

Vansina, Jan, 193
VanStone, James W., 66
Van West, Carla, 332
Vaquero, 124
verb words, in Athapaskan languages, 251–54

vision quests, of Mescalero Apache, 192
volcano. *See* White River ash deposition

Wailaki language, 293, 297
Walde, Dale, 4, 201, 205, 320, 411, 413
Warburton, Miranda, 6, 327
warfare, and abandonment of Four Corners by Puebloans, 332–33. *See also* raiding
Warner, Michel, 157
Warren, Helene, 43
Water Crossing #2 site (Texas), *80*, 85
wave model, of migration, 364
Webster, Anthony K., 3–4, 182, 192, 266
Wedel, Waldo R., 334
West, K. D., 317
Western Apache: adoption of Puebloan traits by, 420; and Apachean languages, 254, 287, 290, 297, 298; and attachment to place, 391; and clan system, 125, 130, 388; distinction between southernmost Apache bands and, 393; divergence date between Kiowa-Apache and, 65; and genetics, 243, 419; historic distribution of, 398; increased sedentism of, 152; and O'odham clans, 388; oral history of and migration, 367; and oral history of Navajo, 161; and personal or group names, 274, 276, 277–78, 279, 280, 282n7, 282n14; separation of Mescalero from, 190; territories of, 384, 394, 395, 396; "traditional homelands" of, 390. *See also* Apache(s); Apachean peoples
Whitaker, Adrian R., 362–63
White Cat Village (Colorado), 25
White Mountain Apache, 289
White Painted Woman (Mescalero Apache), 186
White River ash deposition, 317–19, 359, 417–18

White Shell Woman (Navajo), 139–40, 142n8
"whole cultural" units, 207
Wichita tribe, 192, *230*
wickiups, and similarities between Numic and Athapaskan sites, 325
Wilcox, David R., 319, 320
Wilmeth, Roscoe, 362
Wilshusen, Richard H., 314, 373
Wilson, John P., 91, 396
Wind gods, and rock art, 101, *102*
Windway ceremony (Navajo), 314, 327
Winter River Mountains, 191
Witherspoon, Gary, 161, 168, 169
Wiyot people, 368
women, and Apache personal names, 273, 282n8. *See also* matrilineality
Woosley, A. I., 44
word lists, and linguistics, 262, 267n3, *307–13*
Workman, W., 317–18
worldview, of Navajo, 159
Wright, Gary A., 319
Wyman, Leland C., 164

X-raying, of ceramic vessels and large sherds, 232

Yampa River, 326
Yaqui, 387
Yellowknife Chipewyan dialect, 287
Yellowstone National Park, *189*, 190
Yelm, Mary, 26
Young, Robert W., 126, 163, 254, 298
Yumans, 140
Yurok people, 368

Zolbrod, Paul, 163
Zuazua, Augustina, 296
Zuni, 125, 187, 294–97. *See also* Puebloan peoples

E 99 .A86 F78 2012

**From the land of ever winter
to the American Southwest**